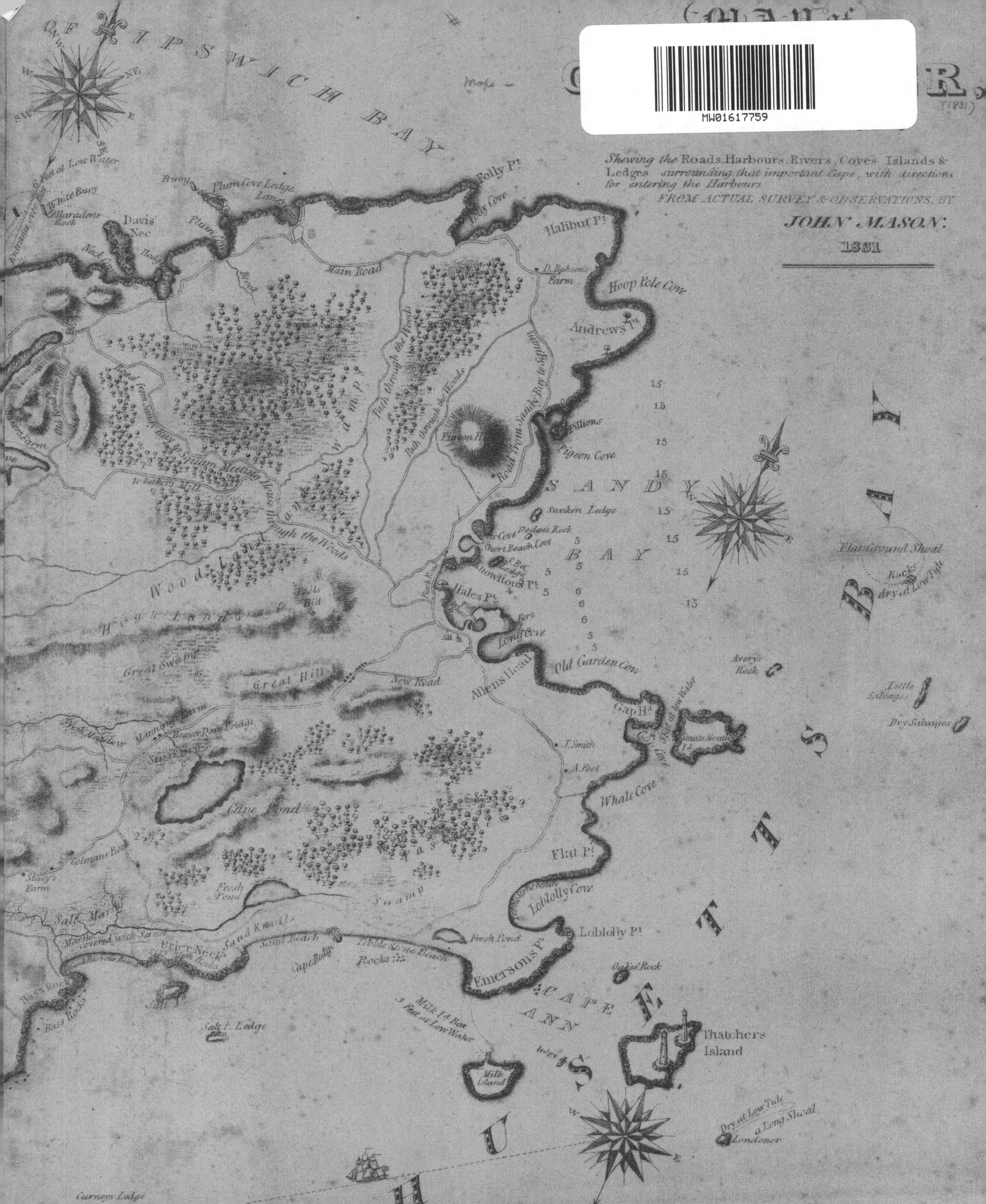

PLAN of CAPE ANN (1831)
Shewing the Roads, Harbours, Rivers, Coves, Islands & Ledges surrounding that important Cape, with directions for entering the Harbours
FROM ACTUAL SURVEY & OBSERVATIONS, BY
JOHN MASON.
1831
MW01617759
IPSWICH BAY
SANDY BAY
Folly Pt
Folly Cove
Halibut Pt
Hoop Pole Cove
Andrews Pt
Pigeon Cove
Sunken Ledge
Short Beach Cove
Knowltons Pt
Hales Pt
Long Cove
Allens Head
Old Garden Cove
Gap Hd
Straits Mouth Id
Whale Cove
Flat Pt
Loblolly Cove
Loblolly Pt
Emersons Pt
CAPE ANN
Thatchers Island
Milk Island
Salt I. Ledge
Bass Rock
Bass Rocks
Brier Neck
Sand Knolls
Sand Beach
Pebble Stone Beach
Fresh Pond
Cape Pond
Great Swamp
Great Hill
New Road
Main Road
Pigeon Hill
Pools Hill
Wood Land
High Lands
Path through the Woods
Road from Sandy Bay to Squam
Davis' Nec
Plum Cove Ledge
Plum Cove
Buoy
White Buoy
Haradens Rock
6 Feet at Low Water
Entrance over Bar
Avery's Rock
Little Salvages
Dry Salvages
Flat Ground Shoal
Rocks dry at Low Tide
Oakes' Rock
Milk Id Bar 3 Feet at Low Water
Dry at Low Tide
a Long Shoal
Londoner
Curneys Ledge
Salt Marsh
Fresh Meadow
Beaver Dam Bridge
Colmans Rock
Stacy's Farm
D. Babsons Farm
J. Smith
A. Poot
Swamp

PAINTING THE INHABITED LANDSCAPE

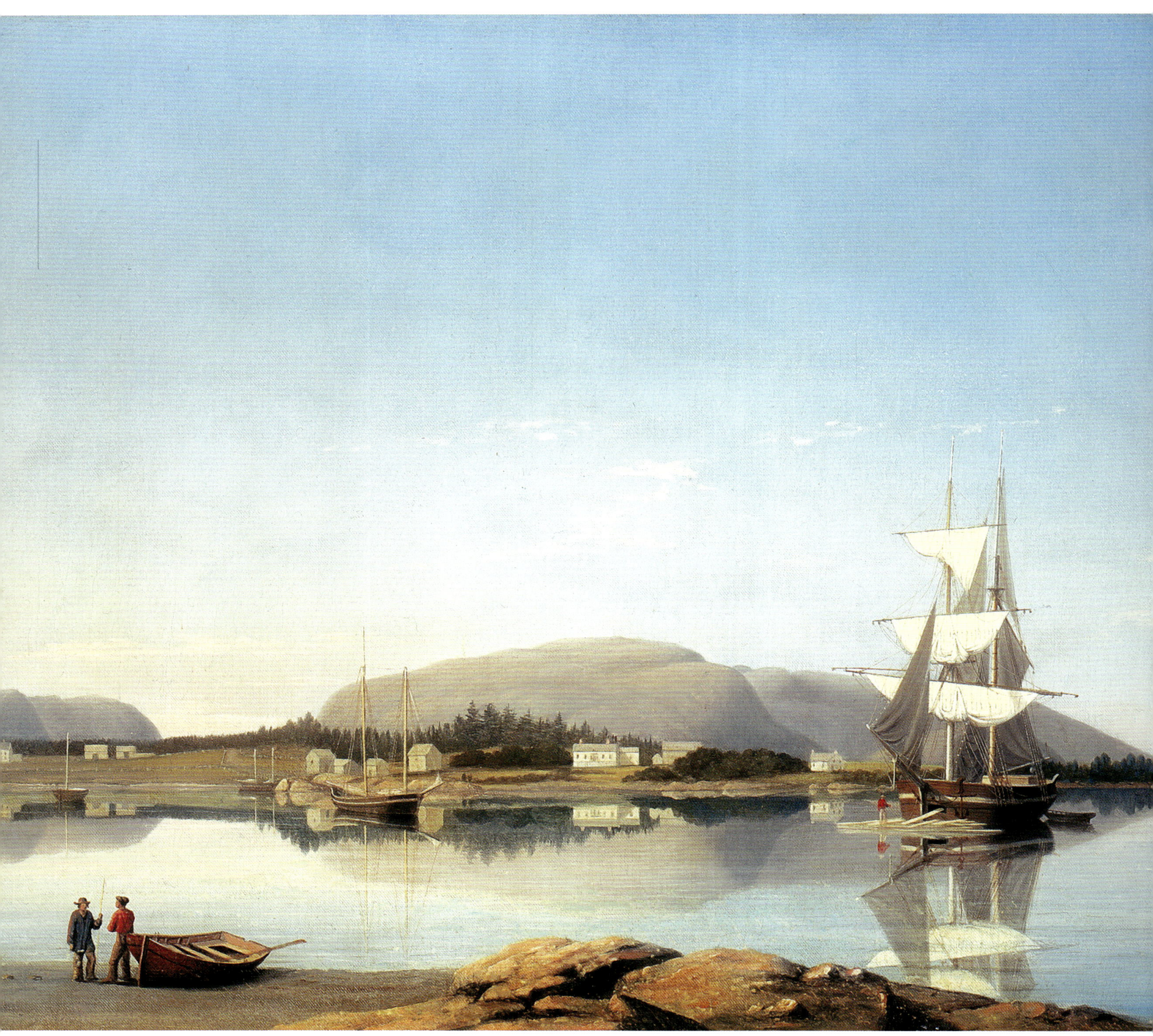

PAINTING THE INHABITED LANDSCAPE

Fitz H. Lane and the Global Reach of Antebellum America

MARGARETTA MARKLE LOVELL

The Pennsylvania State University Press
University Park, Pennsylvania

This publication has been made possible through support from the Terra Foundation for American Art International Publication Program of CAA.

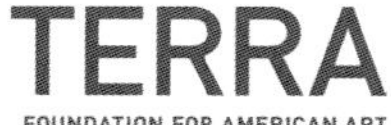

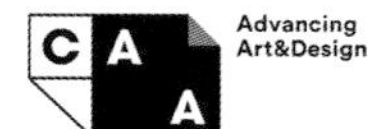

Support for this book has been provided by Furthermore: a program of the J. M. Kaplan Fund.

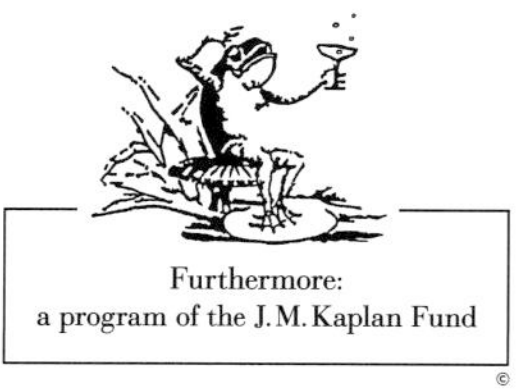

Publication of this book has also been supported by the Jay D. McEvoy, Jr., Fund for American Art at the University of California, Berkeley.

Library of Congress Cataloging-in-Publication Data

Names: Lovell, Margaretta M., author.
Title: Painting the inhabited landscape : Fitz H. Lane and the global reach of antebellum America / Margaretta Markle Lovell.
Description: University Park, Pennsylvania : The Pennsylvania State University Press, [2022] | Includes bibliographical references and index.
Summary: "Examines landscape, harborscape, and seascape paintings by Fitz H. Lane (1804–1865) that comment on agriculture, extraction industries, settlement patterns, trade, and the political economy of nineteenth-century coastal New England"—Provided by publisher.
Identifiers: LCCN 2022041336 | ISBN 9780271092782 (cloth)
Subjects: LCSH: Lane, Fitz Henry, 1804–1865—Criticism and interpretation. | Landscape painting, American—19th century. | Marine painting, American—19th century. | Harbors in art. | Gloucester Harbor (Mass.)—In art. | New England—In art.
Classification: LCC ND237.L27 L68 2022 | DDC 759.13—dc23/eng/20220922
LC record available at https://lccn.loc.gov/2022041336

Printed in Korea
Published by The Pennsylvania State University Press, University Park, PA 16802–1003

The Pennsylvania State University Press is a member of the Association of University Presses.

It is the policy of The Pennsylvania State University Press to use acid-free paper. Publications on uncoated stock satisfy the minimum requirements of American National Standard for Information Sciences—Permanence of Paper for Printed Library Material, ANSI Z39.48–1992.

Additional credits: endsheets, John Mason, *Map of Gloucester, Cape Ann*, 1831 (fig. 9); frontispiece and page 58, Fitz H. Lane, *Entrance to Somes Sound from Southwest Harbor*, 1852 (fig. 31); page xvi, Fitz H. Lane, *Gloucester Harbor*, 1852 (fig. 10); page 20, Fitz H. Lane, *Brig* Cadet *in Gloucester Harbor*, before 1848 (fig. 4); page 78, Fitz H. Lane, *Salem Harbor*, 1853 (fig. 33); page 144, Fitz H. Lane, *Castine, Maine*, 1856 (fig. 104); page 170, Fitz H. Lane, *Coffin's Beach at Sunset*, ca. 1862 (fig. 91); page 192, Fitz H. Lane, *Ships in Ice off Ten Pound Island, Gloucester* (fig. 132); page 218, Fitz Henry Lane, *Baltimore from Federal Hill*, ca. 1850 (fig. 159); page 250, Fitz H. Lane, *Castine Harbor and Town*, 1851 (fig. 164).

CONTENTS

ILLUSTRATIONS

ACKNOWLEDGMENTS

The creation of this book has been a collective enterprise. My debts both personal and institutional are many, and I am pleased to have the opportunity to recognize and thank those who have helped bring the project to fruition.

While I did not know it at the time, *Painting the Inhabited Landscape* began with the development of a course. In 2004, in response to a call by the Hewlett Foundation encouraging the creation of University of California, Berkeley, courses in general education that were conceptually interdisciplinary and team-taught by faculty in Letters & Science and faculty in the Professional Schools and Colleges, Joe R. McBride, professor of Environmental Science, Policy, and Management, suggested we co-teach an undergraduate course that became "The American Forest: Its Ecology, History, and Representation." Teaching that class over the course of a decade enabled me to look closely at theories of and literature on landscape utility, wilderness, and topographic documentation in antebellum America as well as at the history of artworks based on physical aspects of the new nation. Joe's provocative questions prompted me to puzzle over how and why the landscape paintings of Fitz H. Lane are so different from those of the Hudson River School artists. In a single Lane painting, for instance, one can find many different kinds of fences, so unlike the fenceless Nature beloved by New York City–based artists. Lane's paintings prompt questions about what that difference might say about the claims and fictions of ownership, property, sovereignty, and manifest destiny. Initially I thought a study of lumber, lumbering, and milling in Lane's work might make a good, focused article, as lumbering, like other extraction industries, was central to Lane but invisible in the work of landscapists bent on depicting a romanticized "virgin land." So my first thanks are to Joe McBride and the Hewlett Foundation.

By the time I was invited to spend a year at the American Antiquarian Society as Mellon Distinguished Scholar in Residence 2007–8, with further support from a John Simon Guggenheim Memorial Foundation Fellowship, the project had grown into an expansive book, and its shape and character were clear. I am deeply grateful to these two generous institutions for support over the months I was able to pore over maps, manuscripts, diaries, pamphlets, prints, and especially the Gloucester newspapers under the generous dome at the AAS. Two years later I was fortunate in being able to spend the 2009–10 academic year as a Dana and David Dornsife Fellow at the Henry E. Huntington Library and Art Gallery, where I expanded my archive and began writing. There are probably no more idyllic places for an Americanist to work happily and productively than the American Antiquarian Society and the Huntington Library. These two institutions and those who make them work so well for scholars—including Georgia (Gigi) Barnhill, Lauren Hewes, Vincent Golden, and Paul Erikson at the AAS and Shelley Bennett and Roy Ritchie at the Huntington—were incomparably generous and helpful. Gigi lent me snowshoes and a friendly ear. Shelley was a fountain of good ideas and insights. These helpful insiders at these archive-rich research institutions not only provided key bibliographic suggestions and opportunities to try out ideas, they also created an esprit de corps among the resident scholars that enriched the research experience with a festive sense of community and common purpose.

Other institutions with invaluable archives that have been essential to this book include the Houghton Library at Harvard, the Massachusetts Historical Society, and especially the Cape Ann Museum (formerly Cape Ann Historical Association), where Stephanie Buck and Sam Holdsworth were extremely helpful. All of the museums that include Lane works in their collections were welcoming; especially helpful was Erika Hirshler at the Museum of Fine Arts, Boston.

I would also like to thank the institutions whose invitations to present talks drawing on this project gave me an opportunity to try out ideas and receive invaluable feedback: the Pennsylvania State University, the University of Connecticut, Yale University, Stanford University, the Huntington Library, the Freie Universität Berlin, and the University of Southern California. Moreover, I thank the Cape Ann Museum for graciously permitting me to include in chapter 7 material that was earlier published by that institution in "Fitz H. Lane's Marine Lithographs, Robert Bennett Forbes, and the Pirates of the South China Sea," in *Laid Down on Paper: Printmaking in America, 1800 to 1865*, edited by Caroline Sloat.

Of the many individuals indispensable to this project, the late Jay D. McEvoy Jr. looms large. Many years ago he recounted to me his disappointment in not finding art of the United States in the curriculum at the University of California, Berkeley, when he was an undergraduate in the late 1930s. That lacuna remained in place until the 1980s. In order to provide the possibility of studying American art to generations of future students, McEvoy gave a generous bequest to the institution to create a program in American art, an endowment that provides funds for a faculty chair, graduate fellowships, conferences, and library resources to further scholarship in this field. McEvoy funds enabled me to travel to see Lane's works where they are held today, and to the sites where his paintings were created, as well as to hire research assistants to aid in tracking down objects, factoids, and all manner of bibliographic information. McEvoy's concurrent bequest to the Fine Arts Museums of San Francisco has made the Bay Area an important center for the American field.

This book has profited from careful reading and astute suggestions from my Berkeley Americanist colleagues Paul Groth, Richard Hutson, Donald McQuade, Kathleen Moran, Louise Mozingo, Christine Rosen, and Mary Ryan. Over the course of a decade they have read, discussed, and improved each chapter. While I have not always been able to accomplish the mends they recommended, the book is better for the passages and ideas this group of talented and steadfast friends helped me formulate and reformulate.

Other friends who have been a very real help to me in my research include Wai Chee Dimock, who accompanied me on a memorable site visit to Gloucester, and the late Ian Carmichael, who explored Castine and much of New England with me in pursuit of Lane and geology. Marc Simpson and Emily Moore read and responded to specific chapters that needed their experienced eyes; Veerle Thielmanns lent me the perfect attic studio for two weeks in rural France to draft a key chapter. Former student MaryKate McMaster helped me be at home in Worcester during my year there; former student Ellie Hughes kindly teetered on high ladders to check out the canvas weaves of Robert Salmon paintings at Yale's British Art Center; and former student Melissa Trafton, in taking on the massive catalogue raisonné project fitzhenrylaneonlin.org, made my life, and the intellectual lives of all those interested in Lane, much easier. Bryan Wolf, Alan Wallach, Wanda Corn, Bruce Robertson, Sally Promey, Dell Upton, Mimi Gardner Gates, and Laura Wexler have provided long-term scholarly models as well as generous friendship. Reaching way back, I must acknowledge the late David Huntington, who introduced me to American art, to landscape studies, and made my freshman year in college so intellectually exciting. I am particularly grateful to the incomparable Bob Gross, whose intellectual generosity, scholarship on the antebellum period, and leadership skills have few peers. I have also profited from a series of deeply memorable conversations with artist Wayne Thiebaud about landscape, about drawing, about museums, and about the day-to-day business of painting.

The community of graduate students and postdocs with whom I have had the pleasure of working at Berkeley, the Berkeley Americanist Group (BAG), meets informally once or twice a month to discuss the in-progress work of one of the members. It read chapters of *Painting the Inhabited Landscape* when, during the years the book was taking shape, there was nothing else pressing. The group shifts and changes as students and postdocs come into it and depart from it, but it is always vibrant and purposeful, and I am grateful for the careful close reading and responses those in the group have given the chapters on offer. Those members include Mathilde Andrews, Elizabeth Bennett, Will Coleman, Simona Cupic, Seffi Dippold, Elizabeth Bacon Eager, Susan Eberhard, Elizabeth Fair, Diana Greenwold, Eva Hagberg, Edwin Harvey, Can Liu, Meredith Masser, Sarah Gold McBride, Kappy Mintie, Julie Mommeja, Kevin Muller, Mary Okin, Carolyn Riley, Mia Ritzinger, Molly Robinson, Alberto Sanchez Sanchez, Emma Silverman, Jason Vartiker, and Elaine Yau.

Those who have worked as research assistants on this book project include Sylvia Houghteling, Cameron McKee, Justin Underhill, and Elaine Yau. Each has subsequently achieved a distinguished professional identity. As research assistants they were very helpful, sometimes for a few weeks, often for a summer, and I am deeply grateful for their research skills. Cori Schumacher interrupted a summer's research assistantship on another book (concerning the adventures of Lane's Gloucester-based contemporary Nancy Prince) to help with proofreading. Mary Okin is a special case. She has worked on a multitude of research projects for me over five summers, and I am in awe of her resourcefulness and professionalism in locating "lost" objects and difficult-to-find primary sources. She has worked most consistently on the Lane book, securing publication-quality images and managing the unmanageable business of photo permissions. I am deeply grateful for the contributions all these skillful young scholars have made to this project.

I warmly thank the readers for Penn State University Press, editor Eleanor Goodman, and the production team at the press, who embraced the project and have seen it through to realization, especially as they have been dealing with disruptions of all kinds resulting from the social, economic, and personal impacts of COVID-19.

Last, I would like to thank my family. My venerable father, when I mentioned I was investigating the wrecks on the rocks at Norman's Woe in Gloucester harbor, a site memorialized in Henry Wadsworth Longfellow's "Wreck of the Hesperus," quietly recited the whole poem while driving in heavy traffic, having learned it as a child ninety-two years earlier and probably not given it a thought in the intervening decades. Such is the power of art. More immediately, my daughter Stephanie, who shares her three children—Allison, Sophia, and Gavin—with me in my home in Berkeley, is helpful in keeping the household humming smoothly despite a very challenging job. My younger daughter lives at a distance but keeps me in the loop about all the doings in her life on a daily basis; she has been patient about my preoccupation with an era long gone. And I count in this category Debra Pughe and Jon Winet, who are dear friends, neighbors, and, in every sense that matters, family. Debra is a versatile scholar and campaigner for justice as well as a skillful writer and bibliophile both in her field—philosophy—and in more vernacular areas. I am grateful to her for her inventive engagement with the children, her deep knowledge about art, and her warm friendship. I am equally grateful to her husband, Jon, whose wry humor and readiness to give technical support has prevented many a computer meltdown from becoming a psychological meltdown.

Together, the kindness, expertise, and personal and institutional generosity of many people went into the thinking, researching, and writing that resulted in this book. To them all and to my readers I am deeply beholden. It is my hope that others will pick up the points I have missed, the holes I did not see, and carry on with more work on this artist, this era, and this contextualized framing of art, and it is to them, the successors, I offer my last warm thanks.

ABBREVIATIONS

AAS	American Antiquarian Society, Worcester, MA
BET	*Boston Evening Transcript*
CAA	*Cape Ann Advertiser*
CAL	*Cape Ann Light*
CAL & GT	*Cape Ann Light & Gloucester Telegraph*
CAM	Cape Ann Museum, Gloucester, MA, formerly known as CAHA (Cape Ann Historical Association), earlier known as C. A. S. & L. A. (Cape Ann Scientific and Literary Association)
CAWA	*Cape Ann Weekly Advertiser*
"Clippings," CAM	"Fitz H. Lane: Notes & Clippings from Authors & Artists of Cape Ann Scrapbook and other Sources," CAM 759.13/L24.
FHLo	http://fitzhenrylaneonline.org/catalog/index.php
GDT	*Gloucester Daily Times*
GT	*Gloucester Telegraph*
MFA	Museum of Fine Arts, Boston

All of the citations and references to manuscript material by Charles Chauncy Emerson and Edmund Bliss Emerson are courtesy of the Ralph Waldo Emerson Memorial Association deposit, Houghton Library, Harvard University.

PAINTING THE INHABITED LANDSCAPE

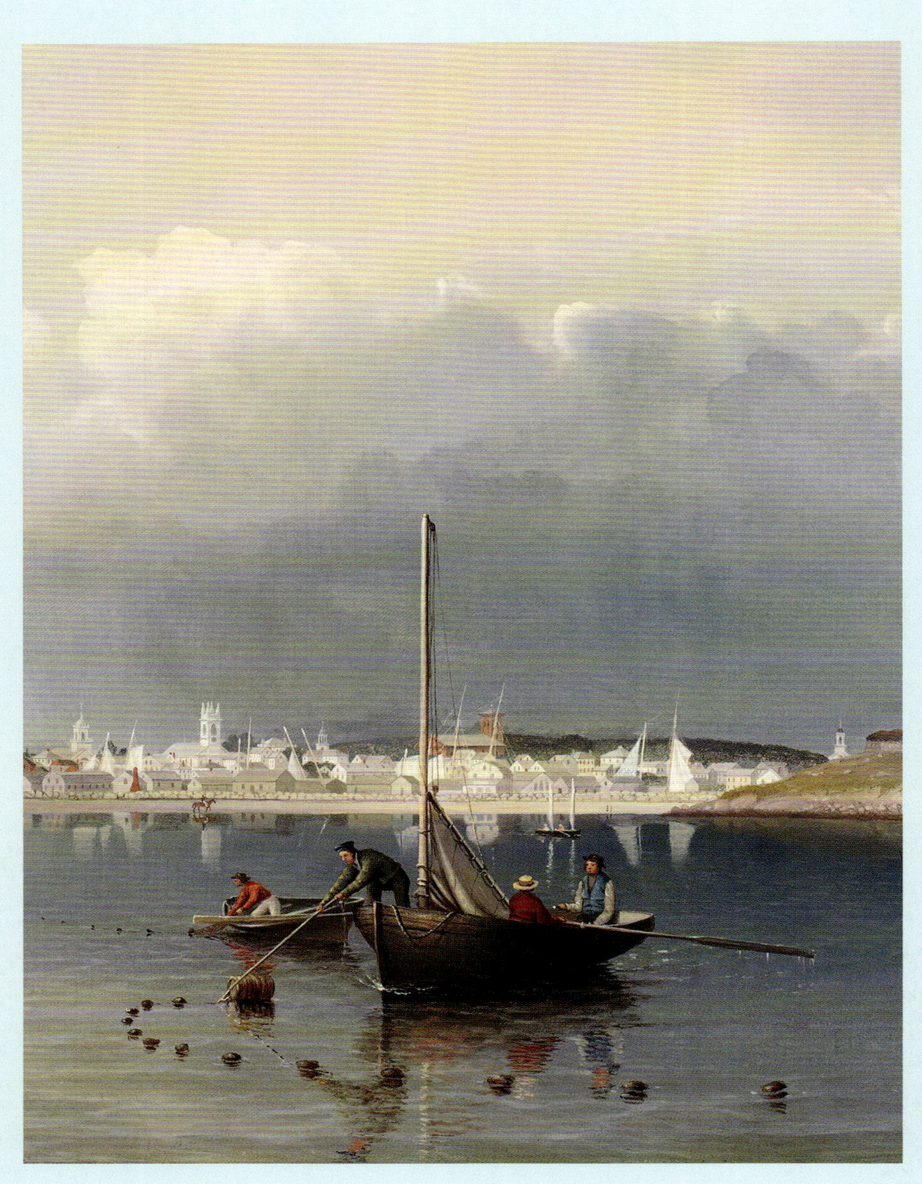

INTRODUCTION

A Small City with a Far Reach

In 1848 Fitz H. Lane designed and had built a stone house perched on a small hill overlooking Gloucester Harbor, the dormer windows of his studio looking out to sea toward Boston, thirty-three miles to the southwest, and beyond, toward the Caribbean and global ports (fig. 1). He was, for the ensuing two decades, the town's artist, painting shop signs, political banners, and fireboards and designing parade floats for schoolchildren, but he was also painting views of Gloucester, New York, and Baltimore, of Maine and Puerto Rico. His works stand out among nineteenth-century American landscape paintings for their attention to cultural landscape—the harbors, ships, sawmills, hay meadows, and shipyard ways that constituted the quotidian spaces of antebellum economic life. Unlike the wilderness views favored by New York City–based artists, Lane's paintings comment on the Atlantic seaboard's agriculture, extraction industries, and settlement patterns, and the workers who labored in these places.

What can we learn about the antebellum United States from Lane? From what he painted and how he painted? Who saw, commissioned, bought, and valued his paintings? For what qualities? What can we learn about canon formation in analyzing the history of Lane's reputation? This study addresses a large and diverse set of artworks depicting labor and habitation in an effort to understand how landscapes painted by Lane were understood by those who commissioned, viewed, and bought them. It also looks "downstream" at how cultural and aesthetic priorities in subsequent generations selected the objects of attention (the canon) and the direction

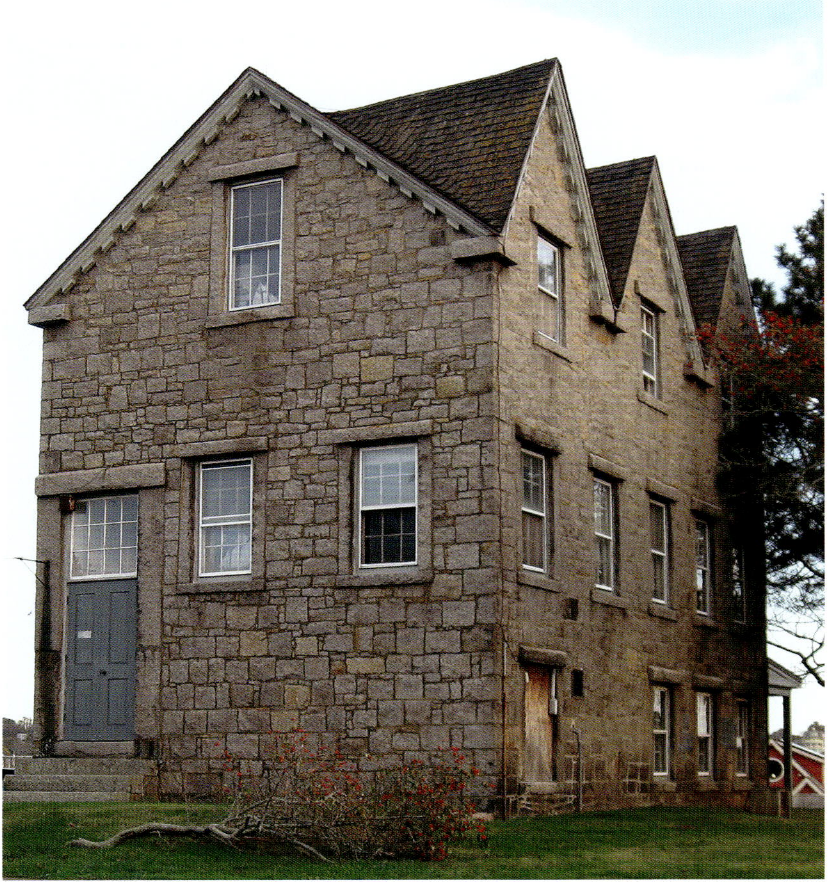

FIGURE 1
Fitz H. Lane, granite house, Gloucester, Massachusetts, 1848–49. Photo: author, 2017.

of scholarly analysis. The project of this study, in other words, is to call attention to the work of a now-celebrated artist from perspectives rather different from those of previous scholars, who have generally celebrated what they understood to be the "sublime," "transcendental," and "luminist" character of some of Lane's works. Instead, this study investigates how Lane's body of work as a whole commented on daily life in the nineteenth century and—through historiographic analysis, provenance tracking, and object biography—how we can better understand canon formation within the field of American art.

The methodological assumption behind this study is that an art object constitutes a text about the context that produced it and, further, that its interpretations provide texts about later contexts that valued and revalued it. This investigation employs the conceptual tools of the cultural historian—thick description, discourse analysis, visual analysis, mobility analysis, and, centrally, deep dives into the archives. This project, above all, aims at a recovery—at reseeing landscapes and their depictions on canvas, insofar as that is possible, with contemporaneous eyes—and it attends to elements of paintings that others dismiss as "incidental detail" but that I believe betray important attitudes toward land, society, history, value, and exchange.[1] The focus is on paintings that emphasize localness and everyday human experience within identifiable settled landscapes, and on the global reach of that localness. It concerns both documentary and nostalgic impulses in nineteenth-century culture; it considers labor, property, money, and economic relations, focusing on the microcosm of coastal New England and the macrocosm of oceanic exchange.

Lane was a Massachusetts artist. This study concerns what he saw in his native Gloucester and in its global marketplace, and what his neighbors saw in his paintings. It is about what Americans for a century after his death declined to see (that is, much value at all in his works), and what Americans in the mid-twentieth century were seeing that spurred them to "discover" and celebrate, buy and exhibit, Lane's paintings. Art objects provide a particularly eloquent kind of cultural touchstone; their reputation is not just calibrated on an absolute scale of accomplishment but responds to broader, unpredictable streams of culture. Time passes, culture changes; paintings on canvas—if they receive adequate care—remain the same. This "sameness" allows us to measure the flow and eddies of public opinion—the opinions of critics, historians, recipients of bequests and gifts, viewers at exhibitions, and bidders at auctions. Each Lane painting has followed a singular trajectory through time and space, yet together they have traced a pathway from modest local renown, through a profound abyss of oblivion in which even the artist's name was forgotten and gifts of his works to urban art institutions were quietly regifted elsewhere, to the heights of national praise and recognition his works enjoy today.

The project of this book is to attend to Lane's depiction of land, water, sky, and ships but also, centrally, to the figures in the paintings, not as scale-giving "staffage" or as actors in the vernacular dramas known as genre painting but as the cocreators of the landscape that the painter records and interprets. These figures are farmers and artisans, mariners and laborers; the paintings are about their work. The artist describes relationships between land and living, between earning and social experience, with canny exactitude. Above all, extractive industries such as lumbering in Maine, fishing in the North Atlantic, and quarrying granite at Cape Ann were, I argue, central to Lane's vision of the geographies he observed and portrayed for his patrons. This study also investigates the artist's participation in the emerging culture of looking—that is, tourism and "summering" in coastal New England. Equally haunting these canvases is an acute awareness—on the part of the artist, his patrons, and his publics—of the threads of commerce that linked Gloucester to Dutch Guiana, Spanish Puerto Rico, and newly acquired Alta California. Unseen in the background of these pictures and in the foreground of the artist's studio, manual and craft labor were compensated; money changed hands, as the surface of the earth and the surface of the canvas record labor and invite looking.

Since David Huntington's groundbreaking *Landscapes of Frederic Edwin Church: Vision of an American Era*, much of the scholarly literature on nineteenth-century American landscape painting has addressed this substantial category of art in terms of the cultural work some of these stunning canvases performed in the interest of tales of national self-definition. Privileging paintings that depict "wilderness" and the wonders of nature—Niagara, the Rocky Mountains, Yosemite Valley—the tendency has been to understand the best-known nineteenth-century American landscape paintings as exemplars of the Sublime and as parables of political ambition. Physically brought into the halls of Congress as evidence, specific paintings in this grand manner and mammoth plate photographs participated actively in the creation of public policy, the invention of U.S. national parks as preserves of nature at its most dramatic, and in the development of national ideologies about wildness, wilderness, and conservation.[2] They also, as Huntington argued, endorsed the rapacious doctrine of Manifest Destiny.[3] Most harshly, landscapes in this vein have been labeled "the 'dreamwork' of imperialism."[4] More recently, Rebecca Bedell, Rachael DeLue, and Jennifer Raab have urged interpretations more scientific than political, calling attention to the points of intersection between theories evolving in the sciences and the minutely observed portrayal of rocks, flora, and fauna incorporated into even the most operatic of canvases.[5] Geology, biology, and period ideas about vision have now been incorporated into our awareness of how ambitious landscape artists thought and worked.

The more modestly scaled paintings focusing on everyday landscapes under uncommon light conditions by some nineteenth-century artists (including Lane) have been consistently interpreted since the 1960s as evocative of the spiritual thrust of contemporary New England philosophers, especially Ralph Waldo Emerson's transcendentalism.[6] This study takes another tack in considering the work of Lane, embracing what many scholars eschew as the merely topographical, or the "distracting . . . narrative elements," in his work.[7] Here I attend closely to the subjects and places depicted (and referenced) in Lane's explicitly *inhabited* landscapes, and to the patrons who supported his career, with an eye to understanding how New Englanders understood their land, their economy, their history, and their links with widely disparate global communities. In this reading, Lane's works depict nature as productive and allied with humans to create a sustainable balanced political economy. As stunning as the grand subjects recorded by Church, Thomas Moran, and other contemporaries, Lane's domesticated landscapes, seascapes, and harborscapes provide insights into issues of patronage, taste, and achievement that revise and temper the lessons of the expansive nature-centered "wilderness" images of Church, Moran, and Albert Bierstadt and potentially turn our assumptions about the relationship between culture and nature, between landscape and ideology, on their head.

David Huntington and his successors have correctly identified the impulse in much nineteenth-century American painting and culture to describe nature as a wilderness on which the young nation might freely inscribe its future: the United States as a virgin land—an unplowed, unfenced, and unpainted land. Insofar as it exhibited evidence of a past, its traces pointed to a geologic or cosmic, not a human, past. But what emerges from a close look at Lane's New England is a picture not only of a land *not* lacking human history (that is, not a "virgin wilderness") but of a land deeply resonant of former uses and human history. While Lane has been interpreted for some decades as a protomodernist, I argue that in his impulse to record landscapes soon to be lost, he is equally an antimodernist. Moreover, his backward glance is toward a history that incorporates rather than excludes Native Americans as shapers of land and as agents of history.

These are the basic facts: Lane was born in 1804 in Gloucester, Massachusetts, on Cape Ann, and died there in 1865.[8] The son of a sailmaker, he was christened Nathaniel Rogers Lane. His two brothers were taught by a noted local mathematician, navigator, and surveyor; he was not.[9] Probably because he was lame (possibly from childhood polio), Lane was trained to the sedentary trade of shoemaker.[10] In 1832, at the age of twenty-eight, he changed his name to Fitz Henry Lane, decided to become a lithographer, and moved to Boston.[11] After an apprenticeship at Pendleton's, in 1845 he established his own lithographic firm in partnership with John White Allen Scott. That same year he was in contact with Robert Salmon, a seventy-five-year-old English marine painter working in Boston, as evidenced by the younger painter's inscription on *The Yacht* Northern Light *in Boston Harbor*: "Painted by F. H. Lane from a sketch by / Salmon / 1845" (Shelburne Museum).[12] By 1849 Lane had acquired an "Esq." honorific, become a proficient painter exhibiting and selling "marine paintings," and moved back to Gloucester, where he designed and built his substantial Gothic Revival granite house, not in the polite part of town, but near the harbor at Duncan's Point, a site surrounded by sail lofts, icehouses, a slaughterhouse, and warehouses in the industrial heart of Gloucester's fish-packing and ship-refurbishing industries (fig. 2).[13] In a town that at times had three women for every man, he never married, sharing his home with his sister, brother-in-law (a window-sash maker), and their eight children.[14] Most of his paintings are of Gloucester and of the coast of Maine where he spent many summers. A solo practitioner in a town with no exhibition space for art, Lane was not a member of a "school"; indeed, after his early years in Boston, he seems to have had little contact with other artists. Probably about half of Lane's paintings were done speculatively, and about half were commissioned, often from pencil sketches made on site and worked up, in oil on canvas, in his dormered attic

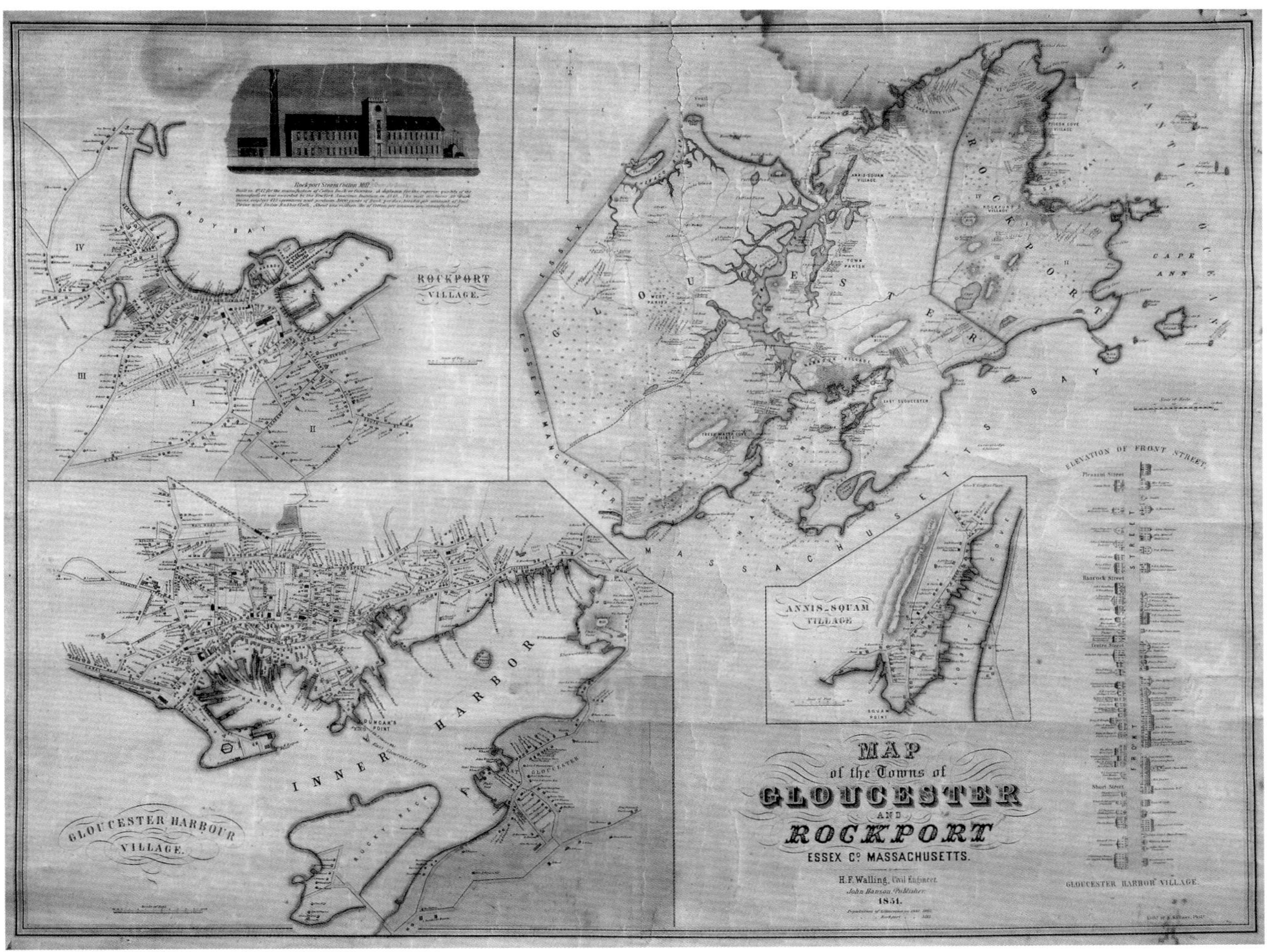

FIGURE 2
Henry Francis Walling, *Map of the Towns of Gloucester and Rockport, Essex Co. Mass.* (Philadelphia: John Hanson, 1851). A. Koliner, lithographer. Colored lithograph on paper, 34½ × 45 in. (87.63 × 114 cm). Cape Ann Museum Library and Archives, Gloucester, Massachusetts.

studio.[15] He exhibited at the Boston Athenaeum and the National Academy in New York, and made a decent living, although the highest price he received for a work was $500 (at a time when Bierstadt, Church, and Moran could command up to $10,000 for a canvas in New York City).[16] Most of Lane's works appear to have sold for $100 to $200. That is nevertheless a substantial sum: about the cost of a saddle horse or the annual wage of a clerk in a Gloucester dry-goods store.[17]

This book focuses on Lane during his brief two-decade career as a painter, when he was a mature and locally recognized Gloucester artist, even a household name, as we learn from one diarist in that community of about eight thousand souls:

> This week our harbor has presented a beautiful and unusual appearance. More than five hundred vessels at anchor during a storm & as it cleared they all spread their snowy sails and glided off like a vapour. I thought few sights on this earth were more glorious than this. We need not go abroad, across the ocean to admire Nature, & the works of God and man—we can see them all around us if we but

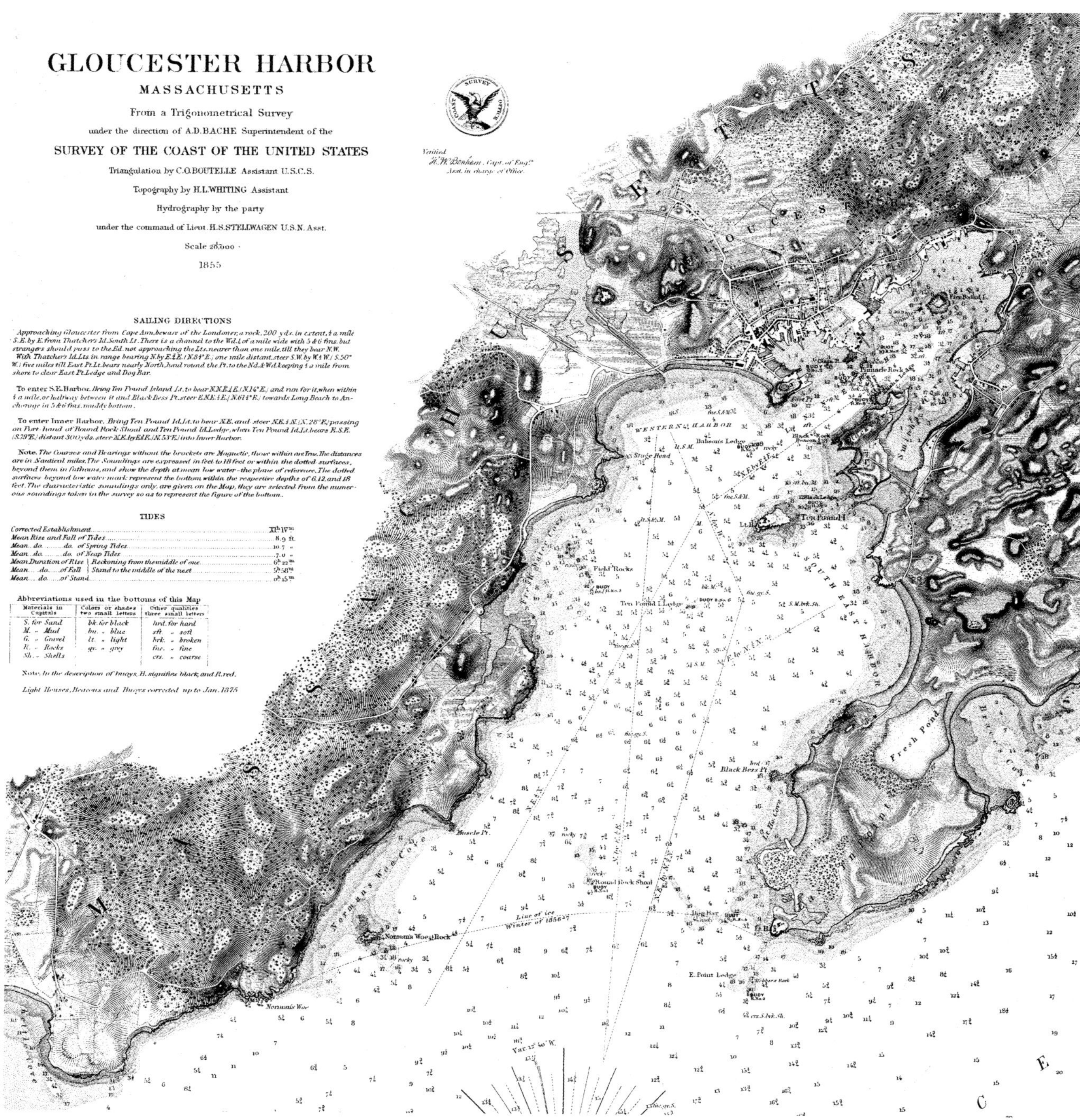

FIGURE 3
A. D. Bache, H. S. Stellwagen, et al., *Survey of the Coast of the United States: Gloucester Harbor, Massachusetts* (1855, updated 1875), detail. Engraving on paper, 30 × 23 in. (76.2 × 58.42 cm). Image: National Oceanic and Atmospheric Administration, Office of Coast Survey Historical Map and Chart Collection, https://historicalcharts.noaa.gov.

> open our eyes. . . . While gathering mosses [at Bass Rocks, on the south shore of Cape Ann], we could not keep our eyes from the broad blue sea covered with myriads of white sails. I wished for the genius of a Raphael or even our own artist Fitz Lane to immortalize this perfect ocean scene.[18]

Gloucester, with its commodious southwest-facing harbor (sheltering ships from the winds of New England's frequent devastating storms that blow in from the northeast), was the economic and social hub of Cape Ann and the fishing capital of the nation in those antebellum years (fig. 3). It was a small city with a long reach. As a commentator reported in 1848,

> Gloucester . . . with a sterile soil, that will raise nothing but *men*, and being insulated in its position, it has been obliged to depend on its *own* resources and enterprise for support. Its people have, from the earliest settlement, devoted themselves to the fisheries and the pursuits of commerce. . . . This port has become the centre and head-quarters of the fisheries in the Union. . . . Nearly two hundred vessels are owned at this place . . . [and] Gloucester's extensive . . . trade . . . is only exceeded in foreign commerce in the State by Boston and Salem.[19]

By 1865, when the town's population numbered about ten thousand, Gloucester's fisheries yielded gross receipts of $3,863,152 and employed 4,767 hands.[20] Thus, the townscape through which Lane and his fellow Gloucesterites daily made their way was busy—with the arrival and departure of ships and schooners, with local commerce victualing and repairing these vessels, and with the movement of goods to and from Calcutta, Odessa, Constantinople, Rio de Janeiro, and Dutch Guiana. In paintings such as *Three-Master on the Gloucester Railway* of 1857, Lane records a moment in which one of these oceanic ships dwarfs the town into which it and a companion schooner temporarily intrude in dry dock for repairs and repainting (fig. 4). Lane's town was *about* these ships and about what they carried—fish gathered from the North Atlantic, lumber cut on the tributaries of the Penobscot River in Maine, granite quarried in the eastern portion of Cape Ann, and pork, beef, and sheep pastured on the untillable, boulder-strewn fields of the peninsula's interior.[21] But mostly, Gloucester's schooners, brigs, barks, and ships carried fish, fish caught on the banks off New England and Newfoundland, filleted, salted, dried, and packed in barrels for consumption in Spain, Portugal, and the Caribbean.

Contemporary descriptions of New England connect its busy industriousness, technological ingenuity, and financial power to wind power, water power, and steam power and to the extraction industries they all facilitated:

> Our manufacturing interest is beginning to wear a shape that will not bear to be tampered with, or trifled with. New England is alive with machinery—the machinery of water-falls, and congregated seas. The whole seaboard is awake to the privileges which have been secured to her by a charter as old as the skies and as secure as the foundations of the earth, and her whole interior is lighting up with a new spirit—a spirit that will not be rebuked. Her woods are beginning to roar like the sea when it moves with a slow, steady, uninterrupted heave along the whole verge of the Atlantic. Her waters are traveling into new channels—and her woods are vanishing as before a storm. A few years more, and the roughest parts of this rude country will be roaring to the blast of furnaces, and sounding with the din of wheels.[22]

Lane's was a noisy, busy town, in a noisy, busy young nation, and the results of that labor, ingenuity, and harnessed power appeared in the fabric of the ships and townscapes he painted and in the vignettes of purposeful economic activity he included in such images as *Gloucester Harbor* of 1847 and *Gloucester Inner Harbor* of 1850 (figs. 5 and 6). According to one Gloucesterite,

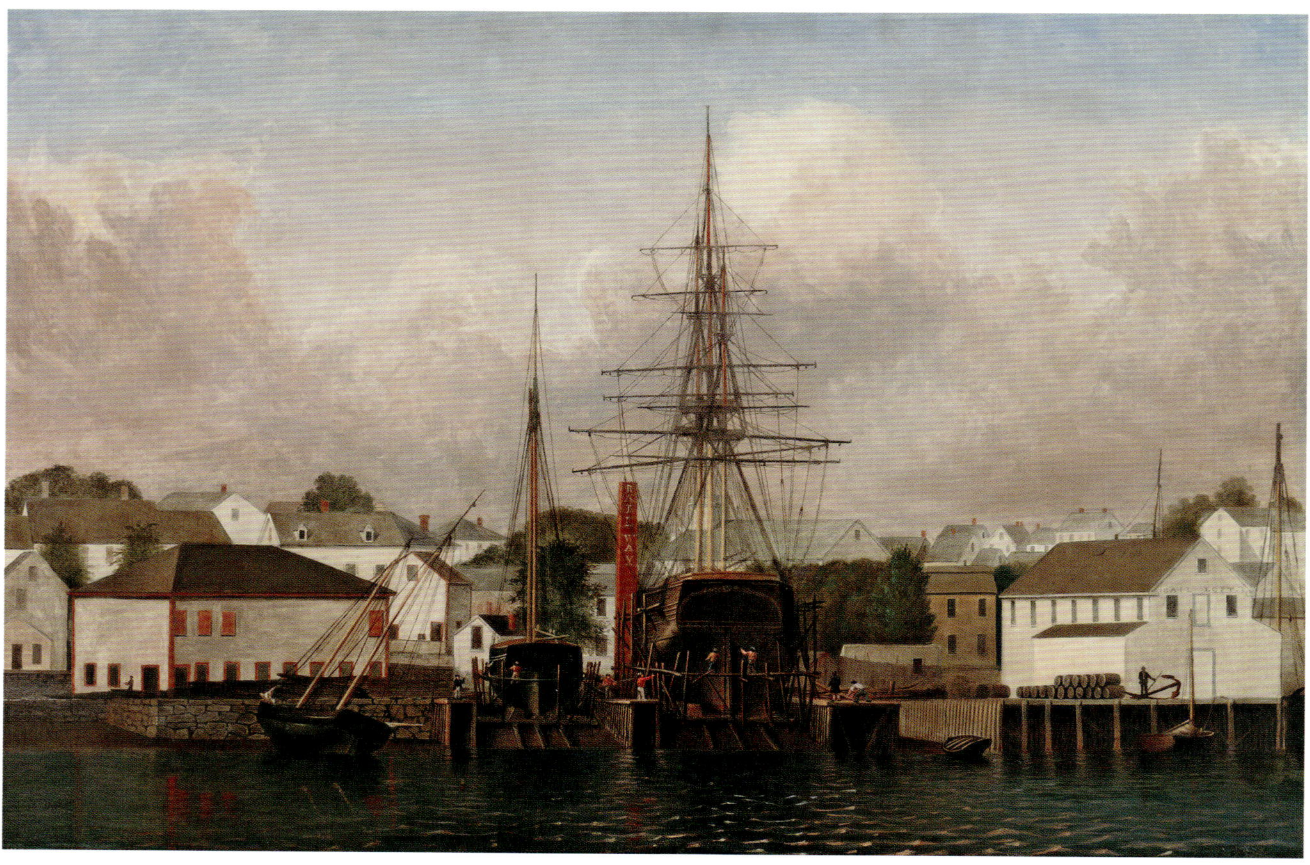

FIGURE 4
Fitz H. Lane, *Three-Master on the Gloucester Railway*, 1857. Oil on canvas, 39¼ × 59¼ in. (99.7 × 150.5 cm). Cape Ann Museum, Gloucester, Massachusetts. Deposited by the City of Gloucester, 1952 (DEP. 202).

the weekday cacophony of the town was "as if noise and confusion had taken everlasting possession of the premises. . . . The hoarse voice of truckmen and waggoners [*sic*] forced by stentorian lungs above the rumbling bass of their wheels,—the discordant song of the stevidore [*sic*], the boisterous mirth of stalworth laborers,—the shouts of seamen and the passionate curses of the profligate,—all blended into one power of sound . . . what a Babel-like confusion." And yet on Sunday, when "[l]abor is at rest;—contention and strife are quieted; man stifles his passions and bows to the spirit of the commandment," the town was invested with a "quietude and almost desert stillness."[23] On Sunday, and on any fair day away from the harbor, Cape Ann, at the edge of a seemingly boundless sea, presented to the leisured wanderer "the vast and sublime solitude of the sea-shore . . . [where] 'the waters touch the beach without a murmur, and our spirit seems, as if it were capable of gliding to eternity, unhurt, upon the tranquil surface of the deep.'"[24] Lane captured his community in both these moods—busy and noisy with the activities of laboring hands and the beasts and tools that aided them in their work, but also quiet and sublime as an unpeopled desert or an endless oceanic expanse.

Gloucester's harbor, as a key hub through which the products of New England's extraction industries passed en route to world markets, was both a small city and a gateway to the globe. With the development of ever more efficient and capacious locally designed and locally built ships, New England's ports became busy and visible sites

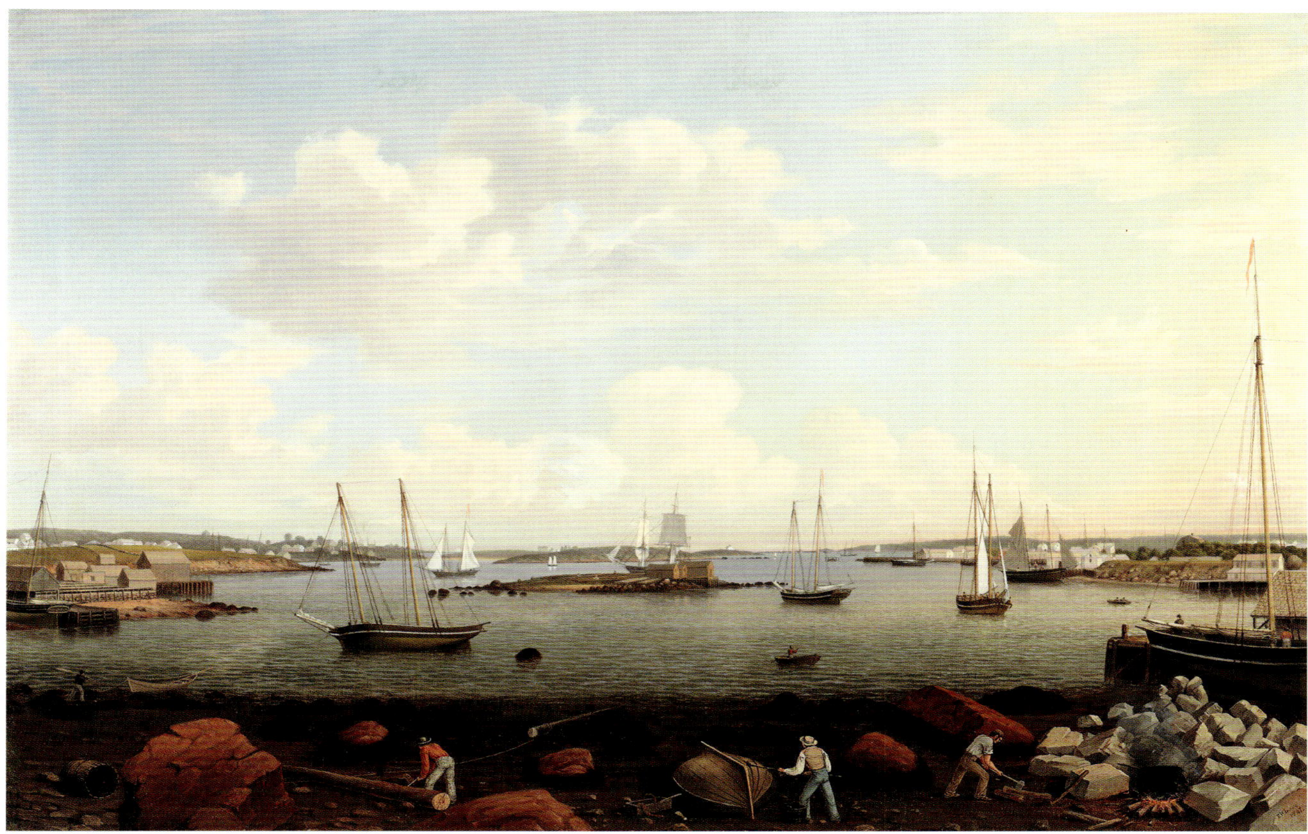

FIGURE 5
Fitz H. Lane, *Gloucester Harbor*, 1847. Oil on canvas, 28½ × 41 in. (71.8 × 104.1 cm). Cape Ann Museum, Gloucester, Massachusetts. Gift of Estate of Samuel H. Mansfield, 1949 (1332.20).

of what its antebellum denizens called "Yankee enterprise." Reading about New England in the January 16, 1830, edition of the *Gloucester Telegraph*, Lane and his neighbors would have recognized themselves and their economy in this brief but pointed article:

> The inhabitants of New England are proverbial for untiring and successful enterprise. They are frightened at no rival—stopped by no obstacle—subdued by no competition. . . .
>
> What people are the most often to be met with on the fishing ground?—The Yankees. What people in the Pacific, in pursuit of oil or furs? The Yankees. Who is he, who barters lumber and onions with the West Indian, beads and red cloth with the Otahetian, rank oil with the Hollander, corn with the Greek, rum, tobacco, snuff, and cast iron muskets with the Africans, cotton with the English and French, pickled fish with the Russians and Danes, flour with the South Americans, opium with the Chinese, and dry knocks [*sic*] with the Algerian? Why, the Yankee. . . . He is every where if a prospect of gain opens that way, and a few days of hard labor is no task for him, if money is to be found at the close.[25]

This robust and positive view of their region and their way of being in the world characterized many of Lane's patrons and, I argue, finds oblique or direct expression in the canvases he painted for them.

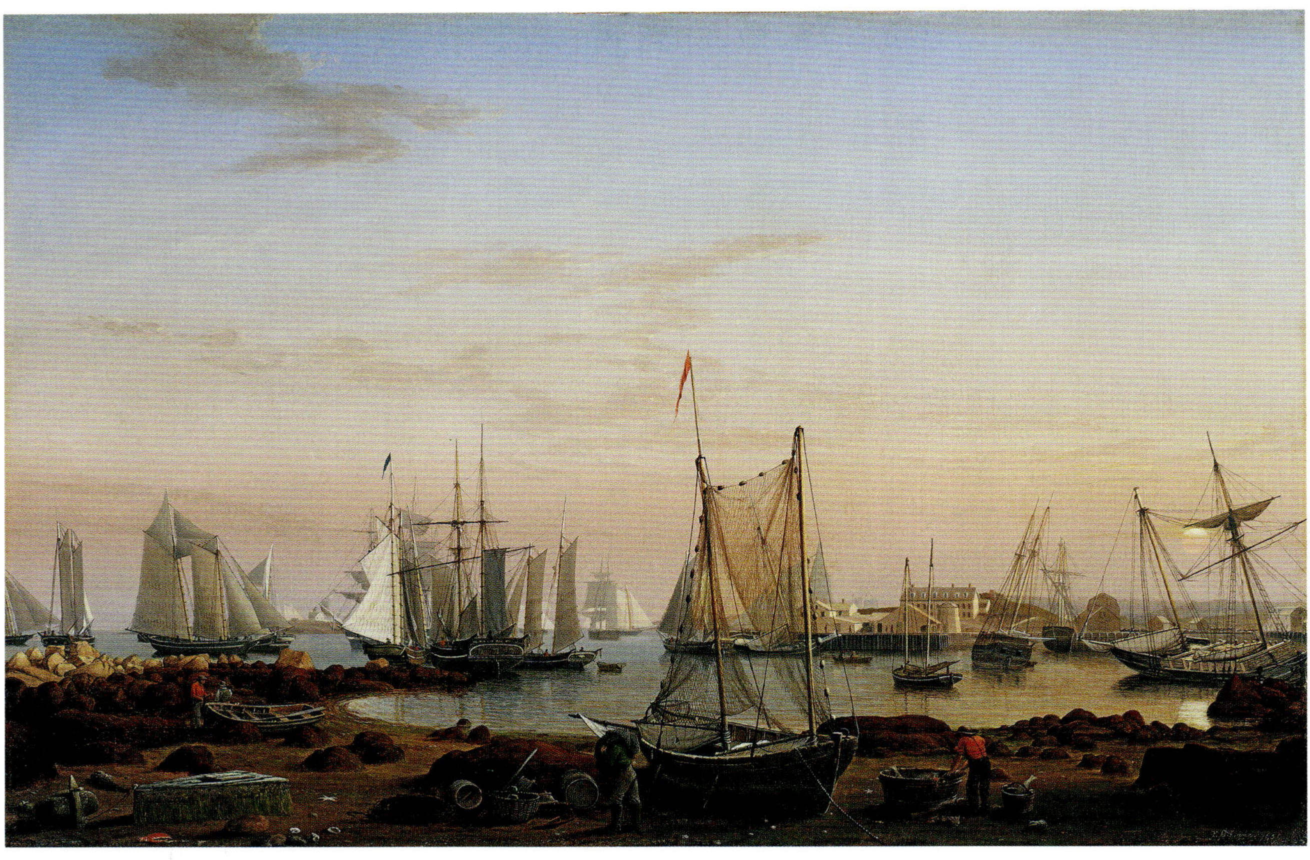

FIGURE 6
Fitz H. Lane, *Gloucester Inner Harbor*, 1850. Oil on canvas, 24 × 36 in. (61 × 91.4 cm). The Mariners' Museum, Newport News, Virginia (1946.0830.000001/QO 0710).

The records of Lane's career as an artist are few—he left no diaries or memoirs, no account book listing works and sales. We have only a few letters to and from him, 110 drawings annotated by his friend Joseph L. Stevens Jr. (1823–1908), some brief posthumous accounts by friends and kin, and several newspaper notices about his works and life (many of these clipped and assembled in a scrapbook by an unknown contemporary).[26] There are also glimpses of Lane in local diaries—such as that of Annette Babson quoted above—in public records such as tax lists, in the exhibition records of the Boston Athenaeum and other art venues (see appendix A), and in the account books of Gloucester businesses, which record, for example, his rentals of horse and gig or sleigh from the local livery stable, presumably for sketching excursions around Cape Ann and inland.[27] We know he spent early years in Boston, many summers in Maine, and probably, from the evidence of paintings and lithographs by his hand, he also traveled to Providence, Norwich, New York, Baltimore, and possibly Puerto Rico. There are several historic inventories of Lane paintings—indicating title and owner in 1892, 1916, 1938, and 1961—that provide useful information concerning his cohort of patrons and the downstream record of his works (see appendix B). These lists are less helpful than one might hope. The titles of Lane's paintings are notoriously unstable, reflecting many misidentifications and reidentifications of the sites depicted—one Lane painting has been exhibited, for instance, in the last four decades under eight different names.[28] But these lists point to one key fact in the history of Lane's reputation and in the survival of his works—while Lane's reputation plummeted within months of his death, one or two individuals in each subsequent generation, convinced of the enduring value of his paintings, drawings, and lithographs, exerted themselves to preserve his memory and his works for a moment of reputation resurrection, which finally arrived in the mid-twentieth century.[29] This is a rather scanty archive, one that sends us to the paintings themselves to find out about the artist, and to a whole host of other primary sources to learn about his social, economic, and artistic context.

There are probably several hundred extant Lane paintings—a partial but very useful online catalogue raisonné of his work has been undertaken by the Cape Ann Museum.[30] Somewhat confusing the picture of determining Lane's oeuvre, there are both signed and not-yet-identified or -attributed copies executed by his students and by contemporary copyists. These include Mary B. Mellen, Salisbury Tuckerman, Harriet Mason, Ada C. Bowles, William Bradford, Jerome Elwell, F. L. Palmer, and Henry J. Pierce; and he is known to have made copies of his own works.[31] Probably about half Lane's extant paintings are signed on the face—sometimes in vermillion paint in the lower right corner, sometimes on the back of a stretcher; but occasionally his signature appears slyly within the fiction of the image—as in *Salem Harbor* (MFA; see fig. 34).[32] Other paintings were signed (and sometimes the locale named) on the reverse, such as *View of Coffin's Beach* (MFA), but many have been relined and these data lost.[33] Of the signed paintings, about half are also dated, and these provide signposts to specific moments in Lane's career. The works that form the basis of the analysis and discussion here are signed by Lane or appear to be well provenanced to his hand. This book is not a life-and-works account of this artist's career, focusing on the artist's "influences," "development," and "achievement." Rather, it looks closely at singular works and at groups of works that speak to central concerns for those living in the Gloucester and New England of antebellum America and, to a lesser extent, a century later, in Cold War America.

The book as a whole considers not only the production and reception of Lane's paintings but also, as noted above, the downstream life of his oeuvre and of his reputation. It positions the paintings as actors instructing generations of viewers in how to see Gloucester and coastal Maine, commerce and labor, extraction industries and summer leisure. Through the eloquent lens of Lane's work, it investigates the roles that memory, time, profit, a sense of local community, and global trade played in antebellum culture. And it also looks at the different concerns of subsequent generations.

What this book emphasizes is not Lane's status as a "Luminist" or his expertise in marine matters but rather the way Lane, unlike any other painter of his day, painted the social economy that revolved around ships, such as that pictured in *Lumber Schooners at Evening on Penobscot Bay* (fig. 7). It attends to what these ships and boats are carrying, to what this working landscape is *doing*. This is a quiet painting about light and an accurate painting about rigging, but it is also a painting about the movement of goods (in this case, lumber) from one place to another, a painting whose convincing magic is achieved through a wonderful rendering of many details and overall mood.

Like the work of mid-nineteenth-century poets of the quotidian and the common such as Emily Dickinson, these paintings are about nonevents, everyday things, things that happen over and over. Lane depicts Time extracted from History—that is, from the notable chronicle of unique events, Important events. He paints the cycles of the day (dawn, noon, dusk), the cycles of the tides, and the cycle of the seasons. In such works as *Lumber Schooners* Lane paints, not the spectacle of "untouched" Nature in the wilderness or the awesome power of unique topographical features such as Niagara Falls, but rather the small details

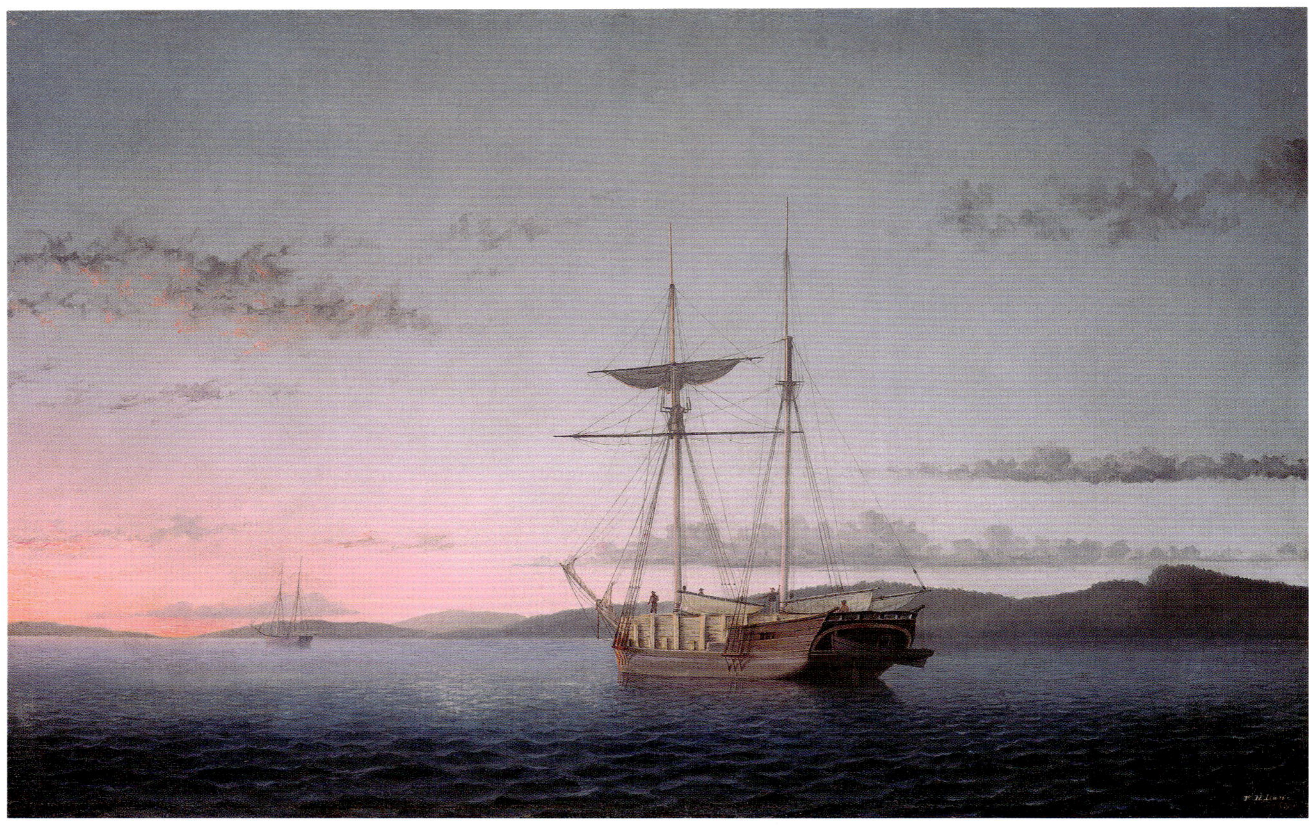

FIGURE 7
Fitz H. Lane, *Lumber Schooners at Evening on Penobscot Bay*, 1863. Oil on canvas, 24 ⅝ × 38⅛ in. (62.5 × 96.8 cm). National Gallery of Art, Washington, DC. Gift of Mr. and Mrs. Francis W. Hatch Sr. (1980.29.1).

that make the cultural geography of the New England coast work as economic geography.

In a rather different but equally characteristic canvas, *View of Gloucester from "Brookbank," the Sawyer Homestead*, one little sloop awaits a higher tide, while another nudges toward a stone pier that marks the point of marine contact between this homestead and the distant town of Gloucester, the larger community with which this farm aligns itself (fig. 8). The social geography of this place, "Brookbank," is interdependent with the economic geography of that place, Gloucester, seen as a line of white buildings and churches in the center distance. In the foreground a complicated but precise assembly of stone walls and rail and picket fencing marks units of agricultural land use. This is a pastoral household—a single cow represents milk, butter, cheese, meat, and hides. The amplitude of rocks and absence of row crops suggest that it is a grazing economy linked to a ready nearby market that keeps a sturdy barn and rolling meadowlands in tidy shape. The key implied ingredients are human labor and ingenuity on the one hand, and linkage to larger communities and economies on the other. Indeed, the owner of "Brookbank" at Sawyer's Hill, on the edge of Freshwater Cove on the western arm of Gloucester Harbor, could commission such a canvas just because he was so well plugged into the local economy.

Gloucester was Lane's primary subject: Ten Pound Island, Dolliver's Neck, Brace's Rock, Norman's Woe, and here Freshwater Cove and Sawyer's Hill—these names are familiar to those who know Lane's work. He painted these sites repeatedly, usually for Gloucester patrons,

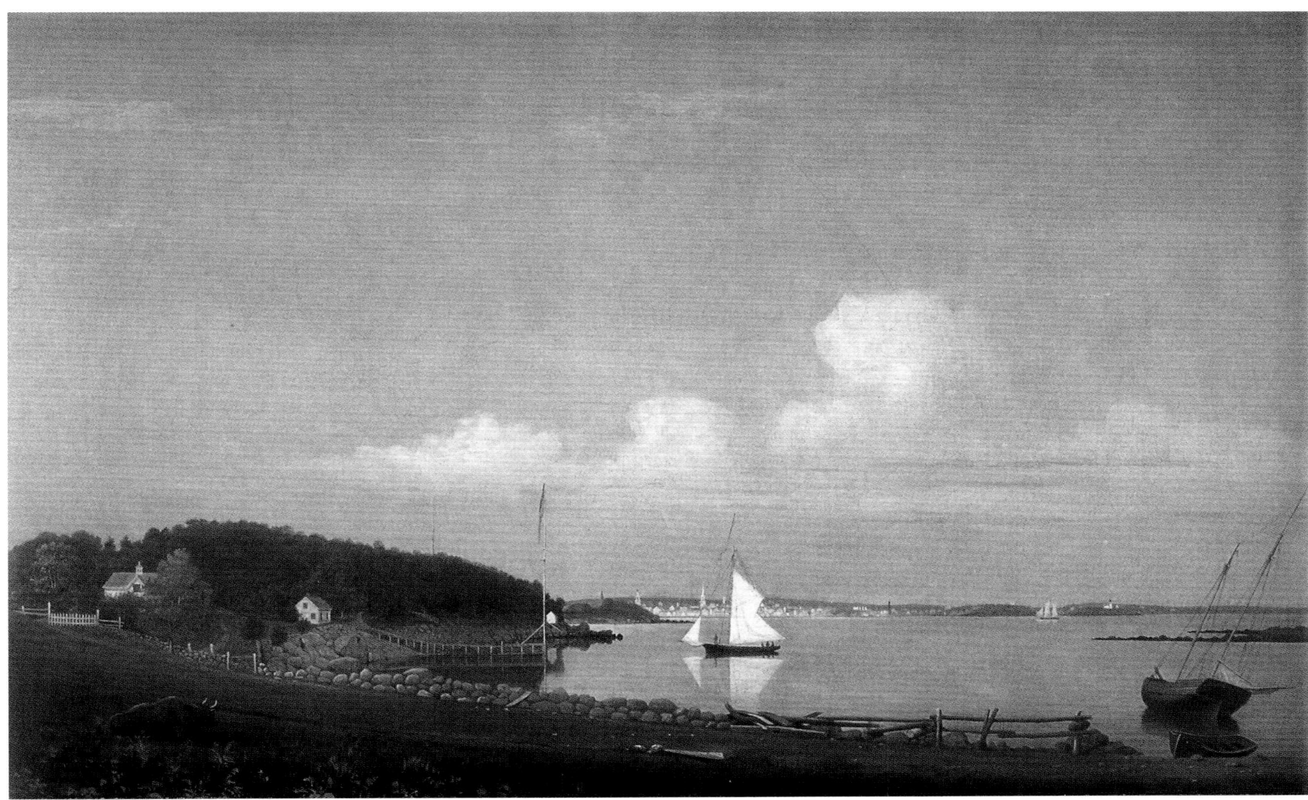

FIGURE 8
Fitz H. Lane, *View of Gloucester from "Brookbank," the Sawyer Homestead*, n.d. Oil on canvas, 18 × 30 3/16 in. (45.7 × 76.7 cm). Carnegie Museum of Art, Pittsburgh. Acquired through the generosity of the Sarah Mellon Scaife Family (77.5). Photo © 2017 Carnegie Museum of Art, Pittsburgh.

sometimes for former Gloucesterites who had established themselves and their businesses elsewhere, in Boston and New York. Lane's principal patron was the son of the surveyor John Mason, who drew a splendid map of Cape Ann and had it printed by Senefelder Lithographic Co. in Boston the year before Lane went to work for that firm to learn the practice of lithography (fig. 9). Here the sheltering coves and harbors, the interior roadways and mills, the sites of wrecks and of summer picnics so familiar to Lane and his patrons are carefully described.

How about Lane himself, how cosmopolitan were his horizons? I am proposing that Lane, like his fellow coastal New Englanders, acted locally but thought globally. He was deeply aware of the webs of money, goods, technology, and mutual interest that bound the farm and the ship to the town, and even the smallest American towns to the most distant ports, in the early nineteenth century. He was a painter of common events but not of isolated instances. Everything in his canvases suggests connection. The universe of tiny unhistoric events Lane paints is a natural world—often, but not always, a benign and hospitable world—in which people have deposited objects of use. Lane—the son of a sailmaker, trained as a shoemaker, sharing his home with his window-sash-maker brother-in-law—was embedded in an artisanal view of his world. If there exists a painter who had what James Elkins has called "an 'unalienated, insider's apprehension of the land' [and] . . . an everyday experience of landscape," it was Lane.[34] And what he apprehended and portrayed was what J. B. Jackson has called "a coherent

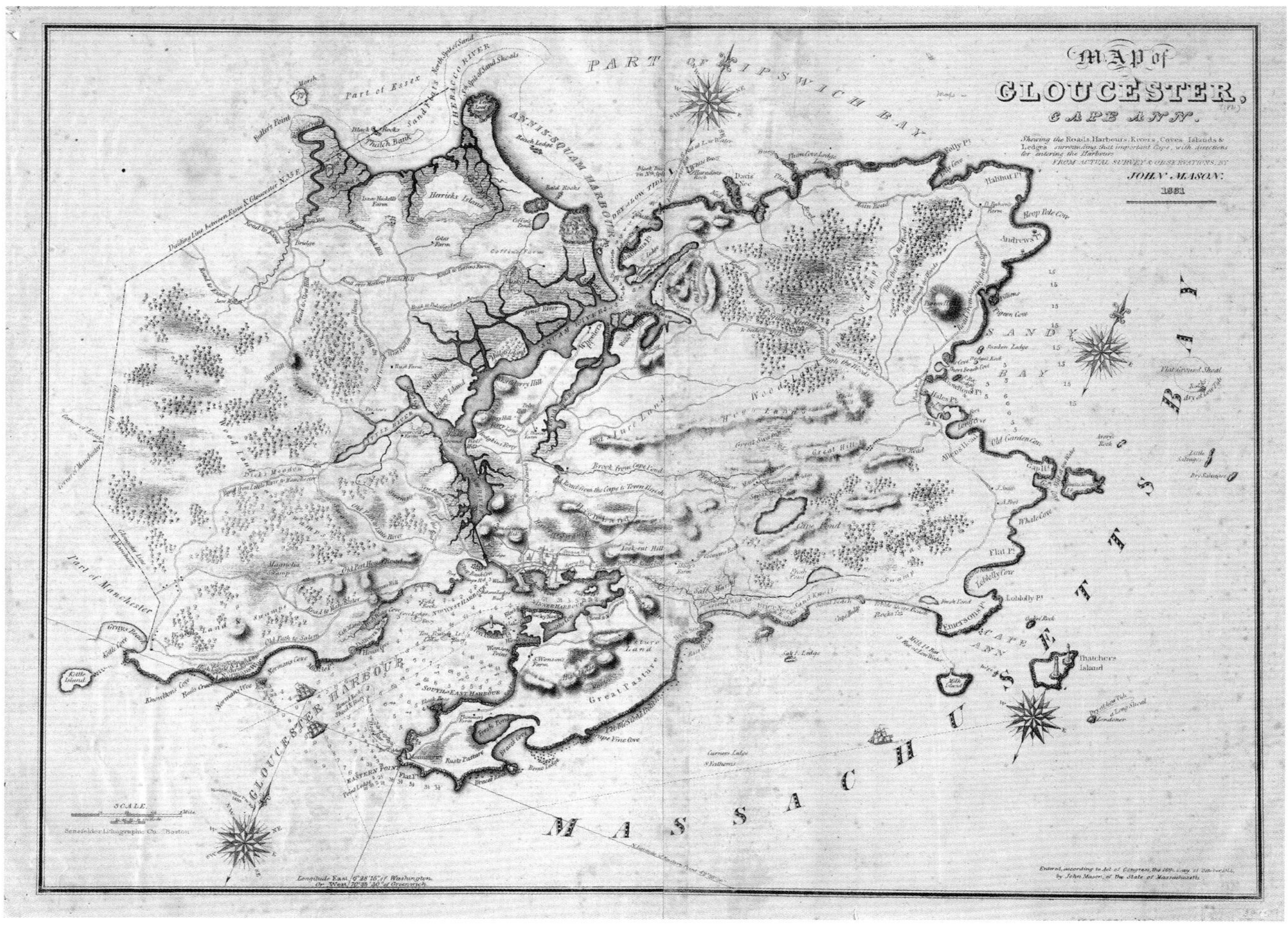

FIGURE 9
John Mason, *Map of Gloucester, Cape Ann* (Senefelder Lithographic Co., Boston, 1831). Lithograph on paper, 20½ × 27½ in. (51 × 70 cm). Sold by W. E. P. Rogers, Gloucester. Courtesy of Harvard Map Collection.

workable landscape [that] evolves where there is a coherent definition of man's relation to the world and to his fellow men."[35]

The objects Lane painted—buildings, fences, ships—were engineered and designed, but not deliberately aestheticized. These are frank, sturdy, geometric structures portrayed in a brushless, seemingly clinical hand. And yet they appear to record two things beyond their straightforward forms. First, they seem vibrant with the artist's visual curiosity; and second, they seem to suggest the record of old places, places inhabited by European Americans for centuries before Lane made his pictorial records.

The facts of daily life recorded in *Gloucester Harbor* of 1852—fishermen setting nets, steeples and sails marking aspirations and ventures, brigs and schooners moving goods and people, the intractable geometry of the fort sitting on a grassy promontory in the middle distance—add up to more than the sum of their parts (fig. 10). Townscapes such as this or farmscapes such as *"Brookbank"* are not the paintings by Lane that appear in twentieth- and twenty-first-century texts on nineteenth-century American painting or that fetch the highest prices on today's market. Those tend to be the emptier canvases, like *Lumber Schooners* (fig. 7), in which ocean and sky predominate, in which there are few reminders of the domestic or

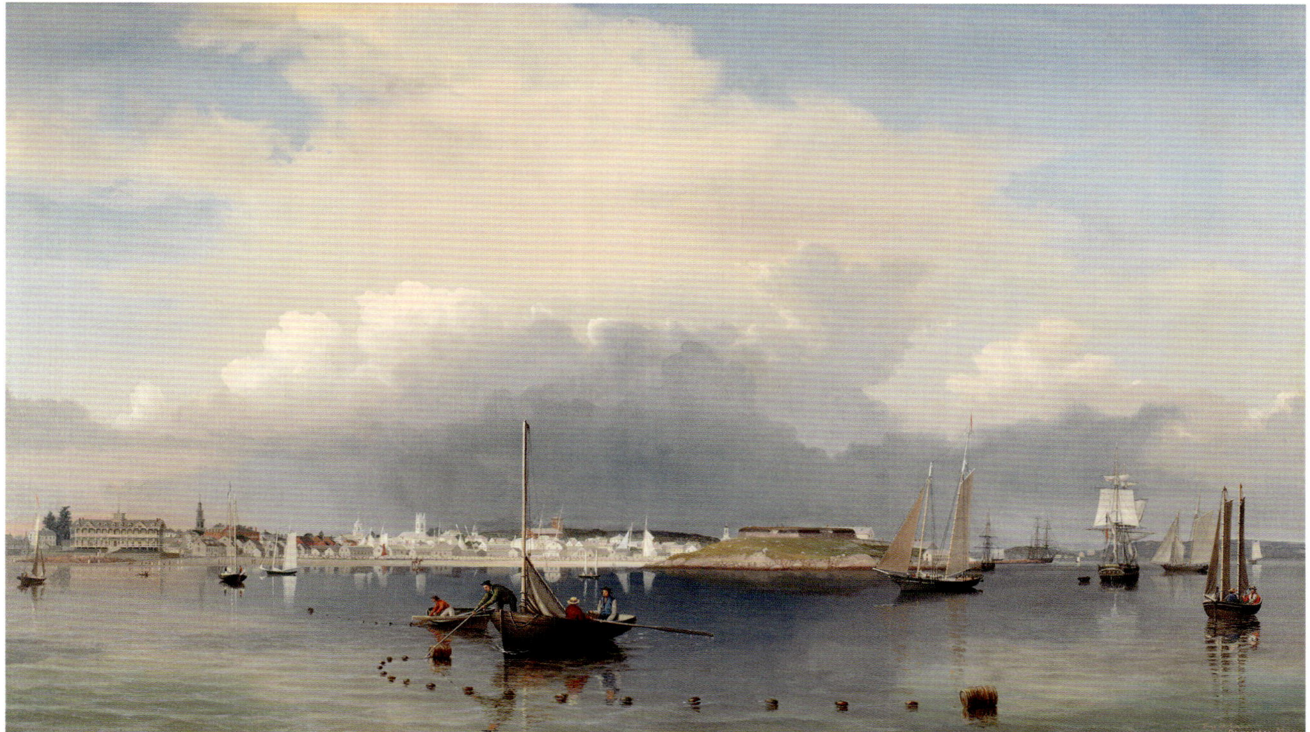

FIGURE 10
Fitz H. Lane, *Gloucester Harbor*, 1852. Oil on canvas, 28 × 48½ in. (71.1 × 123.2 cm). Commissioned by Sidney Mason. Cape Ann Museum, Gloucester, Massachusetts. Deposited by the City of Gloucester, 1952; gift to the City from Cassie Mason Myers Julian-James, 1913 (DEP. 200).

the agricultural, just suggestions of human daring and the haunting depths of the elements. The harborscapes seem too tied to individual facts, to ordinary, unmythic dimensions of daily life for most art historians. But I propose that in these townscape, farmscape, and harborscape paintings by Lane (which I find central to his project), and in the relationships between these canvases and the emptier works, the two kinds considered together, we see, above all, this: a record of relationships between land, individual labor, and broader economic and temporal communities.

Painting the Inhabited Landscape comprises eight chapters; the first, "Reputation," discusses the arc of Lane's self-fashioning as a painter. The second, "Value," is a case study in canon formation. It tracks and analyzes the dramatic reversals in Lane's reputation after his death in 1865 as it plummeted to a nadir of nothingness and then rose—in response to events in American cultural history, including the ascent of modernism and the search for its roots in an American past—to its current extraordinary heights. Succeeding chapters discuss key facets of antebellum America as Lane commented on them in singular paintings or in clusters of related paintings.

"Canvas" investigates Lane's complex personal identity, circling around issues of naming, renaming, and misnaming; Lane's father's canvas-based trade as a crafter of sails for Gloucester's ships; Lane's choices of canvas and his choices of signatures; and the role of canvas factories in Gloucester's local economy. How did this son of a sailmaker, who knew how to trim sails and make shoes, understand his vocation as a painter? Did he see himself as a poet (a keen observer), a craftsman, or an artist in the great Western tradition of Raphael (as invoked by one contemporary noted above)?

"Fish" foregrounds Gloucester's principal industry—the extraction of cod, mackerel, halibut, pollock, and hake from the North Atlantic. Lane models fishing in the foreground of *Gloucester Harbor* of 1852, commissioned by Sidney Mason, son of the mapmaker, and Lane's major patron (fig. 10). Some of Gloucester's fish was sold and consumed fresh, but most was salted, dried, packed in barrels, and exported. In Lane's early lithograph *View of the Town of Gloucester*, he foregrounds the long tables on which the fish were dried in one of the town's many flake yards (fig. 11). Lane's *Gloucester Harbor* includes, on the far left, a portrait of Mason's Pavilion Hotel, the town's first resort hotel, yoking together the long-established fish economy with New England's nascent economy, figured in the foreground, of touring, summering, and looking.

"Lumber" inquires into the nature of Maine's lumbering industry and into its distant markets. By 1850, when Lane was making annual painting trips to the state, the yearly timber crop of Maine was worth almost six million dollars.[36] His seemingly quiet *Lumber Schooners at Evening on Penobscot Bay* depicts one moment in the career of one of hundreds of coasters that carried this profitable crop south: to Gloucester, Boston, Charleston, the West Indies, even Australia. Implicit in all Lane's paintings are the artisanal acts and know-how that used the lumber temporarily afloat in *Lumber Schooners* to construct the houses, barrels, and barns of antebellum America (fig. 7). One feels here and elsewhere in his work the artist's profound respect for the designers of ships, the riggers of spars, but also the loaders of wood, the builders of homes, and the crafters of barrels and buckets. This is a poetic image, but it is also an image of labor and capital at work. This chapter also considers traces in Lane's paintings of seventeenth-century conflicts in Maine between Native Americans and settlers from Massachusetts, including Lane's ancestors.

The primary fact in the life, culture, and economy in antebellum New England is its granitic substrate, the focus of chapter 6, "Granite." Providing building material, discouraging row-crop farming, and creating the region's primary marine hazard, granite is a major subject in Lane's work, and the material of which he—somewhat eccentrically—constructed his home (fig. 1).

The "Travelers" chapters (7 and 8) focus on four distant locales linked to Gloucester, important to Lane's patrons and, in some cases, directly referenced in the artist's paintings: Surinam, California, China, and Puerto Rico. Pointing out the square-rigged three-masted ship on the right in Lane's 1852 *Gloucester Harbor*, for instance, the local newspaper some years later described these vessels as "Surinamers . . . some [of] the large fleet that at that time was engaged in a lucrative business with Dutch Guiana, bringing cargos of sugar, molasses and other tropical goods from that country and taking out cargoes of dried fish and other New England products" (fig. 10).[37] Much of the fish Gloucesterites harvested from the North Atlantic was exported to Surinam to provide protein for the slaves whose labor lay at the base of this profitable economy. California, similarly, was a prominent but abstract presence in Gloucester from 1848, when the names of some of the ships that Lane painted, such as the *Golden State*, marked a major disruptive undercurrent in the culture and pointed to the challenge that California gold leveled at New Englanders, their shipping, their economy, their understanding of the relation between land and labor, and their place in history. In a certain light Lane's work can be seen as an anchor against the seductive siren song of the West, its placer nuggets luring young men into severing their tethers to the lifeways of their fathers. Similarly, distant China was the source of Lane patron Robert Bennet Forbes's considerable wealth, and he engaged the artist to portray vessels he designed and had built to engage in the China trade, as well as to portray his humanitarian mission to Ireland and to illustrate his tracts on naval architecture.

Puerto Rico was a key locale for Lane's primary patron, Sidney Mason, a Gloucesterite who left the town as a twelve-year-old to be trained in a Boston counting house. By his early twenties he owned a plantation in Puerto Rico and was serving as the first U.S. consul there. He married into the local Creole business aristocracy and employed Edward Bliss Emerson, one of Ralph Waldo Emerson's brothers, in his San Juan counting house. In 1840 Mason moved to New York City, where he started one of the first horsecar rail lines, built the first marble mansion on Fifth Avenue, and filled it with paintings, including many by Lane, and elaborate mahogany furniture made from trees on his Puerto Rico plantation. He rode his horse daily, often with the historian George Bancroft and with Frederick Law Olmsted, observing the construction of Central Park.[38] Lane paintings would have served as instruments of memory, shorthand metaphors to mentally transport Mason and family members to whole clusters of associations concerning personal, familial, and national history. The narratives prompted by these paintings make clear that interpretations of nineteenth-century American art need to expand to encompass a much more cosmopolitan view of the role these works played in the complex lives of those who commissioned them. These two chapters also consider the provenance of some of Lane's canvases painted for these peripatetic patrons in their descent to the present, picking up on the central concerns of the opening chapters: reputation, canon formation, and object biography.

The fish, lobster, granite, and lumber Lane painted were netted, trapped, quarried, and cut with methodical skill, moved to local and distant markets (largely by ships and boats), and garnered sufficient profit to allow most of these Yankees to make a living, and some of them to make a killing. Lane's was a world not of stillness but of movement. His paintings do not, I argue, celebrate a "conflict between civilization and wilderness," as some critics allege, but rather offer buoyant vignettes of the complex system that created things (ships, buildings, objects of use) from the boom-time extractive industries of antebellum New England: fish, granite, timber.[39] Nor does this book position landscape painting in the antebellum United States as an account of "uniqueness, purity and difference from the European norm," which some believe might still be a dominant paradigm in the field.[40] While Lane's images appear to celebrate localness, they in fact tell a story about the well-articulated segments of a much larger, very human global marketplace of ideas, art, and goods. Lane's paintings, I would propose, are not empty canvases full of silence but busy seascapes, landscapes, and townscapes full of purposeful activity tied to thousands of other acts of purposeful, useful, knowledgeable, profitable activity. They are about points of intersection between globally understood social and ecological systems.

And yet many of Lane's works, with their sunset tones and chromatic skies, are contemplative, cool in tone. They do not show axes biting into majestic trees clear-cut forests messy with slash, gasping, thrashing fish en route to a profitable market, or desperate attempts at rescue when wrecks like the prototype of Longfellow's *Hesperus* came to pieces on Cape Ann. Violence and destruction are muted. The viewer's focus is directed toward human know-how and finished product. Lane, in such iconic works as *Lumber Schooners*, does not show violence to the forest because he does not see it. Mobile only with crutches, Lane saw what one could from a road, a porch, a dormer window, the deck of a ship. Records of his attempts to join friends hiking inland are full of their alternating patience and exasperation at his disability.[41] Lane was not Henry David Thoreau or Frederick Church, heading off into the wilderness following the faint trails of trappers and Native Americans, pausing to muse at the abandoned remnants of a remote logging camp. The violence in the forest was not his quest. Lane wanted to see (and record) points of intersection, those sites where one kind of labor interfaced with another, where goods in one state were transformed into another: the sawmill, the harbor, the boatyard. And his visual curiosity was unusually democratic—it took in everything and followed few conventions, satisfied few rules. In many of his images sky and water reflect each other in rhyming ombré expanses of glowing air and polished water, suggesting expansiveness and a mood of well-being. But it is the particularized forms of rocks, sails, trees, lighthouses, homes, and silhouetted figures that read as linked elements in a narrative of place—different, disparate in form and color and distance, but all parts of a single local (and extralocal) ecology and economy.

Lane was not, of course, a boatman, lumberman, mill operator, lobster fisherman, or builder. He was a painter—a particularly smart painter. What he was particularly shrewd in perceiving was the fact that his paintings, with their faintly poignant tone of a record of a world about to be lost, also signaled the arrival of a new economy in Penobscot and Gloucester based not on doing but on seeing, based, in other words, on city people summering, touring, looking; people doing, above all, what the artist did—looking intently. The beachfront Pavilion Hotel prominently bracketing Lane's *Gloucester Harbor* on the left marks the establishment of rail lines, followed almost immediately by the establishment of vacation hotels and boarding houses in antebellum Gloucester and Maine. Lane settled in Gloucester just after the arrival of the rail line, and a year before the building of this, Gloucester's first tourist hotel, by Sidney Mason; and on his first trip to Maine, he sailed into Somes Sound on Mount Desert Island about an hour after the first steamboat arrived.[42] With the help of railroads, scheduled packet boats, and well-equipped hotels, urban visitors began summering in areas that locals had regarded as unproductive wastelands: mountains and beaches. They went there for healthful cool air, and they went there for the view. These are the opening years of vacation culture as we know it. The urbanites hiked, they sailed small boats, and they toured through areas they believed to be beautiful. And touring on site was, as the nineteenth century progressed, increasingly replicated in touring by proxy. Books, prints, journal articles, stereoscope views, and paintings, available to an ever-widening public, enabled prospective tourists, armchair tourists, and nostalgic former tourists to conjure views from distant sites. In the case of several of Lane's patrons, it appears that the appeal of his paintings lay in their clear mapping of social and physical relationships that implied seemingly uncomplicated artisanal, pastoral, and maritime geographies of harmony and wholeness suitable to hang in their decidedly more complicated urban homes in Boston and New York.

Overall, I see Lane as an artist who made paintings of the life and the cultural geography around him, as a native of New England who understood, recorded, and analyzed its prosperity and its connectedness with the wider world. But Lane and his generation also had an eye on something else, and that is the past. Repeatedly, he painted scenes and objects reminiscent of pasts long gone. If Pavilion Hotel tourism brackets the town on one side in Lane's *Gloucester Harbor*, the remains of a Revolutionary War fort bracket it on the other (fig. 10). Gloucester's Old Fort, last active in the War of 1812, sat in the middle of Gloucester's harbor and sits in the middle of many of Lane's paintings as a reminder of the stratigraphy of human existence, as a reminder that each layer, each lifetime, owes its being to predecessors only dimly known and rarely acknowledged.[43] Behind these "quiet" harbor scenes of Gloucester and Maine lie memories of wars, hostility, violence, and death. Here the idea of connection and intersecting paths involves the fourth dimension: time. That there is a retrospective, even antiquarian thread in Lane's production is corroborated by his design for his own house. It is exceptional in its context: of granite, adorned with seven gables on the exterior and Gothic vaults on the interior, it sticks out from the vernacular orthogonal streetscape of Gloucester, a singularity among the town's structures. Lane's was the first generation seriously to cast an historical eye over the settled landscape as well as an aesthetic eye over the natural landscape. That it was also the first generation to place a premium on the sequestered silent soul growing in self-awareness, on the one hand, and in awareness of the unity and linkage of all things, on the other, impacted the way Lane painted and the way his contemporaries read his works.

What, then, is Lane's message? Simply that close looking at the small ordinary facts of daily life can teach the observant soul three things: that such looking will be rewarded by epiphanies of beauty and a sense of oneness with the natural and social world; that such looking at even the plainest factoids of an ordinary village will give one a sense of the oneness of social and economic life, a deep sense that each visual fact is part of a complex international social, material, and economic web; and that such looking can and should be captured and the moment frozen, the time and place fixed in amber, so that it will coexist with all future time. The painting, then, above all, is a symptom of that desire to hold a moment of vision.

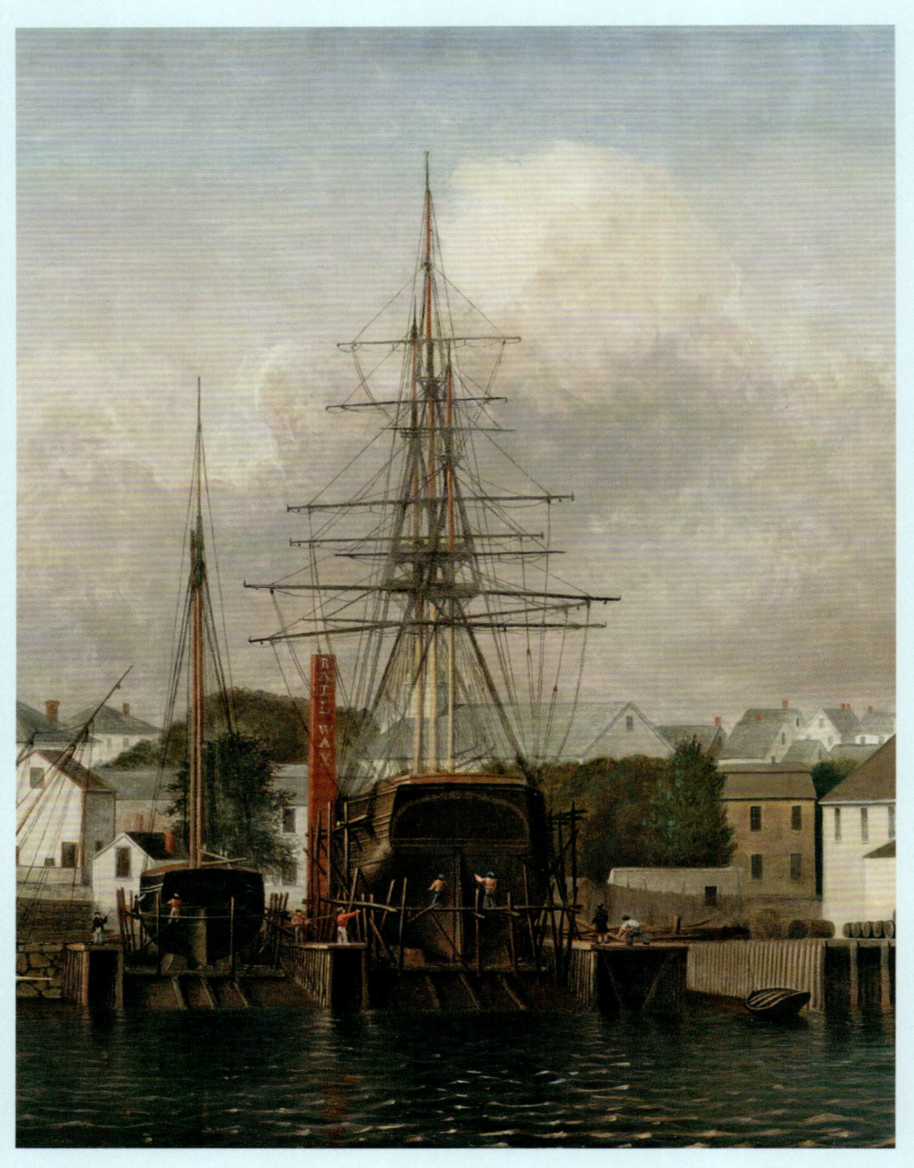
RAILWAY

CHAPTER 1

REPUTATION

Lane, Gloucester's "Own Artist," 1842–1865

Making a reputation as a painter is never easy. In the case of Fitz H. Lane, his reputation was made, unmade, and, eventually, remade. This chapter and the next track that trajectory. Attending to the ways Lane put his work on view, the ways collaborators in shops and in the press helped him keep his name and his work before the public, and the mechanisms by which he sought and executed commissions, this chapter explores the "supply" side of the question during his lifetime. By also attending to the aspects of Lane's work valued by his contemporaries, it begins to explore the "demand" side. Pursuing the issue of value into the later nineteenth century, chapter 2 notes an almost immediate plunge of his reputation following his death, and then, after long dormancy, an equally radical reassessment and elevation of his reputation a century later. My project here is to track this change over time as a narrative of self-fashioning (in this chapter) but also as a history of cultural fashioning (in the following chapter). The forces at work in this making, unmaking, and remaking of Lane include large cultural shifts in markets for art and in concepts of localism and nationalism, as well as in attitudes toward memory, history, and time.

The story of Lane's reputation tracked here is not the narrative of self-expression and inner discovery favored in most accounts of artists' careers. Rather, it embeds Lane's life and work in a social matrix and describes his paintings as responsive to patron desires and cultural developments. It investigates how he understood his art, how his fellow townspeople and urbane knowledgeable critics regarded it, and how his patrons—from modest schoolteacher to grand China trader—thought about it. Unlike most accounts of the artist, this chapter examines Lane's role within his community, the terms his contemporaries used to describe him, and his mechanisms for finding patrons and buyers—in a word, how in the short two decades of his painting career he pursued that career. The prehistory of Lane's painting years, those prior to his embarking on a career as artist in 1848 in his native Gloucester, is taken up in chapters 3 and 8. Chapter 2 pursues the story of Lane's posthumous reputation as an artist, understanding the "career" of his works as embedded in the concerns, values, and intellectual models of subsequent generations. The drama of the vicissitudes in the value of his works over the past century and a half (from $100 to zero to $5.4 million for a single canvas) is extreme; thus, in learning about the fashioning and refashioning of Lane's reputation, we learn lessons potentially applicable to our understanding of other artists, to the history of taste, and to the mechanisms of canon formation.

SEEING LANE

During Lane's lifetime it was not difficult to see his paintings. They were exhibited (and appreciated and bought) at venues for highbrow art that were beginning to appear in the United States in this period, such as the Boston Athenaeum, the National Academy of Design, and the American Art-Union in New York City, but they were also part of the streetscape and daily lives of his fellow Gloucesterites at home.[1] Gloucester (population 7,786 in 1850) had no established venue for the display or sale of art—no art academies, museums, or galleries—but Lane's works were very much on view.[2] They hung in the bank building, in the book and stationery store, in the town hall, and even in the street, as well as in the homes of his patrons. His Gloucester studios, successively on Washington Street, on Elm Street, and in the stone house on Duncan Street, were frequently open to visitors, who were encouraged in newspaper notices to drop by and see the most recent productions of his easel.[3] Lane's paintings are not just attentive records of structures and ships and activity in Gloucester and Cape Ann; they were integrated into the fabric of the town, accessible and visible to his fellows, part of their daily and holiday lives, helping them, through canvas fictions, understand the truths of their time and their place in history.

One of his largest surviving works, *Three-Master on the Gloucester Railway* of 1857, was painted as a shop sign and hung outside the paint shop of John Trask, whose business was to paint ships, literally (fig. 4).[4] Lane had friends in the press, and one cheerily announced the arrival of this work at one of the town's busiest commercial hubs:

> If our readers wish to see something pretty, let them take a walk down to Burnham Bros. Railway [dry dock] and take a peep at the new sign recently hung out over the paint shop of Mr. John Trask. It is a painting on canvas 4½ feet by 5 executed by Fitz H. Lane, Esq., representing a view of the Burnham Bros. Railways, the wharf and stores adjoining. The front view represents the "ways" with a ship and schooner receiving a coat of paint. The workshop and counting-room of Burnham Bros. and the buildings of Mr. Joseph Shepherd, together with the old Parrott and Caswell houses are plainly visible. In the background, a partial view of the residence of Capt. Frederick Norwood on Spring street, the Universalist church on Elm street, Capt. Isaac Somes' residence on Pleasant street and several other buildings on Prospect St. The view is taken from Rocky Neck and makes a very pretty picture.[5]

The author of this announcement takes care to point out the very local and very accurate character of the image. He selectively points to surviving early eighteenth-century homes—the "old Parrott" house is the gambrel-roofed red structure between the dry-docked ship and the sail loft—and to the pyramidal-roofed home of wealthy Capt. Isaac Somes (just under the tip of the taller mast of the canted schooner).[6] The recognizability of the scenes he paints is one of the key elements of Lane's paintings valued by his contemporaries, as is his recording of the antiquities of the place. The painting describes Gloucester at Duncan's Point, but it is also about the massive ship hauled up on the marine railway under repair and the visual jolt of its incongruous size against the townscape. A landscape painting is not usually organized around a central middle-ground vertical—verticals are usually lateral features, while the central portion of the image is opened to lead, by degrees, into deep space.[7] The eccentricity of this composition, together with the scale shifts between, for instance, ship and building, human and anchor, and the juxtaposition of the crisp white orthogonal blocks of the buildings with the weblike intricacy of the ship's rigging rising above the rooftops, gives drama to the work. Lane also includes words—descriptive verbal signs—within this painting-*cum*-sign. He has included "RAILWAY," designating the site of work offered by his client, John Trask—a steel-railed dry dock for large ships. And he also paints "SAIL LOFT" on the large building on the extreme right, a sly reference to what all these vessels are missing, to his sailmaker father's craft, and to the canvas he himself works to such different effect. Framing this descriptive assemblage of the infrastructure of marine traffic and trade are buoyant billowing cumulus clouds, tinged with the pink of a summer evening above, and lapping waves, crested with reddish and white impasto reflections below.

Trask, the painter of ships, valued this signboard, and in 1876, when he was on the common council of the town and its citizens were in a retrospective centennial state of mind, he gave it to the city of Gloucester; they hung it in the council chamber.[8] He also valued his memories of the painter and around 1885 sat down with Emma Todd (Mrs. Howard P. Elwell) to record his memories of Lane, providing one of the few extended first-person accounts of the artist.[9] In 1876, and in the early twentieth century, newspaper articles further explicated details about Trask's sign for generations who did not know the stories as well as Lane's contemporaries: the three-master being caulked and painted was the *California*, damaged in the hurricane of January 18, 1857. It was owned by George H. Rogers—the richest man in town and a Lane patron; built for California voyages in the 1850s, it was subsequently used in the Surinam trade, all matters to which we will return in later chapters.[10]

How long *Three-Master on the Gloucester Railway* hung outside Trask's shop is unknown, but it probably was visible there, advertising both Trask's painting of ships and Lane's painting of pictures, for some years. Lane was not unique among ambitious and accomplished artists to paint shop signs: French artist Jean-Antoine Watteau painted one of the most glorious for his friend Gersaint (1720, Charlottenburg Palace, Berlin); Edward Hicks painted two exuberant signboards for Jacob Christ, a gentleman's hatmaker in rural Pennsylvania (Mercer Museum, Doylestown, PA); William Hogarth—eccentric among London artists for hanging out a sign—also painted a shop sign for a pavior; and George Garrard painted a wonderfully detailed harbor-and-warehouse image for the brewer Samuel Whitbread.[11] All of these signs have survived. A shop exterior is, from a conservation perspective, far from an ideal location for oil on canvas (or on board), but it would vastly increase the painting/sign's audience and—if well done—presumably draw more comment and more business than a perfunctory sign of the usual sort.

Whether Lane painted other shop signs we do not know, but it is notable that he did not eschew the more popular, public, and humble branches of his trade. Among these more vernacular works, Lane is known to have painted at least one fireboard—a decorative board, usually ornamented with a painted bouquet, placed in front of the opening of an empty fireplace in the summer season—an art form that is usually not associated with "fine art" but rather with the efforts of schoolgirls and painters of "fancy work" on furniture, boxes, and wagons.[12] Ambitious though he clearly was for recognition among his generation's practitioners of fine art, Lane seemed to make no such nice distinction when it came to being a good citizen in his family and his community. The fireboard (unlocated) was evidently a gift to his brother, Edward, who was, like all Lane's male relations, an artisan for whom fireboards were likely more usual household furnishings than were framed paintings.

When banners were needed for a firehouse ball or a Fourth of July parade—in a community that turned out en masse to participate and watch these events—Lane apparently happily exerted himself. Although none has survived (at least none recognized as his work), it is clear from public notices of these parades that both his painted banners and the costumed human tableaux he helped orchestrate were highly appreciated.[13] Such activities certainly contributed to the recognition among his townsmen that Lane was, as Annette Babson put it in her diary, "our own artist."[14] It is also notable that in the context of his Independence Day banners and tableaux (and the notice about the very visible Trask shop sign), he is referenced as "Esq.," a courtesy title generally reserved for local nabobs, lawyers, and justices of the peace, a title not supported by his relatively modest place on the town's tax list but rather by his practice of a profession in which he necessarily associated closely with local elites.[15]

Lane painted his first recorded banner in 1840 in support of the continuation of federal bounties to fisherman and of Whig presidential candidate William Henry Harrison, a banner that sported the image of the Gloucester Sea Serpent and the words "The Deep has Felt the Attack Upon her Interests and Sends Her Champion to the Rescue."[16] This banner was painted on silk and, according to two long accounts in the *Gloucester Telegraph*, was conscripted for reuse in the "Floral Procession" in honor of the seventy-third anniversary of Independence, on July 4, 1849. This was a considerable parade, including an equestrian cavalcade, a brass band, numerous floats, dignitaries of all descriptions, ten schools' young ladies bedecked in flowers and carrying floral and moss baskets, and marchers from four distinct temperance organizations. Banners included legends such as "Large streams from little fountains flow; Great sots from moderate drinkers grow." A detailed account of the whole affair signed by John J. Piper and Fitz H. Lane includes the notation that "the Chief Marshall of the Floral Procession, Mr. J. J. Piper [a Lane patron] [was] accompanied by F. H. Lane, Esq. in an open carriage." This pair followed the temperance marchers and preceded the pupils of a private school kept by Lydia Ann Mason, niece of Lane's principal patron, Sidney Mason. The pupils bore garlands and "handsome banners, with a representation of the temple of Science [and] children with an angel." They in turn were followed by a float carrying a tableau of couples dressed in the garb of 1776. A second account, published three days later, underlined Lane's role, noting that "much credit [was] . . . due to Mr. F. H. Lane, for the valuable assistance rendered in preparing designs and banners." The floats included a "laurelled car ornamented with boughs and wreathes [*sic*] containing two paintings appropriately designed and executed by Mr. Lane for the occasion, one representing the effects of Intemperance, and the other a sparkling fountain of pure water." There was also a portrait of Washington "surmounted by an Eagle, so perfectly designed and executed" that, as in the legend of Zeuxis, it was taken for the bird itself.[17] Later that year, in November 1849, Lane extended his design projects to include the decoration of the post office where his friend and future executor, Thomas Sewall Lancaster, served as postmaster.[18]

Lane continued to exert himself as the town's on-call public artist, as evidenced by a news report ten years later, in 1858, concerning a festival to raise money to support the Lyceum Library, which acknowledged "Messrs. F. H. Lane, Addison Center, and John Trask, for their arduous and truly artistic labors in the preparation of Tableaux" (and incidentally demonstrated collaboration between the painter of ships and the marine painter).[19] In 1860 historian John James Babson emphasized in his published comment on Lane that the artist "often contributed a production of his pencil for the promotion of a benevolent enterprise," and Lane's unattributed obituary five years later praised him as "always ready to assist in any charitable enterprise, by contributing his paintings."[20] Overall then, Lane's exertions as artist and designer, both as a painter of the Trask harborscape sign and as the designer of allegorical tableaux and banners, were highly visible in the streets and public spaces of Gloucester. His works participated explicitly in contemporary political and moral discourse on a local level. They would have been seen by the whole population of the town—not just the cognoscenti. The Lane his neighbors knew and acknowledged had a much broader range (including images of eagles, flowers, inebriates, and fountains) than we recognize today.

Gloucesterites would not only have seen Lane's work in the streets as they went about their daily tasks and their holiday frolics, they would also have come across Lane paintings inside shops and public offices. One of Lane's *Boston Harbor* paintings, for instance, had "been placed on exhibition for a few days in the Reading Room of the Marine Insurance Co." (a room that apparently functioned as an informal men's club), as reported in April 1856 by the editor of the *Gloucester Telegraph and News,* who urged his townsmen to go see it.[21] Similarly, a view of the "Old Fort, Ten Pound Island, etc.," spoken of as "one of the finest pictures yet produced by the pencil of our distinguished artist and fellow citizen, Fitz H. Lane, Esq.," was reported to be on view in that same reading room in the summer of 1860.[22] In 1865 this painting of Gloucester Harbor was hanging in the reading room under the bank, at which time it was given to the town by bequest from the artist and was rehung in the large hall of the town house, where it would have been observed by those transacting business and attending civic functions.[23]

Beyond the professional contexts of the bank, insurance company, and town hall, Lane's paintings were on view in local shops. In the fall of 1862 the *Gloucester Telegraph* noted that Lane's painting of Colonel Fremont's encampment at Two Penny Loaf was to be seen at the Procter Brothers store, the town's all-purpose bookstore, stationery supplier, art-materials supplier, and print shop, where engravings, violins, accordions, patent medicines, wallpapers, wheelbarrows, and birdcages were also on offer.[24] Here the painting would have enjoyed the company of works by Hume, Gibbon, Byron, Pope, Wordsworth, and Burns, among other worthies of English philosophy, history, and literature, offered "for 87 cents per vol"; more important, Procter Brothers sold "Picture Frames of any Style Required, Manufactured to Order at the Lowest Living Prices!"[25] And in this last item we see the partnership between artists and retailers who offered picture frames, a connection that became increasingly important as the century progressed. In sum, the citizens of Gloucester would have enjoyed catching sight of, and perhaps gazing attentively at, Lane's paintings in many nonart venues both interior and exterior throughout his productive years among them. His paintings would have been understood to promote local businesses and landmarks and to valorize Whig and temperance platforms, as well as to contribute an aesthetic accompaniment to shopping for books, conversing about marine matters, or celebrating the nation's birthday.

The one context in Gloucester in which Lane's paintings were apparently always on view was his studio. Almost immediately upon his settling in town, in 1849, newspaper editorials urged people to visit his studio, initially a "painting room" in his brother's house and then in his sister's house on Elm Street, where he boarded until his own stone house was completed. In August of that year a long article announced: "Mr. Lane has now on exhibition in his studio on Elm St. four paintings [including] . . . a view in Gloucester Harbor, [and one of] . . . the Old Saw Mill." A long ekphrasis of the latter painting ensues, and the article concludes with: "Mr. Lane's Rooms are open at all hours of the day, and we advise all our readers who have any love of art to call there and look at his paintings."[26] A similarly detailed editorial appearing the next month described Lane's "picture of the Western Shore of Gloucester Harbor, including the distance from 'Norman's Woe Rock' to 'Half Moon Beach.' It was painted for Mr. William E. Coffin of Boston and will be on exhibition in the artist's rooms for only a few days; we advise all our readers who admire works of art, and would see one of the best pictures Mr. Lane has ever executed, to call there before it is taken away."[27] Most of the newspaper notices over the next two decades follow the pattern apparent in these two—a description of and appreciative remarks concerning the works on view, the location of the studio, and a statement of the artist's eager welcome to those "who have [a] . . . love of art." The second one suggests as well that to a certain extent these were exhibitions of bespoke works and not (necessarily) attempts to help sell works painted speculatively. There were also very brief announcements, such as one in 1850 announcing that "Two fine views of Gloucester Beach from Fort Point and Canal Rocks by Fitz W. [*sic*] Lane, Esq. may be seen at the artist's rooms."[28] Part of being an "Esq." and conducting business with gentry in the nineteenth century, as in the eighteenth, was restraint in advertising or hanging out a shingle, but these third-party "news" items were considered appropriate public service announcements, bringing matters to the public's attention that the public wanted to know.

That some Gloucesterites took him up on his proffered hospitality is clear from such newspaper articles as that authored by "Louise" in 1856, in which she gives an exuberant account of her visit with friends to Lane's studio, by then located in the gabled granite house that would remain his home the rest of his life. She frames her description of two paintings—a night scene and a view of Boston harbor—with a comment on the arts in America and a description of "one of those glorious sunsets"—witnessed from the threshold of Lane's harborside home—"which can only be seen in our New England Springs."[29] As Annette Babson had done in her diary entry a decade earlier, "Louise" positions Lane's work within the context of the glories of nature as seen on Cape Ann and the known (but unseen) value of European art: "Many are desirous of seeing rare and beautiful pictures, and take infinite pains to gratify their tastes by going abroad where they can see old castles [and] rich paintings, . . . of which those who have been less fortunate have no idea. Still at home we have many of these, truly American perhaps, but none the less beautiful."[30] In summoning "old castles and rich paintings," "Louise" deliberately evokes the heavy mantle of the Western art tradition and gingerly places Lane in the balance. It is important to remember that both Lane and his immediate audience understood him to be simultaneously "local talent"—with his works actively participating in their everyday lives—and also an artist within and competing against the centuries-long tradition of European fine art.

In this more ambitious orbit, Lane advanced his case by making sure his paintings were also seen in the elite fine arts contexts of his day. From his initial years as an artist practicing in Boston in the 1840s, his works were to be seen not only in vernacular contexts—in the window of a Boston music store and on the walls of Gloucester's commercial establishments, for instance—but also at the annual exhibitions of the Boston Athenaeum, the Boston Artists' Association, and Boston's New England Art Union (see appendix A).[31] From 1841 he also sent paintings to New York—first to the Apollo Association in 1841 and, from 1847, to its successor, the American Art-Union.[32] To this latter venue he sent eight works between 1847 and 1852, and by this mechanism he reached viewing audiences in New York City and Art-Union members as far afield as Indiana, as they acquired his works in the Art-Union lottery.[33] The American Art-Union, established in 1839, was an immensely popular organization, with local chapters all over the nation. Subscribers were entitled to a print, issues of the journal, and an opportunity to win one of hundreds of canvases by living American artists in an annual lottery. Gloucester's chapter secretary was Lane's good friend Joseph L. Stevens Jr., and by 1848 Gloucester had ten members among the 16,475 nationwide.[34]

That Lane was effective in drawing notice by sending his works to the American Art-Union is evident from such favorable comments as those made by the editor of the *Boston Transcript*, who went to New York to review the Art-Union paintings in 1850 and reported back to his New England constituency: Lane's "ships in a squall, his sketches of Cape Ann sea-side scenery, and all his salt water and boating scenes are unequalled in their fidelity to the ocean's varying aspects. For the information of those who are not familiar with the merits of this artist, I would say, he is a resident of Gloucester, Massachusetts, where nautical subjects have been his study from a boy, and that he deserves to be better known." This notice was picked up and reprinted in the *Gloucester Telegraph* under the heading "Lane, the Artist . . . at the American Art-Union Gallery, at New York."[35] Lane also sent one work, *Fishing Schooner on Georges Bank*, owned at that time by a clerk who worked on Tremont Row in Boston's art district, to the National Academy of Design exhibition in New York City in 1859.[36] Participating in these exhibitions, Lane was presenting his works at the premier North American venues for art, where critics, collectors, and potential patrons of all kinds gathered to see, assess, and compare new work by living American artists. In pursuing these national fine-art venues, he was expanding the seeing, viewing, and appraising of his paintings well beyond the face-to-face and face-to-canvas venues of his native Gloucester. But it is important to note that these activities, offering his most serious painting efforts to the most discriminating national audiences, were simultaneous with Lane's painting of ephemeral temperance banners for Gloucester's parades and similar local community projects.

BUYING LANE

What were Lane's sales strategies? How did he find his customers, and how did they find him? Over the course of his career Lane employed all the sales strategies available to artists in his day, including subscription, personal commissions (for painted views, ship portraits, and book illustrations), exhibition at fine-arts venues and local shops, auctions, and the placement of work with a middleman dealer. Some of these strategies proved more important than others in securing a livelihood, but all worked together to generate both reputation and revenue.

One strategy Lane employed throughout his career was the sale of lithographic town views by subscription. These works were offered through newspaper announcements, and when enough takers subscribed to make the venture profitable, the print was made, delivered to subscribers, and overruns were sold through local stationers. Announcements from January 1835, when Lane reintroduced himself to Gloucester as a mature artist, offer a subscription for a lithographed view of the town, published by his former employer, Pendleton's Lithography in Boston (fig. 11). The price was $1, but subscriptions came in slowly, so that it took more than a year and several further announcements before the *Gloucester Telegraph* advised its readers that "subscribers and others may obtain the print at the store of Isaac A. Smith."[37] Lane also sold these 1836 views of Gloucester personally at his Boston studio, as we learn from his friend Joseph L. Stevens Jr., who recounted that his "father brought [home to Maine] a print of Lane's first Gloucester view, bought of the artist at his Tremont Temple studio in Boston. An extra dollar had been paid for coloring it."[38] Lane, then, was introduced to his future "Boswell" through the mechanism of this $2 lithograph, and perhaps these modest views also proved a "gateway" purchase for others who subsequently sought out the artist, his friendship, and his paintings.

In 1846 Lane offered—again through a newspaper announcement—another view of Gloucester, "every house and object being distinctly visible," the price still a modest $1.[39] Although contemporaries note that "there was not very much demand" for these lithographed townscapes, Lane was sufficiently encouraged by the sales figures, or the importance of a continuous presence of his work on offer in the local stationers, that in 1859 he executed a third view of Gloucester. Four years after his death the unsold stock of these views was lost in the burning of the town hall, where the lithographs were stored.[40] That Gloucesterites did not highly value them despite newspaper commendations is suggested by slow sales and by the fact that late in the nineteenth century a prosperous dry-goods merchant, Alexander Pattillo,

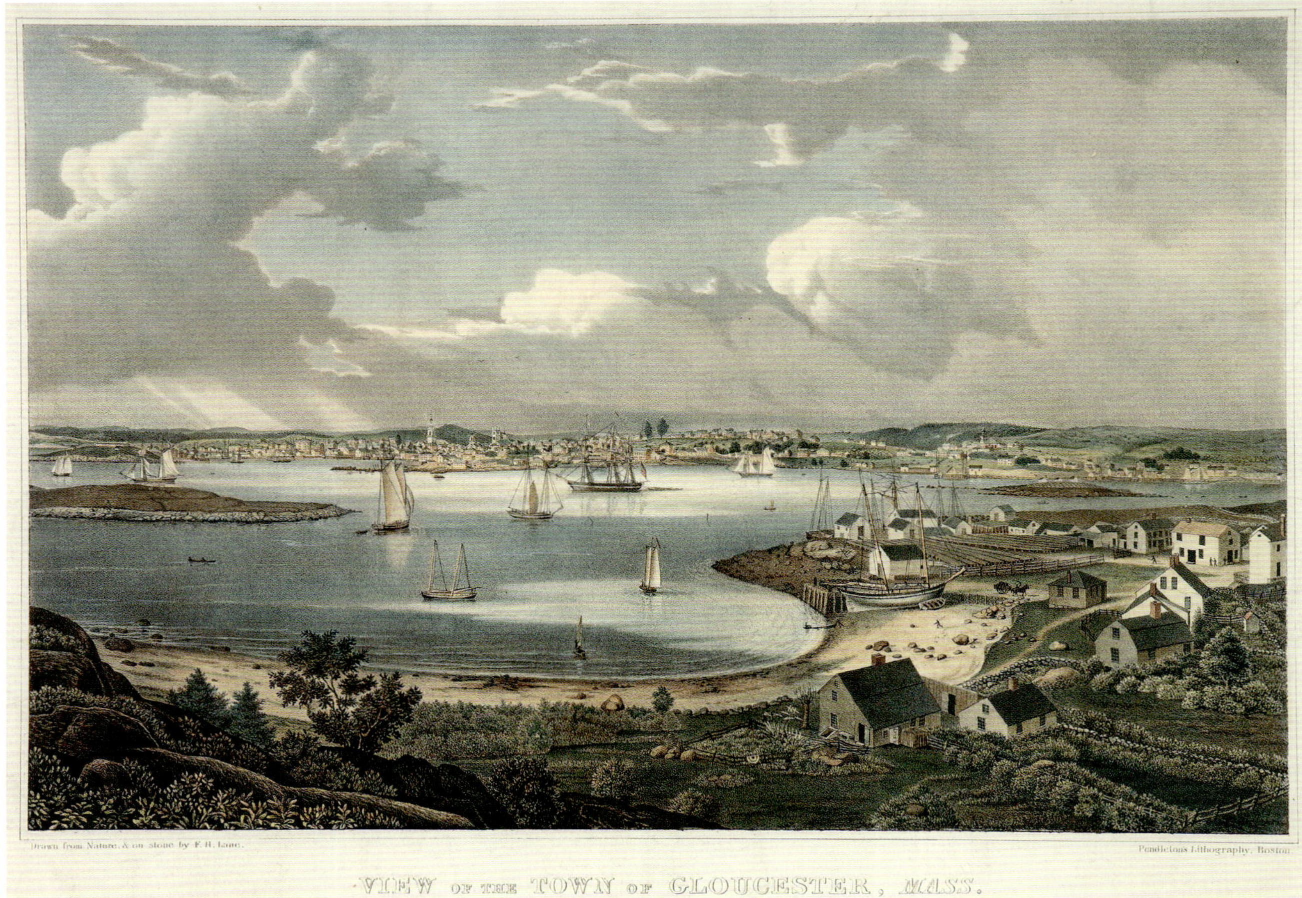

FIGURE 11
Fitz H. Lane, *View of the Town of Gloucester, Mass.*, 1836. Colored lithograph on paper, 18 × 23¾ in. (45.7 × 60.3 cm). Printed at Pendleton's. Yale University Art Gallery, Mabel Brady Garvan Collection (1946.9.1754). Photo: Yale University Art Gallery.

hunting for one, had to settle for a copy nailed to the inside of the back porch door of one of the town's elderly residents.[41] Inventive in the face of indifferent sales, Lane devised an unusual way to vend these lithographed views of Gloucester. As one contemporary recalled: "Mr. Lane had finished a number of lithographs which were sold at a very low price. This did not bring to Mr. Lane much ready money and he was somewhat disappointed so he mounted several on canvas, painted them in oil, and sold them for $25" (e.g., the example in fig. 12).[42] Lane's three-decade effort with subscription sales of lithographed Gloucester views, stretching through his entire career, invites several interpretations. Perhaps he was determined to put low-cost artworks in the hands of many who might not imagine purchasing an oil on canvas, or perhaps he remained hopeful throughout his life that these prints might produce a steady income as sales of paintings proved more sporadic. Moreover, this loyalty to the medium of his initial training suggests Lane's belief that—as described in the (London) *Art Journal* (originally titled *Art Union*), to which he subscribed—unlike copper plate or wood engraving, this new reproductive medium provided purchasers, at a very modest price, access to the artist as skilled draftsman "without the

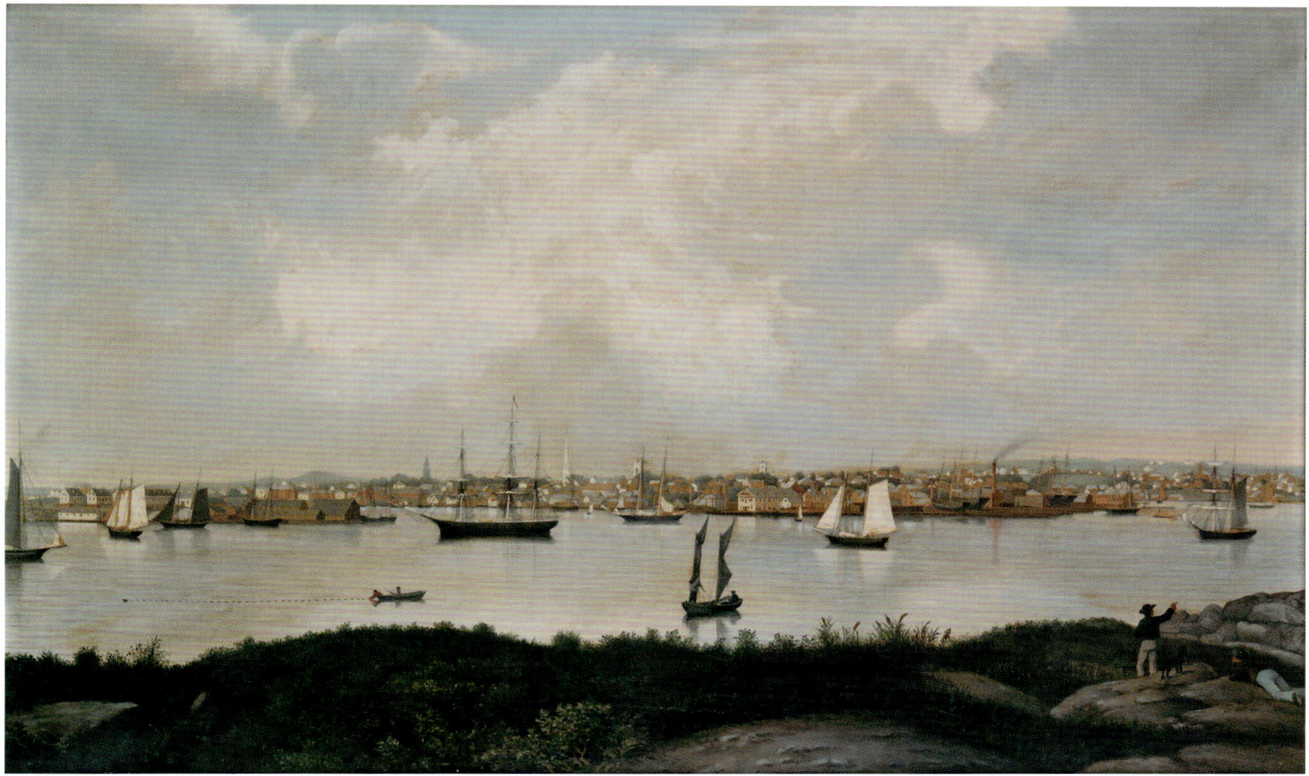

FIGURE 12
Fitz H. Lane, *View of Gloucester*, 1859. Oil over lithograph on paper, 21¾ × 35½ in. (55.2 × 90.2 cm). Cape Ann Museum, Gloucester, Massachusetts (90).

intervention of any other than the artist's hand—the printer's being a merely mechanical process . . . [preserving in the print] the artist's own touch and feeling, each one being as much an original as the actual drawing on the stone."[43] Also of note is that, in spite of scholarly assertions otherwise (discussed in the next chapter), he never "outgrew" his desire to describe "every house and object" in the complicated concentrated settlements of New England's coast. Indeed, he continued to expand his lithographic repertoire during his career, producing views of other towns, including Providence (RI), Baltimore (MD), Norwich (CT), Newburyport, New Bedford, Lowell (MA), and, in 1855, one of his most ambitious and successful, Castine in Maine.[44]

While lithographed city views remained a constant but minor part of his production, providing artworks of local topographic interest to purchasers of modest means, and the paintings Lane sent to such fine arts venues as the Boston Athenaeum and the American Art-Union in New York City helped educate the urban public about his work, increasing his reputation and possibly generating some sales, it appears that Lane depended most heavily on painting commissions to generate income. These commissions were established through personal contact, especially studio visits from potential customers. Certainly the many ways Lane participated in his community as a public artist and the many notices describing his latest works in the local newspaper, as well as the presence of his lithographs at the stationer's and his paintings in the bank, the insurance company, the bookseller, and installed at the door of Trask's paint shop, served to keep his name and his talents before his townsmen. They would also have seen his paintings in the homes of satisfied customers, and the kinship and friendship of many of his patrons suggests that word of mouth was a powerful factor in advancing his reputation and securing him commissions.

Of the several different kinds of commissions Lane took on—ship portraits, book illustrations, depictions of historic events, and views of New England coasts, communities, and shipping—most is known about the views, the largest category of his surviving work. For all sorts of reasons, not the least of which was the fact that the artist was certain of a return for his efforts, protocols familiar from the eighteenth century concerning commissioned paintings were still the preferred sales mechanism in the antebellum period. Artists provided suggestions—such as Lane's surviving topographical drawings—from which customers placed specific orders for paintings. We know about many of these commissions because Lane's friend Joseph L. Stevens Jr., as recipient of the unspecified remainder of Lane's estate, acquired a packet of topographical drawings and annotated them (perhaps in 1865) with the names of the sites depicted and the names of patrons who commissioned paintings based on specific drawings.[45] This is an invaluable resource. We have here the names of more than thirty Lane patrons, almost a third of whom are, surprisingly, women. It is not known why these drawings were preserved beyond their immediate use in securing and executing commissions. Perhaps it was because during his career they served for Lane as *aides mémoire* concerning who had ordered what, or after Lane's death, for Stevens, commemorating their excursions together and with friends, as the presence of those accompanying Lane on each drawing excursion is indicated in initials on the face of the drawings. That they are selective and not the entire corpus of Lane drawings is clear, first, because there are extant Lane paintings of sites not included in this set of 110 drawings, and, second, because Lane certainly made preparatory drawings of ships—as marks on the canvases indicate meticulous transfer of images of vessels—few of which are preserved in this set.[46] Nevertheless, inspection of the drawings themselves makes it clear that at least thirty patrons specifically commissioned paintings based on topographical drawings they viewed in Lane's studio. So it is reasonable to assume that, along with "Louise" and other casual visitors, men and women interested in acquiring Lane paintings availed themselves of the open-door policy announced in the newspaper, "Mr. Lane's Rooms are open at all hours of the day," and came to view these drawings with potential painting commissions in mind.

Beyond identifying the desired sites—many indicated in topographically identifiable land profiles based on relative relief—these patrons would have discussed with Lane the three other principal elements of his compositions: the vessels and their deployment in the composition; the meteorological treatment of the sky and water; and the presence and actions of figures. On these important matters the surviving drawings are almost wholly silent. On one drawing Stevens notes, "This sketch was painted in moonlight effect" (fig. 53 in *Paintings and Drawings*; FHLo inv. 133); and on another, "Sketch made for a picture for J. H. B. Lang in which to introduce a steamer *Harvest Moon*" (fig. 93 in *Paintings and Drawings*; FHLo inv. 159). Beyond that, these drawings include no directives or notations concerning the introduction of the vessels that were the principal characters in Lane's pictorial dramas, or concerning the light and weather effects that have been so remarked in twentieth-century commentary on Lane.

That such matters as site, point of view, and light conditions were discussed with, determined by, and probably often initiated by Lane's patrons is suggested by an undated letter from the artist to his friend Stevens in which he recounts: "I yesterday made a sketch of Stage Fort and the surrounding scenery from the water. [John] Piper has given me an order for a picture from this point of view to be treated as a sunset. I shall try to make something out of it, but it will require some management as there is no foreground but water and vessels."[47] In this instance, which may have been typical, the topographical drawing fixed the subject and the point of view; both were chosen by the patron, who also determined the light effect: sunset. It was left to the artist to "make something out of it."

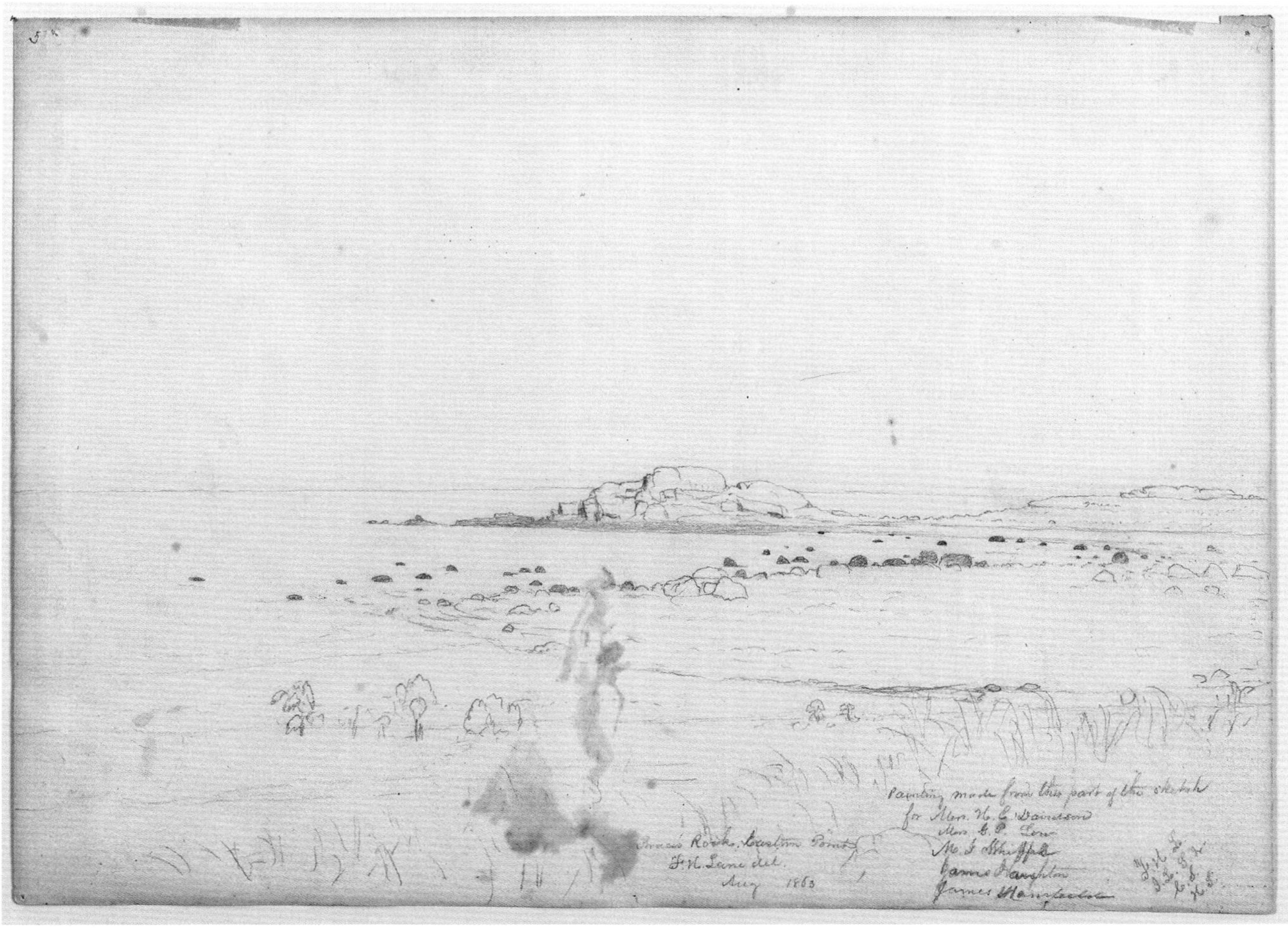

FIGURE 13
Fitz H. Lane, *Brace's Rock, Eastern Point*, August 1863. Pencil on paper, 10½ × 15 in. (26.7 × 38.1 cm). Cape Ann Museum, Gloucester, Massachusetts. Gift of Samuel H. Mansfield, 1927 (485.05).

Perhaps equally often the artist took the initiative, selecting likely sites and producing a number of drawings that were then used as prompts in discussions with potential patrons. Characteristic is Lane's *Brace's Rock, Eastern Point* (fig. 13). Executed in pencil on a 10½ × 15-inch sheet (and later inadvertently splashed by watercolor), this drawing describes a distinctive cluster of large rocks that terminate a spit of land bracketing one side of Brace's Cove on the southern shore of Cape Ann (fig. 14). The horizon line is marked at midpoint on the sheet, below an expressionless sky, while small rocks, cast in shadow, dot the shoreline. A cluster of pencil strokes suggest different kinds of herbage and rocks in the immediate foreground. Among the grasses at the center bottom Stevens has noted, "Brace's Rock, Eastern Point / F. H. Lane del. / August 1863." On a diagonal in the lower right corner he has recorded the initials of those in the party that August afternoon: "F. H. L[ane,] J. L. S[tevens Jr.] C[aroline] S[tevens, and their daughter, eleven-year-old] H[elen] S[tevens]." Between these two annotations Stevens has noted: "Painting made from this part of the sketch / for Mrs. H. E. Davidson / Mrs. G. P. Low / Mr. J. Whipple / James Houghton / James Mansfield." These marginalia indicate that the occasion was a summer family outing, that the sheet included "another part," being originally

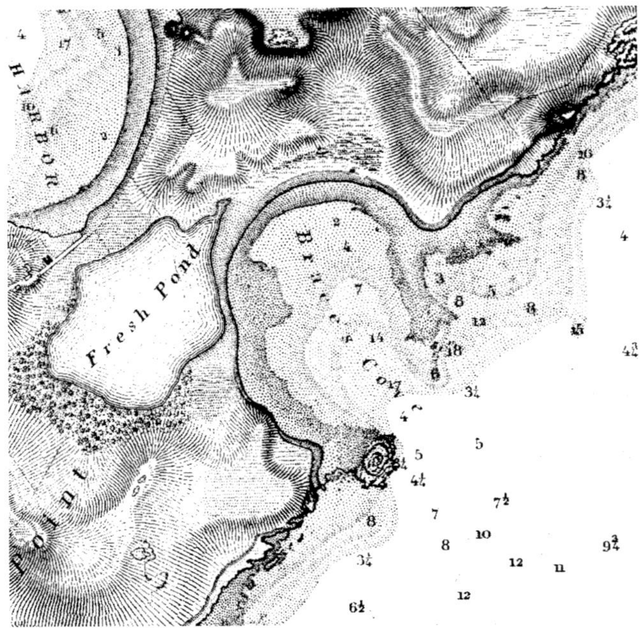

FIGURE 14
A. D. Bache, H. S. Stellwagen, et al., *Survey of the Coast of the United States: Gloucester Harbor, Massachusetts* (1855, updated 1875) (fig. 3), detail.

longer (indeed, many of Lane's drawings are multiple-sheet panoramas as long as 43 inches), and that at least five patrons selected this drawing as the basis for commissioned works.

The site, Brace's Cove, was a distinctive shallow inlet just outside Gloucester Harbor on the ocean side of a long peninsula protecting the town and harbor from the sea, an area used in Lane's day primarily for pasturage (figs. 3, 9, and 14). In realizing the paintings derived from this drawing, Lane characteristically dropped the horizon (to give breadth to an expressive sky), added vessels proportionate to the size of the cove, and adjusted all parts of the coloration to indicate a specific time of day (usually late afternoon) (fig. 15). The "other" part of this drawing is *Brace's Cove, Eastern Point*, recording the less dramatic eastern arm of rock and sand bordering Brace's Cove (FHLo inv. 147). On this second image, Stevens recorded, "Painting ordered from the *entire* [emphasis added] sketch by Mrs. S. G. Rogers of Roxbury / Shortly before his death Lane prepared a canvas 22 × 36 for it and that / was all." The word "entire" suggests the two drawings recombined to give a wide view out of this C-shaped cove looking southeast to the broad Atlantic. In 1864 Lane also painted Brace's Rock from an inlet outside the cove to the southwest, possibly from a drawing made on the same day that he made the other two drawings (Terra Collection, Art Institute of Chicago). Lane's portfolio of drawings enabled the artist to create paintings to suit a variety of customers in a variety of formats while also perhaps enabling him to relive the comradeship of a beach outing that singular August afternoon in 1863.

The evidence in the extant drawings, their inscriptions, and their survival suggests that these modest works in pencil were foundational to Lane's way of thinking about the world, his practice as an artist, his communications with his patrons, and his mechanisms for turning artistic prowess into a professional livelihood. Above all, they formed the basis of his understanding with his customers about what he was to provide and what they would buy.

Much scantier is the documentation concerning the other two kinds of commissioned works Lane made—book illustrations and ship portraits—seemingly minor efforts from the perspective of twentieth- and twenty-first-century value systems but clearly important to Lane in solidifying his reputation with contemporary readers, providing income, and broadening his customer base. For his friend the historian and antiquarian John James Babson, Lane provided drawings of houses for the *History of the Town of Gloucester* (1860), which were the basis for wood engravings included in that volume, contributions Babson acknowledges in his text.[48] Babson was a prosperous Gloucester merchant, town selectman, and member of the Massachusetts House of Representatives. He was one of the sixteen wealthiest men in Gloucester in 1850, eventually moving his business to Boston but, like many after the railroad made it possible, continuing to commute home to Gloucester.[49] More important for my purposes, he was cashier of the Gloucester bank where

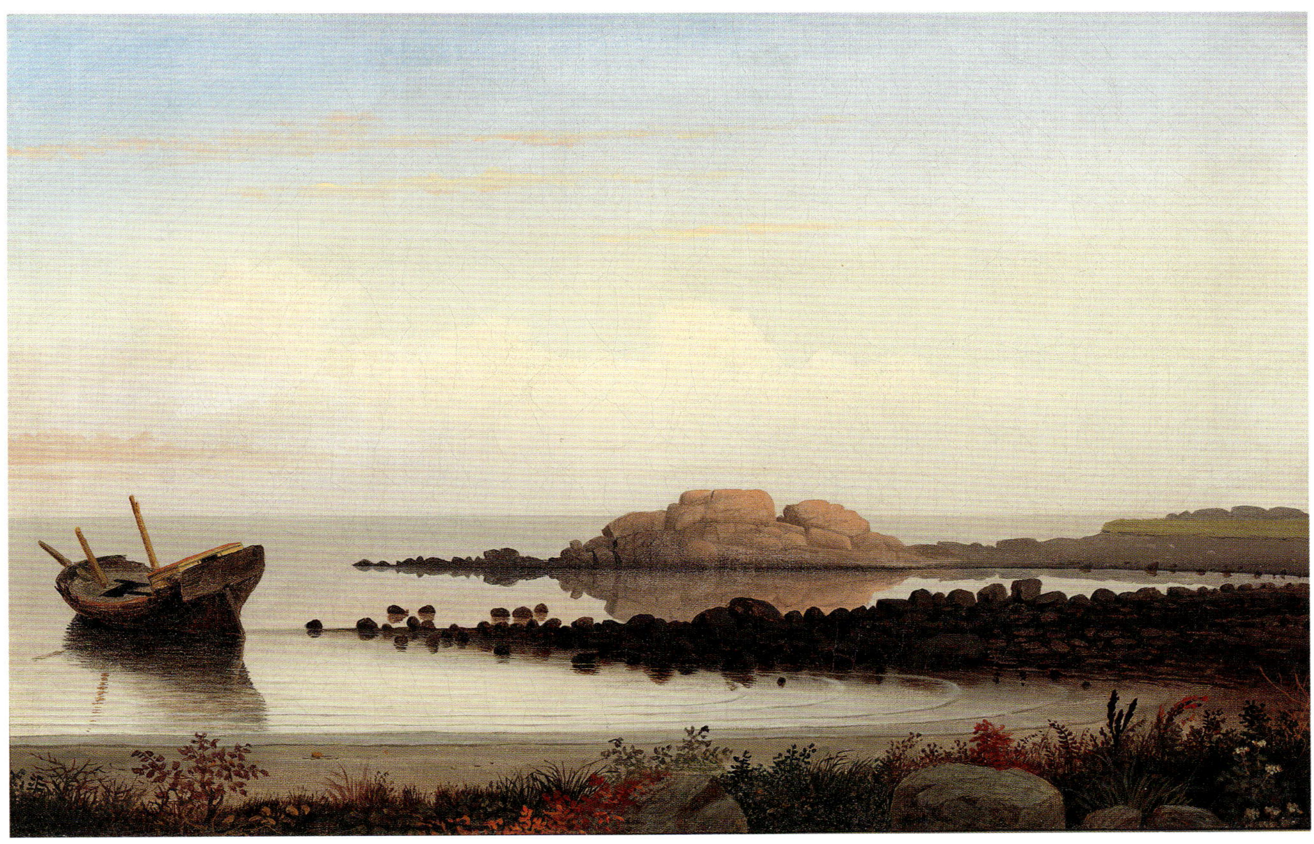

FIGURE 15
Fitz H. Lane, *Brace's Rock, Eastern Point*, 1864. Oil on canvas, 10 × 15 in. (25.4 × 38.1 cm). Cape Ann Museum, Gloucester, Massachusetts. Gift of Harold and Betty Bell, 2007 (2007.10).

Lane's paintings were sometimes on view, brother of Lane patron Edward Babson, cousin of Lane patron Nathaniel Babson, and husband to Lydia Ann Mason, an amateur painter of birds and botanical subjects who was the niece of Lane's principal patron, Sidney Mason.[50] In the case of J. J. Babson, as in that of many Lane patrons, the multiple threads of connection make clear that his art was at the nexus of a broad and interlinked social network.

For an earlier pamphlet commission, Lane provided the lithographed portrait frontispiece of the frigate *Jamestown* for Robert Bennet Forbes's 1847 report, *The Voyage of the* Jamestown *on Her Errand of Mercy* (fig. 16).[51] It records the setting-off of this U.S. warship, under the (civilian) command of R. B. Forbes, loaded with provisions for those devastated by the Irish famine then peaking with the failure of the potato crop that year (see chapter 8). A wealthy merchant, humanitarian, designer of pathbreaking improvements to both sailing and steamship technology, Forbes championed propeller-driven steamboats, one of which Lane has pictured here escorting the warship *Jamestown* out of Boston harbor.[52] Among the handful of small vessels described in Lane's preserved drawings is one of this steam tug—equipped with auxiliary sails—on the bow of which Lane has noted "Tow Boat" (fig. 17). The tug's name was the *Robert Bennet Forbes*. In composing the frontispiece commemorating and describing the *Jamestown* and its mission of mercy, Lane has introduced this apt nautical proxy for his patron, a man who captained both these vessels, one of which

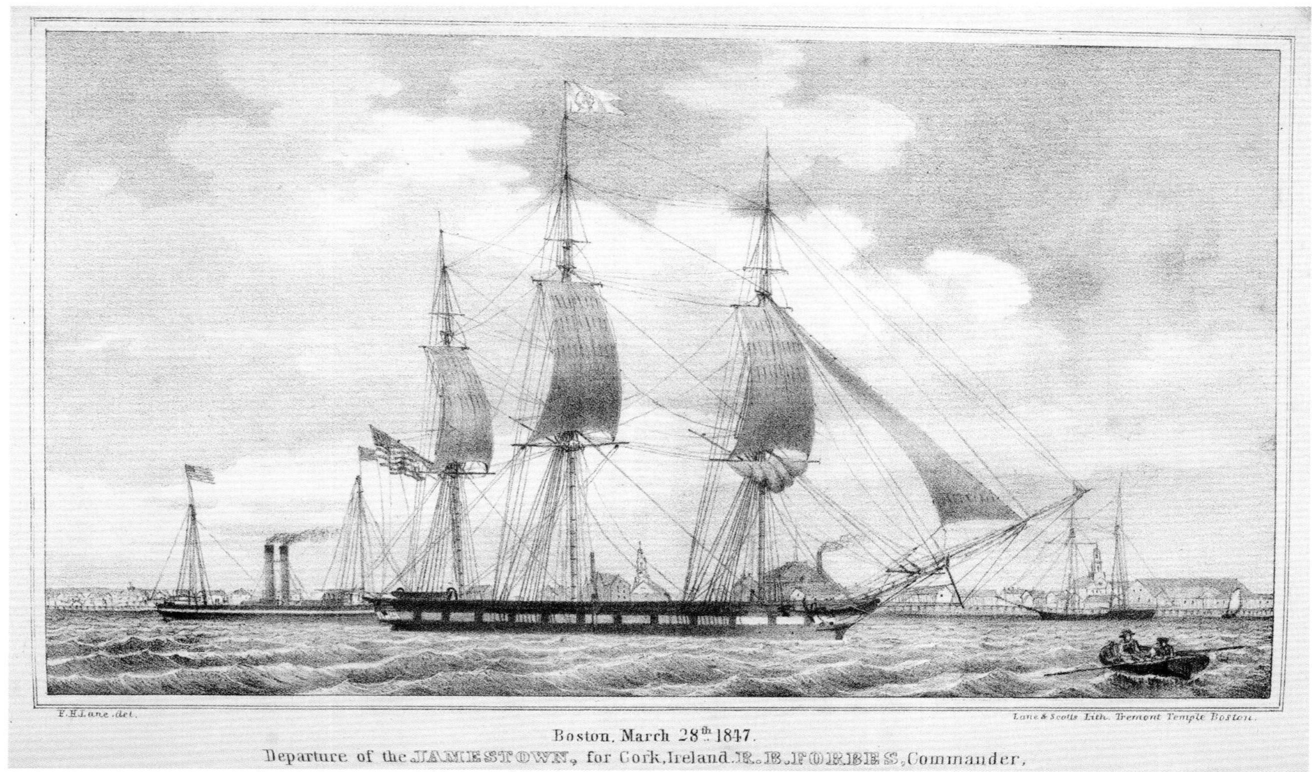

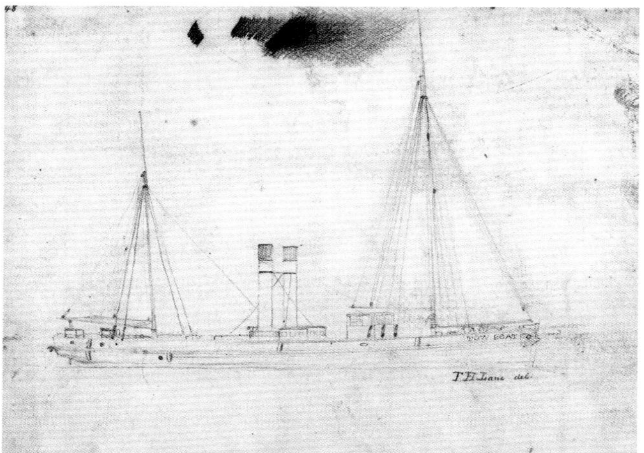

FIGURE 16 (ABOVE)
Fitz H. Lane del., *Boston, March 28th, 1847/ Departure of the* Jamestown, *for Cork, Ireland, R. B. Forbes, Commander*. Lithograph on paper, 4½ × 8 in. (11.4 × 20.3 cm). Commissioned by R. B. Forbes. Lane & Scott's Lith., Tremont Temple, Boston. Frontispiece in [Robert B. Forbes], *The Voyage of the* Jamestown *on Her Errand of Mercy* (Boston: Eastburn's Press, 1847). Graphic Arts Collection, Department of Rare Books and Special Collections, Princeton University Library. Photo: Princeton University Library.

FIGURE 17 (LEFT)
Fitz H. Lane, *Tow Boat* [*The* Robert Bennet Forbes], ca. 1847. Pencil on paper, 8¼ × 11⅛ in. (21 × 28.3 cm). Commissioned by R. B. Forbes. Cape Ann Museum, Gloucester, Massachusetts. Gift of Samuel H. Mansfield, 1927 (485.48).

bore his name. It is probable that many of Lane's paintings include these sly references that would have been clear to his own and his patrons' contemporaries but that are largely illegible to us today. Lane's ability adroitly to work in such references to names, skills, and associations would have been one of the reasons he received such commissions. That he could satisfy such a patron as Robert B. Forbes would have enlarged his reputation in one of Boston's most powerful business and social circles.

Although there is no evidence that he ordered any oil-on-canvas views or ship portraits from Lane, Forbes was alert to art—for instance, in 1825 importing to California from China "some very gaudy pictures of [Christian] saints, got up at Canton . . . for the California

Missions," in the 1830s commissioning paintings from Robert Salmon in Boston, and in the 1840s visiting Rubens's tomb and other art-related sites in Europe.[53] One of Forbes's allies in his efforts to develop and fund safe lifeboats, and a boon companion on hunting excursions to the Forbes family island, Naushon, off the coast of Massachusetts, was George Bruce Upton, owner of clipper ships and railroads and owner of one of Lane's many extraordinary *Boston Harbor* canvases.[54] A subject that neither he nor his wealthy clients seemed to tire of, shipping in Boston harbor against the town's distinctive skyline was the subject of at least nineteen Lane canvases, each somewhat different in character and tone and each an extraordinary, complex achievement.[55] That these two wealthy, influential nautical men were both patrons of Lane is no surprise; for them, seeing images of familiar ships would have served to trigger recall of notable moments and achievements in their eventful lives.

Ship portraits, unlike commissioned views such as the Brace's Rock images, would not have been generated by (although they may have been discussed with) topographical views in hand. In these paintings the identifiable topographic markers of a site were secondary, and the ship—usually in its most descriptive, profile view—was the primary consideration, although Lane often enlivened this somewhat staid genre by placing the vessel in action in a recognizable harbor, with marine traffic providing variety of scale and action. Ship portraits were commissioned—sometimes from the vessel's owner, sometimes from its captain—and what they were "about" was document and memory. The power of ship portraits to focus and give credence to personal, vernacular, national, and family history is suggested by Robert B. Forbes's transcription and publication of his father's *Notes Regarding the Picture of the Schooner* Coquette *Hanging in the Lower Room at Milton*.[56] The painting hanging in the family home—together with his long-dead father's manuscript account of his eighteenth- and early nineteenth-century adventures in the *Coquette* involving war, piracy, imprisonment, and mutiny—clearly prompted the son's curiosity about and sense of connection with a man he had little opportunity to know.[57] For Forbes, himself a veteran of decades of adventures on the globe's oceans, commissioning Lane's lithographed frontispiece of the *Jamestown* with which to add visual evidence to his own published report on a historic mission was clearly a form of communication with his peers and with the future. For Lane, it was an opportunity to associate his name with, and to demonstrate his skills in the context of, Forbes's many well-known enterprises. The primary vehicles of this multilevel communication were the profiles of a tugboat and a warship.

In the case of the *Coquette*, both the painting (unlocated) and Ralph Forbes's vivid account of his nautical adventures were reminders of daring on the high seas in the service of moving goods across oceans and between cultures. For him and for his son, Robert Bennet Forbes, as for all the other mariners and merchants engaged in long and risky voyages, the seaworthiness, defensive apparatus, and speed of ships made all the difference, and their portraits recorded and suggested this prowess.[58] Although important in the development of steamships, Forbes focused much of his design and navigation skill on wind-driven vessels. The *Jamestown*'s Atlantic crossing under his command, for instance, was fifteen days, one of the swiftest ever under sail, and routinely, when ships he designed were launched, he would captain them in trials of speed against the fastest pilot schooners available.[59]

A logical outgrowth of Forbes's competitive attitude toward sailing and his interest in trials of new rigs and hull designs was his founding, with friends, of the Boston Boat Club in 1834, and the introduction of sailing as sport—yachting—to the United States. Decades later, in the mid-nineteenth century, Forbes wrote newspaper articles about yacht races and, like most yachtsmen on both sides of the Atlantic, was particularly impressed with the legendary yacht *America*, a schooner belonging to a New York syndicate; he praised the schooner as "the true thing [in] rough or smooth [water] for superior sailing."[60] This lean craft, with its prodigious expanse of canvas,

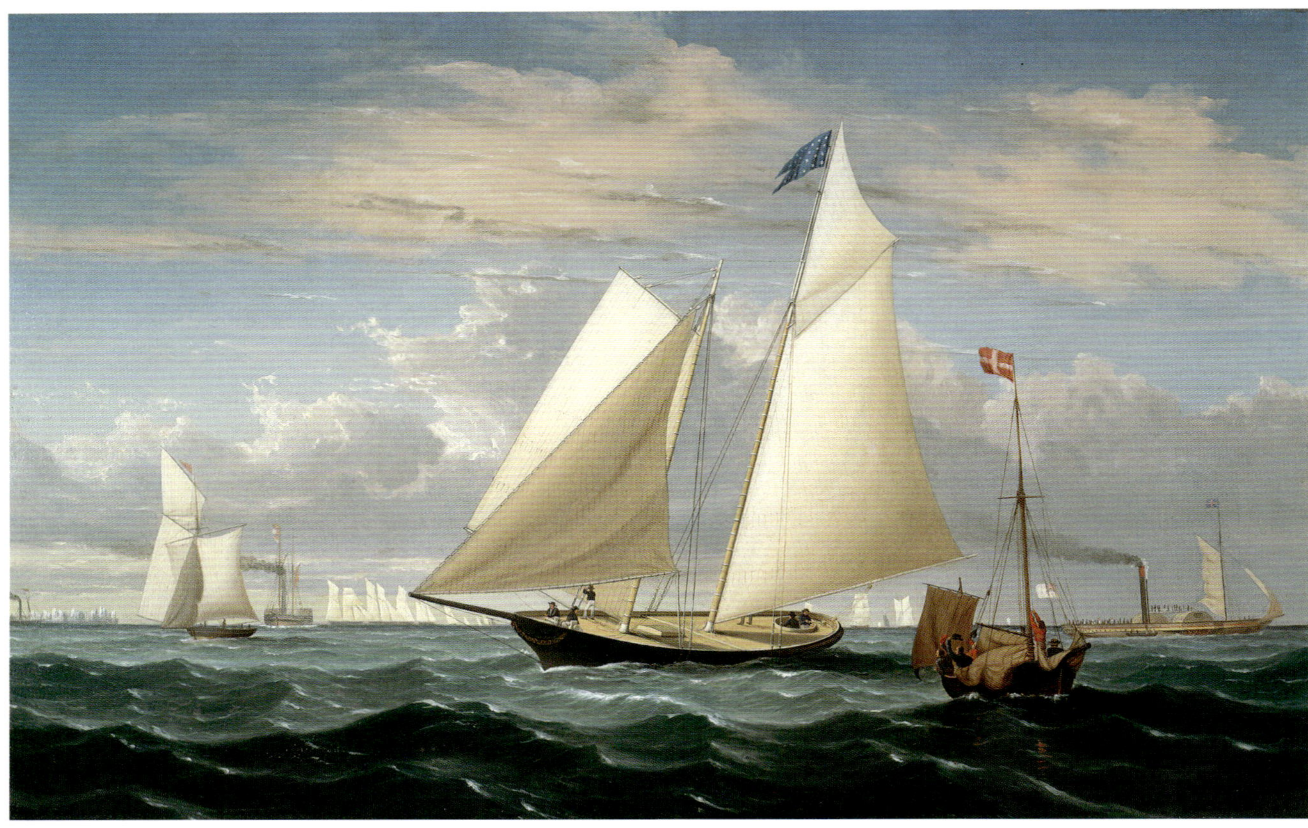

FIGURE 18
Fitz H. Lane, *The Yacht* America *Winning the International Race*, 1851. Oil on canvas, 24½ × 38¼ in. (63.5 × 99.1 cm). Peabody Essex Museum. Gift of Augustus P. Loring Jr., 1949 (M4696). Courtesy of the Peabody Essex Museum, Salem, Massachusetts. Photo by Mark Sexton and Jeffrey R. Dykes.

was the subject of several Lane paintings. Their patron is unknown, but clearly they were commissioned by *America* admirers, and Lane exerted himself to express the speed and elegance of this craft.[61] As in all ship portraits, the subject is centered on the canvas (his views, on the other hand, generally evacuate the center to allow deep visual penetration into space). *The Yacht* America *Winning the International Race*, of 1851, records an event that Lane did not witness, as it took place in the waters off the Isle of Wight in the English Channel, and yet the scene, based on an English print, has great immediacy (fig. 18).[62] Sailing wing and wing before the wind, *America* heels over slightly, exposing its sleek deck as it cuts through heavy swells powered by a stiff following breeze that also catches the pennants, the smoke from the paddle wheelers, and even the low cumulus clouds, while all but one of its competitors beat futilely against the wind on another reach, hopelessly to the rear.[63]

A second portrait of this champion, *Three Views of Yacht* America, is unusual in that, like Van Dyck's triple portrait of Charles I (Windsor Castle, Royal Collection), it presents multiple simultaneous views of its subject (fig. 19). We see in one glance this schooner in action coming, going, and broadside, close-hauled and pointing well with its maximum expanse of canvas—like the almost too-lanky legs of a racehorse. It is performing that act of physics by which wind blowing in one direction can be harnessed to propel a schooner in a different direction with extraordinary speed and precision. It is not known who ordered these portraits of *America*, whether admirers

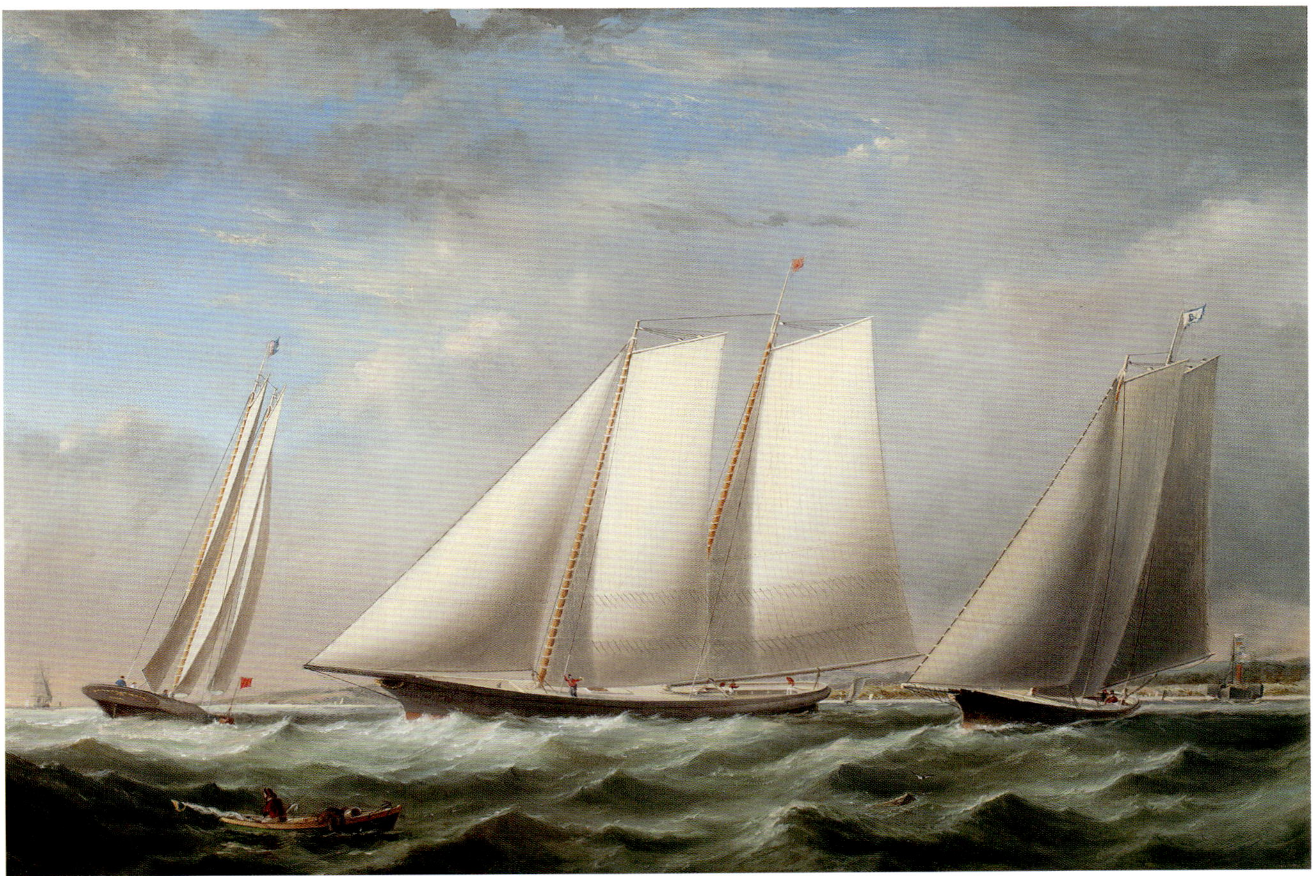

FIGURE 19
Fitz H. Lane, *Three Views of Yacht* America, 1851. Oil on canvas, 18½ × 27½ in. (46.99 × 68.58 cm). William I. Koch Collection.

like R. B. Forbes, who may have wanted to keep a record of this extraordinary "true thing" before his eyes, or one of its New York Yacht Club owners, but yachtsmen paid well, as we understand from John Trask that Lane "painted two yacht races off Newport and received five hundred dollars for each of them," the highest sum in the records paid to the artist for a painting, so Lane must have been pleased to receive these similar commissions and to have his work on view in the homes of those who paid so well.[64] During the Civil War *America* was enlisted as a blockade-runner for the South and then as a blockade-enforcer for the North. It was scuttled, raised, and armed with cannon; after the war it was rebuilt, raced, then given to the U.S. Naval Academy, but, not being maintained, it decayed and was ignominiously scrapped in 1945.[65] In ship portraits—as in portraits of humans—time is frozen and coexists with all future time: in Lane's portrait the schooner remains *America*, the heroic "true thing" in its glory days.

Each of Lane's ship-portrait commissions must have involved considerable communication with the patron and painstaking study on the artist's part. Of these discussions and studies, beyond the evidence of the works themselves, no trace survives. In spite of assumptions by some that on maturity he abandoned this fact-based genre, it is clear he did not; ship-portrait commissions were sufficiently interesting or profitable to Lane that he continued to do portrait work throughout his career. Nor

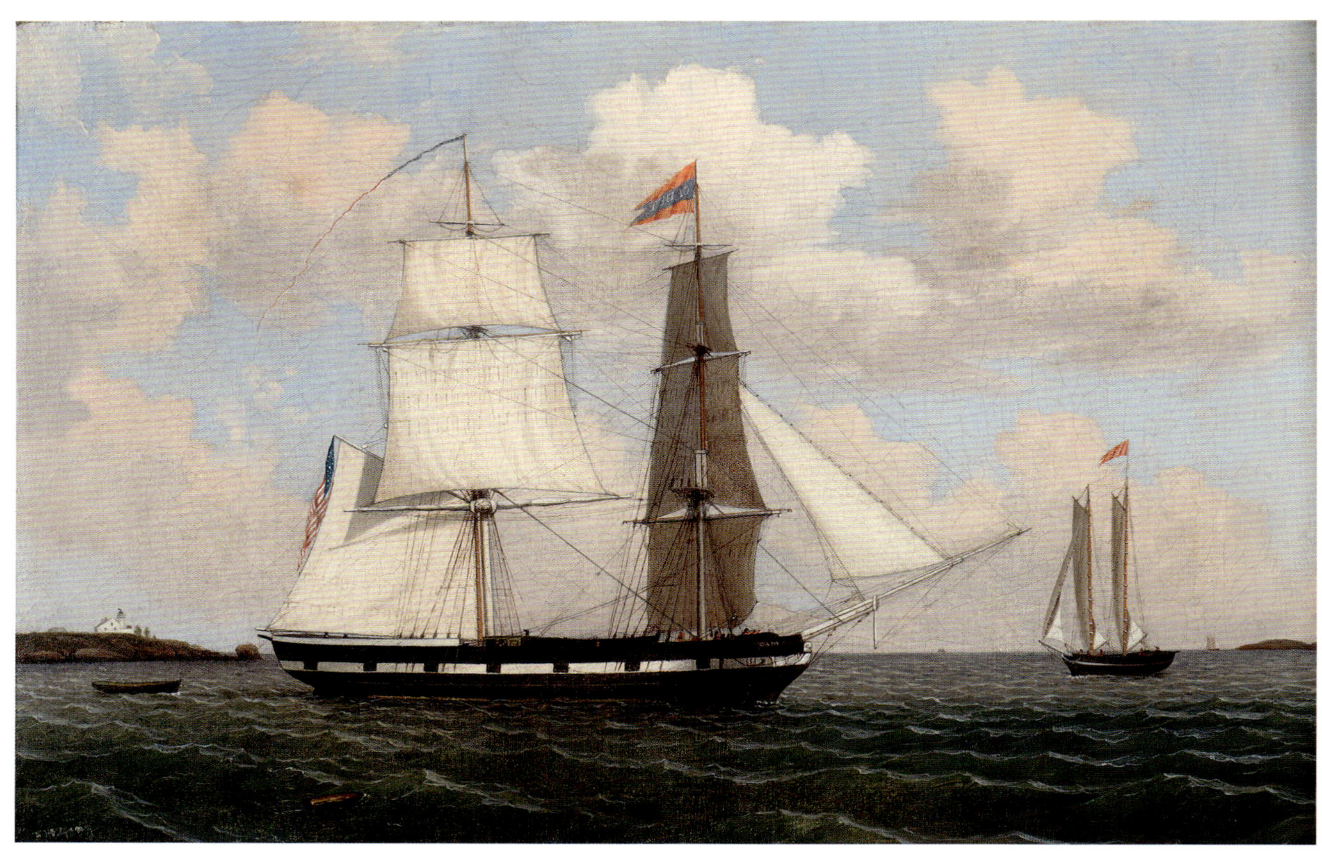

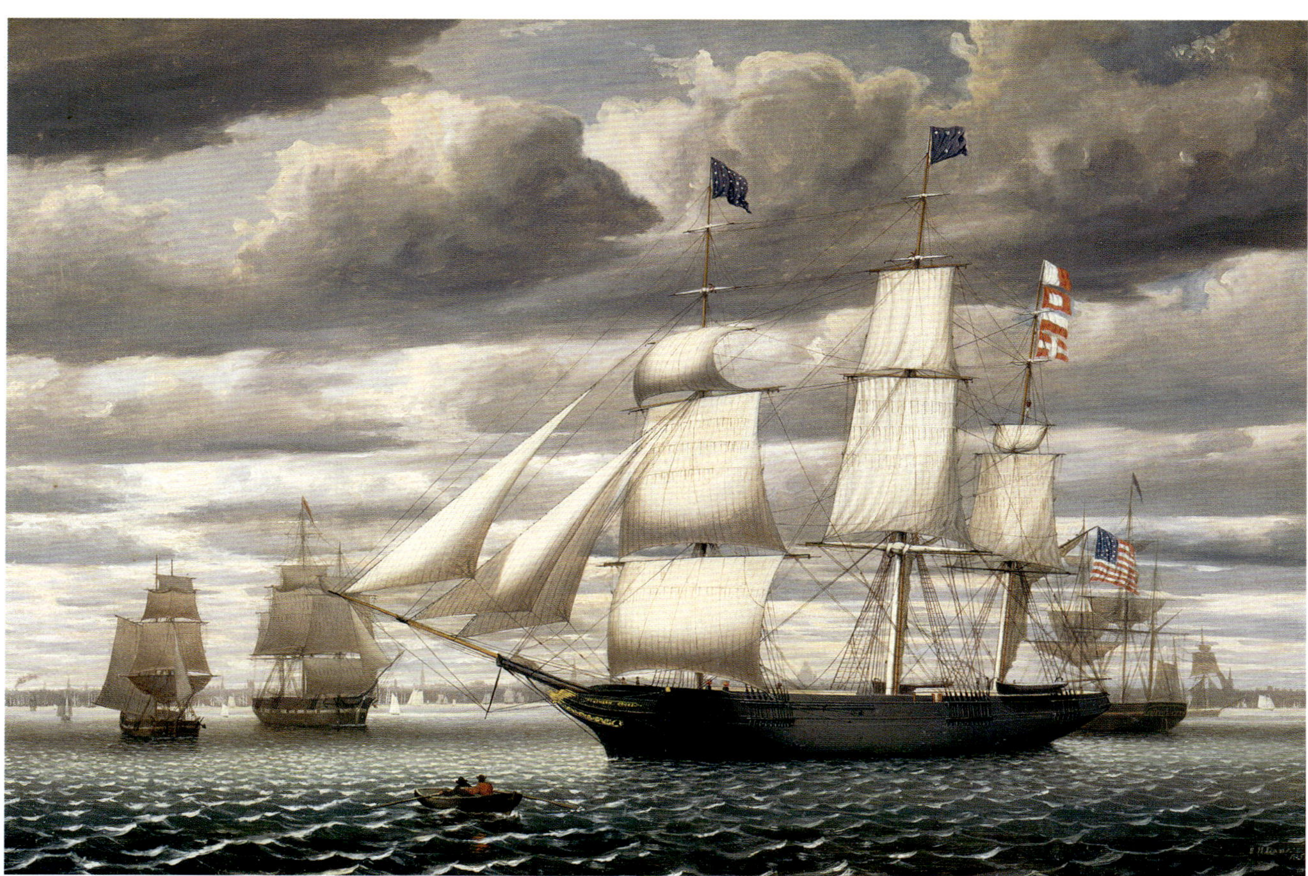

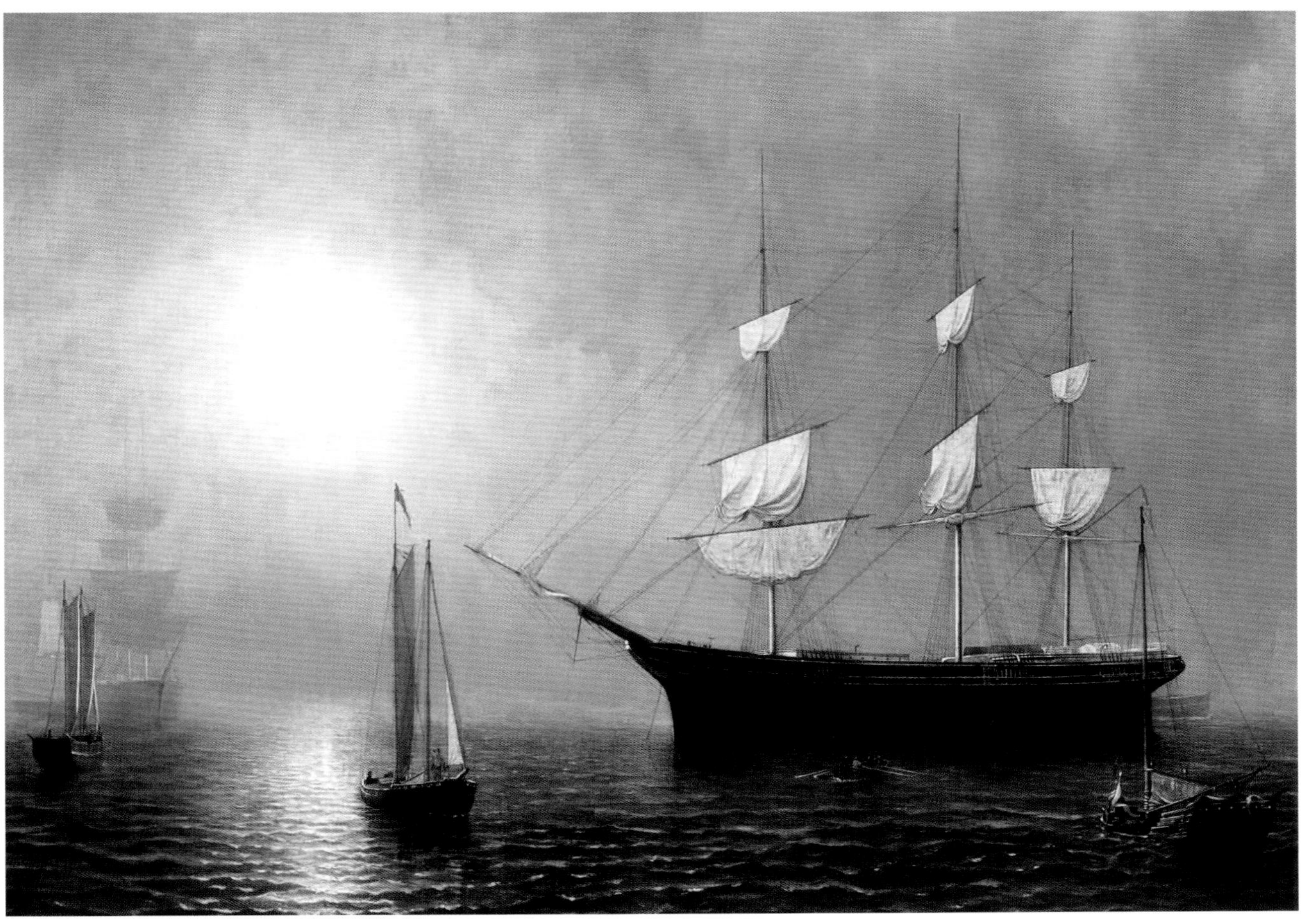

FIGURE 20 (OPPOSITE TOP)
Fitz. H. Lane, *Brig* Cadet *in Gloucester Harbor*, before 1848. Oil on canvas, 17¼ × 25¾ in. (43.8 × 65.4 cm). Cape Ann Museum, Gloucester, Massachusetts. Gift of Isabel Babson Lane, 1946 (1147.a).

FIGURE 21 (OPPOSITE BOTTOM)
Fitz H. Lane, *Ship* Southern Cross *in Boston Harbor*, 1851. Oil on canvas, frame 34¼ × 47 in. (87 × 119.4 cm). Peabody Essex Museum. Gift of the Estate of Stephen Wheatland, 1987 (M18639). Courtesy of the Peabody Essex Museum, Salem, Massachusetts. Photo by Mark Sexton.

FIGURE 22 (ABOVE)
Fitz H. Lane, *Ship* Starlight, ca. 1860. Oil on canvas, 30 × 50 in. (76.2 × 127 cm). Collection, The Butler Institute of American Art, Youngstown, Ohio. Museum purchase, 1928 (S28-o-127).

do they "develop" and change with time. Exemplary are *Brig* Cadet *in Gloucester Harbor* (fig. 20), painted in the first decade of Lane's painting career; *Ship* Southern Cross *in Boston Harbor*, 1851 (fig. 21), from the middle decade of his career; and *Ship* Starlight of ca. 1860 (fig. 22), from the last decade of his career.[66] Although they exhibit variations on a theme, there is a uniformity of approach and treatment in these portraits—the subject vessel is presented broadside, centered or entering the center, with sails set and legible pennants flying; the rigging extends high above the horizon; a smaller foreground boat establishes scale; and the weather conditions tend to be auspicious. That the patrons were pleased is attested by the survival of these works. They point emphatically toward local knowledge and the circulation of local capital (in the commissions for Lane), regional talent and capital (in Massachusetts Bay's masterful shipbuilding industries), and global capital (in the ventures with cargoes to and from distant markets). Throughout his twenty-five-year painting career, Lane continued to take, and satisfy, these portrait commissions; inevitably the presence of these painted documents of personal history, merchant prowess, and financial investment on the walls of the homes of his patrons reinforced his reputation among those whose custom he sought.

The works exhibited by Lane at the Boston Arts Association, the Boston Athenaeum, and the National Academy of Design were landscape views rather than ship portraits. Some had already been sold at the time of exhibition and were, therefore, offered on public view to increase his reputation and generate future commissions rather than achieve direct sales (see appendix A). However, many of the works Lane sent to these annual events were for sale, so it is clear that he saw these high-profile venues as arenas in which to find buyers for unbespoke, or "speculative," works.[67] It is also probable that his placement of paintings at Procter Brother's stationers, booksellers, and printers, at the Marine Insurance Company, at the bank, and at other local venues was, in part, a search for buyers. Indeed, records confirm that one work, while exhibited at Procter's, was bought by John S. Webber, custom's collector of the port and district of Gloucester, town selectman, and ambitious real-estate developer.[68] Some Lane paintings exhibit substantial changes.[69] Whether these were made by the artist, perhaps with a view to improving the chances for sale of a speculative work that did not find a ready buyer, or were initiated by a patron or purchaser who requested adjustments is impossible to determine. In either case, they show an artist who—in spite of careful preplanning—recomposed works to satisfy his patrons or his own desire to make the work better and therefore more vendible.

In one instance, a notation by Stevens on one of Lane's Maine drawings provides a clue to his other strategies for selling noncommissioned works. On one of the Maine drawings Stevens has inscribed "Camden Mountains and Harbor from the North Point of Negro Island made by Lane toward sundown of our second day's cruise"; and he has indicated, as is so often the case, those present when the drawing was made: "F. H. Lane / J. L. Stevens Jr. / J. S. Hooper Sept. 1855" (fig. 108 in *Paintings and Drawings*; FHLo inv. 174). Very unusual, Stevens has also noted, "The picture painted from the sketch was sold by W[illiam] Y. Balch to a gentleman of Maine." On another Maine drawing—done during an excursion in 1850 that included "Lane / Stevens / Tilden / Adams," according to Stevens's notation—he indicates that Lane "painted a small picture from this his first sketch of that scenery / It was sold by Balch to Mrs. Josiah Quincy, Jr." (fig. 112 in *Paintings and Drawings*; FHLo inv. 178).[70] The art sales system dependent on middlemen art merchants that prevails today was only in its infancy in Lane's day.[71] Like so many of these early dealers, the one Lane came to employ to sell at least some of his works—William Y. Balch of Boston—was also in the business of selling art accoutrements such as frames and was located in the heart of Boston's art community at Tremont.

It is clear from these notations (and those on two other drawings on which Stevens indicated he himself used Balch to sell two Lane paintings) that Lane used Balch as a middleman dealer to sell to individuals beyond his immediate acquaintance and outside of the established fine-arts exhibition system.[72] According to Stevens, "Lane was frequently in Boston, his sales agent being Balch who was at the head of his guild in those days. So in my Boston visits I was led to Balch's fairly often—the resort of many artists and the depot of their works."[73] Balch is listed in the Boston city directory as "gilder, 10 Tremont Row," in 1850, although he was also a frame maker and picture dealer.[74] Balch and his wife were both members of the American Art-Union, and Balch served as the Boston agent for that organization.[75] It appears that his wife was also active in the business.[76]

It was by no means inevitable that the dealer system Balch represented would evolve into the dominant mechanism by which artists' new work would find buyers.

Indeed, Lane would have read in his 1840 volume of the *Art Journal* that at least some of his London peers felt art dealers were "a great evil" and that their use resulted in a situation in which "the artist is robbed of that fair reward which is his due; and these men, who for the most part look upon such works in the same light as they would any other articles of merchandise, reap a more golden harvest of the fruits of art than the labourers themselves."[77] This disdain for the art merchant stems at least partially from having to share the "golden harvest" that an artist working directly with a patron had no occasion to share. However, it was through Balch that Lane gained a patron at one remove in Mrs. Josiah Quincy Jr., wife of one of the wealthiest men in Boston, whose good opinion he had every reason to value.[78] In the long run, of course, the dealer system triumphed, evolving earliest in New York City and marked in Lane's day by the establishment in 1840 of a branch of the French firm Goupil, managed by Michael Knoedler.[79] In this transatlantic move we see the seeds of what would become, in the post–Civil War years, a vigorously pro-European art climate that would present obstacles to the reputations of American painters, Lane among them.

Another mechanism that Lane used to vend his wares was the local lottery. Joseph L. Stevens Jr. reported that the Stacys—a Gloucester-based wealthy merchant family—"bought [paintings] direct of [from] him . . . before other residents" and aided him "as time went on in selling paintings by lot. I invested in a view of Gloucester from Rocky Neck, thus put on sale at the old reading room." The event was apparently a raffle of five Lane paintings among the subscribers of his 1855 lithographic view of Gloucester.[80] On at least two occasions during his lifetime Lane paintings were offered for sale at auction in New York.[81] Auctions were popular in Gloucester for the vending of books as well as household goods, including "pictures," and in Boston in Lane's day auctions dispersed paintings along with other goods.[82] In 1837, for instance, nineteen landscape and genre works by Alvan Fisher were auctioned, but no extant evidence suggests that Lane pursued auction sales on this scale.[83]

Lane's primary source of sales appears to have been personal commissions; secondarily, uncommissioned works were offered through vernacular venues in Gloucester and fine-arts venues in urban centers elsewhere. Subscription sales and placement with the dealer Balch seem to have been useful to him as well. Word of mouth appears to have been a major factor in the formation of his reputation and the maintenance of his livelihood. Although a surprising number of Lane's known patrons were women, most were wealthy men representing a wide variety of trades and professions.[84] Many were self-made men, and many knew one another. Of the twenty-five wealthiest individuals in Gloucester in 1850, at least eight were Lane patrons.[85] While it is clear Lane exerted himself to extend his reputation and effect sales by a wide variety of methods, one of the most significant factors in his success was the presence of his works in the homes of those in Gloucester and Boston with a wide circle of friends and kin.

LANE'S "ACCURACY"

According to the editors of the *Art Journal* in 1849, "it may be said of the artist that his first and ruling motive is fame. The idea of value, in the pecuniary sense of the term, or of the legal right incident to the production of genius [copyright], is of an inferior or secondary nature."[86] If this is true—or was true in the mid-nineteenth century—it is equally true that the secondary, pecuniary sense of "value" usually follows fame, so the artist need not have chosen between these goals but rather could pursue them in tandem. Lane had some help from the press in furthering his "fame" (or reputation), and the nature and terms of the public discussion of his career and his works can reveal what his contemporaries and patrons valued (in the most expansive sense) in his paintings. It was this valuing, of course, that enabled him to make a living—that is, to receive pecuniary rewards for his labor.

Exactly what qualities in his technique, subjects, and treatments did his contemporaries valorize and encourage? There are two dominant linked threads in their comments, the first remarking on the accuracy of his works and the second noting with approbation that Lane's paintings serve well as memory triggers. A third quality that finds some mention, however infrequent, is "poetry."

The dominant term in all published commentary on Lane's work during his lifetime is "accuracy." Throughout the recorded commentary by Lane's contemporaries, this term is consistently offered as the chief attribute of his pictures and the primary reason for his reputation. The advertisement for Lane's 1836 lithograph of Gloucester, for example, informs potential purchasers that "the buildings and prominent points, are remarkably accurate and distinct"; that for his 1846 lithograph of the town notes that "every house and object . . . [is] distinctly visible"; and in the 1857 commendation of Lane's new sign for John Trask, the journalist pauses to name seven structures, inviting readers to join him in identifying these paint-transcribed buildings (figs. 4, 11).[87] Characteristically, an unnamed critic in the *Boston Evening Transcript*, speaking more globally, assured readers in 1850 that Lane's "ships in a squall, his sketches of Cape Ann seaside scenery, and all his salt water and boating scenes are unequalled in their fidelity to the ocean's varying aspects," linking "unequalled" and "fidelity" in a tight, authoritative superlative.[88] "Fidelity" presses the more neutral "accuracy" or "distinctness" into a moral valence—faithfulness intimating a potential faithlessness in an inaccurate rendering, a potential betrayal of trust that is here, in the most absolute terms, refuted. Lane's obituary of August 19, 1865, embroidered on this theme: "Mr. Lane was eminently conscientious, never deviating from an accurate copy of nature as presented to his view. . . . He never sacrificed truth of delineation for picturesque effects. . . . The eye was gratified by the exactitude with which individual objects of interest were rendered. His vessel[s] and other maritime objects were perfect portraits."[89] "Conscientious," "accurate," "truth of delineation," "exactitude": these terms line up in a phalanx of assurance. Lane paints "perfect portraits" of his subjects, avoiding a potentially damning untruthfulness or falseness that would follow the introduction of mere "picturesque effects." He is, in other words, above all, praised as a trustworthy narrator of the scenes and objects on offer in his images.

In some commentary accuracy is linked not just to fidelity and trust but also to memory, and this hints at what is so vividly at stake in Lane's "conscientious . . . exactitude." When a contemporary ordered a Lane painting, what he or she imagined was a physical object resonant of a specific kind of recognition, imbued with feeling, often a strong memory. From published comments, it becomes clear that the painting's job was to still time and, through the viewer's recognition, to trigger a cluster of specific associations. In its most direct form this burden is thrust imaginatively upon the painter by a sickly Gloucesterite who journeyed to Surinam in 1860 "to breathe the pure air in these latitudes . . . [to] give . . . the despairing invalid new hopes of life and health."[90] Specifically, this correspondent, signing himself "Junior," opined in his letter to the *Cape Ann Advertiser*: "Would that our fellow townsman and artist, Mr. F. H. Lane, were with us to transfer to canvass some of the gorgeous scenery visible in the tropics, either at the early morning hour, when the God of day arises in his majesty on the eastern horizon, or slowly sinks at nightfall in his rosy bed in the west."[91] "Junior" here imaginatively tasks the artist with creating a still, portable, evocative work that will capture the novelty of Dutch Guiana's "gorgeous scenery" and the evanescent quality of tropical light at sunrise or sunset. He is imaginatively charged with capturing the scene, the impact of the scene, and triggering "Junior's" future memory of a specific time and place imbued with his strong feelings of hope for robust health.

More often, Lane's paintings were praised for their capacity—through their accurate simulation of a scene—to transport a viewer through space or time. Characteristically, in September 1849 the *Cape Ann Light and Gloucester Telegraph* informed its readers that "Lane has just taken from his easel a view of Fresh Water Cove and the beautiful scenery adjacent, painted for a gentleman in Boston, once a 'Cape Ann Boy.' . . . So true to nature is this beautiful picture that the spectator can hardly divest himself of the belief he is standing upon the margin of the meadow to the westward of Stage Rocks, and gazing upon the landscape, which glows with all the warmth and gorgeousness of a summer sunset."[92] This painterly conjuring enables a former "Cape Ann Boy" to step into a Gloucester childhood memory from the perspective of a Boston adulthood.

Accuracy and memory were key ingredients in not only his landscape views but also his ship portraits. His contemporaries particularly valued the recognizability of all his marine subjects—that characteristic of being "perfect portraits," as his obituary writer put it. But for those of us today who are not avid sailors, ship portraits seem a little tedious and redundant, reiterating the conventions of profile hull, swelling sails, and echoing clouds above rippling water and exquisitely detailed rigging. However, if we make an effort to see them as those who commissioned and paid for them saw them, summoning to mind their complex stories of human ambition, know-how, cunning, and achievement, they become mnemonics of human events well remembered; that is, they become portraits in the fullest sense. Robert Bennet Forbes's father's painting of the *Coquette*, for example, hung in the family sitting room at Milton, Massachusetts, and, supplemented by the manuscript account of the vessel's exploits, proved a cynosure of family conversation and knowledge about this adventurous long-gone patriarch.

As a characteristic instance of Lane's ship portraits, *Cadet*, commissioned by Edward Babson, records the outbound brig lying still in the water, awaiting (or discharging) a pilot in Gloucester's outer harbor (fig. 20). It was built in Medford in 1821 and registered in Boston, although owned by consortiums consistently led by Gloucesterites. In 1836 it was bought by the Babson brothers, Edward, William, and John James, together with two other investors; it was captained by Edward Babson, used primarily in the trade between Gloucester and Surinam, and sold in Bahia in April 1848.[93] When *Cadet* was at sea and storms wracked the Atlantic, there were reverberations in the Babson household, as noted by diarist Annette Babson, sister of Edward, William, and John James, who, in a characteristic entry in January 1848, records that "great anxiety is felt for the *Cadet*. I most earnestly hope we shall hear from her."[94] Those distant climes to which the ship routinely ventured sometimes yielded visitors as well as cargo, such as a "Mr. Sanchez, a gent from Surinam, [who] kindly accompanied [Annette] with a low discordant hum" as she was "playing on the piano."[95] The painting of *Cadet*, then, marks one of many departures and homecomings, each beginning or ending a cycle of hope, anxiety, and pleasurable relief focused on the brig. The vessel represented a considerable capital investment, its cargo represented further capital at risk, and the humans whose lives were entrusted to its seaworthiness and to the skill of its commander occasioned further reason for anxiety and relief. A ship's portrait is never, in other words, just a ship. Its commissioning represents regard, gratitude, relief, and perhaps celebration. It implies a narrative of, in this case, more than a decade of concern and confidence at the family hearth, where it would hang as a depository and marker for the vessel's complex history, almost as a member of the family. Accuracy was essential to its role as mnemonic of a specific long-term relationship between humans and this specific object partner. As the *Gloucester Telegraph* put it, quoting James Fenimore Cooper's popular novel of 1828, *Red Rover*, there is a "secret tie which binds the mariner so closely to his vessel, and which often leads him to prize her qualities as one would esteem the virtues of a friend, and almost to be equally enamoured of the fair proportions of his ship as those of his mistress. . . . It is his home, his theme of constant, and frequently of painful interest, his tabernacle, and often his source of pride and exultation."[96] *Cadet*'s portrait remained with the Babsons and descended from Captain Edward (who owned eight other ships but chose this one for Lane's attention) to his daughter Isabel, who married a distant cousin of the artist and, in 1946, gave the painting to the Cape Ann

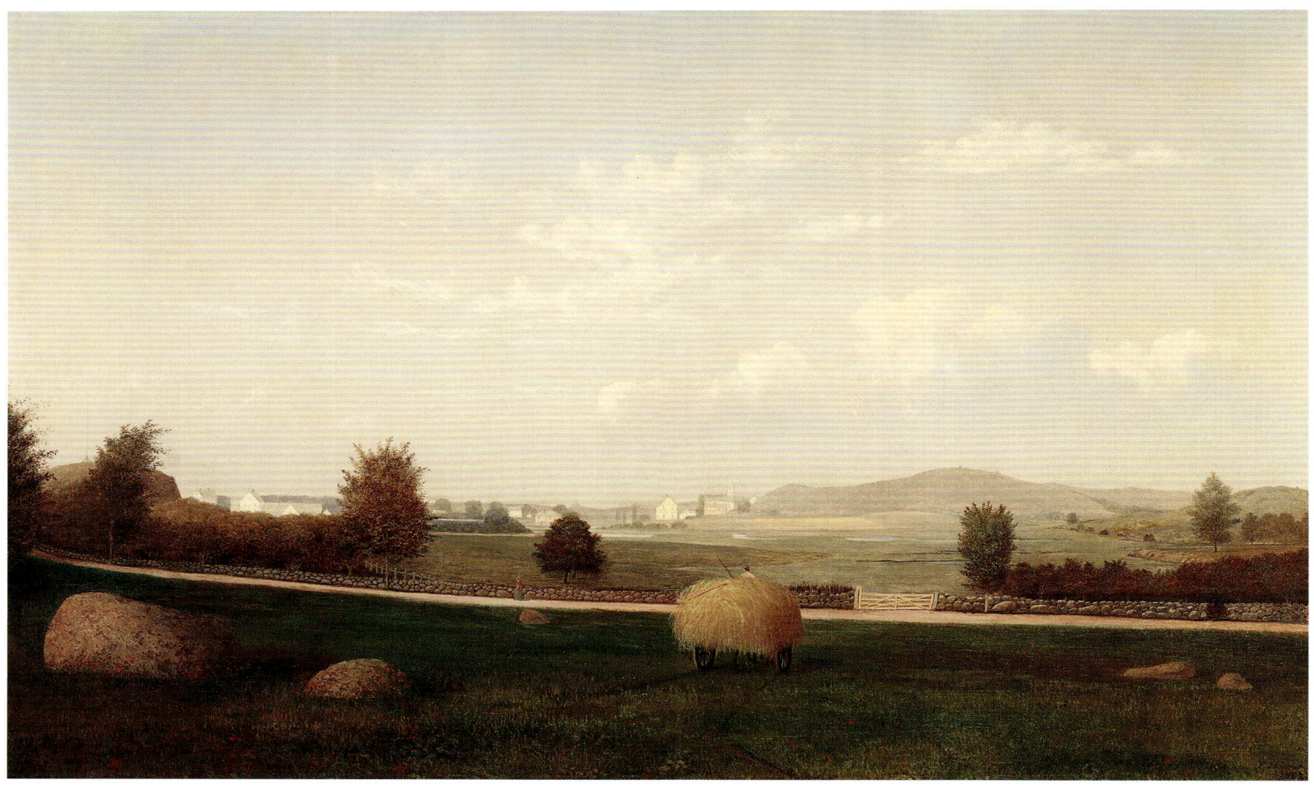

FIGURE 23
Fitz H. Lane, *The Babson Meadows at Riverdale*, 1863. Oil on canvas, 22 × 35¾ in. (55.9 × 90.8 cm). Commissioned by Nathaniel Babson. Cape Ann Museum, Gloucester, Massachusetts. Gift of Roger W. Babson, 1937 (779.03).

Museum.[97] There it became an object on public display needing explication rather than a familiar sitting-room object, a window on long-term memory within the family circle.

While Lane's portrait of *Cadet* as a specific vessel, accurately rendered, memorialized the relationship between a family and a ship, other Lane paintings were commissioned to link another branch of the Babson family to specific and recognizable Cape Ann landscapes and to deep family history. *The Babson Meadows at Riverdale* and *Babson and Ellery Houses, Gloucester* were commissioned in 1863 by Nathaniel Babson, a cousin of Edward, John James, and Annette Babson, as presents for his daughters, Maria Babson and Emma Babson Friend, as they readied to emigrate to California (figs. 23 and 24). Their branch of the family was based on farmland near the inland village of Riverdale, just north of Gloucester on Cape Ann's inland waterway, the Squam River. The girls' grandmother and then uncle maintained a dairy farm and raised a cash crop of English hay on the moderately fertile family land, where their 1738 gambrel-roofed homestead marked more than a century of Low and Babson family inland prosperity.[98] Their father, Lane's patron Nathaniel Babson, was a bank director, a merchant, and a member of the American Art-Union.[99]

Specifically describing a landscape and a set of practices that would become only a memory for the Babson sisters, Lane has created in this pair of images a portrait of the Babson meadows at Riverdale and the capacious Babson farmhouse on the road to that village. In the first,

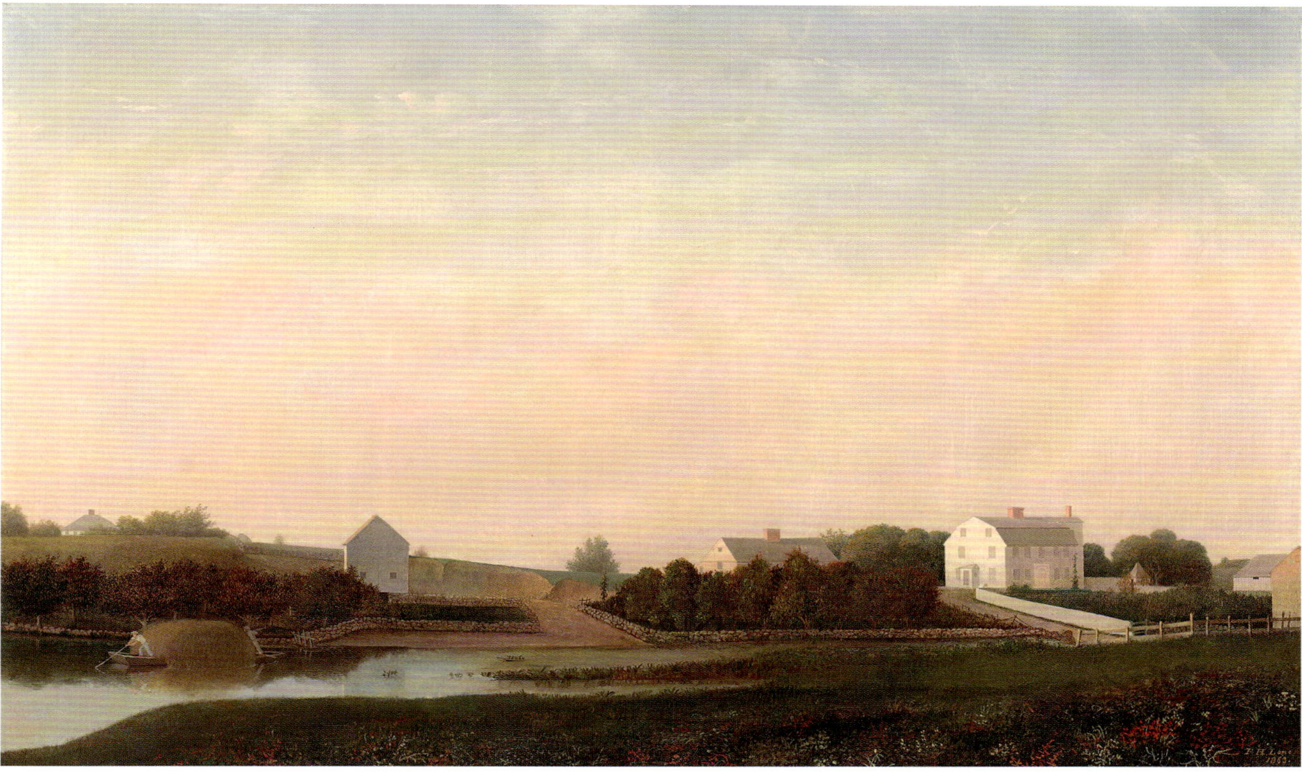

FIGURE 24
Fitz H. Lane, *Babson and Ellery Houses, Gloucester*, 1863. Oil on canvas, 22 × 36 in. (55.9 × 91.4 cm). Commissioned by Nathaniel Babson. Cape Ann Museum, Gloucester, Massachusetts. Gift of Roger W. Babson, 1937 (779.02).

a loose-loaded hay wagon is driven from the boulder-strewn Babson fields toward a road parallel to the picture plane and toward Riverdale's tidy, white-painted wooden houses and steepled church, which a contemporary looking at the painting in Lane's studio referenced as "the old meeting house on the Green with its tall spire as it appeared in days agone. . . . [The painting] is faithful to nature and well executed."[100] In other words, Lane's "faithful" accuracy here includes the painted-in restoration of a tall steeple, a patched memory of a place soon to be entirely only a memory to the painting's intended owner, who would enjoy it in the very foreign landscape of the Sacramento Valley. The archaic use of "agone" and the unbaled English hay point to verbal and technological usages receding into cultural memory by the 1860s. Joseph Wood has made a good case for the sentimental invention of the image of the nucleated whitewashed nineteenth-century New England village, but here the accuracy of Riverdale's specific structures is identifiably certain—Lane's patron and the painting's recipient would have wanted the careful accuracy that Lane's contemporaries attributed to him, a "faithfulness" that included a steeple inpainted to preserve an older memory of a storm-altered landmark.[101]

In *Babson and Ellery Houses, Gloucester*, an "old gundalow [skiff] named, incongruously, the *Royal George*," loaded with salt hay, provides implied movement and a sense of seasonal, integrated rural life as, on an auspicious summer evening, it is poled toward a mid-canvas landing and a capacious barn just west of the historic structure

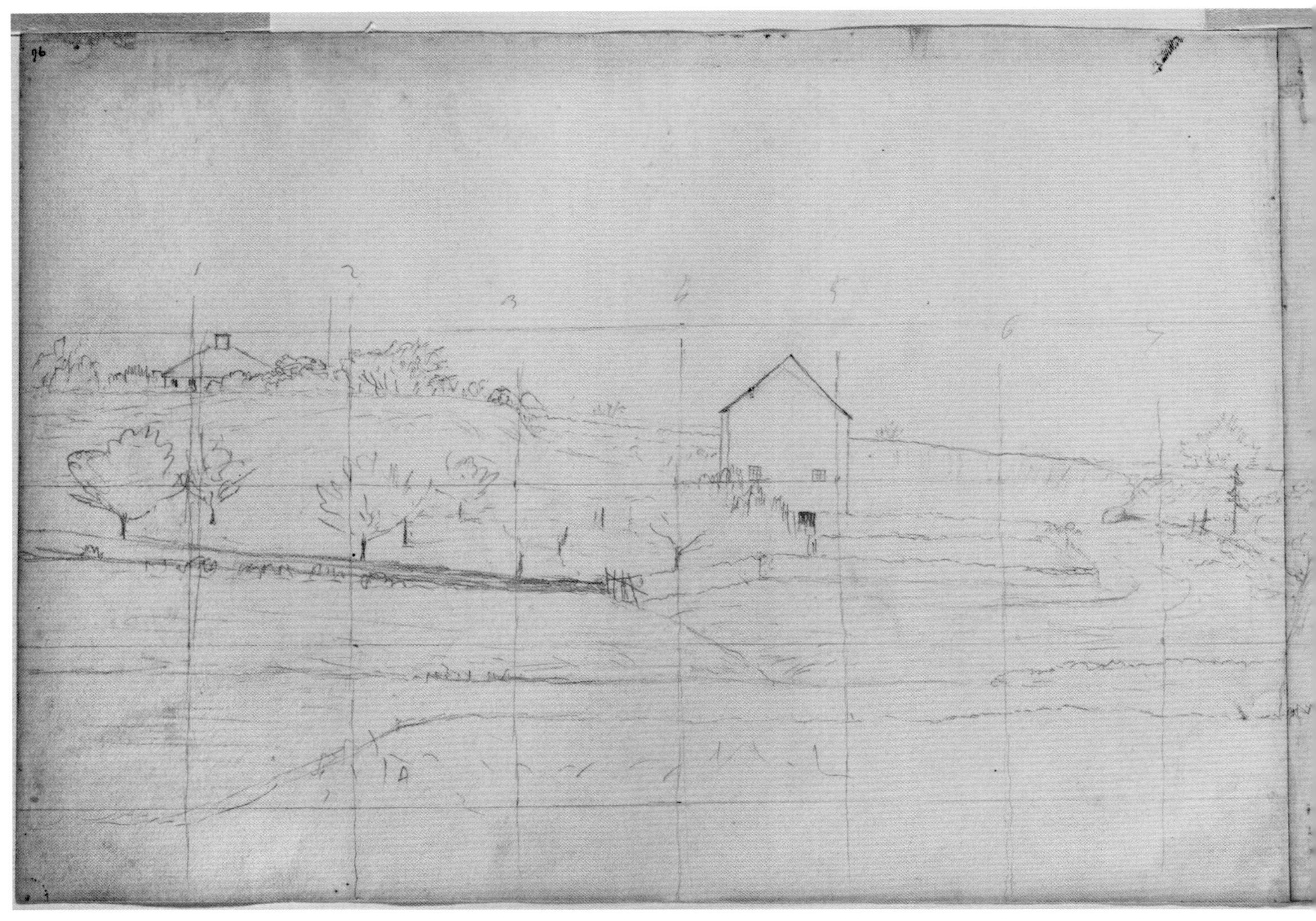

FIGURE 25
Fitz H. Lane, *View in Town Parish*, 1863. Pencil on paper, 10 × 29 in. (25.4 × 73.7 cm). Cape Ann Museum, Gloucester, Massachusetts. Gift of Samuel H. Mansfield, 1927 (485.76).

in which generations of Babsons had been born.[102] This picture and its mate are based on drawings taken on site and, unusual for Lane, squared for transfer to ensure accuracy (fig. 25). The compositions are structured around a homey sense of small-scale pastoral economy (albeit paid for by more urban wealth) and went west as documents of a family line that was broken by the midcentury siren call that drew so many out of New England to the Golden State (see chapter 7).[103] They were commissioned to freeze a memory and preserve a family-land connection. Lane's works, from as early as 1835, were commended and commissioned as appropriate "for those who have gone from among us [Gloucesterites] to other places."[104] This became a leitmotif in Lane's patronage, as many apparently wished to see Gloucester on the walls of the "other places" they chose to live. In the early twentieth century this pair of Babson paintings was retrieved from California, repatriated to Gloucester, and given to the Cape Ann Museum by a Massachusetts-based Babson relative. They

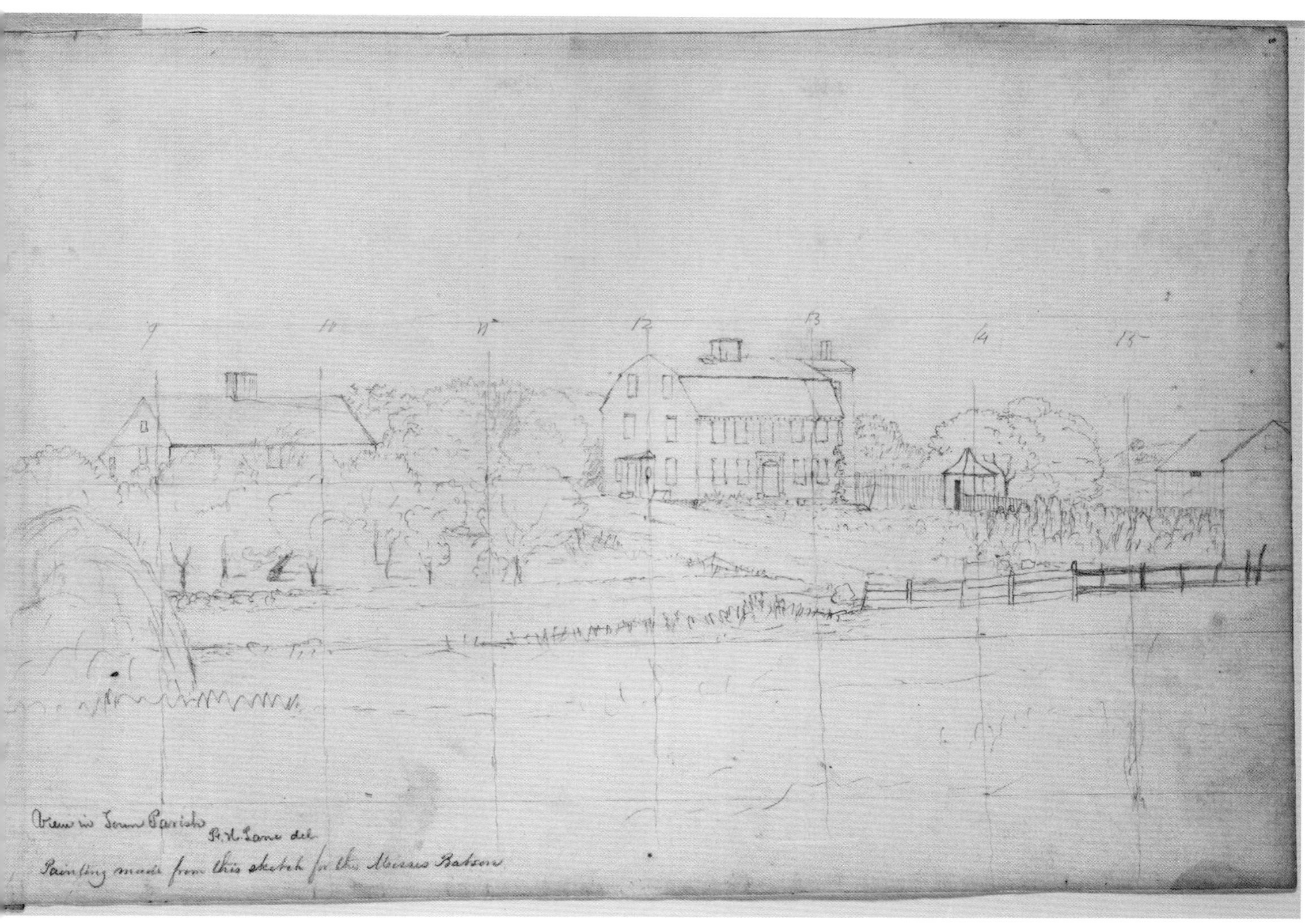

were greeted as documents of Cape Ann landscape but now not as remember-your-roots family admonitions but as historic documents of the Riverdale part of Cape Ann, incorporating its landscape and agricultural practices "in days agone."

Tasking his paintings to retrospectively distill a lost memory (such as that of the lost steeple) or an about-to-be-lost practice (such as that of carting unbaled hay), Lane's contemporaries yoked his "accuracy" and "correctness" to their memories of the built environment. When portions of his images resurrected and revivified lost landscapes and technologies, their job, as this commentary implies, was not only to arrest time but to reverse it. They were intended to faithfully document scenes that *could* have been faithfully recorded had the artist been at his maturity when they were recordable. This subjunctive, synthetic mode of picture making and picture approbation within the context of Lane's "accuracy" is perhaps best seen in the 1860 comment about one of his retrospective Gloucester Harbor scenes, possibly *The Old Fort and Ten Pound Island, Gloucester* (fig. 26):

> There is now to be seen in the reading room in the Gloucester Bank building, one of the finest pictures

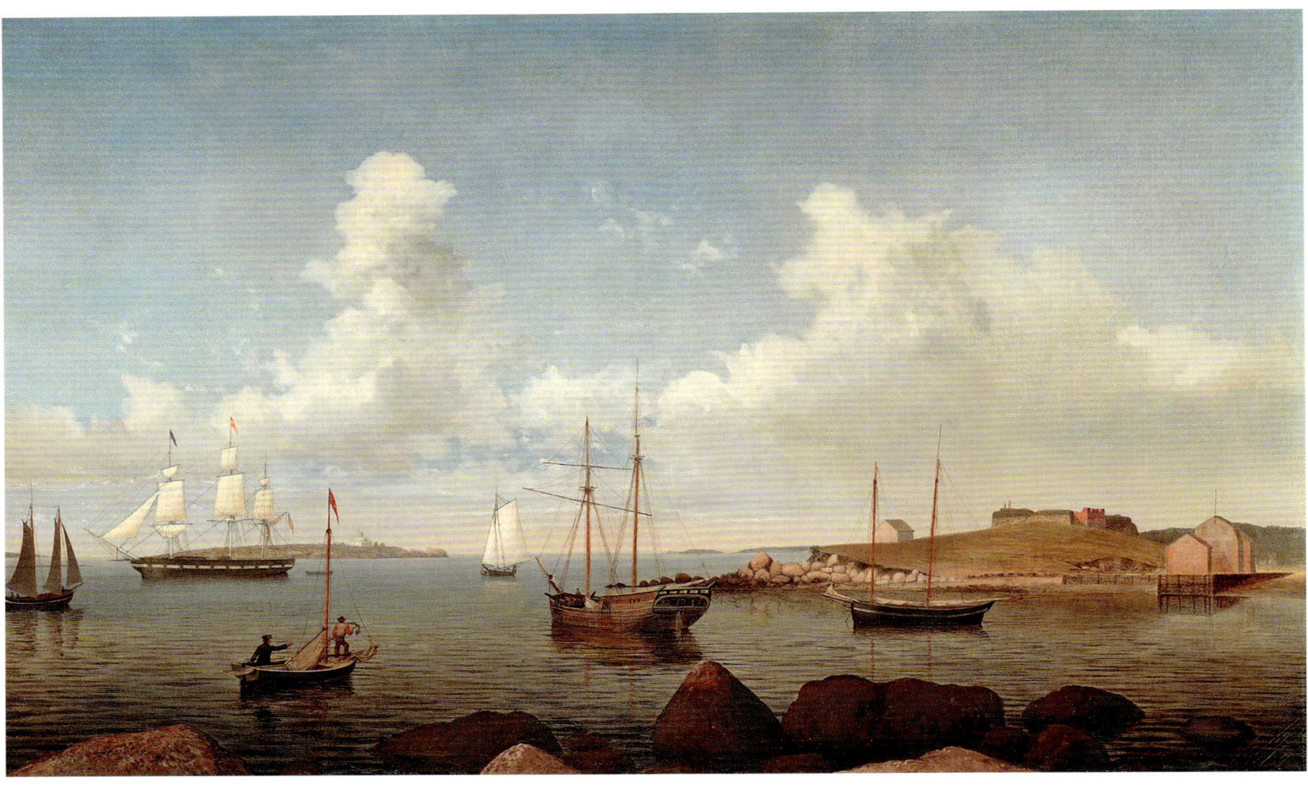

FIGURE 26
Fitz H. Lane, *The Old Fort and Ten Pound Island, Gloucester*, ca. 1860. Oil on canvas, 22 × 36 in. (55.9 × 91.4 cm). Cape Ann Museum, Gloucester, Massachusetts. Deposited by Addison Gilbert Hospital, Gloucester (Bequest of Father Jeremiah Healy), 1978 (DEP. 201).

yet produced by the pencil of our distinguished artist and fellow citizen, Fitz H. Lane, Esq. It . . . [pictures] the Old Fort and immediate vicinity . . . and all who remember this locality, as it then [1837] appeared, will at once admit the correctness of the sketch. . . .

In the foreground are "Cunner Rocks" (now Parkhurst's Wharf). . . . On the top of the hill are seen the old decaying [Fort] ramparts with a distinctness and completeness which brings former times at once to the memory. . . . Then the eye . . . at once recognizes one of the old red-tipped fishing boats that used to frequent our harbor in the days before the breakwater was built at Rockport.

A little way off lies at anchor an old-fashioned banker . . . which presents a good contrast to the modern clippers of the fishing fleet . . . and a Surinam brig is moored in the channel between Ten Pound Island and the Fort. . . .

It is useless to speak of the unsurpassed beauty of the nautical portion of the work. In alluding to a marine painting, to mention the name of Lane is praise enough. His reputation as the first marine artist of the country speaks for that. But this picture is chiefly of interest on account of *its preserving so accurately the features of a view so familiar* to many of our citizens and *which can never again exist in reality* [emphasis added]. We earnestly hope that this picture will not be purchased and carried away from the town. We should be gratified to see its position secured and have it placed in some position where the public can readily have access to it. . . . We would rather forego a whole course of Lyceum lectures

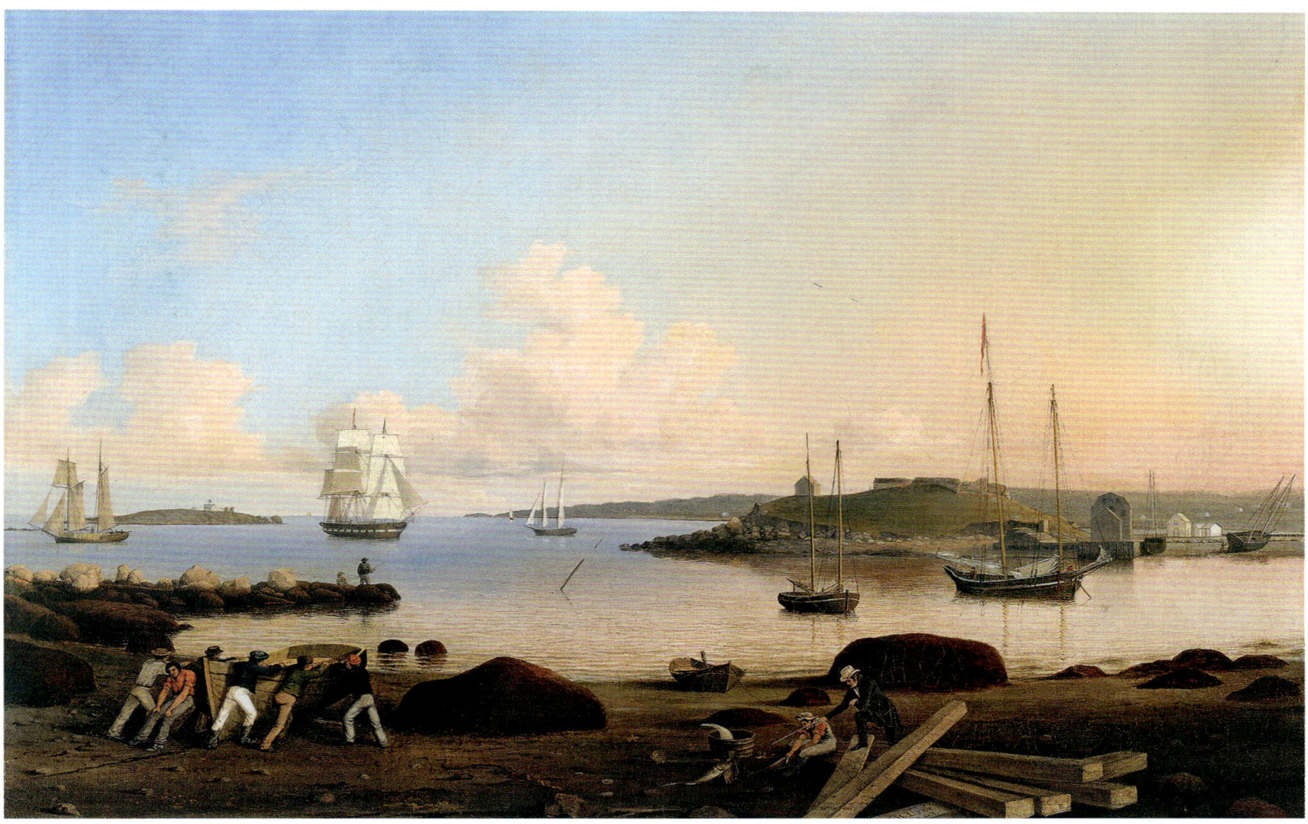

FIGURE 27
Fitz H. Lane, *The Fort and Ten Pound Island, Gloucester, Massachusetts*, 1847. Oil on canvas, 20 × 30 in. (50.8 × 76.2 cm). Museo Thyssen-Bornemisza, Madrid (635 [1982.43]). Photo: Museo Thyssen-Bornemisza / Scala / Art Resource, New York.

> than have this picture taken away from town, if the money were appropriated to retain it among us. It is a lecture and a lesson in itself, and in future years will grow more and more instructive and valuable. Our youth will learn from it the progress of the town, our aged can revive the recollections of their early days.[105]

Here the critic has helped the reader view Lane's imaginative "demolition" of Parkhurst's intrusive wharf, his partial "reconstruction" of the ruined fort, and his restoration to service of archaic types of vessels. Lane has effectively erased a quarter century from the material culture in this view, portraying the harbor's features as he and others had seen it even before he had become a painter. Note that in a similar view painted more than a decade earlier, the fort appears more ruinous (fig. 27). It is unclear why Lane undertook this exercise in temporal subtraction—it is evident from the text quoted above that this painting was not bespoke, and certainly the vast majority of his works are painted in what might be called the present tense—but the critic makes clear that its greatest virtue is its presentation of a view that "can never again exist in reality." The painting is both "accurate" and counterfactual. It is a memory machine, a resource for old and young, and a treasure for the town as a whole. Here, toward the end of his career, Lane has undertaken, and the local press has acclaimed, a painting that fulfills Gloucesterites' expectations for accuracy and their understanding of paintings as memory triggers. Neither of these terms, however, as we will see, figures prominently in the valuing of Lane in twentieth-century commentary.

While "accuracy" and "memory" are the two terms that Lane's contemporaries most frequently used to describe his paintings, in a few instances a third term, "poetry" (or "beauty" or "imagination"), is added to this pair of primary terms. In these passages qualities beyond accuracy of objects (buildings, boats, landscape features), or the burgeoning memories proposed, imagined, reconstituted, or recalled by Lane's images, are underlined, and this "poetry" is usually located in an ineffable quality of color or composition. In the newspaper notice about his 1836 lithograph of Gloucester, for instance, the editor encourages subscribers with "there is a softness and beauty in the design," and thirty years later, in Lane's 1865 obituary, another author states that "his pictures, for accuracy in delineation and beauty of coloring[,] were unsurpassed."[106] Whether this beauty came from "design" or from "coloring," it was clearly a quality that some pointed to with admiration.

The most extensive contemporary commentary on "poetry" or "imagination" in Lane's work was written by Clarence Cook—a twenty-five-year-old New Yorker who would later become a prominent art critic—and published in the *Independent* in New York in 1854.[107] Cook had, some four years earlier, seen some of Lane's paintings and was moved, in the summer of 1854, to compare the work he observed that year to the images he remembered. Concerning the "early pictures," he opines in a paragraph dense with double negatives, "there is no one of them that I have seen, without some valuable passage, showing acute observation and careful, studious execution." But overall these 1840s canvases seemed to him, in retrospect, "too hard and practical." They "delighted sailors by their perfect truth," but they did not delight Cook, who "was doubtful if [he] should find in Mr. Lane the poetical element that must be a constituent in the [first-rate] artist's mind." Here Cook establishes a hierarchy between mere sailors—who delight in "truth" or what its admirers called "accuracy" or "fidelity"—and aestheticians like himself, who could see and appreciate and be delighted by the "poetical." He is articulating, of course, a social hierarchy as well as an aesthetic one, in his invidious distinction between men who work physically and those "higher" individuals who make and comment on art.

On visiting Lane's studio in the granite house (which definitely delighted Cook, a Ruskinian), he discovered a new Lane work and in his essay assures his readers and himself (again with a backward sort of negative) that "there is no longer any fear that he is incapable of imagination." Cook does not parse "imagination," but he does make clear that he feels Lane's patrons have curtailed the artist's potential: "[Lane] has earned his money thus far mostly by painting 'portraits' of vessels for sailors and ship-owners. It is owing to this necessity, perhaps, that he has fallen into the fault of too great literalness of treatment." This is a trope familiar in the analysis of American art from the earliest learned commentary concerning John Singleton Copley before the Revolution: if the painting was too "literal," it was surely literal-minded patrons that made the protogenius do it. Cook, however, feels that, in 1854, in at least one canvas, Lane has transcended his patrons' purported limited vision. He points to an example of what he terms "poetical treatment" in a passage of a painting of the Maine coast (a work currently unlocated):

> The time is sunset after a storm. The dun and purple clouds roll away to the south-west, the sun sinks in a glory of yellow light, flooding the sea with transparent splendor. Far away in the offing, hiding the sun, sails a brig fully rigged, a transfigured vision between the glories of the sky and sea. The clearness of execution and the poetical treatment of this portion of the picture are admirable . . . [especially the] dark-green swells of water, crowned with light and pierced with light. The truth and beauty of the water in this picture I do not believe have ever been excelled. I do not believe deeper, clearer water, or waves that swing with more real power, were ever translated in oil.

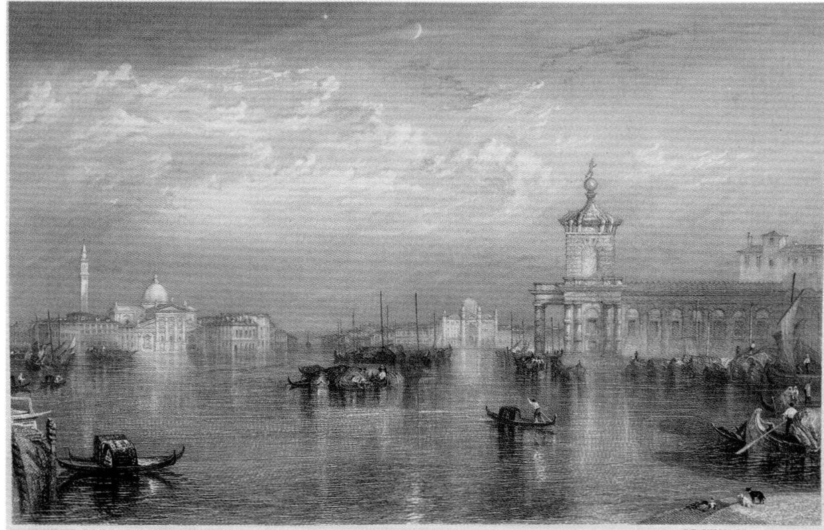

FIGURE 28
James Tibbetts Willmore after Joseph Mallord William Turner, *Venice—The Dogana*. Engraving on paper (first published 1847), sheet: 9¼ × 12½ in. (23.5 × 31.75 cm); image: 6½ × 10 in. (15.24 × 25.4 cm). From the *Art Journal* (London) 1, no. 5 (August 1849), opposite p. 260. Collections of Doe Library (N1.A5), University of California, Berkeley. Photo: The Bancroft Library, University of California, Berkeley.

This enthusiastic ekphrastic passage points to three elements that are characteristic of many Lane paintings: transitional times of day (sunrise, sunset, the gathering or passing of a storm), a source of light facing the viewer and visible (even if veiled) within the image, and convincingly portrayed water (that is, water whose "beauty" is achieved through the "truth," or accuracy, of its portrayal).

Cook describes Lane as "a man apparently of forty years, walking with difficulty, supported by crutches, hard-handed, browned by the sun and exposure . . . [with] an eye that shines clear as a hawk's under over-hanging brows . . . studious, patient, eager to learn," and self-reliant, yet he wonders how "Lane has attained . . . true genius" "without masters, without models, without great encouragement." He provides a clue to how this desirable end has been achieved. Unconsciously recapitulating Benjamin West's advice to the untutored Copley a century earlier, Cook recommends in this article that Lane close up his stone cottage and travel to England and Europe to look at the work of European masters, especially the canvases of J. M. W. Turner and Claude-Joseph Vernet. These, of course, are artists who also frequently painted transitional times of day and included the light source—often a low-on-the-horizon sun—within the picture space; and both often included water (harbor, river, sea) prominently in their paintings. It is not at all unlikely (to take up Cook's double negative locutions) that Lane already did have a model in the works of at least one of these artists through excellent prints, careful descriptions, and critical discussion in the (London) *Art Journal* to which he subscribed.[108] This periodical was an expensively produced large-format monthly that actively carried news of art events not only in England and on the Continent but also in the United States and thus clearly courted American subscribers.[109] It was a cutting-edge periodical, including articles about daguerreotypy and lithography, for instance, from its earliest year of publication (1839) and expensive handsomely produced large-scale reproductions of paintings as well as textual commentary. It carried multiple lengthy articles on eighteenth-century and modern British artists, which Lane would have been able to study with care. While the reproductions are black-and-white engravings, they are extremely high-quality work and are carefully descriptive of the paintings for which they stand in a transatlantic context (fig. 28).

Lane would have been encouraged, for instance, by the *Art Journal*'s coverage of John Constable, for whom, as for the lococentric Gloucester artist, "the scenes of his boyhood made him an artist," one who profitably studied—as Lane did—not only the local habitat of his forebears but also "the 'natural history of the skies.'"[110] The *Art Journal* offered articles, such as "Geology: Its Relation to the Picturesque," that would encourage attention to other forms of scientific visual analysis.[111] It also included careful verbal descriptions of paintings to call attention to effects of color and tone where the engravings were necessarily silent, as with a Thomas Gainsborough landscape described as "resplendent with the rich evening glow which slightly overspreads the whole landscape."[112] J. M. W. Turner's paintings are frequently illustrated, discussed, and offered as a yardstick against which all aspiring modern painters might be measured.[113] Shortly after the American landscape painter Thomas Cole died, for instance, the *Art Journal* carried an extended eulogy, praising his "fine poetic mind" but pointing out that his works fell short of the "high imaginative quality of Turner."[114] Therefore, long before Clarence Cook visited his studio in 1854 to commend "poetry," "imagination," and J. M. W. Turner to him, Lane would have been brooding about the supreme value of these terms and this revolutionary English artist's canvases in the estimation of those whose approbation he would have valued. He also might have noted that Cole was granted "poetry" but not "imagination" and might have found the slippage of these unparsed terms problematic.

What exactly is this "poetry" and "imagination" that urbane cognoscenti urged upon Lane? It seems to be an eschewal of noontime clarity and an embrace of unified tonality (whether warmly pearlescent or golden from the long rays of a rising or setting sun—or cool from the haze of moist air) and, as a character within the image, the introduction of an epiphanic ocular sun. Cook reaches his rhetorical crescendo in evocative descriptions of Lane's depictions of the setting sun's "transparent splendor" and waves "crowned with light and pierced with light." Light (and, by implication, contrast), in other words, is key to achieving what the critic terms "poetical treatment" and "creative imagination," although he is at pains to assure Lane and his readers that particularity, details, and what others call "accuracy" are just fine and in no way hostile to the achievement of "poetry" and "imagination." Above all, his praise suggests awe at Lane's technical skill. But at the end of Cook's extensive commentary the exact meanings of the terms "poetry" and "imagination" remain unclear.

His contemporary and friend the architectural critic A. J. Downing was much clearer in his explication and usage of such terms to bridge between aesthetic phenomena and the humans that construct and experience—and in his case inhabit—them.[115] For Downing there were three types of men (there was apparently only one type of woman, the nurturer of vines and flowers), men of reason, men of feeling, and men of imagination, and each could be suitably domiciled in only one kind of home—respectively, the Greek temple, the Gothic cottage, or the ultimate Gothic villa.[116] Downing's is not a neutral judgment—this is a ranked list of aesthetic capacity, with "imagination" the highest quality and towers the architectural hallmark of these rare "men of imagination." This "poetics" of space may indirectly reflect the *Art Journal* obituary writer's tiered judgment of Cole's oeuvre as evidencing "poetry" ("feeling") but not "imagination," and the supreme compliment that Cook is offering to Lane in declaring in 1854 that he has demonstrated both. The technical skill and the capacity to depict details with "accuracy" represents the state of reason—what Cook calls "studious execution"; the masterful use of specific kinds of light effects he connects with "poetical treatment"; and he points to no specific visual qualities in his ascription of "genuine imagination" but intimates that it is the ensemble of all lesser effects well orchestrated.

Beyond the aesthetic judgments Cook brought to Lane's studio is the larger issue of the critic's judgment about the role of patrons in the oeuvre of an artist—are they an enabling or disabling force? Should the artist be guided by their worldview—their Baxandallian skills at gauging the world and its volumes, for instance—or should the artist march resolutely to an inner drummer ("genius") that hears only itself and the beat of tradition (predecessor artists)?[117] While twentieth-century critics would usually—and, I would argue, romantically—vote for the presumed aesthetic incompetence and negligibility of the maritime-merchant patron group, it is the burden of this book to show that Lane's patrons (Cook's "sailors")—whether benighted or wise—enabled his career, dictated the terms of his success, and helped him create works of extraordinary power, palpable to generations beyond their local horizons. Moreover, these works, tied so intimately to the concerns of those who commissioned, bought, and lived with them, are texts about these contexts in ways that works created *in vacuo* could never be.

The historical record provides little opportunity to look with care at the aesthetic capacities of the "sailors" Cook belittled for having, in his estimation, harnessed Lane to "literalness," but one document suggests Cook saw this class of men as more different from himself than they were. The journal of Solomon H. Davis, future brother-in-law of Lane patrons Edward and John James Babson, opens a window into the mind of one such individual. Captain of the brig *Corporal Trim*, bound from Gloucester for Valparaiso on the coast of Chile, Davis, age twenty-five, was busy with managing the ship, of course, but he also wrote poetry, recorded reading six novels by lady authors, and described the conditions of the night of October 9, 1823, thus: "Calm evening. Grey twilight advances, expands and recedes without a breath from the vaulted heavens. The stars break though the haze as if to dispel the unwelcome visitor, and they finally accomplish their desired object. Unconscious of their duty the sails lay in folds against the masts,—the vessel is unmanageable. Oh, what a melancholy theme."[118] Personification, metaphor, prolepsis, apostrophe: this is hardly the language or voice of a literalist; further, Captain Davis was introspective about the pathetic fallacy: "It is interesting with what facility, we accommodate all the scenes of nature to our state of feeling."[119] A practical engineer, adroit navigator, able manager of men, and crafty businessman, Davis—probably like many other sea captains—was also a poetically minded observer of the world around him, as close an observer of the colors of "twilight, tinged with red, purple, green, grey, yellow, and blue," as any artist or art critic.[120]

We have no way of knowing what stirred Clarence Cook to visit—or, rather, revisit—Lane's Gloucester studio, so far from his usual "beat" in New York. Certainly, during his Harvard years he had spent time in Gloucester, where his stepmother, Ann Trask, had grown up, and perhaps Cook haunted Boston's Tremont Temple area, where studios, framers, and exhibition venues would have drawn a student interested in art, for he recounts that "in former times [he] used to be often in Mr. Lane's painting-room."[121] His having sought the artist out four years later, however, has yielded a singular public document evidencing a young ambitious art critic measuring Lane's 1854 work with his best but youthful professional judgment based on a Harvard education and a few years of experience in what was already the art capital of the United States. Cook would have had the opportunity to have seen only a handful of Lane works in New York—one sent to the National Academy of Design, ten sent to the American Art-Union (see appendix A), and several in private collections, including *Gloucester Harbor* of 1852, installed in Sidney Mason's marble mansion on Fifth Avenue (fig. 10). That he praised Lane as enthusiastically as those writing for Boston and Gloucester papers—although in somewhat different terms—evidences the standing of this artist in a competitive midcentury field. Reading Cook's essay gives us an opportunity to "listen in" on the commendation and advice that the artist received in this very public commentary on his talents, his achievements, and his promise.

One further voice to add to this commentary on Lane's work during his lifetime is that of the artist himself. In an undated letter of about 1857, he wrote to his friends Caroline and Joseph L. Stevens Jr., describing a painting that he had started:

> Since writing you I have painted but one picture worth talking about and that one I intend for you

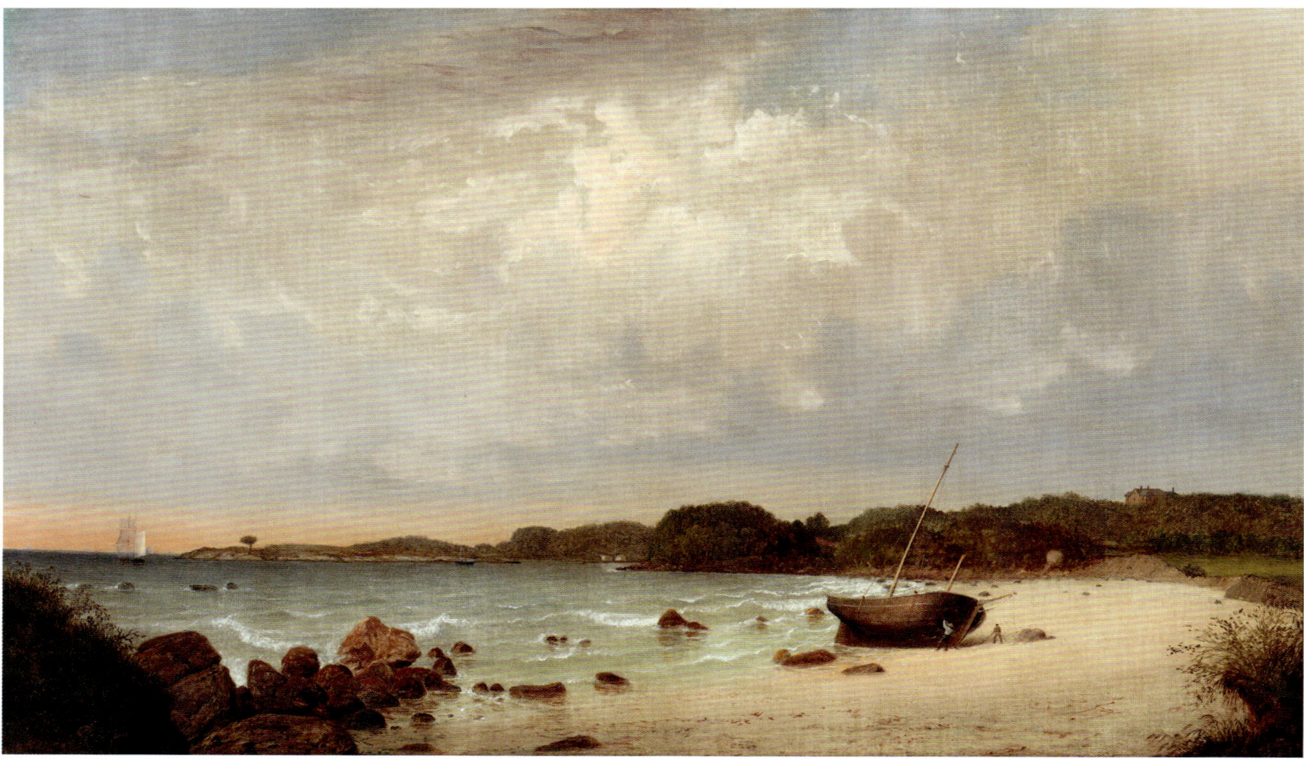

FIGURE 29
Fitz H. Lane, *Dolliver's Neck and the Western Shore from Field Beach*, 1857. Oil on canvas mounted on panel, 18½ × 32¾ in. (47 × 83.2 cm). Cape Ann Museum, Gloucester, Massachusetts. Gift of Helen Stevens Babson, 1933 (678.00).

> if you should be pleased with it. . . . The effect is midday light, with a cloudy sky, a patch of sunlight thrown across the beach and breaking waves. An old vessel lies stranded on the beach with two or three figures; there are a few vessels in the distance and the Field rocks likewise show at the left of the picture. I think you will be pleased with this picture, for it is a very picturesque scene especially the beach, as there are many rocks which come in to destroy the monotony of a plain sand beach, and I have so arranged the light and shade that the effect I think is very good indeed; however, you will be better able to judge of that when you see it.[122]

This letter, written when he was a mature artist and had had several years to think about (or ignore) Clarence Cook's remarks, indicates that the work *Dolliver's Neck and the Western Shore from Field Beach* is uncommissioned and intended as a gift (fig. 29). It survives and was given by the Stevens's daughter to the Cape Ann Museum. What is of interest is the artist's language—that is, what we might call his "theory" of the project. He begins his description with the light—"midday light, with a cloudy sky, [interrupted by] a patch of sunlight"—followed by the setting and action, "beach and breaking waves." Only third does he name the central object—"an old vessel lies stranded"—and the secondary objects, "a few vessels in the distance," modeling what this "stranded" schooner cannot do, and "the Field rocks . . . at the left of the picture," those treacherous obstacles marking the edge of safe anchorage in three or four fathoms of water outside this cove, a comment that finally specifies exactly which beach, rocks, and cove the painting depicts.

He then gives a general estimation of the effect of the work: "It is a very picturesque scene" with rocks that "destroy the monotony of a plain sand beach." Returning to the opening subject of light, he concludes with a comment that the "light and shade" are good.

This rather clinical catalogue of elements affords insight into the artist's thinking about and valuing of the parts and totality of this work and, by extension, of his painting practice. Above all, it indicates that light (and its opposite, shade) is important—the specific weather conditions providing both gray low clouds and an open patch of sky from which the sun spotlights the central features of the work: bright sand and the brighter white of cresting waves. Around this illuminated spot of sky an arc of gray provides contrast, and around the edges of the beach, on both sides and in the distance, dark rocks and landmasses frame the even darker precise hull, about which a few figures labor. Dark rocks punctuate both the white sand and the gray sea. "Picturesque" here points to the variety of forms, tones, and effects, and to their roughness. Lane clearly uses the term as a positive, unlike the cautionary usage by his obituary writer ("he never sacrificed truth of delineation for picturesque effects"), for whom it suggested forced, sentimental passages. Interestingly, the catalogue of elements Lane gives here evidence a stark contrast to his known working methods: while the drawings make clear that he started with topography and then added both movable objects (ships, figures) and atmospheric effects, here his description of the work begins with light and only belatedly names the site. He apparently *constructed* the image with one set of priorities, but once the work was in progress, he *thought* it with another.

Two-thirds of this image is sky, and it is this element that gives the painting its character as much as the human dilemma that he has deposited at its heart but mentions only in brief. Unmentioned altogether are a few houses that point to habitation, indeed to "summering" on this western shore of Gloucester's harbor, structures as oblivious as the rocks to the engineering dilemma and financial drama unfolding on the beach. In short, it is interesting that Lane makes no case for "accuracy" of the topography or the event (indeed, he suggests that while the former is specific and recognizable, the latter is an invention, a fictional beaching standing in for many actual beachings). Stranded vessels were a common engineering, humanitarian, and economic problem in Gloucester, and one that precipitated a legal tangle going all the way to the Supreme Court on the part of one of Lane's patrons, so Lane's laconic treatment here masks substantial turmoil.[123] In his use of the term "picturesque," however, Lane does gesture toward the "poetic" quality valued by Cook and others. Mapped onto Ann Bermingham's political reading of the various British theorists of the picturesque, Lane's practice and his commentary would align more closely with William M. Craig's "British constitution" position, with the "naturalistic . . . ideological implications of its rejection of abstraction and its valorization of individuality, variety, and organic naturalism," than with Gilpin's more abstract, artificial, and politically "French" picturesque, in which the parts are subordinated to the whole.[124] In his letter, Lane does not raise the issue of "imagination," except to suggest throughout his description that this painting is a construction whose parts hang together to create a singular work "very good indeed."

Extrapolating from the corpus of Lane's works, it is clear that what was valued in terms of subject matter by his contemporaries was his capacity to capture vignettes of coastal New England—its familiar harbors, service buildings, daily activities, and ships—as they participated in an exuberant global trade rooted in extraction industries and devoted equally to improvements in daily life and to profit. Horace Mann neatly sums up this the-world-is-our-oyster outlook in a passage from "A Few Thoughts for a Young Man" reprinted in the *Gloucester Telegraph*:

> See how the means of sustenance and comfort are distributed and diversified throughout the earth. . . .

> What textures for clothing—from the gossamer thread which the silk-worm weaves, to silk-like furs which the winds of Zembla cannot penetrate! As materials from which to construct our dwellings, what Quincys and New Hampshires of granite, what Alleghanies of oak, what forests of pine, belting the continent. What coal-fields to supply the lost warmth of the receding sun.[125]

Already engrained in European culture for centuries, this attitude toward nature and toward the globe's riches was embraced by many in the young United States when, in the decades following independence, accumulated capital, technological invention, and aggressive ingenuity propelled resource-poor New Englanders toward the sea. What Lane's paintings reflected back to contemporary viewers was a familiar busy commerce-based well-articulated local-global axis, a world that they understood to be fundamentally ample in its resources for human comfort and often "poetic" in character.

The record indicates that during Lane's lifetime his works were highly valued for their accuracy, their ability to activate memory, their poetic feeling, and sometimes for their suggestion of the artist's "imagination." He himself appears to have been particularly alert to composition in the sense of a unified whole constructed around a dramatic array of light-dark contrasts and a multiplicity of visual incidents—that is, an avoidance of "monotony." His reputation was considerable, and in no instance was his work censured in the press—every notice is positive and encouraging. Equally, in none of these comments is his work compared to, or joined with, that of any other artist. Most of these notices are brief and local, and the one published in New York City (Cook's) is extensive and bruits Lane's name in an important metropolitan art center. All suggest that Lane was an artistic force to be reckoned with; indeed, Cook assured New Yorkers that he was "a man, who in knowledge, feeling, and skill, has had no rival, certainly in America, and I doubt if more than two abroad."

What the foregoing account of the making of Lane's career suggests is, among other things, that there were fewer distinctions between highbrow and lowbrow culture in antebellum America than there are today. Lane's paintings were seen in the streets of Gloucester by everybody and at the American Art-Union by the burgeoning middle class, as well as on the walls of the Boston Athenaeum and Mrs. Josiah Quincy's parlor by New England's elites. Lane worked simultaneously for the very wealthiest of his contemporaries and for those of very modest means. His works were paid for by global capital (Robert B. Forbes, Edward Babson) and by local capital (John Trask). This is not a narrative of unfolding self-expression, as is so often implied by art historians, but rather a tale of a painter making art out of what his patrons wanted. That he succeeded at all is a credit to them; that he succeeded so well is a credit to him.

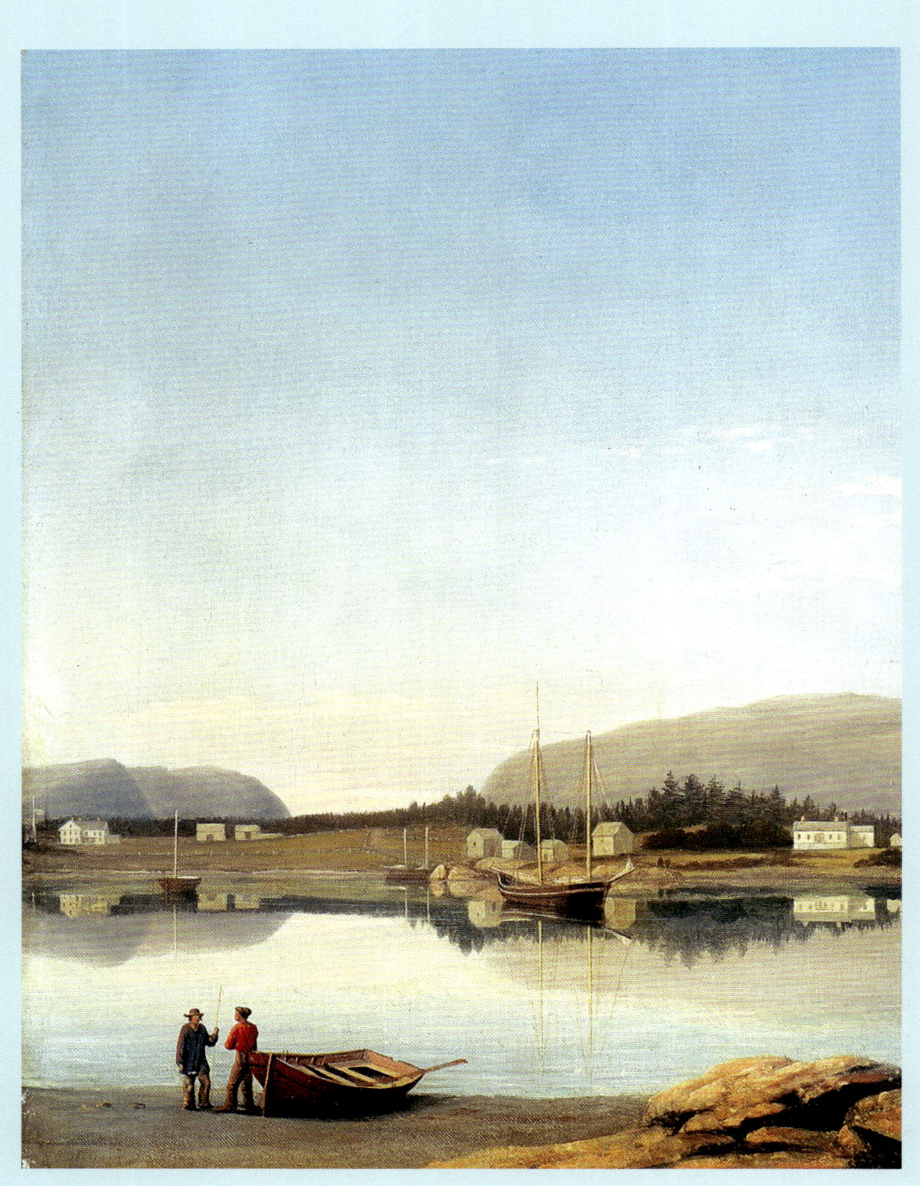

CHAPTER 2

VALUE

Lane, 1865–2020

Today it is assumed that any great museum or private collection of American art that includes nineteenth-century painting must include "a Lane." Those that own multiple examples of his work—such as the Museum of Fine Arts, Boston—are considered extremely fortunate and well served by the curatorial acumen of earlier generations. Competition for the flat-water views, usually considered the finest of his works, is fierce in the rare instances in which they come on the market. Their value is seen by collectors and professionals as almost self-evident, as a matter beyond discussion. They are beautiful; they are important; they are desired. But it has not always been so, and the story of the variant valuing of Lane's paintings, as a cultural narrative, is as remarkable as the canonical status this artist has, belatedly, achieved.

SILENCE

In the summer of 1865, Lane died at the age of sixty. While the finality of death often brings to an artist a flurry of attention in the form of retrospective exhibitions, appreciative career reviews, and higher prices,[1] in Lane's case it signaled the onset of a total eclipse of his reputation and presence in the art world. Several factors intersected to effect this seemingly surprising evaporation of a substantial career, among them the fact that his death occurred four months after Appomattox. His health (and productivity) had been impaired for some years, and the whole country had been embroiled in a devastating four-year conflict that would prove a watershed in many facets of American culture, among them art and its markets.

Lane's paintings, so closely tied to forms of local knowledge about the antebellum extraction industries, trading partners, and vessel types by which his contemporaries organized their world, necessarily spoke less forcefully to a rising generation in the postwar period. Not in a position to judge (or prize) the "accuracy" of his works or to synthesize memories based on firsthand experience, younger viewers of his paintings had less reason to value them by the standards of those who were their primary audience. Those who commissioned or purchased works during the artist's lifetime (as discussed in chapter 1) valued, above all, his fidelity to the world they recognized; they believed that he created "an accurate copy of nature . . . never sacrific[ing] truth of delineation for picturesque effects [in his] . . . perfect portraits" of the places and objects familiar in their daily lives.[2] It was surely harder for belated viewers to value these works in the same way their parents had—that is, as instruments conjoining personal memories with specific places, activities, ships, or people.

Less emphatically but more broadly, Lane's canvases also likely began to be understood as stand-alone narratives told about a broader, more generalized "we" in New England. Personal memory, vulnerable to time and death, was replaced with family—and, to a lesser extent, local group memory—over the course of the second half of the nineteenth century. Certainly it is clear from the record that Lane's paintings receded in prominence even in the patrons' homes where they continued to hang decade after decade, familiar but little-investigated relics of a decisively earlier era. Impacting this pattern of valuation were three types of population changes, the out-migration of young adult Gloucesterites to California in the wake of the gold rush (explored in chapter 7), the in-migration of inland New Englanders and foreigners to Cape Ann, and the seasonal migration of elites from more urban areas. None of these newcomers would have known Lane or the buoyant Gloucester he painted.

While the country as a whole prospered after the Civil War, Gloucester did not. Its fishing fleet continued to scour the North Atlantic, but the more profitable freighting business distributing those fish and other products inland by rail, and globally by ship, was taken over by Boston.[3] From as early as the 1830s, the tendency of Gloucester's most successful merchants to move their businesses and their capital to larger cities—a process accelerated in the second half of the century—transformed Gloucester and all of formerly formidable Essex County into a satellite region. Many of these nabobs retained homes and secondary business interests on Cape Ann, but their wealth and the ties of their children were increasingly located elsewhere.[4] Together these developments served to decenter prewar Gloucester and the Lane paintings that distilled many aspects of that place and that era. On the positive side, although some Lane paintings may have been moved to barns and attics in the period between the Civil War and World War I (there is no sign, for instance, of at least five Lane paintings commissioned by his wealthy patron Sidney Mason in the photographs of his descendants' house interiors taken in the late nineteenth century, although they kept them), others remained in situ in the rooms in which they were first hung, and many were preserved and treated with care.[5] One, a picture of Castine, the Maine village in which Lane summered during the 1850s and into the 1860s, was preserved in a sail loft, nailed over a full-wall collage of 1880s circus and burlesque posters (fig. 30).

Lane's reputation, while secure in Gloucester in his lifetime and bolstered by some press attention and exhibition presence in Boston and New York City, was never as solid or widespread as that of contemporaries who centered their careers in New York. Even before the Civil War it was clear that—although still challenged by other cities for preeminence in trade, education, and global influence—New York was the gravitational center of the art markets in the United States. Beginning with the establishment of a gallery by picture dealers John and Michael Paff on Wall Street in the late eighteenth century, another by P. Beaumont in 1835, and continuing with the founding of a Manhattan branch of the Paris-based firm

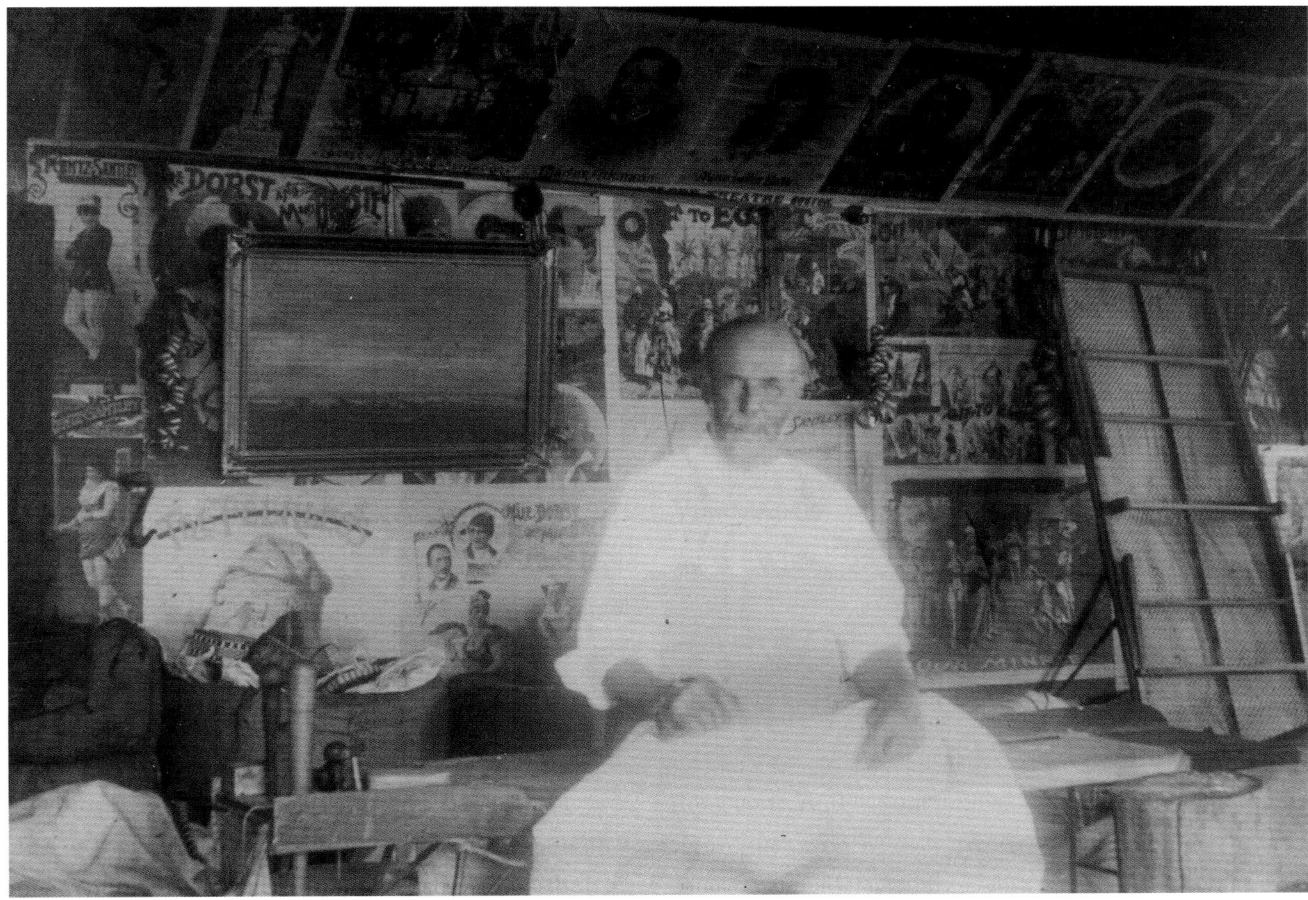

FIGURE 30
Sailmaker in Dennett's Sail Loft in Castine, Maine, with Lane's "Castine, Maine" Hung on the Wall over Circus and Burlesque Posters, ca. 1885. Copy print in the Collections of the Castine Historical Society.

of Goupil in 1840, New York City became the premier North American emporium in which works by living European painters and their Old Master predecessors, as well as many by American artists, readily changed hands.[6] Whether by such middleman-dealer sales, auction sales, or private sales directly from artists in their studios, art sales burgeoned into an important element in the Empire City's economy and identity over the course of the nineteenth century.[7] Related activities—including the formation of private art collections and the establishment of the National Academy of Design in 1825, the American Art-Union in 1840, and the Metropolitan Museum of Art in 1870, as well as the growth of an art press in New York—fostered this development and helped establish the reputation and canonical position of New York artists in general and the Hudson River "school" in particular. While at least two dozen works by Lane found their way to New York during his lifetime, his modest notoriety and his works were peripheral to these developments.

Two of the most important ingredients in the creation and maintenance of artists' reputations in the United States in the nineteenth century were the formation of private collections and the dispersal sales of these collections at auction. Both of these became high-profile activities with considerable press attention, and both were concentrated in New York City. There were, of course, notable private collections formed in other cities—such as those of Robert Gilmor Jr. in Baltimore, William Wilson Corcoran in Washington, and Edward Carey in Philadelphia—but the majority were based in New York.[8] Even collectors located elsewhere routinely bought and sold on the New York market.[9] Artists, logically, were attentive to this pattern, and many migrated to the city, where they could be more certain of attention and sales. After the Civil War the market for American art lost ground against European art, furthering the trend (begun with the invention of photography) toward a concentrated rather than a dispersed art market. Those artists whose fortunes and reputations survived this decisive and economically dramatic turn in the latter half of the nineteenth century, such as Frederic E. Church, Sanford R. Gifford, and John F. Kensett, tended to be based in New York City or Europe or to use New York dealers.[10] Lane and his posthumous "agent" Joseph L. Stevens Jr. were not on this axis.

The art-auction business in New York City was big business, moving individual paintings for sums that astonished onlookers from as early as the sale of John P. Beaumont's pictures in 1850.[11] In the 1870s, for instance, auction prices for individual works include $12,500 for F. E. Church's *Niagara* (in 1876), $6,350 for Frederick Kensett's *Autumn on Lake George* (in 1877), and $10,000 for J. M. W. Turner's *Slave Ship* (in 1872).[12] Dispersal sales following the death of notable American collectors reached considerable aggregate sums as competition for works burnished by the imprimatur of a wealthy connoisseur and the attention of the press, as well as by the reputation of the artists, increased prices—the John Wolfe sale in 1863 netted $114,000; the two Samuel P. Avery sales in 1867 and 1868, $63,100; the two Alexander White sales in 1871 and 1872, $138,700; and that of John Taylor Johnston in 1876, $328,286.[13] There is no record that any of Lane's works were involved in these high-profile exchanges of money for art. Indeed, even in more modest sales he appears to have been a nonplayer. Five of his paintings were offered at A. J. Bleecker Son and Co. over Goupil's on Broadway, February 22 and 23, 1861, but only one found a buyer—at $20.[14]

Throughout the second half of the nineteenth century and well into the twentieth, the records indicate that very few Lane paintings changed hands at auction.[15] A few Lane prints were sold at auction: a colored lithograph of Gloucester sold in 1927 for $60 at a New York sale in which Whistler prints found buyers from $35 to $450 and Mary Cassatt prints from $65 to $160; two Lane & Scott colored prints of New Bedford sold in estate auctions in 1930 (for $165) and 1931 (for $50); and another colored lithograph sold in 1933 for $32.50; but otherwise the auction record is remarkably silent concerning Lane before the mid-twentieth century.[16] From the provenance records of many Lane paintings, it appears that most changed hands by direct descent within the families of Lane's original patrons until the middle of the twentieth century.

While some of this silence may be attributable to the sinking fortunes of American art in general, to the faltering of Gloucester's economy, and to the peripheral position of Gloucester vis-à-vis New York City, the swiftness and profundity of Lane's loss of reputation are nevertheless remarkable. Lane is not only absent from the auction record, he is unmentioned in landmark efforts on the part of scholars and critics to establish a chronology and a canon of American art in the 1860s, '70s, and '80s. In 1867, two years after Lane's death, Henry T. Tuckerman published his 639-page *Book of the Artists*, a New York–based and portrait-heavy account in which some New England artists, collectors, and subjects appear; even the novice Winslow Homer is represented.[17] Artists with whom twentieth-century scholars would later associate Lane—John F. Kensett, Sanford R. Gifford, William S. Haseltine—all appear, but Lane is missing both from Tuckerman's chapter on landscape painting and from his "Appendix List of American Pictures in Public and Private Collections." In his account of marine painting, Tuckerman writes at length about Robert Salmon, who may have been Lane's teacher, and about William Bradford, who a contemporary reports was Lane's pupil, and this encyclopedic author even mentions his own obscure nephew,

"Salisbury Tuckerman of Boston" (actually of Gloucester), who copied Lane works, as having "executed fine coast and craft-scenes," but Lane himself is absent from Tuckerman's account.[18]

Twelve years later, S. G. W. Benjamin published "Fifty Years of American Art, 1828–1878," in the popular journal *Harper's New Monthly Magazine*, and here too Lane is unmentioned.[19] Perhaps most surprising, after his early public enthusiasm for Lane, Clarence Cook, in his benchmark *Art and Artists of Our Time* of 1888, also omits the Gloucester artist altogether.[20] Cook's discussion of landscape painters focuses unsurprisingly on New York artists, including Asher B. Durand, Thomas Cole, Frederic E. Church, and John F. Kensett. He pauses over Kensett: "A small group of men whose names are associated with his appeared at that time and kept alive a public interest in landscape painting by an art that was marked rather by sweetness and delicacy than by strength either of execution or conception," pointing to R. S. Gifford, Samuel Colman, and William Trost Richards, among others.[21] Cook's account of these masters of shoreline landscapes marked by "sweetness and delicacy," with whom he would later be linked, did not include Fitz H. Lane.

LOCAL MEMORIES

By every ordinary yardstick of value and regard—auction sales, critical attention, inclusion in canon-establishing private collections and published narratives—Lane's reputation descended to a nadir of invisibility for the better part of a century after his death. Nevertheless, in Gloucester, in every generation, a handful of individuals—most related to his original patrons—concerned themselves with Lane's memory and the well-being of his works. As noted in chapter 1, John Trask, the painter of ships, gave his shop sign to the city of Gloucester in 1876 and sat down with a local documentarian in the 1880s to record his memories of the artist.[22] Joseph L. Stevens Jr., close friend and residual beneficiary of the artist, kept some paintings and offered others for sale through the framer and picture dealer W. Y. Balch in Boston. He looked after a portfolio of Lane's drawings and, sometime before his death in 1908, turned them over to Samuel H. Mansfield, who was associated with Gloucester's historical society, for safekeeping. In 1904 Stevens wrote an account of his acquaintance with and memories of the artist for Mansfield and offered to sell a *Gloucester Harbor* painting to the town for $150, but there was insufficient interest or insufficient funds to meet this modest price.[23] Most of Stevens's Lane paintings he and his wife gave to their children, Helen Stevens Babson and George Blanchard Stevens. By this turn-of-the-century period, the circle of those who knew something about Lane in his native town had been considerably diminished by the deaths of many of his patrons, but it may also have been somewhat augmented by an exhibition in 1892 of art and historical items held at the local high school in celebration of the 250th anniversary of the founding of Gloucester. Of the 314 items included in the exhibition and listed in the "Gloucester Art and Loan Exhibition Picture Catalogue," twenty-one were paintings by Lane, and two were copies after Lane (one by Salisbury Tuckerman, the other by Mary B. Mellen) (see appendix B).[24] The lenders to (and probably the audience for) this gathering of Lane paintings, thirty years after Lane's death, were largely original owners or their direct heirs. There, among "shoes worn by a Chinese Lady," photos of Copley portraits, needlework, and bric-a-brac, Lane's works provided a window on local history.

Two decades later, in the summer of 1913, Cassie Mason Myers Julian-James of Washington, DC, granddaughter of one of Lane's most important patrons, Sidney Mason, gave the artist's large *Gloucester Harbor* to the city of Gloucester (fig. 10).[25] In their letter of acknowledgment, the city council assured her "that it shall find a place in some public building where its historic value will be appreciated."[26] Possibly prompted by this gift, a flurry of articles concerning Lane started to appear in February 1916 in the "C. A. S. & L. A. [Cape Ann Scientific and Literary Association] Weekly Column on Matters of Local

History" in the *Gloucester Daily Telegraph*, beginning with one entitled "Fitz H. Lane" by Susan Babson (1852–1947) on behalf of "the historical department" of that association. Cousin of the two Babson sisters who took Lane paintings with them to California (see figs. 23 and 24), Susan Babson was born in 1852 and was therefore old enough to have known and remembered the artist herself, although she foregrounds in her article the memories of others. More important, she lists thirty paintings "we have located in town" and fifteen more owned elsewhere, indicating a concerted attempt to learn about the corpus of this artist (appendix B).[27] She invites readers to provide to the newspaper "any further information" they might have concerning Lane. Almost immediately Fred W. Tibbets responded with an article about Lane's house and some of the artist's patrons, noting that he owned "a Sunset Scene off Mt. Desert Maine, which Lane gave to my aunt [Elizabeth C. Procter / Mrs. David Plumer] in 1859 as a wedding present," as well as two Lane paintings of Gloucester "copied by him from the original . . . which was destroyed by fire" in the town hall.[28] Tibbets's article relates personal reminiscences from those who knew Lane and expresses the hope "to have an exhibition of the Lane paintings," as well as Tibbets's desire "to secure for this city in some public building these Lane paintings." He goes on to comment, "I recall seeing an advertisement in the [*Boston Evening*] *Transcript* in very recent months asking for the purchase of paintings by Fitz H. Lane of Gloucester. . . . I think that effort should be made to keep every Lane painting now here [in Gloucester] and [get] every other Lane painting possible."[29] So it appears that by 1916 there was a glimmer of local interest in Lane and that, moreover, an outsider had expressed interest in obtaining his works.

In March 1916, in the "Local History" column of the *Gloucester Daily Telegraph*, short articles appeared by Helen Mansfield, many of whose kin had bought paintings from the artist, contributing some details about her family's pictures.[30] Two weeks later Ada C. Bowles (1836–1928), a well-known abolitionist, suffragist, and temperance worker, responded to Tibbets's article with an account of her memory of Lane having "kindly volunteered to give me some instruction in painting" when she was a teenager.[31] The following week the artist's nephew, Edward Lane, published a long rumination about buildings in Gloucester, including his "Early Recollections of Artist Fitz H. Lane," noting that he would be happy to give his own Lane painting to a suitable Gloucester institution. One further newspaper article in this series, authored by Susan Babson, concerned the encampment of Major-General John C. Fremont at Coffin's Beach in 1862, an event recorded by Lane in a drawing and in a painting that is currently unlocated.[32]

These local stories have preserved several important firsthand memories of the artist, his patrons, and his works, but there is little indication they had any resonance beyond a tight circle of local families. Indeed, soon after their publication, even the local stories stopped, as the generations that knew Lane grew elderly or died and the country entered the turmoil of World War I. In the 1920s Helen Stevens Babson, daughter of his friend and executor, gave to the Cape Ann Scientific and Literary Association a painting that Lane had given to her parents, and her sister-in-law gave another, but a donor wishing to give three Lane paintings to the Museum of Fine Arts, Boston, in 1935 was told that she should place two of them "somewhere else" and that she "will be informed" if the institution decides to accept the third.[33] By the early 1930s Lane had become so obscure that those who wrote and spoke about him became confused about his name and he was inadvertently renamed Fitz Hugh Lane, a topic to which we will return in chapter 3.[34]

In 1937 Alfred Mansfield Brooks (1870–1963), who had been trained at Harvard in European art history, retired to Gloucester after a teaching career at Indiana State University and Swarthmore College.[35] He had been raised in Gloucester by elderly relatives in a family that had done well in the antebellum fishing industry and that had patronized Lane. Lane's harborscapes hung in the sitting rooms of Brooks's grandmother, great-aunt, and great-great-aunt during his boyhood, and as a retiree he turned his attention to gathering in the works of this local artist in a second career as curator at the Cape Ann Scientific and Literary Association, fast becoming a vibrant institution dedicated to collecting and publicizing aspects of Cape Ann's history. Brooks, in spite of his training and career focused on European art, clearly valued Lane's paintings and exerted himself to gather them into the local institution, where they could be seen by the public and cared for by professionals.[36] He was probably "reeducated" and encouraged in this enterprise by Susan Babson and by his cousin, Samuel H. Mansfield. In 1944 Mansfield wrote a long testimonial about the artist and turned over to Brooks the Lane drawings that Stevens had preserved, annotated, and entrusted to him at the opening of the twentieth century.[37] Brooks made a notebook catalogue of the drawings and published an article about them in 1945.[38] Both men gave Lane paintings to the Cape Ann Scientific and Literary Association (later Cape Ann Historical Association and, later still, Cape Ann Museum). The gathering of paintings into an institution open to the public and the publication of commentary in a local newspaper and a historical-society journal signal a modest revival of Lane's reputation in the 1930s and '40s, but it was a very limited, very local kind of knowledge circulation. Brooks evidently contacted the Frick Art Reference Library in New York City, an institution that kept photo files of the work of known artists to aid in art-historical research. As of December 1938 Lane was only known in that institution as the painter of five works, four of which had been formerly owned by Sidney Mason in that city.[39] Outside of Cape Ann, Lane remained deeply obscure.

TIPPING POINT

But something interesting, with far-reaching consequences, began in 1939. That summer the Metropolitan Museum of Art in New York held a loan exhibition entitled *Life in America* as a "special attraction for World's Fair visitors" curated by Harry B. Wehle.[40] The concept was to tell, with paintings, "as varied a story as possible [of life] as it has been lived in our country from the early seventeenth century to about the beginning of the [First] World War . . . to show what America looked like." This was a criterion, according to art critic Forbes Watson, "sufficiently broad and elastic to include primitive efforts of unschooled aspiration together with examples of the most developed craftsmanship in American art."[41] Intended, then, primarily for non–New Yorkers, the exhibition had about it, Watson noted, "an air of good humor and zest" and included, insouciantly, works by artists that "are unknown or practically unknown."[42] Among the works by "unknown" artists was Fitz H. Lane's *Southwest Harbor, Maine* (now known as *Entrance to Somes Sound from Southwest Harbor*) (figs. 31 and 32). Characterized by Watson as "restrained, with a classic serenity and dignity," this work was parsed in the catalogue briefly by organizer Harry B. Wehle: "Southwest Harbor, now a fashionable summer resort, was one of the quiet fishing hamlets dotting the Maine coast when this picture was made" in 1852.[43] Lane, then, made his comeback debut as a national artist with a pearlescent landscape of rural Maine documenting the days before "summering" transformed this settlement from a working landscape into a visited and viewed landscape. Rugged hills, distant conifers, a small cluster of vernacular buildings, and a slack-sailed brig are mirror-reflected in the dead-flat of Somes Sound under a pale blue, near-cloudless summer sky. This combination of elements (flat water, vernacular structures, and vessels under a sky rosy with a rising or setting sun) became, from this moment, paradigmatic of "a Lane." Bruce Robertson argues persuasively in "The Tipping Point: Museum Collecting and the Canon" that "canonization—the moment when the art-historical community accepts a work as essential to its understanding of American art—occurs when an art object enters a public museum collection."[44] However, it was a privately owned work in a temporary exhibition that served as Lane's "tipping point."

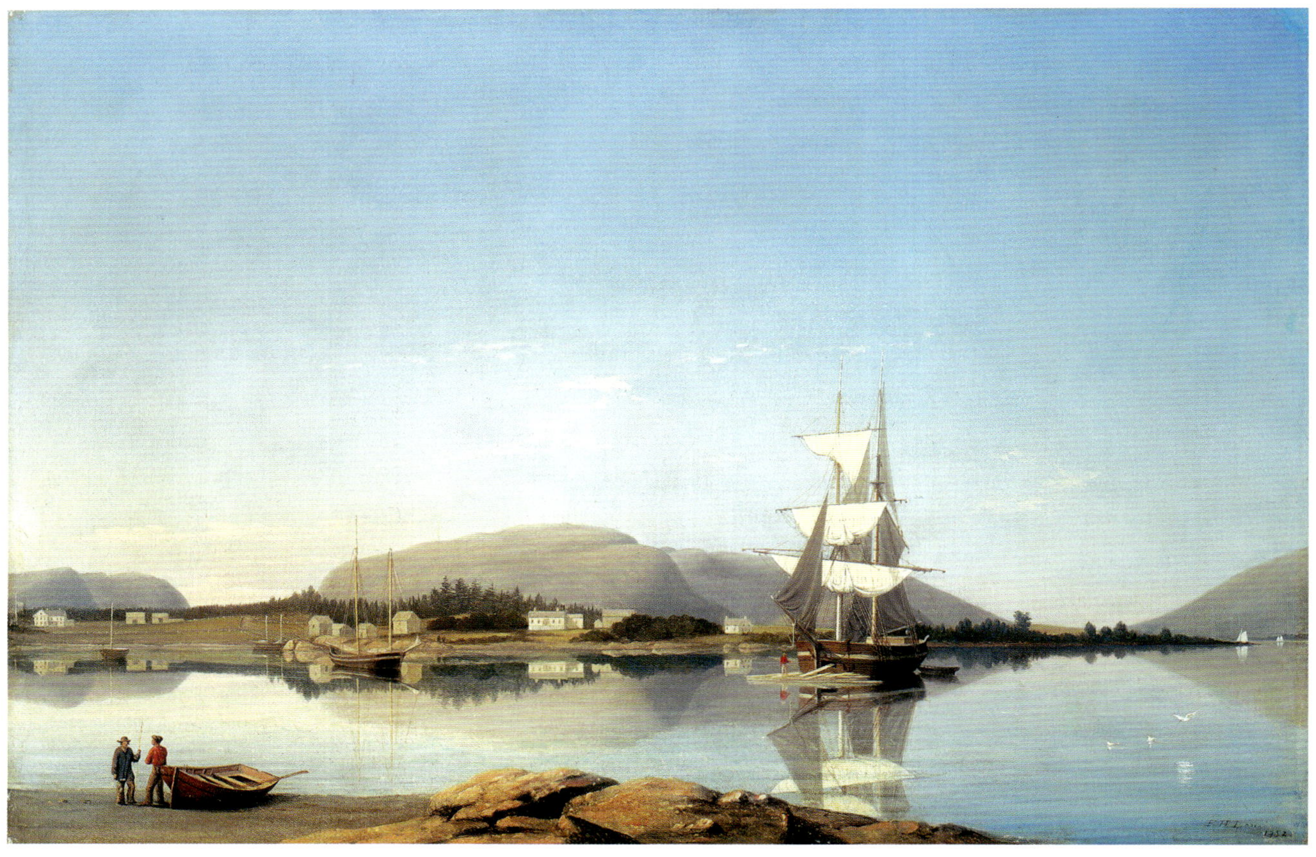

FIGURE 31 (ABOVE)
Fitz H. Lane, *Entrance to Somes Sound from Southwest Harbor* (formerly known as *Southwest Harbor, Maine*), 1852. Oil on canvas, 23¾ × 35¾ in. (60.33 × 90.51 cm). Private collection. Photo © Museum of Fine Arts, Boston.

FIGURE 32 (RIGHT)
Fitz H. Lane, *Entrance to Somes Sound from Southwest Harbor* (formerly known as *Southwest Harbor, Maine*), 1852 (fig. 31), detail.

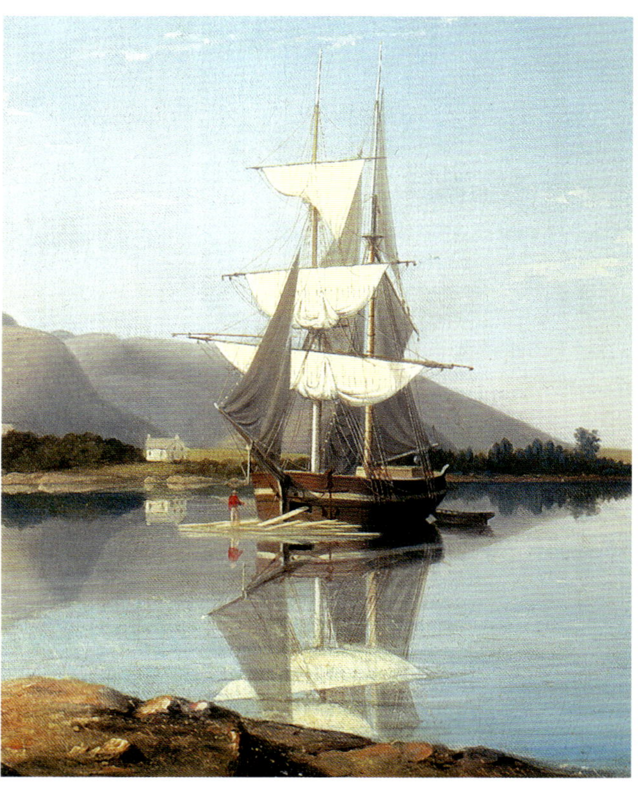

Eight years after *Southwest Harbor* was offered to World's Fair visitors as exemplary of "what America looked like" a century earlier, this same tranquil painting of a "quiet fishing hamlet" was included as one of four illustrated works in "Unknown American Painters of the 19th Century" by John I. H. Baur, published in the *College Art Journal*.[45] Baur notes that at that time "published material on Lane is virtually non-existent" but mentions that, by the mid-1940s, the Boston collector Maxim Karolik had taken an interest in learning about and acquiring Lane's works for the collection of American paintings, which he and his wife, Martha Codman Karolik, would give the Museum of Fine Arts in Boston incrementally from 1945 to 1949.[46]

When *Southwest Harbor, Maine* came to public attention on the walls of the Metropolitan Museum and in the context of a New York–based nationally circulated professional journal, it was owned by Pierrepont Edwards Johnson. Johnson was "well known as a yachtsman," as a twenty-two-year-old sailing his class-A cutter *Flying Cloud*, for instance, in the Bermuda race in 1934, but he was not known as an art collector, and Lane was still virtually unknown outside Gloucester.[47] Yet at the age of twenty-six Johnson loaned *Southwest Harbor* to the Metropolitan and another Lane painting, *Chebacco Boat*, to the Fogg Art Museum at Harvard.[48] It is probable that, like virtually all Lane paintings in the decades before 1945, these were family pictures, not part of an art collection. Johnson's parents had met, courted, and married in Bar Harbor, eight miles as the crow flies from the site of *Southwest Harbor*.[49] The paintings could have descended in the family of either of his parents. Two of Pierrepont Johnson's paternal great-uncles had worked for a large Boston dry-goods store owned by Charles F. Hovey (1807–1859), a wealthy Gloucesterite noted for his generosity to antislavery and women's equality causes and to one of F. H. Lane's known enthusiasms, the temperance movement.[50] It is possible that any of the three Harvard-educated wealthy Johnson brothers bought directly from Lane, but more likely through his Boston dealer, W. Y. Balch. It is equally likely that Pierrepont Edwards Johnson's paintings came from his mother's family. The Edwards family, although British, were in New York City as early as 1833, when Johnson's grandfather, J. Pierrepont Edwards, was born there; and it was an "A. Edwards" who in December 1852 bought a Lane painting, "*Marine View—Coast of Maine* (F. H. Lane)," for $50 at the American Art-Union dispersal sale of "the finest pictures in the Society's possession" in New York.[51] Johnson's Edwards grandparents were wealthy, maintaining properties in Bedford Hills, New York; Bar Harbor, Maine; and elsewhere; although not known to purchase art, they certainly would have had pictures, perhaps inherited, in their homes.[52]

Of course, it is also possible that P. E. Johnson, an avid sailor and lifelong resident of Bar Harbor, on Mount Desert Island, Maine (in the summers), and Newport, Rhode Island, bought both paintings as "marines" from the Newberry Street art dealer, Charles D. Childs, who in 1937 opened his Boston gallery and in 1942 reported having "been much interested in Lane's work for years." Childs, moreover, was instrumental in Maxim Karolik's acquisition of more than a dozen Lane works during the 1940s.[53] Childs knew about the presence of Johnson's Lane in the Metropolitan's 1939 exhibit; in fact, it is possible that Childs was the intermediary who prompted Wehle to include this magisterial work by an "unknown artist" in his benchmark exhibition.[54] Baur, at the time he wrote his *College Art Journal* essay, was young (having received his BA in 1932 and MA in 1934) and had trained in European baroque art, but he clearly was curious, and soon became knowledgeable, about American art.[55] In sum, then, Lane, who outside of Cape Ann was virtually unknown and whose works were uncirculated, was, by 1946, known and valued outside of Gloucester by five individuals well placed to expand his reputation and increase the value of his works: Johnson, Wehle, Baur, Karolik, and Childs—a wealthy owner, two urbane museum professionals, an important collector, and a well-situated dealer.

FORMALISM / NATIONALISM / EMERSONIANISM

John I. H. Baur, the central figure in restoring Lane to visibility, established the twentieth-century interpretive strategies for understanding and contextualizing F. H. Lane's paintings. In a series of essays, including those accompanying the exhibitions of the Lane-rich Martha and Maxim Karolik collection in Boston and New York in the late 1940s and early 1950s, Baur explicated (and illustrated) the newly rediscovered canvases of this "unknown" master for both popular and professional audiences.[56] First, taking *Entrance to Somes Sound from Southwest Harbor* as paradigmatic, he described Lane as depicting "a serene and poetic interpretation of nature through subtle gradations of tone and light" and as seeking "to capture with mirror-like clarity effects of sunlight and atmosphere."[57] In this he emphasized neither the subjects of the works that were of particular interest to Lane's original audience as described in chapter 1 (specific sites, activities and labor, types of ships and boats) nor the manner in which they were painted (which he characterized as "dry, meticulous, sometimes even stiffly naïve"), but rather the coloristic treatment of the sky and the character of reflective water.[58] It was the painting not of objects or place but of air and still water that Baur valorized. Second, he understood Lane to be a participant in a "movement [that] culminated about the middle of the [nineteenth] century," presuming a cohort of like-minded artists that he called "pantheistic realists" in 1949, "Tonalists" in 1953, and—using the name that stuck—"Luminists" in 1954.[59] Third, he attributed national characteristics to what he called their "lyrical feeling for American light." He understood "Luminist" paintings to be "untinged by literary sentiment" and filled with "a kind of intensity of feeling" that suggests "an almost mystical identification of the artist with his subject, a losing of self in the enveloping moods of nature," resulting in paintings that "are hypnotic, trance-like, a moment of poetic insight immaculately preserved."[60] Subsequent authors built substantial edifices on the interpretive scaffolding Baur established here. The long-term influence of his thinking is not surprising as, I argue in this chapter, each of his points of emphasis was characteristic of mid-twentieth-century scholarship in the humanities: formalism, nationalism, and a constructed Emersonian pedigree.

By 1960 the market was rapidly drawing Lane paintings out of the households of his patrons' heirs and into major public and private collections. They were selling for impressive sums—$3,500 in 1960 (then more than the average cost of a new car in the United States), for instance.[61] Substantial offers were even pulling Lane works out of public hands. In 1965 the unique collection of all known Lane drawings at the Cape Ann Scientific, Literary, and Historical Association (now the Cape Ann Museum)—a corpus received by that institution intact from a chain of local Lane "guardians" from the artist's studio—was eroded by the sale of four of the finest drawings to private collectors (and a fifth one was sold to a public institution).[62]

Lane paintings soon began to appear in art auctions and to achieve "serious" figures; his flat-water images track a rise in cost and value from $42,000 in 1979 to $352,000 in 1983, $825,000 in 1989, $3,852,500 in 1997, and $5,506,000 in 2004.[63] Some private sales have been considerably higher. Not unexpectedly, these figures have responded to milestones in public exposure of Lane's oeuvre, notably the publication of *American Painting of the Nineteenth Century* by Barbara Novak in 1969 and *Fitz Hugh Lane* by John Wilmerding in 1971, and two exhibitions organized by the National Gallery of Art, Washington: *American Light: The Luminist Movement, 1850–1875* in 1980 and *Paintings by Fitz Hugh Lane* in 1988.[64] On the occasion of each of these public events (and in the catalogues accompanying the exhibitions), those curious about American art—dealers, collectors, and connoisseurs, together with the general public—were invited to enjoy Lane's "deeply evocative . . . masterpieces."[65] They were also educated in an understanding of the artist derived from Baur's tripartite interpretive schema, which, I argue, is itself deeply rooted in mid-twentieth-century ways of viewing both art and American culture.

One of the two most prominent linked aspects of this interpretive trajectory is its formalism, its insistence that Lane's paintings are fundamentally "about" abstract values—light and geometry. As one scholar put it concerning one of Lane's Boston Harbor views, "the subject of the painting is light itself"; and another described Lane's Brace's Rock paintings as adjustments "of the scene away from the specific toward abstract patterns of shape and thin color" (see fig. 15).[66] Similarly, the latter speaks of *Dolliver's Neck and the Western Shore from Field Beach* as "shed[ding] narrative content for a more abstract formalism" (see fig. 29).[67] A third opines that "the true subjects of his paintings . . . became time and mood" and describes objects within the *Three-Master on the Gloucester Railway* (see fig. 4) as alternating "linear and planar elements" as Lane's art during the 1850s "gives up . . . distracting details."[68] Another scholar observes in Lane's work "that silent, primordial void of light and space where material forms, whether animal, vegetable, or mineral, are virtually pulverized or banished by the incorporeal deity of light."[69] We are urged to read these paintings, with their very specific sites, recognizable rocks and local vessel types, as, in fact, subjectless abstract paintings, their subjects "pulverized" by light. For these scholars, as for others, the material facts of houses and fences, rocks and ships—all that decisively nonabstract evidence of human habitation and quotidian life—are negligible, even embarrassing. Such elements appear in a refrain of disparagement as "bits of incidental detail" or "unnecessary and distracting detail," and Lane is applauded when he apparently "purge[s] his [paintings] of extraneous detail" to create "less cluttered composition[s]."[70] Moreover, Lane is described as evolving over time toward a vision of "a world . . . abstracted by the artist's controlling geometry and purified by the suppression of extraneous detail," creating "compositions gradually diminishing or eliminating the distracting . . . narrative elements of figures at work," even though many of the dated late paintings—such as the Babson pictures—are replete with "detail" (see figs. 23 and 24).[71] It became a truism that "Lane's exploration of light and color . . . transforms his topographical study into a work of art."[72]

What are the implications of the insistent interpretive strategy at work here, and the valence of words such as "purified" in this context? First, it is clear that at least some of the anxiety about the "impurity" of particularity in Lane's painted world—a world potentially "purified" by chromatic light and geometry—evidences concern that Lane's paintings might depict "mere topography" and pedestrian visual facts. The purported erasure of these "incidental details"—by the artist or, most insistently, by these belated viewers—seemed necessary in the mid-twentieth century to make room for some kind of deep universal meaning in these works, on the one hand, and to build a life-and-works narrative toward a Great Late Style, on the other. Central to this interpretive schema is a dramatic leaching over of language and value from that used to commend and valorize abstract expressionism, the newly crowned global avant-garde establishment, and, within that movement, color-field painting in particular. From 1940 Clement Greenberg and others had been successfully explaining and boosting contemporary New York–based artists to collectors, artists, gallerists, and the public. From the pages of the *Partisan Review*, the *Nation*, *Art Digest*, and the *New York Times*, Greenberg valorized a less-is-more aesthetic in the work, for instance, of Barnett Newman, Mark Rothko, and Clyfford Still: "Broken by relatively few incidents of drawing or design, their surfaces exhale color with an enveloping effect." Of these he was particularly taken by "the simple and firm sensuousness and the splendor, of Rothko's pictures."[73] Greenberg described the process of "discarding" the "expendable conventions" of painting in the turn toward modernism as "self-purification," a process in which art is increasingly a matter of geometry, color, abstraction, flatness, simplification, and emptiness, a matter of "relations of color, shape and line largely divorced from descriptive connotations, and [creating] . . . 'situations' in which foreground and background, up and down, are interchangeable."[74] Indeed, looking back at premodern art, Greenberg asserted that the "color and shape relations" were more important than "the extra-pictorial references of old-time illusionist art," and proposed that, in such "old-time art," the "illusion of depth and volume [was] . . . valuable primarily because it enabled the painter to organize such infinite subtleties of dark and light, of translucence and transparence, into instantaneous unity."[75]

Valorizing the virtues of the abstract expressionist artists, then, entailed rewriting the project of predecessor artists. In succeeding decades John Wilmerding, Barbara Novak, Earl Powell, Franklin Kelly, and others implemented this rewriting in their engagement with the paintings of Fitz H. Lane when they proposed, for instance, that "the subject of the painting is light itself." The nouns that Greenberg associated with the work of the artists he endorsed include "honesty," "integrity," "probity," "authenticity," "truth," "intensity," "power," "boldness," "freedom," and "independence," while his adjectives ring similar changes and include "original," "pure," and, importantly, "luminous" (in 1952).[76]

Additionally, Greenberg took it for granted that the history of art was arranged in "movements" and "isms," and that important artists formed congeries of pals (and competitors) pushing each other "forward" by a series of "revolutions" and "great strides" toward an evolving high modernism.[77] Greenberg was not alone. Most twentieth-century art critics and art historians frame their understanding of art, of artists, and, not incidentally, of art markets, as a matter of movements, cohesive "isms," moving in a linear, directional (rather than random) evolution, so it is not surprising that those "rediscovering" Lane would incorporate him into a "movement," one that, in 1954, Baur named "Luminism."[78] Luminism became as concrete an entity as, say, abstract expressionism, and Lane was presumed to hold a leadership role in this cobbled cohort. So while there is no evidence that Lane ever corresponded with, associated with, or even knew any of the artists with whom his name began to be linked in the 1960s (such as Sanford Robinson Gifford, John Frederick Kensett, and Martin Johnson Heade), it became a truism that Lane's "work occupies a central place in luminism, a movement . . . of which Lane was one of the earliest exponents."[79] His works, for some, "stand as quintessential statements of the luminist movement," an assertion that would surely have perplexed this artist.[80] Others have even referenced "a canon of luminism's formal doctrine of color, light, and silence."[81] This "canon" (together with its "formal doctrine") was established in the 1970s and '80s, and it reveals more about that era and its predilection for master narratives than it does about Lane's practice or production.

In retrospect one can understand why this proactive step was so enthusiastically taken by so many, in spite of the contradictions it immediately conjures about Lane's many "less luminist" ship-portrait and choppy-water paintings and his geographical and financial distance from his purported fellow "Luminists."[82] Among the words of critique Greenberg (and others) flung at artists outside the charmed circle of "genuine" practitioners of "advanced" abstract expressionism, one finds "provincial," "insecure," "feeble," "awkward," and "inconsequential," adjectives that those enthusiastic about Lane may have striven to forestall by signaling similarities in his work to the "strong and original talents" of the "triumphantly" successful artists Greenberg (and others) so prominently endorsed.[83] Indeed, it was not long before art critics and art historians explicitly cast the "Luminists" as "precursors of the Abstract Sublime of the Abstract Expressionists."[84] Moreover, virtually all the essays discussing Lane betray anxiety that his topographical and other documentary "extraneous detail" might keep his reputation earthbound. Nor has this tendency abated with time. Even into this century scholars describe Lane's paintings as "purged of extraneous detail."[85]

This "purging" of "extraneous," "unnecessary and distracting" "clutter" is in itself a curious interpretive strategy. Mid-twentieth-century enthusiasts for Lane's painting used these terms only to describe absence; no "early" works are actively tarred with these damning brushes. Rather, it is the works of Lane's probable teacher, the British marine painter Robert Salmon, active in Boston 1828–42, that are conjured to display the "clutter" that Lane's great "late" paintings are presumed to eschew.[86] What this rhetoric of purging accomplishes for these interpreters is a narrative of implied active development over time, on the one hand, and a trajectory similar to the path of notable artists in the Western tradition, on the other. However, while all assert a "steady progression in his art toward a distilled, rarefied vision of the natural world," their tracking of that progression is murky, eliding the reality of extremely topographical and "documentary" late works filled with detail (such as the Babson pictures of 1863 and *The Sawyer Homestead* [Sawyer Free Library] of 1864), while attributing to some dated early works, such as *Somes Sound* of 1852, the "elegant spare style" presumed to be characteristic of his "late" period (figs. 23, 24, 31).[87]

The teleological framework became more insistent once undated works were positioned in the narrative to reinforce the thesis. Early on, Baur was able tentatively to suggest that Lane's later works displayed *more* topographical detail than his early paintings, but this proposal quickly inverted, succumbing to the dominant developmental and evacuative theory.[88] Since Lane's earliest surviving dated oil painting was executed in 1842 and his last in 1864, his career was highly compressed, so the fitful path "he did not consistently pursue" from "crowded busy compositions toward the purified vision of his late style" remains an imposed construct.[89] What it achieves is a life-and-works trajectory for this artist that mimics those presumed (and tracked) in the accounts of the heroes of modernism as they made their way—in association with other artists of their various "movements"—"forward," toward a personal mature (and often a Late Great) style and toward a shared goal of high modernism.[90] For Greenberg, both individual great artists and Western art in general consistently displayed "a readiness to sacrifice and simplify for the sake of large effects."[91] It would have been difficult for art historians of the mid-twentieth-century period to resist the value-laden model so consistently and insistently put before them. For Lane, then, as for other important artists, it was necessary for ontogeny to recapitulate phylogeny. Lane's work had steadily to evolve over time, sacrificing and simplifying to achieve the "large effects" of a "distilled rarefied vision." This interpretive trajectory is consistent with and actively echoes mid-twentieth-century master narratives concerning the history of art, and it is responsive to anxieties concerning the quality of painting produced in the United States before the New York florescence that—with the help of Greenberg and others—suddenly alerted Europeans to transatlantic competition for priority in art production and art markets.

It is true that many artists, especially those with long and highly visible careers like Claude Monet and Winslow Homer, decisively evolved in terms of style, subject matter, and palette over time toward distinctive and masterly works as celebrities in old age. However, others arguably did not, remaining productive in a variety of consistent stylistic "voices" throughout their mature years. The explanatory model offered by one scholar for Lane's presumed evolution from "cluttered" toward "transcendent" canvases hinges on distance from patrons and pecuniary need: "Once freed from the restrictions of such commissions [ship portraits and straightforward harbor views] he began to refine his compositions and gradually purge them of extraneous detail and overt narrative content."[92] But this is also a fiction. As noted in chapter 1, Lane was not painting on spec even in his last years but rather painting ship portraits and satisfying specific commissions (such as the Brace's Rock series, figs. 13 and 15) up to the day of his death. This purging model presumes that it was Lane's patrons who kept him earthbound and that economic success "freed [him] from the restrictions of such commissions." But his works for specific patrons have been judged by twentieth-century viewers as among his most successful works, and the little that is known about Lane's finances suggests that he was at his most affluent in 1849–50, at the outset of his painting career, when he had the resources (or the backing of a wealthy patron) to buy property and build a substantial house. Far from being "freed" from pecuniary concerns in the last years of his life, the evidence suggests that Lane was in financial straits—the property that was his primary asset was mortgaged in 1859 and sold to a benevolent friend for a sum considerably higher than its value in 1862, a friend who allowed him to continue to live there his remaining three years.[93]

If the most prominent aspect of Baur's interpretive trajectory is its alignment with formalism and the invention of "Luminism," the second is its alignment with Emerson and the assertion of nationalism. Beginning with Baur's appreciative promotion of this "unknown" artist, interpretation of Lane's works over the course of the second half of the twentieth century and into the twenty-first has been strongly inflected by values and models imported from major paradigms developed elsewhere. This second leg of the dominant interpretive structure—one intended to underline its Americanness—has been a vigorous campaign to connect Lane (and "Luminism") to Ralph Waldo Emerson and transcendentalism. It is difficult to resist glossing Lane's *Entrance to Somes Sound* with such Emersonian passages as this, from the essay "Nature," of 1836: "There are days which occur in this climate, at almost any season of the year, wherein the world reaches its perfection, when the air, the heavenly bodies, and the earth, make a harmony, as if nature would indulge her offspring; when, in these [often] bleak upper sides of the planet, ... we bask in the shining hours" (fig. 31). With such words, Ralph Waldo Emerson describes "halcyon" days in New England. "Here," he continues, "is sanctity which shames our religions.... The blue zenith is the point in which romance and reality meet." "We penetrate bodily this incredible beauty: we dip our hands in this painted element: our eyes are bathed in these lights and forms."[94] Quoting such passages, many commentators have proposed "parallels," "concurrences," "affinities," and "influences" linking Emerson's beliefs with Lane's paintings.

For Barbara Novak, for instance, "Lane's art concurs with Emerson's concept of light as the 'reappearance of the original soul,'" and it offers the "closest parallel to Emerson's Transcendentalism that America produced: of all the painters of the mid-century, he was the most 'transparent eyeball.'"[95] For Elizabeth Garrity Ellis and others, Emerson offers "the language and meaning of Lane's radiant coastal views," with their "crystalline light and patterned geometries"; for John Wilmerding, Lane's paintings are the "counterparts" to Emerson's prose and suggest "the harmony between the soul and matter, the sublime and the ordinary, the seer and the seen," as articulated by Emerson in "Nature" and "The American Scholar."[96] For Earl Powell, "the quiet stability and mirrored reflections of Fitz Hugh Lane ... illustrate the ultimate influence of ... [Emersonian] transcendental philosophy"; "Lane has depicted the moment when mind and spirit are at one with nature and the universe."[97] There is, in other words, among scholars who have studied Lane's paintings from the 1960s up into the present century, virtual unanimity that Emerson's "transparent eyeball" is the key to understanding them or at least to understanding the "uncluttered" flat-water Lane paintings such as *Entrance to Somes Sound* and *Lumber Schooners at Evening* (figs. 31 and 7).[98] Such observations rest generally on the arguments more convincingly articulated by Michael Baxandall, in the European context, concerning the permeability of boundaries between vision and art, on the one hand, and philosophy, science, and vernacular artisanal practices, on the other.[99]

The best statement by an acquaintance of Lane's concerning the general influence of "advanced" thinking in coastal Massachusetts is probably that articulated by one of his patrons, William Philips Tilden, who recalled his years (1837–40) in Scituate, where he was tutored by Rev. Samuel Joseph May for the ministry: "[William Lloyd] Garrison was one of Mr. May's intimate friends, and A. Bronson Alcott, his brother-in-law, used to spend his summers there.... Transcendentalism, non-resistance, anti-slavery, women's rights, teetotalism, Emerson, Carlyle, Theodore Parker, were my daily meat and drink."[100] Like Lane, Tilden was from an artisanal background and rose to distinction and achievement belatedly and with considerable effort, but of the cosmopolitan movements and individuals he lists here, the only one we know for certain that Lane endorsed was "teetotalism" (temperance). Emerson certainly cast a wide shadow, but how can we know Lane's knowledge of and interest in Emerson's ideas?

Pressing beyond general cultural contemporaneity, some have labored to draw specific lines of personal connection between the artist and the seer of Concord. From 1836, when Emerson published "Nature," and 1838, when he delivered the infamous Harvard Divinity School Address, Emerson was a celebrity and a scandal. Leaving the ministry, Emerson became what we would call a public intellectual, lecturing widely. Emerson's published works were well circulated, and he lectured frequently in Boston when Lane was resident there (1832–48), as well as at the Gloucester Lyceum, an institution in which Lane, some of his friends, and some of his patrons were intermittently active.[101] The strongest, most closely researched argument for "Emersonianism" in antebellum Gloucester is that advanced by Sharon Worley. Her search for "the connection between his [Lane's] luminist style and Ralph Waldo Emerson's transcendental philosophy" led her to one of Gloucester's ministers, Rev. Amory Dwight Mayo, who, she argues, "bridged the gap" between public disdain for Emerson and valuable Emersonian insights concerning the "'wonderful gospel of nature on this New England coast,'" which his parishioners could endorse only if disassociated from Emerson's name and the concept of transcendentalism.[102] But despite her well-researched efforts, the dots do not connect. Nature may be "the present expositor of the divine mind" for Emerson and for many of his contemporaries, but there is little evidence that Lane's paintings were "present expositors" of Emerson's mind.[103] *Entrance to Somes Sound*, with its arching firmament, its mirroring water doubling and inverting each element, its stretched horizon and achingly beautiful summer sunlight, its boards gently clapping as they are moved into the hold of the ship, is the result of many forces and ideas, desires and visions, not the least of which are topographic and documentary (fig. 32).

It is useful to ask exactly what Lane's theological and philosophical inclinations were. A poorly educated man of artisanal background (his father was a sailmaker, and he was trained as a shoemaker),[104] he left no essays or diaries and only a handful of not-very-useful letters to attest to his opinions. We are not even sure which church he attended—if he attended church—during his years working in Boston or the long years before and after that interlude in his native Gloucester. The record is clear, though, that in 1846, during his years in Boston, when he was transforming himself from shoemaker to lithographer to painter, he briefly joined a short-lived group known as the American Union of Associationists, later known as the Religious Union of Associationists and as the First Church of Humanity.[105] Members in that year included refugees from the failing Brook Farm experiment (including George Ripley, an original member and host of the Transcendental Club) and a number of artists and sculptors. As one might expect, this association promoted the socialist principles of Charles Fourier within a Christian framework. But it also leaned toward spiritualism, mesmerism, and phrenology, powerful fringe movements that Emerson did not endorse.[106] Lane's name appears on a handwritten addendum to one list of members in one year, so he was apparently willing to associate himself with this group at least fleetingly, but it is difficult to know exactly which aspect of the association attracted his brief allegiance—socialism, transcendentalism, spiritualism (communication with the dead through mediums), mesmerism, phrenology, or perhaps the companionship of such up-and-coming artists as William Wetmore Story.[107]

It is, of course, possible that Lane was enthusiastic about Emerson's perspectives and sought out his lectures and published essays. Founded in 1841, the Gloucester Lyceum sponsored lectures on a wide variety of subjects of popular and scientific interest; the cost was modest ($1.60 for the course of lectures for men and $1.00 for women in 1861).[108] Emerson's titles in Gloucester, for instance, include "Napoleon Bonaparte" (1845), then "Montaigne" and "Eloquence" (1846), "England" (1849), "The Spirit of the Age" (1850), and "Classes of Men" (1861).[109] We know a good bit about what he had to say in some of these lectures, as they were reported at length in the newspapers. For instance, in his lecture "The Spirit of the Age" he spoke primarily about socialism (ideal, but impracticable) and touched on Goethe's (eccentric) theories of light and color.[110] Lane may have attended, or he may not; he may have read the editorials, or he may not. The interesting point is that opinion among Gloucesterites was by no means uniform and by no means generally positive. In 1849 "Transcendentalism" was the butt of jokes in the *Cape Ann Light & Gloucester Telegraph*, which commented: "[This word] has not its equal in our vocabulary. It is used on all occasions by learned and unlearned, democrat and aristocrat. We hear it in trade, law, letters, politics and religion. . . . We should not be surprised at any time to find teachers . . . complaining of juveniles for stigmatizing the difficult portions of their grammar and spelling book as transcendental." Shortly after, the same paper opined that "transcendentalism" was "a word of fearful import in the estimation of very many worthy old ladies of both sexes."[111] In March 1850 a long editorial in the *Gloucester Telegraph* noted that

> Emerson commands the greatest attention and admiration at New York. He packs the largest halls in the city with hearers almost as closely as we pack our mackerel. He gathers about him the most aristocratic audiences, not the money aristocracy whose station is based upon their knowledge of the multiplication table, but of intellect. . . . But that does not influence his hearers in this place one iota. Many [in Gloucester], probably the majority, do not scruple to denounce him as an unmitigated bore, the quintessence of stupidity and nothingness, who would not be brought hither except by an act of a reckless minority. The Manhattanese are altogether wrong, undoubtedly, and deserve rather to be pitied than otherwise for being so dazzled by "the great eyeball."[112]

A month later the editor reported: "[Nathaniel Parker] Willis says of Emerson's audiences in Gotham, that 'from the great miscellany of New York they come selectively out, like steel-filings out of a handful of sand to a magnet.'" Thereafter followed jibes about "weather transcendentalism" and, in June and September of that year, Emerson's annual income.[113] It is impossible to surmise which side of this clearly polarized debate Lane lined up on, if indeed he took heed of it, so the principal evidence of Lane's transcendentalism is the corpus of surviving paintings. Among these are paintings characterized by, in the words of one scholar, "intense realism in which absolute stillness prevail[s] in compositions resonant with colored light," which he calls "the transcendental sublime" or "the contemplative sublime," or, in the words of another art historian, "formal essays on quiet and light."[114] These canvases constitute a minority of Lane's works. Most of the extant paintings have more the character of *Three-Master on the Gloucester Railway*, works descriptive of particular structures and specific human activities (fig. 4).

However, it should be noted that in the nineteenth century one did not need Emerson to summon visual and verbal poetry about the natural and inhabited world. Many passages published in the Gloucester newspapers that appear to evoke Powell's "contemplative sublime" antedate Emerson's publications and lectures, among them a description from 1830 that quotes an even earlier text concerning the beauties of Cape Ann, its air, roads, villages, harbors, and people, and concludes: "To our taste nothing suits so well, as the vast and sublime solitude of the sea-shore in quick contrast with the dust and toils of the daily labors, strifes and petty rivalries of real life.—'What an idea of a long, unbroken, universal slumber fastens on the mind, when, as we muse along the seashore, the waters touch the beach without a murmur, and our spirit seems, as if it were capable of gliding to eternity, unhurt, upon the tranquil surface of the deep!'"[115] In the late 1840s similar language appears in the diary of Annette Babson, a woman who knew, admired, and frequently visited Lane: "I never saw any thing more lovely than the water with the radiance of a sunset of rare brilliancy reflected 'for thee': earth, ocean and sky mingled in one golden hue; and we glided on in the repose and stillness of twilight like a thing of life."[116] And yet Annette Babson understood transcendentalism to be "entirely beyond the comprehension of anyone," a philosophy with "a decidedly immoral tendency," articulated by a man who seemed to her "half crazy."[117]

In sum, then, Gloucesterites—including presumably Lane—had no need of Emerson to show them the beauties of their region, the qualities of its light, or the reasons to record verbal and visual meditations on beauty that echo English and European as well as American Romanticism. Why, then, have scholars been at pains, over so many decades, to invoke Emerson to explicate Lane? Is it related to why they ask us to overlook the middle ground and attend instead to the ethereal sky and the beckoning geometry of the horizon? Likely the answer lies in the same eagerness evident in the adoption, from the 1940s on, of Greenbergian terms of approbation to validate professional (and popular) enthusiasm for this "dark horse" artist. The strategy was to associate these then–relatively unknown and underappreciated works with the established aesthetic, cultural, and explicitly *American* value of Ralph Waldo Emerson, a strategy, again, of value transfer. In this move, Baur and his successors were not exceptional.

In the 1930s—as Caroline Blinder describes—Lincoln Kirstein and William Carlos Williams, referencing Walker Evans's 1938 exhibition at the Museum of Modern Art in New York, used "Emersonian rhetoric to connect the everyday, the vernacular, with a spiritualized and transcendent idea of vision."[118] For Kirstein and Williams, it was important to validate the medium of photography, the vernacular subject matter of Evans's photographs, and the documentary style that Evans employed, associating these qualities, through Emerson, not only with transcendental depth of purpose but also with "a secular vision of America . . . given sacred implications." By invoking Emerson, they moved Evans's work into a pantheon of non-European aesthetic achievement simultaneously associated with the common, the vernacular, and the American, on the one hand, and with high modernism, on the other.

This strategy for locating an aesthetic pedigree, seemingly independent of Europe, in the person of Ralph Waldo Emerson had been used even earlier by Vernon Lewis Parrington in his *Main Currents in American Thought*, a milestone work of the 1920s establishing the American literary canon.[119] The history of Lane's twentieth-century professional reputation, then, falls into large patterns visible in the historiography of the scholarly analysis of American art, American culture, and American literature. It says perhaps more about the anxieties of belated critics meeting the challenges of modernism and the heavy cultural paternity of Europe than it does about what is actually going on in the works themselves.

"INCIDENTAL DETAILS"

However, Kirstein's and Williams's adoption of Emerson in explicating Evans differs from the Emersonianism of Lane scholars in one major respect: the former's embrace of the vernacular and the documentary. They linked the "transcendent . . . vision" in Evans's photographs to Emerson's rhetoric of the common, the everyday, the local, and the specific; in short, they made a case for documentary photography and "the vernacular as intrinsic to the modernist project."[120] As noted above, the "incidental," "extraneous," and "distracting" details—the topographical and documentary dimensions of Lane's works—have been consistently understood to diminish, rather than raise, their aesthetic value among Lane scholars. Most of Lane's paintings include vignettes of craftsmen, mariners, and laborers going about their chores. While midcentury scholarship downplayed Lane paintings focused on what many called "incidental details," these images of laborers laboring were entirely consistent with Emerson's enthusiasm for the common, the vernacular, the daily details that constituted human experience in his day. Although Emerson is often read otherwise—that is, as privileging the universal over the particular, the timeless over the temporal—it was, in fact, in ocular experience of the *particular* and the *vernacular* that Emerson understood the human capacity to apprehend an "individual relation to the universe" to reside.[121]

Attention to Lane's "details" (and even perhaps Emerson's celebration of the common) leads one both to recontextualize Lane's achievement and also to understand that achievement as even more substantial. It is not, I argue, beside the point that *Entrance to Somes Sound* is a painting about the loading of wood into a brig (fig. 32). Lane's patrons would have understood this painting to reference commerce in the basic material of finished houses, ships, barrels, buckets, and furniture on the whole Eastern Seaboard (see chapter 5). They would have understood it as descriptive of foundational human activities on this continent (craft and commerce) and of the building-block materials of American culture (wood), which together constituted a single system in which ships, people, logs, lumber, and money moved in continuous productive cycles. This painting is also, of course, a record of one of Emerson's halcyon New England days, a scene that catches our souls with its lofty elegance. It does not diminish but rather enlarges our understanding of and appreciation for this extraordinary work to see Lane not as a protomodernist or as an Emerson illustrator but as an artist of his time, recording "the details" of an inhabited continent. Equally, the narrative of this painting, in particular, and of Lane's oeuvre, in general, can help us remember that value is as immersed in culture as it is in the aesthetic object itself.

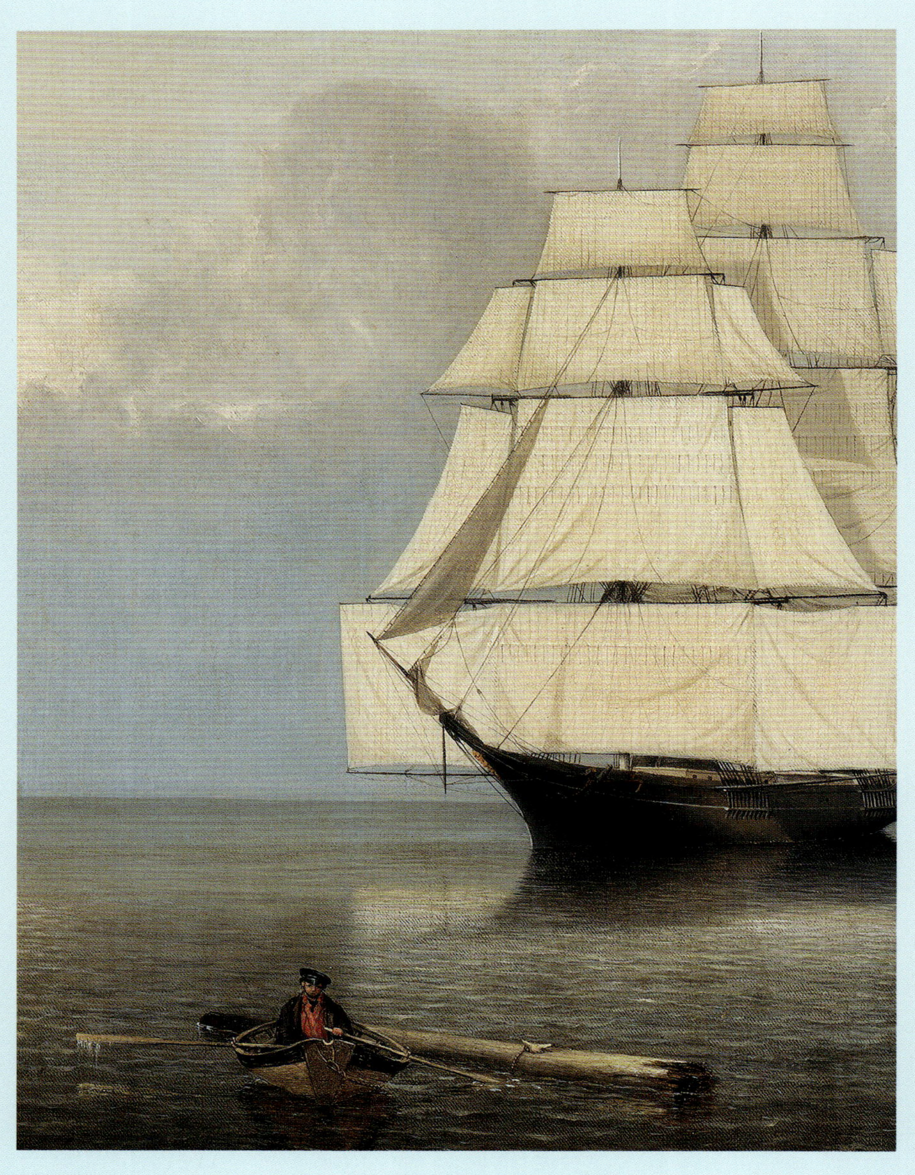

CHAPTER 3

CANVAS

Names, Naming, and Identity

Bracketed by high clouds and still water, maritime traffic in Fitz H. Lane's *Salem Harbor* of 1853 raises issues of artistic identity, cultural geography, and global reach coded within a very local vignette (fig. 33). As is so often the case in discussions of Lane's work, the masterly quality of the atmosphere and reflections in this painting have drawn remark from numerous scholars, who characteristically point to Lane's "glowing light" and his adroit depiction of ripples.[1] But attending to the disparagingly termed "distracting detail" in the image—the ships, boats, and figures—to the material content of this evocative "placid scene" in late afternoon light, a more complex and more interesting painting emerges.[2] Lane's is a narrative told largely in depicted canvas as well as on canvas. This chapter is about the canvas of sails and the canvas of paintings, about words and names, and about identity—in signatures, in signs, in pennants, in figureheads, and emblazoned on the transoms of ships.

Lane was the son of a sailmaker. He was deeply familiar with sails and ships and rigging but particularly with canvas and how it was woven and crafted to harness wind, drive ships, and create the prosperity enjoyed by many in antebellum America. Canvas provided the material link between the globe's most omnipresent renewable resource—wind—and the ambitions of men to move goods and ideas beyond local orbits. In the canvas Lane stretched for his paintings, he appears to have favored the finest, most stable twill weave, as is visible in a detail of this painting (fig. 34).[3] Possibly selected deliberately for works commissioned by his most discerning

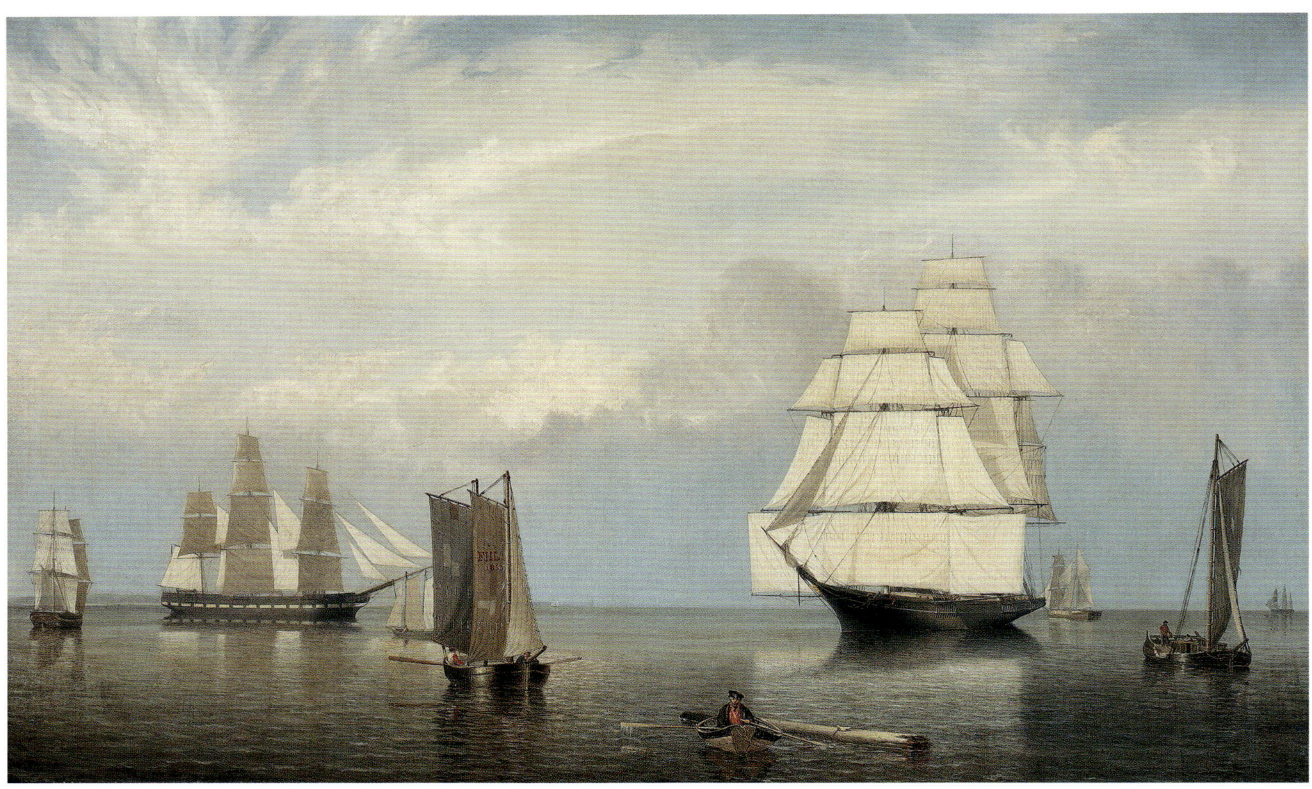

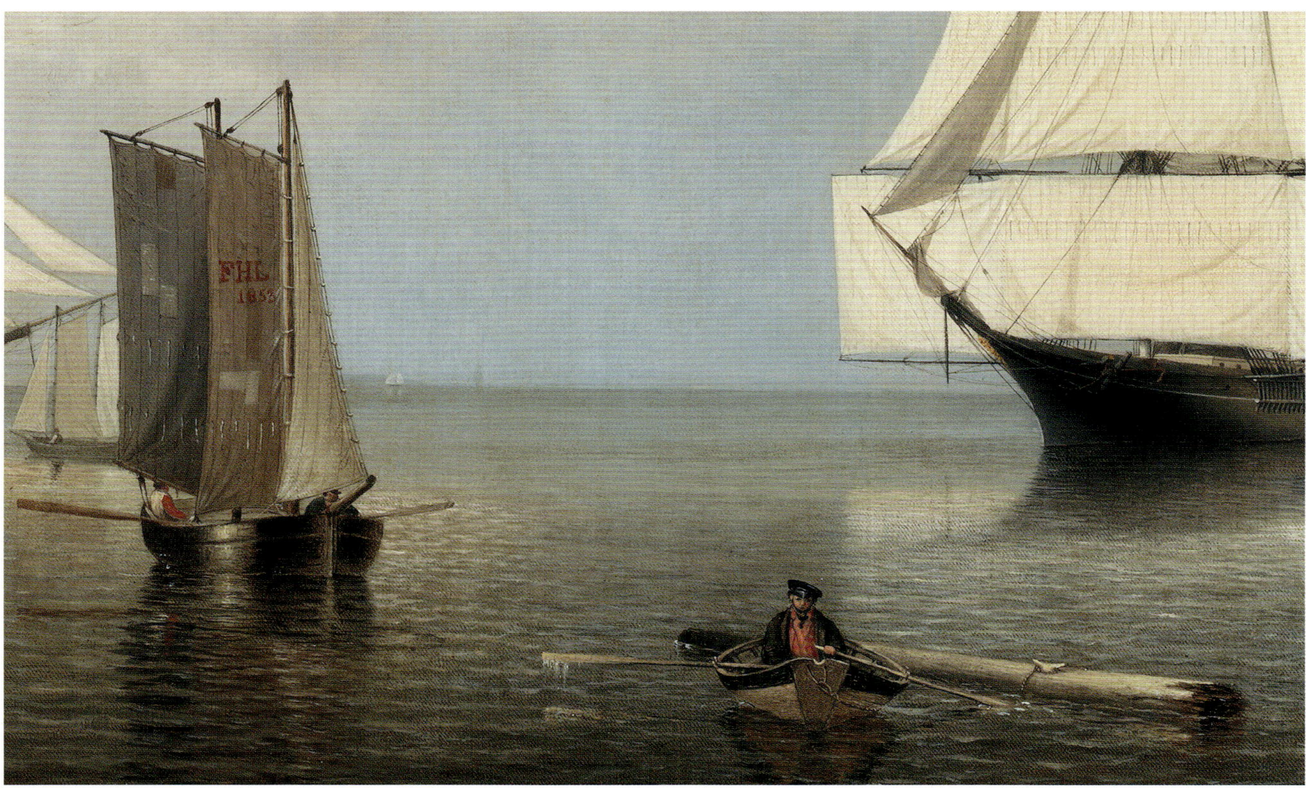

FIGURE 33 (TOP)
Fitz H. Lane, *Salem Harbor*, 1853. Oil on canvas, 26 1/8 × 42 in. (66.36 × 106.68 cm). Museum of Fine Arts, Boston. Bequest of Maxim Karolik (63.465). Photo © 2022 Museum of Fine Arts, Boston.

FIGURE 34 (BOTTOM)
Fitz H. Lane, *Salem Harbor*, 1853 (fig. 33), detail.

patrons, the tight, even weave of the twill canvas gives these generally larger works a distinctive, richer surface than plain-weave canvas.

The setting of this painting is indicated equally by the title—*Salem Harbor*—and by the internal evidence of shipping characteristic of Salem, Gloucester's Essex County neighbor, thirteen miles as the crow flies southwest of Cape Ann. Most dramatically, a majestic clipper ship fills the right side of the image, its broad array of canvas sails drying in the late afternoon sun. Clippers frequented Salem (as well as Boston, New York, and Baltimore); they did not frequent Gloucester.[4] Billowing gray cumulus clouds frame the bright precise trapezoids of canvas on display—at least eighteen sails are carried to extreme heights by this ship's towering masts and extraordinary breadth by the studding-sail booms extending considerably beyond its sides. Everything about this ship, from the yardage of canvas on its superstructure to the trim profile of its bow and raking stern, promises speed and blue-water ambition. It seems sleek and new, and indeed, the class of ship to which it belongs—clipper ships—was novel when this picture was painted, in 1853. Most notably, clipper-ship design sacrificed carrying capacity for extreme speed.[5] In the rush to California for gold, and to China and Indonesia for tea, spices, silks, and porcelain, swiftness trumped cargo space. Capable of traversing 465 nautical miles in a day, outpacing the sturdy merchantmen of the 1840s by doubling or tripling their speed, clippers could beat competition to markets and magnify opportunities by factors of ten.[6] At rest, then, its bright new canvas hanging flat, this ship nevertheless promises exceptional athletic prowess and exceptional profits.

Salem Harbor belonged to, and was probably commissioned by, Nathaniel Silsbee Jr., mayor of Salem, representative in the Massachusetts legislature, treasurer of Harvard University, and partner in Stone, Silsbee, and Pickman, a firm prominent in the Sumatra pepper trade.[7] The ships that Silsbee had built and registered in his name in Salem include *Borneo, Malay,* and *Delphos,* suggesting in their exotic names the far-flung reaches of his imagination and of his commerce. His most focused direct trading partner was, until 1860, Sumatra.[8] Known to Europeans from the sixteenth century and to American ships from 1788, the ports of Sumatra yielded profits for Salem merchants on cargoes of cinnamon, camphor, gold dust, and pepper of as much as 700 percent.[9] One Englishman, recording his experience in the eighteenth century, wrote: "Sumatra, one of the Greatest Islands in the World, is very Populous and has all Necessaries for life. Their Mountains are high, cover'd with Trees, and have Mines of Gold, Silver, Copper, Tin, Iron and Sulphur. They have Sugar, Ginger, Pepper, with which they load many vessels every year. In the Desarts they have Elephants, Tygers, Rhinoceroses, Boars, Porcupines, Serpents, & Monkies. Their Rivers are pester'd with Crocodiles" (fig. 35).[10] The clipper ship pictured in *Salem Harbor,* then, evoked for Lane, Silsbee, and their contemporaries not only the vision of an elegant new, highly efficient ship bathed in the sweet light of late afternoon in its home port but also the scent of exotic spices and the aura of the very distant, different cultures, products, and creatures of an imagined near-Edenic place where, unlike New England, "all Necessaries for life" were plentifully available for harvesting. The name of the clipper ship pictured in *Salem Harbor* has not come down to us, but it certainly was known to Lane and to his patron, who was, most likely, the owner of the ship as well as of the canvas portraying it.[11]

Eight other ships and boats surround and provide contrast to the glorious clipper—a dory, two schooners, two brigs (the hermaphrodite brig on the right carrying lumber), a sloop in the right foreground so low in the water it must be transporting granite, a ship on the far right-hand horizon, giving the composition a sense of deep space, and broadside, on the left, a ship armed (or faux armed) with "Quaker" gunports, its main mast's red pennant limp in the still air.[12] Of these the artist has drawn particular attention to the dory and the little schooner—these two privileged by positioning at the center of the canvas and proximity to the picture

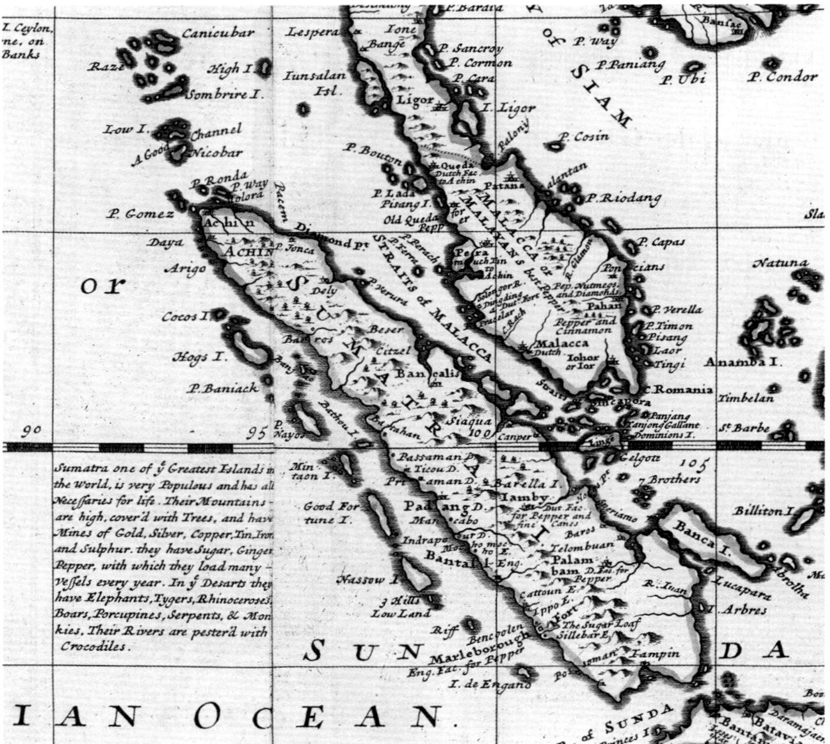

FIGURE 35
Herman Moll, *A Map of the East-Indies and the adjacent countries; with the Settlements, Factories and Territories, explaining what belongs to England, Spain, France, Holland, Denmark, Portugal &c.*, ca. 1709, detail. Engraving. Map 5 in Herman Moll, *The World Described; or, A New and Correct Sett of Maps* [. . .] (London: I Bowles, [1709–20]). Courtesy, American Antiquarian Society (Atlases G1105/.m726/1709 [bound together]).

plane (fig. 34). Lane depicts this harborscape on a windless afternoon, one of Emerson's halcyon New England days, on which a gorgeous vessel catches our souls with its lofty elegance. However, he also expects his viewers to attend to the vernacular, the humble, the narrative note he has injected with these two modest vessels, which—if they do not claim equal status—then at least quietly make a competing, possibly ironic comment on the part of the artist, who brings the ineffable vision of the clipper's prowess to realization.

Closest to the picture plane, a rower appears to have tethered a flotsam broken mast and begins to turn his dory to tow it back to land. This small narrative about salvage catches the viewer's attention not only because it is the closest "event" in the painting, and not only because the red spot of the rower's vest stands out from the prevailing blue gray, but because he appears to fix the viewer with his steady gaze (fig. 34). This gaze, aligned with and emphasized by the dory's position, perpendicular to the picture plane, is unusual in landscape and genre painting. The artist constructs the viewer's subjectivity in this direct address to us, outside the fiction of the picture. It is even a little startling to find oneself thus acknowledged and identified. Water drips from the doryman's lifted oar and suggests the momentariness of this exact conjunction of visual incidents and sightlines.

The shattered floating mast that may soon find another use points toward a second vessel, a small schooner that evidences both repurposed materials and consciousness of another kind. Lane here has included sly commentary not about his viewer but about himself. On the canvas of this modest schooner, with its mismatched, much-patched sails, Lane comments on the canvas of sails and the canvas of paintings, about words and names and identity. A close look at these "incidental details" within many Lane paintings reveals these mime communication devices in the placement of signatures and signs, in pennants and figureheads, in names and ornaments on transoms of ships. Such visual cues were in Lane's world readily legible and pointed to identities of people and vessels that were important to his contemporaries and to the meanings of his pictures. This little vessel, its sails catching just enough air to keep its oars idle, is propelled by sails composed of narrow strips of gray and tan canvas frugally sewn together and then much patched, sails very unlike the broadloom wholecloth matched set that the majestic clipper displays. Lane expects viewers to look closely and recognize his own initials painted in vermillion on the middle of these worn and much-mended sails, identifying himself as local, slow, old-fashioned, and dog-eared in the company of the gallant, new, and elegantly equipped white-sailed ocean trader on the right. The deferential posture of this gesture, however, is somewhat undercut by the centrality and prominence of the artist's claim to authorship and creativity at the very center of his patron's heroic celebration of the Pacific trader, pressed here a bit to the side.

NATHANIEL ROGERS / FITZ HUGH / FITZ HENRY

Lane made his reputation as an artist in Gloucester as a community member integral to its activities and embedded in its economy during his mature years. Earlier, as a teenager and young man, and then later, as a mature artist, he explored and expressed his evolving identity. Something of a chameleon, Lane changed his name, his trade, and his social class before settling on the identity of town artist. Relatively little is known about Lane, and scholarly confusions about his name have only exacerbated this ignorance. We do not know, for instance, how Lane became a painter, how he learned the mechanics of stretching canvas and describing objects in space with pigments, but we can try to reconstruct the Gloucester in which he was raised and in which he made his early decisions to assume and change identities, to learn what art was and might be. And we can look closely at those aspects of his art in which he commented, often slyly within his paintings, on the identity of ships and places and himself.

"F. H. L. / 1853" on the main sail of the little schooner in *Salem Harbor* denotes, in shorthand initials, the name of the painter and the year of the fabrication of the work, but the issue of Lane's identity, quite literally his *name*, has been (and continues to be) a source of confusion and perplexity for scholars, collectors, dealers, curators, and the interested public. As noted in chapter 2, Lane's reputation reached such an ebb in the latter nineteenth century that by the early twentieth century his name was mistaken to be Fitz Hugh (or Fitzhugh) Lane, and this error, through repetition, affirmation, and erroneous corrections, persisted through more than seven decades. Those who had known the artist knew him as Fitz Henry Lane or Fitz H. Lane and used those names in the infrequent local public mentions of the artist into the second decade of the twentieth century. In 1913, for instance, when Carrie Mason Myers Julian-James, descendant of Lane patron Sidney Mason, gave the painting her grandfather commissioned, *Gloucester Harbor*, to the city, the newspaper notice explained that it had been "executed by [Gloucester's] noted native artist, the late Fitz Henry Lane," who had by that date been dead (and largely forgotten) for almost a half century.[13] Two years later a son of Lane's brother died, and the obituary noted that he "was a nephew of Fitz Henry Lane, the famous marine artist of this city, for whom he was named."[14] But as early as 1914 dealers in Boston began referring to the artist as "Fitz Hugh Lane."[15] It is telling that this error seems to have begun outside of Gloucester and among Americana dealers. Fitz Hugh (or Fitzhugh) is not only far commoner than "Fitz Henry" as a name, it is also the name of the border pattern of the most desirable Chinese export porcelain brought into the United States in the late eighteenth and early nineteenth centuries, an object type (and therefore a name) familiar to anyone buying and selling Americana in the early twentieth century. Most notably, the distinctive honeycomb and butterfly Fitzhugh border (named after an English factor in China) was used on the Order of the

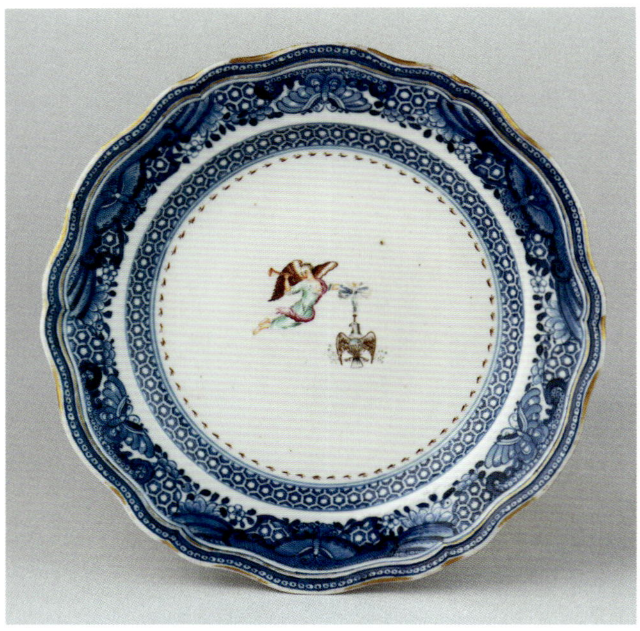

FIGURE 36
Fitzhugh-pattern dinner plate (Order of the Cincinnati Service given to George Washington in 1786), 1784. Hard-paste Jingdezhen porcelain, lime glaze, 9¾ in. (24.50 cm) diameter. Courtesy, Winterthur Museum. Gift of Henry Francis du Pont (1963.700.20).

Cincinnati dinner service presented to George Washington in 1786 (fig. 36).[16] So, given Lane's obscurity and the fact that he usually signed his canvases "F. H. Lane," the error is understandable, almost predictable.

It is rather odd, however, that despite the artist's widespread recognition and the value of his works in the second half of the twentieth century, until 2004 no scholar scoured the records and corrected this error.[17] In fact, when records and paintings inscribed "Fitz Henry Lane" appeared, the records were altered and the paintings or their signatures were deemed suspicious. For instance, the typescript of Emma Todd's account of a conversation she had had with John Trask, friend and patron of Lane, around 1885, regarding his memories of the artist, a conversation that was typed up verbatim by her daughter some years later, begins, "Notes on the life of Fitz Henry Lane," but "Henry" has been struck out and replaced by "Hugh."[18] Similarly, the large *Gloucester Harbor* painted for Sidney Mason and given to the town by his granddaughter had an elegant brass plaque, attached to the frame at the time of the gift, recording information about the artist, the painting, and the donor. "Fitz Henry Lane" on this plaque was overlaid, judging from the typeface, in the 1960s, with a second small brass plaque engraved "Fitz Hugh Lane" covering the artist's name. One art historian brushed aside the repeated resurfacing of "Fitz Henry": "The artist signed his name most often as 'F. H. Lane,' sometimes with 'Fitz H. Lane,' and only rarely with 'Fitz Hugh Lane' or 'F. H. L.' The names 'Fritz H.' and 'Fitz Henry' in some biographers' accounts are mistaken readings of older references or confusions with other members of the Lane family. Lane himself never went by either of these last names nor signed any of his works with them."[19]

As it turns out, it is the reports that the artist *ever* signed his name "Fitz Hugh Lane" that are the "confusions." *A Smart Blow*, for instance, was published as recently as 2004 with the comment "Inscribed 'Fitz Hugh Lane Gloucester,'" when it is, in fact, signed "Fitz H. Lane Gloucester" (figs. 37 and 38).[20] In 1975 the Metropolitan Museum of Art published a compendium of the most recent decade's acquisitions and listed the first Lane to come into the museum's collection, *The* Golden State *Entering New York Harbor* of 1854 (acquired in 1974), as "Signed and dated (on back): 'Painted by Fitz H . . . Lane Gloucester / Mass A. D. 1854,'" eliding the "Henry" and finessing the important fact that this is one of two Lane works signed by the artist with his full correct name (fig. 39).[21] The other painting signed with Lane's full name had entered a New York City collection decades earlier, *Sweepstakes*, accessioned in 1950 by the Museum of the City of New York. It is the portrait of a ship built in New York in 1853 and captained by the artist's kinsman, George Lane, when it made the record-holding time of seventy-four days from New York to India in 1857; it is signed in the lower right of the canvas: "Fitz Henry Lane / Gloucester, Mass. / 1853" (figs. 40 and 41).[22] In retrospect, it seems odd that the rather insistent surfacing of "Henry,"

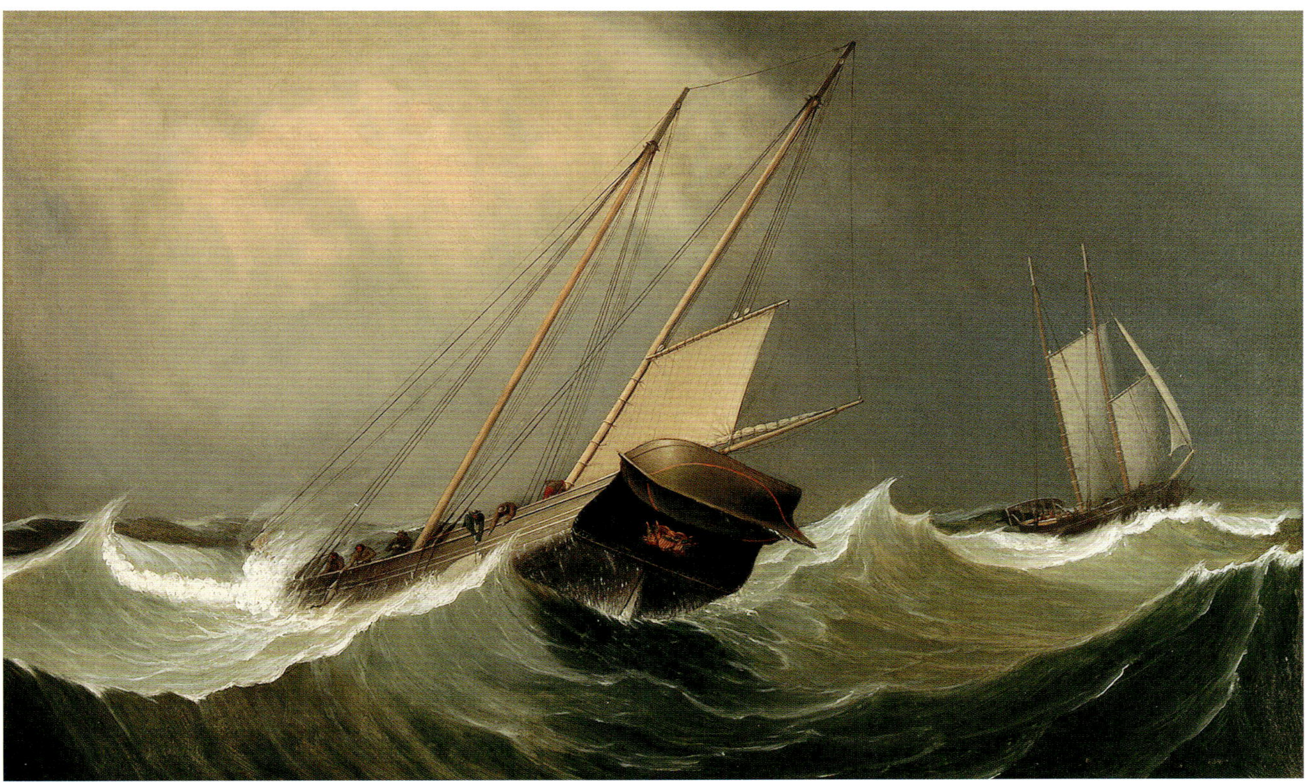

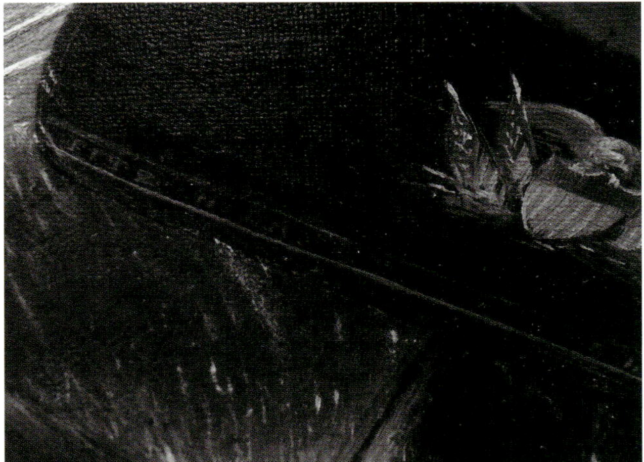

FIGURE 37 (ABOVE)
Fitz H. Lane, *A Smart Blow*. Oil on canvas, 24 × 42 in. (60.96 × 106.68 cm). Collection of Louis Bacon.

FIGURE 38 (LEFT)
Fitz H. Lane, *A Smart Blow* (fig. 37), detail. Signature on stern: "Fitz H. Lane Gloucester."

not in the provinces but in downtown New York City, did not trigger an all-out search of the records earlier. In 2004 Jane Walsh, Sarah Dunlap, and Stephanie Buck of the Cape Ann Museum took on that search and located the document that settled the matter—the list of those in Essex County who were granted permission by the Massachusetts legislature to change their names in early 1832, a list that includes this item: "Nathaniel Rogers Lane, of Gloucester, may take the name of Fitz Henry Lane."[23]

In a well-circulated account of the artist, his friend and patron John Trask introduces this subject: "His original name was Nathaniel Rogers Lane but he said 'Damned if

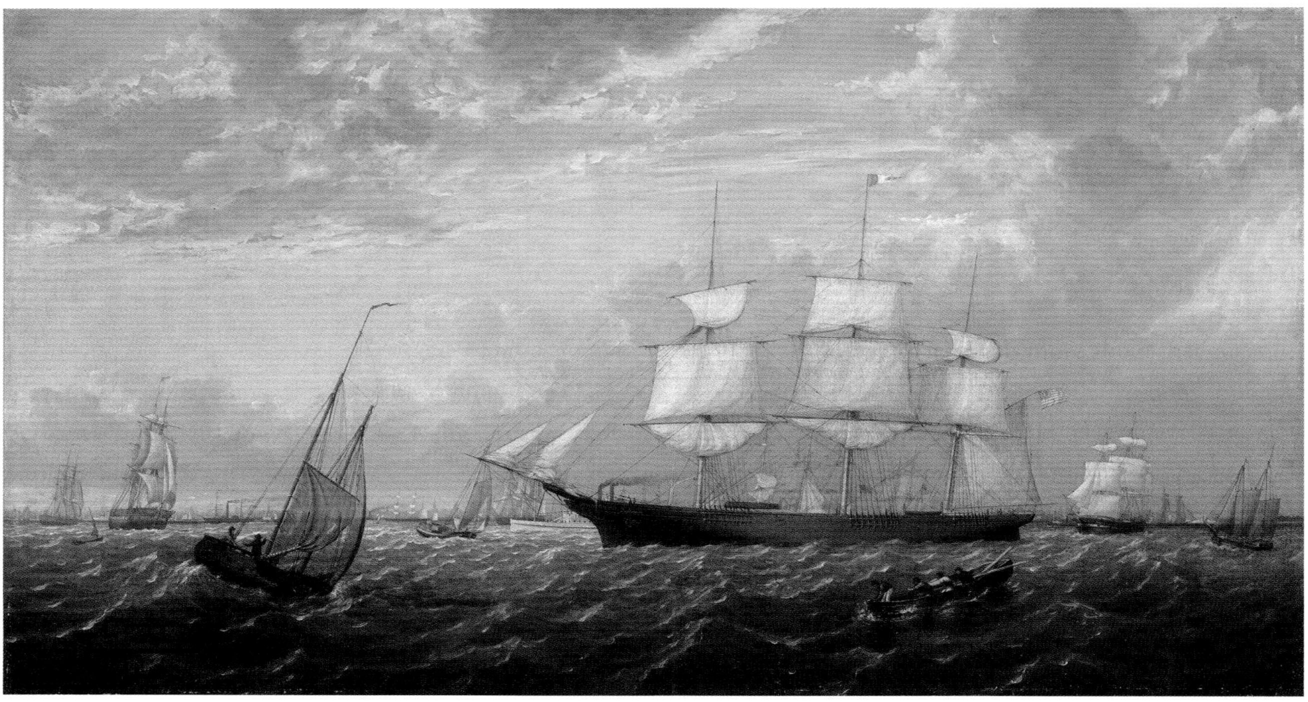

FIGURE 39
Fitz H. Lane, *The* Golden State *Entering New York Harbor*, 1854. Oil on canvas, 26 × 48 in. (66 × 122 cm). Signed and dated (on back): "Painted by Fitz Henry Lane / Gloucester / Mass. A.D. 1854." The Metropolitan Museum of Art, New York. Gift of Hanson K. Corning, by exchange, and Morris K. Jesup and Maria DeWitt Jesup Funds, 1974 (1974.33). Image copyright © The Metropolitan Museum of Art. Image source: Art Resource, New York.

he wouldn't change that name,' and so by legislature it was changed."[24] His petition was written December 26, 1831, shortly after his twenty-seventh birthday; filed January 9, 1832; granted March 13, 1832; and promptly published in the local newspaper.[25] A year before initiating this self-christening, Lane, although working as a shoemaker and evidently uninstructed in art, produced a watercolor recording the burning of a ship at sea, probably for Harvey Coffin Mackay, captain of that ill-fated packet (fig. 42). A wealthy and influential Gloucesterite, Mackay had some years earlier changed his own name; in 1848 he became Lane's landlord and, thereafter, a substantial lifelong patron.[26] Shortly after adopting his new moniker, Lane furthered his transformation from craft to art by exchanging his trade as Gloucester shoemaker for an apprenticeship in the Boston lithography firm of William Pendleton.[27] Sometime in the next decade he completed this radical transformation by morphing from lithographer to marine painter.[28] The name change, then, was part of a mature midlife self-fashioning project as Lane evolved from a worker in leather to a technician producing largely ephemeral images on paper, to an artist creating singular lasting works of art on canvas.[29] From the disabled teenage son of an artisan's widow—whose disability enabled his mother to secure special tax relief—he evolved into an "Esq.," a figure of substance in a community that recognized historical, aesthetic, and monetary value in his works.[30]

Thinking about Lane's self-remaking, it is useful to pause briefly and consider first the renaming project and then the self-fashioning project. While by no means unusual in the early national period, casting off one name

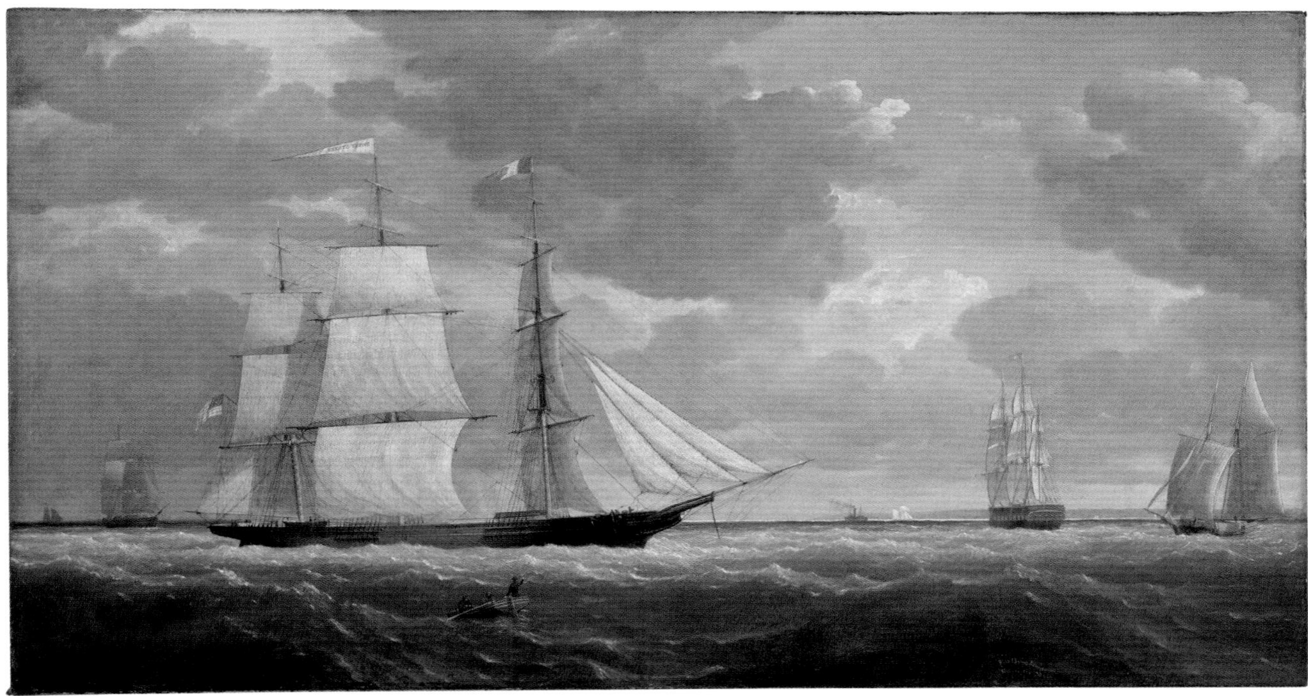

FIGURE 40 (ABOVE)
Fitz H. Lane, *Sweepstakes*, 1853. Oil on canvas, 26 × 48¼ in. (66 × 122.6 cm). Museum of the City of New York. Bequest of Theodore E. Blake (M50.5).

FIGURE 41 (RIGHT)
Fitz H. Lane, *Sweepstakes*, 1853 (fig. 40), signature detail.

and selecting another is foundational to at least one important public dimension of identity. It involved for Lane distancing himself from "Nathaniel Rogers Lane" and imagining himself as "Fitz Henry Lane" or, in the shorthand with which he signed some of his canvases—including, wittily, the ragged schooner sail in *Salem Harbor*—"F. H. L."

In deciding late in 1831 that he would not be "Nathaniel Rogers," he was declining confusion or allegiance with others who had established Nathaniel Rogers identities. These included a Gloucester sea captain of moderate wealth, a not-yet-famous New Hampshire lawyer-turned-abolitionist editor, a seventeenth-century divine that Cotton Mather referred to as "'one of the greatest men that ever set foot on the American strand'" (and possibly the man Lane's parents had in mind when they picked the name), and a contemporary New York artist of that name.[31] It is this last Nathaniel Rogers that, I believe, Lane was deliberately sidestepping, suggesting that even in its infancy Lane's new identity as a lithographic apprentice and artist was a matter of serious forethought. According to historian William Dunlap, Nathaniel Rogers (1788–1844), the New York artist, was born the son of a yeoman farmer and apprenticed to a shipbuilder but, suffering a serious injury to a knee in 1795, became "disqualified for active life" and sought out training as a painter of miniature portraits in New York City.[32] By 1811 he was established independently; in 1818 he married

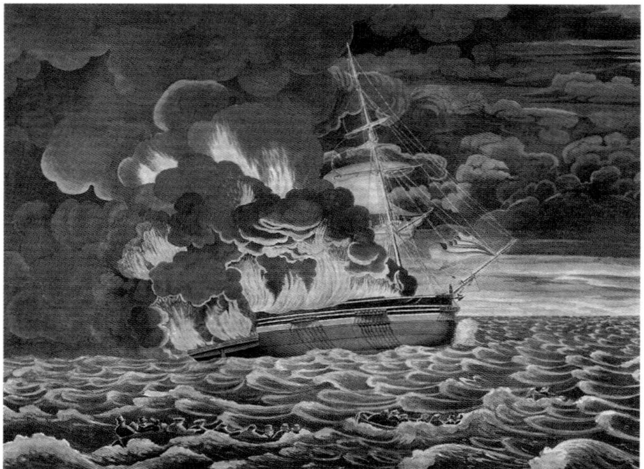

FIGURE 42
Nathaniel Rogers Lane (later Fitz Henry Lane), *The Burning of the Packet Ship* Boston, 1830. Watercolor on paper, 19 × 26¾ in. (48.3 × 68 cm). Cape Ann Museum, Gloucester, Massachusetts. Gift of Samuel H. Mansfield, 1924 (75.00).

Caroline Matilda, daughter of Capt. Samuel Denison, and over a long career enjoyed membership in the National Academy of Design, the regard of opinion makers such as Dunlap, and professional prosperity recording the faces of such dignitaries as Benjamin Silliman, president of Yale College (fig. 43).[33] It is logical that Lane would have striven to avoid confusion with a well-established artist, also lame, and a man twenty-five years his senior, even if Lane were not (yet), in 1831, artistically ambitious beyond achieving the identity of lithographer.

During the months Lane was mulling over his name, his vocation, and his future, the editor of the *Gloucester Telegraph* produced a series of articles concerning obtaining a good name in another sense that Lane could certainly have found thought-provoking:

> The Mechanick. Formation of Character. It is ever to be kept in mind that a good name is in all cases the fruit of *personal exertion*. It is not inherited from parents; it is not created by external advantages; it is no necessary appendage of birth, or wealth, or talents, or station; but the result of one's own endeavour—the fruit and reward of good principles, manifested in a course of virtuous and honorable action. This is the more important to be remarked, because it shows that the attainment of a good name, whatever be your external circumstances, is entirely within your power. No young man however humble his birth, or obscure his condition, is excluded from th[is] invaluable boon. He has only to fix his eye upon the prize and press towards it, in a course of virtuous and useful conduct.[34]

While the unnamed author's concept of "a good name" is an abstract quality of regard in the eyes of others, it is easy to read this passage literally, as a call to create one's own self in all dimensions of identity: name, skill set, and worldly reputation. Part of a continuous journalistic commentary in the antebellum period about the salt-of-the-earth mechanic, who constitutes the backbone of the country and its economy, these articles would have bolstered Lane's resolve to enact a series of bold moves. Having decided he needed a name of his own making, Lane fixed on one of rather different resonance from that of his birth. "Nathaniel" was a classic New England name, and "Rogers" the patronymic of one of the most ancient, respectable, and well-to-do families in Essex County; together they recalled the Ipswich minister so admired by the even more distinguished Cotton Mather. "Fitz," on the other hand, denoted in early modern England the illegitimate son of a king and therefore suggests both positive and negative qualities, royal origins and bastardy: the raw materials of romance. "Fitz" was also, by 1831, an established given name and family name in Gloucester, so it is possible that the valence he sought went no further than oblique reference to those he admired among his neighbors. These included Fitz William Sargent (owner and part owner of many vessels from 1805 to 1825); Fitz William Winter (West Indian goods merchant from at least 1831); and Fitz J. Babson (carpenter, builder, and inspector of customs in 1850, 1859, and 1860).[35] However, there appear to be no local "Fitz Henry" prototypes.[36]

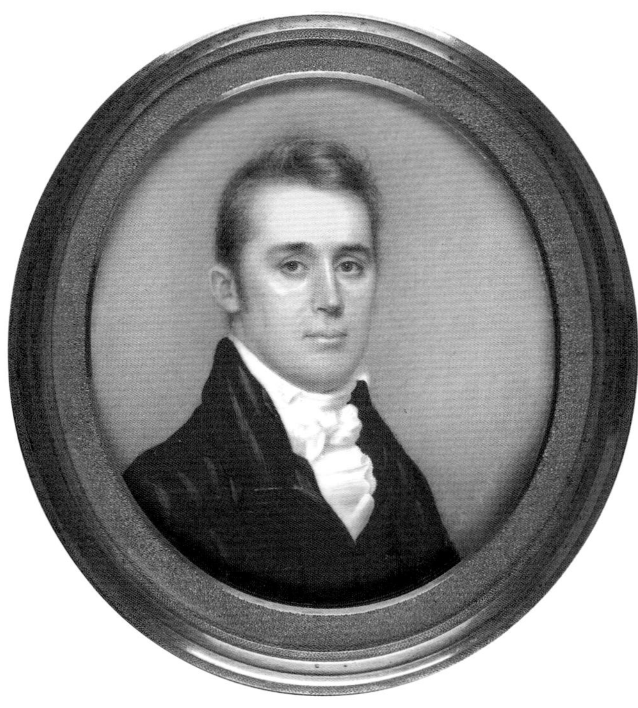

FIGURE 43
Nathaniel Rogers, *Benjamin Silliman* (1779–1864), B.A. 1796, M.A. 1799, ca. 1815. Oil on ivory, 3¾ × 3⅛ in. (9.5 × 7.9 cm). Yale University Art Gallery. Gift of Miss Maria Trumbull Dana (1954.34.1). Photo: Yale University Art Gallery.

Among the many "Fitz" names, "Fitz Henry" (or "Fitzhenry") is rare, so it is notable that it was selected for the principal character of a popular novel published in England in 1828: *Fitzhenry, or A Marriage in High Life: A Story of the Heart*.[37] Fitzhenry, the twenty-seven-year-old only son of an earl, with "the manners and conversation of an intelligent man-of-the-world," cuts a "graceful, manly figure . . . [characterized by] indescribable *elegance*."[38] There is "a peculiar liveliness and originality in all he [says]," and he sports a "handsome, manly countenance"; in short, he represents model masculinity in virtually all respects.[39] But his fatal flaw—infatuation with the wrong woman—is his undoing. The narrative is about emotional turmoil and psychological thrust and parry, about love, honesty, dishonesty, pride, honor, endurance, duty, and suffering against a backdrop of social conventions and behaviors. The plot turns on the interpretation of two drawings glossed by a passage from Lord Byron.[40] In sum, it is a lively tale about an admirable young man with a romantic name, and the legibility of art.

Might Lane—with both a sense of aspiration and irony—have adopted this hero's name? Certainly such novels were read with gusto in Gloucester not only by women but also by young men, as indicated in the journal of Capt. Solomon H. Davis, who in 1828 recorded his pleasure in reading *Flirtation* (an earlier novel by the author of *Fitzhenry*), as well as *The Three Perils of Women*; *Love Without a Doubt*; *Emily, or A Wife's Affection*; *Hobomok*, by "Miss Francis of Duxbury, authoress"; and other romances.[41] Others, however, disapproved of such reading, including the unnamed author of a Gloucester newspaper article published in 1829 celebrating the innocent pleasures of old-fashioned husking parties, where rustic youths were "under no constraint to imitate the ridiculous actions of this or that heroine, or hero; they never read or sighed over the pernicious pages of . . . Byron."[42] Of course, such sentiments are evidence that both the author and the author's readers were well acquainted with the "pernicious" texts in question and the tendency of the young to model themselves after fictitious heroines and heroes.

Whatever Lane's motivation in adopting a new name, he did so shortly after producing his first marine painting (of the *Boston* aflame), and the year before he took steps to radically retool his identity in other ways. Although the records are scanty, it is clear that Lane's first adult identity was that of shoemaker.[43]

SHOEMAKER/LITHOGRAPHER

In the decade between 1820, when Lane's mother's taxes were abated in consideration of his disability and presumed marginal employability, and 1830, when he was referenced in a deed as "Nathaniel R. Lane, shoomaker [*sic*]," it is evident that he found training and useful employment in that trade.[44] According to John Trask,

Lane was "apprenticed to one Haskell to learn a shoe-worker's trade."[45] As the local paper enunciating the local ethic put it: "It behooves both parents and children to learn the proper channel for their industry, which, if followed steadily, will as certainly lead to comfort and competence, as time leads to eternity"; and so the widow Lane endeavored to situate her son in an appropriately sedentary and respectable trade.[46] In Massachusetts the making of shoes was a common form of employment—often seasonal when winter weather impeded fishing—from the eighteenth century.[47] The goal of Lane's apprenticeship, of course, was to give him the skills to be self-reliant. As the editor of the local paper put it concerning the training of youth: "The success of individuals in life is greatly owing to their early learning to depend upon their own resources. . . . Teach young men to rely upon their own efforts, to be frugal and industrious, and you have furnished them with a productive capital which no man can ever wrest from them."[48] Knowledge of shoemaking, together with self-reliance and frugality, was to be Lane's "productive capital."

During the years when Lane's identity was that of shoemaker, the production and sale of shoes in Massachusetts was a changing economy. No longer a seasonal family-centered cottage industry, it was increasingly organized in shops of full-time workers. Of the several master shoemakers in Gloucester, the one that appears steadily in the records is John W. Haskell. In 1827 he advertised the sale of inexpensive shoes "just received," which had clearly been made elsewhere, and also noted his readiness to take orders for bespoke shoes "at the shortest notice."[49] The following year he advertised for "a Journeyman Shoemaker, to work on Ladies heel'd Pumps, to whom good wages will be given," suggesting that his was a shop with at least some specialization and multiple workers.[50] Haskell's store burned down in the fire of September 1830 that destroyed sixty buildings in Gloucester's business district, but within two months he had opened a new store and was offering a wide assortment of ready-made shoes as well as "shoes made to order."[51] His shop was still in business in 1850 and 1860, long after Lane had moved on to other activities.[52] Haskell's competitors in selling ready-made shoes included Jacob Parsons (1828, 1830), George H. Rogers (1849), and Mary Rogers (1830), although bespoke shoes were apparently understood to be generally better: "The shoe must be made to the foot—and not the foot to the shoe."[53] Exceptional feats of speed in shoemaking and boot making by remarkable craftsmen were reported in the news, like that of the Maine man who in 1829 single-handedly cut out and made up "16 pair of thick cow hide boots" in six days.[54] In the 1820s it was a trade that everyone patronized and that could be a source of pride in individual achievement.

Presumably, then, Lane embraced his identity as shoemaker and applied himself to making shoes, earning a respectable living; but having enjoyed drawing from an early age, he no doubt was alert to the many local opportunities to learn about the various categories of art, public taste, and the ways in which art was valued in his culture during that third decade of the nineteenth century. He may have begun to imagine an identity as an "artist," as that term was locally understood. He could have read the articles on Apelles, Giotto, Michelangelo and Raphael, Francis Danby, George Moreland, and the sculptor Canova in the local papers (many picked up from other urban and even distant London papers).[55] He may have been attentive to the cautionary message in the long and largely accurate account "Diseases of Painters," underlining in detail the chemical composition of the "preparations of copper, lead, mercury, [and] arsenic" in standard paints, materials that are "unfriendly to the human constitution."[56] On a more positive note, he no doubt took notice of the articles reporting on the extraordinary sum paid for Gilbert Stuart's *Washington* in 1827 (£1,000), the even more extraordinary size of the estate of the English sculptor Joseph Nollekens (£240,000), as well as the thousands of paintings and sculptures imported to and warehoused in London.[57]

In his spare time he would have found a new and important way to learn about art closer to home in the high-quality engravings that suddenly, amply, and competitively became available to popular audiences in these years. The decade between 1820 and 1830 saw an unprecedented flood of illustrated journals and gift books, rivaling one another in their claims to artistic perfection in the copper-plate, steel-plate, and wood engravings that were their chief ornament. Many were available at Procter's bookstore in Gloucester (where Lane's own prints would later be sold), and others, available by subscription, were advertised in the local paper. Virtually all vendors made claims to the *art* quality of these images, and some ads, such as those that appeared in the *New York Mirror*, described the engravings (views of New York and its harbor, for instance) in considerable detail. The ad for the *Repository of Polite Literature* in the *Gloucester Telegraph*, for instance, promised "splendid Engravings of Steel, Copper, and Wood," including "super-royal Quarto Views" as well as a "Vignette Frontispiece of uncommon beauty, designed and painted by [Robert W.] Weir, and engraved on steel by [Asher B.] Durand. . . . [All the journal's] Embellishments . . . [have] been placed under the sole direction of Robert W. Weir, Esq."[58] In reading such an account—even before he saw the plates themselves—Lane would have learned the names of notable artists and received an excellent education in the importance of the new reproductive media, the centrality of artists in these popular commercial ventures, and the eminence of those artists suffixed "Esq." Closer to home he would have read that the *Ladies Magazine and Literary Gazette*, produced in Boston, promised "either copperplate engravings, or lithograph drawings" done "by Pendleton," signaling the arrival of the newest reproductive medium in the shop where Lane soon would find training and employment.[59] Generally these images were portraits, landscape views, and genre images (or subject pictures), often commissioned specifically for these popular publications, although sometimes they reproduced well-known or newly finished paintings. They were both art and ephemera, and Lane could have learned all about them in such local newspapers as the *Gloucester Telegraph* in the 1820s and 1830s even if he could not afford the journals, gift books, or prints themselves.

The same "soft" line between fine arts and popular visual culture that one can see in the illustrated monthlies and gift books offered for sale at the general store in Gloucester was evident in other dimensions of Lane's culture. He would have had the opportunity during his shoemaking decade to see or read about, for instance, exhibitions of many kinds. Some came to Gloucester, others to nearby Boston, and still others he would have known only through secondhand reports from distant cities. At John Mason's hotel in Gloucester, for instance, Lane could have seen, for $.25, the Papyrotomia exhibition—that is, "Military, Architectural and sporting subjects, Flowers, trees, Landscapes," and portraits, executed in cut paper—the cost of admission including a cut-paper portrait of oneself by the "young Artist, Master Hankes."[60] A year earlier he could have seen, for half that price, an exhibition of "100 Living Rattlesnakes . . . [up to] four and a half feet in length" at that same venue.[61] In nearby Newburyport he could have seen an exhibition of paintings in 1827 that included copies of Rubens's *Descent from the Cross* and *Christ Showing His Wounds* as well as "Schulkes' [*sic*] *Rape of the Sabines*" (fig. 44).[62] One can only imagine what Lane and his compatriots made of these exhibitions. Probably equally foreign to them would have been the exhibition of Rembrandt Peale's enormous *Court of Death* in Boston in 1822, part of a yearlong tour that proved exceptionally profitable for that artist (fig. 45).[63] If the teenage Lane missed seeing this work on its tour, he would later have had an opportunity to purchase a chromolithograph of it in Gloucester for a dollar, puffed in a local advertisement that put the value of the painting at "TWENTY-FIVE THOUSAND DOLLARS," a sum fifty times the sale price of Lane's highest-priced work and a value, no doubt, astonishing to him and to his peers.[64]

The conjunction of art, showmanship, and sheer size in the *Court of Death* exhibit is characteristic of the antebellum era. Gloucesterites would not have been surprised, for instance, reading about the "five thousand square

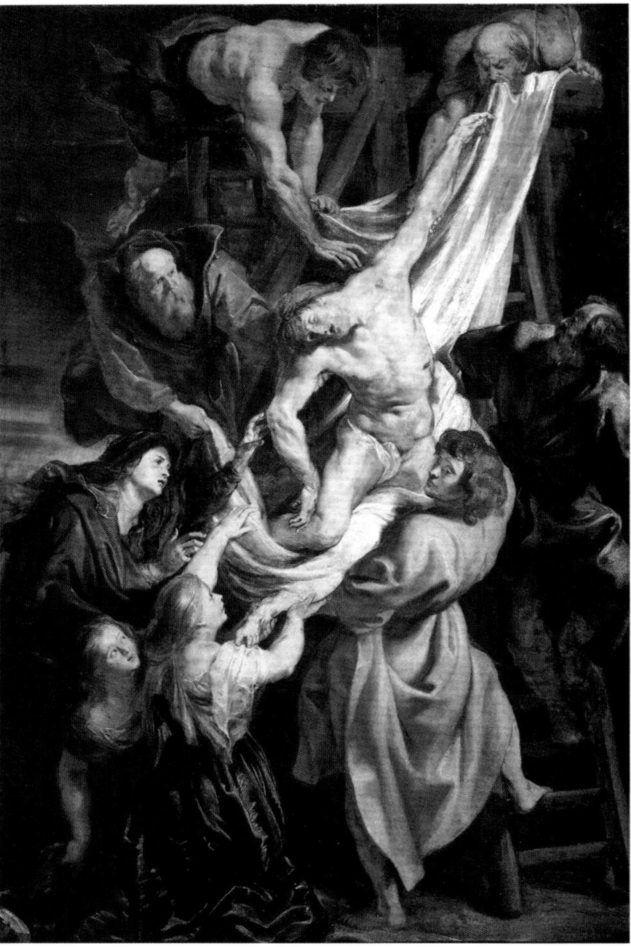

FIGURE 44
Peter Paul Rubens, *The Descent from the Cross*, 1611. Oil on panel, 45.35 × 30 in. (115.2 × 76.2 cm). The Samuel Courtauld Trust, The Courtauld Gallery, London.

feet of canvass" that constituted "Ford's panorama of the Falls of Niagara" when the *Gloucester Telegraph* included a notice of its exhibition in Washington, DC, in 1828; or the 12 × 16–foot dimensions of a picture of Lafayette landing at Cincinnati, "the fruit of eighteen months' labor" by "Hervieu, an artist of the west," also on view in Washington in 1830—both canvases given nationwide press coverage as much for their size as their aesthetic quality.[65] Lane could also have read in the *Gloucester Telegraph* about a "Curious Painting" in Baltimore, apparently installed out of doors "at the corner of Baltimore and Charles Streets . . . [that,] when approached on the one side, . . . appears to be the likeness of a *female*, when directly opposite, . . . resembles a horse's head, when on the other side, . . . presents a good likeness of the immortal Washington."[66] This agglomeration, then, of art journalism, engravings in illustrated monthlies, and exhibitions of art and other marvels would have served to inform (or confuse) the young journeyman shoemaker about the nature and purpose(s) of art in his culture and about opportunities newly opening in the new reproductive media, in panoramas, and in the public taste for all kinds of art.

It is probable that during his shoemaking decade Lane would have continued to practice drawing, watercolor, and perhaps oil painting. Supplies were readily available in Gloucester, where several vendors advertised paints, not only for ships, houses, and signs but also for painting on velvet; others offered paint boxes for amateur watercolorists.[67] One article reminded Gloucesterites that "the art of painting" was something a "young man well educated, according to Locke, should learn," and local vendors of appropriate equipment were happy to further this goal.[68]

In the early national period, the shoemaker was often offered up as the archetypal "mechanic," a craftsman whose trade involved relatively little capital and whose wares were useful to—indeed essential to—the whole community. Shoemaking was also seen as the trade of humble beginnings that talented men who applied themselves vigorously could rise above. Americans recognized "degrees" of men, or social strata, but the rhetoric (and, to some degree, the reality) was that nowhere else in the world was a man as free to fashion his own destiny—that is, to rise to achieve fame and fortune from modest beginnings—as in the United States. In an article titled "Value of Reading" published in Gloucester in 1830, the author asks rhetorically: "What forms the principal difference between men, as they appear in the same society?—Knowledge! What raised Franklin from the humble station of printer's boy to the first honors of his country? Knowledge! What took [Roger] Sherman from his

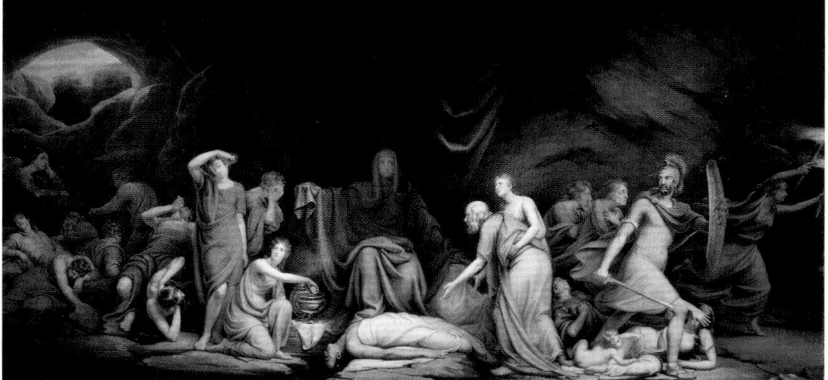

FIGURE 45
Rembrandt Peale, *The Court of Death*, 1820. Oil on canvas, 138 × 281 in. (350.52 × 713.74 cm). Detroit Institute of Arts. Gift of George H. Scripps (85.3). Photo: Bridgeman Images.

shoemaker's bench, gave him a seat in Congress, and there made his voice to be heard among the wisest and best of his compeers? Knowledge!"[69]

Similarly, a long obituary published in the *Gloucester Telegraph* in 1828 records the life and passing of one Zenas Coffin of Nantucket, who "left his shoemaker's bench and engaged in the whaling business . . . [becoming] one of the first merchants of Nantucket."[70] Such brief narratives might easily have impacted Lane's strategies for defining and redefining himself—that is, understanding himself as a man who might rise "above" his shoemaker's bench by acquiring knowledge of art as it was understood, practiced, valued, and seen in popular culture.

On a larger scale New Englanders were remarkably organized in their efforts to encourage "mechanics" with limited formal schooling to rise in the world. The decade of the 1820s saw the establishment of lyceums and mechanics' institutes explicitly to continue the education and broaden the horizons of young men starting out in the world: "The proposed Lyceums will furnish [our] sons with every study, or pleasure or company[,] . . . [learning] French, Geography, Statistics, History, Mathematics, [and] Political economy . . . in continued pursuit of knowledge by study and conversation."[71] More down-to-earth, the already popular Boston Mechanics' Institution, with 634 members and 240 minors, provided lectures in 1829 "on Architecture, the elements of Mechanics and Chemistry, the process of Fermentation and Distill[at]ion, and on some branches of Civil Engineering, Optics and Accoustics [*sic*]."[72] Such developments, investing in knowledge transfer and the development of "judgment, memory, temper, and imagination" for a population that generally left school and began trade apprenticeship at fourteen, were invaluable in a world increasingly complex in its application of physics, chemistry, metallurgy, and navigation, as well as increasingly complex and global in its outlook and activities.[73]

Beyond this general encouragement, a substantial article in the *Gloucester Telegraph* in 1829 encouraged Lane, in a somewhat backhanded way, not to let himself be defined or limited by his disability and his dependence on crutches:

> Deformity of Body.—Deformities and imperfections of our bodies, as lamenesse, crookednesse, blindnesse, be they innate or accidental, torture many men—yet this may comfort them, that those imperfections of the body do not a whit blemish the soul, or hinder the operations of it, but rather help and much increase it. Seldom, said Plutarch, honesty and beauty dwell together. How many deformed Princes, Kings, Emperors, could I reckon up, philosophers, and orators. Hannibal had one eye . . . Aesop was crooked; Socrates purblind, long-legged, hairy; Democritus withered;—Seneca lean and harsh, ugly to behold; yet show me so

> many flourishing wits, such divine spirits. Horace, a little blear-eyed contemptible fellow—yet who so sententious and wise? Galba the Emperor, was crook-backed; Epictetus lame; that great Alexander, a little man of stature; Augustus Caesar of the same pitch . . . commonly your great vast bodies, and fine features, are sottish, dull, and leaden spirits. . . . A little diamond is of more worth than a rocky mountain.[74]

On an almost weekly basis Lane and his peers were exhorted in the *Gloucester Telegraph* to understand themselves as self-fashioning and encouraged to be ambitious and original: "A self-relying confidence, untinged with arrogance, must animate our efforts, . . . [and] lead the mind to act for itself. . . . he who communicates a single new thought[,] or an original combination of old thoughts, exerts a power over the empire of mind, which will outlive all time; he who shews his countrymen a new resource of knowledge, a new method of increasing it opens a new avenue to happiness."[75] In sum, the culture in which Lane found himself in the late 1820s encouraged him to learn new skills, think broadly, and be ambitious—in every sense to make a name for himself. But there might equally have been "push" factors as well as "pull" factors in his desire to follow the example of Roger Sherman, to "leave his shoemaker's bench" and rise in the world.

During the decade that Lane practiced the trade, the business of shoemaking was changing rapidly. First, it appears Gloucesterites were beginning to travel to Boston to buy their shoes—Boston vendors advertised in the *Gloucester Telegraph*, and editorials fought back, urging shoe purchasers to buy local products: "Our own money would thus be kept in town."[76] Second, new mechanisms were being devised to raise the volume of production, differentiate tasks, and lower the value of skill and experience in the making of shoes and boots.[77] But most destructive to the concept of the local shoemaker equipping his town or village, the way the local farrier continued to shoe its horses, was the pressing fact that shoemaking had become industrialized and centralized. The town of Lynn, south of Boston, with a population of 3,300 in the 1820 census, was reputed to manufacture and "export" a million pairs of shoes a year by 1828.[78] Three years later there were "from sixty to seventy shoe manufactories in Lynn, Massachusetts which employ more than 1500 mechanics and as many females, and make nearly 2 million pairs of shoes every year . . . mostly distributed in the United States."[79] Regardless of how skilled a small-shop craftsman might be at this trade, it is clear that by 1831, when Nathaniel Rogers Lane, shoemaker, began to imagine himself Fitz Henry Lane, lithographer, it was a good time to get out of the shoemaking business. And it is telling that he picked a line of work—lithography—that not only allowed him to use and perfect the drawing skills he is reputed to have demonstrated since childhood, but also represented a "horizon" niche in the newest media of the new economy of illustrated printing.

Encouraging Lane to make this leap were a series of long articles in the local paper about the history of printing technologies, highlighting recent important developments, and minibiographies of self-transforming high-achieving figures like soon-to-be-president "Martin Van Buren . . . once a poor, friendless boy. He has been the architect of his own fame."[80] Taught about the importance of new printing technologies, encouraged to be "the architect of his own fame," and assured that "almost every individual of the human family has by nature a particular talent, which, when brought into requisition and applied to some exclusive object, cannot fail to be attended with a commensurate success," Lane had a ready-made template for the transitions in identity and locale that he undertook in 1831 and 1832.[81] The specific catalyst, allegedly, was the decision by William Edmund Pearson Rogers, manager of the *Cape Ann Light* and the *Gloucester Telegraph* from 1827 to 1833, to show one of Lane's drawings to William S. Pendleton, securing for the young man a berth in the shop of this pioneer Boston lithographer.[82] This negotiation occurred at a time when multiple links connected Gloucester with Boston's pioneering lithographers, exemplified by the excellent map of Cape Ann drawn by Major John Mason (proprietor of the Gloucester House hotel, where paper-cutting art and rattlesnakes were exhibited), which was produced in Senefelder's (soon to be Pendleton's) Boston shop in 1830.[83] Mason's map is one of the best extant documents of the Gloucester of Nathaniel Rogers Lane, shoemaker. Mason's son Sidney would prove to be one of Lane's most important patrons. Pendleton's was the place where both substantial large-scale projects, such as maps and books, as well as ephemeral ads and sheet music were turned out by a team of ambitious young men eager to achieve not just "comfort and competence" but also, if possible, "fame."

Pendleton's lithography business—the first of its kind in Boston and one of the first in the nation—was established in 1826 by two brothers, William and John Pendleton, who had managed the tour of Rembrandt Peale's *Court of Death* and who gathered a singularly talented group of young men in their shop, men who would become well-known artists, sculptors, and architects in the next decade, including Alexander Jackson Davis, George Loring Brown, Benjamin Champney, David Claypoole Johnston, William Rimmer, and Lane.[84] According to contemporary authority, "the art [of lithography] is founded on the property which stone possesses, of imbibing fluids by capillary attraction, and on the chemical repulsion which oil and water have for each other.... The drawing on the stone ... is done either in ink, with steel pens and camel's hair pencils [brushes], or with crayons made of lithographic chalk."[85] The superiority of this technology over the older copper- and steel-engraving techniques was understood to reside in greater yield (upwards of ten thousand impressions before degradation was visible in the impressions struck), more tonal richness, and the fact that it preserved the immediate gesture of the artist, who drew directly on the stone without the intervention of a technician transferring the design, as was the case in engraving.[86]

John W. A. Scott, as quoted in an obituary for William S. Pendleton in 1874, gives an excellent account of early lithography in Boston, the activities in the Senefelder shop (bought out by Pendleton in 1831), and the artists working there. He remarks that "Fitz Henry Lane, who later became a somewhat celebrated marine painter succeeding Salmon in this respect in Boston, ... was a good all-round draftsman, especially on 'views,' but his natural liking for the water and his knowledge of boats turned him wholly to marines."[87] Scott married the sister of another artist in the shop, Robert Cooke, and formed a partnership with Lane when they both left Pendleton's in 1844.[88] Cooke was, according to Scott, "the ablest draftsman in Boston," but he died in Paris tragically young when traveling with landscape painter Benjamin Champney.[89] A close-knit group of emerging artists, this cohort was undoubtedly important in Lane's development of skills and his evolving identity as "artist." Recalling his early years from the perspective of the 1890s, Benjamin Champney, who entered the Pendleton shop the year after Lane, wrote that "F. H. Lane, afterwards well known as a marine painter, did most of the views, hotels, etc. He was very accurate in his drawing, understood perspective and naval architecture perfectly ... and was a good, all-round draughtsman."[90] As discussed in chapter 1, recognizability of specific structures in his images was a source of comment and approbation among Lane's audiences in later years. Lane's *View of the Old Building at the Corner of Ann St.* memorializes one of the few remaining seventeenth-century structures in Boston together with one of the city's eighteenth-century landmarks, Faneuil Hall, and, in the distance, the more recent Quincy Market (fig. 46). All three of these structures, as well as the street activity Lane has included, suggest commerce, entrepreneurship, and exchange—the hallmarks of Boston's burgeoning economy in the decade Lane was associated with Pendleton's. The legible two-dimensional signs on the near buildings, along with the show windows cut into the walls of the ancient structure on the left, bespeak a Boston of business and enterprise and seize the viewer's attention as firmly as do the distinctive architectural century-specific buildings to which they are affixed.

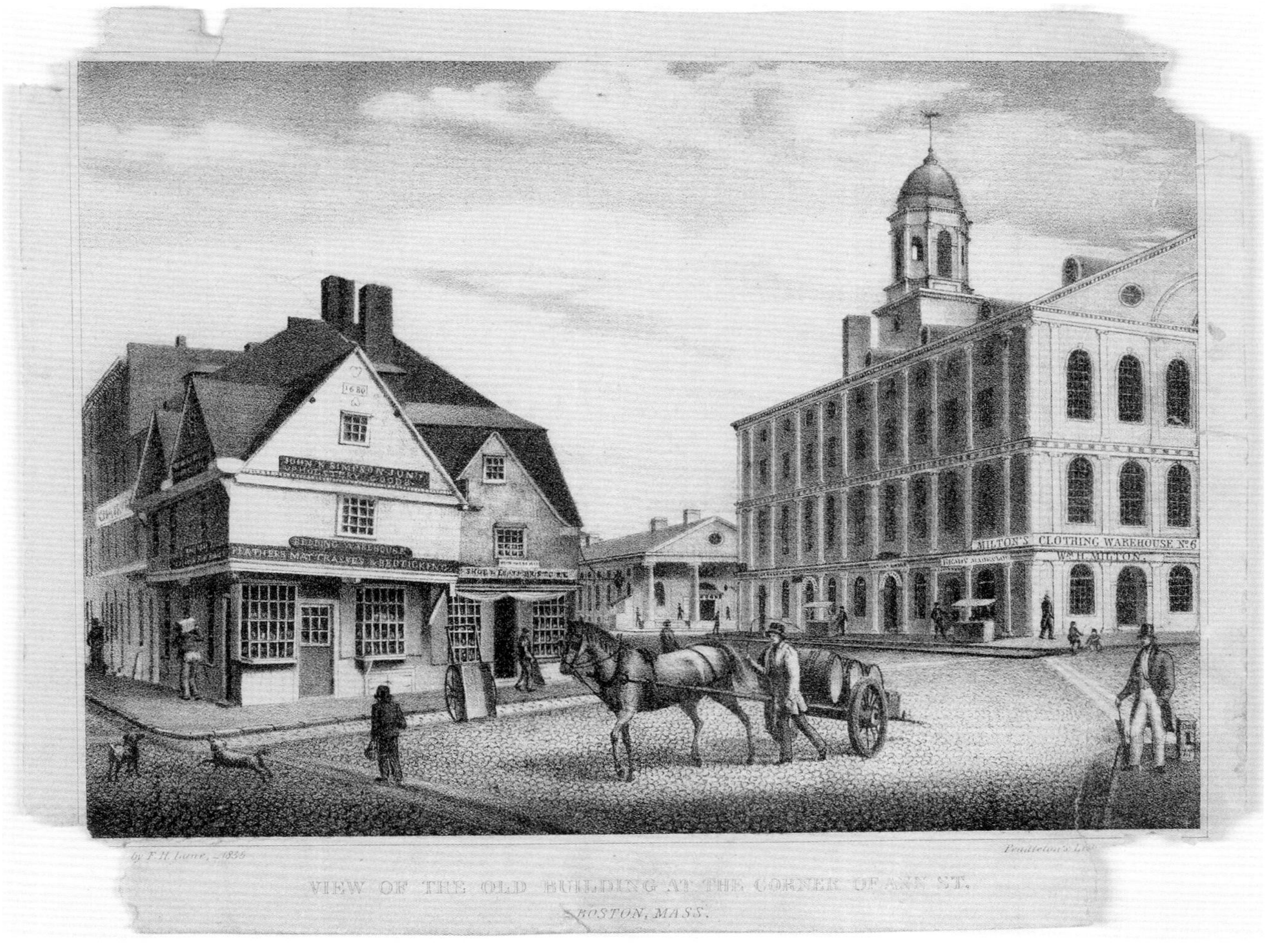

FIGURE 46
Fitz H. Lane del., *View of the Old Building at the Corner of Ann St., Boston, Mass.*, 1835. Lithograph on paper, 10½ × 13 in. (26.67 × 33.02 cm). Printed at Pendleton's. Courtesy, American Antiquarian Society. Gift of Charles Henry Taylor.

A lithograph executed in 1844, when Lane was in partnership with John Scott (and also transitioning to his third professional identity, that of marine painter), was created to frontispiece a pamphlet advertising, as the bold lettering below the busy seven-bay-deep interior view indicates, "George W. Simmons' Popular Tailoring Establishment, 'Oak Hall,' Boston" (fig. 47). By the time he made this image, Lane had been working as a lithographer for more than a decade. In each of the lithographic images shown in figures 46 and 47 he demonstrated his skill at perspective drawing and locating structures, figures, and other visual events in deep space. It has been argued that the on-the-job training Lane and the other aspiring artists received in Pendleton's shop was the equivalent of "entry-level academic training."[91] The firm's artists had also worked on, indeed apparently initiated, a number of drawing books aimed at instructing aspiring artists in descriptive line, shading, and especially the fine points of perspective, so Lane was in a context rich in resources and information concerning art as well as lithography.[92]

Undoubtedly Lane took advantage of all opportunities offered to him at Pendleton's and, from 1844 to 1847, when

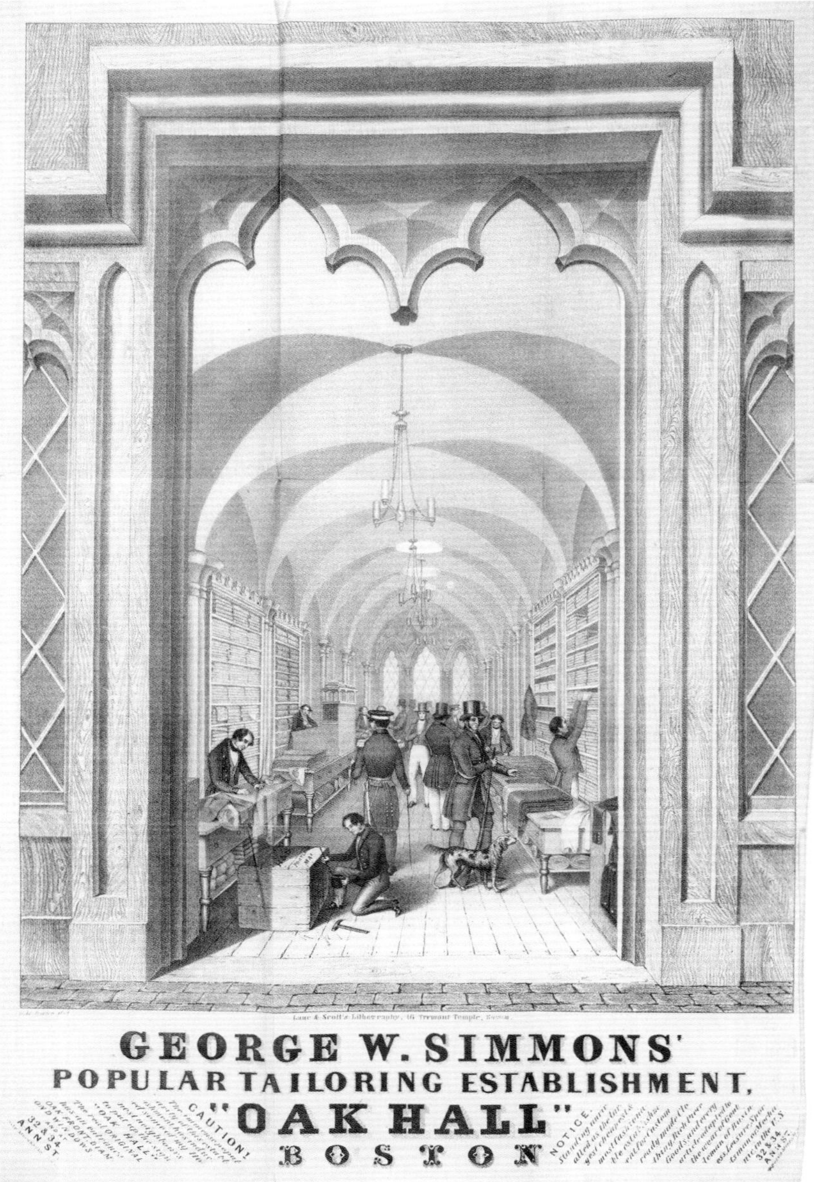

FIGURE 47
Fitz H. Lane del., *George W. Simmons' Popular Tailoring Establishment, "Oak Hall," Boston.* Lithograph on paper, 16 × 12¼ in. (40.6 × 31.1 cm); sheet, 19½ × 13 9/16 in. (49.5 × 34.5 cm). Lane & Scott's Lith., Tremont Temple, Boston. Frontispiece from the pamphlet *Oak Hall, or the Glory of Boston: A Poem in Four Parts* (Boston: Mead & Beal, 1844). Courtesy, American Antiquarian Society.

he was in an independent lithography business in partnership with John W. A. Scott. One of the projects the firm of Lane & Scott undertook, an illustrated abolitionist tract by Charles C. Green, *The Nubian Slave* (1845), suggests not only the strong antislavery sympathies of the artists but also the ambitious scope of some of the firm's projects.[93]

Little is known about Lane's transition from lithographer to painter, but it is probable that he found encouragement and possibly instruction from Robert Salmon.[94] It was in the context of his partnership with Scott that Lane did the lithographic project for Robert Bennet Forbes, *Departure of the* Jamestown (fig. 16, discussed in chapters 1 and 8). He was also painting in oils during his last years in Boston and clearly doing well in this new medium, as by 1848 he had secured sufficient capital and a sufficiently strong patron base to move back to Gloucester, purchase property, and build himself a substantial granite house. His transition, then, from lithographer to artist was relatively meteoric, and it is probable that, having secured the patronage of Forbes and other wealthy men by 1847, he was in a position to take on the bold new identity of a substantial property owner, artist, and "Esq."

Coincident with his move back to Gloucester—and probably not coincidental—excellent rail service between Boston and Cape Ann was established in 1848, permitting, for instance, "a citizen of Gloucester to 'set off' for Boston after breakfast, spend a fair portion of the forenoon there, and return in season for [midday] dinner."[95] Equally important, his sister, Sarah Ann Lane Winter—who probably kept house for him as well as for her husband and their children during at least some of Lane's years in Boston and would keep house for him for most of the rest of his life—moved back to Gloucester in 1848 as well.[96] Although he continued to produce a few lithographs and to paint ship portraits of the classic type (such as *Cadet*, discussed in chapter 1) throughout the seventeen remaining years of his career, he developed an extraordinarily imaginative range of work, including contextualized ship portraits (such as *Salem Harbor*) and a wide variety of landscapes and harborscapes, all evidencing curiosity about the inhabited landscape and an amplitude of Geertzian "local knowledge" well beyond the usual definition of "marine painter" (figs. 20 and 33).[97]

ART IDENTITIES AND SLY SIGNATURES

During the years that Lane was working as a lithographer, he was also beginning to paint, exhibit, and sell oil paintings. From as early as 1841 his offerings appeared in the Boston Athenaeum art exhibitions, and from 1842, at the Boston Artists' Association (see appendix A).[98] But it was not until 1847–48 that he left the field of commercial lithography to adopt the identity (and risks) of a producer of fine art. At that time many forms of art and entertainment were competing for the attention and support of the public. In 1848, 1849, and 1850, for instance, newspaper advertisements and articles enticed Gloucesterites to see acres of scrolling canvas in artistic entertainments known as panoramas, including Donnavan's panorama of Mexico, twenty-one thousand feet of "moving canvass" at Boylston Hall in Boston; Curtis's competing "Panoramic Painting of Mexico and Its Battles," in Gloucester's town hall; a "Botanical and Poetical Panorama of the Garden of Eden, with Adam and Eve . . . the most splendid work of art in the United States," also seen in Gloucester's town hall; "A Panoramic Excursion to Europe"; a six-thousand-foot-long twelve-foot-wide panorama of the Holy Land (unfortunately burned in Philadelphia before it could be seen in New England, where it had been advertised and was eagerly awaited); a "Panorama of Mammoth Cave lit by 500 torches"; and a "Mammoth Panorama of the Mississippi River," exhibited in nearby Salem, for which special rail fares were on offer.[99] All of these popular entertainments brought to Lane's immediate neighborhood art as spectacle and hints of distant parts of the globe, competing with the exhibition of live lions from Africa in Salem, more lions and a tiger in Boston, and elephants and giraffes in Gloucester in 1854.[100]

When the circus came to town, it included a presumably educational and certainly patriotic "Grand living Tableau in which the Father of his Country, Mounted on his Charger, is borne Aloft in triumphal procession."[101] At permanent venues in Boston, such as the Melodeon, one could see "wonders of modern Optical Science" that "make the sun stand still, magnify nothing into mountains, and compress infinity into a nutshell."[102] At the Boston Museum the public could see "One thousand costly paintings" as well as "Giants, Dwarfs, [and] Orange Orangutans . . . Witty Comedies, Thrilling and Ingenious Dramas, soul-Inspiring Operas, . . . Sully's great picture of Washington Crossing the Delaware . . . and a magnificent marble Venus, the finest piece of statuary in the country, together with Indian, Egyptian and Polynesian relics."[103] Like the names of Silsbee's ships, the listings of these entertainments in the newspapers conjured a world well beyond New England, promising visual first-person experience of exotic animals and artistic representations of distant lands. All of this energy to place art and objects of instruction and curiosity before the public pales before the spectacle of Jenny Lind, whose activities were in the press daily and who was reputed to have been paid $1,000 a night for 150 nights for her celestial singing on her U.S. tour in 1850, a venture financed by P. T. Barnum.[104] The pliant line between art and entertainment, and the wide variety of types of visual experience on offer, framed both Lane's sense of vocation and the "art" expectations of his audiences.

The heterogeneity and global character of "art" events in Lane's Gloucester were mirrored in the interiors of Lane's patrons' houses. Mixed in with inherited Copley portraits and eighteenth-century mahogany furniture, Lane paintings shared the parlors, back rooms, and bedrooms for which they were intended with "quantities of blue and white Canton china," Icelandic bedspreads, "bell glasses of stuffed birds from Brazil and the Guianas," Delftware, and Dutch silver candlesticks. Vivid vignettes of the domestic material culture of some of Gloucester's homes, filled with the physical residue of the town's global reach, survive in the voice of Alfred Mansfield Brooks, who was an unusually observant child in the 1870s. He was kin to most of these families and was raised by elderly relatives who were contemporaries of Lane and his patrons.[105] For them, there was no dissonance in the conjunction of such disparate objects from such disparate cultural contexts.

Annual art and design exhibitions available to the public and to Lane included those of the Massachusetts Charitable Mechanic Association in Faneuil Hall and Quincy Market in Boston, where one could see, in 1850, "cloth goods . . . pianos . . . a very handsome billiard table and some wax statuary by Mrs. Pelby . . . some paintings and statues, a great number of fine daguerreotypes, by various artists, and some curious specimens of artificial limbs."[106] In May 1850 an explicitly fine-arts exhibition circulated—a group of "upwards of a hundred" paintings by the artists of the Düsseldorf Academy that opened in a church hall on Broadway in New York City, then traveled to Boston.[107] Lane may have made an excursion to New York to see it there, perhaps also visiting the American Art-Union exhibition nearby, where several of his own paintings were on view that month. Certainly at some point he journeyed to New York to discuss the commissions of paintings for patron Sidney Mason and to make preparatory studies for paintings of New York harbor. Whether he traveled to New York on this occasion remains unknown, but seeing the German works there or in Boston was an important event for Lane, as his friend Joseph Stevens wrote that "the coming of the Dusseldorf Gallery to Boston was an event to fix itself in one's memory for all time. What talks of these things Lane and I had in his studio and by my fireside!"[108] Among the Düsseldorf paintings—"all of rare merit and extraordinary finish"—he would have seen some landscapes and marine paintings, but many were figurative works; genre paintings of poignant peasants were particularly remarked by reviewers.[109] This event would have permitted Lane to study many examples by accredited European modern masters and learn from their handling of paint, glazes, and pigments as well as their selection of subjects and management of composition.

During the years of his resettlement in Gloucester, from 1848, Lane was building his house, solidifying his new identity as a practitioner of "fine art," and beginning to branch out well beyond the ship-portrait business. Given the "soft" lines of demarcation between art, design, and popular amusement in mid-nineteenth-century America, it is not surprising that Lane painted political banners, street signs, allegorical tableaux about temperance for community parades, a firescreen for his brother, and other objects now lost, as well as the easel paintings for which he is so well known today. It is clear, however, that as he imagined and took on a broader range of "fine-art" projects, he decided not to do certain kinds of art that were highly valued, such as the explicitly allegorical paintings by Thomas Cole, whose *Voyage of Life*, "estimated to be worth between four and five thousand dollars," was offered as the most valuable prize in the American Art-Union drawing of 1849, or historical tableaux, such as Sully's *Washington Crossing the Delaware*, on view at the Boston Museum.[110] Nor did he pursue the pathos-rich genre paintings reviewers praised in descriptions of the Düsseldorf exhibition. Equally, he did not venture into the wilderness paintings that garnered such remunerative rewards for his contemporaries Frederic Church and Albert Bierstadt. Rather, he painted what he saw often, studied easily, and knew well—the ships, buildings, farms, and land profiles of coastal settlements. Not just a surrender to the limitations of his disability—his friends recorded their alternating concern and exasperation at the slow pace with which he was able to follow them while hiking—this decision to fabricate his painterly fictions from materials close at hand was, in fact, deliberate.[111] In the early years of his ambition to become a marine painter, he undoubtedly read tracts on the art and would have found passages, such as this by Dominic Serres and John Thomas Serres, that underlined the importance of painting from detailed personal knowledge of technological and structural facts: "Many are the obstacles to the attainment of a proficiency in drawing Marine Subjects, particularly as it is not only requisite that a person desirous of excelling in the Art should possess a knowledge of the construction of a ship or what is denominated 'Naval Architecture' together with the proportion of masts & yards, the width, depth & cut of the sails, &c; but he should likewise be acquainted with seamanship."[112] That he heeded such advice is evident from the brisk business he did all his life in supplying marine paintings to ships' captains, those most knowledgeable—and critical—about such matters.

Expanding beyond marine painting in the late 1840s and early 1850s, Lane would have found encouragement to look to the local, the everyday, and the deeply familiar to find the materials with which to create extraordinary art. In "The Career of an Artist," for instance, a tale published in Boston in 1850, Francis A. Durivage recounts efforts of a country lad, Julian Montfort, who goes to New York City to learn how to be a history painter but, after much discouragement, "he found vent for his home feeling in painting some of the scenes of his earliest life—the rustic dances, the huskings, the haymakings, and junketings with which he was so familiar." These works are discovered by an appreciative connoisseur who laments, "why don't our artists study to produce life as it exists around them, and as they themselves know it and feel it, instead of giving us the gods and goddesses of a defunct and false religion . . . ?"[113] Julian wins success with canvases about the rural "life as it exists," the life with which he is deeply familiar. The real-life version of this story was reported in the public accounts of the career of George Caleb Bingham, Lane's celebrated contemporary. The unnamed author of an article that Lane undoubtedly read in the 1849 *Bulletin of the American Art-Union* concerning "the career and success of Bingham, the Missouri artist," commends his paintings for their "fidelity of the representations of Western life and manners," asserting that they are "thoroughly American in their subjects and could never have been painted by one who was not perfectly familiar with the scenes they represent."[114] Bingham's Missouri was recognized to be simultaneously local and national, modest and iconic (fig. 48). Bingham is described in this article as an artistically talented youth who labored for a decade on a remote Missouri farm before boldly undertaking portraits as a self-taught artist. Making his way to Philadelphia and Washington as a portraitist, he was persuaded to attempt "delineations of Western life" and, with the encouragement of the Art-Union, achieved singular success.[115] Such narratives clarify the strong strain in mid-nineteenth-century American art validating the potential of regional, common subjects. Lane embraced this perspective and, returning to his hometown, produced a Gloucester-eyed view of the world, a view at once factual and iconic, local and global.

Once committed to his new vocation, Lane exerted himself to maximize his opportunities and to keep his work—identified as *his* by signatures—before the public eye. Lane's *Lumber Schooners at Evening on Penobscot Bay*

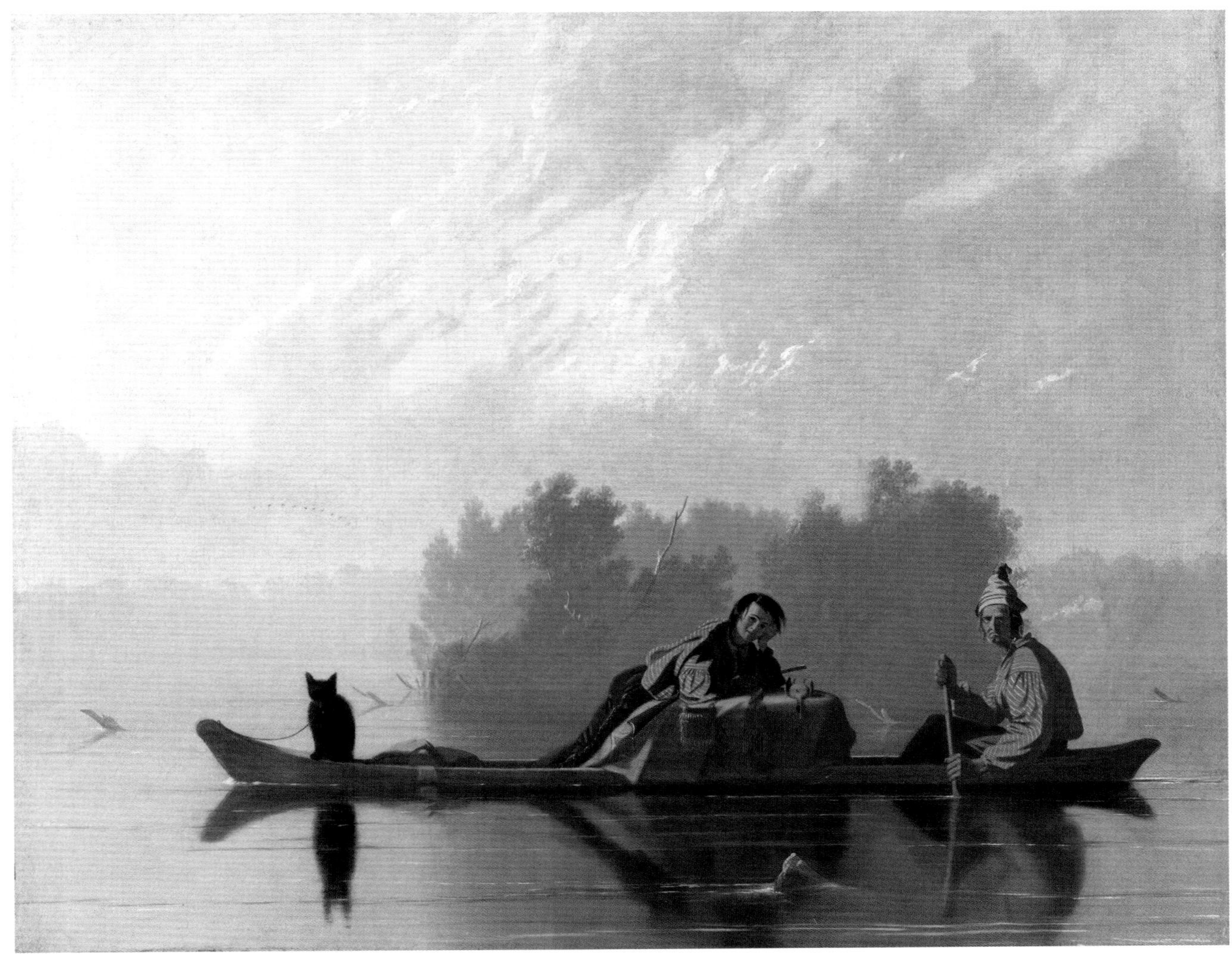

FIGURE 48
George Caleb Bingham, *Fur Traders Descending the Missouri*, 1845. Oil on canvas, 29 × 36 in. (73.7 × 92.7 cm). The Metropolitan Museum of Art, New York, Morris K. Jesup Fund, 1933 (33.61). Image copyright © The Metropolitan Museum of Art. Image source: Art Resource, New York.

is signed "F. H. Lane / 1863" in block letters using light paint on a dark ground, the initials emphasized with thin serifs, on the surface of the painting in the lower right corner (see fig. 7). This is the manner in which he signed (although sometimes in dark paint on a light ground) perhaps a third of his works from as early as 1844 (*Gloucester from Rocky Neck*, CAM) to as late as 1863 (*The Babson Meadows at Riverdale*): initials, last name, and date, in the lower right-hand corner (fig. 23). It is likely that this terse signature on the lower right of his larger, more ambitious, and more expensive works might have been designed to prompt kin or visitors of the owners to recognize the name and to order paintings for themselves. In a few cases, when he knew the painting was going to a site far from his Massachusetts orbit, he added further data, such as his first name—so "Fitz H. Lane 1859" appears on *The Blood Family Homestead* (private collection), a work for out-of-town associates; and he added his hometown to his name—"Fitz H. Lane / Gloucester, Mass"—for the *Gloucester Harbor* of 1852, painted for Sidney Mason's

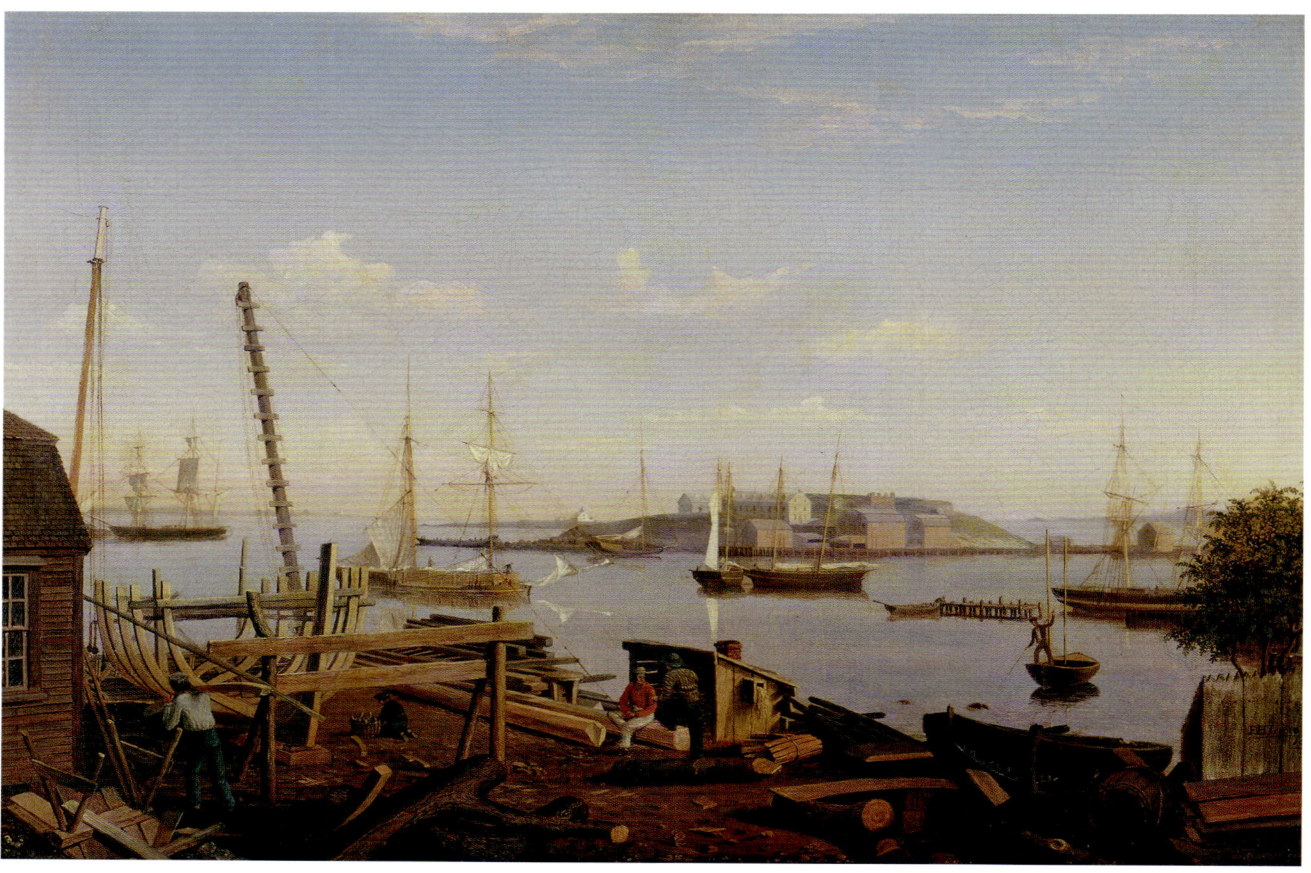

FIGURE 49
Fitz H. Lane, *The Fort and Ten Pound Island, Gloucester (Harbor Scene)*, 1848. Oil on canvas, 20¼ × 30 in. (51.4 × 76.2 cm). The Newark Museum. Gift of Mrs. Chant Owen, 1959 (59.87). Photo: The Newark Museum.

marble mansion on Fifth Avenue in New York City (fig. 10). Similarly, *Sweepstakes*, the portrait of an extreme clipper launched in 1853 from a New York shipyard and almost certainly painted for one of *Sweepstakes*'s New York owners, is inscribed "Fitz Henry Lane / Gloucester / 1853" (figs. 40 and 41). Based on the known examples, it is reasonable to conjecture that the more information provided, the further the painting was sent from Gloucester.

In some instances Lane's paintings were signed on the back of the canvas with more complete information: *The* Golden State *Entering New York Harbor*, for instance, which was inscribed on the back "Painted by Fitz Henry Lane / Gloucester / Mass / A.D. 1854," not only giving his full name and place of residence but also adding the superfluous flourish of "A.D." to the date (fig. 39). It is probable that many of these works with fulsome information were sent for exhibition in Boston, New York, and other venues. At least one inscription records a bestowal signature: *View of Coffin's Beach* was inscribed on the back of the canvas "View of Coffin's Beach, from the rocks at the Loaf, after a sketch taken, August, 1862. / by Fitz H. Lane. / Presented to Dr. H. E. Davidson and Lady / by the Artist."[116] Unfortunately, with the relining of these canvases—a prudent and common conservation measure—this information has been lost. However, most of Lane's signed works display his name on their faces.

On a substantial subset of Lane canvases the lettering of his signature appears within the fictive space of the

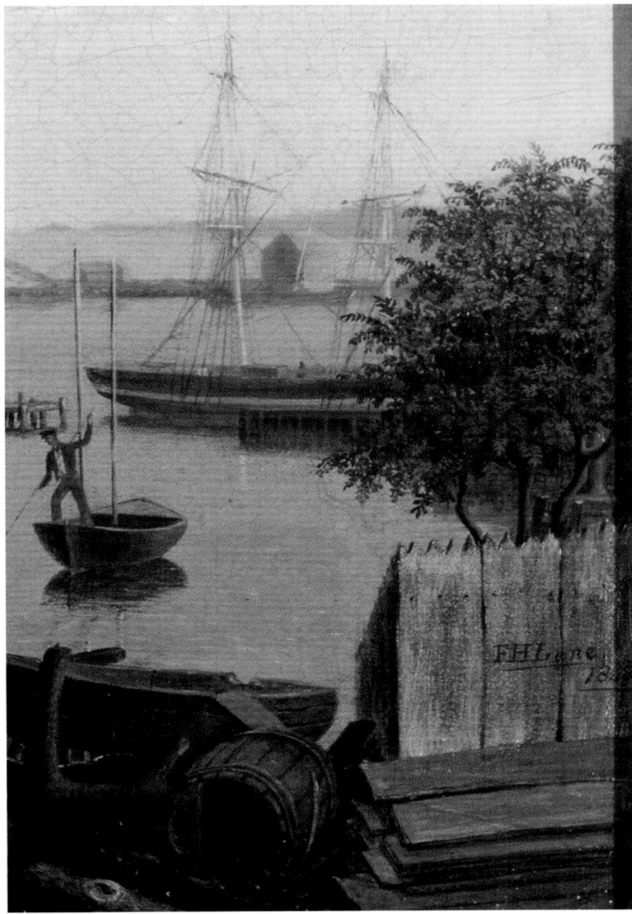

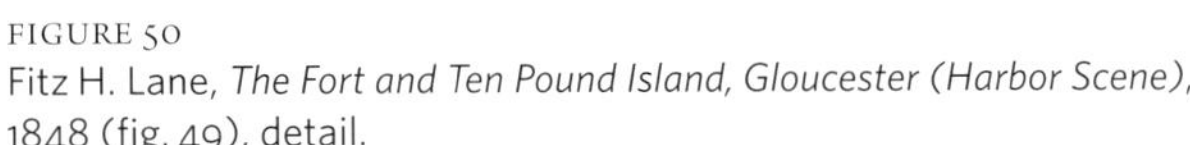

FIGURE 50
Fitz H. Lane, *The Fort and Ten Pound Island, Gloucester (Harbor Scene)*, 1848 (fig. 49), detail.

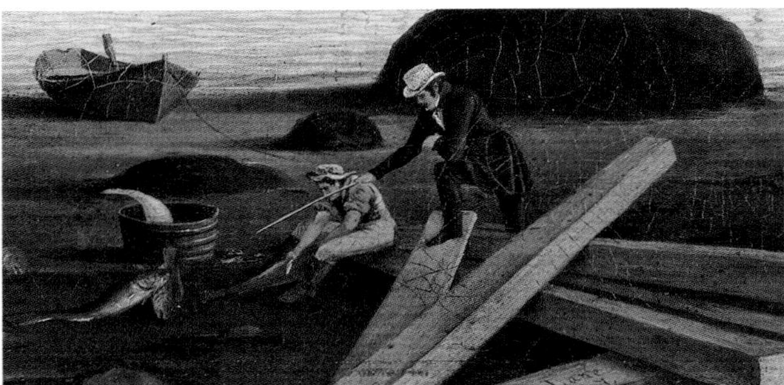

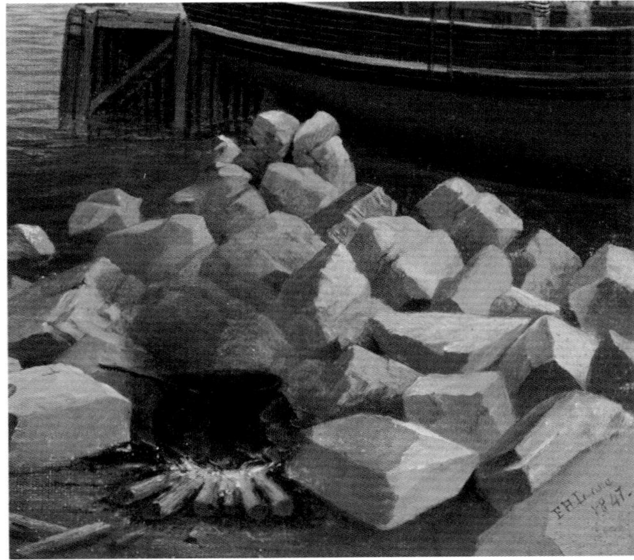

FIGURE 51 (TOP)
Fitz H. Lane, *The Fort and Ten Pound Island, Gloucester, Massachusetts*, 1847 (fig. 27), detail.

FIGURE 52 (BOTTOM)
Fitz H. Lane, *Gloucester Harbor*, 1847 (fig. 5), detail.

painting rather than floating, colophon-like, on the surface, as is the more customary usage. Most prominent among these is *Salem Harbor* (with which this chapter opened), where the artist's initials and the work's date appear as notations on a canvas sail (figs. 33 and 34). Most of the signatures that figure within the fictive space of Lane's paintings are more reticent, requiring close examination and rewarding that attentive scrutiny with the pleasure of discovery. The identifying initials and/or name of the painter in these works follow the surface of sails, waves, rocks, and boards. In *The Fort and Ten Pound Island, Gloucester* of 1848, for instance, Lane's signature is "chiseled" into the palings of a board fence on the far right of the picture (figs. 49 and 50). In another harbor scene done a year earlier, Lane's signature appears in perspective on a squared beam at the lower edge of the canvas (figs. 27 and 51). In the *Gloucester Harbor* of 1847 it is "chiseled" on a rock face in the lower right (figs. 5 and 52). Although this device appears most often in 1840s works, it also appears in late works, such as *Stage Fort Across Gloucester Harbor* (Metropolitan Museum of Art), where "Fitz H. Lane / 1862" clings to the face of a large rock on the extreme right margin. On two occasions

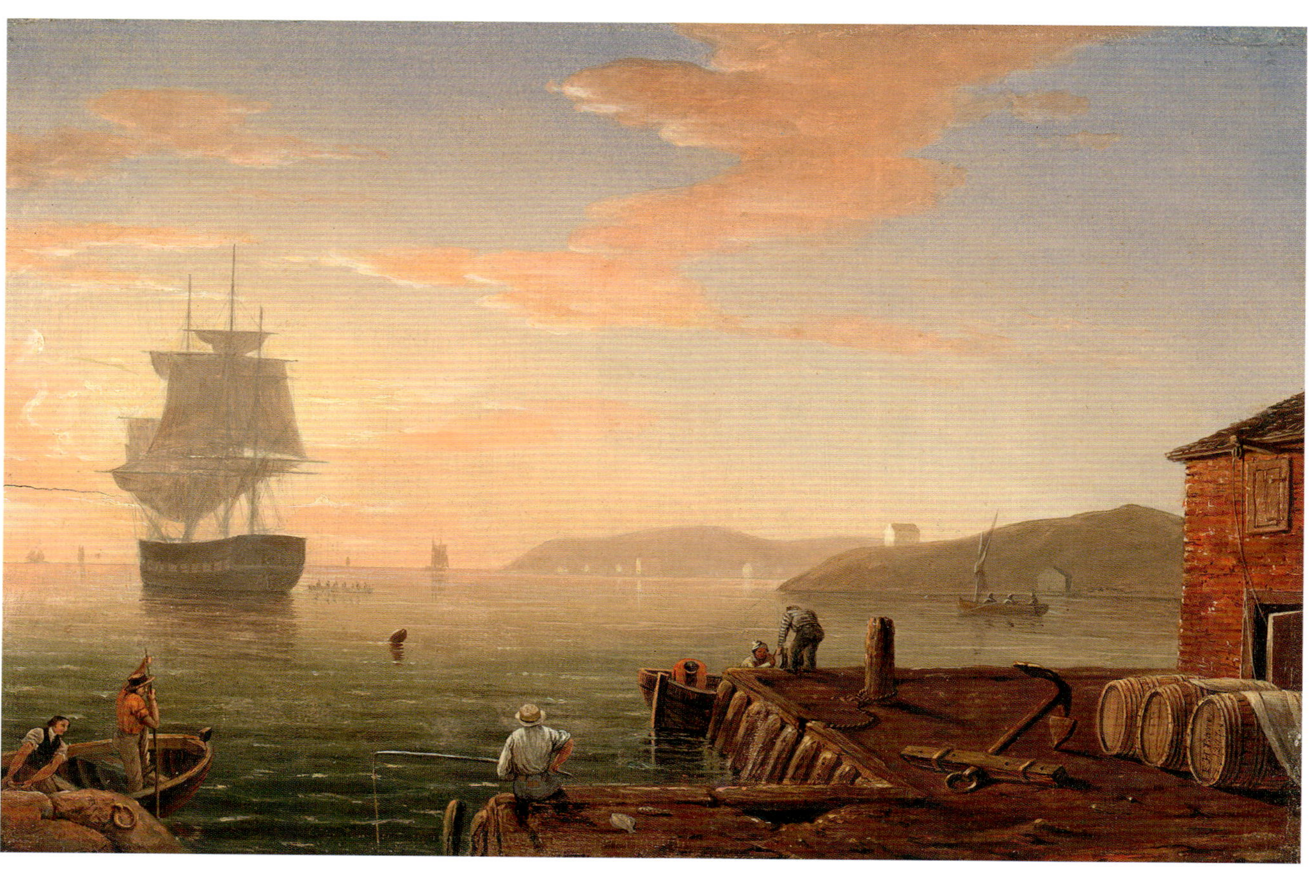

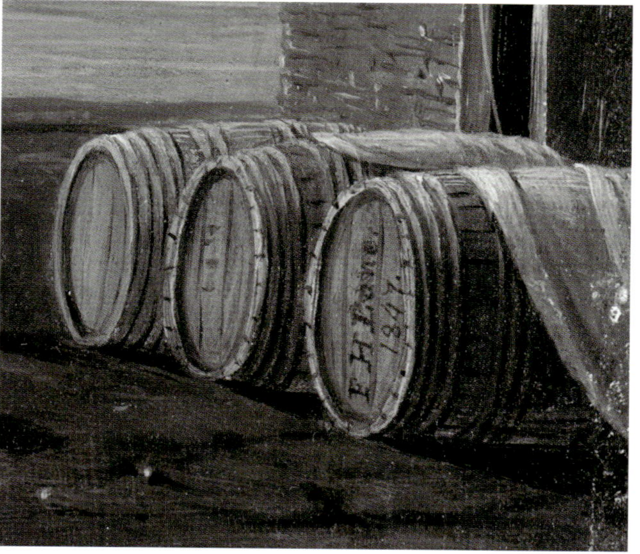

FIGURE 53 (TOP)
Fitz H. Lane, *On the Wharves, Gloucester Harbor*, 1847. Oil on panel, 13 × 18 in. (33 × 45.7 cm). Cape Ann Museum, Gloucester, Massachusetts. Gift of George O. and Jane Parker Stacy, 1948 (1289.1b).

FIGURE 54 (BOTTOM)
Fitz H. Lane, *On the Wharves, Gloucester Harbor*, 1847 (fig. 53), detail.

his signature rides the curve of a wave—in *The* Britannia *Entering Boston Harbor* (MFA) and *Sweepstakes*. In this latter case, the painting of an extreme clipper, the wave carries generous information for the work's out-of-town owner: "Fitz Henry Lane / Gloucester / 1853" (figs. 40 and 41). Another work carries an abbreviated signature on a barrel, where, in the nineteenth century, the initials of the owner of a barrel's contents were often branded, *On the Wharves, Gloucester Harbor*, of 1847 (figs. 53 and 54).[117] Last, *A Smart Blow* is signed on the transom of a fishing schooner, simultaneously "naming" the vessel and the author of the painting (figs. 37 and 38). All of these sly signatures reward close looking and suggest that, as a general practice, the "incidental details" of Lane's paintings contain clues of all sorts that the artist understood to be legible and of interest to those who viewed his canvases. In integrating his signature into the perspectival fiction of his images, Lane was using visual wit to foreground his presence within his art, while associating his name and himself with rocks, boards, barrels, and waves as well as canvas.

NAMES WITHOUT WORDS

Beyond the artist's lettered signature, testifying to authorship, Lane's paintings also include nonverbal references to the identities of his patrons, their ships, and himself, deliberately triggering recognition and "decoding" in the well-informed contemporaneous viewer. *Salem Harbor*, as noted at the outset of this chapter, points directly to the artist in its "FHL / 1853" inscription, but it also comments indirectly and wryly on the artist in the association of that inscription with a much-patched set of sails on a modest schooner in juxtaposition with a majestic clipper (figs. 33 and 34).[118] This modest vessel is positioned as the artist's proxy, a vessel offered as an extension of and a comment on his identity. Such playfulness with his identity emerges again in the *Gloucester Harbor* of 1856 (fig. 55). Although the view here of the town is from the western shore of the outer harbor (near the residences of two of his patrons), Lane's studio windows, in the distinctive three gables of his house, are visible, "looking back" at the viewer from the center of the canvas, just peeking over the rise of Fort Point (fig. 56). More straightforwardly, *New England Inlet with Self-Portrait*, of 1848, includes the image of a young artist seated on a rock, sketching on a large tablet (larger than Lane is known to have used), near the Anisquam River just north of Gloucester's harbor (figs. 57 and 58). Whether this is a self-portrait or the record of a *plein air* expedition with an associate, it certainly highlights artistic production within an artistic product. These three paintings include direct references to the artist through proxy vessels, buildings, and figures.

More frequently Lane's works include small but easily legible vignettes that point to the identity of others, to specific well-recognized sites, ships, and patrons. The many Boston Harbor views, for instance, are decisively Boston Harbor as viewed from the shipbuilding yards of East Boston, because in each case the busy marine traffic obligingly parts to reveal Charles Bulfinch's domed Massachusetts State House of 1795–97, a structure as iconic in the present day as it was in Lane's (fig. 59). *Three-Master on the Gloucester Railway*, however, is more obscure in its key nonverbal information; it was painted as the shop sign for John Trask, but it does not say so (fig. 4). Although it includes less-important verbal information as signage within the image, it only mimes the business that it was commissioned to mark and advertise: the caulking, waterproofing, and painting of ships. Lane and Trask expected the denizens of Gloucester to "read" its message and the identity of the shop whose front it ornamented, a message and identity that would be lost to twenty-first-century viewers but for the preservation of contemporaneous records (see chapter 1).

Other kinds of visual information that Lane expected his audiences to "read" include figureheads, pennants, and specific vessels or vessel types, all of which can be illegible or seem negligible to viewers today. I have already discussed (in chapter 1) the witty inclusion of a tow boat (tugboat) named the *Robert Bennet Forbes* in

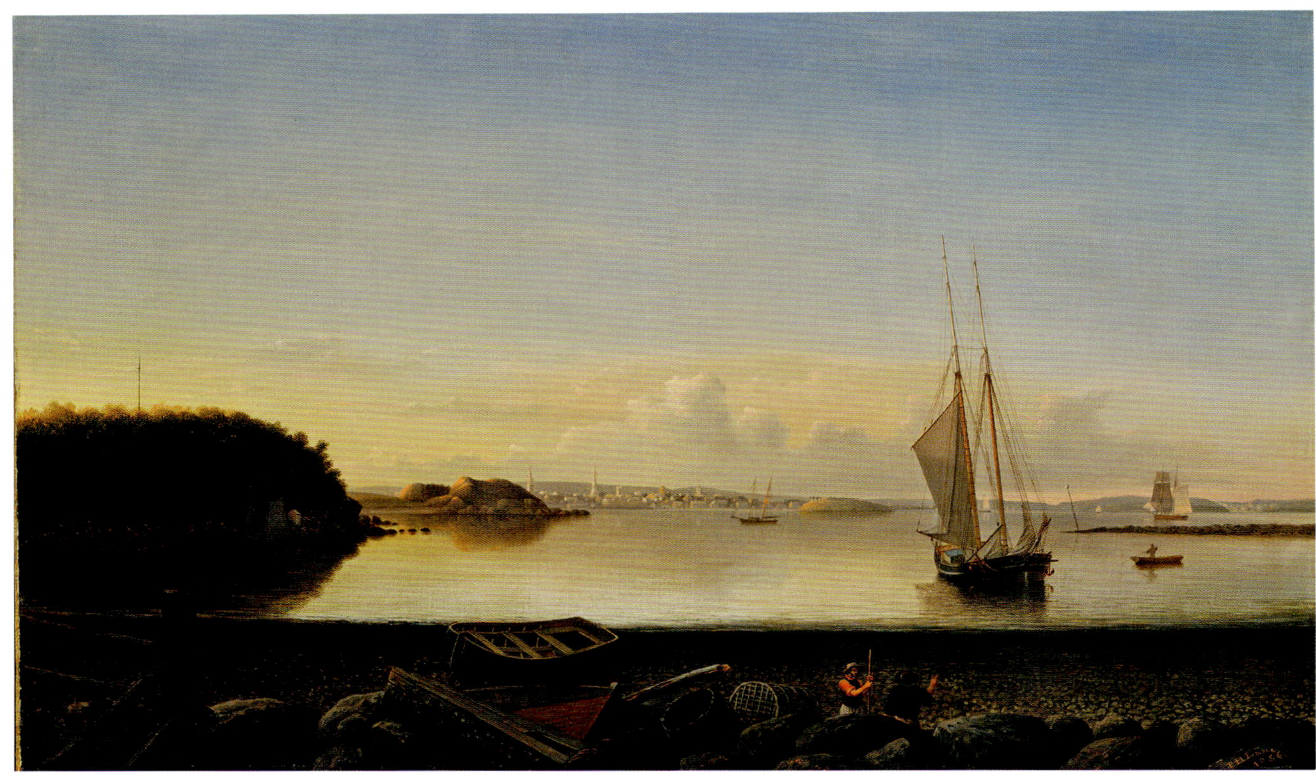

FIGURE 55 (ABOVE)
Fitz H. Lane, *Gloucester Harbor*, 1856. Oil on canvas, 22⅜ × 36¹⁄₁₆ in. (56.8 × 91.6 cm). Daniel J. Terra Collection, Terra Foundation for American Art, Chicago (1993.21). Photo: Terra Foundation for American Art / Art Resource, New York.

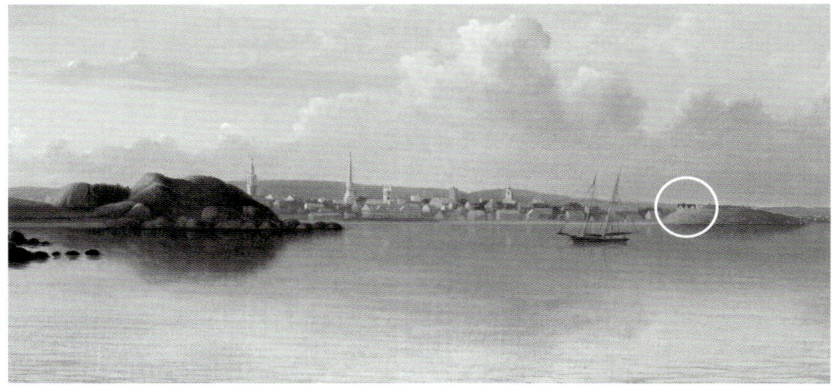

FIGURE 56 (RIGHT)
Fitz H. Lane, *Gloucester Harbor*, 1856 (fig. 55), detail.

Lane's lithograph drawn for Forbes's pamphlet, published in 1847, recording the voyage of the *Jamestown* (see fig. 16, also fig. 17). Here the man captaining the heroic naval ship is also personified in the much smaller well-known tug assisting the *Jamestown* in its epic departure. In other instances, the name and ownership of ships are indicated in the pennants they fly, the figureheads they carry, and, infrequently and more straightforwardly, in writing on the bow or stern.

Exemplary of the coded systems of identity found in Lane's paintings and in the marine models he memorialized is the *Portrait of the* National Eagle, of 1853 (fig. 60). The ship's name is visible on its bow, and to underline its identity, its figurehead is a gilt eagle, wings spread majestically, with talons trailing golden ribbons (fig. 61). Figureheads were not just ornaments—they were nonverbal signs that could be "read" by a spyglass at sea or by an illiterate mariner looking for a ship in a crowded harbor.

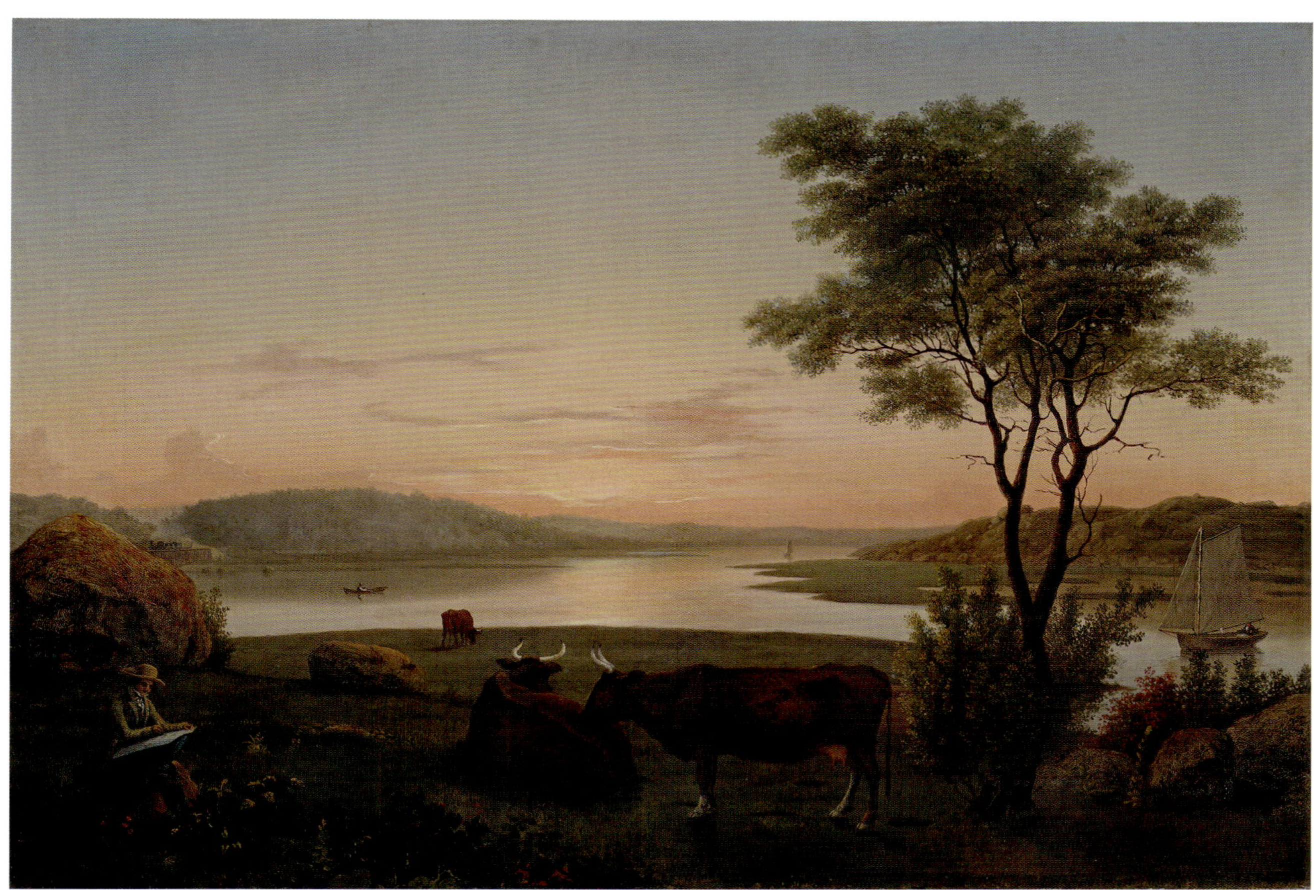

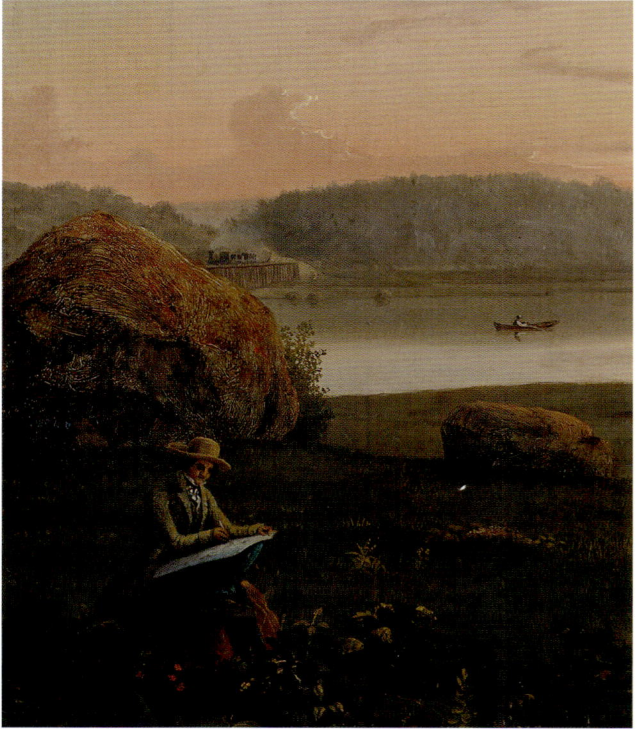

FIGURE 57 (ABOVE)
Fitz H. Lane, *New England Inlet with Self-Portrait*, 1848. Oil on canvas, 17¾ × 25⅞ in. (45.1 × 65.7 cm). Yale University Art Gallery. Gift of Kenneth A. Householder, B. Arch., 1947, in memory of Royal A. Basich, and partially purchased with the Stephen Carlton Clark, B.A., 1903, and John Hill Morgan, B.A., 1893, Funds (1992.107.1). Photo: Yale University Art Gallery.

FIGURE 58 (LEFT)
Fitz H. Lane, *New England Inlet with Self-Portrait*, 1848 (fig. 57), detail.

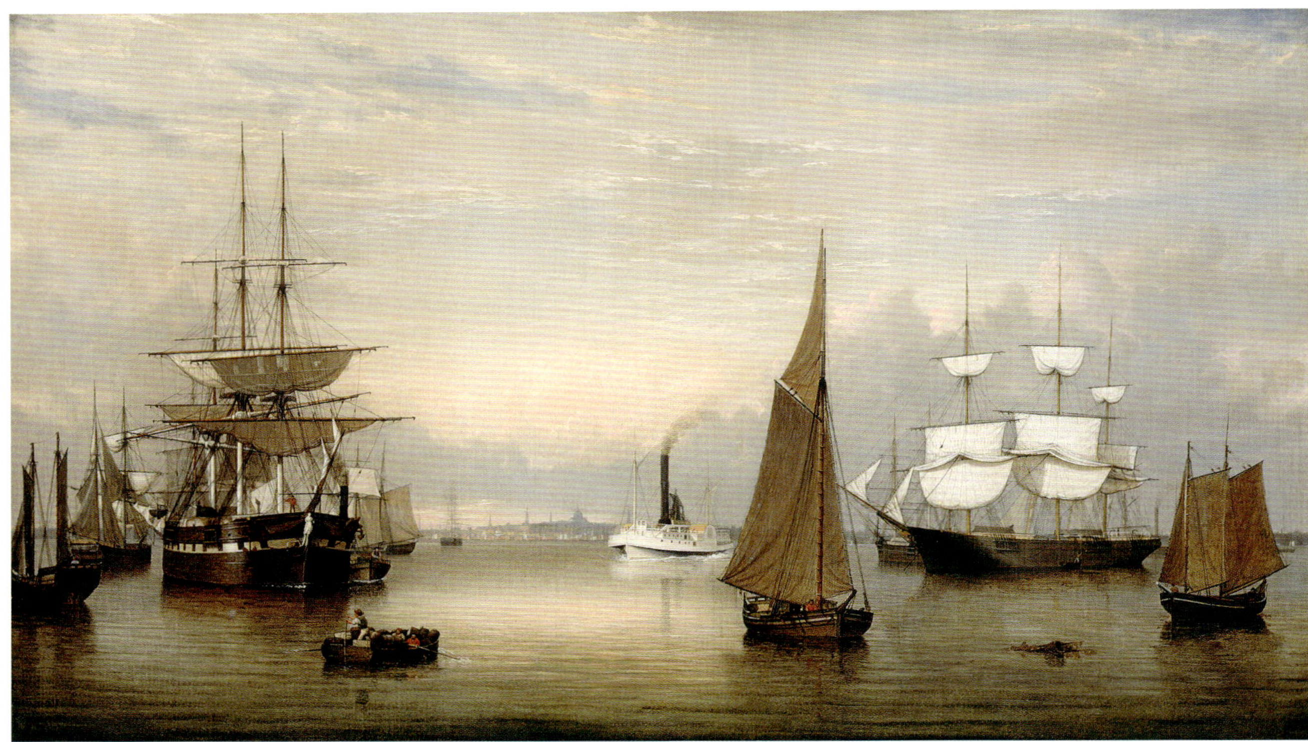

FIGURE 59
Fitz H. Lane, *Boston Harbor*, 1856. Oil on canvas, 25½ × 42½ in. (64.8 × 108 cm). Amon Carter Museum of American Art, Fort Worth, Texas (1977.14).

Flying above the vessel's foresails, red-and-white flags reiterate its identity to those familiar with the conventions of the Marine Telegraph System, generally known as Elford's signals; the white flag with a medallion in red, white, and blue announced that this noble ship was owned by Francis Fisher of Boston.[119] (The schooner approaching the *National Eagle* is identified by its blue-and-white flag as a Boston Harbor pilot schooner.)[120] Its name announced in linguistic, sculptural, and signal-code signs, the *National Eagle*'s identity is triple marked in this painting commissioned by Fisher to commemorate this clipper ship. It is in redundancy, of course, that a culture signals its deepest concerns. The name of the vessel referenced more than the object itself; it pointed to a narrative of national, global, and personal import. This ship and others like it were capable of extraordinary feats and represented extraordinary investments, all of which are concentrated and evoked in their painted facsimiles.

Flags were particularly important in marine communication, where national flags quickly announced either "friend" or "foe"—or, deceptively, faux friend.[121] Among mariners, signal flags were particularly important where verbal communication was impossible and passing ships might have much data to exchange. The marine flags that Lane deployed in his paintings indicate ownership and much else. In the nineteenth century the systems that had been developed for marine communication were complex and extensive, consisting of thousands of flags and flag combinations; indeed, these systems—the Parker System and Marryat's Universal Code of Signals, for instance—constituted discrete and powerful languages that Lane deployed in many paintings.[122]

Flags were also a common and important communication system on land in the antebellum period. The *Gloucester Telegraph* reported in May 1850, for instance,

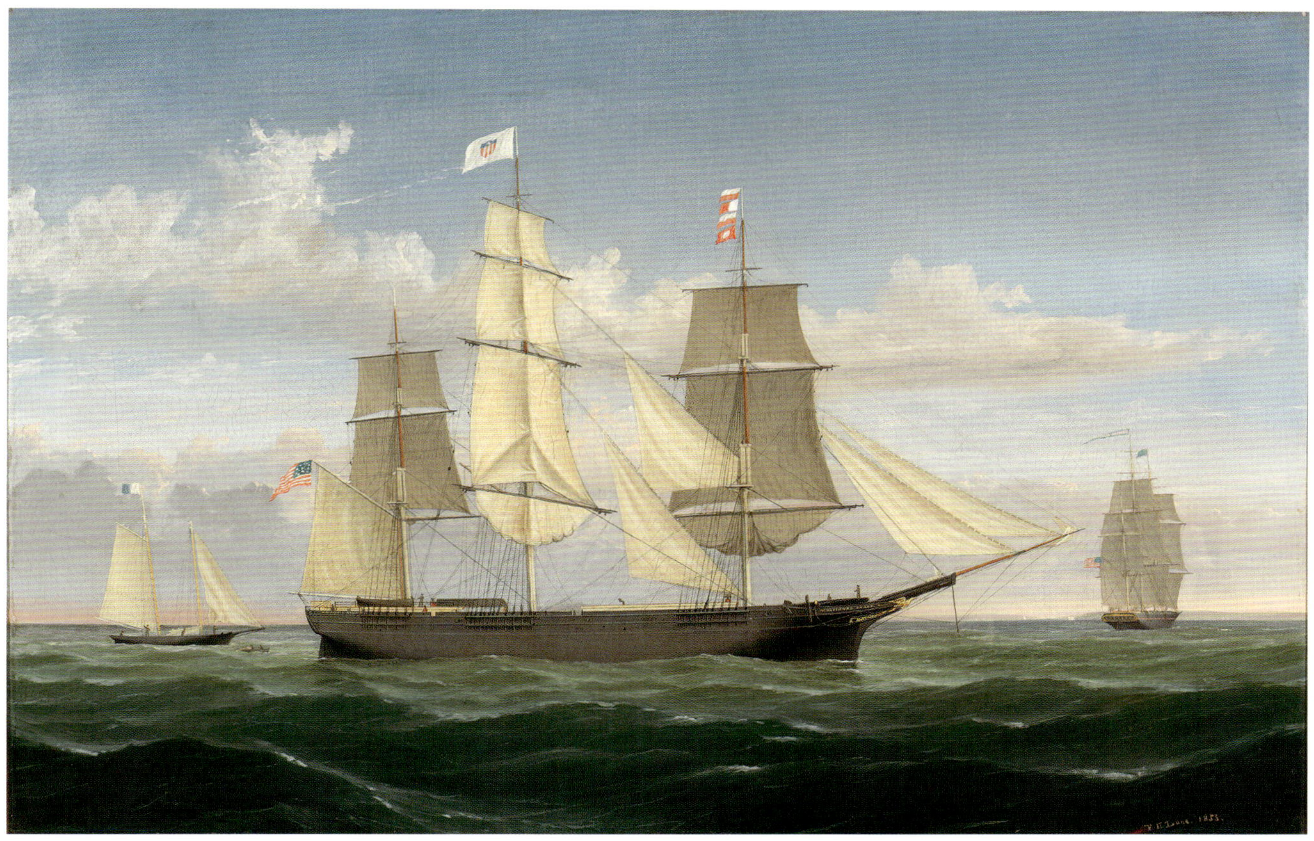

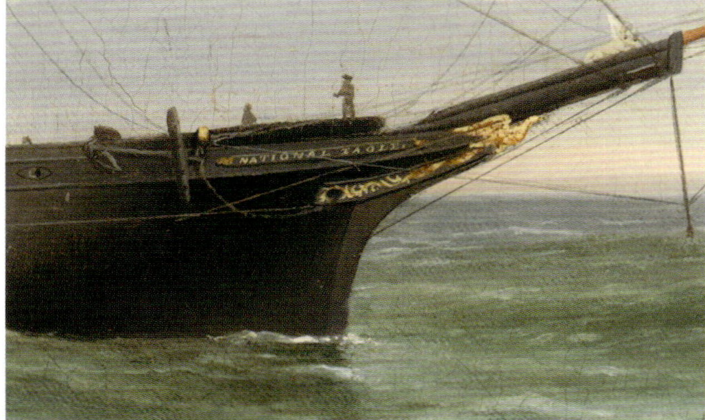

FIGURE 60 (TOP)
Fitz H. Lane, *Portrait of the* National Eagle, 1853. Oil on canvas, 23½ × 36 in. (59.7 × 91.4 cm). Cape Ann Museum, Gloucester, Massachusetts. Gift of the Estate of Marjory A. Johnson, 1988 (2612.00).

FIGURE 61 (BOTTOM)
Fitz H. Lane, *Portrait of the* National Eagle, 1853 (fig. 60), detail.

that in nearby Salem "the Board of Health . . . have ordered a yellow flag to be attached to houses where small pox exists, instead of red ones, as the latter have frequently been taken for an auction flag."[123] By this we learn some of the purposes of flags on private homes provided an urgent warning of contagious disease and a beckoning banner to advertise a public sale. Such signs were vital—intended to be nonlinguistic, quickly attached, ephemeral markers of matters of public importance. Their legibility could be a matter of life and death.

Perhaps the most important nonverbal but generally legible communication system that Lane incorporated into his canvases, a system that is much less legible to us today than to his fellow Gloucesterites, was cloud formations. In Lane's culture clouds were meteorological indicators of grave importance to mariners and all those whose ships, cargoes, and livelihoods were dependent on favorable weather for safety and prosperity. Giving almost two-thirds of his picture space to sky, Lane used that expanse to add inflection to, and comment on, the landscape or seascape incidents below. He included feathery cirrus clouds, five or six miles up (as in *Gloucester Inner Harbor*, fig. 6), to indicate "calm sea" and give the subject an air of well-being. More often he combined high-flying cirrus with puffy cumulus, as in *Salem Harbor*, a combination that described the weather to cognoscenti as benign, with moderate winds, and that gave him the opportunity to juxtapose white sails against low-hanging gray cumulus (fig. 33). Occasionally he would use clouds to heighten drama, as in *Ship* Southern Cross, where he described the vessel setting out under twisted stratocumulus, a low-hanging cloud formation that nevertheless showed a good deal of blue sky and augured fair weather and thus a prosperous voyage (fig. 21).[124] When he sought to underline the tempestuous nature of adverse conditions, Lane overlay his turbulent sea with threatening gray altostratus or thick dark nimbus, as in *A Smart Blow* (fig. 37). For Lane's patrons, his knowledge and rendering of the appropriate legible sky was as important as his expertise in the rigging of ships and the deployment of lines in governing the canvas sails on which safety and speed depended.

Lane would have learned to be mindful of skies from his youth in maritime Gloucester, but he would also have learned the value of skies to an artist from reading such essays as that by W in the *Bulletin of the American Art-Union* in 1850 in which the author praised many of J. M. W. Turner's paintings for their attention to clouds, on which W, too, lavished much attention: "one of these mist-filled, luminous skies, in which the cumuli are piling sluggishly up, wasting away and mingling themselves into the vapor which grays the blue sky in the light of the noonday sun."[125] Lane's contemporaries were publishing folklore about clouds and scientific studies about weather prediction, but it is apparent that artists and mariners were in the forefront of studying and understanding these phenomena, and more or less everyone in the antebellum period could "read" clouds.[126]

The expressive expanse of ever-adjustable sky in the upper portion of his paintings—which could, with color and emotionally charged weather-specific cloud formations, give dramatic character to the scene—provided an advantage that was not available to the rising generation of photographers, rivals to Lane in picturing Gloucester's landscapes. One advertised "Views of Half Moon Beach, Rockport, Long Beach, and other scenery 'round the Cape'" in the town's newspapers from midcentury, but unless clouds cooperated during the shoot or were synthetically added by double exposure or other artificial mechanisms, photographers' much cheaper wares lacked the expressive skies that were so much a part of the palette Lane deployed to give strong interpretive valence to his sites and his subjects.[127]

A CANVAS ECONOMY

Canvas was a relatively inexpensive but essential commodity in the antebellum period. Although some desirable types were imported from such distant ports as Russia, good canvas was made right on Cape Ann starting in 1847, when steam power enabled sites lacking strong river flows to build mills and factories.[128] Isinglass, manufactured from hake sounds (air bladders, a by-product of the fisheries), was essential in the sizing of cotton goods and had been manufactured on Cape Ann from 1824.[129] Tightly woven of cotton, linen, or hemp, canvas was the flexible, adjustable, compactable, and infinitely reusable material that enabled the ships and schooners of antebellum New England to harvest fish and to trade with China. Canvas sails were the alchemical agents that put the skills of shipbuilders and seamen, the acumen of merchants and artisans, into motion. Lane, who knew the material from infancy, would have understood well its transformative properties in moving commodities and knowledge. His

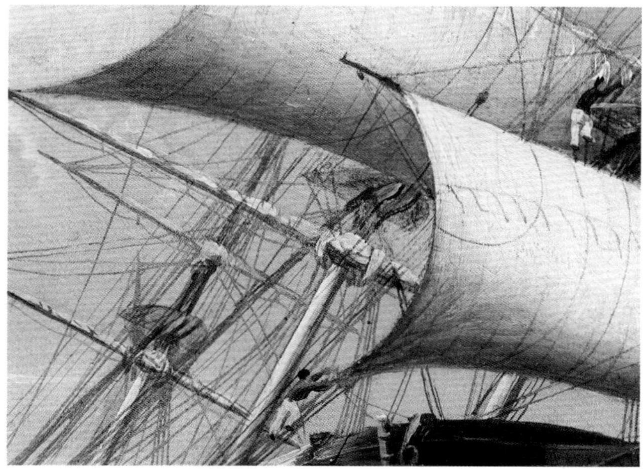

FIGURE 62
Fitz H. Lane, *Three-Master in Rough Seas*, 1856, detail. Oil on canvas, 10½ × 15¾ in. (26.7 × 40 cm). Cape Ann Museum, Gloucester, Massachusetts. Gift of George O. and Jane Parker Stacy, 1948 (1289.1c).

respect for those who managed the canvas of sails is clear from his inclusion of small figures engaged in this skilled and perilous work, reefing and setting sails, especially in dangerous circumstances (fig. 62). He may in fact have identified with these seamen, wrangling canvas in their way as he did in his. It is no wonder that his most prominent signature, his most dramatic assertion of identity, is on the canvas of a modest but sturdy schooner (fig. 33). Unusually conscious of issues of identity and the power of mime communication, Lane, through imagination, application, and hard work, consciously evolved as a member of his community from a disabled, marginally employable shoemaker into a self-christened figure of regard and accomplishment. His culture was rich in opportunities, useful information, and models for self-fashioning in a wide variety of highbrow and lowbrow artistic activities. Indeed, it is clear from his recognition within the community as a polymath—as ready to paint political banners, shop signs, fireboards, and ship portraits as the landscapes so valued in our culture today—that he enjoyed lowbrow community engagement as much as highbrow "art."

The decisions Lane made strongly suggest that he was a bit of a romantic (in adopting the moniker of Fitz Henry), that he had a sense of humor (in, for instance, including his studio windows "looking back" in *Gloucester Harbor*), and that he felt a sense of deep alignment with the materials of his workaday world (in his integration of his proxy signatures into fence palings, lumber piles, granite blocks, and waves). Moreover, the mime shows of his canvases demonstrate his (and his culture's) rich local knowledge of the nonverbal but eloquent communication systems encoded in figureheads, pennants and signal flags, "Quaker," or faux, gunports, and cloud formations. Most decisively, however, it is clear that Lane understood his own alchemical magnification of value in turning canvas into art as a counterpart to the larger culture's vigorous embrace of canvas as the critical element in enabling the ingenuity of ship designers, the acumen of ships' captains, and the skill of common seamen to harness the wind so that clippers such as that celebrated in *Salem Harbor* yielded seemingly magical sevenfold profits.

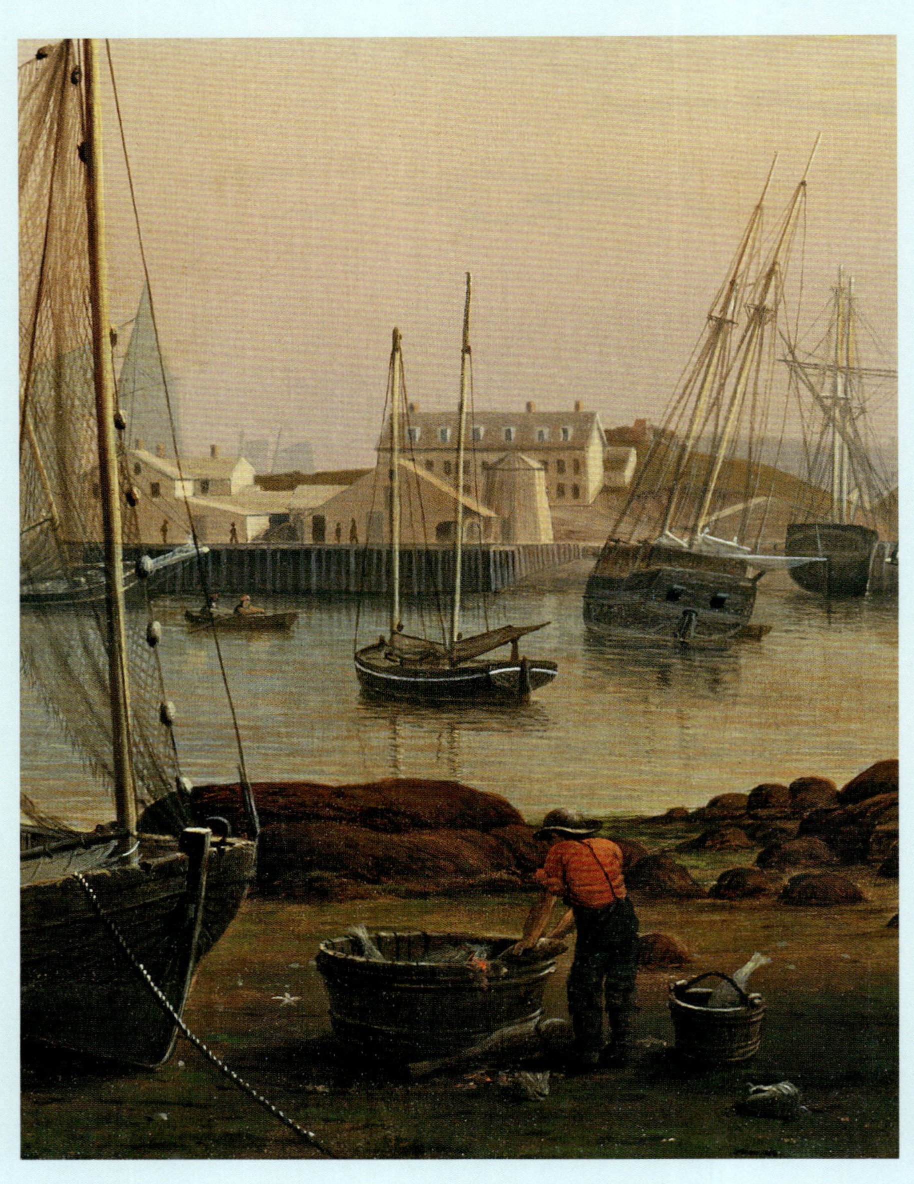

CHAPTER 4

FISH

Lane's Gloucester

"When we speak of business prospects in Gloucester we of course refer to the fishing business, for all others here rest upon that," opined the editor of the *Cape Ann Advertiser* in April 1861.[1] This had been true when Lane was a boy at the opening of the nineteenth century, and it continued to be true throughout his lifetime. Gloucester's fisheries, decade after decade, were at the center of a complex far-reaching business network involving the procurement of salt from Cadiz, canvas from Russia, barrels from Maine, baitfish from Canadian waters, and ice from local ponds; schooners built in neighboring Essex and ships, barks, and brigs built in East Boston; and markets in Surinam, Lisbon, and Montreal. It involved fresh, frozen, salted, dried, and smoked fish, primarily cod, halibut, and mackerel. Gloucester's fisheries dominated the local economy, loomed large in the region, and played a major role in international trade. Lane and his fellow Gloucesterites understood this intricate and global antebellum economy as central to their lives, so it is not surprising that fish, and the vessels dedicated to their capture and circulation, figure prominently in so many of his canvases.

Simultaneous with the booming of the fish economy, a new economy was developing in Gloucester, one in which Lane was a notable actor, and that is the economy of looking. Touring, vacationing, summering, and excursioning began in earnest early in the nineteenth century, and with the building of beachfront hotels and summer cottages, the commencement of scheduled rail and steamship service, and the development of such amenities as pleasure-boat and gig hires, a steady, if seasonal,

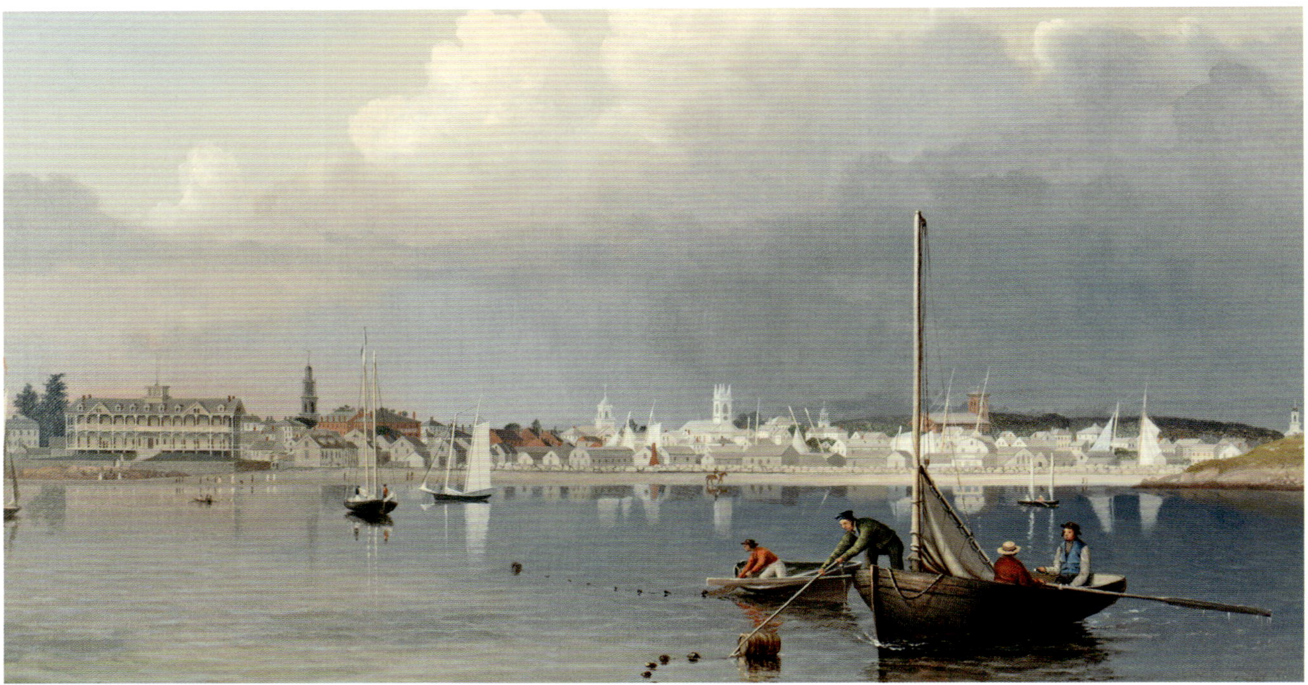

FIGURE 63
Fitz H. Lane. *Gloucester Harbor*, 1852 (fig. 10), detail.

secondary but also far-reaching economy grew. To this economy Lane contributed directly. When he sent his views of Gloucester to Boston, New York, and elsewhere for exhibition and sale—often including "Gloucester, Mass." by his signature on the face of these "export" works—Lane was enhancing the reputation of his region as a source of visual pleasure and contemplation, as well as building his own reputation as an artist.

These two seemingly incompatible economies—one based on fresh sea air and the other on the necessarily coarse redolence of thousands of fish and the by-products of their processing—coexisted, and in fact, it is probable that the appeal of Gloucester to outsiders was as much in its very visible and seemingly quaint extraction industry as in the region's cool breezes and verdant drives. A Boston reporter gave an account of the first steamship excursion from the metropole to Gloucester on a beautiful day in September 1828: "Yesterday morning at half past 5 o'clock with some fifty or sixty Bostonians" on board, the *Franklin* steamed up to Salem, where it took on "a party of four or five hundred people of both sexes . . . [bound for the] ragged rocks and briny waters" of Gloucester, where "we landed amidst a cloud of fishermen and wharfloads of Mackerel—promenaded through the town, which appears to be wealthy, purchased all the gingerbread we could find," and returned home by mid-afternoon. The locals, according to this Bostonian, took note of the event: "Along the whole coast, the population swarmed forth in great numbers, covering every bank and ledge and rocky promontory"—the artist, then a twenty-four-year-old shoemaker named Nathaniel Rogers Lane, perhaps among their number.[2] Seeing the wharfloads of mackerel, the cloud of fishermen, and the huzzahing locals apparently contributed as much as the gingerbread and sea breezes to the excursionists' pleasure.

The inhabitants of Cape Ann swarmed the rocks because excursionists on that scale, transported by steamship, were a novelty, not because marine contact with

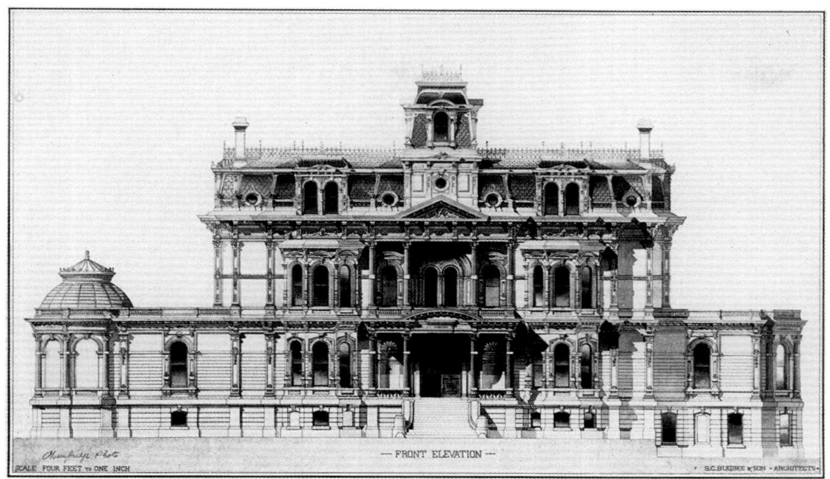

FIGURE 64
Samuel C. Bugbee and Son, *House for Charles C. and Mary Ann Deming Crocker, San Francisco*, ca. 1876. Elevation drawing. Photograph by Eadweard Muybridge. Lone Mountain College Collections of Stereographs by Eadweard Muybridge (BANC PIC 1971.055:36—AX), The Bancroft Library, University of California, Berkeley. Photo: The Bancroft Library, University of California, Berkeley.

outsiders was a novelty. In the previous year Gloucester's harbor had provided home anchorage to 13 ships, barks, and brigs trading to such foreign ports as Lisbon, Surinam, Odessa, and Calcutta, as well as 55 schooners in the coasting trade, and 165 schooners in the cod fishery.[3] For a town that would not reach a population of seven thousand for two decades, this fleet of 233 vessels suggests the Atlantic focus of Gloucester's interests and manpower and what might be called its piscatorial cosmopolitanism.

Two decades later Lane depicted these two economies side by side in one of his most ambitious paintings, the *Gloucester Harbor* of 1852, commissioned by Sidney Mason (see fig. 10). In the center foreground a vignette of seine (net) fishing is set off on the left edge by a portrait of Mason's Pavilion Hotel, Cape Ann's first resort hotel, built directly on the harbor beach in 1849 to attract summer visitors (fig. 63). Mason's family also owned the older brick hotel, Gloucester House, in the heart of the town and identifiable in Lane's painting as the nearby large red building with a sign reading "... HOUSE." Gloucester House, built in the business district of the town in 1810, had solid walls pierced by windows to light interior spaces, while the very different Pavilion was oriented to the ocean view and to promenade opportunities on the wraparound verandas and the beach.[4] Its designer, Samuel C. Bugbee, was also, according to one account, "the well known architect of most of the summer residences built along [the Cape Ann] coast [in the] Italian ... [style], giving the house[s] a plain but rich and beautiful appearance."[5] He was exceptionally sensitive to the fresh-air requirements of his patrons and, when he emigrated to California, designed for railroad magnates Leland Stanford and Charles Crocker elegant urban hilltop mansions with porch and deck extensions affording capacious views (fig. 64).[6] Lane has taken care to suggest in his painting white-frocked summer visitors on the beach and near the entrance of the hotel. The seventeen vessels with which Lane populates this *Gloucester Harbor* include a yawl boat and a dory setting the net, fishing schooners of various sizes associated with coastal and blue-water fisheries, as well as square-rigged freighters poised to transport barrels of dried fish to distant ports.

Taken together, Lane's paintings of Gloucester Harbor and Gloucester vessels describe three kinds of fishing: the international Banks fisheries; the coastal fisheries including the extraction of lobsters, clams, and baitfish; and recreational, noncommercial fishing—this last, what might be called symbolic fishing, linked to the culture of looking and the recreational experience of nature. These three fisheries involved different species, different fishing grounds, different technologies of capture and processing, different vessel types, and different economic circuits.

Lane painted vignettes of each kind of fishing and of the points of intersection between the fisheries and other economies.

THE BUSINESS OF FISH

Gloucester's economic orientation to the sea and its "free" resources was not entirely voluntary. As one commentator put it: due to the combination of its "splendid harbor . . . with a sterile [thin rocky] soil that will raise nothing but *men*, . . . [i]ts people have, from its earliest settlement, devoted themselves to the fisheries."[7] There were fisheries of international scope at Gloucester even before there was European settlement. In the early seventeenth century the Dorchester Company—an English consortium—erected stages (or long temporary tables) at Gloucester Harbor to dry their catch for sale in the West Indies and continental Europe, and it is clear from early maps of North America that the underwater precincts of St. George's Bank, Jeffrey's Ledge, and what was termed "the submarine mountain known as the Grand [or Great] Banks" of Newfoundland, and other fish-rich invisible shallows in the North Atlantic, were much better known and better mapped than the New World's continental interior until well into the eighteenth century (figs. 65 and 66).[8] These fixed banks, ledges, and shoals were the areas of the Atlantic where the sea floor was rich with marine life and shallow enough to permit successful fishing. The methods of capturing the cod and preparing them for market were well established early on and sufficiently important economically to warrant a detailed illustration in Herman Moll's landmark world atlas published in London in 1709 (fig. 67). Here twenty-five men engaged in hooking, landing, cleaning, salting, dressing, and drying the fish, and extracting the cod liver oil, are framed by a warmly clad fisherman exhibiting a baited handline on the left and four others fishing with handlines off the sides of their ship in the distance on the right. Between these framing figures the fish are moved from one operation to the next

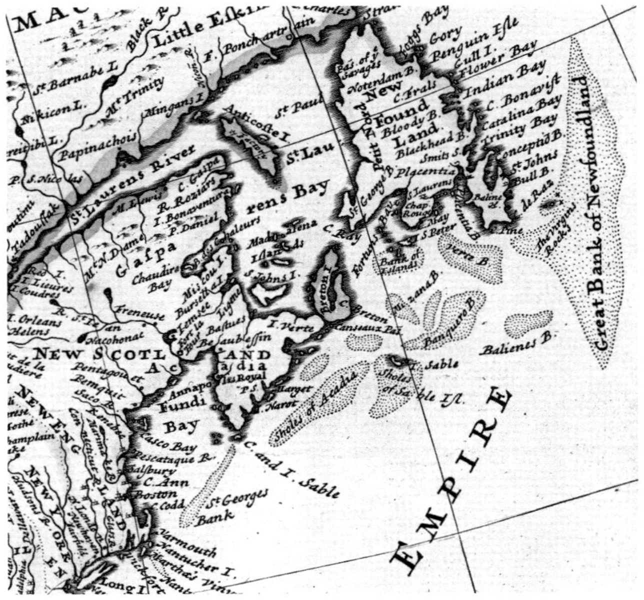

FIGURE 65
E. Kirkall sculp., *North America*, detail. Engraving. Map 7 in Herman Moll, *The World Described; or, A New and Correct Sett of Maps* [. . .] (London: I Bowles, [1709–20]). Courtesy, American Antiquarian Society (Atlases G1105/.m726/1709 [bound together]).

on pallets. These practices, originating in the sixteenth century, were largely unchanged and were familiar to Lane's audience more than two centuries later.

Reoriented to local capital by the mid-eighteenth century, the international importance of New England's (and especially Gloucester's) fisheries was recognized by such public figures as Edmund Burke, English statesman, political theorist, and philosopher, who was quoted in the *Cape Ann Light & Gloucester Telegraph* as having remarked in the House of Commons shortly before the American Revolution that there was "no sea, but what is vexed by their fisheries. No climate that is not witness to their toils," and surpassing "the perseverance of Holland, the activity of France, and the dexterous and firm sagacity of English enterprise," these New Englanders were worthy of great respect.[9]

Fishing was big business. Briefly curtailed by the Revolution and the War of 1812, Gloucester's fish-based prosperity recovered in Lane's youth and—despite some

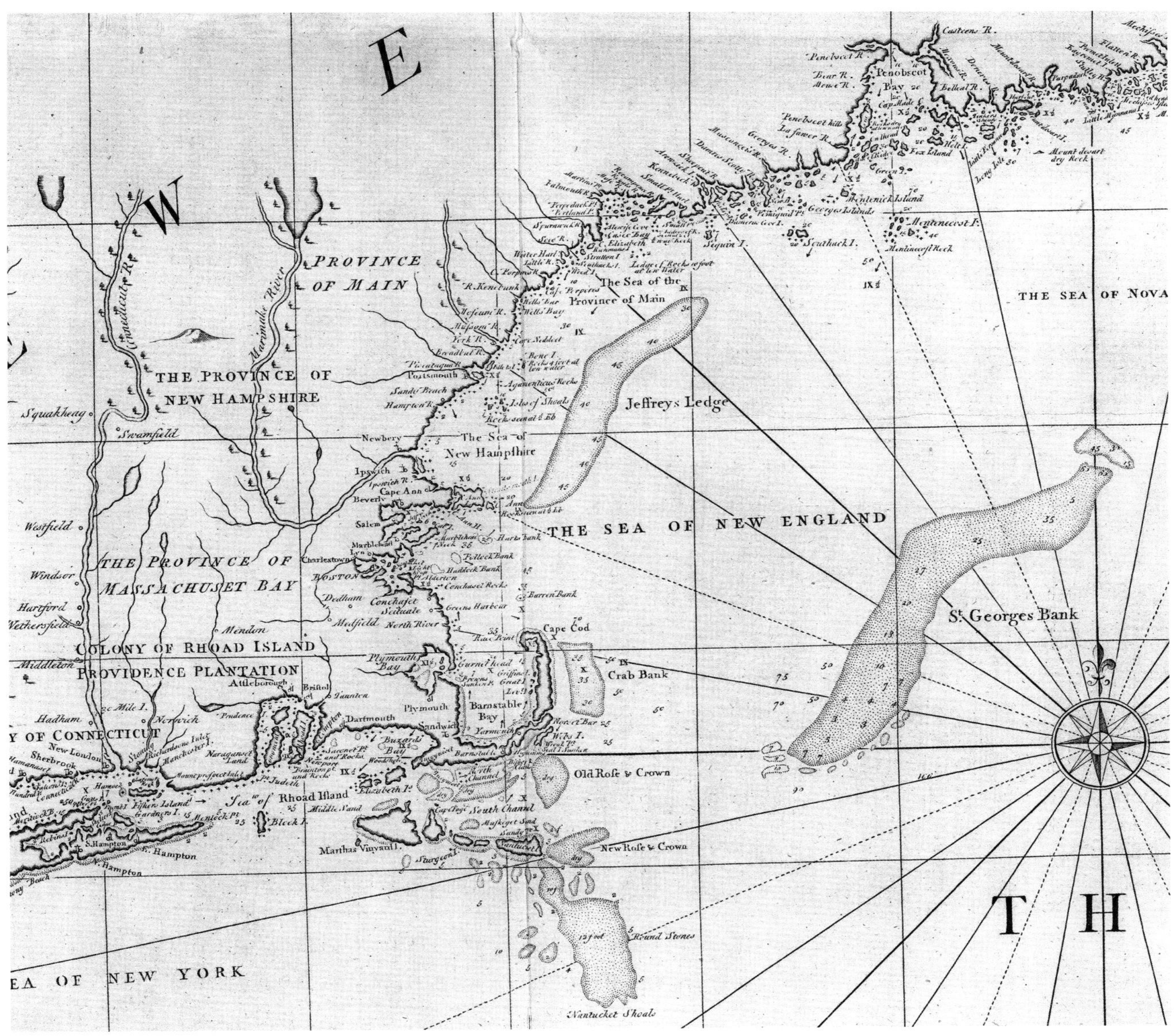

depressions—continued largely unabated during his lifetime. In 1849, just after Lane had reestablished himself in Gloucester and the Eastern (later Boston & Maine) Railroad had opened the town to new inland markets to the north and west, the winter months saw eight tons of iced fresh fish shipped every day to Montreal, upstate New York, and the Mississippi watershed by rail, followed by 3,584,000 pounds of cod and halibut brought into the port by 173 schooners in March, April, and May for drying and shipment eastward by sea.[10] A like quantity of fish would

FIGURE 66
Capt. Cyprian Southack, *A Map of the Coast of New England from Staten Island to the Island of Breton, as it was actually Survey'd by Capt. Cyprian Southack* ([London], 1744, reprinted 1794), detail. Engraving on paper, 17 × 21½ in. (43.18 × 54.61 cm). Courtesy, David Rumsey Map Collection, David Rumsey Map Center, Stanford University Libraries.

have arrived during the summer mackereling months and into the fall. Dealers from Montreal, in particular, understood to be "one of the greatest markets for fish on this continent," conveyed quantities of Gloucester's

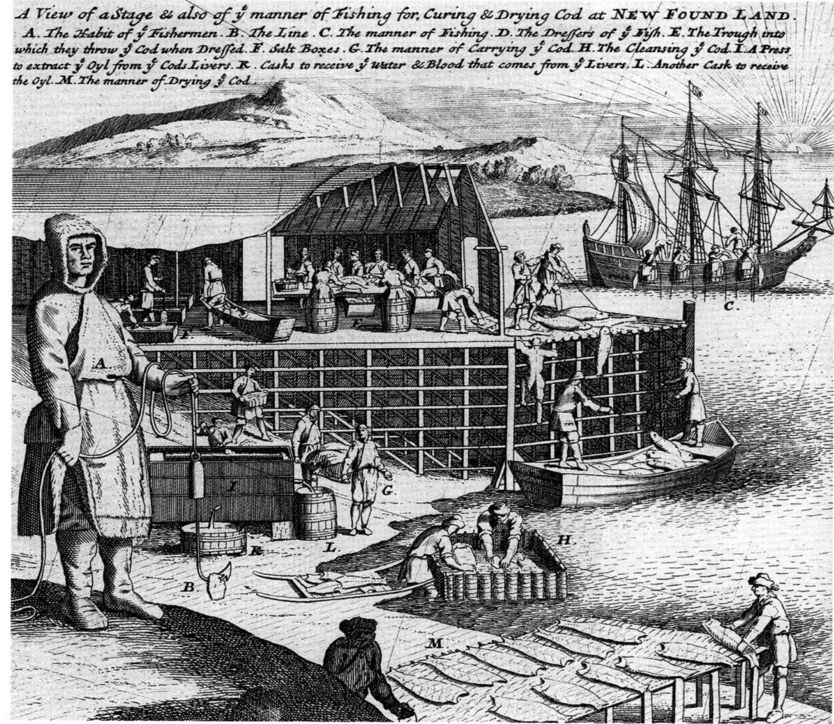

FIGURE 67
Herman Moll, *A View of a Stage & Also the Manner of Fishing for, Curing & Drying Cod at New Found Land*. Engraving. Inset in *North America* (fig. 65).

fish, shipped fresh in ice in winter, by four- and six-horse teams, a "weary and toilsome journey," but after 1849 they were shipped by rail to northern New Hampshire, substantially easing and speeding the journey.[11] Although much of the dried fish was shipped out in American ships, barks, and brigs involved in the Surinam trade, a surprising 147 foreign vessels, many from the Canadian provinces, arrived in Gloucester with wood, lumber, salt, and coal and left with fish and West Indian products.[12] Between 1840 and 1850 ships from the Canadian Maritime provinces also brought about one thousand immigrants to Gloucester to work in the fisheries, underlying the pivotal position of the town in employing seamen and its financial dominance of the North Atlantic fisheries.[13]

The activities and successes of the fishing and freighting fleets were the major forces governing daily life in antebellum Gloucester and were the major factor in the capacity of the town's population to support an artist. The surprising thing is that Lane painted these activities at a moment when most American artists, in their efforts to celebrate the natural wonders of an expansive and seemingly untouched virgin land, were suppressing evidence of economic activity—especially extractive industries—in their landscape paintings.

Gloucester's newspapers convey the scale, complexity, capital investment, and annual cycle involved in the town's antebellum fisheries. The schooner fleet's year began in January when several Gloucester vessels departed for Newfoundland to catch herring to be used as baitfish.[14] While awaiting their return, the main cohort of Gloucester fishermen took onto the schooners ice that had been cut from Cape Ann's freshwater ponds and provisions of salt pork, molasses, rum, and hard bread to supplement their largely fish diet.[15] A report in the January 13, 1860, edition of the *Cape Ann Advertiser* states that "about one hundred sail are now ready" to embark for St. George's Bank and "will start as soon as the first fresh herring arrive from Newfoundland." The following week the paper reported that the fishermen were "cutting a channel through the [sea] ice," which locked the schooners in the inner harbor, and that "the arrival of bait has set the fishermen to work in good earnest" on the ice channel. On February 3 the reporter announced that there were now "four vessels in port with herrings," apparently enough to furnish the fleet of schooners with bait. Clearly this was an organized, well-articulated, large-scale, cooperative (if also competitive) venture. That it also involved a majority of the town's capital and a large proportion of its manpower is also apparent. At that date a secondhand schooner (such as that Lane pictures with ruddy sails in *Gloucester Harbor* of 1852) sold for $1,515, nearly the cost of a very substantial house, and the one hundred schooners headed out for cod were managed by crews of eight or nine men and boys and so represented fully a third of the town's male population (fig. 10).[16]

In early February those one hundred schooners then embarked for St. George's Bank, 150 miles southeast of Gloucester, or for the Grand Banks, 750 miles northeast, in search of halibut and cod in the first of as many as nine trips over the course of the year.[17] In June the schooners turned their attention to hake (a subspecies of cod) and pursued them at night on Jeffrey's Ledge, just six miles off Gloucester, until mid-October (see fig. 66).[18] Other schooners took up the mackerel fisheries from July through mid-November, using lines, then seines, and after 1861, trawl fishing from dories on the Bay of St. Lawrence and the Bay of Chaleur in Canadian waters.[19] Others fished for haddock and pollock in the summer and fall on a part of Jeffrey's Ledge twelve miles off Cape Ann's Eastern Point.[20] This calendar was not arbitrary but responded to the behaviors of the quarry, including the itineraries of migrating mackerel and the feeding habits of hake, which brought them into shallow water only at night.

The North Atlantic's banks were, in those decades, teeming with fish, so these fisheries were, most years, very profitable. In 1849, during the cod and halibut season, 173 vessels employing 825 men brought more than one million pounds of fish into Gloucester each month.[21] For the year ending May 1, 1865, for instance, 341 Gloucester vessels engaged in the cod and mackerel fisheries brought in 154,938 barrels of mackerel (each barrel weighing 200 pounds) valued at $2,190,562, as well as 113,025 quintals (a little less than 25 million pounds) of codfish valued at $706,420, and cod oil that sold for $90,420.[22] The cod fishery, the largest branch of the fisheries, employed 4,600 men that year. The costs included $230,025 for salt.[23] Beyond these salted and dried cod and mackerel, Gloucester's fisheries brought in 6,000 tons of fresh fish valued at $360,000, 115,000 lobsters valued at $3,450, 14,000 barrels of baitfish, and 3,000 barrels of cod tongues and sounds.[24] These "tongues" were actually a muscle in the cod's neck, considered a delicacy, and the sounds were the fishes' swimming bladders, which were processed into isinglass, an essential ingredient in sizing fabrics and softening leather, in the satellite community of Rockport.[25] The only segments of Gloucester's economy that came even fractionally close to the value of the fisheries that year were construction (a church, a bank, 36 new stores, and 18 dwelling houses together costing $175,000 and employing 85 men) and sail manufacture. Eight sail lofts converted $106,550 worth of canvas into 425 new sails worth $127,800.[26] The new church, shops, and houses were a result of earlier profits from fish, and, of course, sailmaking was in demand because of the fisheries. The centrality of the fisheries to life on Cape Ann extended to remote details of life, including an ordinance exacting a $100 fine for damaging ice on freshwater ponds, essential for preserving the catch, and a bounty on crows, presumably because they foraged on the drying fish.[27]

Not a small part of what I term the cosmopolitanism of Gloucester's fisheries is the key factor of demand. Fish were most keenly desired elsewhere, especially in places that were culturally alien to Gloucester. While much of the town's fish was consumed in familiar Protestant locales such as Vermont, the main engine that drove this industry was the requirement for fast days (that is, meatless days) in Roman Catholic Spain, Portugal, Montreal, and the Spanish Caribbean islands such as Cuba.[28] Associated with abstinence and penance at the core of Catholic belief, fast days made up nearly a third of the calendar

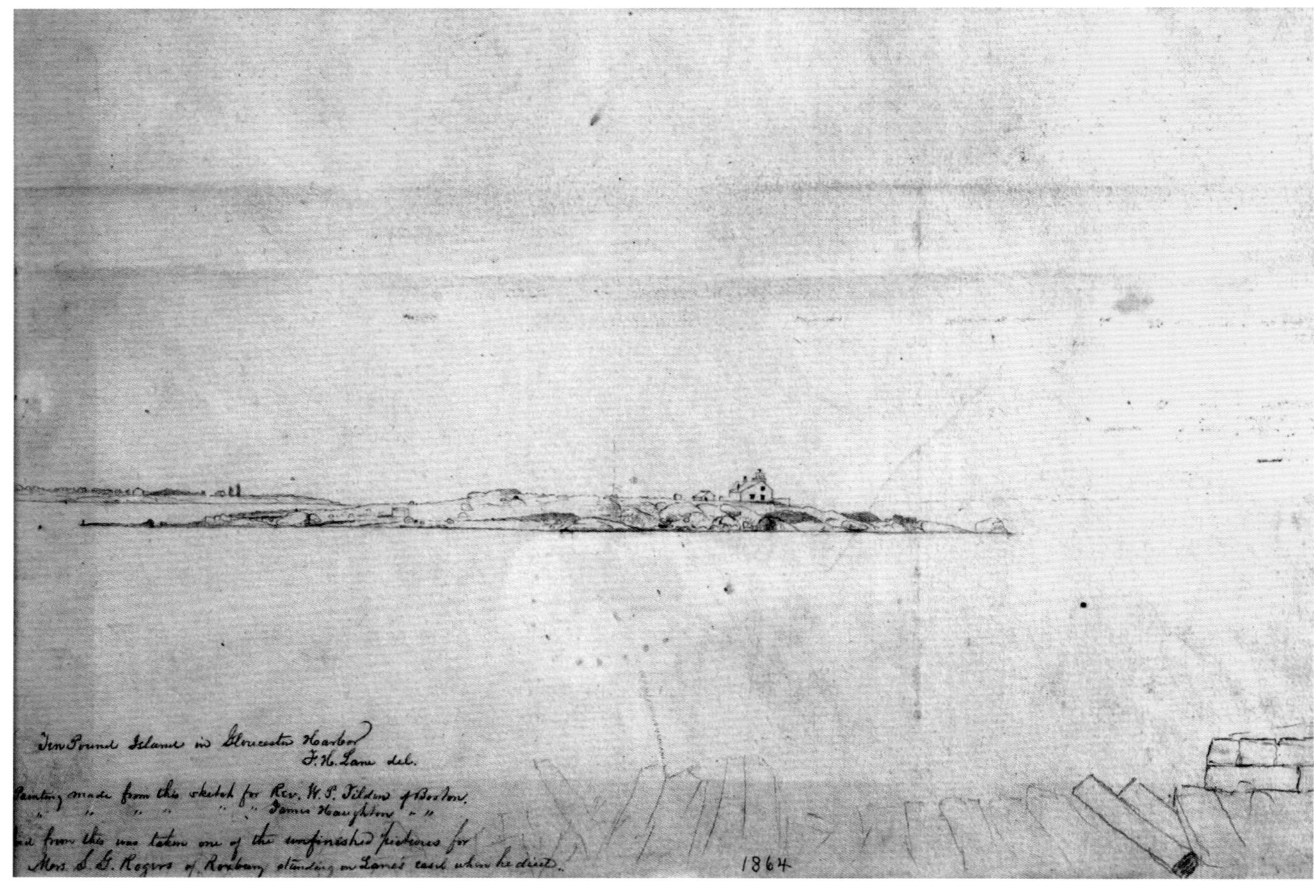

FIGURE 68
Fitz H. Lane, *Ten Pound Island in Gloucester Harbor*, 1864. Graphite on paper, 10 5⁄8 × 14 7⁄8 in. (27 × 37.8 cm). Cape Ann Museum, Gloucester, Massachusetts. Gift of Samuel H. Mansfield, 1927 (485.2).

year.[29] European and Caribbean fisheries were depleted, and the first-run fish caught in the western North Atlantic were understood to be superior to (as well as larger and more abundant than) those locally available.[30] Even more culturally alien was the tropical slave society of Dutch Guiana, which was Gloucester's primary trading partner through the first half of the nineteenth century. Here the third-grade salted dried fish was bought by the planters to provide necessary protein (until 1863) for the enslaved workforce on vast sugar plantations.[31] Of these distant cultures there was little direct visible impact in Gloucester beyond advertisements in the newspapers for Spanish wines and "West Indian goods," especially sugar, cocoa, and molasses.[32] But the result of the fisheries and their hungry markets was a town that, on the whole, appeared to the Boston steamship excursionists of 1828 as "wealthy." Every year new wharfs were run out; new churches, houses, and ships built; and fifteen or sixteen new schooners added to the fleet—all signs of fish-driven prosperity.[33]

The owners who commissioned the construction of new schooners and put up the capital to outfit voyages to the banks took half the gross, while the crew shared the other half.[34] For the fairly large cohort of owners (there were thirty-three, for instance, in the mackerel fleet that fished in the summer of 1862), their investment was at risk; for the fishermen, their livelihoods and lives

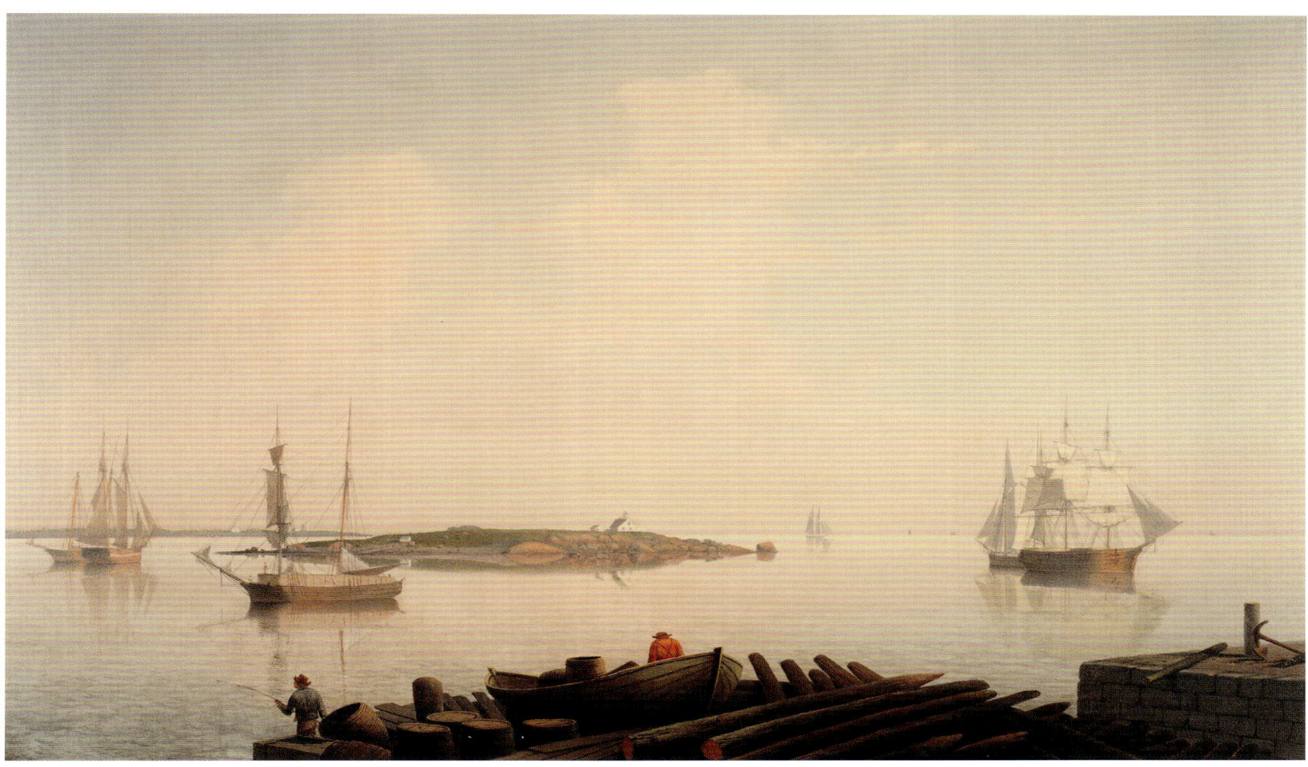

FIGURE 69
Fitz H. Lane, *Ten Pound Island, Gloucester*, n.d. Oil on canvas, 18½ × 30¼ in. (46.4 × 76.8 cm). Cape Ann Museum, Gloucester, Massachusetts. Gift of Bessie Stanwood, 1948 (1238).

were at risk, so care was taken by all concerned to return safely and with good fares.[35] The Atlantic was fecund. One schooner, for instance, returned from the Western Bank, four hundred miles north of Gloucester, off the coast of Nova Scotia, in 1860 with a halibut catch that sold for $1,135.[36] Another returned from the Grand Banks in 1865 with 75,000 pounds of halibut and 6,000 pounds of codfish, netting $3,468 for a four-week trip.[37] Generally speaking, these prodigious numbers continued during Lane's lifetime, but there is good evidence that this was the result of increasingly more effective technologies, not sustainability, as, after four centuries of concentrated fishing, the complex ecology of the North Atlantic was partly or wholly depleted of some species even before the start of the nineteenth century.[38] From the perspective of the inhabitants of Cape Ann, the alternatives to fishing were few. Over the course of Lane's lifetime, many formerly fish-oriented New Englanders found alternative livelihoods with the harnessing of river flows for manufacturing, but Gloucesterites without these resources or arable land actually increased their fisheries and developed larger, swifter schooners and new strategies for maintaining good fares.[39]

The autobiography of William Phillips Tilden (1811–1890) provides a rare glimpse of a common fisherman's experience. According to Joseph Stevens Jr.'s helpful annotations, Tilden, a patron of Lane's, was one of three individuals who commissioned paintings of Ten Pound Island from a drawing the artist made in 1864; one of these paintings survives (figs. 68 and 69). Like Lane, Tilden rose to distinction from a humble background with little education. He worked in the mackerel fleet from the time he was thirteen, in 1824 (when he

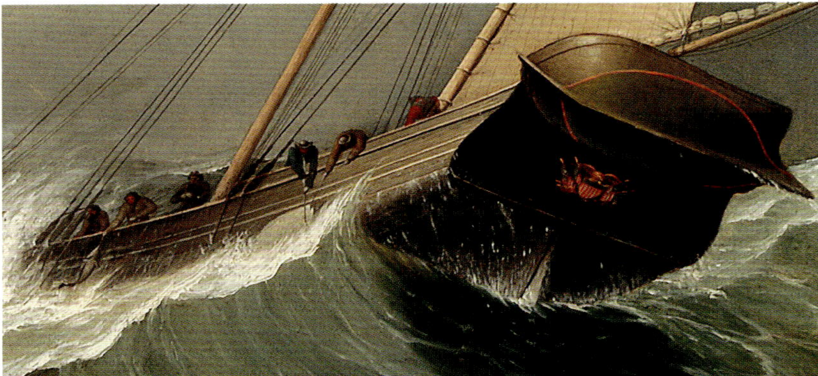

FIGURE 70
Fitz H. Lane, *A Smart Blow* (fig. 37), detail.

was the boat's "monkey," or most junior member), until he was sixteen (when he was "high line," or the most productive member, "for the season, taking with my own hands a hundred and thirty-four barrels"). He recounts, "On packing day the owners gave the whole crew a dinner at the hotel on shore. And such a dinner! . . . finishing up with plum pudding . . . *celestial*."[40] The mackerel fishery was particularly upbeat, involving fair-weather summer tours on the inner banks and the more sheltered Bays of St. Lawrence and Chaleur.[41] Gloucesterites appreciated not only the monetary rewards of mackereling but also the aesthetic. Lane was praised, for instance, for capturing in one of his paintings (now unlocated) "one of the most beautiful of all sights on the ocean—a large fleet of mackerel catchers" in the "glow of dawn, just moving from their night's anchorage, in every direction" off Good Harbor Beach.[42]

PAINTING FISH

Lane's strategy in painting the fisheries was not to suggest its massive scale and multiplicity of forms but to focus on single vignettes of activities that would have been familiar to his audience and would have, even in singularity, conjured the hundreds of schooners, thousands of men, and millions of fish involved. Characteristic is *A Smart Blow*, which depicts a half dozen fishermen using handlines—just as their predecessors had more than a century earlier—one to hook a cod (toward the bow of the schooner) and another a man-sized halibut (toward the stern), which necessitates the assistance of a second man with a gaff to land (figs. 37, 38, 70, and 71). The sea is tempestuous and the working conditions rough, but the whole enterprise—involving the design of schooners, the production of sails, the sawing of ice, the importation of salt, the sounding of shallows, the investments of owners, and the know-how of mariners—achieves its payoff in this moment Lane depicts of a successful catch. The cod in particular was regarded as "a wonder of nature," its population seemingly "inexhaustible by human skill or avidity."[43] It provided a "wholesome article of diet," "tongue" and roe delicacies, sounds to be made into isinglass, oil pressed from livers for many uses (including lighting Cape Ann's massive canvas factory), and gills that served as bait to catch more fish.[44] Lane shows just one cod and one halibut, but beyond the singular event, these represent a model for the three hundred catches that a single expert fisherman could land in one day and the thousands of other catches on the hundreds of schooners fishing that day.[45] In 1872 Lane's *Smart Blow* was engraved by portraitist Capt. Addison Center in the central portion of his design for the town seal of Gloucester, summing up the narrative that the town told about itself—its fisheries, its granite industry, its maritime trade, and, most centrally, its cod-based prosperity.[46]

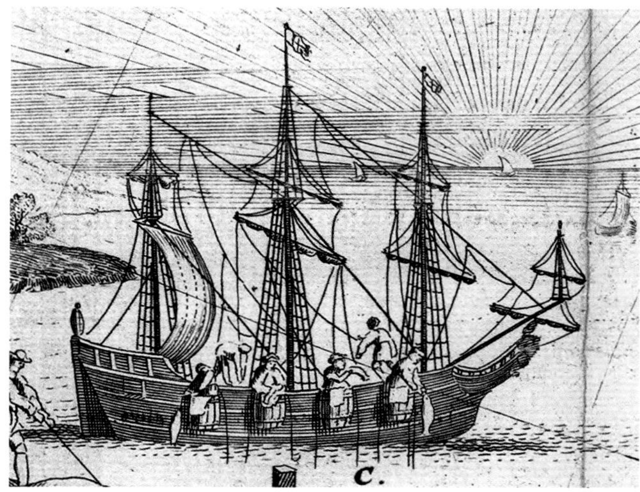

FIGURE 71
Herman Moll, *A View of a Stage & Also the Manner of Fishing for, Curing & Drying Cod at New Found Land* (fig. 67), detail.

But before the potential of the caught fish could be realized as family meal or commodity, this perishable cargo needed immediate and expert attention until fully stabilized, as the possibility of its spoilage before reaching market loomed large. Before 1846 the schooners did not carry ice; rather, seamen kept the fish alive on the fishing craft in watertight bins that admitted seawater, on return to land "bringing in the fish fresh and dressing them from the boats on the beach," according to a contemporary.[47] Lane frequently records this "dressing," a process in which the fish were gutted, beheaded, and cleaned. This practice, however, began to be supplanted with the cleaning of the fish at sea as early as 1831, and after 1848, when commercial ice became available and wharfs were constructed in Gloucester, fish were routinely cleaned, partially processed, and packed in ice at sea and then disembarked directly onto the wharfs, near the flake yards and packing houses.[48] In Gloucester, they were sold fresh or salted, often dried in the sun, always graded, and usually packed in barrels for sale and shipment.[49] Of these processing steps, the beachfront cleaning particularly interested Lane.

Many of Lane's paintings depict small-scale, quiet vignettes of what were actually very large-scale, busy fisheries as he would have known them in his childhood and early adulthood. Eschewing the opportunity to describe the "wharfloads of mackerel" that were a part of Gloucester's daily landscape, remarked on by the Boston and Salem visitors in their inaugural excursion in 1828, *Near Reef of Norman's Woe* pictures a small catch of moderately sized fish that appears to have been landed from the sloop in the right foreground; the fish are being cleaned by a workman sitting on an overturned tub at the edge of the water (figs. 72 and 73). The cleaned fish, in the narrative of the painting, are then placed in a fish basket and carried to a waiting cart. This is a two-man, one-horse operation, a kind of microview of the business, but the two larger fishing vessels in the mist offshore suggest more ambitious fisheries. It is morning if the silvery fish awaiting processing are hake, and evening if they are mackerel, the oculus of a rising or setting sun hanging in the mist at the dead center of the painting. Lane has turned the scene of industrial-scale everyday labor into poetry, but the ingredients of that poem are common incidents pared to essentials, distilled by the action of deep memory, and inflected with admiration for J. M. W. Turner, whose heliocentric works Lane would have seen praised and engraved in the London *Art Journal*, to which he subscribed.[50]

In *View of Gloucester Harbor* of 1848 a series of similar fish-centered vignettes occupy the foreground and the viewer's attention. An old-fashioned pinky schooner is drawn up on the stony beach where two men talk over a large basket of clams and a third sits at an impromptu trestle table cleaning cod, the fishes' discarded heads and entrails conspicuously littering the ground (figs. 74 and 75). Two other men carry a heavy load on a fish pallet that appears to have changed little from that illustrated by Moll in 1709 (fig. 67). Since by 1848 the fish were generally cleaned at sea and only the vendible parts of the fish came to Gloucester, it is clear that this is a retrospective look at the uses of Harbor Cove, an area that was, by midcentury, congested with wharves (see fig. 2). Similarly, the artist has tidied up the area of the

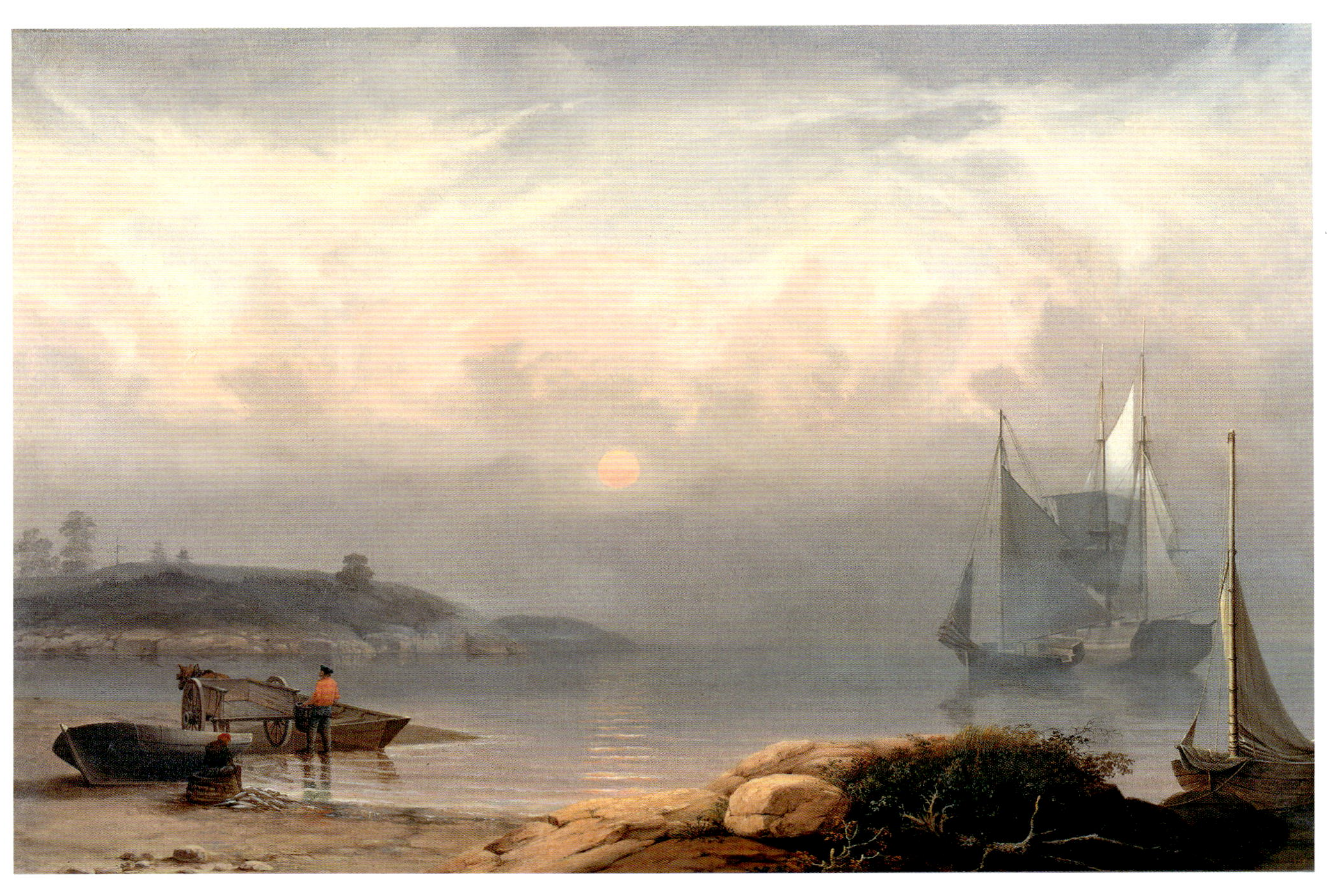

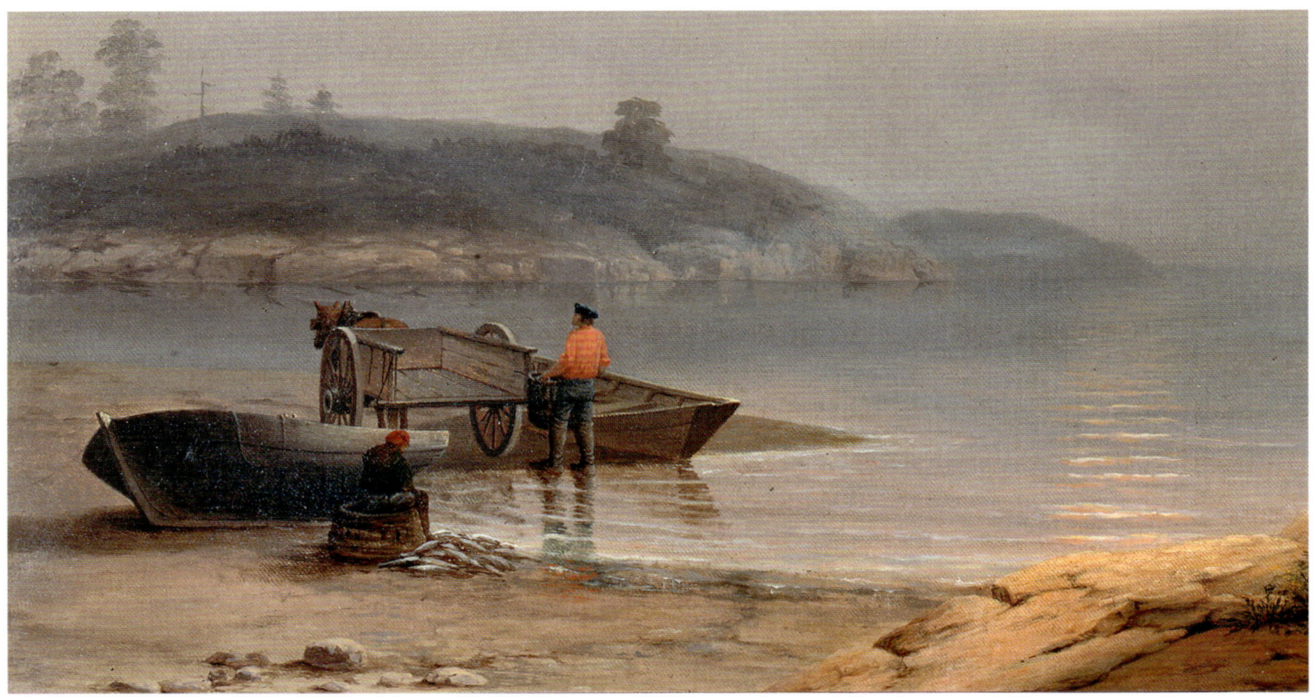

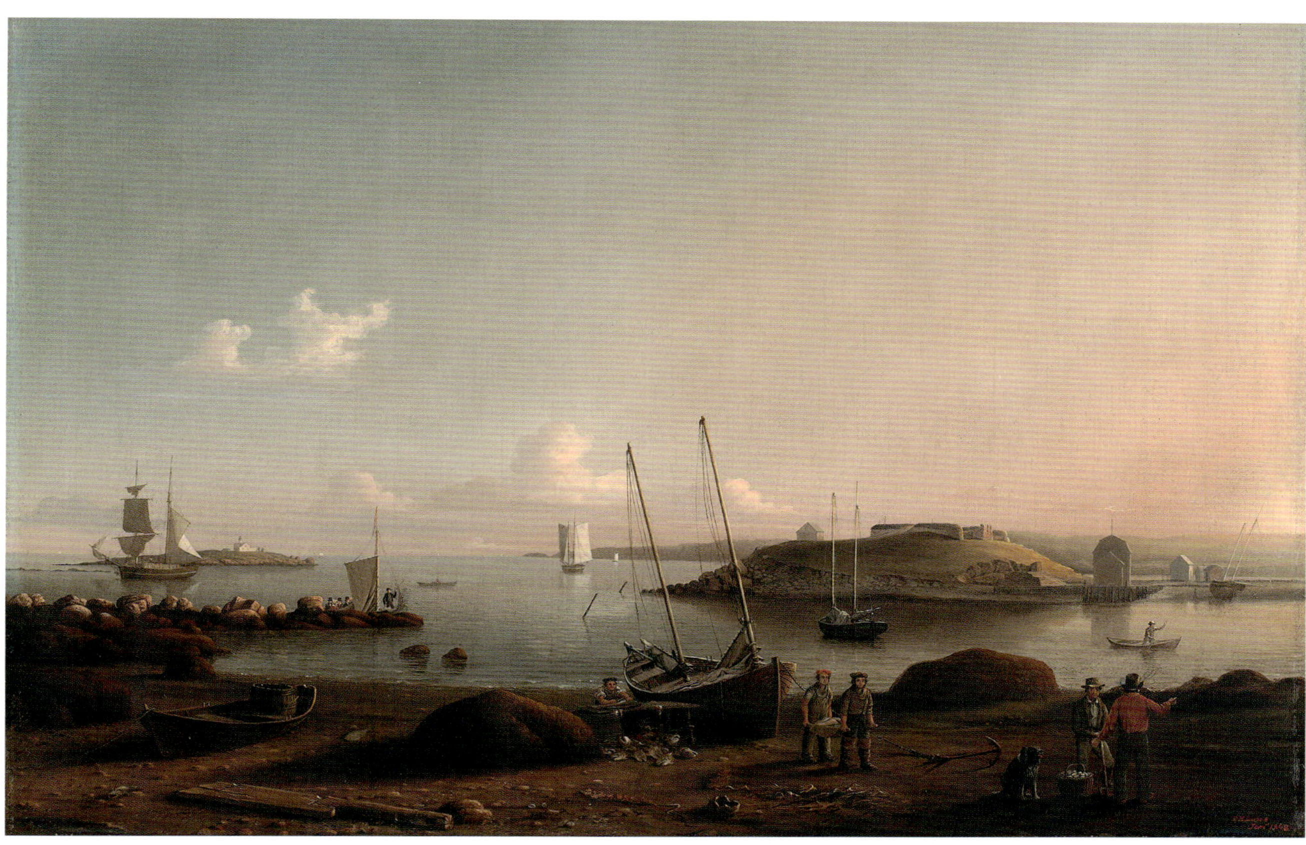

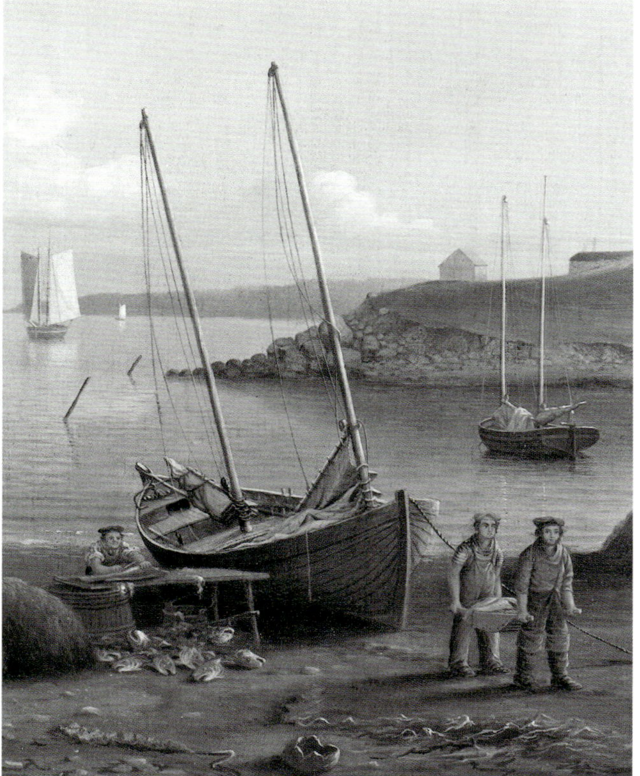

FIGURE 72 (OPPOSITE TOP)
Fitz H. Lane, *Near Reef of Norman's Woe*, n.d. Oil on canvas, 33 × 44 in. (83.8 × 111.8 cm). Commissioned by Sidney Mason. Rough Point Collection, Newport Restoration Foundation, Newport, Rhode Island (1999.382).

FIGURE 73 (OPPOSITE BOTTOM)
Fitz H. Lane, *Near Reef of Norman's Woe*, n.d. (fig. 72), detail.

FIGURE 74 (TOP)
Fitz H. Lane, *View of Gloucester Harbor*, 1848. Oil on canvas mounted on panel, 27 × 41 in. (68.58 × 104.14 cm). Virginia Museum of Fine Arts, Richmond. Adolph D. and Wilkins C. Williams Fund (62.32). Photo: Katherine Wetzel © Virginia Museum of Fine Arts.

FIGURE 75 (LEFT)
Fitz H. Lane, *View of Gloucester Harbor*, 1848 (fig. 74), detail.

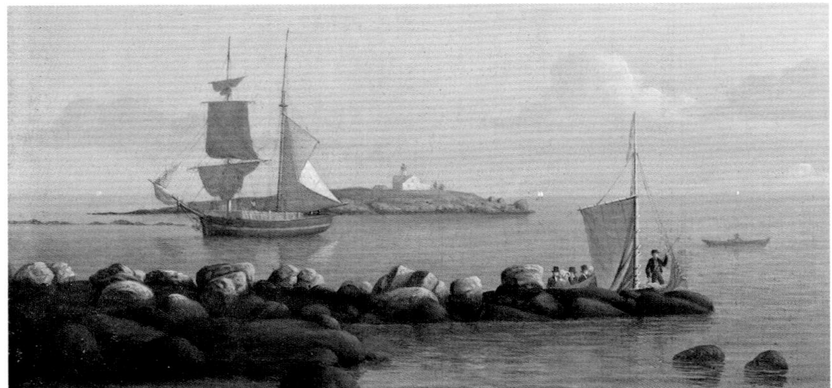

FIGURE 76
Fitz H. Lane, *View of Gloucester Harbor*, 1848 (fig. 74), detail.

Revolutionary-era fort, a structure that by 1848 had largely crumbled and was obscured by surrounding buildings, not grandly commanding its eminence as Lane has remembered it and depicted it here.[51] One wonders what this beachfront would have looked like if even a fraction of the one million pounds of cod and halibut that were landed at Gloucester each month in the late 1840s had been cleaned in the harbor, the waste from this process left to ornament the landscape. This question becomes more immediate when we note the small pleasure craft filled with top-hatted and bonneted excursionists coming around the small jetty (fig. 76). How compatible, really, were these two economies? After all, fish heads were not understood to be anything but refuse in Lane's day; indeed, the *Gloucester Telegraph* included a ribald article that described boys who, taking umbrage at a group of peddlers in nearby Provincetown, "pelted the rascals out of the town with cod fish heads."[52] It is apparent that the dressing of fish continued to occur at least in outlying parts of Cape Ann into the second half of the nineteenth century, as attested by a complaint registered in the newspaper in the spring of 1860: "The numerous pleasant drives about the Cape are rendered odious by the piles of fish offal putrefying by the road side . . . [in the vicinity of] Little Good Harbor Beach. . . . And these offences against good taste, decency and the public health, continue year by year."[53] But in Lane's portrayal the fish refuse—at this scale—is more matter-of-fact local color than alarming. It appears as a blunt reminder of the facts of the fisheries, but portrayed at the scale of a cottage industry.

Clearly for Lane, the fish and those who caught and cleaned them were foreground or middle-ground material, while the touring, excursioning locals and visitors were usually positioned as they are in this painting and in Sidney Mason's *Gloucester Harbor* of 1852—that is, as recessive elements (fig. 63). The somewhat awkward stocky fish tenders in their overalls, flannel shirts, over-the-shoulder suspenders, sturdy boots, and soft non-descript caps are of interest to Lane. They also appear, together with the fish they knew so well, in other works of the 1840s and 1850s, for instance, *The Fort and Ten Pound Island, Gloucester, Massachusetts*, and *Gloucester Inner Harbor* (figs. 6, 27, 51, and 77). A recurring figure is that of a man whose head has been "replaced" by the material burdens of his work—a bundled fish net in *Gloucester Inner Harbor* and a heavy cask in *Castine Harbor* (figs. 78 and 79). By this device Lane subsumes the worker's personhood in his labor and marks him as an embedded participant as well as active agent in this world of physical work within the marine economies. Lane was not a genre painter, and his mastery of the human figure does not approach his capacity to render vessels, water, and atmosphere, but he almost always includes these denizens of the sea—in the rigging of ships, on the beach cleaning fish, or at the oars of small vessels.[54] These are the crafters

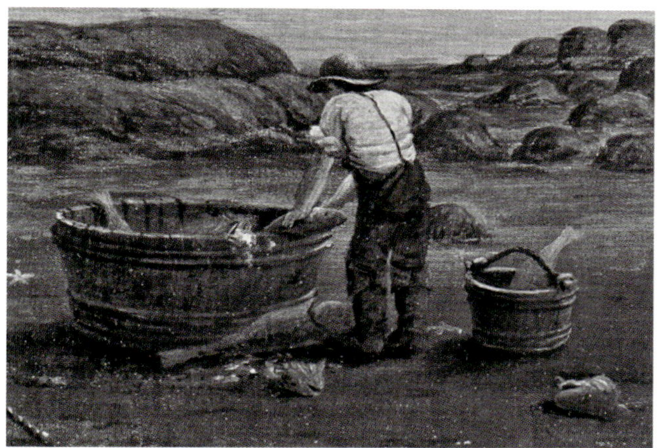

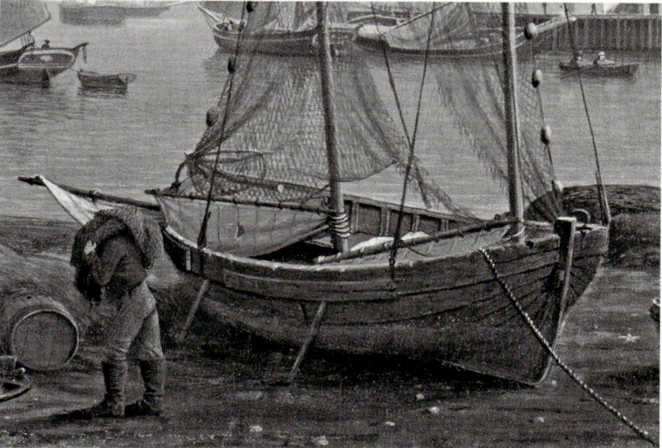

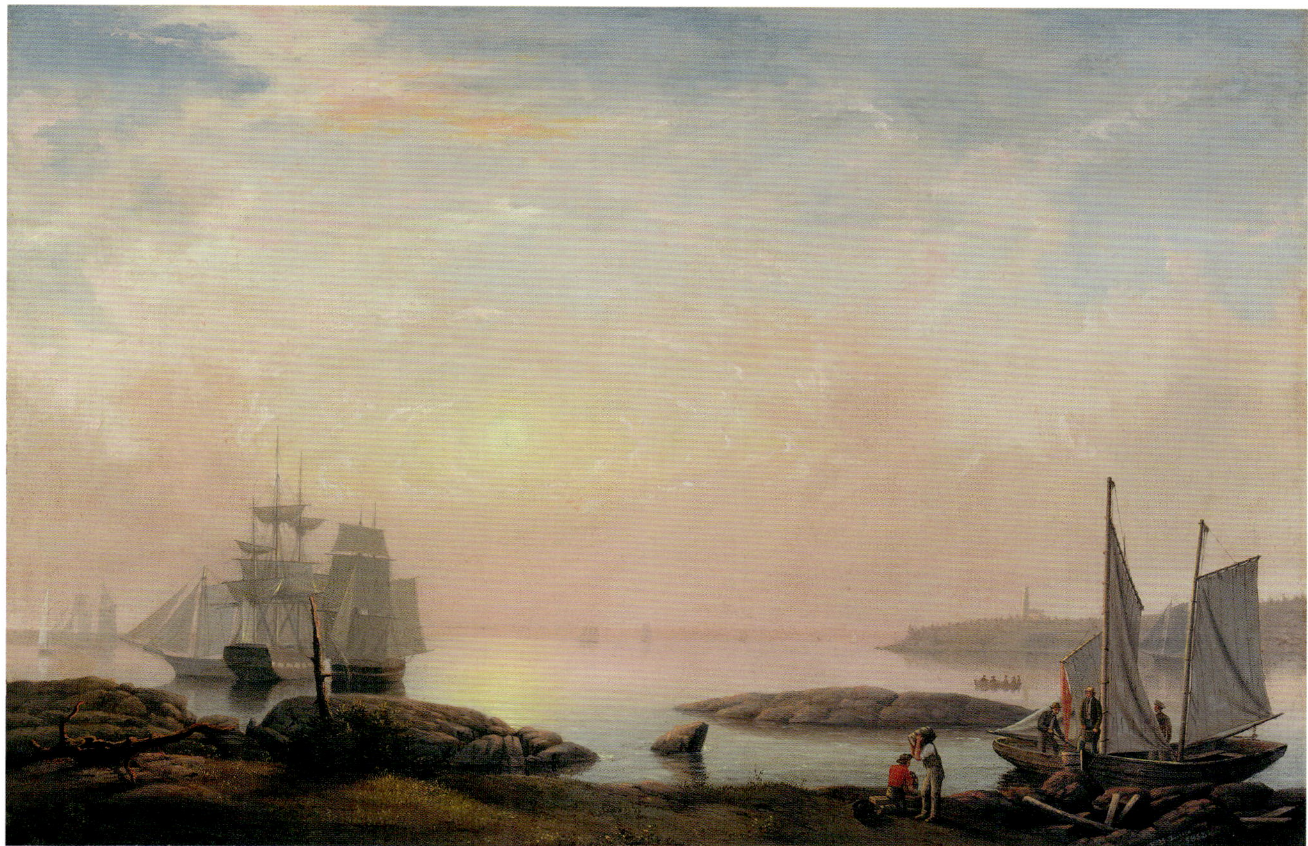

FIGURE 77 (TOP LEFT)
Fitz H. Lane, *Gloucester Inner Harbor*, 1850 (fig. 6), detail.

FIGURE 78 (TOP RIGHT)
Fitz H. Lane, *Gloucester Inner Harbor*, 1850 (fig. 6), detail.

FIGURE 79 (BOTTOM)
Fitz H. Lane, *Castine Harbor*, 1852. Oil on canvas, 20⅛ × 30⅛ in. (51.1 × 76.5 cm). Portland Museum of Art, Maine. Bequest of Elizabeth B. Noyce (1996.38.29). Image courtesy of Luc Demers.

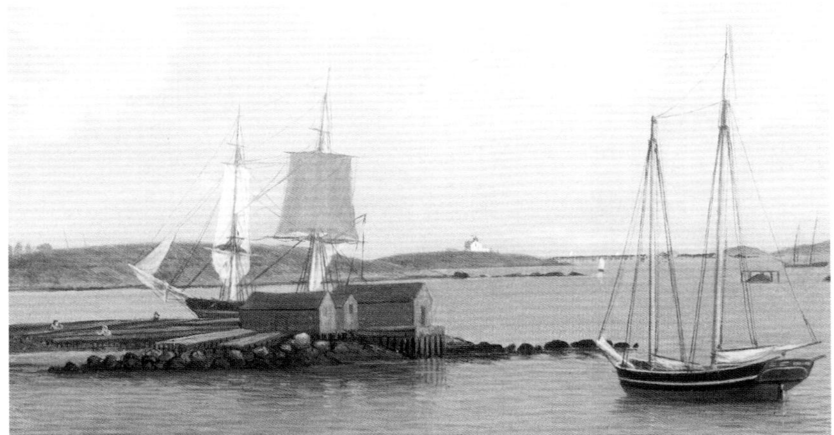

FIGURE 80
Fitz H. Lane, *Gloucester Harbor*, 1847 (fig. 5), detail.

of the landscape and the men who make the economy of Gloucester work; with these figures he reminds us that this is not a "found" unpopulated landscape but a thoroughly inhabited one created by many hands, made and remade daily by cooperative, coordinated, knowledgeable, laborious, and often stoic efforts.

The last venue in which Gloucester's fish were visible on the landscape was the extensive flake yards, where the split fish were dried, and thus preserved, and readied for packing in barrels and shipping abroad. In *Gloucester Harbor* of 1847 and his 1836 lithograph of the city, Lane depicts the long tables on which the flattened fish lay for days drying in the sun, and the adjacent foursquare vernacular buildings that were the packing establishments in which they were barreled for shipment (figs. 5, 11, 80, and 81).[55]

In short, from hooked catch on the schooners at sea through cleaning and salting, washing and drying, in town, Lane chronicles the fisheries of his native place in evocative, summarized, and sometimes historic form. Not only is this the narrative of many of his paintings taken together, it is also suggested within individual works; for instance, Five Pound Island, in the central middle distance of *Gloucester Harbor* of 1847, is flanked by a fishing schooner of the type that caught and delivered the fish on the right, largely covered with the drying tables and packing plant where the fish are readied for export, and backed by a two-masted brig that will take the fish to distant markets around the globe—the fisheries in a tightly compressed but also picturesque narrative nutshell (figs. 5 and 80).

PERILOUS SEAS

An upbeat *Gloucester Telegraph* article from June 1850, about the handsome new schooners being built in Essex to augment Gloucester's fishing fleet, concludes: "We wish them all quick voyages, full fares, and ready sales at good prices."[56] This benediction calls to mind the unpredictability of fishing: sometimes the fish were scarce, and sometimes a returning schooner found the market glutted, reducing profits. But as financially precarious as the fishing business might have been, these were not the major perils of the fisheries.[57] George H. Procter, whose family's store carried artists' supplies and Lane's lithographs among its diverse merchandise and, on at least one occasion, exhibited a Lane painting, begins his account of Gloucester's fisheries thus:

> To watch the pretty crafts when they sail away on their summer cruises for mackerel, gives one an idea

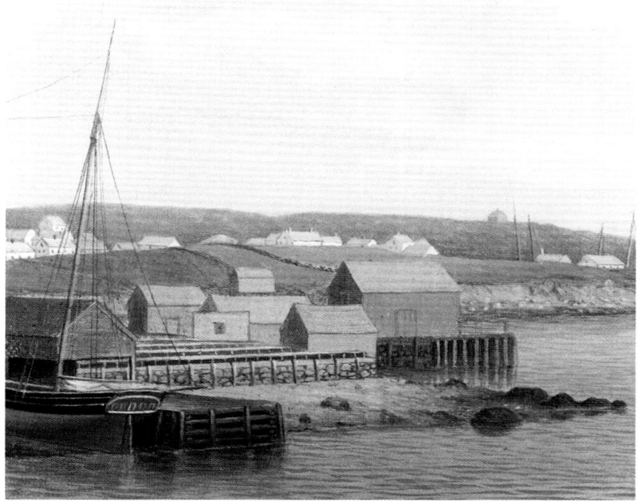

FIGURE 81
Fitz H. Lane, *Gloucester Harbor*, 1847 (fig. 5), detail.

> that such an avocation is replete with enjoyment. These trips are in reality very pleasant, affording considerable excitement, much jollity, and agreeable labor, which yield good returns; this may well be called the sunny side of the picture. . . . [But when] winter comes, and the necessities of the fishermen, many of whom have large families [to support], render it imperative that they must follow winter fishing on Georges [Bank] or to the [Grand] Banks, then is presented a far different aspect . . . keen blasts, piercing cold, boisterous winds, murky sky and raging waters . . . thick driving snow-storm[s] . . . [and] terrible gales with all their accompaniments of disaster and discomfort.[58]

Lane's *A Smart Blow* conveys some idea of the harsh conditions verging on "disaster and discomfort" under which cod and halibut were caught in the winter months in the North Atlantic in the period of Lane's maturity as an artist (figs. 37 and 70). The hazards included not only "smart" (tempestuous) winds, which created turbulent seas, but also dark nights, which exposed the schooners anchored for hake fishing on Jeffrey's Ledge, "directly in the track of steamboats and coasters," to collision.[59] Subsequent to the introduction of trawl fishing from dories in the 1850s, "another peril [was] added to the fisheries, viz.: that of [the schooners'] being lost from the dories while [men in these small open boats visited] trawls, or strayed during the fog which oftentimes shuts in on the fishing grounds . . . [resulting in] death by starvation, or . . . [being] swallowed up by the waves."[60] Francis Bennett, a teenage dry-goods clerk working for Samuel Stevens, noted with some dismay such an event in his diary on May 25, 1854: "A vessel got in from George's [Bank,] having left four of her men in open boats on the banks. They went out in the boats to attend to their trawls . . . [then] a thick fog [descended] and it is supposed they could not find their vessel."[61] Such incidents created a sense of anxiety, pity, and dread in the population of Gloucester, as virtually every family had members at risk on the sea and accounts of accidents and catastrophes were frequent. Empathetic Annette Babson, whose brothers were Lane patrons, noted in her diary on January 22, 1847: "Tis the most bitter day we have had yet. The snow flies in clouds and the house totters to its foundations. How I pity our poor fishermen on Georges [Bank] and homeward bound mariners [from the West Indies]. What lives of peril, anxiety and suffering are theirs."[62]

In some cases the newspapers gave matter-of-fact accounts of marine losses with strong undercurrents of pathos. When four fishing schooners on George's Bank disappeared without a trace, for instance, the *Cape Ann Advertiser* on March 16, 1860, listed not only the value of the vessels, and when and where they were built, but also the name of each of the crew members, his marital status, and the number of now fatherless children.[63] Less than a month later, near a buoyant article on Gloucester's imminent role as "the head quarters of the fishing business, and the largest market of the sale of fish in the world," appeared a brief notice of the death of "the fortieth man lost overboard or otherwise on Georges Bank this season" (fig. 82).[64] Indeed, one reason that Gloucester became the center of North Atlantic fisheries was that communities with options bowed out. Marblehead, for

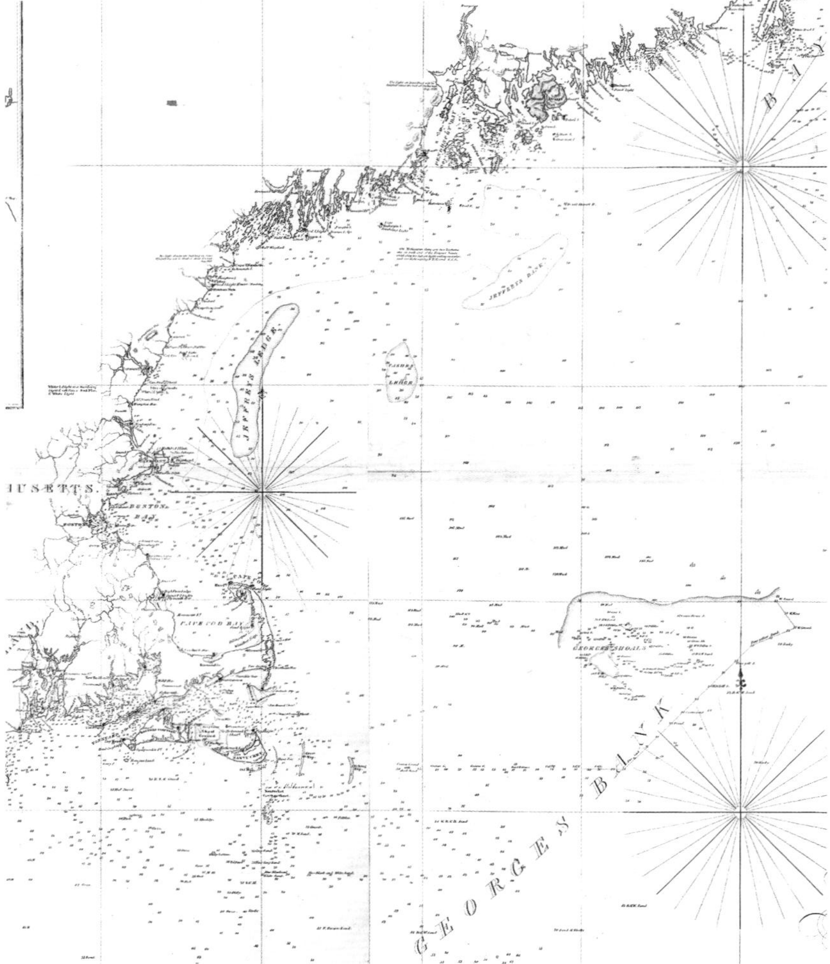

FIGURE 82
Edmund M. Blunt, *The North Eastern Coast of North America from New York to Cape Canso* [. . .] (New York, 1828), detail. David Rumsey Map Collection, David Rumsey Map Center, Stanford University Libraries.

instance, formerly a competitor, gave up serious fisheries in the wake of a gale in September 1846 that destroyed 10 vessels and killed 65 men.[65] By the end of 1860 Gloucester, with a census count of 10,904 that year, had lost 73 men and 7 vessels. But this figure pales in comparison to the record of 1862, when 162 Gloucester men and 19 vessels were lost at sea.[66] In a single "terrible gale" in February 1862, "there were about seventy sail at anchor very near to each other" on George's Bank when a storm of "terrible violence" created "fearful collisions" and "thirteen vessels [were] lost with their entire crew, and two [schooners] abandoned. . . . Nearly every [surviving] vessel [of the seventy] met with more or less disaster, losing cable and anchors, booms, masts, or were so badly stove up hardly to be able to get back [to] port." In sum, "There were lost in this gale *one hundred and twenty men and fifteen vessels, leaving seventy widows and one hundred and forty fatherless children*" (emphasis in the original).[67] Two years later, in 1864, another disastrous year, 85 men died, and 13 schooners were lost, making of "Georges [Bank] a vast burial ground . . . [a] vast sepulcher, swallowing up many a young man in the pride of his youth, many a middle-aged toiler upon whose earnings a loving family were dependent, and many an aged one whose voyage of life" would have continued a few years longer, a "fearful record . . . of woe and bereavement."[68] Yet each year they returned to fish.

Procter calculates that in the midcentury decades Gloucester's fisheries each year, on average, lost twenty-eight men and six vessels and created ten widows and twenty fatherless children.[69] Such loss of life among those in the fishing fleet contributed to an impressive gender disparity in Massachusetts, reported to have fourteen thousand more females than males in the 1830 census.[70]

Indirectly, the fisheries also contributed to the loss of property in the town during Gloucester's periodic disastrous urban fires. In 1830 about twenty houses and forty stores, shops, and other buildings burned to the ground. In spite of the fact that "the females exerted themselves in removing goods and furniture and also in passing water, for 6 or 8 hours," the fact that about six hundred of the town's "most efficient men" were absent on the schooners contributed to the loss of so many buildings.[71] Surprisingly and fortuitously, "a party of Penobscot Indians were in town, who also exerted themselves [in fighting the fire] with great bravery," preventing an even worse outcome.[72]

Living in proximity to death and disaster created in Gloucesterites, according to one observer, "intrepid mariners" characterized by a "noble fearlessness" and "unstinted generosity which ministers to the wants of the sufferers."[73] Called upon not only to support one another, they periodically extended their aid to outsiders. In December 1839, for instance, when Gloucester's fishing fleet was hauled up for a few weeks between fishing campaigns, a severe gale, perhaps a hurricane, forced sixty-five coasters from other ports to take refuge in Gloucester's capacious harbor, where they anchored in view of the town (fig. 3). Within a few hours the storm became so furious that many of these out-of-town vessels had been ripped from their anchorages, thirty were dismasted, and "twenty wrecks were strewn along the shore"; as well, "twenty lives were known to have been lost."[74] The locals rescued those they could reach, and "everything that sympathetic men and women could do was done for the comfort of the living and for the recovery of the bodies of the dead."[75] A similar severe gale in 1849 brought "upwards of four hundred vessels inside of the Point," with happier results, but knowledge of the destructive force of the sea, even within the precincts of their harbor, must have been a matter of personal observation and daily concern to all in Lane's Gloucester.[76]

Many scholars who have written about Lane's Brace's Rock paintings executed in 1864 and featuring a ruined sloop or dismasted schooner in a quiet cove associate these works with the Civil War (see figs. 13, 14, and 15). Characteristic is the art historian who speaks of the Brace's Rock works as "the extreme of the sublime of silence . . . painted during the American apocalypse," and another scholar who includes these paintings in an extended discussion of pictures of stranded boats as expressive of "the issue of the fate of the national enterprise. . . . The Civil War . . . was tied to the motif of the wrecked or stranded boat."[77] But sometimes a wrecked schooner is just a wrecked schooner. Cape Ann was, every year, the site of many fatal wrecks of vessels large and small. Many of these misfortunes happened in the vicinity of Brace's Cove as vessels missed the opening to Gloucester's harbor in a fog or mistook the cove for the harbor entrance. John J. Babson, a Lane patron and brother of Annette, mentioned above, in his *History of the Town of Gloucester*, describes the particularly "melancholy shipwreck" of the brig *Persia* on the night of March 5, 1829, in a violent snowstorm en route from Trieste to Salem; the vessel was cast ashore near Brace's Rock, and "all on board were lost. . . . [N]ine bodies were found on the shore. Four of these were delivered to their friends, and the remainder were buried from the Universalist Church [in Gloucester]."[78] The residents, in other words, not only mourned their own but had occasion to witness such disturbing scenes of the loss of strangers. Lane and his fellow residents of Gloucester had every reason for melancholy at Brace's Cove, even on the bright summer day in 1863 when Lane did his drawing of the site in the company of the Stevens family, which resulted in five commissions (see fig. 13). There was considerably more immediate reason to mourn the disasters of the sea than the disasters of war.[79] As George Procter, the statistician, from the perspective of the 1870s, put it: "Notwithstanding the large number [of] men, from this town, who served in the army and navy during the rebellion, the loss of life from the casualties of war was far less than the losses at sea for the same period of time. There were two hundred and eighty-two lives lost in the fishing business from this port during the four years of the war, while the record of those who have been killed, or died in the service, is less than half that number."[80]

Of course the Civil War was disruptive as it siphoned off manpower and resulted in its own dismaying record of both local and national loss, but it reduced the cod fleet by only 7 percent and appears to have touched Gloucester less immediately and less forcefully than the town's quotidian tragedies.[81] The fishing fleet was disrupted by a Confederate bark that harassed Gloucester's fishermen, capturing crews and burning four schooners on June 24, 1863, prompting owners to visit the governor and naval command in Washington, requesting naval protection for the fishing fleet.[82] Washington responded by seizing fifty-three acres on Eastern Point, constructing earthworks, and equipping this impromptu fort with seven cannon and a company of artillerymen.[83] As traumatic as the events of the war were for Gloucester—and the rebels certainly did hit home by making it clear that they could and would harass the fishing fleet at sea—the tone of pathos and loss apparent in Lane's Brace's Rock paintings is more certainly linked to the immediate disasters associated with the fisheries with which Gloucesterites lived year in and year out than to the political upheaval and military losses of the Civil War.

THE CULTURE OF LOOKING

The major cultural shift that moved New Englanders in all walks of life to seek day trips, vacations, excursions, or hours after work out in nature had occurred long before the Civil War, and the miseries of that prodigious national conflict did not diminish this enthusiasm. The *Cape Ann Light and Gloucester Telegraph* reported in August 1862: "The war does not affect the number of visitors to our fashionable watering places. The influx of visitors at Newport is unprecedently [*sic*] large, every cottage and room has been taken. At Saratoga, there is full as large a number of arrivals as for several years past."[84] Cape Ann was not in the same league as Newport or Saratoga, but it did have a substantial summer "influx" from early in the nineteenth century, a trend accelerated by the ease of access provided by the extension of the Eastern Rail line into Gloucester in 1848 and on to Rockport shortly thereafter. But it is important to note that, at least in Gloucester, this tendency to valorize nature, including sea bathing, and the admiration of "scenery" (and, by extension, landscape painting) was not confined to outsiders or to the local elite. While fishermen surely did not see the need to balance their work lives with stints in the fresh air, other working Gloucesterites did.

What brought locals and "strangers" alike to Gloucester's beaches and other sites of recreation was the dawning of new ideas about health, exercise, and fresh air. Cape Ann was understood to offer respite from Boston's summer heat, the threat of cholera, and the increasingly enclosed and anxious nature of urban employment.[85] Locals were encouraged to "take regular exercise in the open air," to relieve "the dust and toils of daily labors, strifes and petty rivalries of real life," and, especially, to "plunge into the limpid wave after a day's confinement to business."[86] They were advised to remedy the ill effects of "sedentary employments" and consider "rowing a boat" or engaging in the "far more gentle exercise" of managing a sailboat, in other words, to engage in activities for pleasure that others in Gloucester did to make a living.[87] The local papers abound with reports of pleasure parties and sailing picnics, and schooners are advertised as boats for "Pleasure or Fishing," suggesting a certain interchangeability of these vessels' functions as Gloucester's workers seized on outdoor activities and owners of resources saw reason to be flexible in accommodating either the dominant economy or this new taste for boating parties.[88]

In several of his paintings—including *On the Wharves, Gloucester Harbor* and *Ten Pound Island, Gloucester*—Lane depicts vignettes of local workingmen fishing for

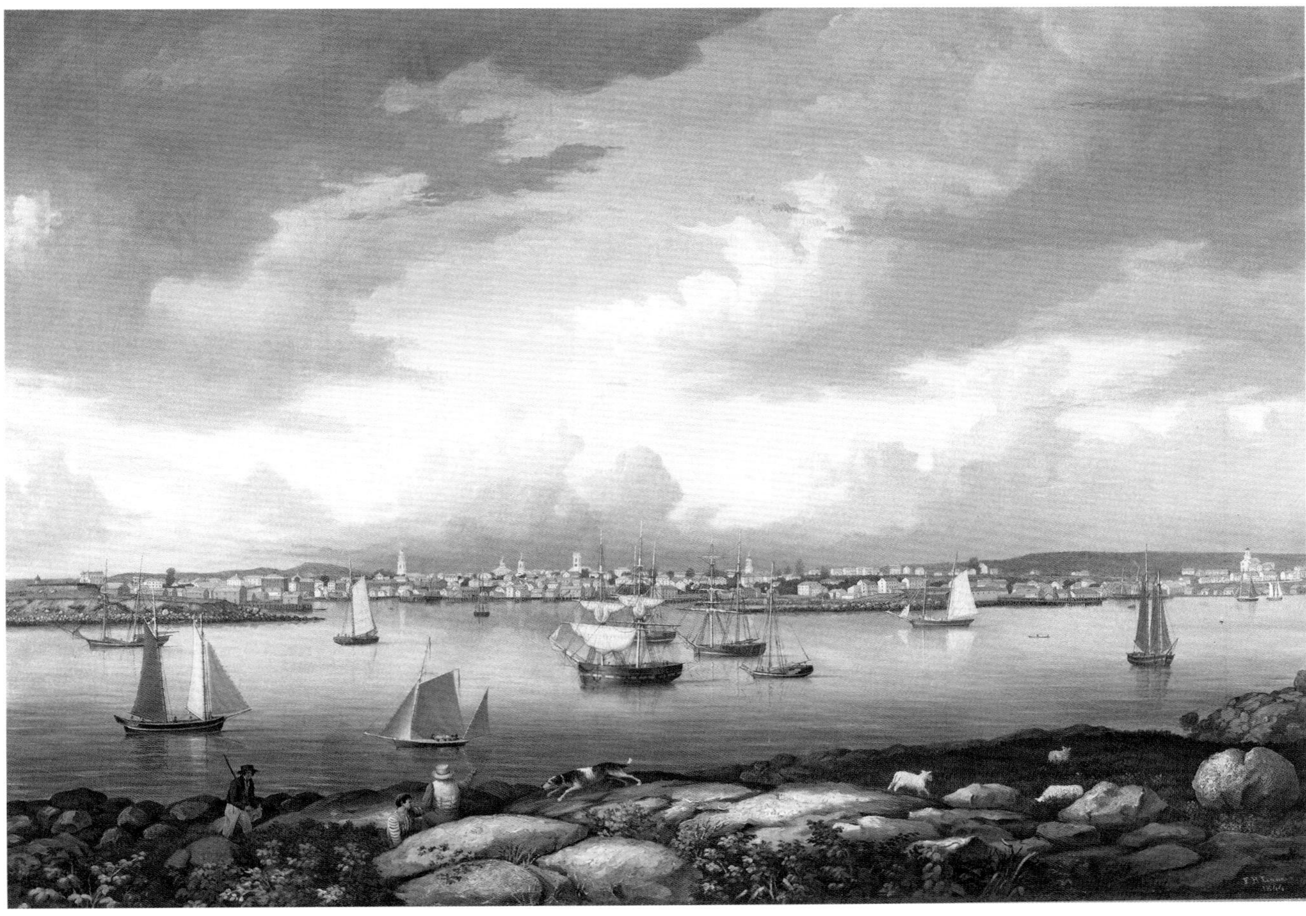

FIGURE 83
Fitz H. Lane, *Gloucester Harbor from Rocky Neck*, 1844. Oil on canvas, 34 × 45¾ in. (86.4 × 116.2 cm). Cape Ann Museum, Gloucester, Massachusetts. Gift of Mrs. Jane Parker Stacy (Mrs. George O. Stacy), 1948 (1289.1a).

recreation within scenes dominated by the more serious commercial fisheries (figs. 53 and 69). Each of these fishermen sits, pole in hand, at the edge of the water, his back to the viewer and his attention on both the leisure task at hand and the panorama of harbor activity spread before him. Unlike the cod-catchers in *A Smart Blow*, who are completely absorbed in their difficult task under dangerous conditions, these dockside fishermen not only are part of the artist's tableau; they also model quiet, reflective absorption in the scene—that is, the culture of looking.

Gloucesterites from all walks of life also enjoyed boat parties, picnics, and "chowdering," especially on holidays, hiring schooners for excursions to day-trip destinations around the cape.[89] Lane includes these vessels and their mixed-gender, brightly clothed participants packed "like mackerel" in sloops and schooners within several of his harborscapes (e.g., figs. 74, 76, 83, and 84). These excursionists, men and women, both locals and summer visitors, are tertiary elements in Lane's works, as they were in the economy of Gloucester. Two rare departures, however, bring these recreational sailors into the foreground, in paintings Lane executed in Maine, where, tellingly, he was himself a summer visitor (figs. 85 and 86). In the

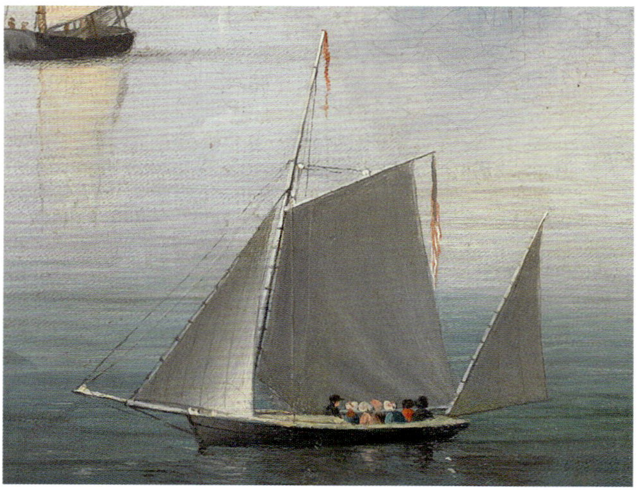

FIGURE 84
Fitz H. Lane, *Gloucester Harbor from Rocky Neck*, 1844 (fig. 83), detail.

nocturnal *Fishing Party*, Lane includes two figures with handlines leaning over the gunwale of a crowded vessel in a festive recreational reprise of the deadly serious cod fishers in *A Smart Blow* (fig. 70). But these fish are small (a second catch is being admired by a young man on the far side of the boat), the conditions benign, and they will soon be supper, cooked on the open fire on the beach in the background rather than commodities within a global marketplace. These sailing parties, with their foraging activities and sociable chowders and fish-fry culminations, were a feature of coastal New England life enjoyed by both locals and visitors.

The influx of vacationers from Boston and inland Massachusetts was first accommodated in boarding houses in town and on campgrounds on peripheral farms.[90] Charles Sawyer's farm at "Brookbank" in Freshwater Cove is of particular note. Sawyer had cows, two wharves, a granite quarry, and two pinky schooners participating in the commercial fisheries.[91] He also cured and sold fish, ran a retail fisherman's outfitting store, sold exotic West Indian goods, and, from the early 1830s, rented out one of his waterfront fish houses to a businessmen's club, the Boston Pioneer Seashore Club, which summered in tents on his property and entertained neighbors with evening concerts.[92] Successful in managing the mixed use of their largely untillable farm and the retail demands of a dry-goods store in Boston, Sawyer family members commissioned at least three paintings of "Brookbank" by Lane, including *Fresh Water Cove from Dolliver's Neck, Gloucester* (figs. 87 and 88).[93]

In early September 1849 journalist Mrs. Nowell published in the local newspaper a long article about Gloucester's character as a "famous resort," noting with approbation that "[i]n the months of July and August, an entire new population throngs the narrow and somewhat crooked streets" and praising the newly opened Pavilion Hotel, "situated most romantically on the very edge of the seashore . . . [where] are daily performed swimming feats of incredible skill" (fig. 63).[94] By the late 1840s the Pavilion (probably named after the fanciful seaside royal residence in Brighton completed in 1823) was the primary place where visitors and locals mixed—both populations promenaded on the beach by day and danced and listened to music by night.[95] But growing distinctions separated these two groups in their understanding and use of real estate, and Lane records these distinctions and quietly comments on them in his paintings.

Mrs. Nowell mentions among the town's notables "Fitz Henry Lane, an artist who has acquired no little well deserved fame by the spirited execution of his marine views,—and who has also transferred to his canvas many of the wild and romantic spots which make up the rude grandeur of his place of birth."[96] In this allusion to his depiction of "rude grandeur," she is explicitly associating Lane's paintings with the scenery and viewing activities of what I am calling the economy of looking. Most historians of tourism in the young United States tend to associate leisured looking with wilderness and the development of the Hudson River School coincident with the opening of the Erie Canal and good roads into the White Mountains.[97] Sounding the dominant note, English transplant Thomas Cole asserted that "the most distinctive, and perhaps the most impressive, characteristic of American

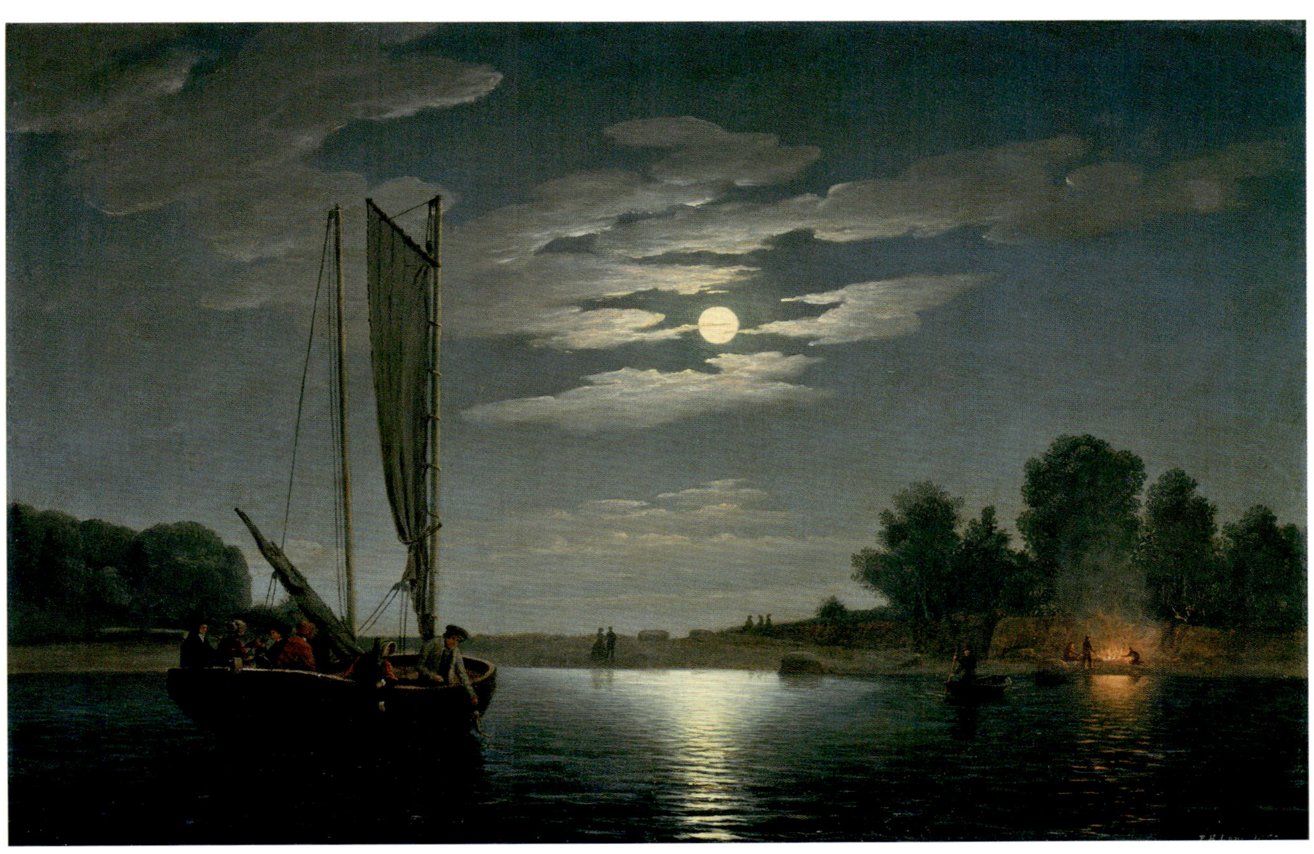

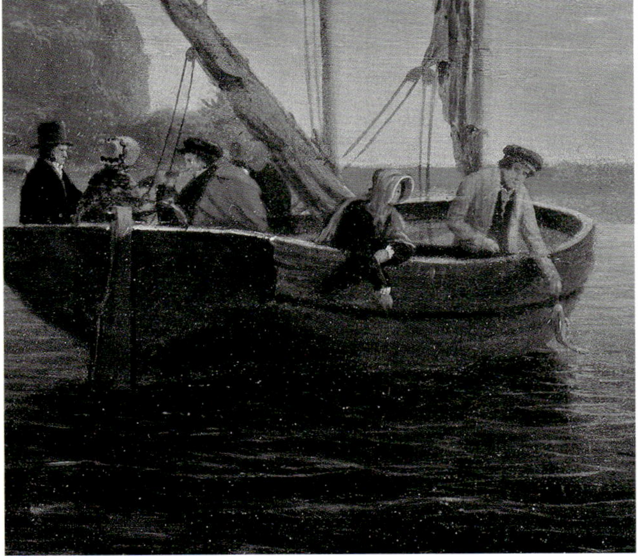

FIGURE 85 (ABOVE)
Fitz H. Lane, *Fishing Party*, 1850. Oil on canvas, 19 ⅝ × 30 ¼ in. (49.85 × 76.83 cm). Museum of Fine Arts, Boston. Gift of Henry Lee Shattuck (69.405). Photo © 2022 Museum of Fine Arts, Boston.

FIGURE 86 (LEFT)
Fitz H. Lane, *Fishing Party*, 1850 (fig. 85), detail.

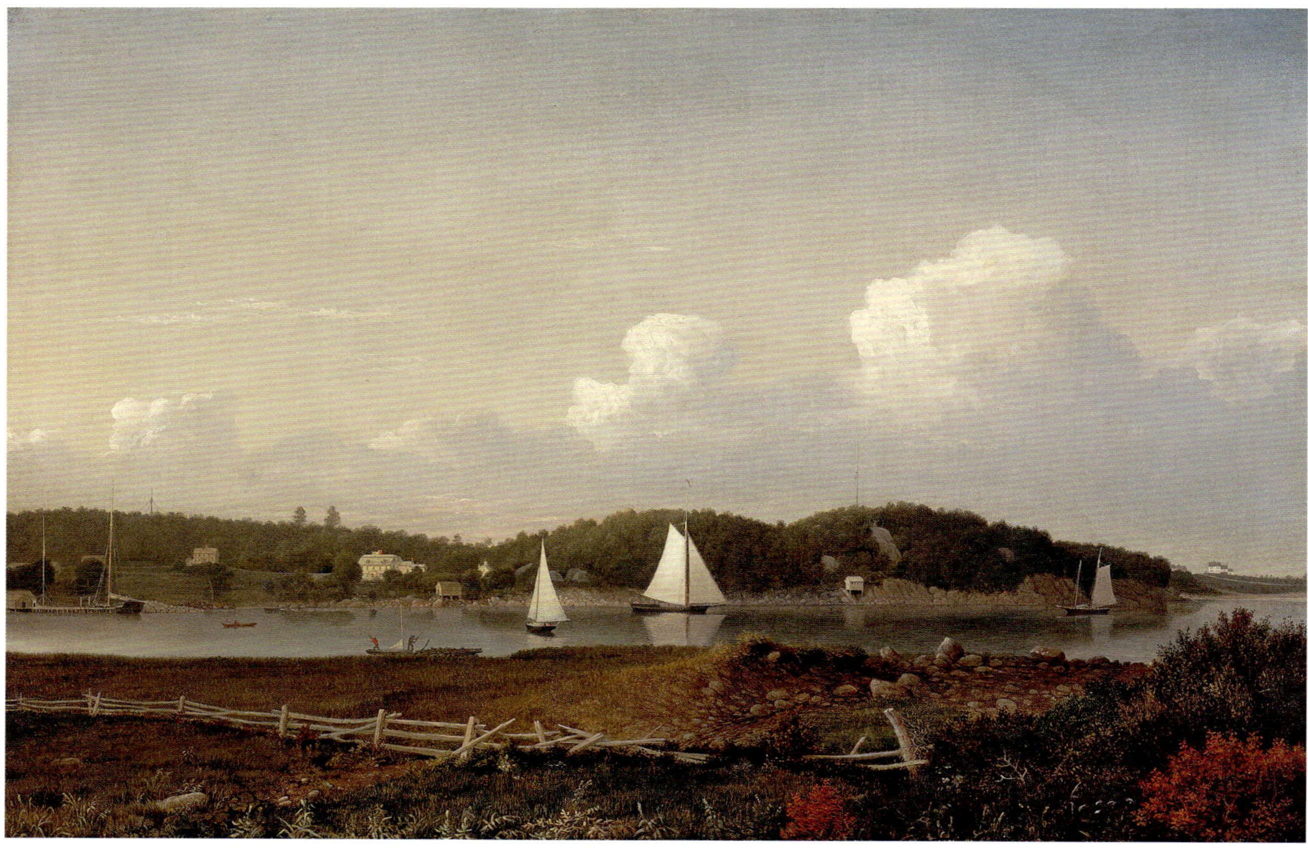

FIGURE 87
Fitz H. Lane, *Fresh Water Cove from Dolliver's Neck, Gloucester*, n.d. Oil on canvas, 24 1/8 × 36 1/8 in. (61.28 × 91.76 cm). Museum of Fine Arts, Boston. Bequest of Martha C. Karolik for the M. and M. Karolik Collection of American Paintings, 1815–1865 (48.445). Photo © 2022 Museum of Fine Arts, Boston.

scenery is its wildness."[98] But those traveling east to Gloucester, rather than north and west, were not seeking (or promised) wild, unpeopled expanses of vertiginous mountain vistas and trackless forests.

Descriptions of the pleasures of Cape Ann tended to emphasize "good fishing, fowling, and eating . . . hills, valleys, beaches for promenading . . . cool breezes night and day."[99] Commentators also promised excursions through "rural scenery, woods filled with aromatic flowers, and frequent and ever varying views of the wide expanse of the waters and coasts of Massachusetts Bay . . . [including] marine views truly magnificent."[100] An 1831 editorial in the newspaper of nearby Lynn, fast evolving into the industrial shoemaking capital of the country, encouraged residents to take a trip to Gloucester to "inhale from her promontories the cool and invigorating breezes that continually fan the rough and rock-bound peninsula." Further, they were encouraged to enjoy "the ocean scenery: at times peering through the foliage of umbrageous pines [one can see] . . . laden with the fruits of industry, the returning fisher's tiny bark flitting swiftly up the bay."[101] In other words, Cape Ann's visitors were promised not sublime wild nature but delights of scent, taste, healthy activity, and scenic vistas of a poetic working landscape. They were encouraged by another enthusiast writer-illustrator, F. A. Durivage, to see Cape Ann as

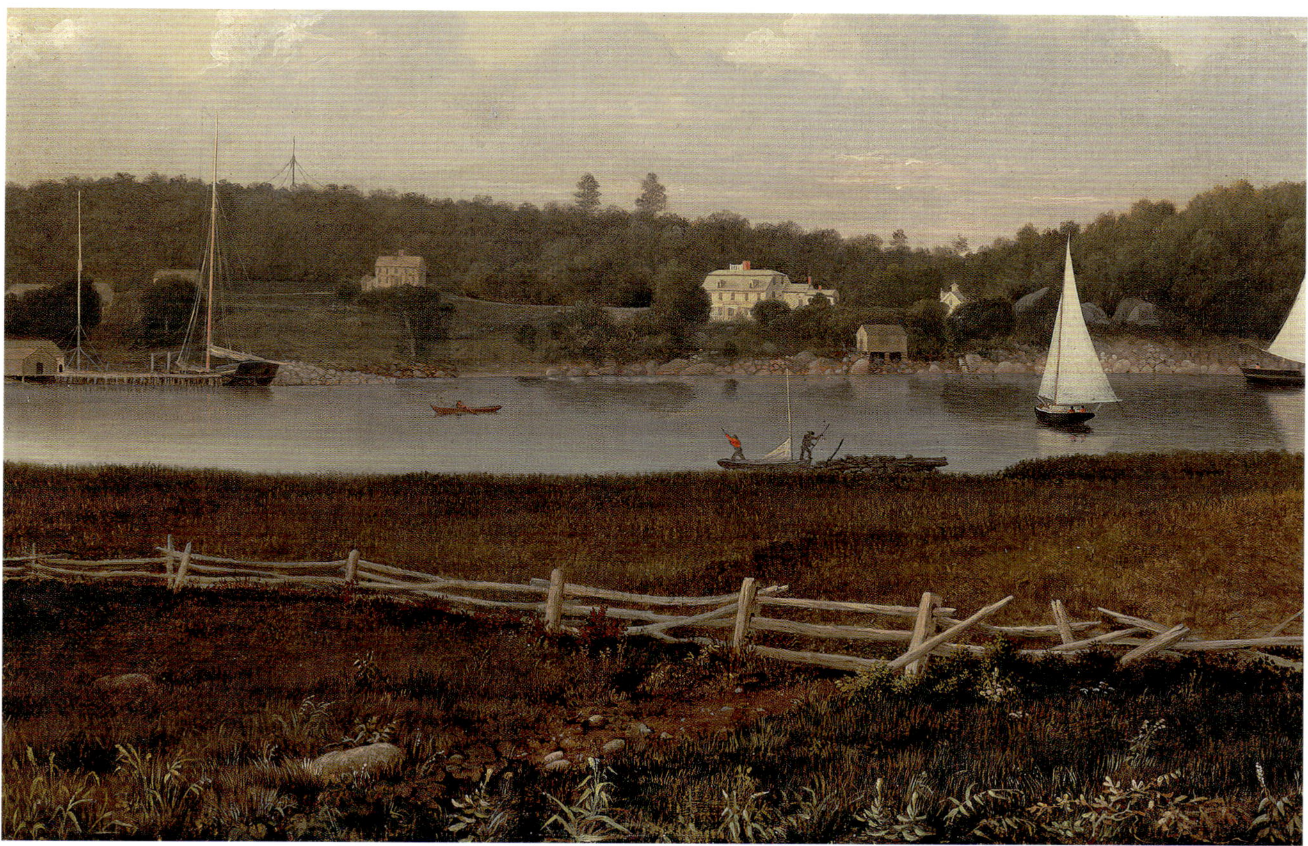

FIGURE 88
Fitz H. Lane, *Fresh Water Cove from Dolliver's Neck, Gloucester*, n.d. (fig. 87), detail.

a long-inhabited, if "rough and unpolished," place where ancient houses and barns dot a landscape of "bold headlands, pleasant valleys and delightful prospects," peopled by "intelligent, industrious, moral" New Englanders at work.[102] But reminding his readers that all nature is not beautiful, picturesque, or sublime, Durivage warns potential visitors that "several hundred acres [of Cape Ann is] almost entirely covered with rocks . . . [and is] revolting to the eye from its utter barrenness and desolation."[103]

Lane, like these commentators, was selective in the sites on Cape Ann he chose to paint, or, to be more precise, chose to draw and offer to potential patrons as prospective painting subjects.[104] One of his few "prospect" paintings, *Annisquam Marshes, Near Gloucester, Massachusetts*, answers Mrs. Nowell's description of a "wild and romantic spot" characterized by "rude grandeur" (fig. 89). Although it includes tidy stone walls, a barn, a cow, and a herder, it foregrounds rough nature in huge granite boulders and the shattered end of a broken tree. The visual pathway to a distant schooner bathed in pearlescent light is obstructed by screens of "umbrageous" trees giving this upland pasture both drama and poetry. The fact that Lane included a modest farm's stone walls in this and other images of the farmsteads on Gloucester's periphery separates him decisively from most nineteenth-century American landscape painters. Those walls underline the fact of property as well as habitation, moving his works in

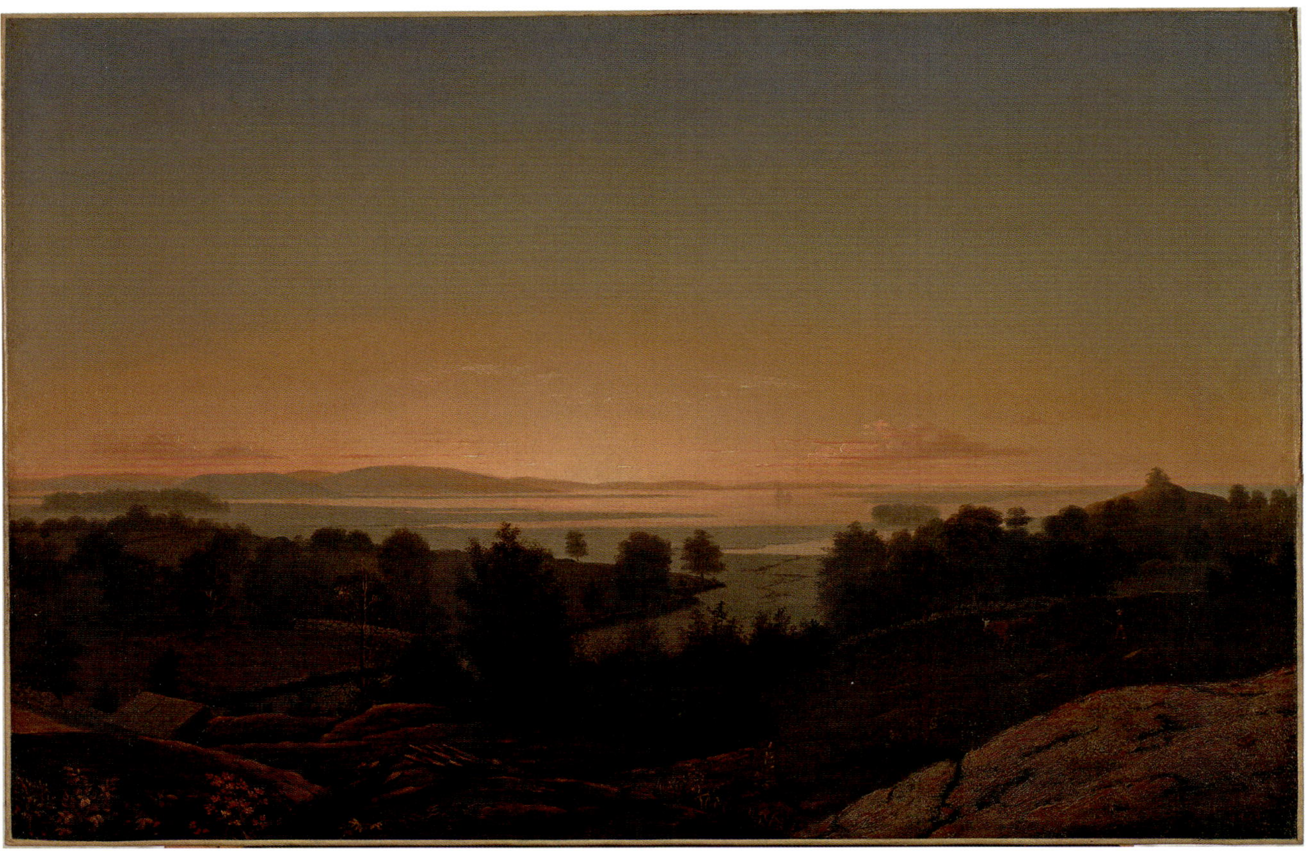

FIGURE 89
Fitz H. Lane, *Annisquam Marshes, Near Gloucester, Massachusetts*, 1848. Oil on canvas, 20 1/16 × 30 1/8 in. (51 × 76.5 cm). Portland Museum of Art, Maine. Gift of Elizabeth B. Noyce (1995.56). Image courtesy Luc Demers.

the direction of description and topography and seemingly away from poetry and national ideology. Productive ownership of land is usually understood to be too prosaic a subject for the poet-artist. While our eyes are famously free to roam and "own" the agricultural view in both Emerson's and Thoreau's formulations, our feet are not.[105] Fences signal the containment of cattle and sheep and the separation of livestock from crops, as well as specific private ownership of land and its improvements, such as the walls themselves, a sturdy kind of visible capital at work. Ownership and its markers tend to bring viewers' flights of warm appreciation for "rude grandeur" back to earth, so most ambitious antebellum American landscape painters, such as those identified with the Hudson River School, eschewed fences as well as signs of extraction industries in their canvases.

In Lane's day, livestock and hunters (and, by extension, other humans) had the right to cross unfenced land.[106] On Cape Ann unfenced property included unproductive land such as the remote beaches—Coffin's Beach, near the Coffin family farm to the north of the town, and Good Harbor Beach, to the southeast (fig. 90). Beaches were a source of seaweed fertilizer for Cape Ann farmers but, since they were generally not highly valued as land and required no fences for crops or livestock, were not enclosed. Contemporary diaries are full of accounts of local boys, girls, and women gathering mosses, flowers, and berries and picnicking on the open fields and rocks

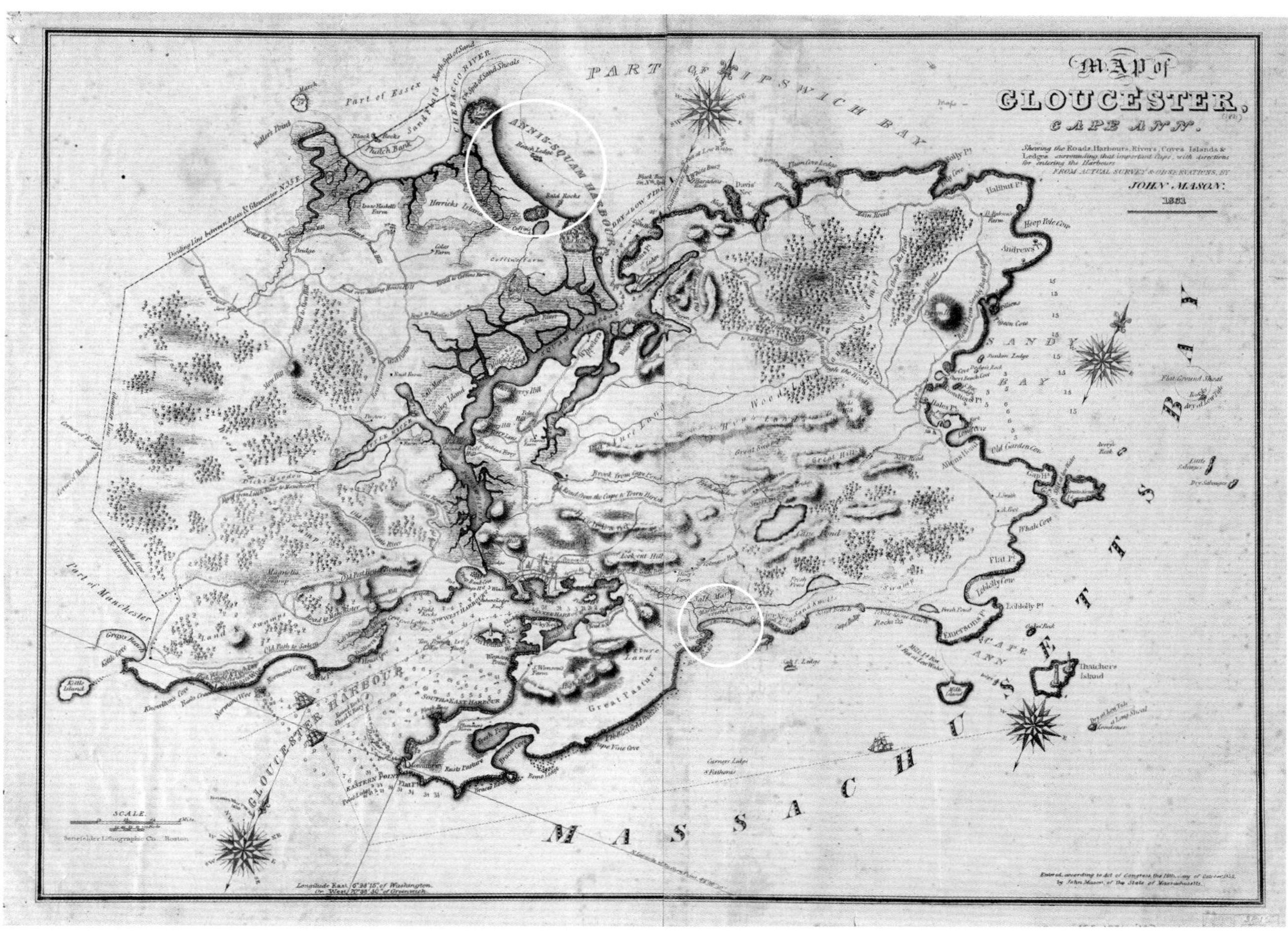

FIGURE 90
John Mason, *Map of Gloucester, Cape Ann* (Senefelder Lithographic Co., Boston, 1831) (fig. 9). Coffin's Beach and Good Harbor Beach indicated.

near Gloucester's remote beaches.[107] Francis Bennett, the fifteen-year-old dry-goods clerk introduced above, reports sledding at night on private property, including on the hill beside Lane's house, in winter and frequently swimming and berrying at Good Harbor Beach during his days off or after work in summer.[108] On August 24, 1854, with two men and three other boys, he "went over to Coffin's Beach to have a chowder. . . . After dinner [one of the boys] and I went way across the beach a gunning. I carried the wadding and shot and also the birds. He killed 6 plovers going and coming. He and his father killed about 2 dozen. . . . About 4 o'clock we had a [fish and plover] fry."[109] Remote enough from settlement (and livestock) to make "gunning" possible, Coffin's Beach offered a patch of wildness, if not Natty Bumpo's wilderness, for Gloucesterites with a taste for open-air exercise and hunting. When he moved to Boston, shortly after this companionable foray into nature, to work in Charles Hovey's remarkable department store, the adolescent Francis reported venturing onto the Boston Common on a moonlit autumn evening, where he "sat down beside the frog pond and viewed the loveliness of nature" in an urbanized and miniaturized version of the nature he had known in Gloucester just weeks before.[110]

Lane's *Coffin's Beach at Sunset* is an evocative image of this remote site, about a six-mile walk from the harbor by

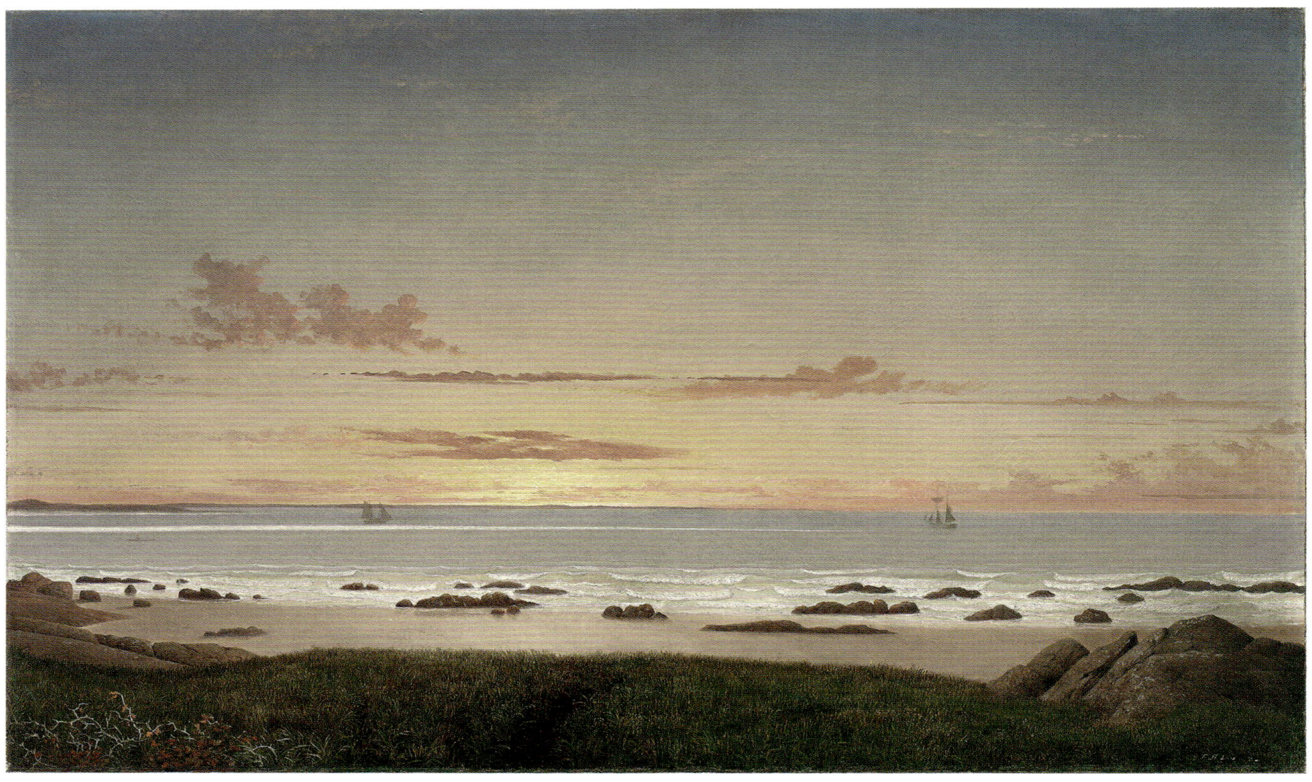

FIGURE 91
Fitz H. Lane, *Coffin's Beach at Sunset*, ca. 1862. Oil on canvas, 22½ × 36¾ in. (57.2 × 93.3 cm). Cape Ann Museum, Gloucester, Massachusetts. Gift of Frederic Friend Low through his niece Martha F. Low (2150.00).

a roundabout route through a sparsely populated marshy part of Gloucester (figs. 90 and 91). It was as close to a "wild" place as Cape Ann had to offer, and this is one of the very few Lane paintings that includes no sign of human habitation, although the distant schooners mark the site as "maritime" rather than "wilderness." It is clear, from looking at his more than one hundred surviving drawings, that Lane, despite his disability, frequently accessed such remote sites. At times he rented a gig, at times rented or borrowed a boat, and often excursioned, perhaps for assistance as well as society, in the company of Joseph Stevens Jr. and his family.[111]

Beginning in the 1830s and with increasing frequency and impact in the 1840s as the railroad linked the town into the national overland transportation system, two important changes occurred in Gloucester real estate related to the culture of looking. Formerly unproductive and minimally valued coastal farms and rough hilltop sites were bought up by wealthy Bostonians, with far-reaching consequences, including, first, the closing of what had functionally been commons and, second, the arrival of architecture (as distinct from building) on Cape Ann. Leading a trend that would leave most of the fifty-mile arc of seacoast from Boston to Cape Ann in the hands of wealthy entrepreneurs by midcentury, China trader John Perkins Cushing in 1831 bought three hundred acres at the western end of Eastern Point and had built a stone boundary wall across the peninsula from Southeast Harbor to the Atlantic, embracing Brace's Cove.[112] At the time, an ad described the property as a working farm with a harbor suitable for commercial cod and mackereling schooners, but the ad also noted that the property had the potential for use as "a place of Entertainment for genteel company."[113]

In 1844 Cushing sold the property to Thomas Niles, a well-to-do, curmudgeonly livery-stable proprietor from Boston, who asserted ownership rights against neighbors gathering seaweed at Brace's Cove and picnickers alike; taking the matter to court in 1859, he won his case.[114] So four years later, when Lane, accompanied by Joseph, Caroline, and eleven-year-old Helen Stevens, spent the day at Brace's Cove making the drawings that resulted in his iconic Brace's Rock paintings, he was probably officially trespassing.

At the other end of Eastern Point, and more accessible to town, Gloucester-based (later Boston-based) Surinam trader George H. Rogers, who frequently ranked highest in Gloucester's tax list, began buying up the coastal land and "cow rights" to Good Harbor Beach, Bass Rocks, and pasturage in that area.[115] One farm bordering the beach was advertised in 1850 as furnished with productive fruit trees and hay meadows, but it also offered "advantages of sea bathing and ocean scenery rarely found, and cannot fail to attract the attention of the capitalist, man of leisure or the farmer; for the latter purpose, its proximity to the seashore where seaweed is abundant [for fertilizer], renders it highly advantageous."[116] So just as schooners were advertised for sale or rent as suitable for the fisheries or excursionists at midcentury, real estate was offered as suitable for farming or leisure-oriented pastoral gentry homes. When a farmer in nearby Beverly sold his 101 acres with a half mile of ocean frontage to a Boston attorney in 1844 for a sum he felt exceeded the land's worth, he is said to have remarked, "These Boston fellows don't know anything about values," reflecting the difference between the value of acreage as productive of sellable crops and the value of seacoast as a source of visual pleasure in the new economy of looking.[117] What Lane offers in *Coffin Beach* is a formerly almost valueless piece of property

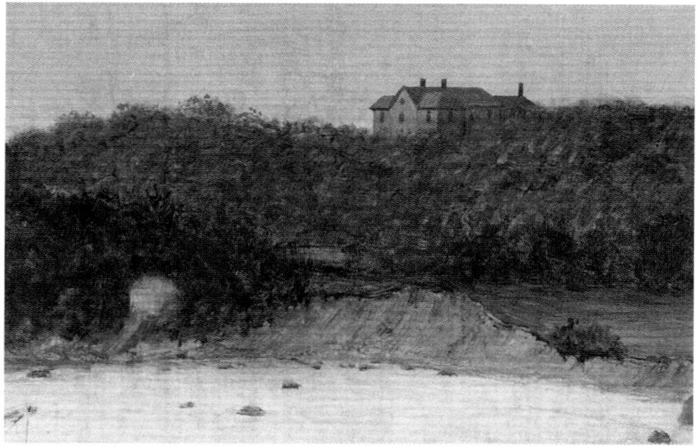

FIGURE 92
Fitz H. Lane, *Dolliver's Neck and the Western Shore from Field Beach*, 1857 (fig. 29), detail.

that, lacking good anchorage or forage for livestock, was useful only for sport hunting of the fauna that flourished in landscapes humans avoided. To help us understand the new value of the place as a site for contemplative looking, Lane has devoted the center third of the canvas to the soft pyrotechnics of a rising sun. The array of receding pink-mauve clouds and the diminutive scale of the schooners pull the eye to the horizon so that it registers distance and expanse. The viewer is simultaneously aware of the obdurate permanence of the foreground herbage, rocks, and sand at the border between land and sea, and the fleeting character of opalescent light at the border between night and day.

If the first shift in the valuation of Cape Ann real estate occurred in the substantial revaluing of formerly "waste" landscapes such as beaches and marginally profitable coastal farms, the second major shift in Cape Ann real estate that followed the arrival of wealthy Bostonians began when one of the summer tent campers on the Sawyer farm at Freshwater Cove, George Hovey, bought the hilltop above the Sawyer property in 1845 and built a summer home, Pine Cottage, on the site.[118] Where formerly the most desirable locations for homes tended to be in town or near the harbor, where good access to social

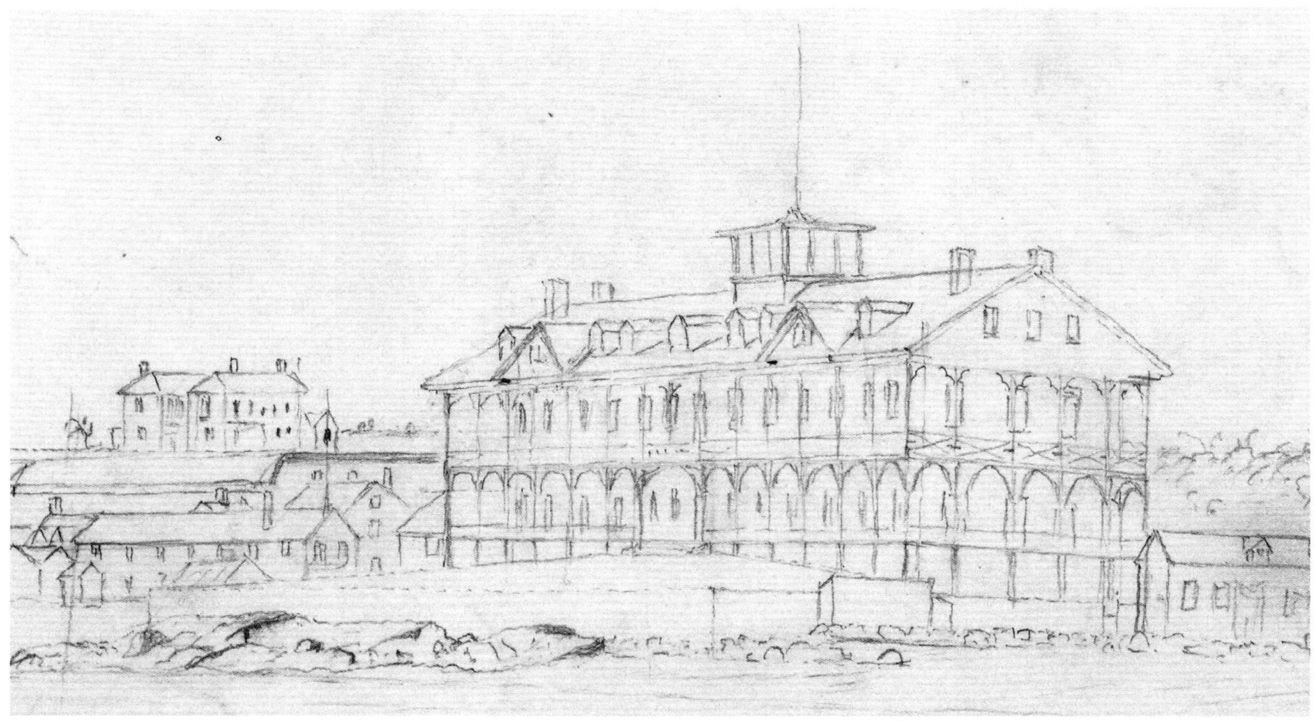

FIGURE 93
Fitz H. Lane, *Pavilion*, after 1849, detail. Graphite on paper, 10 3⁄16 × 16 1⁄8 in. (25.9 × 41 cm). Cape Ann Museum, Gloucester, Massachusetts. Gift of Samuel H. Mansfield, 1927 (485.100).

amenities, shelter from winds, and good transportation were to be had, Hovey prioritized vision and situated his summer residence on an eminence commanding expansive views of the harbor and the Atlantic. The architect may have been Samuel C. Bugbee, who is credited with designing the Pavilion and, in 1851, a nearby summer home on the road to Manchester for James Eddy of New York City, as well as other summer cottages in the vicinity.[119] Hovey also bought Dolliver's Neck, affording him good access to yachting activities.[120] Lane includes Pine Cottage in three paintings, most prominently in *Dolliver's Neck and the Western Shore from Field Beach* (figs. 29 and 92).[121] Perched in a clearing and peering above the trees in all directions, Hovey's house signals the arrival of the culture of looking on the domestic scale that the Pavilion Hotel had done on a commercial scale. A rare letter from Lane, addressed to his friend Joseph Stevens Jr. in 1857, describes this painting, mentioning "Hovey's Hill and residence," and indicates that he intends to give the canvas to Stevens if his friend likes it.[122] The drawing Lane executed in preparation for the painting—like so many Lane drawings—does not include the vessels, but it includes a carefully and emphatically delineated portrait of Hovey's new house, presumably as a new kind of conspicuous landmark.[123] Since the resulting painting was subsequently given to the Cape Ann Museum by Stevens's daughter Helen, he evidently did like the work and accepted the gift. Not surprisingly, George Hovey's brother also built a summer cottage on an eminence commanding views out to sea, visible to the left of the hotel in Lane's drawing of the Pavilion (fig. 93).

In including a vignette of George Hovey's summer residence in *Dolliver's Neck*, Lane has introduced this new kind of real estate and a new kind of house, located with a new kind of address to the topography and social geography of the region in his paintings, which nevertheless foreground Gloucester's accustomed maritime activities. This work is about the transportation of lumber, the deliberations about a beached schooner, the movement of fish and granite, but with Pine Cottage surveying the panorama from across the harbor and looking back at the artist and the painting's viewers, it is also a kind of acknowledgment of the privileging of view over utility. What Lane has achieved in these images of Gloucester's fisheries and the region's burgeoning economy of "summering" is the creation of a visual language that alludes to global economies rooted in individual acts of labor and singular objects on the landscape. These small visual anecdotes intimate large stories that would have been familiar to Lane's immediate audience, both the narratives of "disaster and discomfort" in the background of Gloucester's prosperity and the poetry of a "rough and rock-bound peninsula." What Lane takes care to picture is both a working landscape and "scenery." The first would have been familiar to Lane's audience, and the second was a taste that his canvases helped develop. Involving the full social spectrum—workers, capitalists, and the evolving middle class—Lane's small rectangular canvas fictions rooted in time and place comprehend the global networks that he was in a privileged position to observe, both by his trade as a distiller of visual experience and by his choice to build his own house in close proximity to the businesses equipping the fishing fleet and processing the catch but also situated, like those of the Hovey brothers, on a promontory facing out to sea.

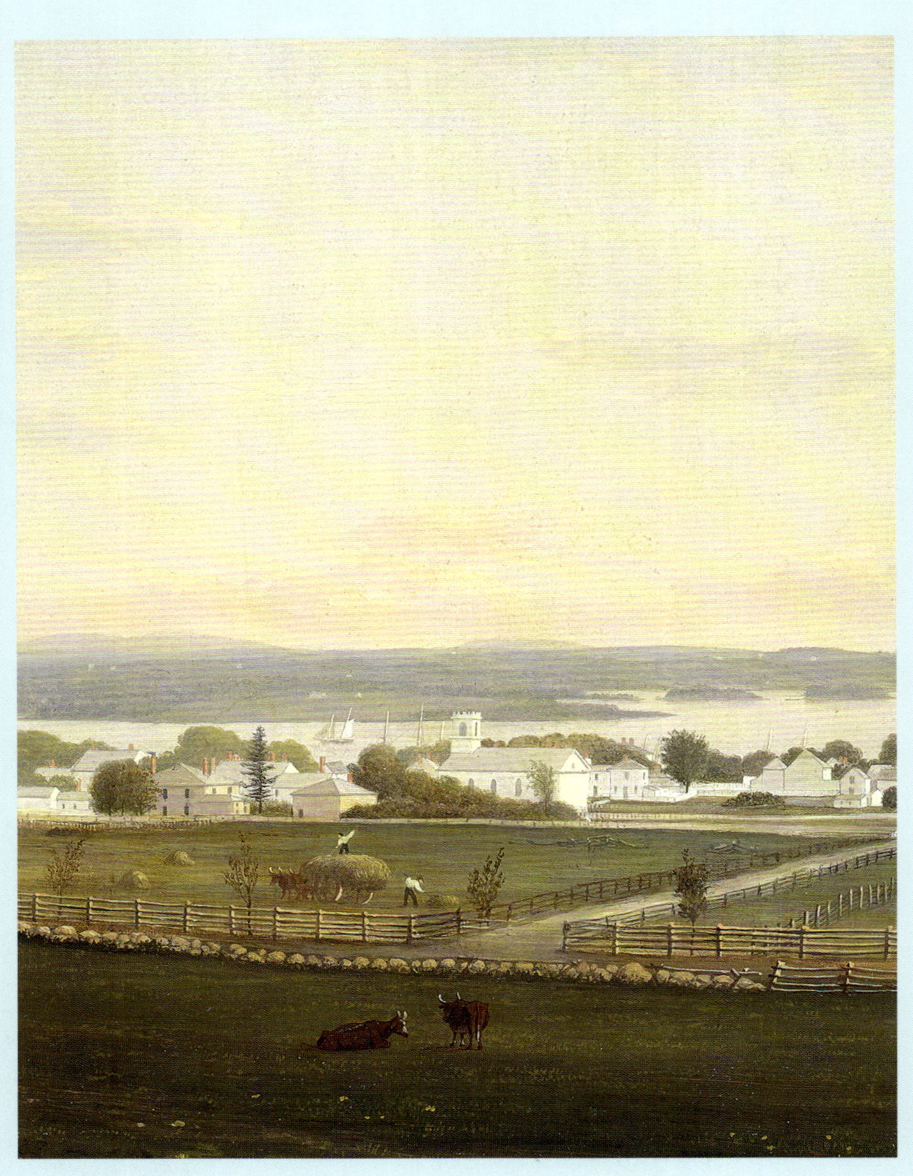

CHAPTER 5

LUMBER

Lane's Maine

Fitz Henry Lane's Maine paintings of the 1850s and 1860s are among his most celebrated. Scholars looking at them (as at the Cape Ann paintings) have had little to say about the human activities pictured, however, tending to see and remark upon "formal patterns and contrasts, of dark against light, diagonals against horizon line," or "elevated formal aesthetics ... revealing a sense of ordered, mathematically conceived composition[s]," or a "scene of stasis and calm," an uninterrupted "sense of order ... purified by the suppression of extraneous detail."[1] *Entrance to Somes Sound from Southwest Harbor*, for instance, is understood to be "a masterpiece of structural harmony and balance" that includes "bits of incidental detail" (see figs. 31 and 32).[2] It is exactly these seemingly undiscussable "bits of incidental detail" in the Maine images that I wish to foreground, attending carefully to what these ships and boats are carrying, to what this working landscape is *doing*. Equally, I investigate here indications of disharmony and imbalance in Lane's selection of these sites and within his images.

Lane made at least six seasonal trips to the Penobscot Bay area of Maine, three hundred miles northeast of Gloucester, in 1848, 1850, 1851, 1852, 1853, and 1863.[3] In the company of others participating in the culture of looking and in "discovering" the Maine coast in these years, Lane spent these summer months sociably, staying with the parents of his friend Joseph L. Stevens Jr. in Castine, at the mouth of the Penobscot River, excursioning by sloop, camping out, sometimes hiking, and always sketching (fig. 94). He was not the only artist in the area.

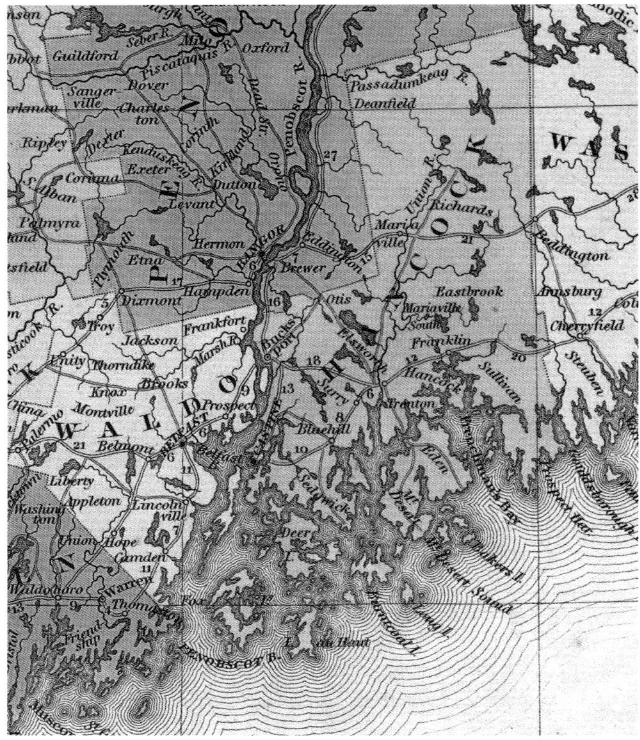

FIGURE 94
Henry S. Tanner, *A New Map of Maine*, 1836, detail. Hand-colored engraving, 14½ × 11½ in. (37 × 29 cm). In Henry S. Tanner, *A New Universal Atlas* (Philadelphia: self-published, 1836), 5. David Rumsey Map Collection, David Rumsey Map Center, Stanford University Libraries.

As reported in the *Gloucester Telegraph*, the island of Mount Desert, while formerly understood to be "barren and desolate," frequented only by fishing craft, became, to an eye reeducated in looking, a site that could "boast of scenery so grand and beautiful as to be unsurpassed by any on the whole American coast," and it thus quickly became a novel magnet for midcentury artists. This detailed account of a company of Gloucesterites who sailed to, camped out on, and hiked the uplands of the island in September 1850 concluded with a description of painters on Mount Desert that month: "We heard of [George] Bonfield and [Virgil] Williams who had reluctantly left but a short time before, [Alvan] Fisher had spent several weeks there. [Benjamin] Champney and [John] Kensett were then in another part of the island, and we have reason to believe that [Frederic] Church and some others were in the immediate vicinity.—Lane who was with us, made good additions to his portfolio."[4]

While the scenery sought by these other artists was generally wild nature, often seen from an eminence, Lane turned his attention to the harbors and townscapes, and to the activities of the region revolving around lumber. As in his Gloucester paintings of the fishing industry, Lane portrayed focused vignettes of specific lumbering activities rather than attempt to portray the vast scale of Maine's primary extraction industry. Wood was big business. By 1850, when Lane was making annual painting trips to Maine, lumbering in the Penobscot watershed employed ten thousand men, and the yearly timber crop of the state in 1866 was worth close to $20 million.[5]

The loading of planks into the hull of a single brig on glass-smooth water in *Entrance to Somes Sound from Southwest Harbor* evokes an activity that was omnipresent, and a single outbound topsail schooner loaded high with dimensioned lumber in *Lumber Schooners at Evening on Penobscot Bay* stands for the hundreds of coasters moving south with this valuable cargo throughout the spring, summer, and fall months (figs. 7, 31, 32, and 95). These vignettes of the lumber industry are offered as singular examples, meticulously articulated portraits of everyday activities characteristic of that place and that time, often set in poetic frameworks of transitional times of day. These pictures are about a working landscape—brigs and schooners and the workers and mariners who loaded and managed them—and about the larger economies and connections in which these activities participated. While describing particular activities and cargoes, they also reference the cutting of thousands of trees deep in Maine's remote forests, vast log drives, thundering sawmills, treacherous journeys through tempestuous seas, and eventual consumption in the production of houses and barns, wharves and ships, barrels and buckets, in cities near and far. Were these brigs and schooners not included in these compositions, were these canvases indeed "about a sense of emptiness" or just assemblages of abstract geometric forms and gestures, the paintings would be of little interest and import.[6]

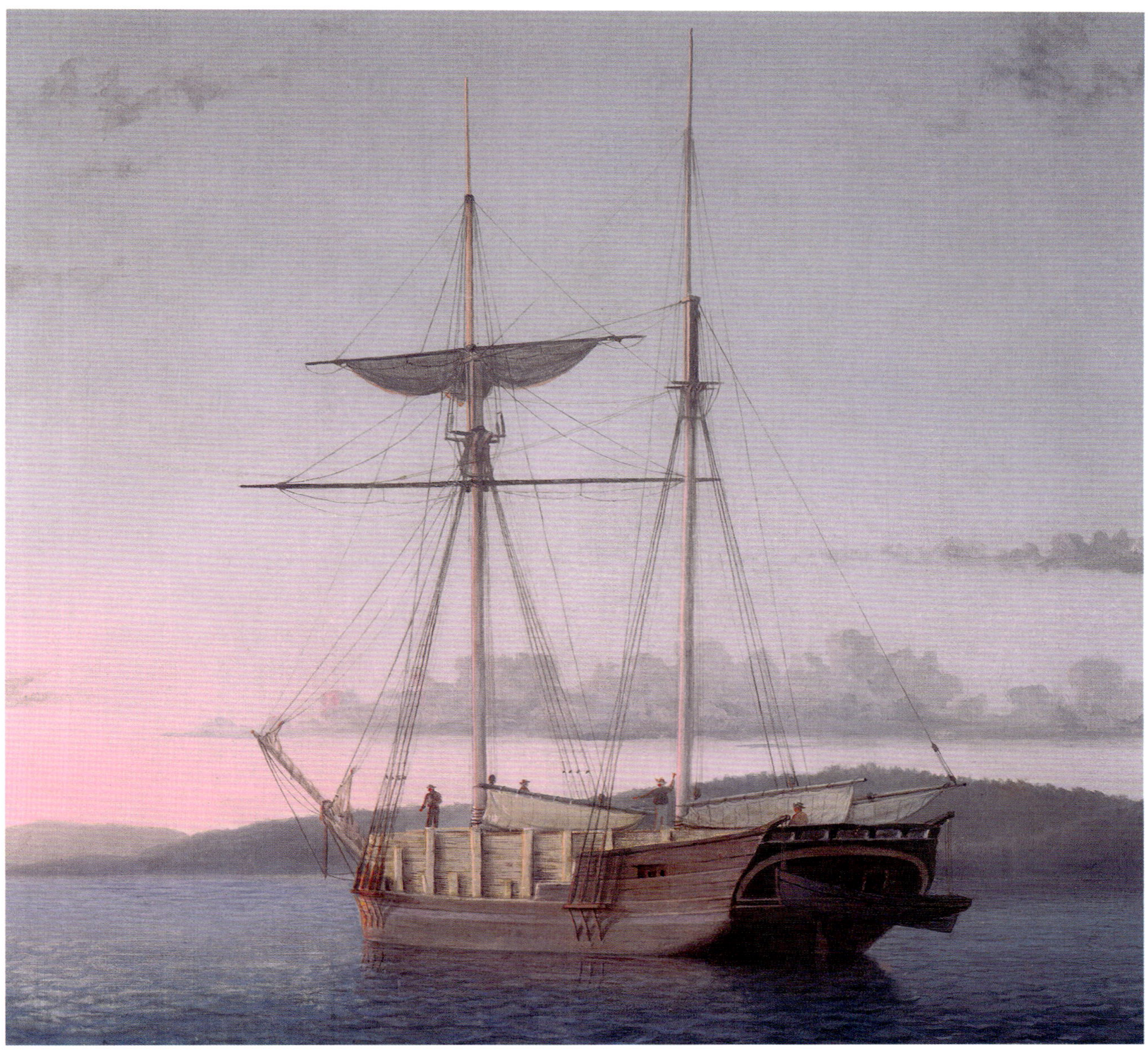

FIGURE 95
Fitz H. Lane, *Lumber Schooners at Evening on Penobscot Bay*, 1863 (fig. 7), detail.

The reporter for the *Gloucester Telegraph* who described the adventures of Lane and his associates from Gloucester exploring Mount Desert Island in the summer of 1850 also made clear that there were substantial historic links between Cape Ann and coastal Maine. Somes settlement, for example, took "its name from the early settlers . . . [who] went from Gloucester eighty or ninety years ago," and the current population bore names like Babson, familiar in Gloucester. There is, in other words, a Gloucester-Maine backstory of migration and remigration that is of interest, and that is a narrative of dislocation, loss, and aggression as well as adventure, success, and apparent harmony.

LUMBER, LUMBERING, BUILDING, AND BURNING

Lumber Schooners at Evening on Penobscot Bay, of 1863, is a poetic image, but it is also an image of labor and capital at work (figs. 7 and 95). An outbound vessel is carrying an overflowing load of milled wood from the Penobscot River area, where it was cut deep in the inland forests, floated downriver as logs to a mill, sawn into dimensional lumber, and then loaded into and onto vessels to be transported to distant urban markets. The painting is a scene both of completion (twilight) and of inception (an outward-bound journey). Its protagonist is a vernacular vessel, cunningly constructed and managed to produce specific motion, to enact human will—its technologically complex fabrication of wood, rope, canvas, and metal fittings harnessing the wind to move a heavy cargo through the resistant medium of water toward some far distant place. This topsail schooner and its cargo, so lyrically poised against an ombre sky, are part of a vast national, even international, market for the primary building material in North America. The seemingly quiet scene portrays one moment in the career of one of hundreds of coasters that carried this profitable crop south to Gloucester, Boston, Charleston, the West Indies, even Australia, each coaster averaging three to seventeen round trips a year.[7] Lane's paintings appear to be eventless, depicting quotidian moments of no consequence, but their "details" point to international as well as local concerns, and to the integration of humans into both environment and a global economy. The three key implied ingredients are valuable extractable resources, human labor and ingenuity, and linkage to larger communities and economies.

From the forests and harbors of Maine, such as Somes Sound in Mount Desert Island and nearby Penobscot Bay, to the finished houses, ships, and furniture of the Eastern Seaboard and the Caribbean, human activity and its material culture constituted a single system in which ships, people, logs, lumber, and money moved in continuous productive cycles. Lumbering, an extractive industry, began with the shaggy forests Lane portrays in the middle and far distance in these two paintings: the hills of Mount Desert Island and of the Penobscot watershed, on the cusp between the fir-spruce forest of northern Maine and the beech-birch-maple-hemlock forest of southern Maine. The trees were felled by axe and dragged to waterways by teams of oxen. They were then floated downstream to a boom, where they were sorted by owners and harnessed together in rafts (as seen in the right foreground of Lane's *Twilight on the Kennebec*), then floated on to the sawmills (fig. 96).[8] Northern New England had many powerful dammable streams, and wood was more easily, more compactly, and more economically transported as dimensional lumber than as logs. In the mills, the force of the dammed water powered reciprocating or circular saws that tirelessly, accurately produced a predictable measured orthogonal product with a minimum of human labor. From the seventeenth century, in what was to become the United States, where labor was always more expensive than in Europe, mechanical force and technological ingenuity substituted for expensive hand-driven pit sawing and contributed to the vast scale of lumbering activities. The census of 1840 reported 1,381 busy sawmills in Maine.[9] Mount Desert, for instance, with a population of only two thousand in 1828, already kept six sawmills busy, and it was "not unusual to see in [Somes Sound] at once 700 vessels" involved in lumber transport or in the offshore fisheries.[10]

The most prized New England tree was the white pine (*Pinus strobus*), flourishing especially near riverbanks within old-growth forests between the 43rd and 47th parallels.[11] Reaching two hundred feet or more with a straight smooth trunk, it yielded a wood lighter, softer, freer of knots, more durable, and with a greater proportion of heartwood (that is, interior wood from former years' growth, more stable than newer, outer sapwood) than any other. When protected by white lead paint, white pine lumber was "incorruptible," and, since it was easier to work than other woods, it involved lower labor costs.[12] It was particularly prized for ship masts and was thus embroiled in political and military as well as economic

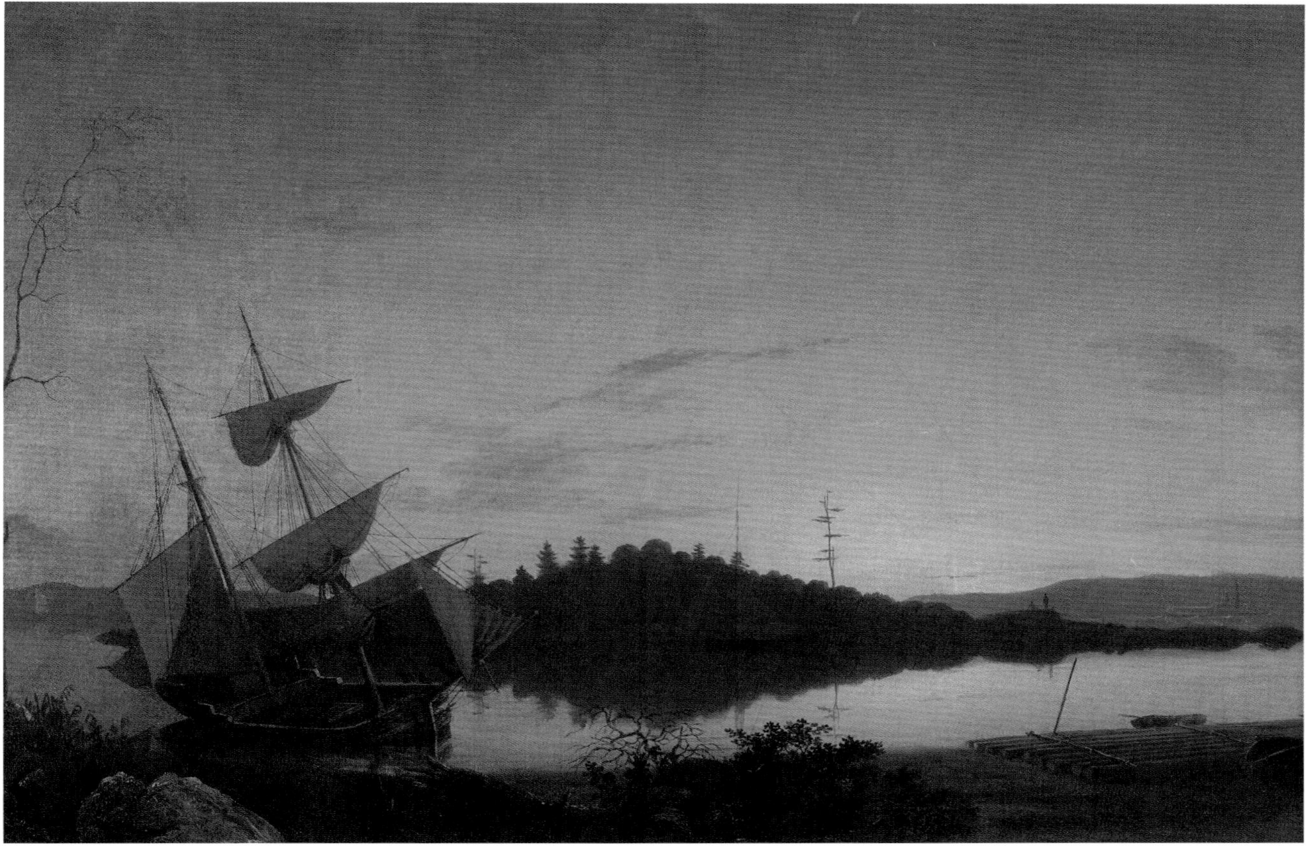

FIGURE 96
Fitz H. Lane, *Twilight on the Kennebec*, 1849. Oil on canvas, 20 × 30¼ in. (50.8 × 76.8 cm). Peabody Essex Museum. Gift of Serena M. Hatch in honor of Francis W. Hatch, 2014 (M22672). © 2011 Peabody Essex Museum, Salem, Massachusetts. Photo by Walter Silver.

and artisanal narratives from the sixteenth century. Most structures in antebellum America and many abroad were framed and clapboarded with white pine timbers and boards, and the major bridges in early America—such as those over the Schuylkill at Philadelphia, the Delaware at Trenton, and the Charles at Cambridge—were built of white pine.[13] In *Camden Mountains from the South Entrance to the Harbor* of 1859 Lane gives a précis of the life of white pine from immature trees (on the island behind the topsail schooner) to mature trees (on the distant hills), to dimensional lumber (loaded for shipment on that vessel), to houses (in the distance), to the scantlings burned in the steamboat (in the center distance) (figs. 97 and 98).

The boards (and to a lesser extent the timbers, posts, palings, lath, barrel staves, mast trees, compass timbers, and cordwood) were transported in beamy brigs and schooners by sea—on often perilous journeys—to towns where such lumber was scarce or to sites where sawmills had not yet been established, such as midcentury California (fig. 99).[14] Implicit in Lane's paintings are the artisanal acts and know-how that used this lumber to construct the houses, the barrels, and the barns of antebellum America. One feels in his paintings a sense of respect not only for the designers of ships and the riggers of spars, but also for the loaders of wood, the builders of homes, and the crafters of barrels and buckets.

In a few cases, Lane explicitly describes the transformation of this lumber into objects of use. Against a

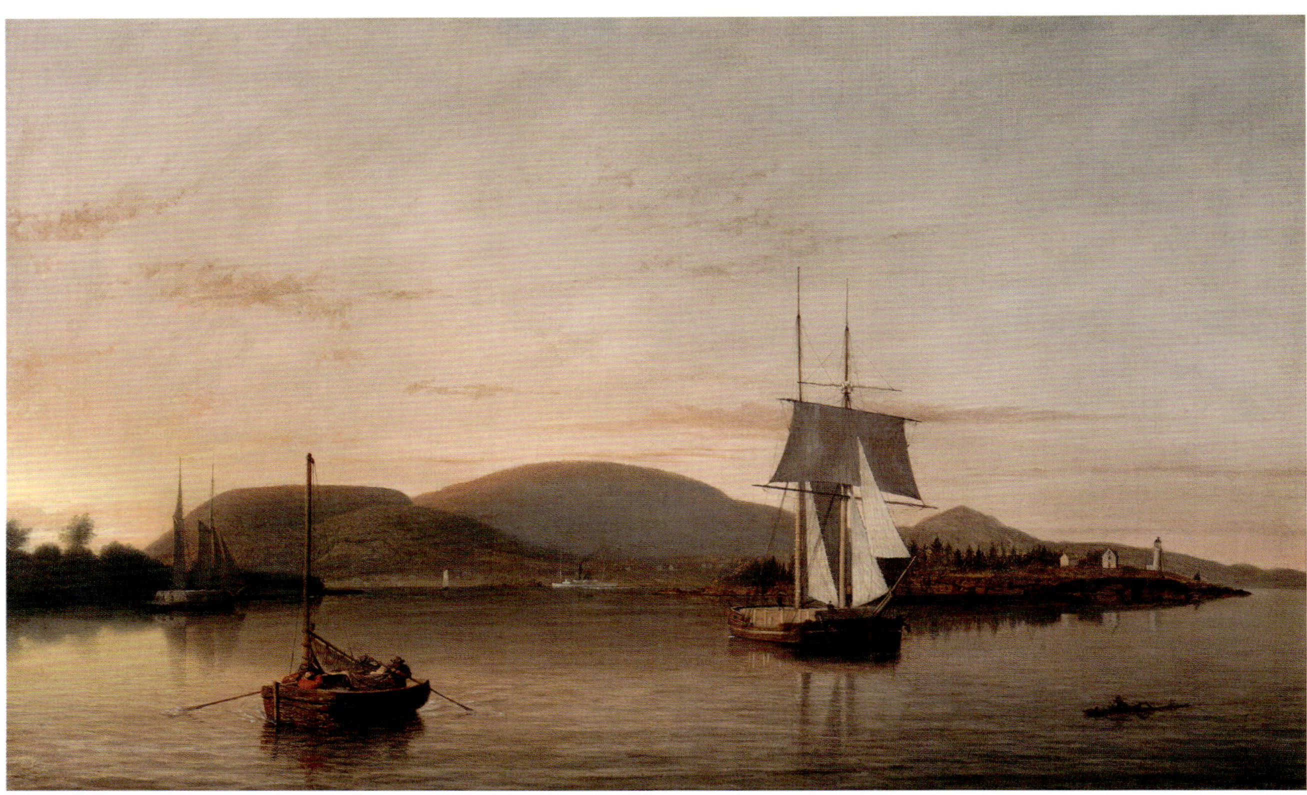

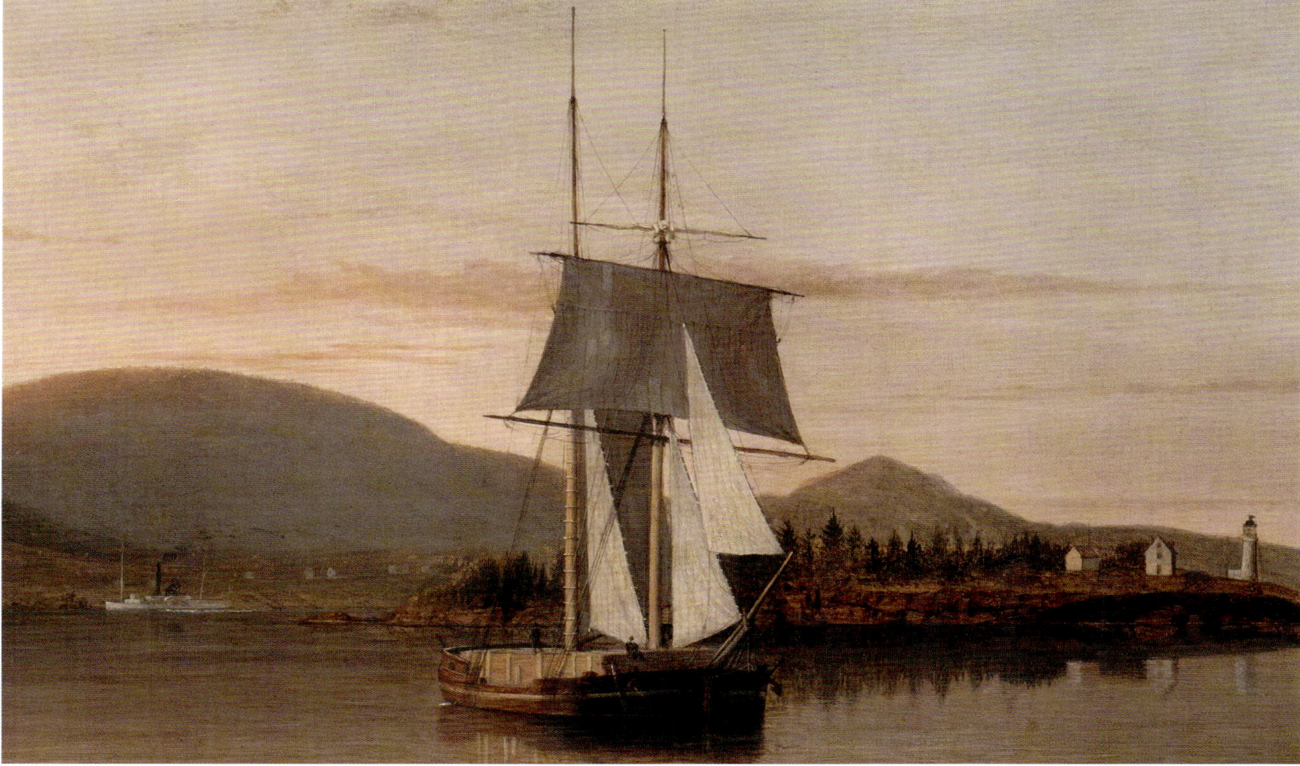

FIGURE 97 (TOP)
Fitz H. Lane, *Camden Mountains from the South Entrance to the Harbor*, 1859. Oil on canvas, 22 1/8 × 36 1/4 in. (56.2 × 92.1 cm). Collection of the Farnsworth Art Museum, Rockland, Maine. Bequest of Mrs. Elizabeth B. Noyce (1997.3.30).

FIGURE 98 (BOTTOM)
Fitz H. Lane, *Camden Mountains from the South Entrance to the Harbor*, 1859 (fig. 97), detail.

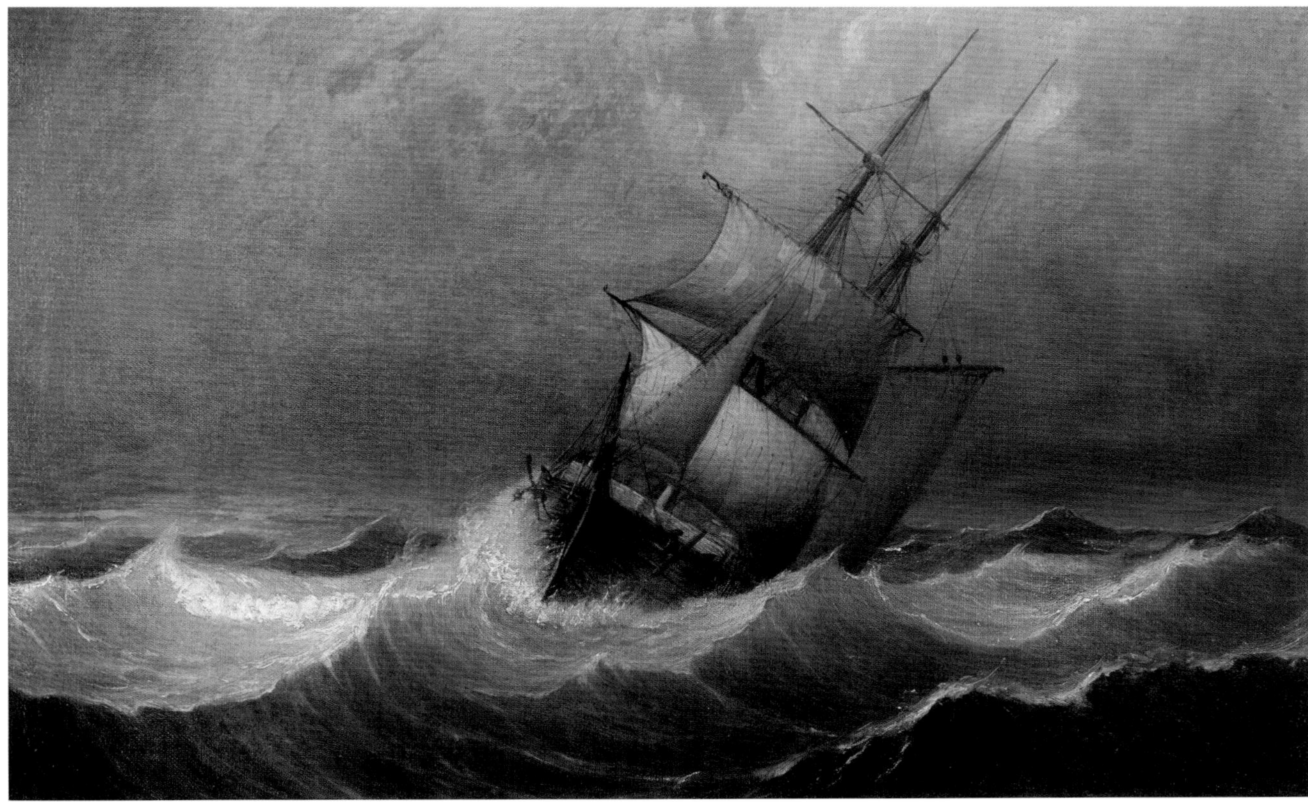

middle-ground scene of a lumber-laden topsail schooner of the type seen in *Lumber Schooners at Evening on Penobscot Bay* (fig. 95) arriving in Gloucester Harbor, *The Fort and Ten Pound Island, Gloucester* foregrounds the ingenuity of shipwrights fashioning a vessel from an array of forest products as they form each part of the craft from the most appropriate tree to serve its role in the complex engineering of even a small seaworthy vessel (fig. 49). It took many trees to make a ship, as many as two thousand mature trees to make a single ship of the line (or warship), and a wide variety of woods from disparate forests—live oak, pine, chestnut, locust, and cedar being commonly used in the construction of American vessels.[15] Lane's paintings, in other words, are not empty canvases full of silence, abstract geometry, or images accidentally overreplete with "extraneous detail," but busy seascapes, landscapes, and townscapes full of purposeful activity tied to thousands of other legible acts of purposeful, useful, knowledgeable, profitable activity.[16]

FIGURE 99
Fitz H. Lane, *Lumber Brig in High Seas*, n.d. Oil on canvas, 10⅛ × 16 in. (25.7 × 40.6 cm). Cape Ann Museum, Gloucester, Massachusetts. Gift of the Estate of Anne K. Garland, 1990 (2676.00).

A single lumber schooner and a single boatyard in *The Fort and Ten Pound Island* gesture in the direction of the "60,000 Boards" unloading in Gloucester from a single shipment and the seventeen schooners leaving Gloucester for Maine ports on a single day in 1859 (fig. 49).[17] Maine harbors were even busier; the *Gloucester Telegraph* reported that on a single day in June 1827, sixty-four vessels actively loaded lumber in Bangor.[18] John Stevens, brother of Lane's host in Maine and uncle of his closest friend, was in the lumber business in Bangor and kept in close touch with his kin, so evidence of this key industry was not only everywhere in view in Maine waters and in urban harbors to the south but also integral to

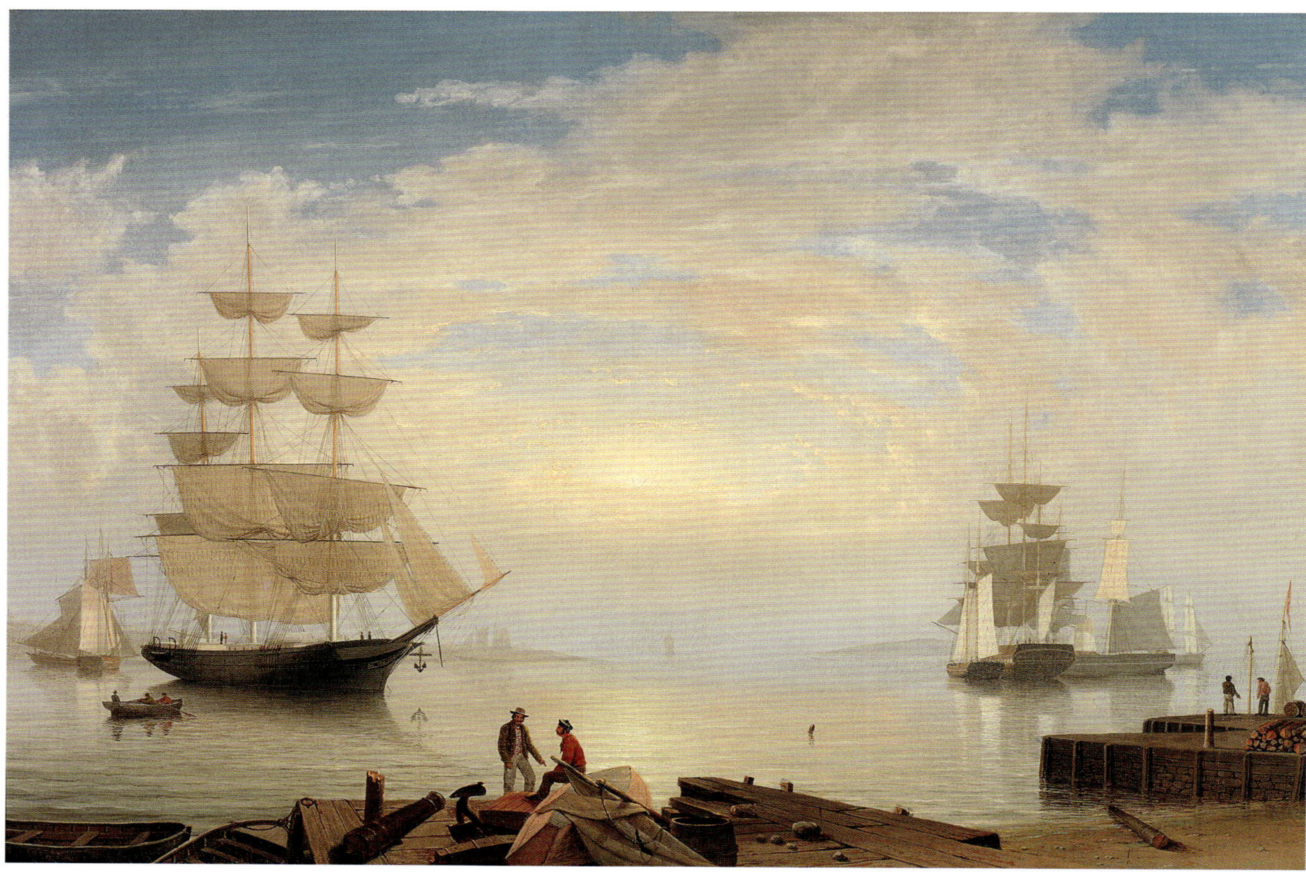

FIGURE 100
Fitz H. Lane, *New England Harbor at Sunrise*, ca. 1850. Oil on canvas, 24¼ × 36¼ in. (61.6 × 92.1 cm). Cape Ann Museum, Gloucester, Massachusetts. Gift of Judge Lawrence Brooks, 1970 (2020).

the daily conversation among and financial well-being of Lane's closest associates.[19]

Lane was a craftsman respectful of craft knowledge, a traveler well acquainted with the travel of wood: trees to logs, logs to lumber, lumber to finished, serviceable, sellable product. He was a traveler who knew well that the tall straight white pines sprinkled through the spruce-fir forests of northern Maine and through the birch-beech-maple-hemlock forests of the rest of northern New England made the best ships' masts and house frames, that the oak of the oak-chestnut-poplar forest of southern New England and Pennsylvania made the best hulls, and that chestnut made the best rail fences. In other words, Lane was someone for whom a landscape was legible not just as geometry, or as a geography of place, but as a geography into which trees have been brought, trees grown in distant forests, each type of tree enlisted to do the job it was best suited to do. He himself may have made a trip to the Caribbean to paint a view that foregrounded mahogany logs, the Atlantic world's most expensive lumber (see chapter 8). A maker of shoes and of paintings, he would have known what it was to craft his town and his culture's fleets of vessels from all kinds of wood. While Lane's images focus on the specific and appear to celebrate localness, they also tell a story about the well-articulated segments of a vast, very human, wide-ranging oceanic marketplace.

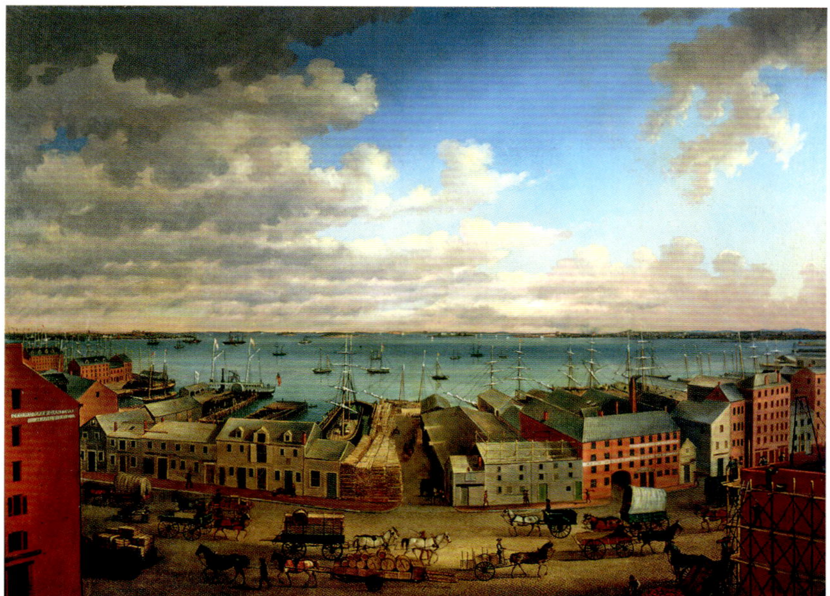

FIGURE 101
John White Allen Scott, *Boston Harbor*, 1853. Oil on panel, 38½ × 50½ in. Courtesy of the Bostonian Society. Museum purchase (1884.0209).

The trade in wood was not, however, just a straight trajectory from tree to finished product. Wood was one of many products circulating in a complex map of exchange including extraction commodities (lumber, fish, furs, salt), agricultural commodities (cotton, salt pork, sugar), and processed commodities (rum, whiskey). The 1829 log of one Gloucester-based vessel, a bark, reveals the complex patterns of trade in which lumber was a key commodity; it records a detailed picture of "tramping," starting with a load of lumber. The venture involved a continuous string of trades in St. Thomas, Savannah, Liverpool, Portland, Mobile, Havre de Grace, Philadelphia, Norfolk, and Gibraltar exchanging lumber, logwood, cotton, coal, salt, hay, potatoes, more lumber, mackerel, skins, pipe staves, molasses, and pine planking, endeavors undermined by drunken and AWOL crew members, mutiny, and hurricane—all in the conduct of one voyage throughout the Atlantic.[20] Nor did all wood have the dignity of becoming a crafted product—more was burned as fuel for heating, cooking, driving steamboats and steam engines, than was employed as dimensional lumber during the 1840–60 period.[21] Lane includes a small stack of cordwood on the right edge of one of his most poetic paintings to intimate this extremely important use of the vast forests of the eastern portion of North America (fig. 100). By contrast, one artist who actually attempted to depict the scale of the antebellum trade in wood products was Lane's partner in the lithography business from 1845 to 1847, John White Allen Scott, whose very descriptive *Boston Harbor* of 1853 gives a view opposite to that chosen by Lane for his many Boston Harbor paintings, its central feature a warehouse-sized stack of cordwood destined to help heat the metropolis over the winter (fig. 101). It is estimated that at midcentury the average American family used 17.5 cords of wood per annum (a cord being a wood stack 4' × 4' × 8').[22] Lane, predictably, just gestures to the substantial trade in this commodity, implying but not describing the volume of cordwood consumption in antebellum America.

In his paintings depicting cordwood piles, the building of ships, the transport of lumber, or the processing of fish, Lane's strategy is, like the creator of any fiction, to present a coherent focused narrative, only gesturing to the scale of the industries in which his fictional characters are engaged and with which his audience is understood to be familiar. In Herman Melville's *Moby-Dick* a single whaler, the *Pequod*, is the setting for a novel of expansive proportions; the reader recognizes this ship as evoking hundreds of such vessels vigorously engaged in securing essential lamp fuel and lubricating oil in an intensely industrializing nation. Against these very real sets of facts, well known to his readers, concerning a valuable commodity, Melville constructs a fiction in which the quest morphs into an artwork "about" a single ship with an entirely separate aesthetic value. Lane's fictions make the same moves with the same presumptions about the substitution (and elaboration) of the single fictional instance in a forest of facts and assumptions about realities at the center of the culture's powerful economic and technological forces and thousands of quotidian enactments furthering those goals. My project here is to parse those facts for an audience for which they are unfamiliar, not to critique Lane for portraying single modest instances instead of describing the large-scale human activities his pictures evoke. What is rare about Lane is that these human activities are at the heart of paintings usually described as "landscapes" even though they might more aptly be described as "harborscapes" or in similar terms intimating the central role of humans, their constructions, and their motivations. He is not a documentarian; rather, he is a "poet" whose fictions—unlike those of most nineteenth-century landscape painters—allude to human craft, creativity, ingenuity, and, sometimes, destruction.

Frederic Church's paintings of the Maine coast from the years when he was reportedly sketching and planning paintings on Mount Desert Island at roughly the same time Lane was there are very different in character from Lane's. Church's paintings depict the lonely, dangerous, rocky shore or broad expanses of majestic wilderness, offering a view of Maine that suggests no utility and little comfort for human inhabitants. Although at this date "immense tracts of land all along the coast of Maine, from the St. Croix to the Penobscot," were clear-cut and thus presented "a desolate and forbidding aspect," Church and others steadfastly averted their eyes from extraction activities and from commerce.[23] Church was by far the more celebrated artist—the expansive virgin forest was the Maine his New York patrons wanted to see and, in portable landscape-painting form, to buy. This is Maine pictured as though he were the first human to see this vision of pure nature. Characteristic is the oil sketch *Eagle Lake Viewed from Cadillac Mountain, Mount Desert Island, Maine* (fig. 102). Frederic Church's fiction of a virtually "untouched" natural landscape was (and remains today) an extremely powerful force in the making and selling of images. It was an important vehicle in promoting the doctrine of Manifest Destiny, the myth of an empty continent—"virgin" land voided by retreating or deceasing Native Americans.[24]

At about the time that Fitz Henry Lane, Frederic Church, and other artists began to explore coastal Maine, Henry David Thoreau made the first of several forays into the interior of the state. He paused en route to Mount Ktaadin to describe metropolitan Bangor: "fifty miles up the Penobscot [River], at the head of navigation for vessels of the largest class, [this city is] the principal lumber depot on this continent, with a population of twelve thousand, [like] a star on the edge of night . . . , still hewing at the forests of which it is built, already overflowing with the luxuries and refinements of Europe, and sending its vessels to Spain, to England, and to the West Indies for its groceries."[25] In 1830 an unnamed writer for the *Gloucester Telegraph* corroborated Thoreau's analysis:

> These eastern [Maine] vessels poke their bowsprits into almost every port in the known world, with an outbound cargo that cost them nothing but the demolition of their own forests, and a freight home that builds towns and cities where those forests grew. With truth they are the most enterprising portion of a most enterprising people. The state of Maine has, for the last fifteen years, carried on a trade with the Spanish West India Islands, to a greater extent than any nation in the world and during the first five years, exchanged a cargo of lumber for a cargo of molasses, without the aid of a single dollar in cash. They have crossed every

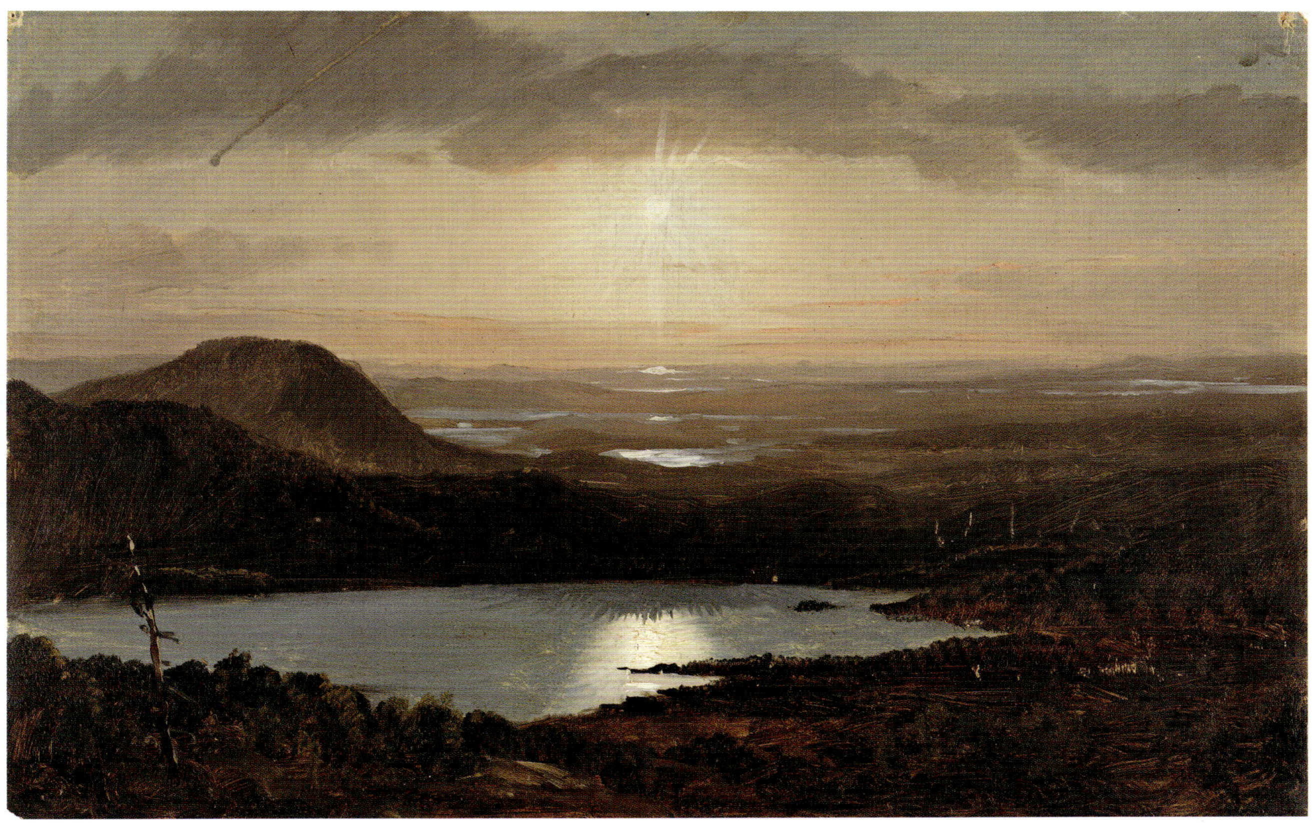

FIGURE 102
Frederic Edwin Church, *Eagle Lake Viewed from Cadillac Mountain, Mount Desert Island, Maine*, 1850–60. Brush and oil paint, graphite on paperboard, 11⁹⁄₁₆ × 17½ in. (29.4 × 44.5 cm). Cooper Hewitt, Smithsonian Design Museum, New York. Gift of Louis P. Church, 1917-4-324. Photo: Cooper Hewitt, Smithsonian Design Museum / Art Resource, New York (Matt Flynn).

> ocean—traversed every sea—visited every people in search of a market . . . to peddle lumber and fish, and become wealthy.[26]

The reader can imagine Thoreau, noticing but averting his eyes—like Frederic Church—from town and from lumber, setting out for the wilderness, and for the values it represented as a corrective to society, civilization, and their faults, as a place of potential refuge and redemption. Unlike Thoreau, who celebrated the living tree and decried lumbering in Maine as a "a war against the pines," the painters made no complaint and, except for Lane, made almost no reference to this enormous industry.[27]

Lane was not Thoreau or Frederic Church, heading off into the wilderness following the faint trails of trappers and Native Americans, pausing to muse at the abandoned remnants of a remote logging camp or the majesty of the remaining first-growth white pines. His disability and his inclination kept him near waterways, roadways, and harbors. Lane's paintings picture activities downstream from winter logging in the forest. Although his works allude to lumbering, violence and destruction are muted. His focus is directed toward human know-how and finished product. Lane does not show the violence in the forest because that was not his quest; Lane wanted to see (and record) those sites where paths intersected, where one kind of labor interfaced with another, where goods in one state were transformed into another: the sawmill, the harbor, the boatyard.

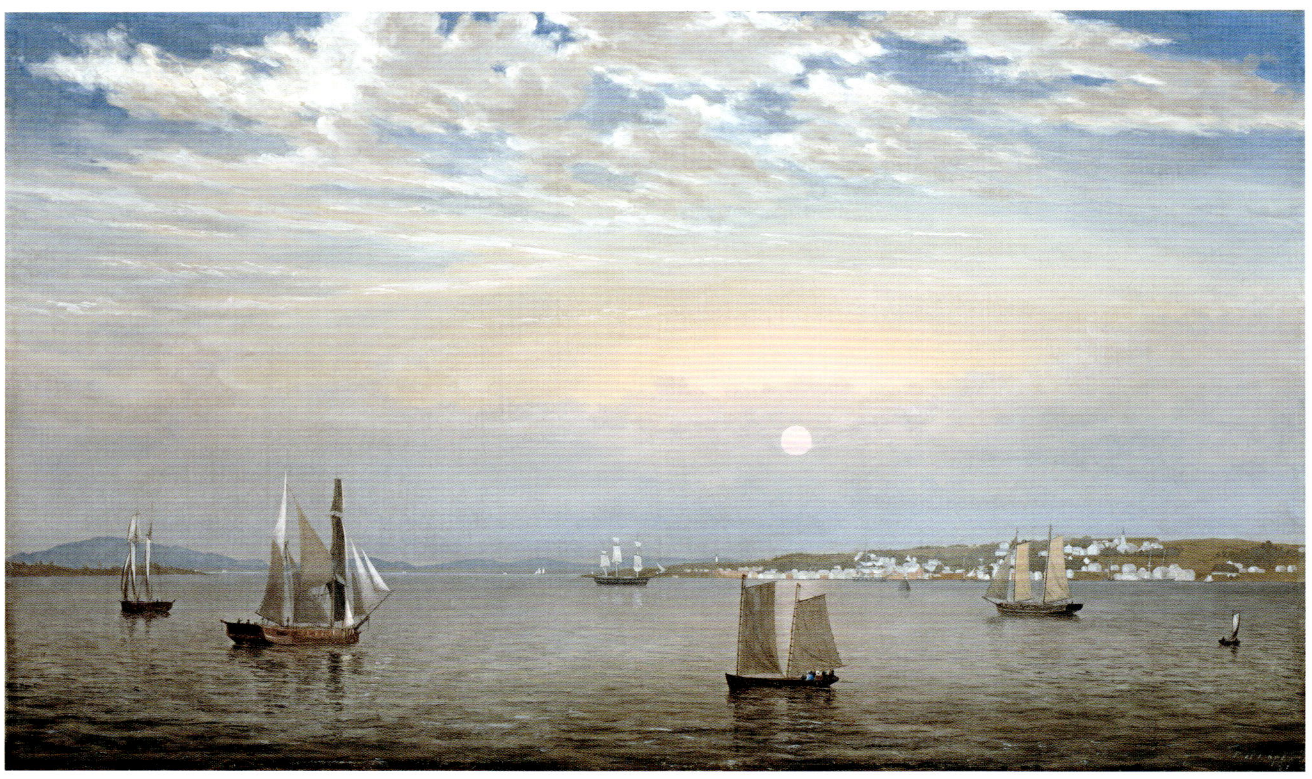

FIGURE 103
Fitz H. Lane, *Castine Harbor and Town*, 1851. Oil on canvas, 20 × 33¼ in. (50.8 × 84.5 cm). Putnam Foundation, Timken Museum of Art, San Diego, California (1986.001).

This, then, is the link so many have intuited between Walden Pond and Penobscot Bay: both Thoreau and Lane presuppose a solitary viewer with intense viewing skills and deep knowledge of social, historical, and physical ecology, as well as intense curiosity about the multiple interdependent links between them.

CASTINE WITH INDIANS

According to one art historian, Lane saw Maine as "a more purified and untroubled place conducive to resting and uplifting the spirit."[28] From such a perspective, one could see *Castine Harbor and Town* of 1851 as exemplifying Nathaniel Hawthorne's view of the young United States as "a country where there is no shadow, no antiquity, no mystery, no picturesque and gloomy wrong, nor anything but a commonplace prosperity in broad and simple daylight" (fig. 103).[29] The lumber brig on the left, with the crisp late-afternoon light catching the edge of its sails, the grand white-sailed square-rigged ship in the distance, and the day-trippers in the little schooner in the foreground, as well as the foursquare white-painted wooden buildings of the town of Castine, appear to represent an "untroubled place" of "commonplace prosperity" seen in the clear descriptive light of day. But Lane's paintings of the town of Castine and Penobscot Bay, I would suggest, in fact contain intimations of Hawthornian "shadow," "antiquity," and "gloomy wrong" that bear investigation.

Lane's *Castine, Maine* of 1856 depicts the town in which Lane spent many summers as guest in a house on the hill that shelters the settlement's principal asset, its

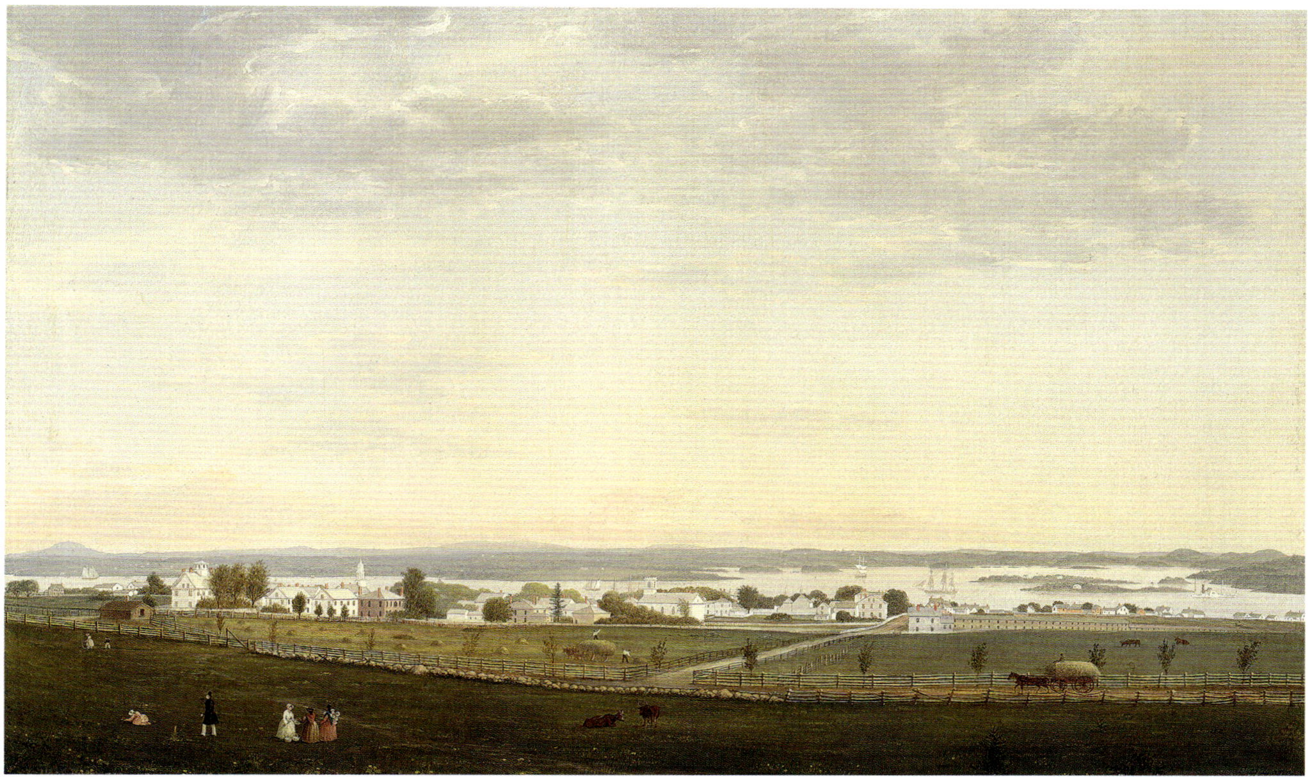

FIGURE 104
Fitz H. Lane, *Castine, Maine*, 1856. Oil on canvas, 21⅛ × 33½ in. (53.66 × 85.09 cm). Museum of Fine Arts, Boston. Bequest of Maxim Karolik (64.437). Photo © 2022 Museum of Fine Arts, Boston.

deepwater harbor (fig. 104). The buildings cluster near the water's edge, and a scene of haying occupies the sunny middle distance. This is not just picturesque pastoral summer farm work; it is a crucial aspect of the logging industry. There was little meadowland for haying in nineteenth-century Maine, and yet the oxen that provided the muscle of the logging industry could not survive their winter work without hay. It took as many as fourteen oxen to draw a single log from the place where it grew to the nearest river or navigable tributary. Hay to feed the oxen was valuable. Without hay the oxen would starve; without the oxen the logs could not move.[30] The making of hay in Lane's painting signals the linkage of meadow to forest and the making of profit, not a pastoral subsistence economy. Here, as elsewhere, Lane has underlined relationships between land, individual labor, and broader economic and temporal communities.

In the distance an orderly array of brick-chimneyed, white-clapboarded buildings—homes, churches, schools—give a sense of a well-ordered community. The long low gray ropewalk to the right underlines the maritime character of the town's economy, and a small steamship approaching from the right suggests regularly scheduled passenger and freight service between Castine and larger urban areas in the region and beyond.[31] In the distance, the forests of northern Maine stretch seemingly endlessly to the horizon.

Against the darker green grass sprinkled with wildflowers in the foreground, a transaction is taking place. A bonneted Euro-American woman, parasol or umbrella in hand, turns from her family and pauses in her walk to look at baskets proffered by two darkly clad women, their wares bundled in the grasp of the blue-shawled figure

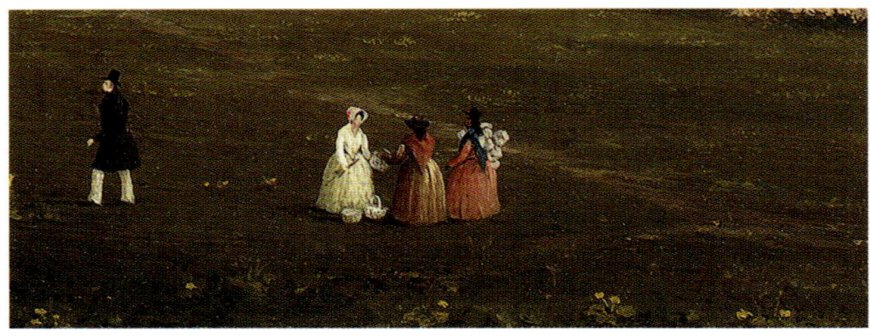

FIGURE 105
Fitz H. Lane, *Castine, Maine*, 1856 (fig. 104), detail.

on the right and on the ground at their feet (fig. 105). Their untied hair, flat-brimmed hats, and copious shawls identify them as Native Americans. But these are not the befeathered warriors poised majestically with bow and arrow that figure in the romanticized landscape paintings of such contemporaries as Thomas Cole or the nubile Indian maidens of midcentury dime novels;[32] they are stolid women in the matter-of-fact hybrid clothing of Native Americans living in physical and cultural proximity to Euro-American mid-nineteenth-century settlements. Sturdy baskets made of brown ash splints—a forest product fabricated from beaten ash logs—had long been crafted by the Indigenous people of Maine, and they were sought after, prized, and used in the majority culture as indispensable, sturdy carryalls.[33] Indeed, George A. Wheeler, historian of Castine and successor to Joseph L. Stevens's medical practice, describes such a basket at work in the hands of Dorothy Stevens, Lane's hostess in Castine:

> Dorothy Little Stevens, a veritable grandmother to the host of patients of the good old doctor, her husband . . . trips down Main street from her house at the corner of Stevens [Street]; beneath the shadow of the nodding plumes upon her bonnet bob her soft white curls, which lend a halo to the calm serenity of her face. Within that basket so carefully guarded on her arm, it is an easy wager, is concealed a bowl of calves foot jelly, fine rye bread and a soft custard, to be left beside the bed of some little sick girl.[34]

Like so many of her contemporaries, Mrs. Stevens did her errands with the aid of what was almost certainly a Native American basket on her arm.

What Lane intended to suggest with the inclusion of these figures and these baskets is a useful question to pursue. Perhaps he sought to describe the everyday character of contact with Native people in Castine or the persistence of their very useful arts and crafts, or the deep history of not-always-so-benign cultural contact in coastal Maine. In 1830, according to "Indians in Maine and Massachusetts," a report based on the census and published in the *Gloucester Telegraph*, "in the State of Maine there are three tribes of Indians—the St. John's, 300 in number; Passamaquoddies, 379, which claim 100 acres of land; and the Penobscot tribe, 277 in number, and claiming 92,160 acres. In Massachusetts, there are the Marshpee tribe of 320 persons; Herring Pond tribe of 40; Martha's Vineyard of 340; and the Troy tribe, of 50 persons."[35] Lane's basket sellers are presumably among the Penobscots who lived inland and camped in summer near Castine.[36]

Lane may equally have been querying how Native Americans fit into the larger economies he references in his canvases. His friends and hosts, the Stevenses, visited nearby Wabanaki seasonal camps, perhaps to purchase articles of use.[37] But there were also, apparently, year-round Indigenous residents making and selling baskets. An article published in 1850 described a white man of "gentlemanly bearing" living with a Native American wife "in a beautiful cove on the Bagaduce peninsula" near Castine, where, "making baskets, moccasins, bows and arrows, fishing, and shooting, they seem to live as contentedly and happily as human beings could desire; the neighboring village [Castine] affords a ready market for their products and thence they supply themselves with many of the necessities and luxuries of life."[38] On a larger scale, contributing to the relative prosperity of the local Native Americans, the valuable river frontage above

Bangor, in the area of the Penobscot River Boom, where annually thousands of logs were caught, sorted, rafted, and held until sold to mill operators, was owned by the Penobscots and rented for substantial fees to the boom's proprietors.[39]

Although they held tribal lands, Native Americans also moved freely—if conspicuously—through the townscapes of antebellum New England. In September 1849, for instance, "a party of Ojibway Indians, who have visited various parts of the United States and also Europe," visited Gloucester, and one, "Maungwudaus in his own native costume," gave "a lecture on the manners and customs of their tribe . . . [to a] very large audience."[40] The next year he returned, having visited the president in the interim, and assured his Gloucester audience that "the money which he now receives at his lectures and entertainments, will be appropriated for the support and education of his sons at Dartmouth College."[41] Also recall the party of Penobscot Indians who were in Gloucester on the occasion of the disastrous fire of 1830 and were credited with having valiantly helped extinguish the conflagration.[42] Francis Bennett, the teenage diarist who worked in Samuel Stevens's dry-goods store in Gloucester, noted that on August 25, 1854, he had gone to the depot in nearby Manchester "to see a Company or tribe of Penobscot Indians about 20 in number" come in on the train.[43] Bangor apparently was frequently visited by "Indians . . . from [the permanent settlement nearby at] Oldtown, in their canoes. . . . [They] promenade the streets in light and airy attire of blankets and paint" (fig. 106).[44] Records indicate that Indigenous Americans worked in the lumbering industry; Joshua Cooper, an Indian, died of cholera in Boston in 1849; and three Indians were among the 262 convicts incarcerated in Massachusetts jails in 1829.[45] These scattered comments suggest populations of somewhat urbanized Native Americans moving freely, individually and in groups, seeking employment, selling their craft products, and giving lyceum-type lectures throughout the townscapes Lane and his patrons inhabited.

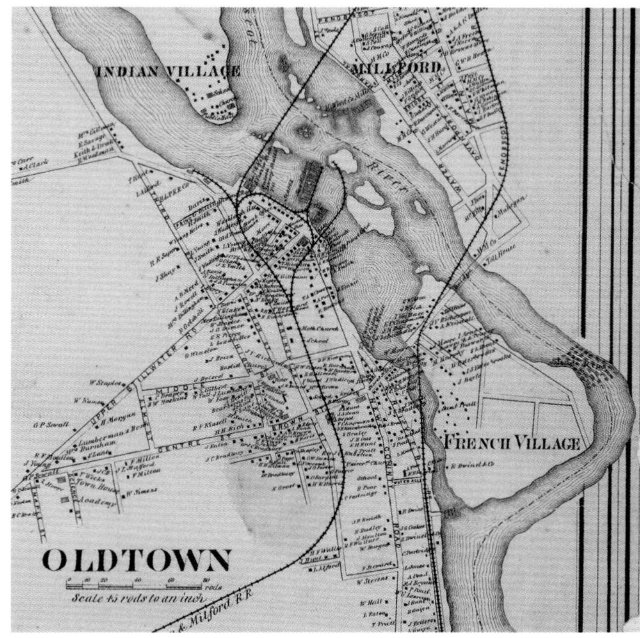

FIGURE 106
Henry Francis Walling, *Topographical Map of the County of Penobscot Maine, from surveys under the direction of H. F. Walling*, 1859, detail. Field work under the direction of L. H. Eaton, Bangor, Maine. Printed at H. F. Walling's, New York. Courtesy, American Antiquarian Society.

The eighteenth-century distinction made in the majority culture between "neighbor-Indians," or "Settlement Indians," and "foreign Indians," or "back nations," appears to have persisted into the nineteenth century, allowing members of the dominant culture to hold simultaneously contradictory views on Native American matters.[46] The *Cape Ann Light and Gloucester Telegraph* on successive Saturdays in May 1848, for instance, reported "the death of the famous Osage Chief *Black Dog* . . . courteous in his manners, warm hearted, and generally beloved. As a warrior he had no equal" (reprinted from the *Cherokee Advocate*), followed a week later by "news of a battle between 500 white settlers and 2000 Indians in Oregon after missionaries [were] massacred."[47] These and similar contemporary documents suggest widely disparate understandings of the current contentions, the substantial disadvantages, and the ideal future for Native Americans in New England and in the United States.

In the background of Lane's young adulthood, Indian removal—the forced relocation of Native American tribes from their treaty lands in Georgia, Florida, and Mississippi to the trans-Mississippi West from 1830—roiled not only the dislocated Native Americans themselves but also those watching from afar, stirring a controversy that was constantly before the public and that must have prompted all citizens to examine their understanding of Native peoples in the national future. A congressional report of 1826, for instance, opined: "Their tracts of land are mostly situated near flourishing [Euro-American] villages. They seem (as now situated) to contract the evil without pursuing the good habits of white men. . . . Locating themselves in a body sufficiently compact for agricultural purposes, and sufficiently remote . . . [is] the only course that can save these sinking people from annihilation."[48] Such sentiments, sympathetic with the idea of removal, were followed up in the *Gloucester Telegraph* with positive news reports on the prospect of the military relocation of Georgia's and Florida's Native Americans, one of which reassuringly stated: "Arriving in Arkansas, each warrior will receive thirty dollars, a rifle gun, beaver trap, brass kettle, and be supported at the expence [*sic*] of the United States for twelve months. The country selected for them is said to be fertile and desirable, abounding with game, and in every respect adapted to the habits and pursuits of such a people."[49]

Four months later the same Gloucester newspaper reprinted from the *Cherokee Phoenix* (a newspaper published by the Cherokee Nation) an editorial sharply critical of President Andrew Jackson's removal enterprise, eloquently pleading, "Where have we an example in the whole history of man, of a Nation or tribe, removing in a body, from a land of civil and religious means, to a perfect wilderness, in order to be civilized!"[50] Taking another tack, Rep. Edward Everett of Massachusetts was reported to have argued against the removal on the grounds of expense, which he estimated to be $24 million, to cover "purchase of the Indian title [to Georgia and Florida lands], Improvements to be paid for, Transportation, subsistence one year, cost of new lands in the West, military force to protect them."[51] In January 1831, the *Gloucester Telegraph* quoted without comment Thomas Jefferson's forceful statement, from 1791, that "the Indians have a right to the occupation of their Lands . . . until they cede them by treaty," and "that the [federal] Government [during his administration] is determined to extend all its energy for the patronage and protection of the Rights of the Indians."[52] Nevertheless, the Seminoles, Creeks, and Cherokees were displaced, and Supreme Court Chief Justice John Marshall was reported to have "declared that the treatment of the Indians by the present Administration [of Andrew Jackson], has shocked the moral sense of the American people."[53] In sum, Lane, then a shoemaker in Gloucester, and other adults in New England distant from these events would nonetheless have read many newspaper articles on the subject and would have been alert to the rights and fates of Native Americans, especially those embroiled in removal but also those who remained near "flourishing villages" such as Castine and sold baskets to their neighbors.

By midcentury, when the country had expanded to the Pacific, the newspapers frequently reported not only murderous clashes among settlers, the military, and trans-Mississippi tribal groups but also occasional narratives of harmonious coexistence.[54] In other words, beyond public-policy debates with real-world consequences, reports of massacres, treachery, and destruction of property, livelihoods, and lives frequently reached Lane and the communities of which he was a part. These alarming incidents occurred far away, but they were constantly in the background of Lane's adult life, and subsequent to the annexation of, and discovery of gold in, California, the bloodshed increased as, in the 1850s, pressure on the "back nations" accelerated, with aggression and resistance leading to atrocities and vengeance, which were reported weekly. These news reports inevitably brought to mind similar events distant in time from the artist's sojourns in Castine but close in geography.

Lane, hosted by Dr. Joseph L. Stevens, who had an antiquarian bent, would not have been unaware of the

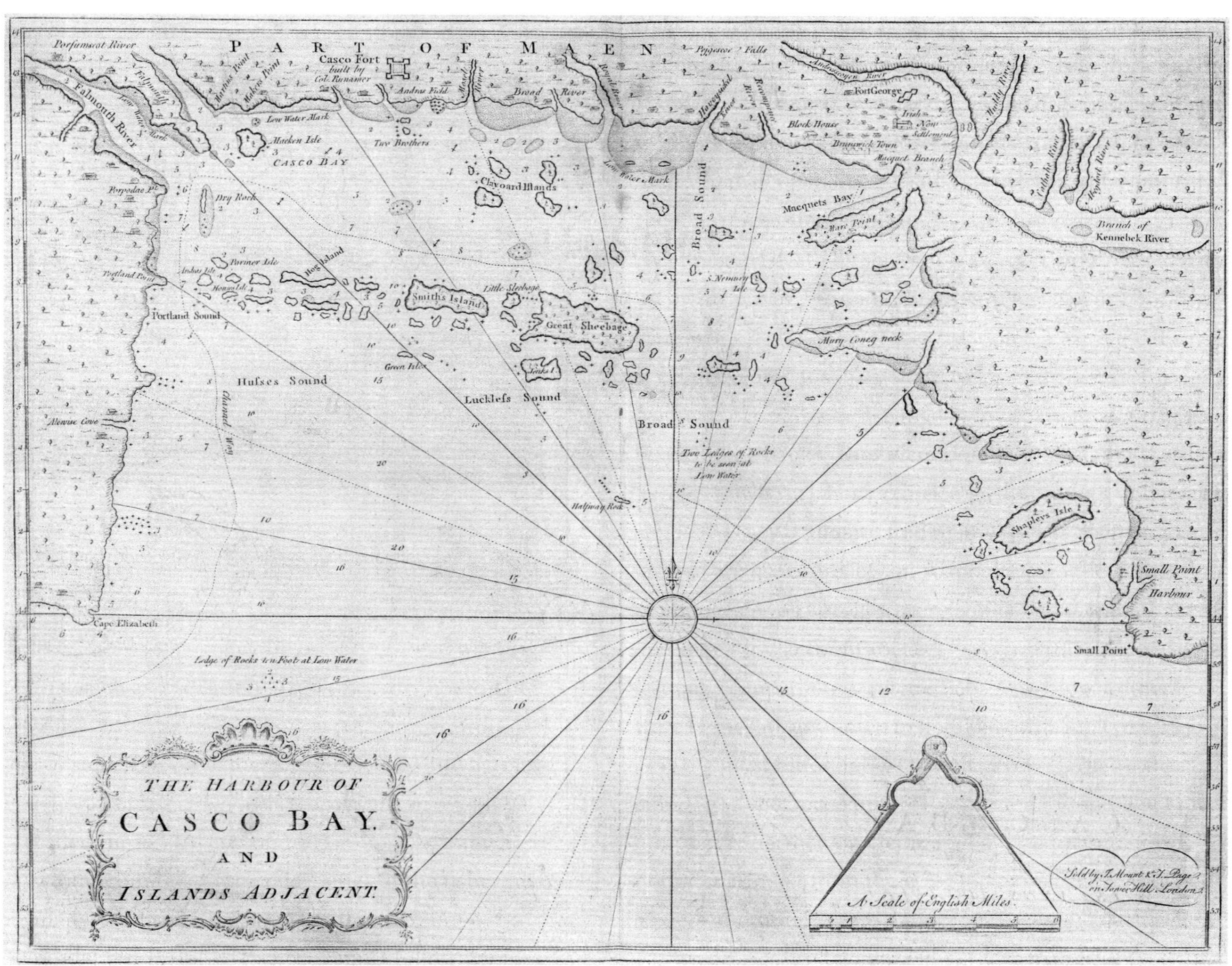

FIGURE 107
Capt. Cyprian Southack, *The Harbour of Casco Bay, and Islands Adjacent* (London: Mount & Davidson, ca. 1720, reprinted 1794). Engraving on paper, 17 × 21½ in. (43.18 × 54.61 cm). Courtesy, David Rumsey Map Collection, David Rumsey Map Center, Stanford University Libraries.

history of coastal Maine, where, between 1675 and 1745, Euro-American settlement had twice been curtailed as Native Americans—often prompted by the French in Canada—eliminated some Anglo-American communities. Lane's family was directly impacted, as he would have learned from family narratives.

James Lane, the family's American progenitor, was a woodworker, specifically a turner, by trade, and he emigrated from London to Malden, Massachusetts, just north of Boston, in 1655. Five years later he moved with his young family to Casco Bay, Maine (near present-day Portland), a landscape of farms and forts, where he acquired considerable land (fig. 107).[55] In September 1688, in what one scholar has termed "a tragedy of errors," James (Fitz Henry Lane's great-great-great-great-grandfather), together with other settlers, was killed by Wabanakis.[56] The same month, two of James's sons—Henry and Samuel—were attacked by an Indian who spent the night in their home in North Yarmouth, but the brothers survived and retreated to Gloucester.[57] Fitz Henry Lane was descended from Samuel (born around 1664), a blacksmith who, abandoning his Maine properties, obtained a land grant in Gloucester in 1708.[58]

John Lane, a third son of the immigrant James, abandoned his property in Falmouth, Maine (also in the Casco Bay region), in the wake of the second destruction of that settlement by Native Americans, and he settled in Gloucester around 1693.[59] He was awarded ten acres at Flatstone Cove on Cape Ann, property named for him and subsequently known as Lanesville. John raised his family on Cape Ann; his third son, also John, born around 1688, became a mariner, owning half a coaster and half a fishing vessel. On June 22, 1724, during a fishing trip with the husband of his sister and two other kinsmen, he put in at Owl's Head or adjacent Fox Harbor at the mouth of Penobscot Bay (for fresh water or to make repairs), where they were killed by Native Americans (fig. 108).[60] John's grandson William Lane was also killed by Indians at Owl's Head on an unspecified date before 1760.[61] Altogether, six of Lane's antecedents were killed by Native Americans between 1688 and 1760, some at Falmouth (Portland) but most near the mouth of Penobscot Bay, where the artist summered, and painted, and sojourned in a household steeped in history.

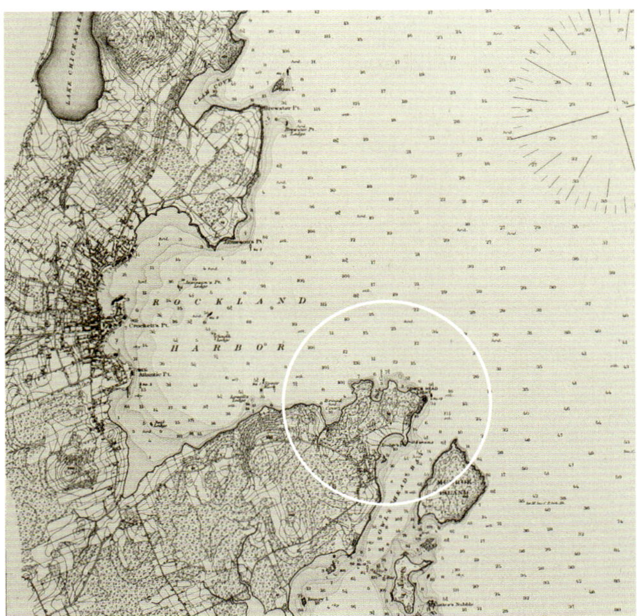

FIGURE 108
A. D. Bache, *U.S. Coastal Survey, Penobscot Bay, Maine*, 1876, detail. Courtesy, American Antiquarian Society. Owl's Head indicated.

These were not isolated incidents (there were many deaths, captures, and abandonments), nor were they simply acts on the part of an Indigenous population resisting intrusion. After decades of more or less mutually accommodating trade relationships based on the exchange of furs for European metalwares and armaments, global forces impacting mutual trust and tribal alliances disrupted a fragile trade-based status quo on the border between the English and French imperial projects in the New World.[62] These local conflicts were, in other words, localized chapters in larger European wars and religious hostilities. They concerned ideology and also derived from utilitarian motives such as Native American impatience with traders withholding arms and ammunition as much as from international upheavals or individual bad acts and ill will.[63] Keeping the seventeenth-century past, including relations between Native Americans and New Englanders, in view, Gloucester's newspapers periodically published notes from the archives, as did, for instance, the *Gloucester Telegraph* in 1827, in an article that described how in 1631 one Josias Plaistow, as punishment for purloining corn from the Indians, was fined and stripped of his honorific "Mr."[64] Among those with strong antiquarian interests were Lane himself, his friend Joseph Stevens Jr., and Joseph's father, Lane's host in Castine.[65]

For Lane, then, the landscape of Maine was not the "untroubled place" twentieth-century visitors to Maine experienced and valued but a landscape in which grim historic events had happened that directly impacted both the ancestors of the basket makers he painted and his family's five-generation life of retreat in Gloucester.[66] The dramatic landmark Owl's Head, a distinctive pair of steep hills on a prominent point at the mouth of Penobscot Bay where the majestic estuary meets the Atlantic, had a private and ominous character for Lane as the site of the

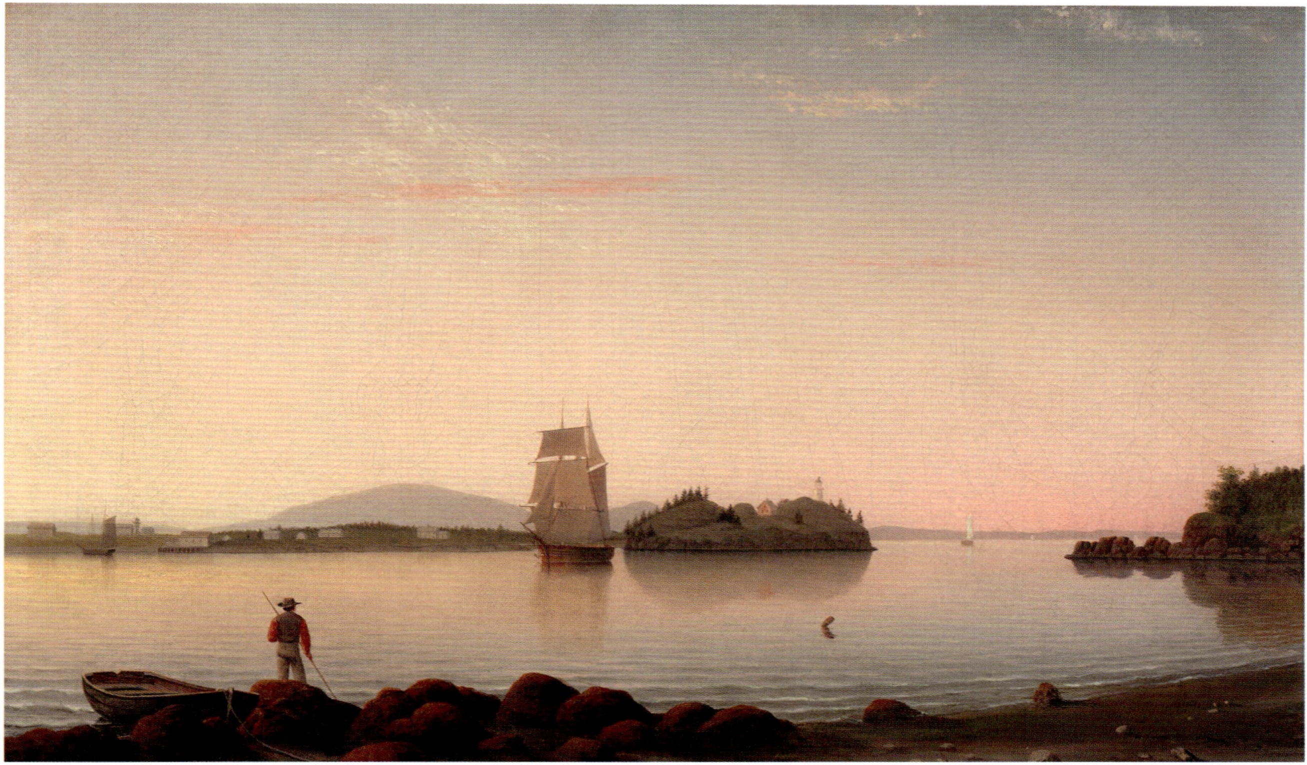

FIGURE 109
Fitz H. Lane, *Owl's Head, Penobscot Bay, Maine*, 1862. Oil on canvas, 15¾ × 26⅛ in. (40 × 66.36 cm). Museum of Fine Arts, Boston. Bequest of Martha C. Karolik for the M. and M. Karolik Collection of American Paintings, 1815–1865 (48.448). Photo © 2022 Museum of Fine Arts, Boston.

murder of a kinsman as well as a more public character as a prominent public landmark (fig. 108). Lane painted it repeatedly and gave a dark nocturnal view of the site to his Maine hostess, Dorothy Stevens.[67] Most of Lane's views of Owl's Head depict a turbulent sea and windy sky as vessels of all types pursue their individual errands (for example, *Off Owl's Head, Maine*, 1852 [CAM]; *Owl's Head Light, Rockland, Maine*, n.d. [Farnsworth Art Museum]).[68] But his best-known view of Owl's Head is that at the Museum of Fine Arts in Boston, showing the prominent hills and lighthouse set off against a flat sea in the strait between the promontory's peninsula and Munroe Island in the pearly light of early morning (fig. 109).[69] Lane's flat-water views have usually been interpreted by scholars today as more contemplative, intellectually "deeper," than his choppy-water paintings, which were favored by his contemporaries, and Lane invites that introspective interpretation here by including a prominent turned figure in the foreground. This man is not rowing or cleaning fish or taking in sail or loading lumber; he is looking at the landscape and thinking, inviting the painting's viewer to look and think as well. The nature of that thinking has been glossed as reflection on "the place of man in nature—man as solitary [in] . . . the limitless wilderness of the New World," and that site has been described as a portrait of "natural outcroppings of rock and shore . . . transformed into an abstract sequence of planes . . . [evoking] timeless stability," a scene from which "the artist's self is purged from the canvas," suggesting that "the continuous connection with the fundamental and simple

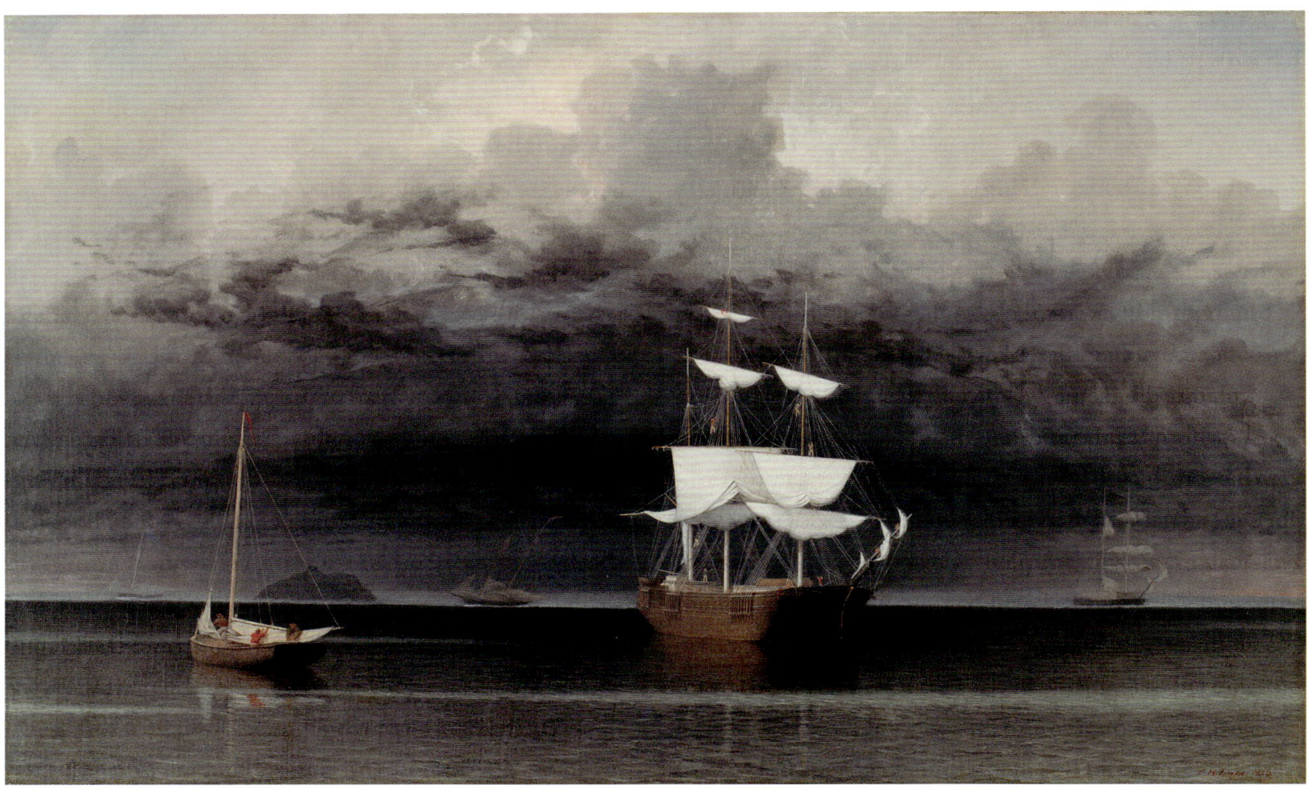

FIGURE 110 (ABOVE)
Fitz H. Lane, *Ships and an Approaching Storm off Owl's Head, Maine*, 1860. Oil on canvas, 24 × 39 ⅝ in. (60.96 × 100.64 cm). Private collection.

FIGURE 111 (OPPOSITE)
Fitz H. Lane, *Ships and an Approaching Storm off Owl's Head, Maine*, 1860 (fig. 110), detail.

element in life will lead man to that kind of illumination, knowledge, and faith which enables him to recognize that '[e]very vessel is an ark.'"[70] Extremely unusual in Lane's oeuvre, this contemplative figure, a viewer surrogate, most obviously suggests, however, that the specific object of his attention—Owl's Head—is of particular import. The site of Lane's kinsman's unforeseen death and the larger historic scene of deadly antagonism throughout centuries of Maine's history, it is a worthy object of contemplation.

Equally unusual in Lane's oeuvre and equally masterful is Lane's *Ships and an Approaching Storm off Owl's Head, Maine* of 1860 (figs. 110 and 111). Of the suite of paintings Lane did of this site at the entrance to Penobscot Bay, this is the most ominous. Seven sailors scramble in the rigging of the three-master in the middle of the painting and on the sloop to the left to furl sails and secure canvas as the blackening sky and dangerous winds already in evidence in the background threaten to carry these vessels onto the rocks. Even more beautifully painted than the chromatically subtle skies for which he is so celebrated, this monochrome blanket of dark air with a sliver of light-blue water at the horizon, interrupted by the dark mass of Owl's Head between the vessels, has astonishing depth and weight, at once fearsome and sublime.

Few other subjects received such sustained attention from Lane as Owl's Head. He pictured the distinctive promontory from the north and from the south, during night and during daytime, in gusty conditions and in dead calm, as well as here shrouded in a tempestuous

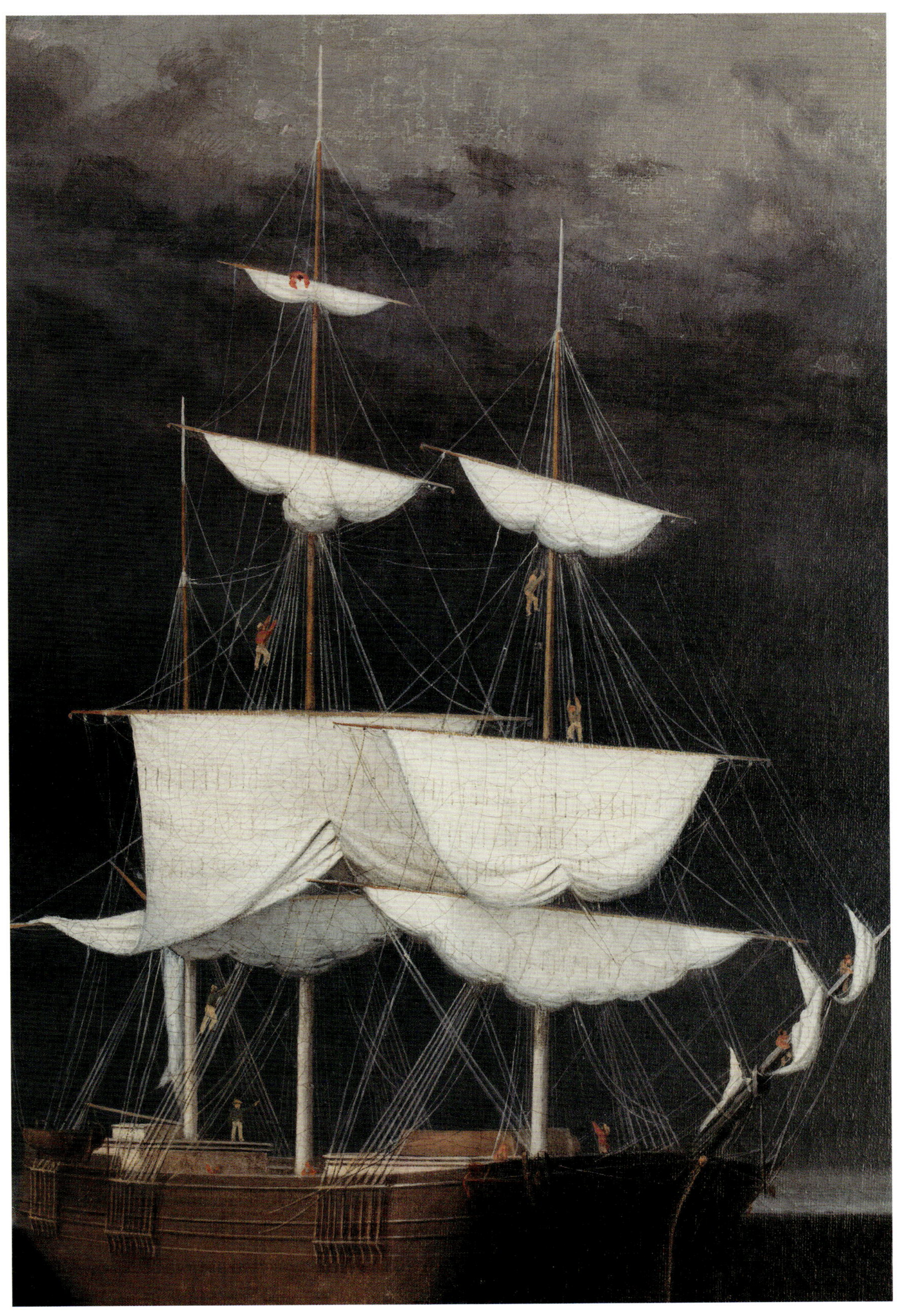

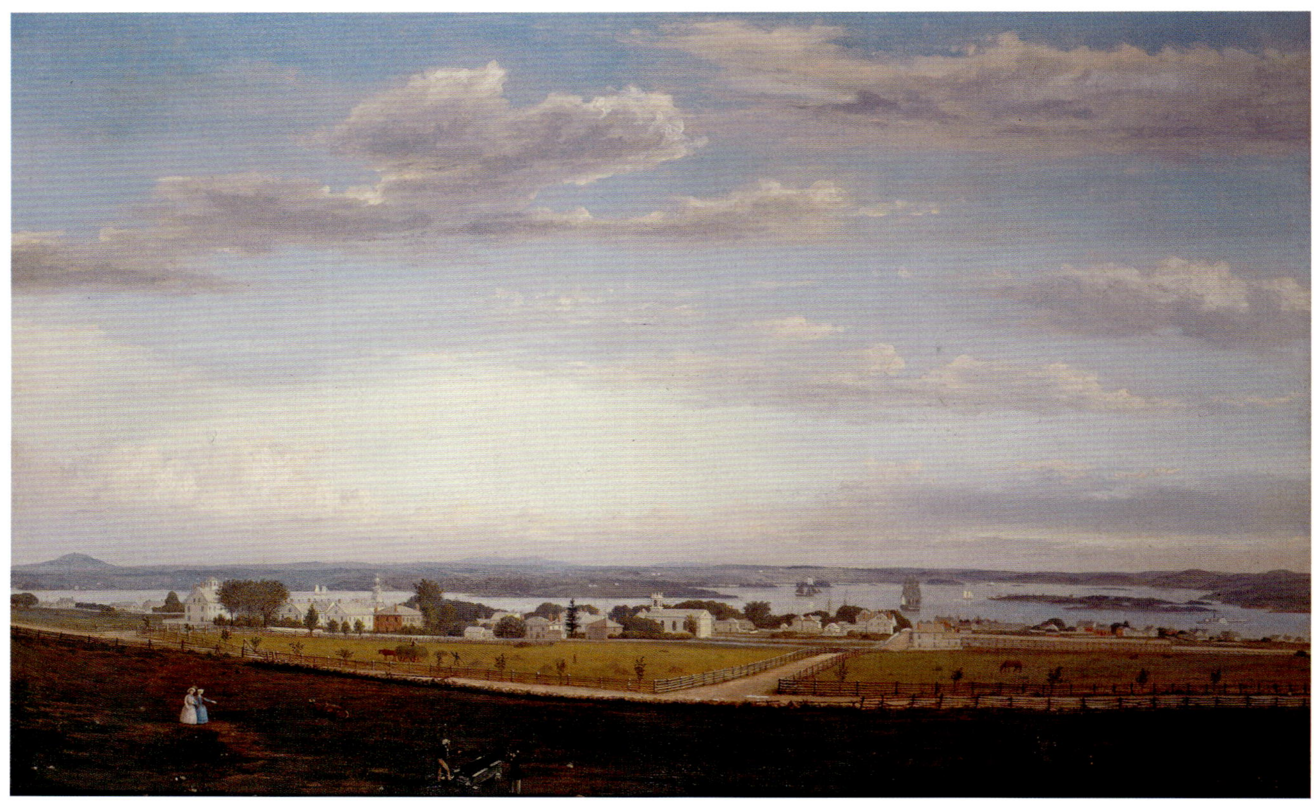

FIGURE 112
Fitz H. Lane, *View of Castine from Fort George*, 1856. Oil on canvas, 20 × 32 in. (50.8 × 81.4 cm). Thyssen-Bornemisza Collections.

blackness. As a trope for memory and history, death and disaster, this double-humped promontory does well, inviting the viewer to see time—that is, the events it has witnessed—as well as geography of place. While the bounty of Maine's forests passed this landmark outbound as lumber and fur to service the needs and desires of a global market, the quarrels and wars of European monarchs were transported inbound to roil Maine's coastal inhabitants, leaving an aura of Hawthornian "shadow" and "gloomy wrong" in the air more than a century after the antecedents of Lane's basket makers faced the antecedents of his basket buyers with mutual suspicion, animosity, and sometimes murderous intent.

CASTINE WITH CANNON

Lane painted a second view of the town of Castine in the same year, 1856, that he painted *Castine, Maine*, at the same size, with almost the same prospect (fig. 104).[71] But this second version, known as *View of Castine from Fort George*, points not to interactions between Native Americans and Euro-Americans but to the embattled history of the town of Castine as a strategic player in the imperial power struggles of rival Europeans throughout the seventeenth and eighteenth centuries and into the nineteenth (fig. 112). In lieu of the basket-bartering figures, here Lane foregrounds a cannon. In his *Pictorial Field-Book of the War of 1812*, Benson J. Lossing reports on his research visit to Castine in 1860 in preparation for writing that account (and sketching the scenes of action): "Near the fort [Fort George] lay a 24-pound iron cannon—a relic of the war of 1812—on a decayed carriage, which the citizens on some occasion had dragged up from the old half-moon redoubt (Fort Porter) on the shore, where two of the same kind yet lay."[72] Lossing's engraved illustration of the cannon comports with Lane's portrait of this armament and indeed with the character of the cannon on the site today. Lossing acknowledges in his text the assistance of two local informants: "Dr. Joseph L. Stevens and Samuel T. Noyes, Esq. (the former a physician and the latter a ship-builder of Castine)"; both were antiquarians deeply interested in local history, its objects, and its documents.[73] Stevens, who began his medical career as surgeon on a privateer in 1814, was, as noted above, Lane's host during his summers in Maine, and traces in the records suggest that they discussed history together, specifically military history.[74] According to a notation on the preparatory drawing now in the collection of the Farnsworth Museum, Lane gave this painting, with its foreground cannon, to Dr. Stevens, no doubt as a souvenir of these conversations and as a gracious gift for the Stevens family's ongoing hospitality.

"Twenty-four pounds" indicates the weight of the round stone or iron ball the cannon was equipped to fire, at a muzzle velocity of about 590 mph.[75] Such a cannon, cast of iron, brass, or bronze, typically weighed about five thousand pounds and was intended to fire from a fortification on land or from a gunport on a ship, its objective to bring down rigging and thereby destroy the maneuverability of an enemy vessel, puncture the hull, or start fires.[76] This cannon, a defanged, inert object of curiosity when Lossing, Lane, and Stevens saw it in the 1850s, was a serious instrument of death and destruction in its career as a weapon in a highly militarized town. Castine's harbor was the site of five naval engagements, and the town itself was besieged, occupied, razed, and fortified many times, a zone of shifting sovereignty that saw, in quick succession, conquest and reconquest by four different nations keen to control and exploit highly sought-after resources.[77]

Castine, seemingly so modest in scale and quiet in outlook to modern eyes, was the object of long-term global geopolitical rivalries and military action because of its deepwater natural harbor at the mouth of the Penobscot River, its concentration of major importers and dealers in salt (the key ingredient in preserving marketable fish), and its proximity to major lumber resources (especially the white pines coveted for masts by all the major European naval powers), to rich offshore fishing grounds, and to a vast beaver-rich hinterland populated by Native Americans eager to exchange pelts for trade goods.[78] Lane includes the cannon in this image as an unmistakable relic of turbulent historic times characterized by aggression and hostility, as well as prosperity based on the three key extraction industries in early North America—fur, fish, and lumber. In another image, *New England Harbor at Sunrise*, Lane includes another cannon, this one brass, not mounted on a carriage but lying on a high wharf, almost poignantly immobile, seemingly stranded, pointing out to sea (figs. 100 and 113). Perhaps it awaits mounting in one of the merchantmen frequenting this place en route to the pirate-infested South China Sea; more likely it is one of the two that Lossing mentions lay abandoned at Fort Porter, at the water's edge on the western side of town—certainly the shipping Lane has depicted in this painting is appropriate for Castine and global trade.

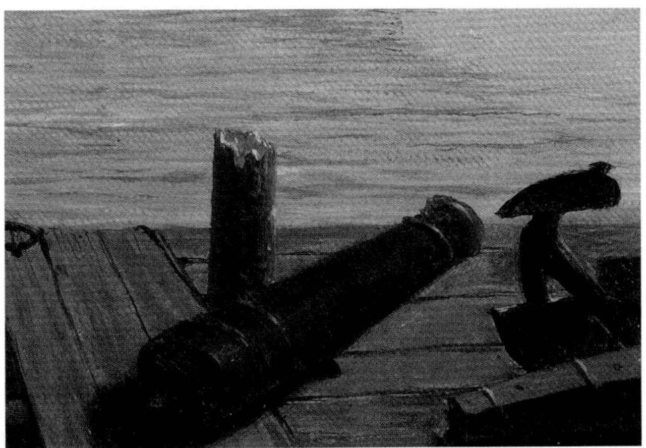

FIGURE 113
Fitz H. Lane, *New England Harbor at Sunrise*, ca. 1850 (fig. 100), detail.

According to Lossing, Castine (in 1860) was "said to be the wealthiest town in Maine in proportion to its size," maintaining its prosperity even as it was bypassed by the railroad.[79] Others claim that it was, from 1830 to 1840, the second-wealthiest town per capita in the country.[80] But Lossing's errand was not to investigate the present but to "visit the theater of the stirring historic scenes on the Penobscot Bay and River."[81] Those "stirring scenes," according to local historian Joseph Williamson, writing in 1859, who credits Dr. Joseph Stevens as a key informant, began when French fishermen in the mid-sixteenth century established, on the site of a Native American settlement, a European foothold at what was then known as Pentagoet. This community was supplanted in 1626, when the Plymouth Colony established a trading post there, which was itself soon taken by the French, and then, after a decade during which rival French interests contested the site, reconquered by the English in 1654. The Treaty of Breda in 1667 affirmed French control, and a retired military commander, Baron de St. Castin, built a fortified home there in association with thirty-one white persons, including soldiers and priests.[82] Castin took a Native American wife and claimed to realize 80,000 livres annually in the beaver trade.[83] In 1674 the valuable peninsula and harbor were taken by Dutch privateers, who razed the French fort, but in 1677 Castin was again in possession, and he built a new home located beside an Etchemin village two miles up the Bagaduce River.[84] In 1688 the English governor of Massachusetts seized the contents of Castin's home—armaments, merchandise, and furniture—initiating the Maine phase of King William's War, in which Lane's progenitor James Lane was killed, precipitating the flight of his sons to Gloucester.[85] Castin incited the Indians against the English, and the English burned all the buildings on the peninsula; Castin rebuilt and the English replundered. The site was ceded to the English by the Treaty of Utrecht in 1713. In 1759 the governor of Massachusetts took formal possession of the peninsula, which he found deserted and in ruins.[86] Rebuilt, Castine during the Revolution was the site of the Penobscot Expedition, a dramatic ignominious loss by patriot forces, including Paul Revere.[87] The particular interest to the British in taking and keeping Castine was to control access to timber for the Royal Navy and to establish a base to keep prizes and harry patriot privateers.[88] Episodes in the chronicles of the Revolution kept alive in the retelling include one in which the ship *Harriet*, lying in Gloucester Harbor with valuable cargo in March 1781, was captured by the British and carried to Castine, only to be recaptured by Gloucesterites sailing in "*Betsy* of 20 guns" within a matter of hours.[89] Castine was again occupied by British forces in 1814 and held until 1816, months after the treaty of peace dictated its surrender.[90]

Williamson's essay focuses on a treasure trove of gold and silver coins, "four or five hundred pieces of the currency of France, Spain, Spanish America, Portugal, Holland, England, and Massachusetts" dated as early as 1625 that were found in 1840 in the riverbank six miles up the Bagaduce River, in all probability secreted by Castin or his associates during one of the English raids. In 1841 Dr. Joseph Stevens was present at one of the excavations of the site by the property owner and bought nineteen of the coins; the rest were probably melted down.[91] When Lane began his summer visits to the Stevens household seven years later, it is probable that his host shared this lively story and its larger narrative of international strife and enormous wealth based on the extraction of local natural resources. In the years Lane was the family's repeat visitor, his host's son, Joseph Stevens Jr., was also active in antiquarian matters, taking oral histories from elderly residents concerning Castine during the Revolution, narratives that were shared with his father's successor, Dr. George A. Wheeler, and incorporated into Wheeler's 1875 *History of Castine*.[92] Lane, in other words, was certainly well versed in the turbulent early history of conquest and reconquest by rival European empires, the Revolutionary siege of the town, and the historical material culture of the place he visited and painted. His interest in the Revolution and in the War of 1812 in Gloucester parallels his interest in those conflicts in Castine.[93] The cannon included in *View of Castine from Fort George* is no "incidental detail" but a pointed reference, not only to the ramparts of the Revolutionary-era fort on which the artist sat to make the preliminary sketch but also to the whole complex, international history of violence and contested possession literally underfoot.

The amplitude of natural resources of interest to the European powers in Massachusetts (which until 1820 included present-day Maine), especially the forest bounty of lumber and furs, was a matter of celebration and remark from early on, as noted in Capt. Edward Johnson's *Report*, published in London in 1654: "Everything in the country proved a staple-commodity. . . . Timber, masts, tar, . . . plank-board, frames of houses, clabboard [*sic*], and pipestave. . . . Nor could it be imagined, that this Wilderness should turn a mart for merchants in so short a space, Holland, France, Spain and Portugal, coming hither for trade."[94] But while this abundance in natural resources led to wealth and all the earmarks of prosperity for many, it also prompted the most powerful nations on earth to engage in an international land grab that resulted in turbulent and bloody centuries of strife on this site. Not only was Lane's family history embroiled in these events, but the physical evidence left behind received Lane's close attention. Earthworks, cannons, a trench across the neck of the peninsula dug by the British to prevent desertion, and a cache of ancient coins insisted on the physical presence of the past within the present that Lane inhabited during his summer visits in Maine. Lane's closest friends were keenly interested in this material culture and in oral histories, and in such works as *View of Castine from Fort George* we can see that local history also received Lane's close attention. From the relative calm of the 1850s, the artist and his associates had a good view of not only the scenery of coastal Maine newly accessible by steamship and train but also the deep past of the landscape they viewed. History and a historic consciousness are aspects of the culture of looking as much as "views" were, allowing the attentive to peer into the fourth dimension: time.

Lane was embedded in a culture that was daily grappling with the present situation and future of Native Americans within a rapidly evolving nation. When he was born, the Louisiana Purchase was scarcely a year old, and when he died, the continental United States, newly reconsolidated, extended to its current boundaries. What he pictures is not on its face the clash of cultures precipitated by this unprecedented expansion or the historic background of centuries of global discord that was a key factor in his own family history, but a matter-of-fact quotidian exchange of forest products made into baskets, objects of universal human utility, and a derelict cannon beside a crumbling military rampart—these objects pointing obliquely but steadily to deep and divisive chapters in the history of this place.

It has been said that Lane's canvases depict a "conflict between civilization and wilderness," but there is little evidence that Lane was interested in anything as grand as "civilization" or as wild as "wilderness."[95] His paintings evidence an artist interested in how humans have used resources, built community, and retained memory of the past. He makes no plea for the forest in *Entrance to Somes Sound* or for the dark forces of nature in *Ships and an Approaching Storm*, except as sites for ordinary activities and incidents with which humans deal as they inhabit the corner of the world they understand, using the technologies they have mastered and the economies that sustain them. His paintings are neither grand celebrations nor national elegies. Their narratives are most often of small events he, his friends, and his patrons recognized as representing quotidian occurrences that happened thousands of times in their daily lives—the loading of boards, the reefing of sails, the cutting of hay—all resonant of a deep human history and complex economic and social webs. These are not "incidental details" over which Lane invites his viewers to skim; rather, he wishes, above all, to call attention to quotidian life in a resource-rich time-deep world seen attentively, resonantly.

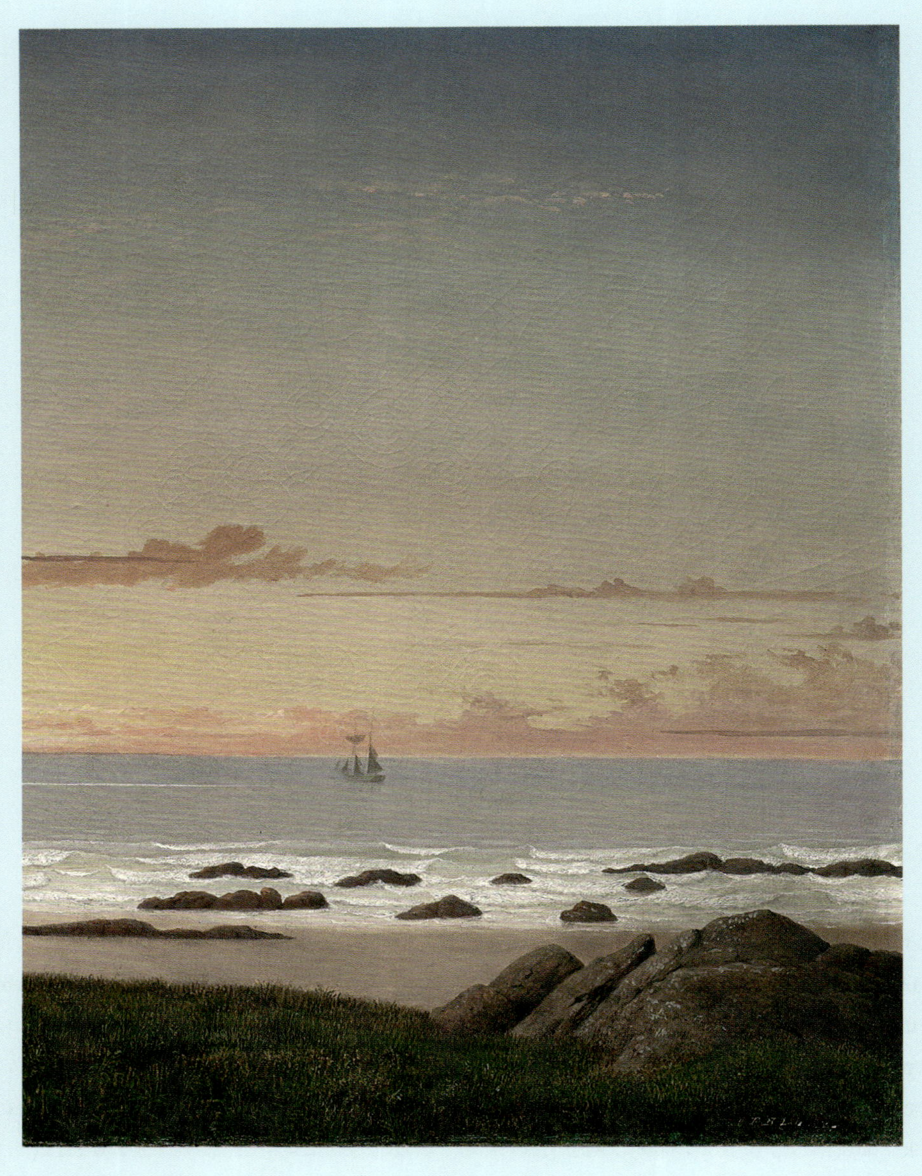

CHAPTER 6

GRANITE

Shipwreck with Spectators

A "gentlewoman" in Massachusetts in 1637, reporting on her situation in the New World, summed it up as follows: "The air of the country is sharp, the rocks many, the trees innumerable, the grass little, the winter cold, the summer hot, the gnats in summer biting, the wolves at midnight howling, &c. Look upon it as it hath the means of grace, and, if you please, you may call it a Canaan."[1]

Of all the regions of New England in which "the rocks [are] many" and "the grass [for grazing and hay] little," none fits this description better than Cape Ann, the bold northeastern headland in a crescent of obdurate granite framing the city of Boston and Massachusetts Bay (fig. 114).[2] The major attributes of the peninsula were a landscape strewn with "bowlders of every size" and a seascape marked by a "granite rim of shore."[3] These omnipresent rocks obstructed agriculture and endangered shipping, but they added drama to the local scenery and provided a seemingly inexhaustible natural resource to those willing to blast and hew rock to human service. Born in primordial heat and scraped clean by advancing ice sheets, Gloucester's granite is a hard stone that dictated the terms of life in Fitz H. Lane's community, and it appears in all its many guises in his paintings. He knew granite as a thing to paint but also as a thing to think about, to use, to fear, and to inhabit.

"VERY ROCKY AND FULL OF STONES"[4]

Granite is an exceptionally hard, often smooth, variably colored rock. The cooled igneous substrate of continents,

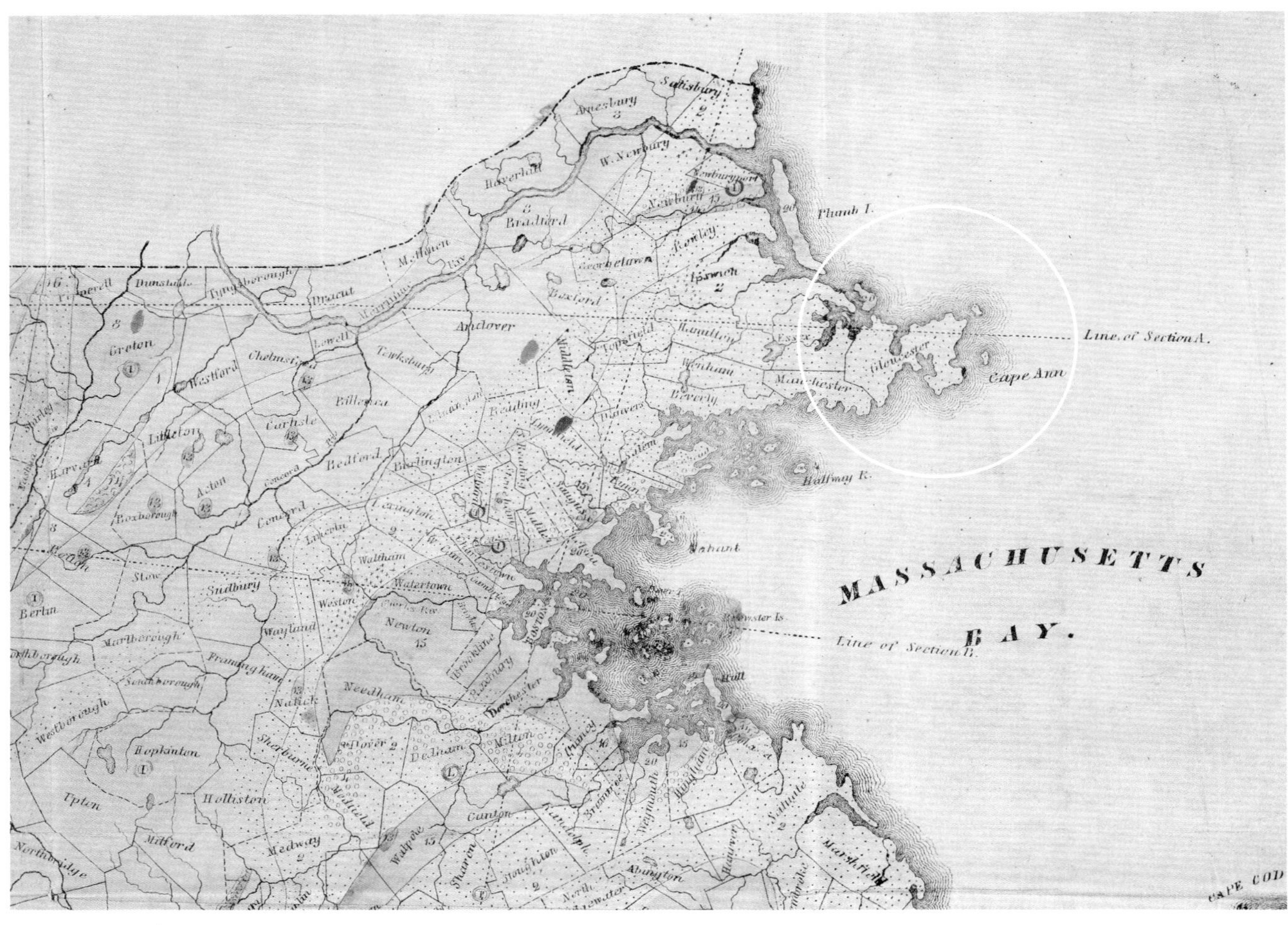

FIGURE 114
Edward Hitchcock, *Geological Map of Massachusetts*, detail. In *Final Report on the Geology of Massachusetts* (Northampton: J. H. Butler, 1841), 147. The Huntington Library, San Marino, California, RB477575. Granite and synite indicated in pink; Cape Ann indicated.

it rises in mountains, deflects voracious rivers, and until the application of gunpowder and the development of railroads, it defied human mastery. And as one geologist describing the granite of Massachusetts said, "Cape Ann is little else than a vast block of it."[5] Yet even on Cape Ann, where it seriously obstructed agriculture, it provided materials for sturdy rock walls and caught enough soil to provide some grazing and haying, and its declivities sheltered wild berries; these quotidian and local features appear—together with enormous obstructionist boulders—in many of Lane's landscape paintings (e.g., figs. 23 and 83).[6] Even visitors from nearby towns marveled at the size and omnipresence of Cape Ann's rocks. A journalist from Salem ventured wryly that he "never before saw a soil so productive—not of crude, watery vegetables, to be sure, but of bona fide bowlders—none of your small potato pebbles, either, but huge stones."[7]

Farms on Cape Ann, mostly lining the riparian zone along the Squam River, where thin silt deposits made agriculture possible, were unusual in that they required a wide variety of skills and offered (modest) profit from multiple economies. Characteristic is the farm advertised in 1829 that provided its proprietor with "about 15 acres of Tillage Land, and pasturing sufficient for six Cows, with

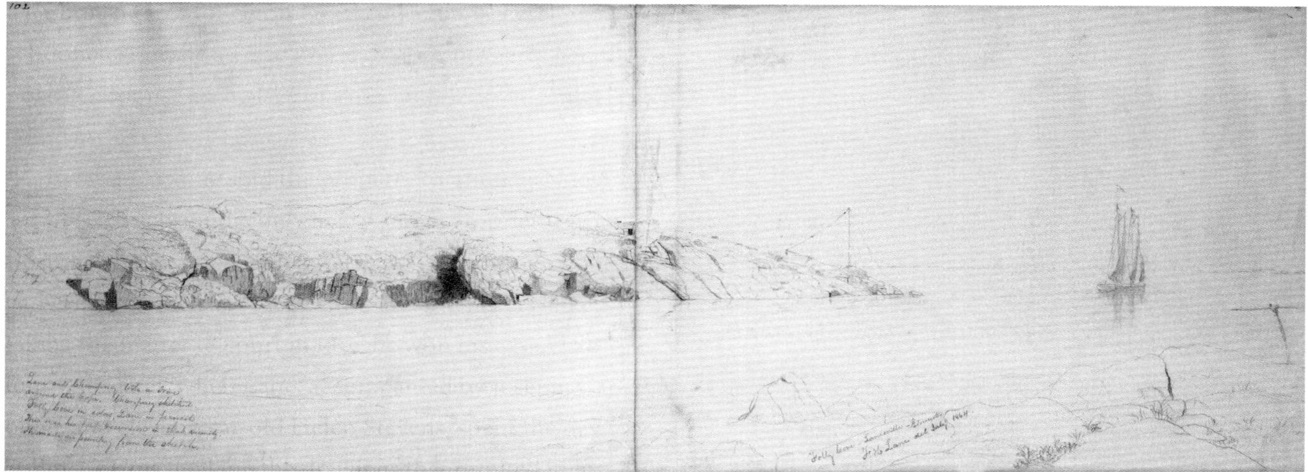

Salt Marsh which usually cuts six tons of Hay. Also a small Wood Lot. . . . It is a convenient place to carry on the Cod or Mackerel Fishery, and also worth the attention of Stone Cutters."[8] Here the multiskilled owner was presumed to be a fisherman and a stonecutter as well as a plowman and a dairy farmer. This is the landscape Lane describes poetically and sympathetically in his *New England Inlet with Self-Portrait* of 1848 (see fig. 57). Three cows point to modest dairying, a middle-ground skiff suggests river fishing, a distant schooner gestures toward offshore fisheries, and the abundance and scale of rocks describe quarrying potential. These attributes are bracketed by a sloop on the right and a locomotive on the left, pointedly establishing the connections of this place to both local and distant communities and markets. It is summer; the blush of a sunset is echoed in the wildflowers at the artist's feet as he positions himself within a world that is rockbound but green, productive, and habitable as well as picturable.

FIGURE 115
Fitz H. Lane, *Folly Cove, Lanesville—Gloucester*, 1864. Graphite on paper, 9 ¼ × 28 ¼ in. (23.5 × 71.8 cm). Cape Ann Museum, Gloucester, Massachusetts. Gift of Samuel H. Mansfield, 1927 (485.102).

Lane convincingly describes rocks in *New England Inlet*—both boulders on the left and a substantial bare granite hill on the right in the middle distance—but it is clear that his visual interest in the structure of rock is not as keen as his appetite for the details and workings of ships and boats, or skies and meteorology. It is also less keen than that of some of his contemporaries, most notably William Stanley Haseltine, whose intense lithic curiosity (and university education, including geology) is evident in his amazing rock portraits, eloquently parsed by Marc Simpson.[9] Although it is unlikely that Lane was acquainted with Haseltine, he did know, and in fact taught, William Bradford, who was praised for his "almost photographic delineations . . . of rocks . . . so faithfully drawn and colored are they, that each stone seems a magic memorial."[10] While Lane was not focused on portraits of rocks, he was clearly interested in the juxtapositions of rocks with other materials, such as, in *New England Inlet*, the boulders with the cattle-cropped greensward on the left, and the abruptly vertical granite hill with the horizontal expanse of marsh vegetation and river on the right. This interest in sharp contrasts also appears in the sandy expanse of beach interrupted by dark bulky boulders in *Coffin's Beach at Sunset* and the heavily shaded craggy coast against the faint linearity of a derrick for loading granite blocks in *Folly Cove, Lanesville—Gloucester*, a rare pencil portrait of rock for a painting that is currently unlocated (figs. 91 and 115).

Lane's contemporaries echo this taste for dramatic contrast in texture and material, as indicated in the

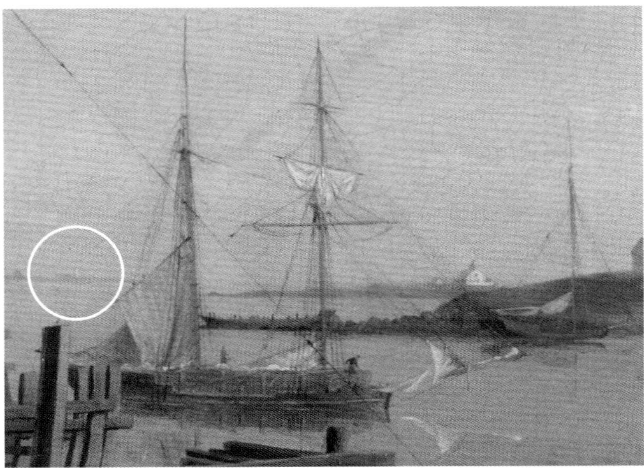

FIGURE 116
Fitz H. Lane, *The Fort and Ten Pound Island, Gloucester (Harbor Scene)*, 1848 (fig. 49), detail.

account of Massachusetts's midcentury state geologist, Edward Hitchcock, who took as much interest in what he called "Scenographical Geology" as "Economical Geology." The former concerns "the connection between geology and scenery," and scenery's paradigm for Hitchcock is the granite "headlands and promontories" of Cape Ann, where "in vain have the waves for thousands of years spent their fury."[11] This conjunction of disparate materials—sea and headlands, horizontals and verticals—creates visual interest and excitement. English theorists agree: undulating mountain and valley granite formations create "many a romantic and beautiful scene . . . [exhibiting] in a striking manner the dependence of the picturesque in nature upon great geological phenomena [and creating] . . . the picturesque beauties which render the districts of primary rocks especially favourites with the landscape-painter."[12]

Masses of rocks by themselves, however, like the "hundreds of acres" in the interior of Cape Ann, constitute for Hitchcock "perfect barrenness and desolation . . . the planet in its nakedness."[13] Another contemporary agreed, describing the "centre of the Cape [as] a wild, deserted district . . . several hundred acres, almost entirely covered with rocks, and revolting to the eye."[14] Lane did not elect to paint this sea-of-rocks landscape, undoubtedly agreeing that "scenery of this kind . . . [was] extremely dreary," as well as inaccessible.[15] Likely, however, Lane found the interior of Cape Ann unpicturable not only because it was "dreary" and lacked the kinds of striking contrasts seen everywhere in his work but because it was completely outside of the zones of human activity that were the focus of his artistic project.

Given this granitic context, it is not surprising that, as a Boston journalist put it, "the people of Gloucester and other villages on the Cape, . . . [who were] distinguished for intelligence and enterprise," early on began to use this obdurate material as a resource. Not only gathering portable rocks into useful walls, "firm, high, and close [to prevent] . . . cattle in the corn . . . [and] pigs in the peas," they undertook major public works using this durable but intractable material.[16] Residents of Sandy Bay (Rockport), a village of fewer than three thousand on the eastern edge of Cape Ann, with no safe natural harbor for fishing schooners but eager to participate in the fisheries, built an artificial harbor of "blocks of stone of great weight." As building with stone was very costly in terms of labor and engineering, the artificial harbor—begun in 1811 and completed in 1817—cost $33,542.50 when an exceptionally large stone Shaker barn cost $3,000.[17] At the same time, a massive forty-foot-high monument was erected of "split granite" on a ledge on the dangerous eastern shore at the mouth of Gloucester's harbor, "to serve as a beacon to those who approach this coast," and another similar massive aid to navigation was erected of granite at Squam Harbor, on the north side of the Cape Ann peninsula.[18] Lane includes the former monument at Gloucester Harbor's gateway in the middle of *The Fort and Ten Pound Island, Gloucester*, the "finger" of a lumber upright pointing to it as a bright tall tower on the distant horizon, catching the light of the morning sun (fig. 116).

The townscape of Gloucester was apparently as plagued by boulders as its more rural parts, and efforts to remove them during Lane's early adulthood produced mixed results. In the autumn of 1827, for instance, the

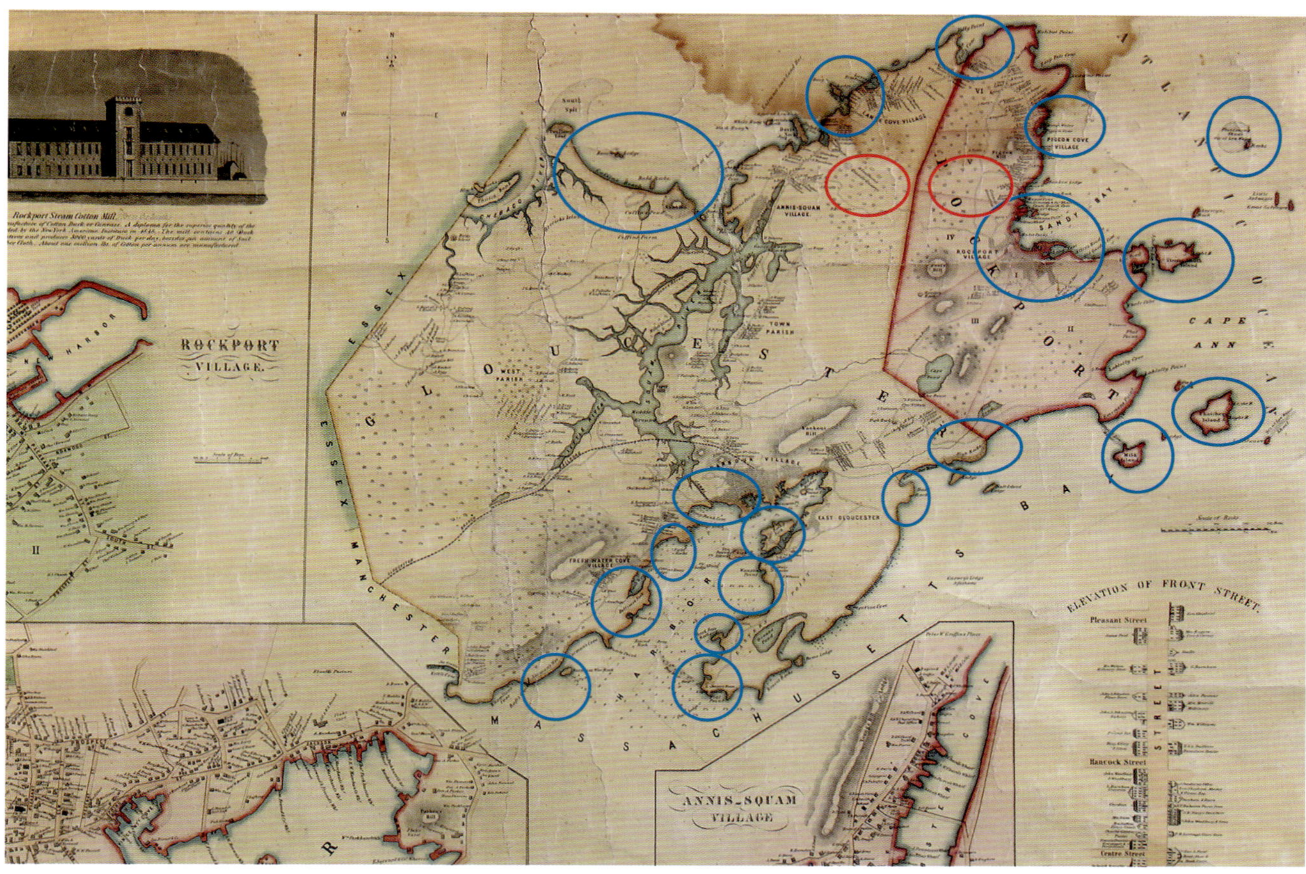

FIGURE 117
Henry Francis Walling, *Map of the Towns of Gloucester and Rockport, Essex Co. Mass.* (Philadelphia: John Hanson, 1851), detail. A. Koliner, lithographer. Colored lithograph on paper, 34½ × 45 in. (87.63 × 114 cm). Cape Ann Museum Library and Archives, Gloucester, Massachusetts. Large quarries indicated in red; sites of major shipwrecks indicated in blue.

Gloucester Telegraph reported difficulties caused by "the custom of blowing [blasting] rocks near dwelling houses," specifically when "an experiment was made on the great rock at Whittemore's corner": "A stone weighing, as near as we could judge, at least 3000 pounds, entered the side of the house of the Misses Whittemore, making a hole of uncomfortable dimensions, and lodging in the centre of the parlour, to the utter dismay of sundry tables, chairs, looking glasses, portraits and clocks. Another, weighing about 5000 pounds entered the room used as a shop."[19]

Lane's family moved into this house, presumably well repaired, in 1839, and his nephew left a description of open-fireplace foodways he experienced in this ca. 1700 structure during the Lane-family occupation.[20] In the same newspaper as that recording the accident at the Whittemore house, an advertisement appeared for "Gunpowder and Glass," an incongruous pairing of wares, and another, directed at "Rock Blowers, Sportsmen and others," offered three kinds of gunpowder.[21] Most of these "Rock Blowers" were not urban boulder-removing "experimenters" but probably were associated with the commercial quarries that began operation on Cape Ann in 1823 (the largest granite quarries are circled in red on figure 117).[22] Facilitated by wooden "railways" and the artificial harbor at Rockport, massive blocks of granite were extracted and shipped by sloops to Gloucester for local

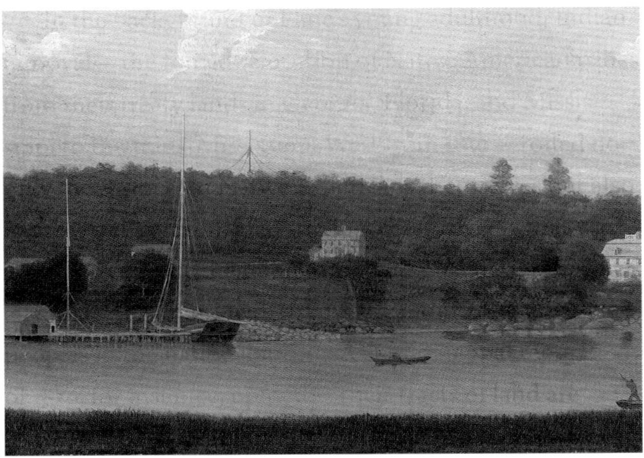

FIGURE 118
Fitz H. Lane, *Fresh Water Cove from Dolliver's Neck, Gloucester*, n.d. (fig. 87), detail.

use (as in the construction of the seawalls and stone piers visible in many Lane harbor views) and to Boston and elsewhere for cobblestones, curbstones, and building projects.[23] Lane includes one of these stone sloops moored to a wharf in *Fresh Water Cove from Dolliver's Neck*, its mast echoing a quarry derrick just over the hill to its right and a granite hoist on the dock to its left (fig. 118).[24]

Underlining the presence of granite as an extracted commodity, he includes a load of rough-quarried granite used as an ad hoc windbreak for a pitch-kettle in the *Gloucester Harbor* of 1847 (figs. 5 and 52). Unlike the reddish-brown seaweed-stained rounded granite boulders "native" to the place, which Lane depicts erupting from the beach, this quarry-broken rock exhibits the light-gray color of unexposed Cape Ann granite. This pile of sharply broken blocks clarifies one of the reasons it was a favored building material—unlike many rocks, it does not cleave preferentially but will break along any face. These stones may be used as they appear here for rubble fill or riprap, or a stone mason may dress them to orthogonal regularity with a smooth ashlar face appropriate for architectural use. Lane inserted himself onto these rocks with his perspectival signature "chiseled" on the face of one of the granite blocks in the lower right (fig. 52).

As a portable commodity, the most significant aspect of granite is its extraordinary weight. Lane exerted himself to describe the maritime challenge of moving a load of rock in his *Coasting Schooner off Boon Island* (also known as *Schooner Hauling Granite in Rough Seas*) (Sawyer Free Library). A two-sentence article titled "Disaster" in the *Cape Ann Light & Gloucester Telegraph* sums up the most obvious problem: "Sloop *Pigeon Hill*, laden with stone, foundered in Rockport Harbor on Thursday night, in about six fathoms water, just as she was getting under way for Boston. The crew barely escaped with their lives."[25]

Blowing, cutting, and transporting granite were all difficult and dangerous operations involving substantial numbers of skilled workers. Engineering tools for its extraction, movement, and construction involved a generation of experimenters as the demand for granite increased through the nineteenth century. Wood remained the most important building material in the early national period, especially in rural and vernacular contexts, but as stone found favor for major building projects, Cape Ann's entrepreneurs found themselves sitting on a resource highly valued in urban contexts. All they needed to do was quarry it and transport it.

By midcentury, granite was an important element in Gloucester's economy, although, of course, it never rivaled fish. According to an account of Cape Ann's quarry works in 1850, "the business of cutting stone is extensively carried on at . . . [Rockport on Cape Ann] where are quarries of granite of excellent quality. In these, 175 men are employed, and 80,000 tons of stone were in 1849, quarried and shipped to various parts of the United States, employing in their transportation, 20 sloops and 100 men."[26] The gross amount received for these eighty thousand tons "was over $200,000." Part of this harvested granite "crop" was sent to Boston and used in paving the streets of that city, in building the foundation of a new jail, and in the erection of the Cochituate Waterworks.[27] Gloucesterites were proud of their granite business and conscious of both the skilled labor it involved and the notoriety it brought to their locale: "By the application of hardy industry, persevering labor, and mechanical skill, the stout-hearted and iron-armed stone-cutter is converting the granite rocks of our bettling [*sic*] cliffs, barren mountains, and rugged pastures, into sources of wealth; fashioning their rude and shapeless masses into symmetrical and beautiful forms; and rearing them, in all parts of the land, into durable elegant, and noble structures of domestic and public architecture."[28]

Granite was in demand for paving, for curbs, for jails, banks, and large infrastructure projects where great strength, long-term durability, and resistance to fire and escape or intrusion were important considerations.[29] It was also used for the new large-scale factories that were being built in New England, such as the 210-foot by 60-foot four-story cotton-duck textile mill built at Rockport, where fire resistance was sought.[30] Perhaps the largest users of granite in the antebellum period were the burgeoning railroads, where dressed blocks for embankments, bridges, viaducts, culverts, drains, and crushed rock for the roadbeds accounted for a considerable part of the $13,544.48 average cost per mile.[31] Despite the laudatory comments about "the stout-hearted and iron-armed stone-cutter," it is clear that the fashioning of granite was not entirely voluntary: at the top of the list of employments for the convicts incarcerated in the Massachusetts State Prison at Charlestown in the 1840s was stonecutting.[32]

Probably the most impressive, influential, and public use of granite in Lane's lifetime was the 221-foot obelisk of the Bunker Hill Monument designed by Solomon Willard and erected on the site of that memorable Revolutionary War battle. It was constructed of Quincy granite, and transportation of the blocks to the site from Quincy, south of Boston, to Charlestown, across the Charles River to the north, involved the design, engineering, and construction of one of the United States' first railroads.[33] Although construction on the Bunker Hill Monument began in 1826, it was completed and dedicated, after many delays, only in 1843.[34] A landmark in every sense of the word, it appears as it looked, an unfinished pyramidal/trapezoidal stump, on the distant horizon in Lane's 1840 lithograph *View of the Battle Ground at Concord, Mass.* (figs. 119 and 120).[35] While it is improbable that one could actually see even such a mammoth structure from fifteen miles away, the trope of its inclusion in Lane's view of the Concord Monument brought together the two most memorable conflicts at the outset of the Revolutionary War and the two obelisks erected a half century later in commemoration of those battles and the men who fought them. Moreover, since the Bunker Hill Monument Association helped to pay for the Concord obelisk—intended to be a smaller version of the granite memorial at Bunker Hill—there were important financial, design, and philanthropic links between the two projects.[36] The youth pictured in the skiff on the river in Lane's lithograph is John Shepard Keyes, who, in his autobiography, records Lane's on-site visit to draw the spot, probably in 1838, and attests to the accuracy of the view: "That was a very correct picture of the place as it then looked, and I can point out on it my boat in which the artist was carried by me across the river to make his sketch while I paddled about waiting his return."[37] In commending the artist's accuracy in recording "the place as it then looked," Keyes is referencing not just the neatly ordered array of specific rock-fenced meadows and pastures of rural Concord but the fact that Lane drew the image before the citizens held a "tree bee" and planted "in four long straight lines to the river nearly a hundred elms, buttonwoods, pines, maples, and spruces" on April 19 of 1838 or 1839.[38]

The turn to the use of granite on the part of the institutions and architects of Boston in architect-designed buildings as well as monuments during the 1820s, 1830s, and 1840s was sufficiently revolutionary and citywide that the architecture it engendered has been dubbed the Boston Granite Style. It was a shift in more than building material; it was an expression of mastery of previously impossible engineering and design feats, as the preference was not just for granite but for monolithic granite blocks. The courses of the Bunker Hill Monument, for instance,

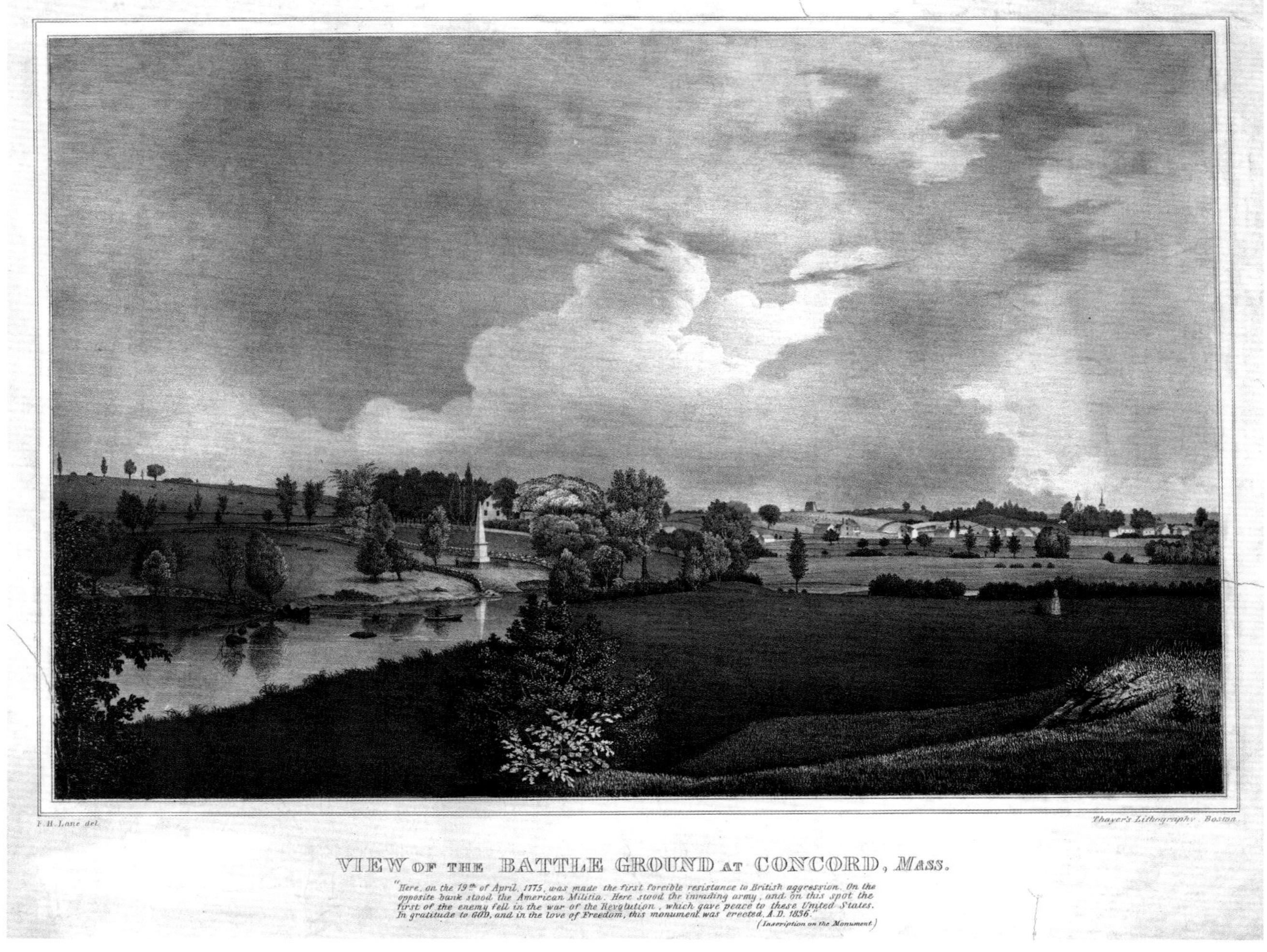

FIGURE 119
Fitz H. Lane, *View of the Battle Ground at Concord, Mass.*, 1840. Lithograph on paper, 15¾ × 20¹⁄₁₆ in. (40 × 51 cm) (sheet). Printed at Thayer's Lithography, Boston. Courtesy, American Antiquarian Society.

are composed of granite blocks twelve feet long, two feet six inches high, and two feet deep, each monolith weighing five tons.[39] Equally ambitious, Boston's new granite structures themselves were built on an unheard-of scale: the two-story granite ropewalk at the Boston Naval Yard (completed 1838), for instance, was more than a quarter mile long.[40] County courthouses, business blocks, banks, markets, jails, churches, military fortifications, and university buildings were fashioned of massive granite blocks, many involving novel engineering and maneuvering devices. Transport of the material for the columns of the Suffolk County Courthouse, designed by Gridley Bryant, for instance, involved the construction of special wagons drawn by sixty-five oxen and twelve horses through the streets of Boston.[41] Such a spectacle was a display not just of engineering prowess but also of capital. Building with granite was far more expensive than building with wood or brick, and a granite building was, in its completed form, an assertion of that wealth as well as engineering, invention, civic pride, and architectural skill.

Several distinguished designers worked in the Boston Granite Style—among them Alexander Parris, Isaiah

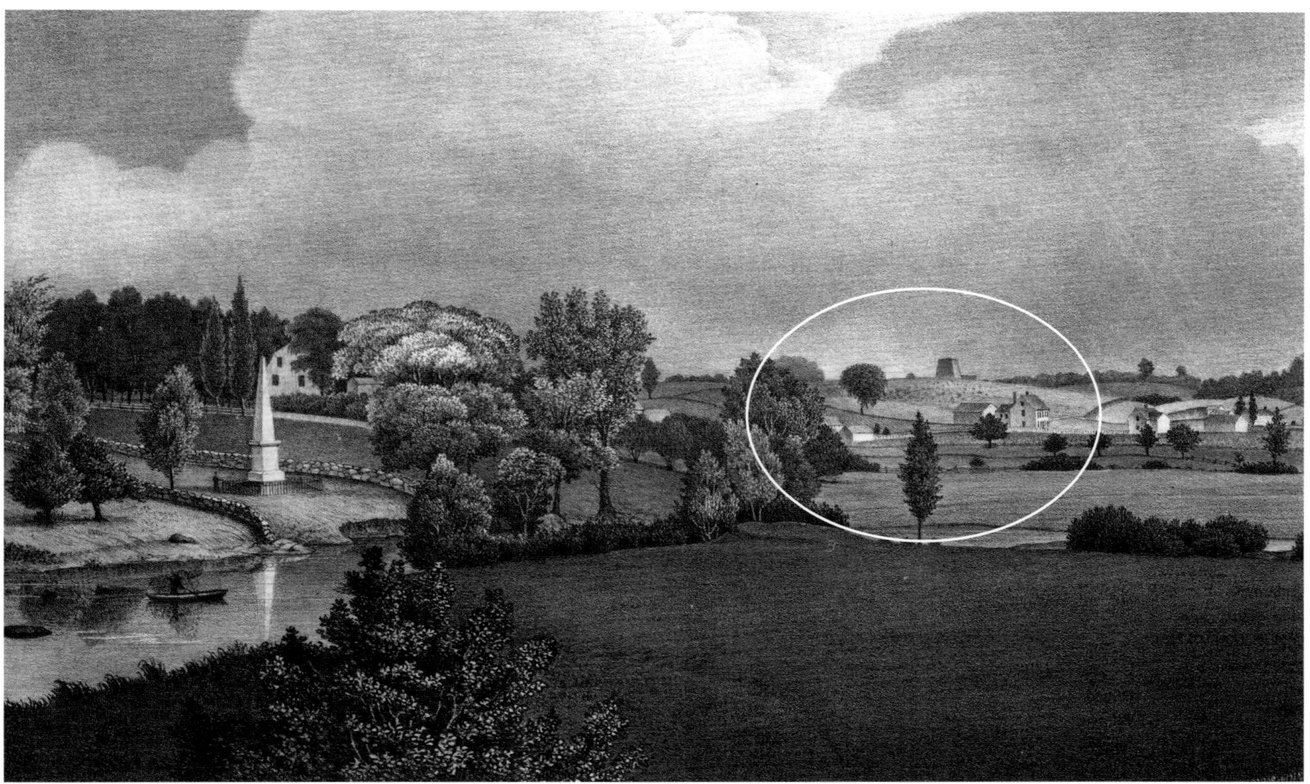

Rogers, Solomon Willard, and Gridley Bryant. They came from artisanal backgrounds and combined the skills of engineer and mason as well as architect.[42] During the years that Lane was in Boston working as a lithographer, 1832–48, they refashioned the skyline and the character of the city with the erection of many notable granite buildings—most in the Greek Revival taste, and Lane, whose lithographs indicate a keen interest in architecture, would have been attentive to these developments. But these Boston Granite Style buildings were almost entirely structures raised for public, philanthropic, military, or business purposes. Very few private, domestic structures were built of granite in Boston or elsewhere in New England, probably because of its great expense and a lack of domestic-builder expertise, but also because of its resistance to modification and enlargement and perhaps because of its association with grandeur, permanence, and public purpose.

FIGURE 120
Fitz H. Lane, *View of the Battle Ground at Concord, Mass.*, 1840 (fig. 119), detail.

A STONE COTTAGE

In September 1849, the year after Lane left Boston, moved back to Gloucester, and bought land on a hillock at Duncan's Point for $369, the *Cape Ann Light & Gloucester Telegraph* included this short unattributed article on the use of rock for domestic construction:

> The piled wealth of rocks is the grandest feature of this ancient town. They are of beautiful white granite, slightly grained with a bluish tint,—totally unlike the muddy-looking yellowish rocks of Marblehead. They split easily, and form a beautiful

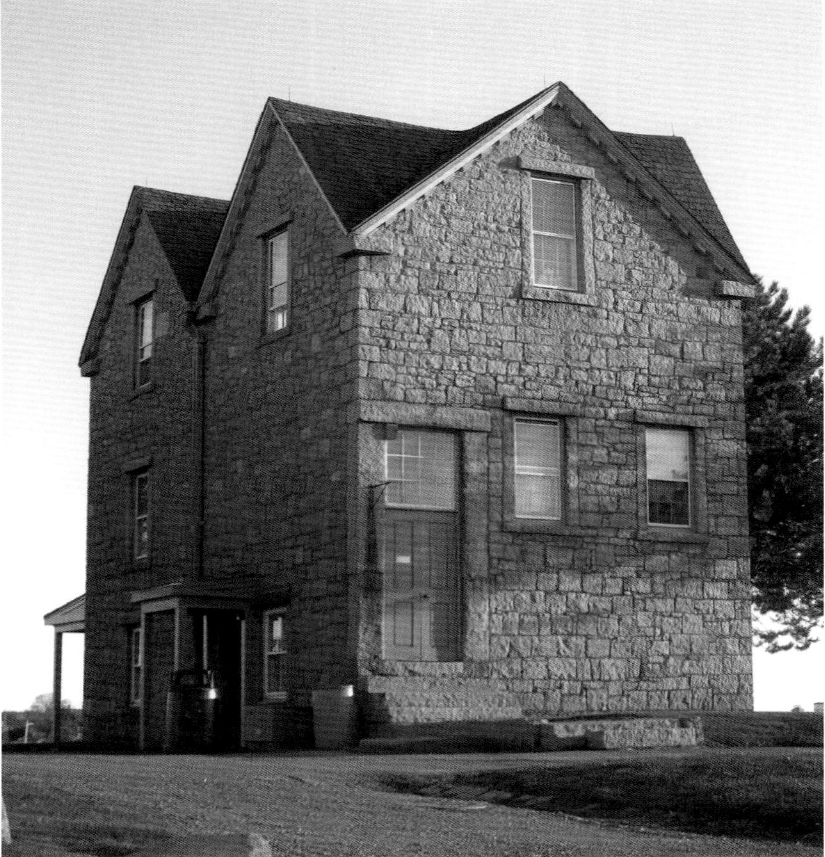

FIGURE 121
Fitz H. Lane, granite house, Gloucester, Massachusetts, 1848–49. Photo: author, 2017.

> material for building purposes. Yet, although nature has been so lavish of her favors in this respect, few have availed themselves of her liberality; and the magnificent blocks of granite are carried off to beautify other places. With the exception of the Bank and a few brick stores, the inhabitants [of Gloucester] cling pertinaciously to the ways of their grandfathers, and go on erecting their wooden tinder-boxes. He would be a bold and venturous man who would brave the tide of public opinion so far as to build a stone cottage.[43]

Lane proved to be that "bold and venturous man." Gloucester was a burgeoning city in 1849, with new streets laid out and thirty dwelling houses and stores built that summer, all of wood, the material that had proved so disastrously flammable in multiple Gloucester conflagrations, including the one in 1830 in which sixty buildings were burned; losses in that fire included the store in which Lane was probably employed and the home, store, wharf, and other buildings belonging to the Stevens family, who would later become his closest friends.[44] Whether anxiety about fire was the artist's primary consideration is not known, but Lane was a man willing to build a fire-resistant stone cottage where such a thing was almost unheard of (figs. 1 and 121).

Lane's house is a singularity in Gloucester not only in its use of granite but also in its dramatic inclusion of Gothic elements—ganged gables on the exterior and Gothic vaults on the interior. It was equally unusual in its conspicuous position on the "working" side of the business district rather than in the residential neighborhood where the grander homes had been built by sea captains, merchants, professional men, and others who shared the "Esq." designation with which he returned to Gloucester from Boston.[45] Almost certainly unknown to Lane, the house he built as his home and studio is one of a group of unusual structures designed or substantially renovated by a handful of American painters all on distinctive sites central to their practice, including John Singleton Copley, Albert Bierstadt, Samuel F. B. Morse, Thomas Cole, and Frederic Church.[46] Untrained in architecture, these successful artists developed clear but widely disparate ideas about design features, the arrangement of interior rooms, and the integration of building and site that were unusual in their communities. The record confirms that Lane designed the house: art critic Clarence Cook, who interviewed the artist and praised the building in an essay published three years after its completion, specifies that this house was "built from his own design."[47] Lane might have thought about hiring one of the Boston architects known for their work in granite, but that was either not his inclination or beyond his means. Moreover, it is more in keeping with his artistic exploration of the activities of artisans and workers that his was a local, vernacular project despite its use of this newly fashionable, labor-expensive, urbane material. It has been reported that Lane built the house "in conjunction with Mr. Ignatius Winter," his brother-in-law, who was a window-sash maker by trade, and as a woodworker, Winter would have had links with local builders skilled in cutting stone, if not in building with it.[48] Winter, with his wife, Lane's sister (who presumably was the linchpin "keeping house" for the whole household), and the couple's seven surviving children, shared this house with the artist for fifteen years.

Lane's house is a severe rectangular block with its main entrance on the north side facing the city, three cross gables on the western front, and two on the eastern. It sits on a hilltop site, a rise so visible it was used in the eighteenth century for signal bonfires; so, by extension, its rooms afford panoramic and distant views in all directions.[49] The walls are coursed rubble granite, the rocks roughly squared, and the window jambs, projecting lintels and sills are granite monoliths. Clearly not the polished work of the urbane stonemasons of Boston, the walls of Lane's cottage seem to have more in common with the stone walls built to curb cattle and the riprap used to contain spring freshets on local streams. Some of the blocks are smaller in size in the irregular courses that frame the windows. The stone is of a warm gray hue with dark specks of biotite and hornblende embedded in the lighter quartz and feldspar. Even apologists speak of the architecture of Lane's house as "rugged," "harsh," "peculiar," "frowning," "forbidding," appropriate for a "bleak Scottish moor."[50] Even if there were no other evidence, one would think that Lane's design and habitation of such a structure might give scholars pause before they enlisted his paintings in "Luminism," characterized by a presumed "all-pervading light . . . standing in for the divine," and expressive of a "radiant . . . sunny-side up" ideology of national culture.[51]

Art critic Clarence Cook admired Lane's house overall but faulted it for "a want of depth in the eaves," clearly influenced in his expectations by the illustrations in A. J. Downing's popular *Architecture of Country Houses*, where shadows cast by projecting eaves add to the drama of steep gables.[52] A wooden dentil course, evidently painted white in Lane's day, zigzags along the eaves, emphasizing the staccato gables. The main door, up a short set of steps, opens directly onto a narrow staircase, lit by twelve transom panes, that winds up to the third floor. This is evidently the stair Lane and visitors to his studio used. A second staircase directly abuts this stair and winds up two stories from the partly below-grade lowest floor—accessed by secondary exterior doors on the eastern and southern fronts. This was probably the stair that Lane's sister, brother-in-law, and seven children used to move between the ground floor and the middle floor. While it is not unusual for a house of this period to have a main and a secondary stair, Lane's arrangement is decidedly eccentric; its goal was probably to keep the semipublic access to the studio separate from the domestic space of the busy household.

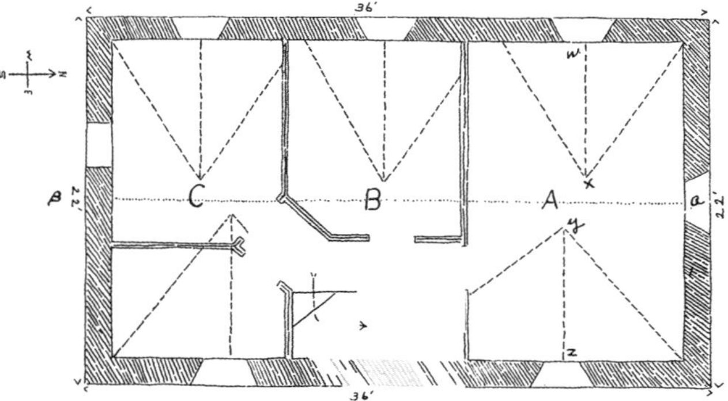

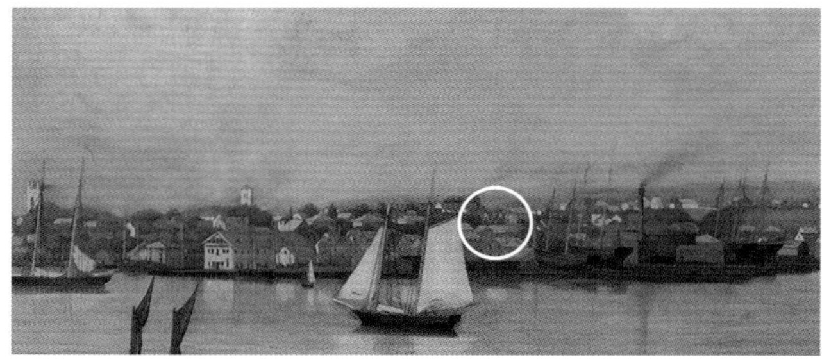

FIGURE 122 (ABOVE)
Fitz Henry Lane House, Gloucester, 1848–49, plan of third floor, with reflected ceiling plan indicating the vaulting pattern interrupted by subsequently installed partition walls. From Alfred Mansfield Brooks, "The Fitz Lane House in Gloucester," *Essex Institute Historical Collections* 78, no. 3 (July 1942), opposite p. 283. Courtesy Phillips Library, Peabody Essex Museum, Salem, Massachusetts.

FIGURE 123 (TOP RIGHT)
Fitz Henry Lane House, Gloucester, 1848–49, vaulting on third floor. Photo: author.

FIGURE 124 (BOTTOM RIGHT)
Fitz H. Lane, *View of Gloucester*, 1859 (fig. 12), detail.

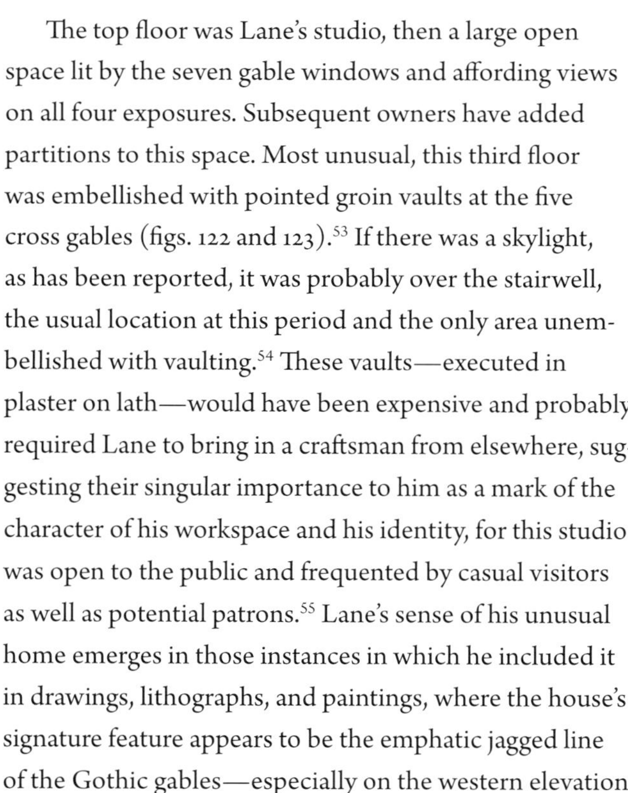

The top floor was Lane's studio, then a large open space lit by the seven gable windows and affording views on all four exposures. Subsequent owners have added partitions to this space. Most unusual, this third floor was embellished with pointed groin vaults at the five cross gables (figs. 122 and 123).[53] If there was a skylight, as has been reported, it was probably over the stairwell, the usual location at this period and the only area unembellished with vaulting.[54] These vaults—executed in plaster on lath—would have been expensive and probably required Lane to bring in a craftsman from elsewhere, suggesting their singular importance to him as a mark of the character of his workspace and his identity, for this studio was open to the public and frequented by casual visitors as well as potential patrons.[55] Lane's sense of his unusual home emerges in those instances in which he included it in drawings, lithographs, and paintings, where the house's signature feature appears to be the emphatic jagged line of the Gothic gables—especially on the western elevation (figs. 124 and 125). The sharp pitch of these staccato gables, their dentil courses painted white under a dark roof, stand out boldly from the community's vernacular white wooden buildings with their generally plain, flattish, two-plane gable and four-plane pyramidal roofs. Lane built this unusual structure very soon after his arrival from Boston with sufficient skills and capital won in that city to establish a painting career and to build a home. It is likely that he also brought with him architectural design ideas, interest in granite as a building material, and a taste for the Gothic, as a style but also as an idea, a willingness to look at the darker side of human experience and history.

Two of the lithographs that Lane had produced in Boston before his permanent return to Gloucester may provide some idea of the development of his thinking: *View of the Old Building at the Corner of Ann St., Boston, Mass.*, printed at Pendleton's Lithography in 1835, and *George W. Simmons' Popular Tailoring Establishment, "Oak Hall," Boston*, the frontispiece to a pamphlet Lane

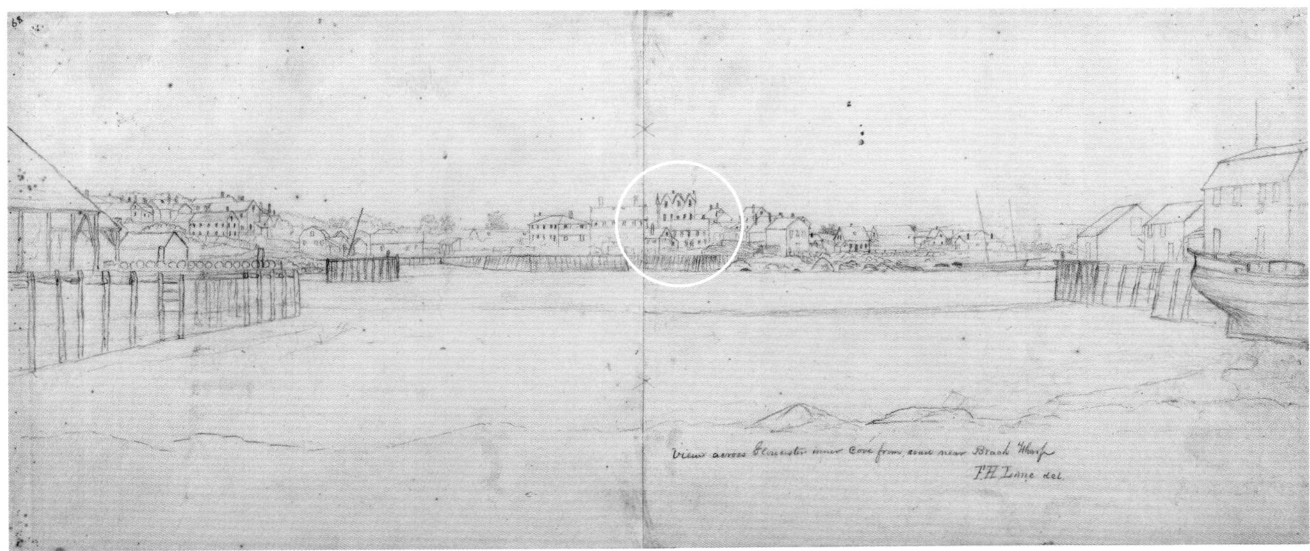

FIGURE 125
Fitz H. Lane, *View Across Gloucester Inner Cove, from Road near Beach Wharf*, n.d. Graphite on paper, 9¼ × 22 in. (23.5 × 55.9 cm). Cape Ann Museum, Gloucester, Massachusetts. Gift of Samuel H. Mansfield, 1927 (485.68).

produced while working in partnership with Scott in 1844 (figs. 46 and 47). The first is a view of a First Period building that survived in Boston from the seventeenth century until demolished in 1860 (on the left in his print). Commonly referred to as the Old Feather Store and known to scholars as the Stanbury House, it was built in 1680, right after a devastating fire in Boston. Although built of timber, its surface was rough cast—that is, sheathed in a kind of thick fire-resistant cement skin that looked like masonry.[56] Like most surviving First Period buildings in Massachusetts, it was characterized by steep cross gables, both in the main structure and in the ell.[57] Beside it in the lithograph is the venerable brick Faneuil Hall, and in the distance Lane offers a glimpse of the new granite Quincy Market of 1824. But the main subject is the ancient structure in the foreground, bespeaking the history of building, settlement, and community in this place. There were other First Period (that is, vernacular late medieval) buildings surviving in the area, such as that known as the House of Seven Gables, more formally known as the Turner House, in Salem, which would be made famous by Nathaniel Hawthorne's novel sixteen years after Lane published this print and a year after Lane erected his own seven-gabled house in Gloucester, but this lithograph shows that the Stanbury House in Boston is the one he studied minutely.

The second Lane print that demonstrates his engagement with Gothic elements in architecture during his Boston years is a threshold view of a fashionable tailoring business housed in a large wooden faux-medieval structure built in 1840.[58] It had all the earmarks of the newly popular Gothic Revival style, including elements of surviving European castles and churches. What is key in this image for Lane's house are not the diamond casements or shaped aperture-surrounds (or the crenellations and ganged pointed windows that the building's facade sported) but the groined vaults that make the interior space simultaneously majestic and medieval.[59] As Lane carefully studied the interior of this business to make this lithograph, he would have had plenty of time to think about the advantages and the character of a vaulted ceiling. And in practical terms, he could have

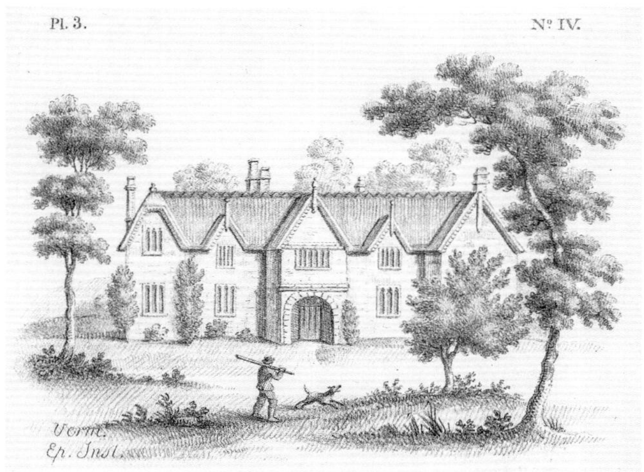

FIGURE 126
Gothic house, lithograph on paper, Pendleton Lithographic Co., in John Henry Hopkins, *The Vermont Drawing Book of Landscapes; Designed and Executed at the Vermont Episcopal Institute, Burlington; For the Use of Schools* (Burlington, VT, 1838), plate 3. Lithf Pend Verm 4. Courtesy, American Antiquarian Society.

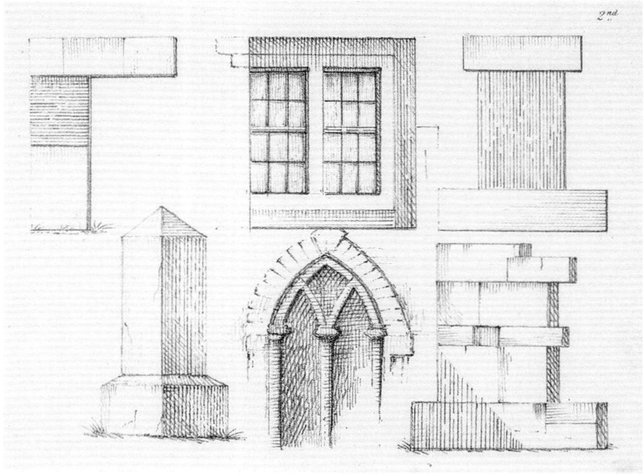

FIGURE 127
Stone architecture details, lithograph on paper, Pendleton Lithographic Co., in John Henry Hopkins, *The Vermont Drawing Book of Landscapes; Designed and Executed at the Vermont Episcopal Institute, Burlington; For the Use of Schools* (Burlington, VT, 1838), plate 2. Lithf Pend Verm 4. Courtesy, American Antiquarian Society.

asked the proprietors who in Boston might be skilled in doing this work. His house, then, combines two kinds of "Gothic" features that he would have studied and drawn, one derived from seventeenth-century vernacular New England building (the ranges of steep cross gables) and the other (groin vaulting) from European church and elite domestic interiors, all of these elements popularized by the Gothic Revival.

While Lane was working at Pendleton Lithographic Company, the firm produced several drawing books intended to help novice artists by providing models for them to copy, one of which included a Gothic house with a suite of impressive cross gables (fig. 126). Another depicted details of architectural stonework and monolith window surrounds (fig. 127).[60] It is possible that Lane observed these projects in production, worked on them for the firm, or actually used them in his program of self-instruction as he perfected his drawing skills and evolved into a painter. Most likely these drawings were produced by Thomas Edwards, who was employed at Pendleton's and is known to have authored drawing books produced by the firm.[61] Edwards also offered drawing lessons (for 75¢ each). The future granite architect Gridley Bryant, for instance, took twenty-four lessons from Edwards in 1833, and Lane—who is known to have taken drawing lessons in Boston—may have benefited from his instruction, perhaps even garnering ideas about the architecture of his future home.[62]

At the end of the 1840s, when the Eastern Railroad extended its line to Gloucester and Lane traveled that route frequently, he would have seen Bryant's massive Gothic granite Eastern Railroad Station in Salem, completed in 1847, on each trip.[63] But in Gloucester there were few signs of interest in the Gothic taste beyond notice in the papers about the publication of Sir Walter Scott's novels and specific mention when two Cape Ann churches were built with rare Gothic embellishments.[64] So while Gloucester did not embrace the Gothic Revival, Lane had models, both in drawing books and on the landscape, for building in granite and in the Gothic taste, which he imported to the coastal city when he returned there as a professional artist with urban design ideas. The art critic

Clarence Cook, who admired Lane's house as much as his paintings, predicted that it would become a model and, because "good examples win followers," "in ten years no man [will] . . . think of building with timber."[65] But Cook was wrong. Lane's house was imitated in neither its stone structure nor its Gothic form, remaining a telling singularity. Others did not follow his lead into granite domesticity. Lane's "English stone cottage, covered with ivy and [approached through] beautiful grounds and terraces," as one admirer put it, is a unique object of his imagination and intentions, and it offers important insight into his mind.[66] He was not interested in settling in the part of town where the merchant elite and other professionals built, and he was not interested in local vernacular building models. Clearly attracted by the romantic associations of the Gothic, the fire-resistant qualities of stone construction, and presumably its assertive permanency, Lane built his house using a local rock on a granite knob where he could daily see and hear from his elevated aerie the busy activities of the port, its denizens, and the ocean that was their highway to prosperity and peril. Granite must have been important to him, as it was much more labor-intensive and therefore more expensive than lumber brought in from Maine; the Gothic aspects of the structure were also important to him, as they were rare in Gloucester and necessarily expensive as well. As is evident from the three-gabled "face" of his house included within several of his artworks, this structure and these Gothic gables became a kind of proxy for Lane as observer and artist. But he was not alone in thinking about the rocks. Granite was always there, always to be reckoned with, the material that forced generations of his townsmen to the sea for a living and that proved their fiercest enemy as mariners.

"A GRANITE RIM OF SHORE"[67]

"In 1635, the first disastrous shipwreck occurred on our rock-bound shore. A bark belonging to a Mr. Allerton was cast away, and 22 persons were drowned."[68] This two-sentence newspaper article reminded the citizens of Cape Ann in 1830 that while the losses of their vessels, cargoes, and mariners far out at sea had been formidable (as discussed in chapter 4), the granite rocks that ringed the cape at home had done as much damage over two centuries of seafaring. According to the calculations of one historian, 109 ships and boats were wrecked on the rocks of Cape Ann before 1865, and many more were damaged but recoverable.[69] Figure 117's map shows, with blue circles, some of the sites of these wrecks, the size of the circles indicating the relative number of wrecks at specific sites. So while "shipwreck" is often understood metaphorically, at Cape Ann it was a very real fact of life and something that every man, woman, and child knew from personal experience and traumatic observation.

The power of the word "shipwreck" derives from the calamity that ensues from the sudden, terrifying destruction of a ship, loss of life, or ruination of cargo, and often all three.[70] So it is a poignant and powerful metaphor for destruction, often with assignation of blame. Lane himself used the term in this manner in his 1842 lithograph *Alcohol Rocks*, in which the sober mariners from the ship *Temperance* exert themselves to rescue those who have wrecked their ship (i.e., become public wrecks) through drink (fig. 128). Given Lane's support of the temperance movement in Gloucester, putting his artistic prowess to work in the design of temperance floats and banners for parades, the use of the metaphor in this context is consistent with the public position he took within the community (see chapter 1). This lithograph conjoined two references that would not be lost on New Englanders, for seafaring touched most lives and rum was a major trade commodity.

Lane also used shipwreck as both a literal and a metaphorical disaster early in his painting career in a series of five paintings, portraying a sequence of events, that he exhibited and offered for sale at the Boston Artists' Association in 1844: *The Voyage—The Departure*, *The Voyage—Fine Weather*, *The Voyage—Stiff Breeze*,

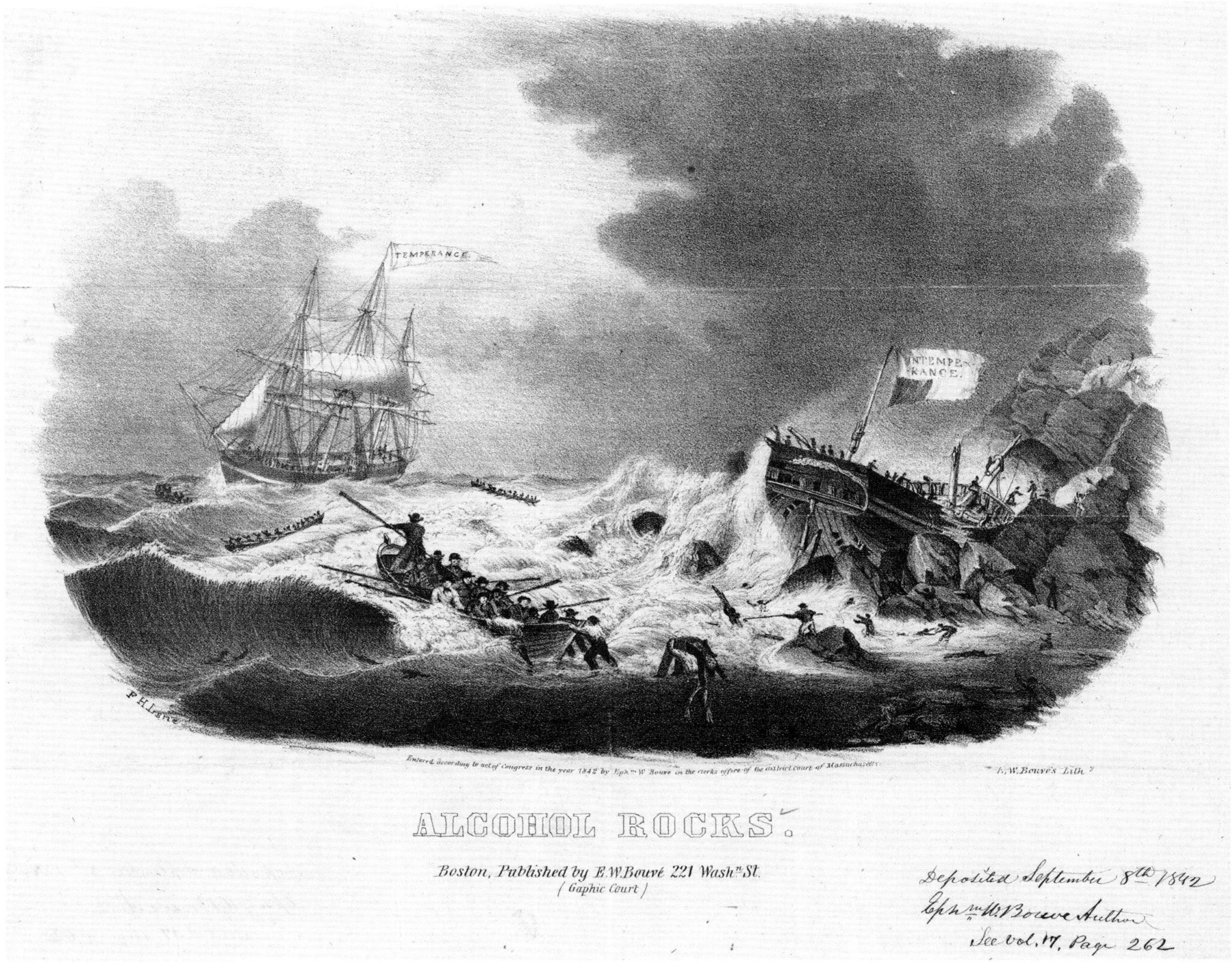

FIGURE 128
Fitz H. Lane, *Alcohol Rocks* (Boston: Ephm. W. Bouvé, 1842). Lithograph on paper, 9 7/16 × 13 in. (24 × 33 cm). Library of Congress, Prints and Photographs Division, Washington, DC (852,207).

The Voyage—Storm and Wreck, and *The Voyage—Calm After the Wreck*.[71] In this set of paintings Lane describes the journey of a ship with a nadir event and a consolation finale, perhaps taking a cue from Thomas Cole's well-received *Course of Empire* series commissioned and exhibited a decade earlier. While individually Lane's five *Voyage* works—which have not been identified—could probably be understood as classic "marines," together they set out an allegorical trajectory with moral overtones. Generally speaking, this is the way paintings of shipwrecks tend to be read—that is, as really about something else, often a human failing or a political debacle. This leap to the allegorical and metaphorical is both an aspect of nineteenth-century Western culture and an important dimension of human nature in its search for patterns, causes, and meaning. The very fact of looking at an image of a shipwreck prompts the viewer to find meaning in the catastrophe on view or, at the very least, feel pity for those fictionally but immediately in peril and perhaps a sense of the sublime in experiencing a fearful situation at a safe aesthetic remove.[72] Shipwreck was a powerful metaphor because of the very real and very sudden financial, emotional, and human devastation it created when it occurred. It occurred frequently on Cape Ann.

Shipwreck was not an abstraction for Lane. His agnate grandfather was lost in a shipwreck on the rocks at Scituate, on the southern edge of Massachusetts Bay, before his father was born, leaving his grandmother a widow with children and without support, a situation that necessarily had long-lasting impact on Lane's family.[73] And he certainly would have seen from the west- and south-facing windows of his hilltop house dozens of collisions and shipwrecks unfolding like spectatorial dramas when violent storms caused havoc among vessels seeking safety in Gloucester's harbor. Accidents occasioned by the harbor's rocks were frequent, as confirmed by an article in the *Gloucester Telegraph*: "The harbor of Gloucester is visited every year by upwards of five thousand vessels, and from the numerous and dangerous rocks which are scattered over it, disasters are almost constantly occurring."[74] On October 26, 1860, for instance, the *Cape Ann Advertiser* reported the results of a hurricane:

> Those who were on the Fort or at any other place wherein a good view could be obtained of the harbor, witnessed a lively time, last Saturday morning. Some three hundred sail of fishermen were running in, to escape the storm and make a harbor. Several collisions occurred and numerous were the cases of bulwarks stove, boats smashed, sails torn, and broken booms. Several vessels adopted the novel idea of placing empty barrels over their rails to ward off the blows, and when a vessel would strike these, a report could be heard nearly as loud as a cannon. It is a lively scene to see these fishing schooners coming in, and the dexterity with which some of them are handled betoken good seamanship.[75]

Lane would have had a good view of these events from any of his west- and south-facing windows, but he did not paint these events. Nor did he paint grim pictures of more calamitous storms, such as those of December 1839, one of which was so eloquently "pictured" by an unknown author:

> [Gloucester's] harbor was supposed to be very secure, and at the commencement of the [December 15] storm a great many vessels, especially coasters, put in there for shelter. Unfortunately, instead of anchoring in the inner harbor . . . they generally anchored just North of Ten Pound Island and Ten Pound Ledge, where they were right in the teeth of the current of wind. . . . Such a scene of terrific and horrible ruin has not been witnessed in that harbor within the memory of the oldest resident. . . . More than FIFTY vessels were either driven ashore, dismasted, or carried to sea, and the loss of lives could not have fallen much short of FIFTY. From one end of the beach to the other, nothing could be seen but pieces of broken wrecks; planks and spars, shattered into a thousand splinters; ropes and sails, parted and rent; flour, fish, lumber, and a hundred other kinds of lading and furniture, soaked and broken; with here and there a mangled and naked body of some poor mariner; and in one instance that of a woman lashed to the windlass-bitts of a Castine schooner, lay all along the beach, while off, thirty yards, with the surf breaking over them every moment and freezing in the air, lay nearly a score of lost vessels; all together forming a picture which it is in vain to attempt to copy in words.[76]

Lane did not attempt to "copy" in paint this catastrophic chaos; he elected to reference such events in his paintings in the calm-after-wreck mode, on the model of the early *Voyage* series—that is, as an image of peaceful normalcy restored after the event, prompting memory and meditation rather than terror and dismay. He referenced and alluded to shipwreck but—beyond the metaphorical vignette in his temperance lithograph—made no images of active catastrophe or of mariners and other

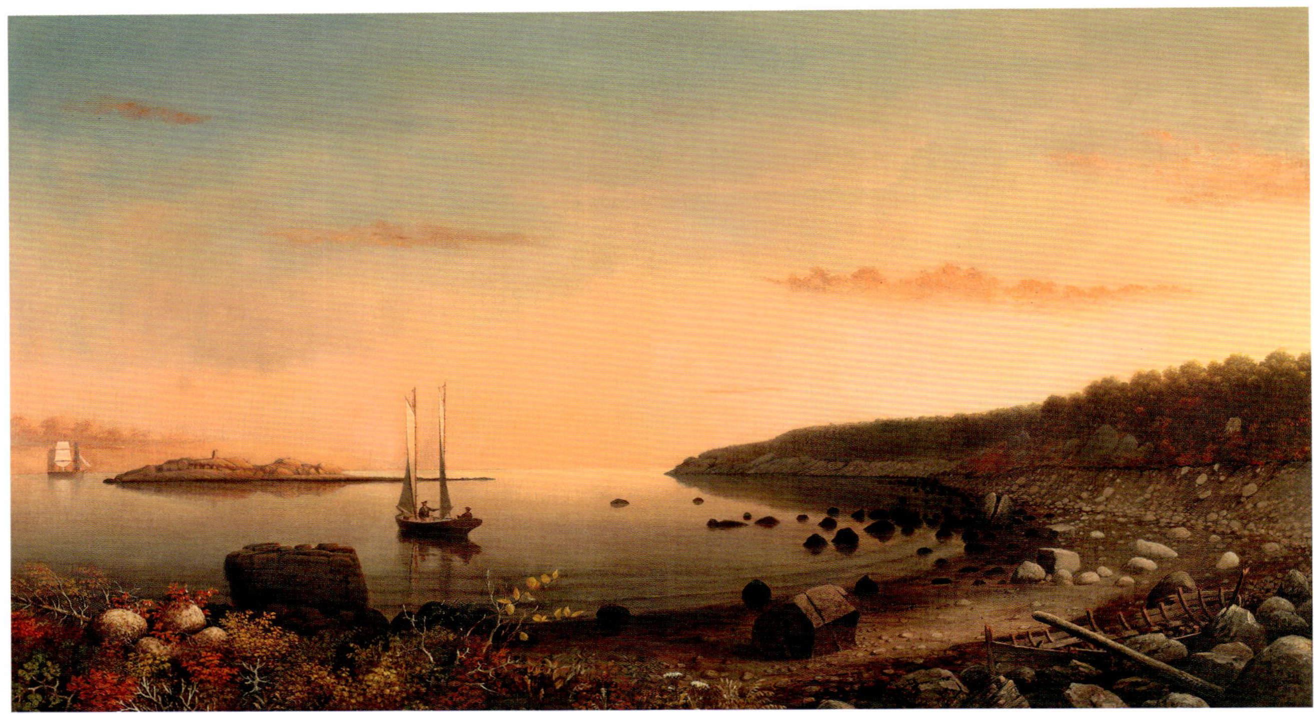

FIGURE 129
Fitz H. Lane, *Norman's Woe, Gloucester Harbor*, 1862. Oil on canvas, 27¼ × 49¼ in. (69.2 × 125.1 cm). Cape Ann Museum, Gloucester, Massachusetts. Bequest of Margaret Farrell Lynch, 1999 (1999.76).

victims being "suddenly hurried into eternity."[77] As in the fishing images discussed in chapter 4, he did not try to describe the magnitude of the activity, in this case Cape Ann's devastating shipwrecks within view of the shore, but rather painted or alluded to individual paradigmatic events.

The spectrum of shipwrecked relics Lane painted range from the large schooner of *Dolliver's Neck and the Western Shore from Field Beach*, which has been damaged and driven ashore but appears salvageable and therefore is chiefly an engineering problem, to the dismasted vessels of *Brace's Rock, Eastern Point* and *Dream Painting*, which appear to be abandoned, to the small vessel of *Norman's Woe, Gloucester Harbor* which has been long abandoned and rests decaying among the rocks (figs. 15, 29, and 129).[78] In each case the drama circulates around a sharp contrast between the now-invisible but implied extraordinary destructive force of a storm-driven sea against a rocky coastline and the benign moment of the painting's present. In other words, the painting contains a narrative of past (implied) and present (described), which stand in stark paradoxical contrast. What Lane asks is that viewers summon their memories of schooners at sea—productive and buoyant, crafted and guided by skilled artisans and mariners—and combine that picture with the one before them. The carcass of the rock-damaged vessel also references the bodies of those who suffered and perished with the vessel. In these and similar events, when hundreds of coasters came into Gloucester Harbor for shelter, the bodies found included those of strangers, which were bereft not only of life but also of identity and the solicitous care and mourning of family and friends. Accounts make clear that Gloucester's citizens gave them church burials and did not plunder their salvageable belongings, but the bodies often remained unidentified. The "past"

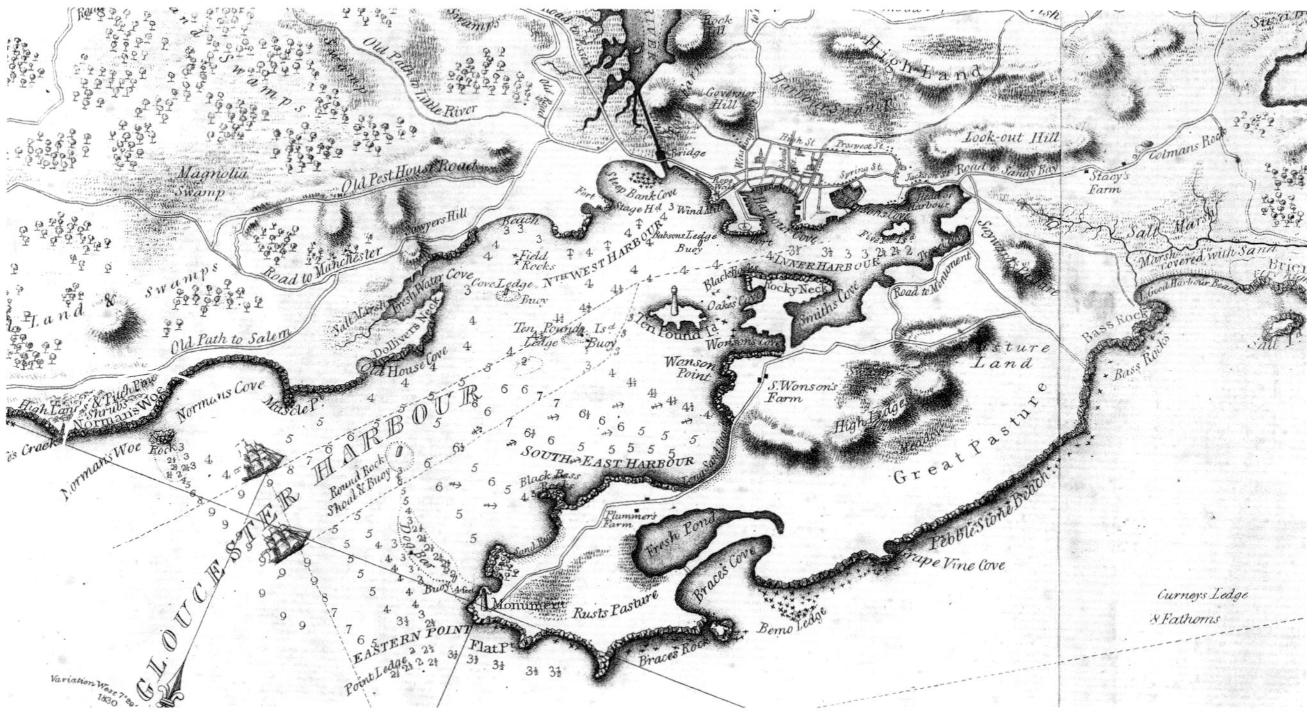

FIGURE 130
John Mason, *Map of Gloucester, Cape Ann* (Senefelder Lithographic, Boston, 1831) (fig. 9), detail. Site of Norman's Woe Rock, Cove, and Ledge indicated.

image was vibrant with life, purpose, and skill; the present is an empty vessel carcass inhabited by ghosts of those lost in this place during a catastrophic event. Lane counts on viewers' knowledge and their capacity to see the contrast as poignant or tragic, to trigger an intellectual and emotional response to the juxtaposition of a calamitous "then" and a reflective "now."

Cape Ann's rocky shore and Gloucester's commodious but also treacherous harbor were covered with well-known shipwreck sites, but none was more infamous than Norman's Woe, a site Lane portrayed twice and also included in the wider views of other works (figs. 129 and 130). This is a rock that is as much a memento mori as a boulder of Cape Ann granite. Norman's Woe Rock is, according to a contemporary of Lane's, named for a captain "Norman [whose vessel] was wrecked here [in the distant past, with] . . . the total destruction of life and property." It rises "about twenty feet high from the surface of the water. The water is very bold here, the ship channel running quite near."[79] It is the most visible part of a "ledge of rocks extending nearly a mile in length. As most of [Cape Ann's] heavy gales are from the eastward, vessels coming into the harbor are liable to be driven on this ledge and dashed to pieces."[80]

In the three hurricanes of December 1839, the arc of Massachusetts Bay from Cape Ann to Scituate was battered:

> It appears that 1 barque, 17 brigs, 68 schooners, and 4 sloops, were lost in the three gales; and the estimated number of lives destroyed at the same time is from 150 to 200. It was supposed 50 were lost at Gloucester alone in the first storm. Besides this, 23 ships and barques, 22 brigs, 168 schooners, and 5 sloops, were dismasted, driven ashore, or greatly

> injured in some other way. The destruction of property must have been near $1,000,000. . . . What wide spread ruin and desolation . . . [in] the short period of fourteen days.[81]

Inspired by this natural catastrophe, which included Boston and the whole Massachusetts coast but was most severe in Gloucester, Henry Wadsworth Longfellow, celebrated poet and professor at Harvard, wrote a poem about a single vessel: "The Wreck of the *Hesperus*," published in 1842.[82] Here he concentrated widespread loss of life and property into a brief narrative about a single wreck. In this memorable poem Longfellow offers the consolation of art, by which I mean he circumvents our tendency to suspect that devastation is random and meaningless by introducing exactly what we seek: meaning, causation, and closure, but in this case mostly causation. The captain of Longfellow's *Hesperus* belittles the folk wisdom of an experienced sailor who sees classic warnings in the clouds and implores him to take the vessel to safety ("Last night the moon had a golden ring, / And Tonight no moon we see!"), and displays hubris ("I can weather the roughest gale"), so the *Hesperus* wreck is not inexplicable suffering but the result of human failings, pride and poor judgment:

> And fast through the midnight dark and drear,
> Through the whistling sleet and snow,
> Like a sheeted ghost, the vessel swept
> Tow'rds the reef of Norman's Woe.[83]

Even the rocks display intention toward the schooner: "the cruel rocks, they gored her side / Like the horns of an angry bull." The poignancy on which the poem depends for its power is the fact that not only the captain pays the price for his folly, but the crew are swept "like icicles from her deck," and an innocent—his young daughter—perishes as well. The reader's perspective is that of the "spectator" fisherman who finds her body at daybreak, "lashed close to a drifting mast."

When Lane painted *Norman's Woe, Gloucester Harbor* in 1862—one of two versions made for different patrons—with, in this version, the skeleton of a small skiff or dory decaying among the rocks above the high tide line in the lower right-hand corner of his image, he expected viewers to bring to their viewing experience their knowledge of dozens of wrecks at this site, the December 1839 hurricanes, and their memory of Longfellow's poem (fig. 129). Unlike Longfellow's "*Hesperus*," Lane's painting of the site assigns no blame, but it does—in its sense of completion and wholeness, its very fact as art—move to achieve a consolation.

From the viewers' position in the sand "elbow" of Norman's Woe Cove, the line of the water's edge sweeps back in a smoothly geometric curve to a point—a finger of brush-topped gray rock that is Norman's Woe. The bare island of granite that this gesturing hemicircle points toward is Norman's Woe Rock. The western sun fills the sky with sunset tones, and the distant Atlantic—still as a millpond—reflects a bright golden sheen. There is scarce enough wind to bring the distant ship to a mooring or the small schooner away from this place. While the beach rocks are white and gray, those below the high tide line are an ominous black, numerous, and random, suggesting myriads of fellows lurking dangerously below the surface of the now-placid water. Wildflowers are blooming along the line of the cove, and a woody tangle of brush and fallen trees in the foreground displays an array of red, orange, and yellow leaves among the rocks. The broken ribs of the ruined dory in the right foreground are tipped with red as though freshly broken, exposing new red wood like wounded fingers. This is not a well-frequented place or a cared-for place. It appears to offer no utility, and one begins to worry about the small schooner becalmed here with night coming on. What the site does offer is opportunity for the artist, as for the poet, to make something of a negative, to make art out of what we see conjoined with what we know. Triggering memories of the many deaths in this place—both real ones and Longfellow's fictional ones—the small granite "monument" on Norman's Woe Rock, which was designed to make that hazard more visible and hence less deadly, may in this image lead viewers to reflection and hope.

Cape Ann's granite was the omnipresent substrate of life in that place, a material that the inhabitants of Gloucester understood to have agency in their lives. In obstructing agriculture, it pressed them to the sea. It proved extractable and yielded revenue, but it also was a constant danger to life and livelihood. The rocks, for the inhabitants of Gloucester, contributed to a sense of pride in overcoming the difficulties of living in an inhospitable place. In selling granite blocks to Boston entrepreneurs they were reaping profit from a seemingly intractable obstacle to prosperity. Lane in his own way made art out of this seemingly barren rock-bound landscape; none of his views of Gloucester fail to include rocks, boulders, cliffs. They are actors in every Cape Ann scene.

Granite was a material that Lane knew personally and well—he drew it and painted it, thought about what it meant for those damaged by it, and enlisted it in building his home. He even built a garden beside his house with fruit trees and magnolias on granite-walled stepped terraces, defying the barrenness of his promontory boulder. Like fish and lumber, granite was a "free" natural resource awaiting ingenious and determined extraction efforts and major capital expenditures, and affording substantial rewards. But it made the coast a treacherous place. Lane was a sharp-eyed observer of all the efforts by members of his community to wrest a living from their improbable circumstances on a "vast block of granite." He was not only fully integrated into the community—participating in their parades, painting campaign banners, teaching painting to those who asked, seeking and executing commissions—but also self-consciously a kind of keen-eyed nonparticipatory observer. With an acute sense of history and singular self-confidence, for fifteen years he gazed upon, recorded, and interpreted the activities of his townsmen from a boat rowed by his friend Joseph Stevens Jr., from hired gigs he took on excursions around the cape, and from the seven Gothic gables in his stolid granite house.

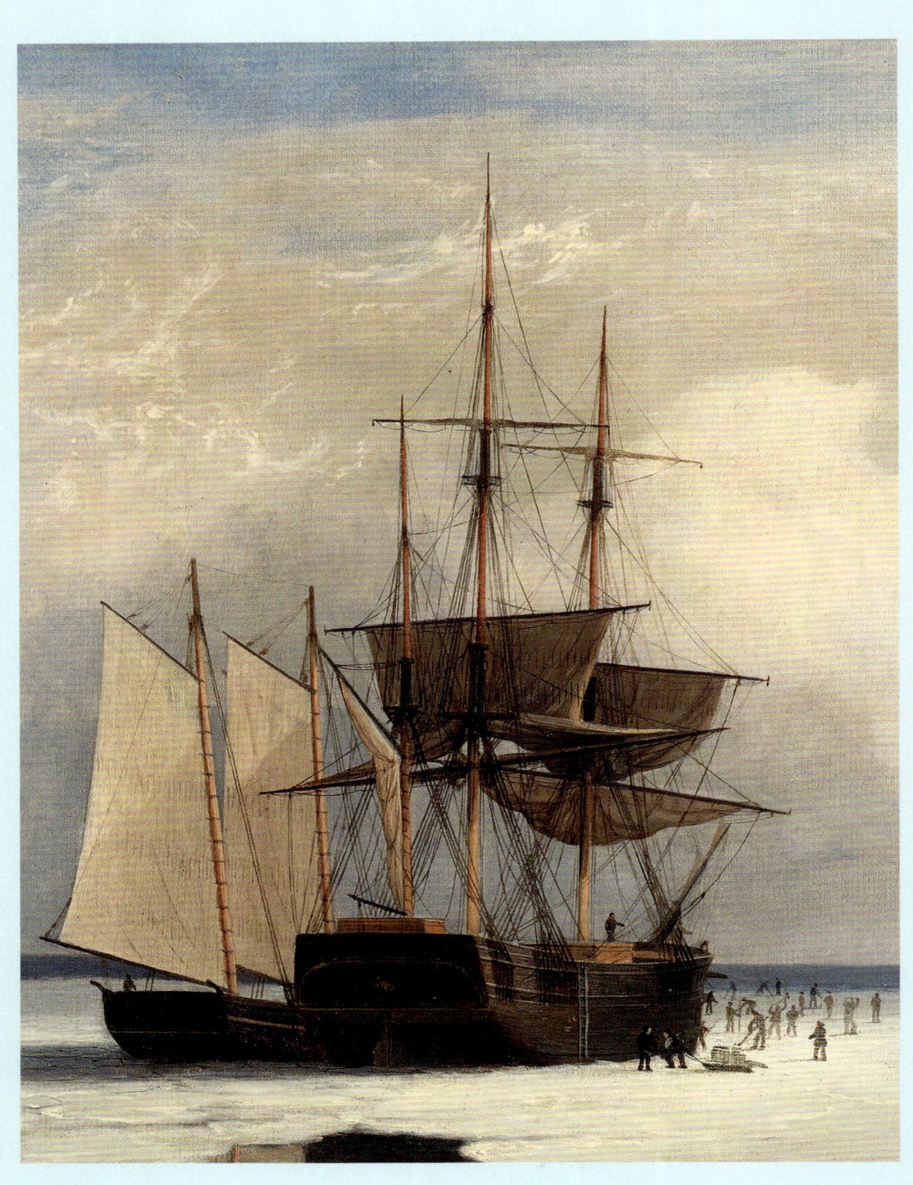

CHAPTER 7

TRAVELERS I

Surinam and California

Those who purchased or commissioned paintings from Fitz H. Lane represented a wide social spectrum—they included a newspaper editor, a grocer, a clerk, a lawyer, a clergyman, a house painter, a physician, and several widows, as well as ship's captains, ship owners, merchants, and bank directors.[1] Since the prices for Lane's paintings were relatively modest (records indicate sales ranging from $41 to $500, with the average being about $100, at a time when a good milk cow cost $125–$150 and advertisements in Gloucester offered pianos "from $55 to $350"), they were affordable to much of the middle class as well as the elite.[2] Only one of Lane's known patrons, Thomas Wigglesworth (1814–1907), a Boston-based "India merchant," would qualify today as a connoisseur or collector of art.[3] His Lane painting, *A (Foggy) Morning* (currently unlocated), kept company in his collection with works by Gustave Courbet, William-Adolphe Bouguereau, Jean-Baptiste-Camille Corot, Charles-Francois Daubigny, Théo Rousseau, and Samuel Colman.[4] This was not the destiny of Lane's other works. They were purchased and commissioned by men and women as household objects that helped them remember or imagine familiar scenes, figures, and ideas.

Of particular interest among Lane's patrons is the group of men from Boston and Gloucester who, while not in the usual sense collectors of art, were repeat customers of his, acquiring four or more of the artist's works during his lifetime. All of these men—George Homans Rogers, Nathaniel Babson, Robert Bennet Forbes, and Sidney Mason—were also deeply involved in trade with, travel to, and residence in distant parts of the globe: Surinam, California, China, and Puerto Rico. Lane's representations of scenes familiar to his customer group often appear to be distilled vignettes of fixed moments, but they also imply dynamic sets of people, objects, and circumstances, and specific ideological positions concerning distance, contact, and mobility. This chapter, focusing on Lane's incorporation of Gloucester's links to Surinam and California, is followed by a companion chapter in which China and Puerto Rico play equally active roles. Indeed, while on the surface of Lane's canvases there appears to be little trace of the off-stage activities of this highly mobile customer group, close inspection of his paintings provides glimpses of these adventurers' far-flung travels (and investments), a sense of their motivations, and hints of the disparate cultures they visited embedded within the artist's decisively local views of New England. Implied in his paintings are links between and among fish, sugar, slavery, drunkenness, temperance, abolitionism, the looming Civil War, and serious conflicting ideologies about labor, prosperity, and patriarchy. These four Lane patrons and their kin were players in what literary historian and mobility theorist Stephen Greenblatt evokes in his description of the "complex 'flows' of people, goods, money, and information across endlessly shifting social landscapes" that characterized the highly mobile lives of some in the premodern period.[5] Looking closely at their decisions about paintings and about trade provides an opportunity to see what it was about Gloucester and maritime life—beyond ornamenting a life of profit—that brought these globally-entwined men repeatedly to Lane's studio door, and what they saw in the works Lane painted for them.

In period terms, stated positively, "There is certainly nothing which speaks louder in praise of human ingenuity, than that art by which man is able to forsake the land, contend successfully with winds and waves, and reach, with unerring certainty, his destined port in some distant part of the world."[6] But of equal interest is the insight of new materialist historian James Cook "that antebellum markets *mattered*—not simply as economic engines driving the movement of bodies, goods, and aesthetic forms across borders, but also, simultaneously, as the very networks through which transnational counter-publics and oppositional ideas frequently took shape."[7] These "oppositional ideas" emerged as distant places, unfamiliar resources, and foreign cultures washed back ashore to impact Lane's New England.[8] Recognizing unintended consequences as well as "the fierce compulsions of greed, longing and restlessness" also helps in explaining these mobile actors, their fields of action, and the artworks that Lane provided for them.[9]

One of the Salem owners of a late eighteenth-century brig named *Cadet* noted that it was "the first American vessel at Bencoollin, Tappannooly, Moco Moco, Padang, and many other ports on that west coast [of Sumatra], where I bought and traded for Cassia, Cinnamon, Gold Dust, Pepper, Camphor, Gum Benjamin, and other goods, and opened a trade with that island, that has been so beneficial to the United States."[10] That catalogue of exotic place-names and exotic goods only begins to suggest the lodestone these distant ports were for every individual and country that could muster the technology and capital to build and send ships to trade for rare and desirable commodities. The United States had only recently joined that group of nations when *Cadet* was first outfitted for this trade in 1788.[11] One can vividly see this European (and Euro-American) vision of the world by paging through *The World Described*, published in London by Herman Moll a century earlier (1709–20). In this set of twenty-seven two-sheet maps, England is drawn by the author-cartographer with accuracy and detail, with place-names carefully specified. The rest of the world, however, is drawn as accurately as its seacoasts were known, and place-names orient the reader, but the majority of the text on every continent is a grand inventory of the world's goods and resources, lists of what is plentiful in those places but rare in the North Atlantic (see fig. 35). An uninformed reader might mistakenly interpret these indications of absence and plentitude as mapping "centers" with no goods or resources and "peripheries" replete with both.

But in fact the notations about pepper, cinnamon, pearl divers, and precious stones outline filaments of desire radiating from the maritime ports throughout the globe and suggest contentions with peoples and unanticipated consequences as well as with "waves and wind." Moll helps us understand the mental maps and transnational networks, and begins to conjure the "oppositional ideas," experienced by these peripatetic global merchants, including Lane patrons.

G. H. ROGERS'S "SURINAMERS"

In November 1828, when Lane was a young Gloucester shoemaker, George Homans Rogers was a twenty-year-old shopkeeper who offered for sale in his drug and grocery store on Front Street "Huse's [*sic*] celebrated Cigars, Snuff and Tobacco . . . 50,000 Long Cigars . . . 5,000 half Spanish do. [ditto], Maccaboy, Rappee and Yellow Snuff; cut and Keg Tobacco; Flint's Havanna Cigars."[12] Two weeks later he advertised "patent medicines, fancy articles and family groceries . . . Old Cognac Brandy, Jamaica and St. Croix Rum; Holland and American Gin, Old Port, Sicily Madeira, Lisbon, Cette Madeira and Malaga Wines," as well as lard, candles, butter, cheese, and shoe blacking.[13] In December the inventory of goods on offer included "superior Hyson, Common do., Young Hyson, Hyson skin, and Pouchong [tea] . . . Single Refined Loaf [sugar], double do.; White Havana, Brown do., Brazil and New Orleans do. . . . Mace, Nutmegs, cloves, Cinnamon . . . Pepper . . . Malaga Raisins . . . currants, figs, Dates . . . Almonds, Filberts, Shagbarks, Chesnuts [*sic*], Pea Nuts . . . Sperm Candles, Sperm Oil, St. Domingo and Porto Rico Coffee."[14] These three advertisements indicate that Rogers was well capitalized and that a wide palette of consumable foreign goods that could not be raised or made in New England were imported to Gloucester from the Caribbean, Europe, China, and Brazil. Indeed, most New Englanders probably knew Madeira, Malaga, Hyson, and Havana as goods and tastes better than as places. Such a listing tempers any temptation to think of Gloucester as an insular place and intimates how efficiently the barrels of dried fish from the North Atlantic translated into global goods of every description.

Toward the end of December in 1828 Rogers advertised a variety of papers, tablets, inks, and "Osborne's Water colours, in boxes, six sizes . . . [and] Camel's Hair Pencils [brushes]."[15] These Osborne's boxes were handsome portable boxes of mahogany or rosewood made in Philadelphia, comprising a complete kit packaged for watercolor painting, including palette, brushes, solid blocks of watercolor pigments, dishes for water, and a drawer for papers or a tablet—at six different price points. Lane would have needed a set of this sort to produce his first surviving painting, *The Burning of the Packet Ship* Boston, a few months later (fig. 42). If he purchased his watercolor kit from Rogers, the encounter gave him an opportunity to speak with the proprietor of this emporium of exotic wares, who, two decades later, would become one of his best customers.

Among the nonconsumables in his shop Rogers sold gunpowder, crown window glass, and, importantly, paints ("75 Kegs Ground White Lead—10 do. Verdigris—Yellow Ochre—Whiting, Venetian Red—Umber—Red Lead . . . Spanish Brown—Linseed Oil, spirits Turpentine") and paint brushes.[16] These oil-based paints were essential for protecting the wooden sides of ships and buildings, but they also were essential for artists painting images on canvas, and Lane may have made note of these materials as well.

Beginning in the early 1830s Rogers broadened his business interests, buying a ship, eight barks, and sixteen brigs (as well as two lighter schooners) and trading directly with merchants in Surinam, three thousand miles away on the Caribbean coast of South America.[17] In the 1840s his vessels were taking shiploads of dried fish, barrel staves, and shooks for sugar boxes south and unloading hundreds of hogsheads, barrels, and bags of sugar, molasses, coffee, and cocoa from the Dutch colony onto the wharfs he built at Fort Point, together with storehouses,

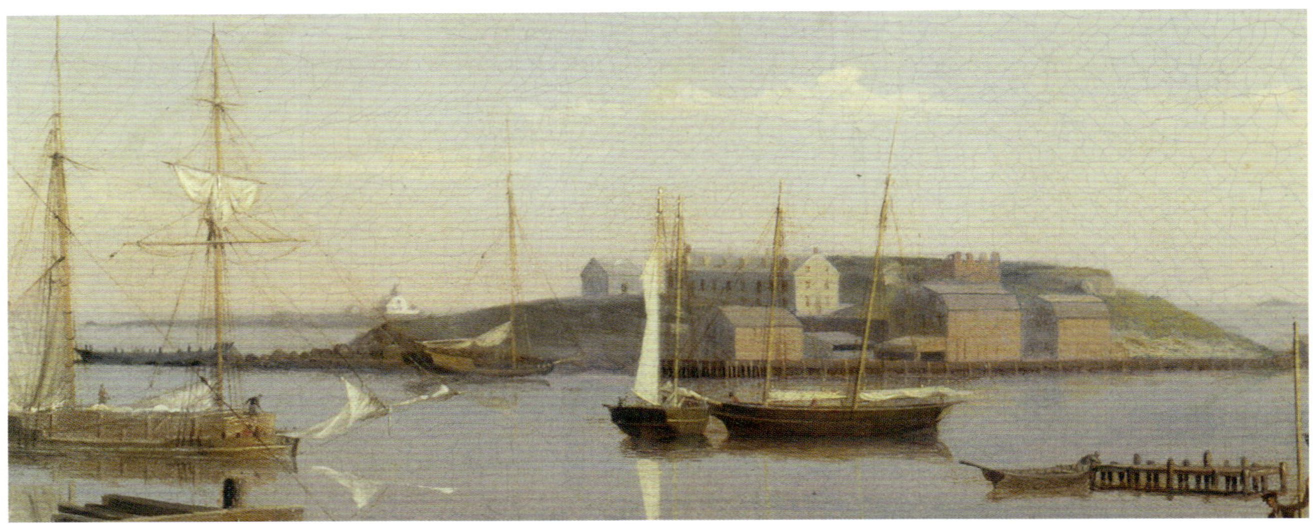

FIGURE 131
Fitz H. Lane, *The Fort and Ten Pound Island, Gloucester (Harbor Scene)*, 1848 (fig. 49), detail.

a factory, and a sail loft (fig. 131).[18] He also owned a business block on Front Street and other real estate. By 1848 he was at the top of Gloucester's tax list, a position he maintained through 1860, when he moved his business and winter home to Boston.[19]

Rogers's extensive business enterprise based at Fort Point appears in many of Lane's views of Gloucester Harbor, although the artist also painted historical views of the fort as it had appeared before its eighteenth-century walls crumbled and became almost invisible behind Rogers's burgeoning business structures (fig. 26). In Lane's contemporary views Rogers's large four-square buildings and extensive wharves dominate the skyline on this prominent peninsula associated with the Revolutionary War and the history of Gloucester before it became defined as Rogers's business hub (fig. 131).[20] His property even makes cameo appearances in other views. For instance, the extension of Rogers's Fort Point wharf out into the harbor (on which two figures stand) is visible on the extreme right in *Ships in Ice off Ten Pound Island*, suggesting that the ice-imprisoned ship is Rogers's and that its picturesque predicament is impeding the usual flow of goods and capital on the Surinam route (fig. 132). As with so many Lane paintings, the image today seems still, silent, and poetic. But that is not what Lane's contemporaries would have seen, or at least not *all* that they would have seen. The world on view in *Ships in Ice* is frozen but not still. The vessels are trapped, held fast by ice, but this is the problem, not the point, of the picture. Characteristically precise, the central actor in this work—a bark with sails partially and forlornly furled—is rendered in dark hues, but sunlight piercing the low clouds brightly lights its masts (and those of the lighter schooner on its port side). The crisp lines of its rigging are taut with potential for action. More than a dozen figures labor with tools of all kinds to break a passageway through the harbor ice, to free the hulls and set all in motion. One of the two diminutive figures standing on the end of the wharf on the right edge of the painting extends his arm above the horizon in a gesture directing the attention and labor of others. This may be Rogers or his surrogate. His energies are bent on solving the problem, on freeing the bark and its cargo to move out into the Atlantic, to contend with "wind and wave" and actively participate in the network of international contact and trade that it was built to serve.

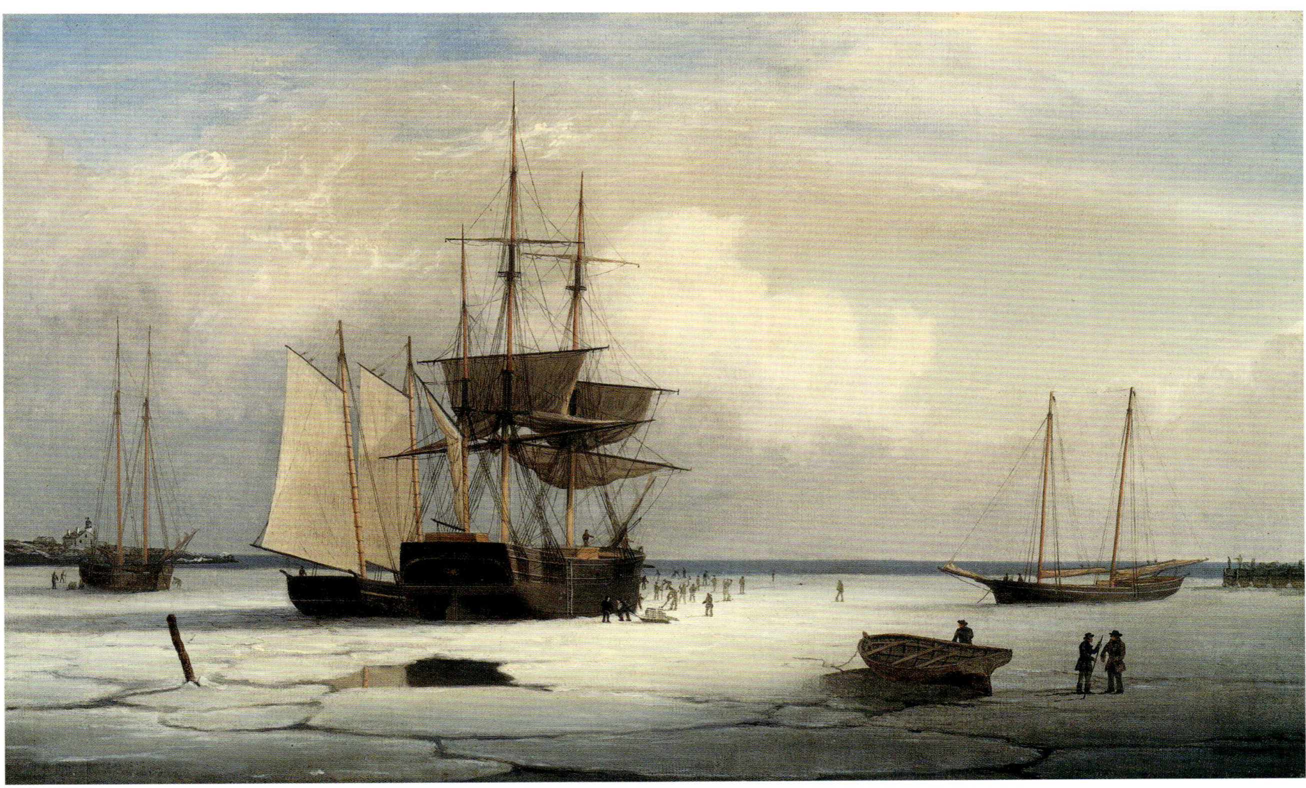

FIGURE 132
Fitz H. Lane, *Ships in Ice off Ten Pound Island, Gloucester*, n.d. Oil on canvas, 12⅛ × 19¾ in. (30.8 × 50.16 cm). Museum of Fine Arts, Boston. Bequest of Martha C. Karolik for the M. and M. Karolik Collection of American Paintings, 1815–1865 (48.447). Photo © 2022 Museum of Fine Arts, Boston.

Most prominently, it is Rogers's ship the *California* (a "Surinamer"), along with a companion schooner, that Lane painted so dramatically in the shop sign he made for ship painter John Trask (fig. 4).[21] While Rogers had partners and competitors in the Surinam trade, such as Obadiah Woodbury, James Mansfield, and the Babson brothers—who were all also Lane patrons—it is probable that many of the "Surinamers" in Lane's Gloucester Harbor views were Rogers's.[22] As summarized by an old-timer discussing Lane's *Gloucester Harbor* of 1852, these large vessels were a very familiar sight from the late eighteenth century to the mid-1860s: this painting includes "three 'Surinamers,' brigrigged, representing the large fleet that at that time was engaged in a lucrative business with Dutch Guiana, bringing cargos of sugar, molasses and other tropical goods from that country and taking out cargoes of dried fish and other New England products. . . . [One has] its topsails spread for drying" (fig. 10).[23] Many "Surinamers," like Rogers's *California* and the Babsons' *Cadet* (discussed in chapter 1), were older vessels on their second careers.[24] In the vernacular these square-sailed oceangoing vessels were known as "molasses jugs."[25]

Shortly after George Homans Rogers, who had no children, died in 1870, his goods, including four paintings by Lane, were auctioned. These are described as a beach scene, a view of Ten Pound Island, a ship at sea, and "a scene in Gloucester Harbor representing the old Fort and its surroundings, with one of the Surinam fleet at anchor."[26] Although none of these works has been positively identified, it is clear that the Gloucester Harbor scene is one of several that include portraits of Rogers's extensive structures at "the old Fort" and his vessels,

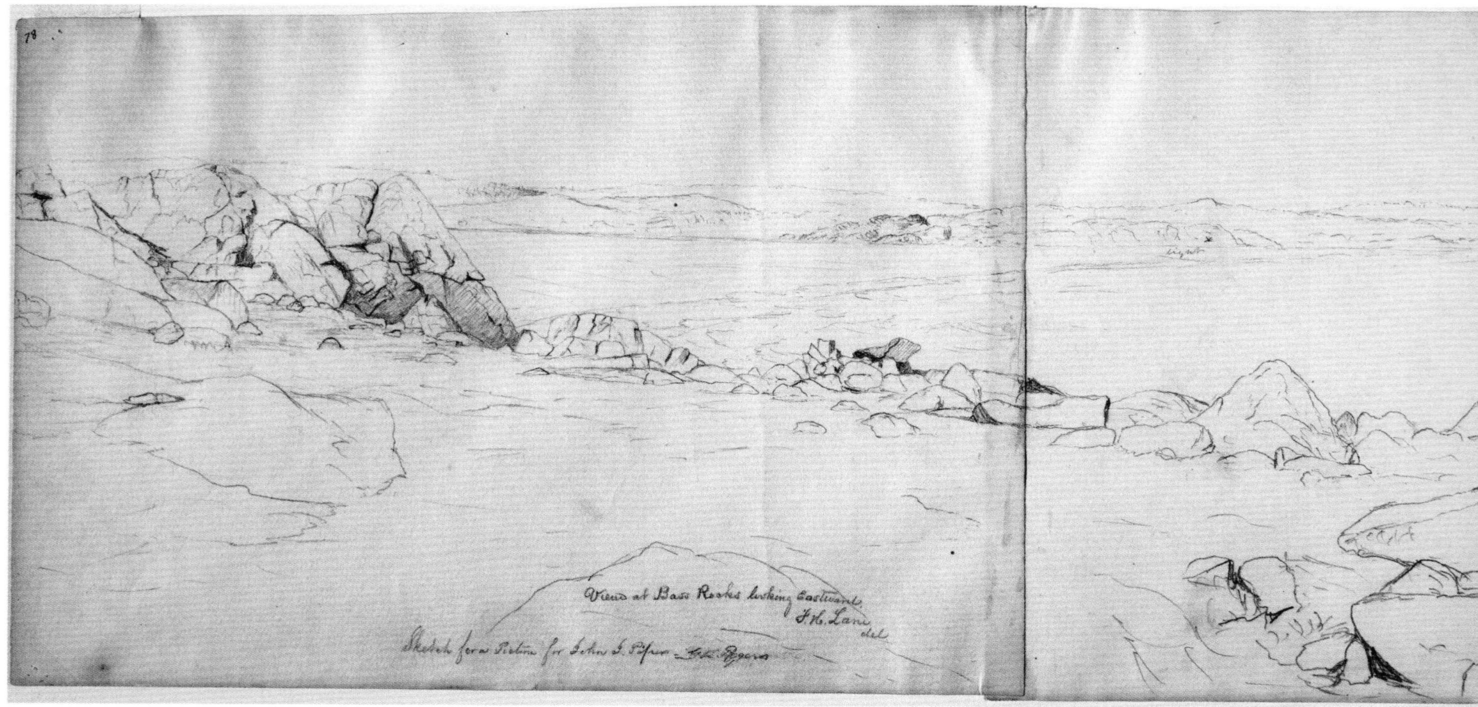

FIGURE 133
Fitz H. Lane, *View at Bass Rocks Looking Eastward*, n.d. Graphite on paper, 10¼ × 43½ in. (26 × 110.5 cm). Inscribed "Sketch for a Picture for John J. Piper / G[eo] . . . Rogers." Cape Ann Museum, Gloucester, Massachusetts. Gift of Samuel H. Mansfield, 1927 (485.78).

such as *The Fort and Ten Pound Island, Gloucester (Harbor Scene)* (figs. 49 and 131). In addition to the four auctioned works, a fifth painting had been commissioned by Rogers. Although the finished work is unlocated, a drawing Lane or Joseph Stevens Jr. annotated "View at Bass Rocks Looking Eastward" and "Sketch for a Picture for John J. Piper / G [. . .] Rogers" indicates that this view, taken on the eastern undeveloped side of the peninsula that frames Gloucester Harbor, was selected by both Piper and Rogers to be worked up into paintings (fig. 133). Among his other activities, Rogers was a real-estate speculator and developer, and among his investments were extensive purchases in the Bass Rocks area of Eastern Point.[27] So tempted as belated viewers might be to see hints of spiritual longing in such horizontally stretched scenes of a calm Atlantic punctuated by distant islands and picturesque foreground rocks, it is probable that this drawing and the painting based on it were as much "about" property and real-estate prospects as about transcendence.

SUGAR, RUM, TEMPERANCE, ABOLITION

Although cargoes brought to Gloucester from Surinam included coffee, cotton, cacao, indigo, vanilla, pineapples, and oranges, the major commodity that George H. Rogers and his fellow Surinam traders imported was sugar in solid form or molasses, including as many as 590 hogsheads in a single shipment (a hogshead is sixty-three gallons, weighing twelve hundred pounds).[28] Some of this went into confections, ice cream, and patent medicines, but most was distilled into rum.[29] And some of this molasses became a kind of medium of exchange, used, for instance, by Lane's father to pay school fees for the

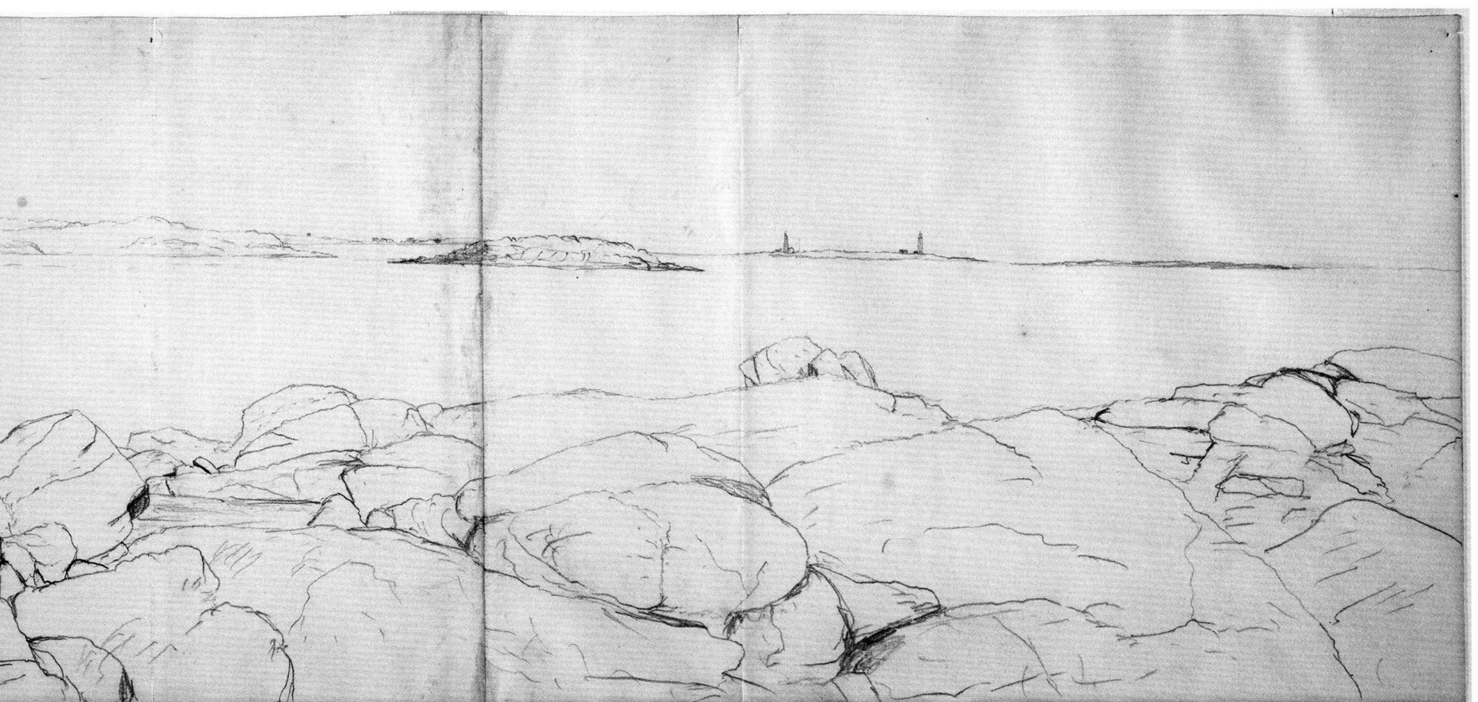

artist's brothers.[30] The plentitude of rum in Gloucester was a direct result of the town's busy trade with Surinam. In 1827 William Pearce & Sons, owners of ships, barks, and brigs engaged in foreign trade, advertised the sale of rum "at their Distillery on Central Wharf."[31] In the great conflagration of September 1830, this distillery and adjacent stores burned down.[32] Either there were multiple distilleries in Gloucester, or the Pearce establishment was quickly rebuilt, as six weeks later the newspaper reported that during dynamiting on the construction site for a new bank, a three-hundred-pound rock "was thrown through the roof of the Distill-house."[33]

In 1828 a whopping fifty-one individuals were licensed to retail "Spiritous liquors" in Gloucester, then a town of 7,510.[34] In 1850 the *Gloucester Telegraph* printed an article entitled "Drunkenness Defined," purportedly "copied from an old Magazine." It comprises a list of sixty-nine terms, including "high," "half-cocked," "breezy," "groggy," "tipsey," "smashed," "slewed," "salted down," "on the lee lurch," "all sails set," "three sheets in the wind," "well under way," "screwed," "stewed," "soaked," "all over the bay," "bamboozled," and "a passenger in the Cape Ann Stage."[35] The nautical and local character of these terms—some still familiar today—suggests that just as Inuit peoples have many words for snow, Gloucesterites needed even more to describe inebriation. That a good deal of rum was consumed on Cape Ann, as elsewhere in New England, is not surprising, since—beyond personal recreational drinking—mariners and workmen of all trades expected it as part of their daily due. Liquor, it seems, was the lubricant of all work. As William Tilden, a former Gloucester fisherman and later a Lane patron, put it in his autobiography, concerning the period 1824–32, when he was a common seaman: "In the ship-yard as well as on board the fishing vessel, rum was a common beverage in those days. All hands were called at eleven o'clock and at four for grog. Besides this, many kept a private bottle in their tool-chests."[36] And of course when sailors came ashore, they apparently took full advantage of the many retailers of "spirituous liquors" in Gloucester. On one midweek evening in September

1848, for instance, when "it was estimated there were five hundred vessels inside Eastern Point" seeking mooring and safe shelter from a gale, the behavior of the sailors "all over the bay" evidently caught the attention of the townspeople. The following Saturday edition of the *Cape Ann Light and Gloucester Telegraph*—a newspaper with a masthead clarifying that it was an organ "devoted to Patriotism, sound Morals, Temperance, Literature and News"—included a short editorial comment: "We wonder if the 'Fathers of the town,' considered that their constituents were amply protected . . . amid all the drunkenness and riotism which occurred in our streets? We have but two policemen."[37] The following summer this editor pointed not to the drunkenness of out-of-town sailors but to Gloucester's own citizens: "Intoxicating drinks appear to have assumed a new fascination among us. . . . Not only men but women stagger under the influence of the liquor from the still, and come with pestiferous breath and haggard looks to ask advice, sympathy, assistance."[38]

To be fair, it should be noted that Gloucester did not install a municipal freshwater system until 1881 or a centralized sewer system until 1928, so in a town serviced by wells, brooks, and springs adjacent to outhouses, stables, and other sources of potential contamination, it is reasonable to think that rum was probably a safer beverage than water.[39] Perhaps understanding the advisability of precautions, vendors of consumables like Rogers also promoted boiled-water drinks, tea and coffee, and Gloucesterites probably spoke with good reason of temperance enthusiasts such as Lane as "teetotalers." It appears that those who eschewed liquor were, in Lane's day, a minority, albeit a very vocal one.

It is difficult to surmise the amount of rum made and consumed in Gloucester, but it was considered exceptional for workmen to forgo their rum and a matter of note when "the timber for a ship of 350 tons has been hewn . . . and was . . . raised . . . [in a nearby Haverhill shipyard] entirely without the use of ardent spirit."[40] That temperance—a movement in which Lane participated with enthusiasm—would gain such a strong foothold in Gloucester by the 1840s is probably an "oppositional idea" directly attributable to the inexpensive and ubiquitous availability of rum in the town resulting from the booming Surinam trade. Networks, of course, are multidirectional and as likely to cause "unintended consequences" as sought-after profit.

Not just a matter of newspaper editorials, lectures, conferences, and parades of artistic floats and schoolgirl assemblages with badges, banners, and music (which Lane helped organize), temperance in Gloucester created the kind of wry dissembling seen in such news items as the following: "Mr. McCoy is a bar-keeper at the Gloucester house, or would be if it was admitted that there was a bar in that house of entertainment. . . . The existence of bars is not for a moment to be supposed—Mr. McCoy is clerk. . . . Powers called him a liar and the son of a female dog. His genealogy not being pleasing to McCoy he extended his arm rather suddenly in the neighborhood of Powers' face, . . . the cause of the present complaint."[41] Attempts to restrict to licensed vendors all sales of liquor and to curtail public nuisances were noted by Francis Bennett Jr., a dry-goods store clerk whose father was a mariner, largely in the Surinam trade, but who attended frequent temperance lectures and meetings. Francis as an observant fifteen-year-old recorded in his diary that police officers had seized liquor on January 7, 1854; and a week later he reported, "This noon I saw some Liquor destroyed in front of the Town house."[42] Temperance in Gloucester also had a violent streak. A Bennett diary entry for May 1854 states: "In the night a mob tore the front and part of the side off of Moses Gilbert's building in Beach St. which was used for a rum shop & kept by an Irishman. They also destroyed the contents of the shop."[43]

Temperance was a widespread movement, evident in the travels of John H. W. Hawkins, whose portrait Lane lithographed in 1842 (fig. 134). Hawkins, based in Boston, devoted years of his life to preaching the gospel of temperance and collecting pledges of sobriety in cities all over the eastern states and provinces, as far south as Alabama and as far north as Nova Scotia, on land and

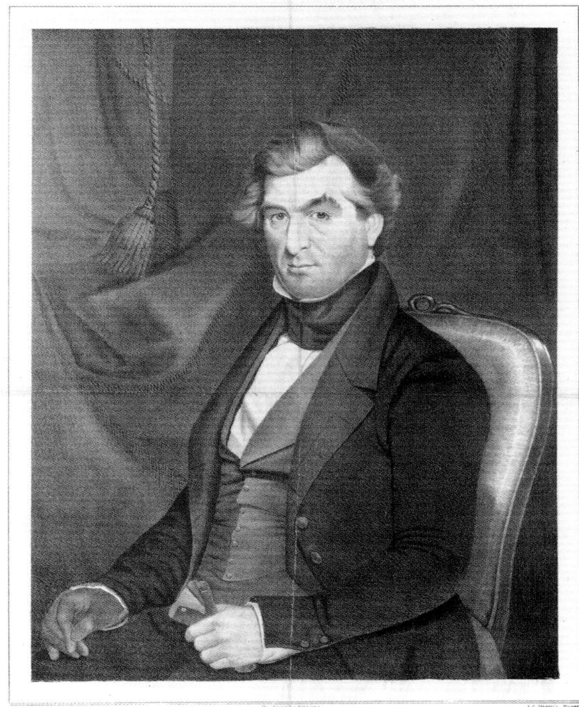

FIGURE 134
Fitz H. Lane, *John H. W. Hawkins*, 1842. Lithograph on paper, 15 3/16 × 11 5/8 in. (38.6 × 29.6 cm). Printed by J. C. Sharp's Press. Below the image: "On stone by F. H. Lane." Below the title: "From the original Portrait Painted & Presented to the Washington Total Abstinence Society of Boston by T. M. Burnham." Library of Congress, Prints and Photographs Division, Washington, DC (2003670213).

on board ships. He assured audiences that liquor is "the deadly destroyer of industry and thrift, upon the farm, in the shop, on the ship, behind the counter, in the office and wherever there are hands to work or work to be done; the foe of agriculture, of manufactures, of art, and of learning . . . [whose] effects . . . may be seen in the brutal wallowings of debased men, in the shameful spreeings of drunkenness, in the turbulence of mobs, in the abominations of the brothel." With such declarations he hoped to enlarge at every stop "the Cold Water Army" of teetotalers.[44] Despite this passionate movement, particularly vigorous in Gloucester, George H. Rogers and others continued to exchange dried fish for vast quantities of distillable molasses from Surinam, and Lane, the temperance advocate, continued to supply him with pictures.

Dutch Guiana—a fertile tropical country slightly bigger than New York State, whose principal city, Paramaribo, was situated near the mouth of the Surinam River—was originally inhabited by the Arawaka, then discovered by the Spanish, taken by the French, settled by the English, traded to the Dutch (in exchange for Manhattan), peopled by Portuguese Sephardic Jews (expelled from Brazil) and British loyalists (fleeing the American Revolution), populated by imported African slaves, and Christianized by Moravians; this polyglot place was the principal trading partner of Gloucester (fig. 135). They had developed a mutually profitable exchange of molasses (to make rum) for dried fish (largely to provide protein to slaves) in the late eighteenth and early nineteenth centuries, when New Englanders sought foreign trading partners because Britain was making trade between its Caribbean colonies and merchants in the rebellious North American colonies difficult.[45] Surinam was described as an "earthly paradise" tainted by "oppression and . . . sin, [inhabited by] . . . men without mercy, women without modesty, the black man a slave to the white man's passions, and the white man a slave to his own."[46] It was a "low and marshy" place, "far from being favourable to health," where malaria and leprosy were serious problems, but its extremely fertile soil attracted investment, for, as one observer put it, "the spirit of gain is a very powerful principle."[47] Unlike neighboring French Guiana, which was a penal colony and thus populated largely by involuntary European settlement, Dutch Guiana's vast sugar plantations were dependent on the importation of 294,000 enslaved Africans, more than the total imported to all of North America between 1501 and 1865.[48]

George H. Rogers would have known about Dutch Guiana through accounts from his ships' captains, but like most Europeans and Euro-Americans, he could have learned about the country through the documentary

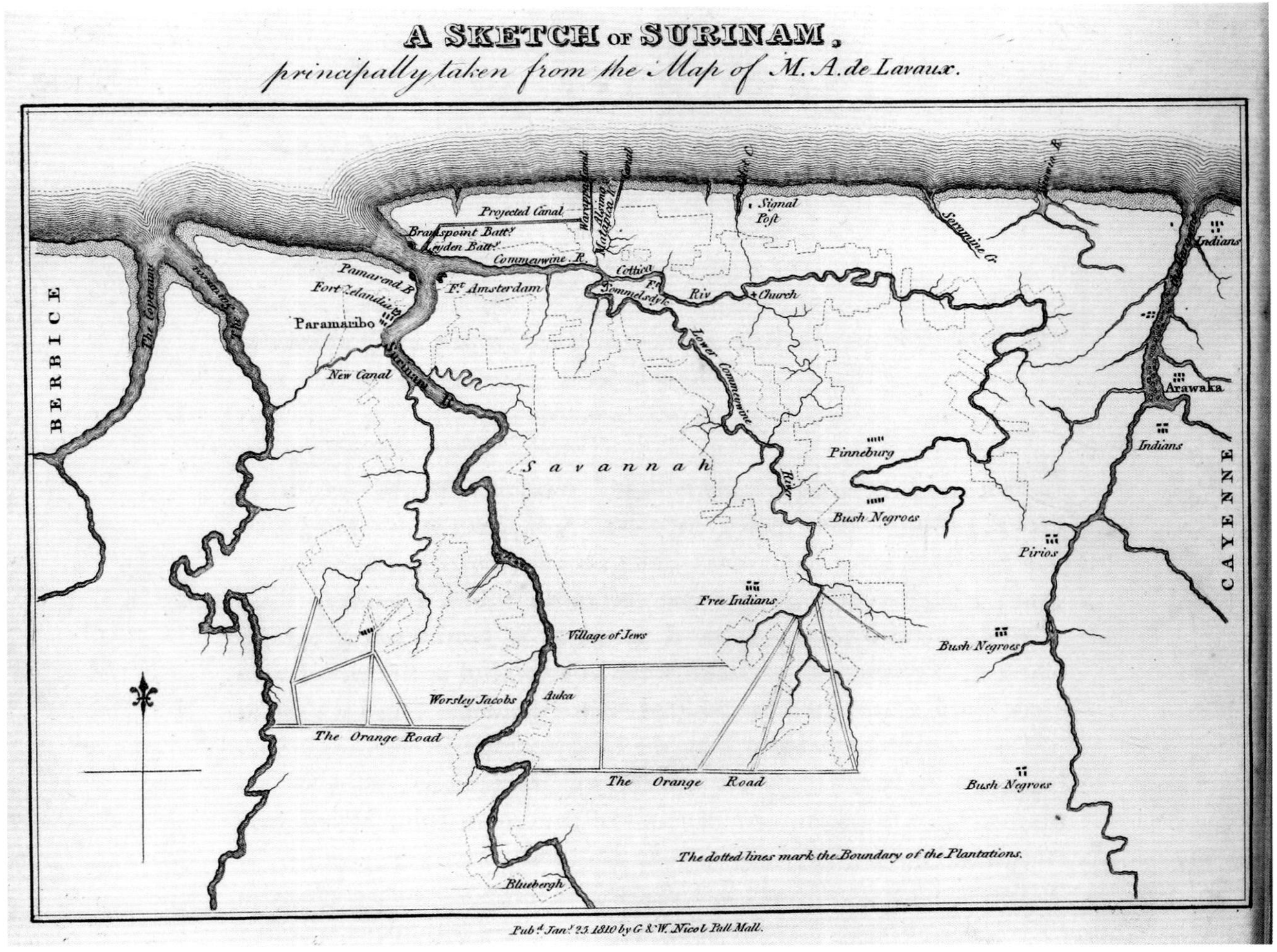

FIGURE 135
M. A. de Lavaux, *A Sketch of Surinam*. Frontispiece in Baron Albert von Sack, *A Narrative of a Voyage to Surinam* (London: Printed for G. and W. Nicol by W. Bulmer, 1810). The Wellcome Trust.

novel *Oroonoko: or, The Royal Slave: A True History* by Aphra Behn (1688) and through the popular account of Capt. J. G. Stedman, resident in the country 1772–77, whose regiment of Scots guards was hired by the Dutch to pursue and recapture slaves who had revolted and fled to the interior.[49] Stedman's narrative was bowdlerized by his publisher, and his drawings were redrawn by his friend William Blake and others, but his book nevertheless gives an in-depth eyewitness account of the natural history and late eighteenth-century social conditions of the country and conveys his dismay at the "diabolical barbarity" he observed there as sugar plantation owners and overseers sought, with only intermittent success, to control their reluctant workforce.[50] At the time of his writing, "the whites or Europeans in this colony, and who reside principally in town [Paramaribo], are computed at five thousand, including the garrison. The negro slaves at about seventy-five thousand."[51] He describes the town of Paramaribo as having "a noble road [harbor] for shipping, the [Surinam] river before the town being above a mile in breadth, and containing sometimes above one hundred [oceangoing] vessels."[52] Its streets are "crouded [*sic*] with planters, sailors, soldiers, Jews, Indians, and

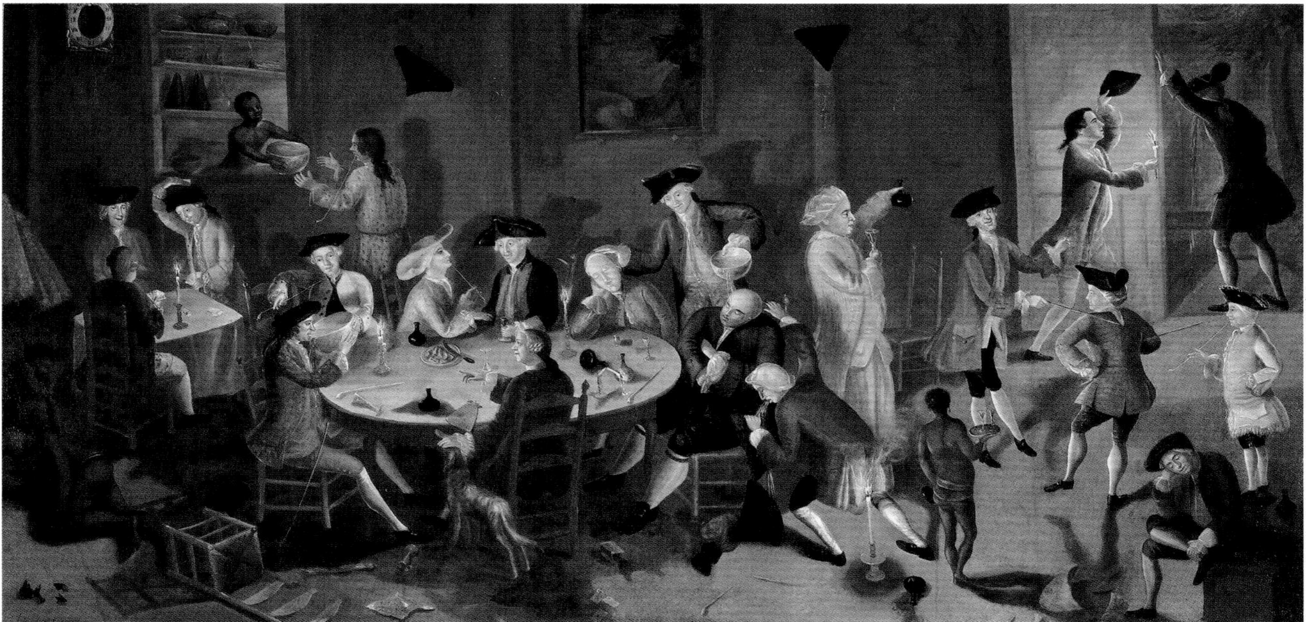

FIGURE 136
John Greenwood, *Sea Captains Carousing in Surinam*, ca. 1752–58. Oil on bed ticking, 37¾ × 75 in. (95.9 × 190.5 cm). Saint Louis Art Museum. Museum purchase (256:1948).

Negroes, while the river is covered with canoes, barges . . . often accompanied with bands of music."[53] The houses, he recounts, "are elegantly furnished with paintings," and the elite dress in "silk embroidery, Genoa velvets, diamonds, gold and silver lace."[54] But overall his impression of the population is that they were a pack of "despotic and despiseable [*sic*]" rascals, and he is not chagrined that his regiment's five-year mission to recapture escaped slaves was entirely unsuccessful.[55]

Stedman records buying "a barrel . . . of salted mackerel . . . imported from North America," which he found delicious, but most of these fish were bought by the planters for the slaves.[56] Contemporaries recount that slave rations included—besides salt fish—vegetables, bananas, and "a glass of rum, on their return in the evenings from their work."[57] It was illegal to make rum in the country, so Surinam's sugar, distilled elsewhere, was apparently reimported as rum.[58] That this common beverage was enjoyed there is indicated in many records, including a mid-eighteenth-century satirical painting by American John Greenwood, *[New England] Sea Captains Carousing in Surinam* (fig. 136).

All the Gloucester newspapers carried news of events in Paramaribo, including an account of a Grand Gala Day celebrating the Dutch king's birthday in 1860 that suggests the polyglot nature of the populace. The rowing races were won by a "Crew of bush negroes" (i.e., escaped slaves with whom the government had made a truce); the contest for climbing a greased pole was won by a man-of-war crewman, while a Native American came in second.[59]

Charles A. Homans, later U.S. consul at Surinam, as a teenage second mate on George H. Rogers's vessel the *Izette*, the bark captained by Nathaniel Rogers on voyages between Gloucester and Surinam in 1848–49, kept a journal (which survives) of his time aboard the *Izette*. In it he gives a good indication of the tempo of this trade: the trip south from Gloucester took about five weeks, followed by two and a half to four months in Paramaribo discharging and selling cargo, repairing rigging and painting the ship, acquiring and loading new cargo, and provisioning the ship, then five to six weeks returning to New England.[60] Beyond the master and two mates there were eight crew members, including the cook. From notations on a loose sheet in the log, it is clear Homans was exerting himself to learn about a hundred words in Sranan, the Creole tongue combining English, Dutch, Portuguese, and some African terms that was used by the slaves, free blacks, and many whites and that the Moravians had systematized into a grammar.[61] The log of the *Amazon*, in 1854, a brig belonging to the Babson brothers, gives more detail concerning activities in port: "Discharging Fish," "Landed some Mackerel," "Took 18 casks of molasses." "taking in sugar." It also details the crew members' "getting Drunk . . . put in prison."[62]

Just as the vigor of the local temperance movement in Gloucester was undoubtedly related to the volume of rum available from distilled Caribbean sugar, so was the fact of slavery in Surinam related to the strong abolitionist position of many in Gloucester. By 1840 slavery had been all but abolished in the northern states, and news of slavery elsewhere (in central Africa, in Constantinople, in Cuba) was frequently discussed in the local newspapers with a tone of consternation.[63] Articles concerning the strenuous efforts by the British to curtail the trade—through treaties with "kings in the interior of Africa" to "stop the [interior] slave trade," the burning of the coastal forts and "factories," and the interdiction of 1,575 slave ships by British naval vessels and the return of their captives to Africa—were much in the news.[64] Wendell Philips, William Lloyd Garrison, and other noted abolitionists lectured at the Gloucester Lyceum and preached in the churches.[65] In 1850 the *Gloucester Telegraph* included a profile of a man named "Bacchus, stolen from Guinea," within a vehement anti-Southern tirade.[66] When, in the summer of 1854, a fugitive slave, Anthony Bunns, was apprehended in Boston and "carried off with some difficulty," "back into bondage," by U.S. soldiers, the Boston police, and the Boston militia, "the streets of Boston were dressed in mourning and the infuriated populace hissed."[67] In Gloucester two effigy figures were hung on the public wharf, one labeled "Judas Iscariot" and the other, "dressed as a Negro Driver [overseer of slaves]" with a whip, was labeled "Benedict Arnold."[68]

No direct record documents how Lane or his patrons felt about abolitionism beyond the fact that the firm of Lane & Scott published Charles C. Green's abolitionist book, *The Nubian Slave*, in 1845, but it seems very probable that the dramatic rift between Lane and the brother-in-law with whom he had resided most of his adult life, Ignatius Winter, could have been prompted by a quarrel about slavery. Winter, whose work as an artisan in the construction trades was unrelated to foreign or Southern trade, early in 1861, in the heated weeks before the outbreak of the Civil War, introduced to the Gloucester town meeting a resolution that stated, in part, that the town's "[Massachusetts] Representatives in General Court be instructed to use their utmost endeavors to repeal any . . . unfriendly acts, and especially the Personal Liberty Bill [that protected fugitive slaves] . . . [in a] spirit of conciliation and compromise."[69] Perhaps, as the father of draft-aged sons, anxiety about the meaning of war to his family was in the forefront of his mind, but it is clear that Winter was, if not a Southern sympathizer, then an active Southern conciliator.[70] If, as is likely, Lane was, like many temperance advocates, a firm abolitionist, this serious disagreement concerning the principal social, political, and moral issue of the day would have made daily life within the same household extremely difficult. In the summer of 1862 Lane moved out of the stone house and in with Dr. Herman and Mrs. Davidson, selling his house to his lifelong friend Joseph Stevens Jr., a staunch abolitionist who promptly evicted Ignatius Winter—together with Lane's sister and his many nieces and nephews—in an acrimonious event that resulted in unsuccessful lawsuits on the part of Winter.[71] Of course, the rift could have been about something else, but it seems probable that the strength of feeling about the inappropriateness of chattel slavery on the part of its opponents was in the order of magnitude necessary to result in such a decisive and public family schism.

Slavery was abolished in Dutch Guiana in 1863, shortly after Lincoln's Emancipation Proclamation effected that result in the United States. With the ensuing abandonment of Dutch Guiana's sugar plantations by the planters and their workforce, Gloucester's Surinam trade collapsed. Seeing the writing on the wall, George H. Rogers had moved his increasingly diversified business interests to Boston in 1860. It is probable that he hung his Lane paintings, including a scene of Fort Point in Gloucester Harbor "with one of the Surinam fleet at anchor," in his Boston parlor, reminders of his financial acumen and meteoric rise on nearby Cape Ann but also, unintentionally but necessarily, reminders of the drunkenness of rum-soaked sailors and the "diabolical barbarity" of the slave-raised sugar at the base of this prosperity.

CALIFORNIA GOLD, NEW ENGLAND "GOLD"

During the two decades of Lane's painting career in Gloucester, no subject occupied more space in the town's newspapers than California. From 1848, the year Lane moved back to his native place from Boston and gold was discovered at Sutter's Creek, one and often two full front-page columns of every issue of the town's newspapers were devoted to news about, and news from, the Golden State.[72] California as a place and as a state of mind loomed ever present as an alternative to the facts and the ethos of life on the substrate of granite that characterized their home for New Englanders during these years. Although Lane himself went east (to Maine, as discussed in chapter 5) and south (as we will see in chapter 8) rather than west, several of his close kin, many of his neighbors, some of his patrons, many of the ships he painted, and a few of his paintings made the journey to California during the artist's lifetime. Lane did not picture California, but the pressure of this dark star, this alternative utopia, is evident in his works and their itineraries. Arguably many of Lane's paintings could be said to embody what Cook calls an "oppositional idea"; they were engaged in a rearguard action to bolster the social fabric of coastal New England as its patriarchy, its social economy, and its pride were threatened by the alternative universe that California represented.

The gold-rush exodus was prompt and massive. Eager gold seekers from the Northeast crowded west by sea and by land on conveyances of all types, with an eagerness that was astonishing and easy to parody (fig. 137). On a sample day, September 9, 1849, the *Boston Shipping List* noted that 154 ships, 145 barks, 87 brigs, and 69 schooners were on their way by the Straits of Magellan or Panama to California.[73] The following summer the *St. Louis Republican* reported that "42,000 souls and 9,700 wagons" had registered in that city on one of the most popular overland routes and were "on the trail" (fig. 138).[74]

The spoils were immediate and enormous. By June 1849 the *Lexington* had arrived in New York with 1,676 pounds of California gold; by November gold valued at $3,700,000 had reached the U.S. Mint in Philadelphia, and $6,000,000 worth, weighing seventy tons and packed in 1,400 boxes drawn from the port by eighty horses, had reached the Bank of England in London.[75] During the first months of 1849, $350,000 in gold was received in China, triggering strong interest there, and fearing depopulation, the emperor prohibited emigration to California.[76] It was estimated that in the first year of the gold rush, more than $40,000,000 in gold was shipped out of San Francisco.[77] Gold was recognized as a metal with unique and astonishing characteristics and uses; it also represented a steady value in an antebellum economy rife with counterfeit paper bills and flimflam con men.[78] Gloucesterites, including Lane, read every week in the local papers about this all-out migration and the unheard-of wealth being rapidly unearthed; no doubt their emotions were mixed: excitement, greed, pathos, and longing for the pre-1848 status quo, so quickly and completely upended. Side by side with news of gold, they read unsettling accounts of disasters—cannibalism, cholera, urban fires, disease, lawlessness, and vigilantism en route to and in California—and, just as often, articles reinforcing New England pieties, established social hierarchies, and time-honored

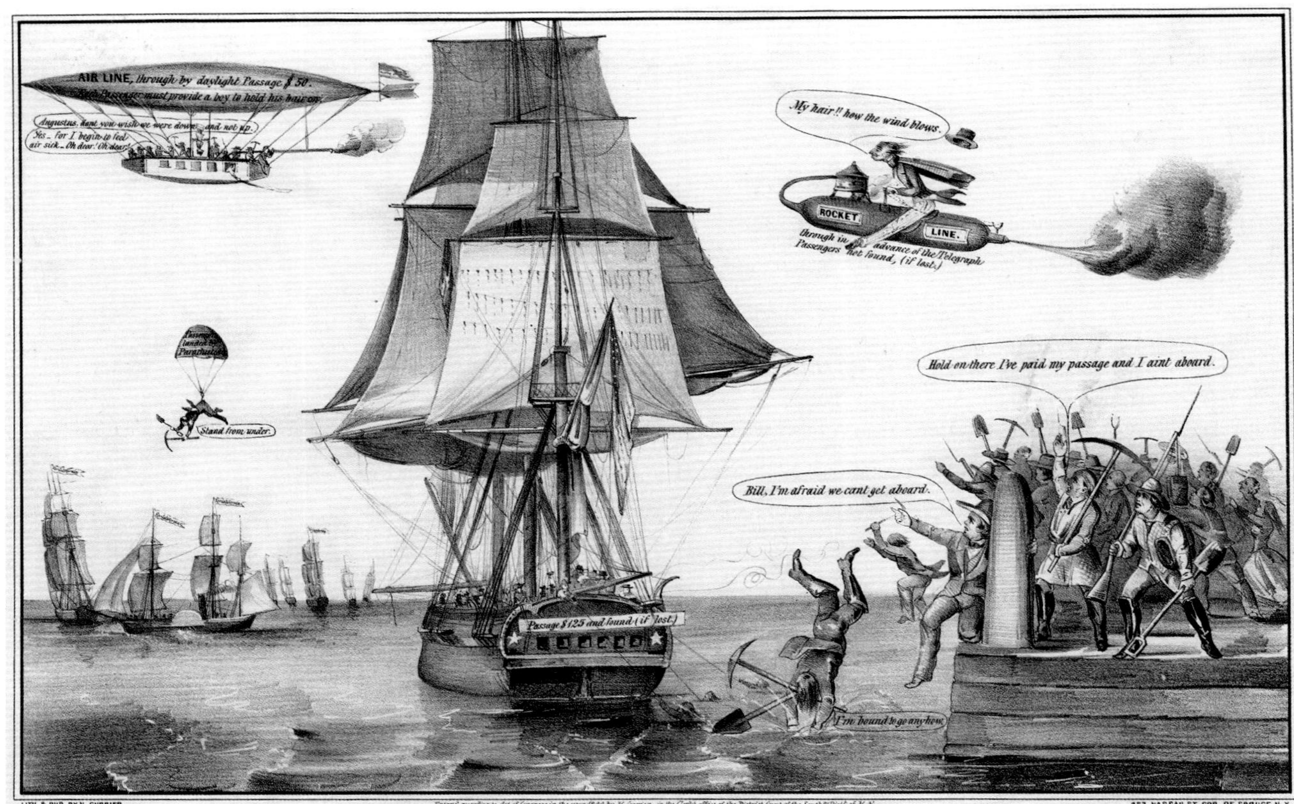

FIGURE 137
N[athaniel] Currier, *The Way They Go to California* (New York: Currier & Ives, ca. 1849). Library of Congress, Prints and Photographs Division, Washington, DC (91481165).

relationships between labor and wealth, between the individual and the community.[79]

Gloucester as a whole during the period between the gold strike and the Civil War—the years when Lane was painting—continued to be publicly imagined as having a balanced social economy composed of a network of intersecting nodal points. As one apologist put it: "Were we endued with power to discern the subtle threads of connection running through society, binding its members together, each individual would be seen to occupy the center of a circle more or less extended, and to and from that center, would appear influences and attractions extending like silken cords, connecting all within its circumference of affection or interest. This is true in a wider or narrower aspect of every person in his moral, religious, and business relations."[80] But gold was a great disrupter of webs and silken cords. Among the "California items" reported in Gloucester in January 1849 was this poignant tale: "The thirst for gold severs all domestic ties. A widowed mother whose son was about leaving New Haven for California, in the schooner *Montague*, offered him, with all the persuasion in her power, any sum to the amount of 20,000 dollars, if he would remain at home, but in vain. How many ties of affection are thus rudely snapped by the prevailing mania!"[81]

Lane's landscape paintings in general, and his canvases commissioned by Nathaniel Babson in particular, participated in the regional effort to maintain threads of social cohesion and to imagine just relations between labor and

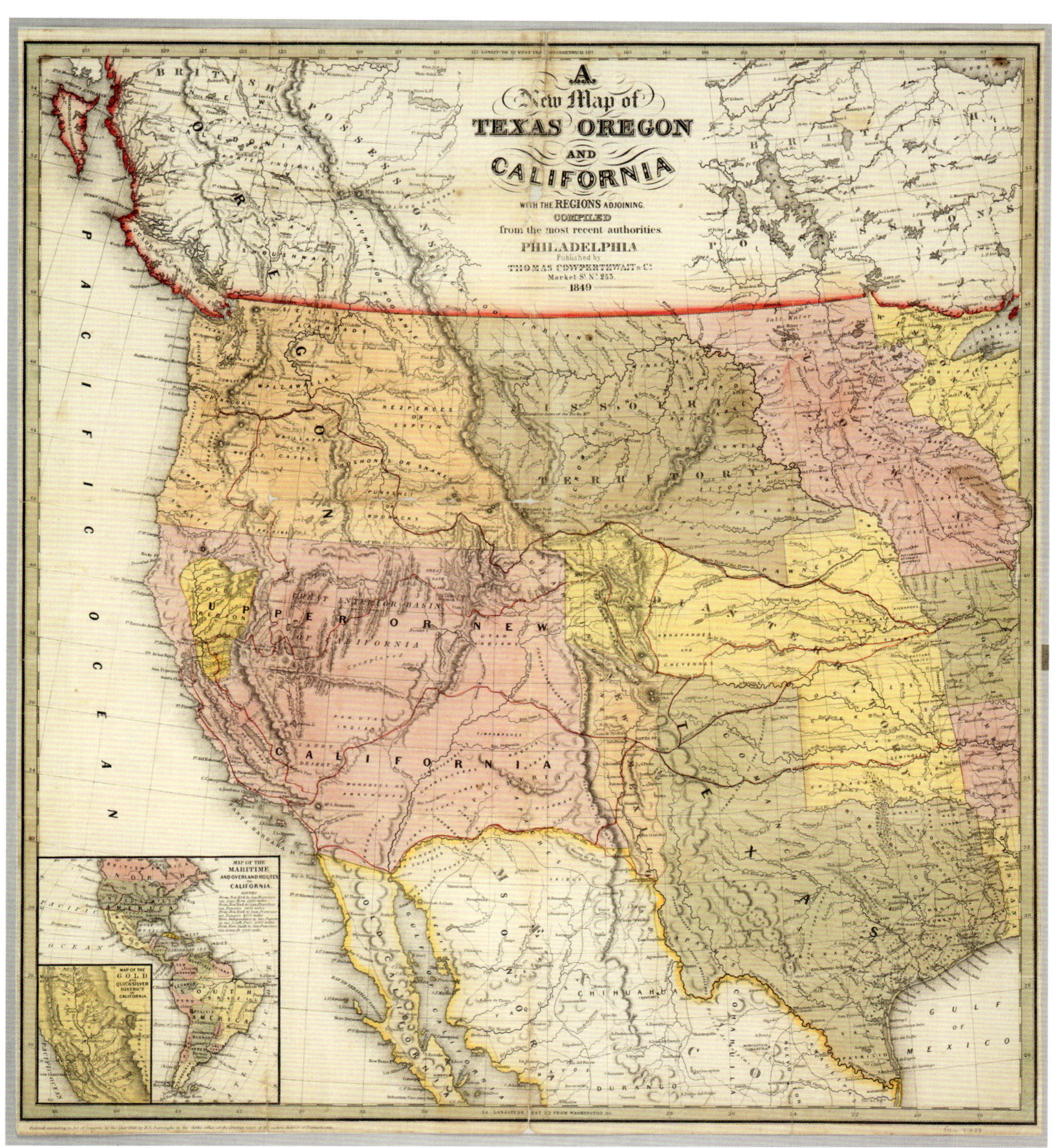

FIGURE 138

A New Map of Texas, Oregon, and California with the Regions Adjoining. Hand-colored lithograph, 21¼ × 19⅝ (54 × 50 cm). From Samuel Augustus Mitchell, *Description of Oregon and California, Embracing an Account of the Gold Regions* (Philadelphia: Thomas, Cowperthwait, 1849). The Huntington Library, San Marino, California, RB41388.

prosperity, land and productivity, parents and children, memory and aspiration. Nathaniel, cousin of the siblings Annette Babson, John James Babson, and Capt. Edward Babson, bought three, possibly four, Lane paintings, two of which were commissioned specifically to travel to California, *The Babson Meadows at Riverdale* and *Babson and Ellery Houses, Gloucester* (figs. 23 and 24). Unlike the harborside Babsons, who were focused on marine matters and commerce, cousin Nathaniel maintained the farm established by Babson and Ellery ancestors a century earlier on the inland portion of Cape Ann.[82] One of his two surviving children, Emma, became affianced to William Hovey Friend, who left for California that year to seek his fortune and returned in 1863 to marry her and bring her west.[83] It was decided that his other child, Maria, would go as well, so Nathaniel Babson asked Lane to paint gifts for them—a landscape that included the family's eighteenth-century gambrel-roofed house and another with a view of the Babson meadow properties fenced with stout stone walls and, in the distance, the local nucleated community dominated by a church's spire.

The activity pictured in both these canvases is bringing in summer hay—in the one case by wagon, in the other by gundalow, or punt. This pair of paintings are matter-of-fact, but they also express a kind of parable about the virtues of New England life as it had developed over two centuries. The aquatic load is probably salt hay (fine fodder for the herd of dairy cows that were the center of production on the Babson farm), and the wagon load is probably timothy, or English grass, for horses and likely a cash crop.[84] Both are images of good husbandry—the summer's bounty and the farm's labor resources have been utilized to prepare for the five lean months of winter when pasturage will not be available to feed stock. In short, these are pictorial sermons on the essential elements of what one might call a New England ethos: a deep religious and domestic history, a prosperous present, and a solid future ensured by diligent labor in a familiar seasonal round of tasks, ever mindful of future consequences. The outcome was not wealth but rather comfort and prosperity in proportion to the work, care, and ingenuity expended, even on a farm, as Lane's paintings make clear, plagued by boulders.

From the earliest decades of the nineteenth century the citizens of Cape Ann had labored to frame and reiterate the virtues on which their way of life depended and to admonish one another concerning the consequences of not hewing to the model: "Industry," one editorial promised, "crowns us with health. . . . Industry brings wealth. . . . The only way to secure riches is by industrious habits."[85] "Order and regularity, punctuality . . . truth and virtue. . . . [as well as] diligent and persevering application . . . [are] absolutely necessary to success."[86] Early in the century the dangers to the individual and to society as a whole seemed to be located in worldliness ("the plough has been exchanged for the insignia of professional life, and the spinning-wheel for the piano") and in the tropics ("Man is no where found more degraded, than in climes the most delicious, and upon a soil that produces, spontaneously, an abundant supply of his wants").[87] There was also some uneasiness about potential emigration to farms in the Midwest when the Erie Canal opened, but locals assured one another: "the industrious habits of the people, and our moral, religious, and literary institutions . . . are very strong inducements for our population and their descendants to remain within the limits of their native State. . . . Our young men . . . choose to live here, die and be buried by the side of their fathers."[88] These anxious minisermons allude to the many pressures on the status quo and suggest some of the roles Lane's paintings were asked to play in recording what his patrons wanted to fix in memory as well as on the wall. Certainly the two Babson paintings were about fixing a memory of an ideology as well as a place.

The Babson Meadows and the *Babson and Ellery Houses* depict landscape as fenced—that is, owned, managed, ordered space. The stone walls assert division between and hierarchy among agricultural activities (containing grazing animals, marking off garden, orchard, grain and row crops from pasturage and from the public right of way) and among humans. In such a landscape it is clear who owned, made decisions about, and garnered sustenance and profits from these fields and structures. The West and the wild areas of upper New York State depicted by Hudson River landscapists, by comparison, were understood to be unfenced, disordered, representing an alternative set of unmarked and disruptive spatial and social relations.

Agriculture is offered in mid-nineteenth-century New England's advice literature as the paradigmatic activity for the householder-patriarch. The average Massachusetts farm of about a hundred acres and worth about $3,300 yielded a profit of about $400 a year.[89] Those living on such a farm, it was asserted, "want no reasonable comforts of life, and can bring up their children to their own healthy and honorable occupation."[90] Sentiments like these gained a new urgency and a new antimodel in 1848 when gold in California offered a very different career path to seemingly unearned prosperity. Farming in New England was specifically held up as having a "soothing, purifying ennobling influence on the heart and mind."[91] Such a life cultivated men of "dauntless energy and perseverance [who]. . . . have given New England its character. . . . [They have] made this cold and barren soil to blossom like the rose and the rock-bound coast to yield that which has enriched our country more, and [is] of greater value than all the gold of California."[92] The character of the region being invoked was one of generational order and patriarchal authority prevailing among successive generations of "orderly, sober, and industrious" citizens contributing to a mutually sustaining, family-oriented, historically framed, modest, virtuous, harmonious community.[93] A characteristic editorial in the *Cape Ann Light and Gloucester Telegraph* of December 1, 1849, two days after Thanksgiving and in anticipation of Christmas, gives Gloucesterites a rousing paean to their region's social and historical wholeness:

> Glorious New England! Full of good people, good things, [and] good times. . . . A few more days and the poor girl at service and the hired man, and the little dapper clerk, and the newly married pair and their new baby will all go home, and sit down at the old table, tell long yarns, and call up old times. . . . Give us New England for a home. There is no place like it in all God's great earth. Give us the Yankee Thanksgiving; the old stony hearth warms on its cheerful fires. It is the most precious gem set in the golden circle of the year.[94]

Note that both these tributes to New England—published in the months after the discovery of gold upended local pieties—explicitly reference value and "gold" only to suggest its higher metaphorical value at home than its literal material value in the far West.

Lane's paintings that Nathaniel Babson ordered for his two daughters participate in this warm emotional defense of New England. They were sent west, no doubt, as reminders to these young women to hold fast to the virtues and the memories of their patrimony as they entered a region notoriously unhinged from the core idea that "the only way to secure riches is by industrious habits." But the vigor of these pleas for the utopic metaphorical "gold" of New England paled before the strength of the lodestone California from fall 1848, when the old order appeared to collapse more or less overnight as the reality of easy gold was confirmed. Placer gold, picked up as nuggets in streams or sifted flakes (dust) from gravel beds, was to be found and owned by anyone fast enough to see it first and stake a claim. Unlike the rich mines of precious metals in Spanish America, which were monopolies and royal property, the gold-bearing real estate in California was available to all takers.[95] Certainly in the second, later, phase of gold extraction, highly capitalized, industrially equipped companies were formed for hydraulic extraction and for hard-rock mining, but it took many months to develop these financial structures and technological innovations, during which time there was a remarkably democratic scramble. Suddenly, in light of California gold, all the pieties about the appropriate relation between steady effort and prosperity appeared to be undone, all loyalty to family and community and "forefathers" dissolved, or at

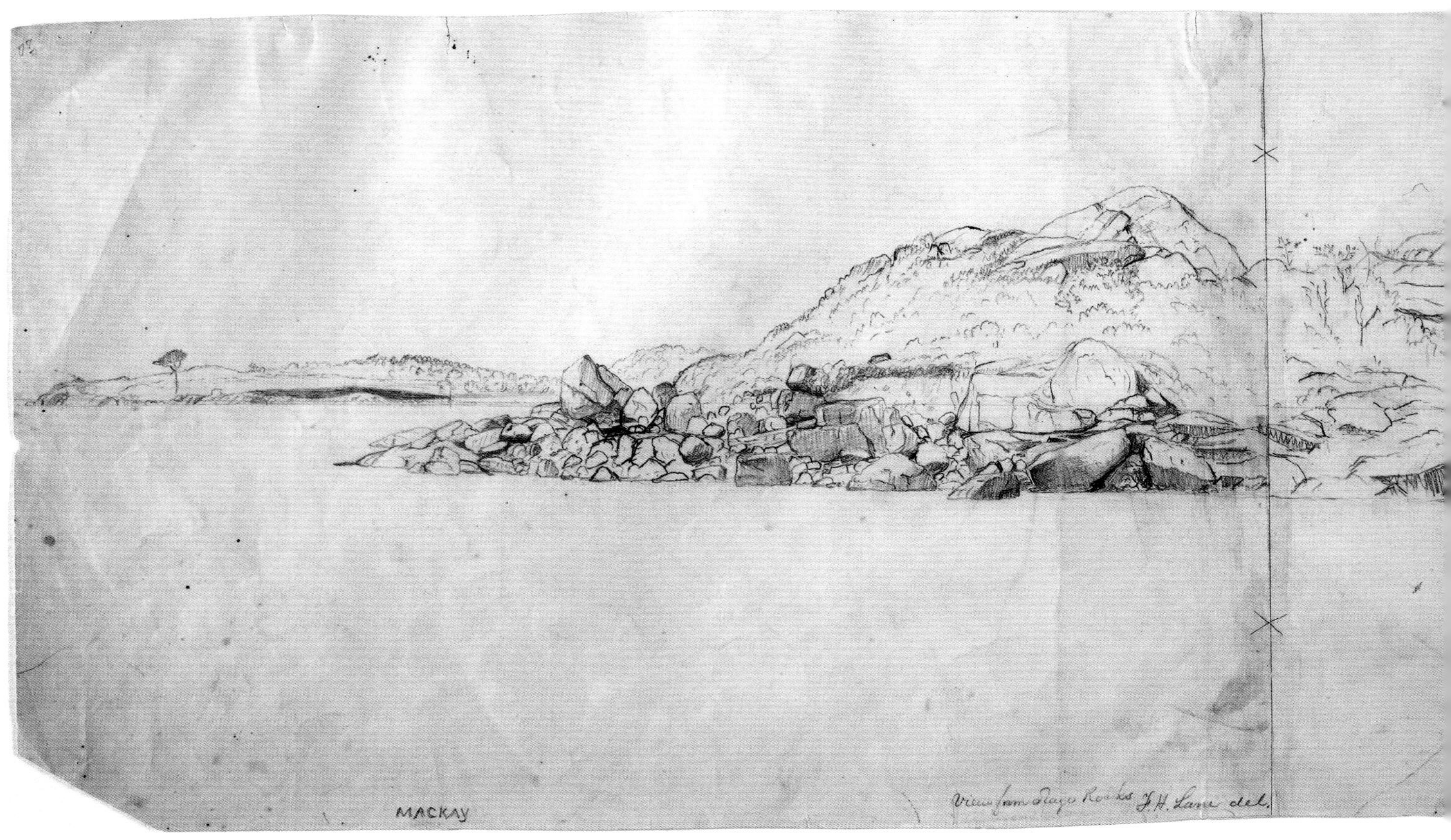

FIGURE 139
F. H. Lane, *View from Stage Rocks, Gloucester*, n.d. Graphite on paper, 10 × 36 in. (25.4 × 91.4 cm). Inscribed "Picture from this sketch painted for Nathaniel Babson." Cape Ann Museum, Gloucester, Massachusetts. Gift of Samuel H. Mansfield, 1927 (485.77).

least in need of vigorous reinforcement. The outcome was, on the one hand, a headlong rush for riches and, on the other, a stream of vigorous public exhortations about the importance of industrious habits, the blessings of labor, and the rewards of steady work, as well as the creation of documents such as Lane's sweet backward glance at an ancestral homestead and a rooted community clustered around the beacon of a church spire.[96]

A third painting commissioned by Nathaniel Babson prominently portrays Stage Rocks in the harbor; while the painting has not been located, it is clear from the drawing from which Babson ordered it that it is, above all, about rocks, specifically the hulking islands of granite that were associated with the earliest years of settlement on Cape Ann (fig. 139). These rocks represented cultural memory; they were marine landmarks—steadfast, unchanging, useful only aesthetically as triggers to a historic and picturesque sense of place. A long article in the *Cape Ann Light and Gloucester Telegraph* published in September 1849, when gold fever was at its height, praises the beauties of Gloucester and the skill "of Fitz Henry Lane, an artist who has acquired no little well deserved fame by the spirited execution of his marine views,—and who has also transferred to his canvas many of the wild and romantic spots which make up the rude grandeur of his place of birth, [where] . . . people possess a hardy independence and self-reliance as impregnable as their own rock-bound coast."[97]

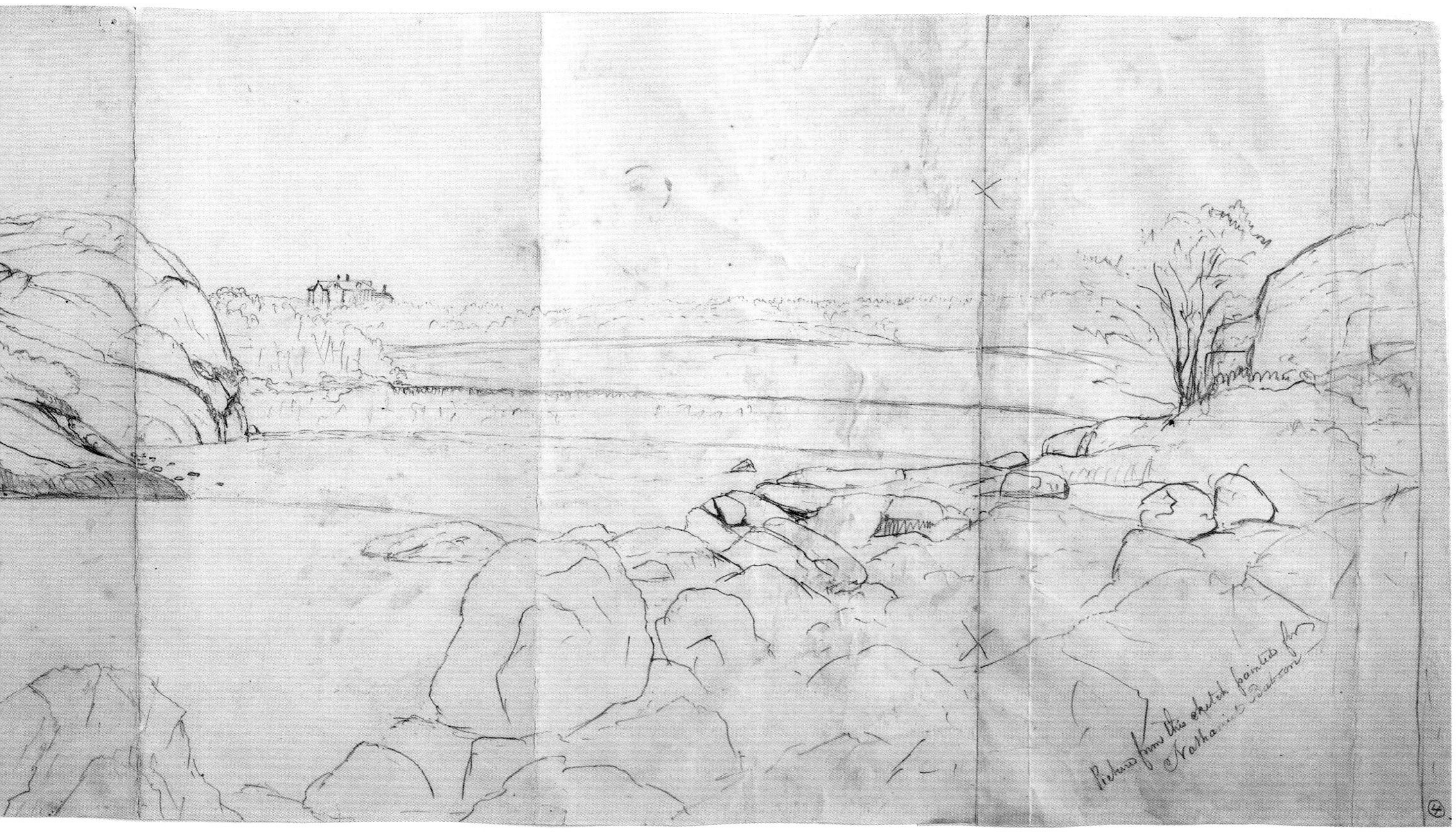

This “rock-bound coast” and its “rude grandeur” captured on canvas by Lane are associated with “the noble fearlessness . . . and the unstinted generosity” of Gloucester’s citizens, explicitly linking the artist with an ideology of New England manhood.[98] However, the same issue of the *Cape Ann Light and Gloucester Telegraph* includes a notice that trees belonging to Lane patron James Mansfield had been surreptitiously sawn down and stolen for lumber—a distinctly unnoble, ungenerous act of theft. Another article that day describes a wonder beyond the magnificence of anything seen in Massachusetts, a twenty-chandelier, $100,000 hotel shipped in pieces from New Orleans to San Francisco that month.[99] So Gloucesterites were aware of the two realities bracketing the mythic New England ethos so often and firmly repeated—locals actually behaving badly, on the one hand, and the enormities of instant unfathomable wealth elsewhere, on the other. By mid-1849 early young adventurers had returned to the East Coast with hundreds of thousands of dollars in gold in their pockets, instantly refuting ancestral wisdom about slow accruals through virtuous labor. But tales of hardship, banditry, and disease, especially at the Isthmus of Panama; shipwreck of those who went around the Horn; Native American hostilities, misery, and cannibalism experienced by those who traveled overland; and strange inversions of value in San Francisco provided cautionary tales, illustrating not only that chasing gold was, in fact, *not* a matter of “secur[ing] riches by industrious habits” but that it was gambling, and gambling for very high stakes.[100]

Many gambled. In the first flush of 1849 young men from Gloucester (and elsewhere) formed companies and went west as fast as they could, while older, well established men quickly revised business models. George H. Rogers, for instance, redirected his bark *Izette*—a vessel profitably engaged in the Surinam trade—to California in the fall of 1849 with a cargo of lumber, as San Francisco had a desperate housing and materials shortage.[101] Capt. Simon P. Burnham, husband of Lane's first cousin Susan Haskell, took the forty members of the hastily formed Mattapan and California Trading and Mining Company (each paying $200) to San Francisco in April 1849 in the Gloucester-owned brig *Ann*.[102] Robert Bennet Forbes, whose earlier efforts had been concentrated in China, on hearing of the gold strike, chartered a ship in New York in January 1849 for $25,000 and sent it to California, and also that year had a river steamer, *Mint*, built to his specifications and shipped on the deck of one of his clippers to San Francisco, where it served as the first steamboat transporting eager prospectors inland from that city to Sacramento and the gold fields.[103] There was a huge premium on speed among the vessels built for and redirected into the California trade. Sacrificing cargo space for lean hulls and carrying enormous acreage of sail on vast superstructures, these ships were understood to be handsome and extremely fast but fragile. However, in one of those strange inversions of value that so startled people in 1849, such vessels as the *Izette*, the *Ann*, and Forbes's clipper were worth little in San Francisco, and their officers had to offer enormous sums to secure crews for the return voyage—even naval vessels' crews were deserting to head for the gold fields.[104] And of course not all miners prospered. George Babson, cousin of Nathaniel Babson, Lane's repeat customer, left Gloucester in 1849 in company with John Baker for California.[105] Babson dropped out of the records almost immediately, possibly returning to Massachusetts, while Baker made it to the gold fields in Eldorado County by 1850, where he was ensconced with fourteen other men in their twenties, all "miners of gold," in a boarding house.[106] But the 1860 census lists Baker as a disabled "mariner" living alone in Placer County with no personal estate. In short, California, by divorcing prosperity from traditional labor, had a considerable effect on Gloucester—it drained manpower, especially the rising generation of bachelors, and it undermined the established ideas about generational order and patriarchy even while clearly destroying the hopes and fortunes of many who responded to its siren call.

However, many did prosper in California, most by providing goods and services that the miners needed. Lane patron Capt. Edward Babson, cousin of Nathaniel Babson, had retired from the sea in 1846 and became a land-based merchant with offices in many cities, including San Francisco.[107] It is uncertain whether he himself made the trip to California, but many of his close kin did. Babson's son, Edward Babson, was a twenty-year-old clerk living in San Francisco in a boarding house in 1860, probably engaged as his father's agent. Twenty years later the younger Edward, then forty, having returned to Massachusetts between 1866 and 1870, was prospering, running a commission and shipping business and living in Chelsea with his wife, two daughters, his widowed sister Amanda, her daughter, his half-brother George Friend Babson, and two Irish servants.[108] He had done well in California but, reembracing the land of his youth, returned with California wealth to New England.

Two of Capt. Edward Babson's brothers-in-law were established in California by 1860, and like the children of his cousin Nathaniel Babson, Emma and Marie, they included Lane paintings of Gloucester in their luggage or sent for them soon after arrival.[109] Joseph Sayward Friend, Edward Babson's eldest brother-in-law, through his second wife, Julia Friend, was living in Sacramento by 1860, where he was a lumber merchant with considerable real estate and personal wealth.[110] Lumber was a good business to be in near the gold fields in these years. The timber in California's forests was plentiful, the technology for its extraction was quickly developed, and the mining operators needed enormous supplies of dimensional lumber to construct flumes for hydraulic mining and to support mine shafts for hard-rock mining. An inscription on Lane's drawing titled *Gloucester Outer Harbor from near the Cut* (fig. 140), dated 1864, reads: "Picture painted from this sketch for Joseph S. Friend, Sacramento California. This was probably the last of Lane's sketches from nature."

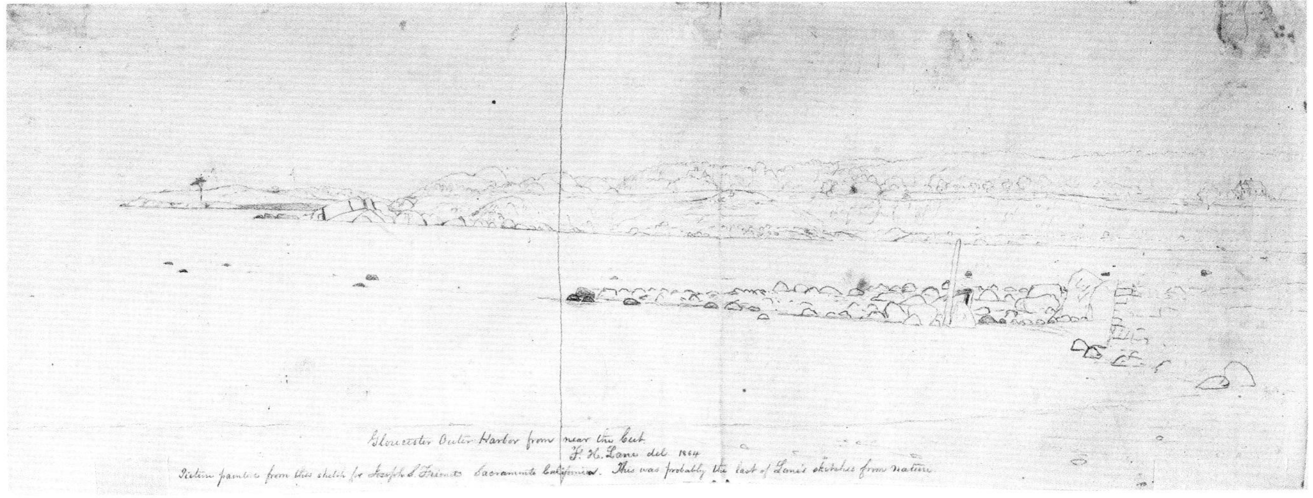

FIGURE 140
Fitz H. Lane, *Gloucester Outer Harbor from near the Cut*, 1864, detail. Graphite on paper, 9 × 34 in. (22.9 × 86.4 cm). Inscribed "Gloucester Outer Harbor from near the Cut. / F. H. Lane del. 1864. / Picture painted from this sketch for Joseph S. Friend, Sacramento California. This was probably the last of Lane's sketches from nature." Cape Ann Museum, Gloucester, Massachusetts. Gift of Samuel H. Mansfield, 1927 (485.62).

So we can imagine Joseph Sayward Friend prospering in California and, wishing to recall the familiar scenes of his early decades, writing to Lane in 1862 or 1863 requesting a painting. One of Lane's last completed works, the painting was likely delivered by sea on a journey of several weeks, probably facilitated by Capt. Edward Babson's maritime business. The painting made from this drawing has not been identified, but the resonance it must have had for the recipient is easy to imagine—its view of the broad Gloucester Harbor, looking out on the Atlantic, with the "rock-bound" coast illuminated by the warm hues of a setting sun and a chromatically enlivened sky. In Sacramento, a key provisioning center for miners, Joseph Sayward Friend remained engaged in the life and work of a very different harbor town. While Sacramento is a seaport, it is deep inland and located in the extensive fertile flatness of the Central Valley. Described by a contemporary as a "country [that] has no winter . . . [where] all the products of the United States, from apples to oranges, from potatoes to sugar cane, may be produced in . . . the richest, most picturesque and beautiful region . . . upon the face of the earth," with the Sierras on the distant horizon, it represented a topography very different from Cape Ann's.[111] Lane's painting of Gloucester Harbor would have performed a different social function in California than similar works did in New England, offering a permanent historic and perhaps nostalgic view of Gloucester for Friend and family members seeking to keep memories alive of a remote native place while embracing this wondrous Western Eden.

Another brother-in-law, Richard Goss Stanwood, was Capt. Edward Babson's eldest half brother-in-law through his first wife, Amanda Stanwood. He had a son of the same name who grew up in Gloucester and emigrated to California in the 1850s. Richard Goss Stanwood Jr. was established as a twenty-nine-year-old clerk in Marysville, north of Sacramento, at the confluence of the Feather and Yuba Rivers, in the heart of gold country, by the time of the 1860 census. By 1880 he was a prosperous lumber dealer in that city.[112] His son, Edward Babson Stanwood (1872–after 1961), also of Marysville, was apparently named after the redoubtable Gloucester captain, and when the Frick Art Reference Library did an inventory of

Lane paintings in 1961, Edward Babson Stanwood, a lifelong Californian, indicated that he owned a F. H. Lane painting. It is likely that this painting, which remains unidentified, came with his father, Richard Goss Stanwood Jr., directly from Gloucester.[113]

It may seem odd that young people bent on making their fortune and willing to endure the strain and hardship of emigration and marginal living conditions would think about ordering paintings to include in their luggage, let alone actually bring them, but the fact that they did lends insight into the roles these canvases—documents of carefully selected, framed, and toned views of the world—were asked to play. It sheds light on art's social role. In this context paintings that in themselves seem quiet, fixed, and self-contained were introduced as a kind of powerful elastic adhesive charged with binding the travelers and their descendants over thousands of miles to their kin, their memories, and their social values. Other migrants carried pictorial anchors in their baggage. In 1850 Gloucesterites read about a full-length picture of George Washington painted by "a daughter of [Gilbert] Stuart, the celebrated painter . . . for which she received $700. It is to go to California."[114] Vision, it may have been assumed, can trigger memory, emotional attachment, loyalty, and exemplary behavior even better than more pointed sermons and other verbal exhortations.

How conscious was Lane of the dynamic upending of his culture by the remote but powerful lodestone California? The newspapers were full of California, tableaux on floats in Gloucester parades included gold-mining scenes, maps of California and newfangled pistols were suddenly available in local shops, and the dry-goods store of the Stevens family—his closest friends—titled their ads "Dry goods for California."[115] Conditions in distant California stimulated Massachusetts industries large and small. One of the artist's kinsmen, Capt. Oliver Gideon Lane, for instance, set off in the *Deucalion* for San Francisco in June 1849 with his wife and a cargo of fifty prefabricated houses.[116] And sizeable amounts of gold dust—that powerful physical trace of California—were seen in Gloucester by early 1850.[117] California affected how people in Gloucester thought, acted, planned, and related to one another. Many of Lane's patrons redirected their businesses, and every young and unattached man with some capital had a major decision to make: to stay in New England or head westward for gold.

Because travel to California was expensive, it was beyond the means of workingmen (unless they were mariners employed on California-bound ships). It cost at least $200 to join a company journeying to California, even if one walked the two thousand miles between St. Louis and Sacramento (fig. 141). The middle-class young man ambitious to emigrate had to reimagine himself ready not only to engage in difficult physical activities but also to clothe and present himself differently; indeed, he needed to undertake a kind of social cross-dressing. In this regard the Boston emporium that Lane portrayed in a handsome lithograph in 1844, Oak Hall, was preeminent: "for all kinds of goods suited to those who are preparing Outfits for California, from Clothing to a six-barrelled Revolving Pistol, Oak Hall, Boston seems to keep the lead, as the cheapest and greatest place in the Union" (fig. 47).[118] But instead of the dapper clerks and customers in tight-fitting elegant clothing that Lane portrays in this impressive Gothic-themed interior, the extensive and frequent notices in the Gloucester papers for Oak Hall after October 1848 imagine a very different, more feral kind of sartorial masculinity:

> To the Travelling Public. Visit Head Quarters for your Outfits. As many of our citizens and New-Englanders in neighboring towns, are about starting for the New El Dorado, or California Gold Diggings,—and having no experience as to what they will require for their convenience and comfort, . . . [we offer] a good, suitable Outfit [at] Oak Hall, Boston. Having made the Outfitting business our study—(three-fourths of my entire force, numbering some fifty clerks, being all engaged in this new branch of our trade,)—and having fitted out a

> number of extensive companies, we are prepared to furnish our patrons with . . . information concerning the various routes to the Gold Regions [as well as] . . . Feather River overcoats—Spanish or California Cloaks, adapted to the double purpose of Cloak by day, and Blanket at night—Sutter's Long Mining Waistcoat—Linen Sacks— . . . Life Preserves—Isthmus Bags, for pack mules—Canteens—Travelling Bags—Boots—Gold Bags—Tents, . . . Fancy Striped Travelling shirts—Red Flannel shirts and Drawers . . . El Dorado Caps—California Hats—Bowie Knives—Pocket Knives— . . . Pistols. . . .
>
> We hope that all who are going will succeed to their anticipations, but they will not unless they lay in a good supply of the above-named articles. . . . Together with the above, we have an extensive stock of every grade of Clothing adapted to those who have not caught the "Gold Fever," and prefer to remain at home.[119]

ESTIMATE OF AN OUTFIT.

The following estimate of an outfit, for one year, for three persons, with ox teams, is copied from "*The Emigrants' Guide to California*," by Joseph E. Ware, published by J. Halsall, St. Louis, Mo.:—

Item	Weight	Cost
Four yoke of oxen,* $50 each		$200 00
One wagon, cover, &c.		100 00
Three rifles, $20		60 00
Three pair pistols, $15		45 00
Five barrels flour,	1080 lbs	20 00
Bacon,	600 "	30 00
Coffee,	100 "	8 00
Tea,	5 "	2 75
Sugar,	150 "	7 00
Rice,	75 "	3 75
Fruit, dried,	50 "	3 00
Salt, pepper, &c.,	50 "	3 00
Saleratus,	10 "	1 00
Lead,	30 "	1 20
Powder,	25 "	5 50
Tools, &c.,	25 "	7 50
Mining tools,	36 "	12 00
Tent,	30 "	5 00
Bedding,	45 "	22 50
Cooking utensils,	30 "	4 00
Lard,	50 "	2 50
Private baggage,	150 "	
Matches		1 00
One mule		50 00
Candles and soap		5 30
Total	2,583 lbs	$600 00

NOTE.—Estimated cost for one person, $200; those having families, with children, will find it necessary to make nearly as large an estimate for children as an adult. Make no calculation on game, you will need that in addition; as men, women, and children require much more food on the road than usual.

☞ Do not leave home, or St. Louis, without possessing the above GUIDE, also the best *map* of California, &c., that can be procured.

* The teams for the journey should be oxen or mules, either of which can be purchased at the frontier towns. Cows are often taken along for their milk, being sometimes the only dependence for drink.

FIGURE 141
John Disturnell, "Estimate of an Outfit," in *The Emigrant's Guide to New Mexico, California, Oregon* (New York: self-published, 1849), 6. The Huntington Library, San Marino, California, HM-RB41390.

Lane, of course, stayed home. Having easily observed the effects of California on his hometown, he would also have heard firsthand about life in that distant place from his cousin Elizabeth Haskell Gabcar. He must have been close to her, as she was the only relative to whom he left a bequest, and she, her husband, and their daughter were buried with the artist in Joseph Stevens Jr.'s Oak Grove Cemetery plot.[120] Elizabeth was in California by 1853 with her husband, sister Susan, brother-in-law Capt. Simon P. Burnham (who had taken a shipful of hopefuls to San Francisco in the first weeks of the gold rush four years earlier), and her niece.[121] But after a decade in California, she and her husband returned to Gloucester, and he enlisted in the Union Army. She was widowed in 1864, and it appears that she and her daughter moved into Lane's stone house and she kept house for him (as his sister had most of his life, until the Winter family were evicted).[122] What tales she had to tell about the not-always-golden state remain unknown, but the fact of her family's return to Massachusetts in itself speaks of disillusionment and a reembrace of the ideology and community on Cape Ann, where "people possess a hardy independence and self-reliance as impregnable as their own rock-bound coast." It should be noted that the ideology so often summoned in similar terms actually described and dictated male virtues rather than those of "people" in general. Exhortations concerning women did not speak of independence or self-reliance. They were often intended to "inspire [a woman] with a desire to make all around her comfortable and happy, and teach her that not self-gratification, but the

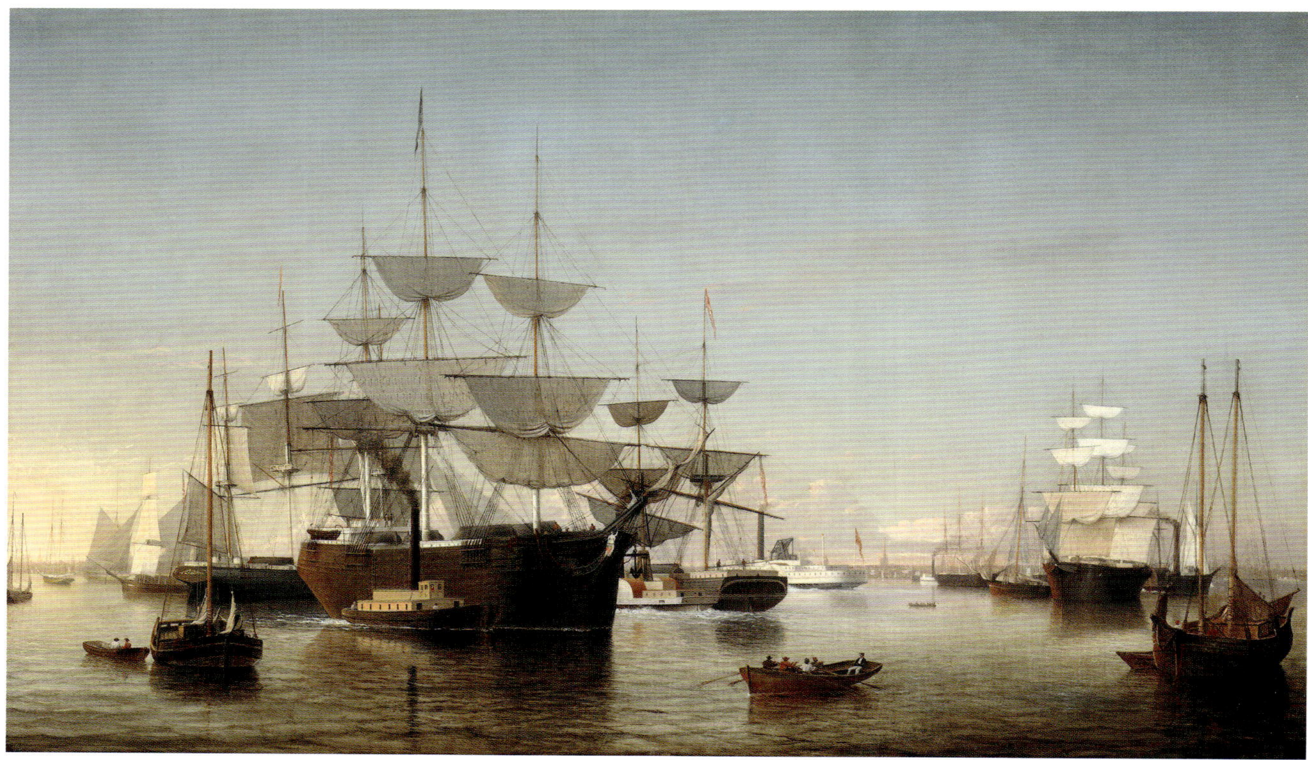

FIGURE 142
Fitz H. Lane, *New York Harbor*, ca. 1855. Oil on canvas, 36 × 60¼ in. (91.44 × 153.03 cm). Museum of Fine Arts, Boston. Gift of Maxim Karolik for the M. and M. Karolik Collection of American Paintings, 1815–1865 (48.446). Photo © 2022 Museum of Fine Arts, Boston.

good of a household, the improvement of even the humblest dependent, is the business of her sex," encouraging her especially "to sit by the side of the sufferer."[123] Schooled in such sentiments, newly widowed cousin Elizabeth would have been well chosen as companion for Lane's last months. Thus his cousin's narrations of California as the abandoned place would have been as much in the artist's consciousness as California the sought-after place.

While Lane did not venture west, in the 1850s he traveled to New York City possibly several times and possibly at the behest of one of his very best patrons, Sidney Mason, and in connection with his most lucrative commissions, scenes of the New York Yacht Club races in Buzzard's Bay. His New York paintings include portraits of two clipper ships built in that city and owned by the same New York firm, Chambers & Heiser—*The* Golden State *Entering New York Harbor* (1854) and *Sweepstakes* (1853)—on which he indicated his full name and the town and state of his residence (Gloucester, Mass.) as artists were wont to do when working out of town (figs. 39, 40, and 41).[124] While in the city he also painted (or made studies in preparation for painting) several works describing activity in the port, including a large canvas depicting marine traffic in New York Harbor (fig. 142). Even busier with myriad vessel types than his scenes of Boston Harbor, this painting captures the congestion and variety of ships and boats of all kinds carrying people and goods and gold. While the vessels part obligingly to give the viewer a place-establishing glimpse of Trinity Church's spire, mapping the seemingly random and potentially colliding trajectories of these vessels suggests a kind of

New York social and economic free-for-all expressed in aquatic terms.

In the 1850s two kinds of exceptional arrivals in New York Harbor were of such particular note that they circulated nationally in the press, the oceangoing steamers from Chagres (Panama), where passengers and freight crossed the Isthmus on mules from the Pacific with literally tons of gold, and the packet ships from Europe. On one day in May 1850, for instance, three steamers—the *Cherokee*, the *Georgia*, and the *Empire City*—arrived in New York harbor with $3 million in gold dust.[125] In June the *Cherokee* returned to New York with another $1,152,000 in gold, and in a single week that July the steamships *Philadelphia* and *Oregon* arrived in New York with "$2,920,000 in gold dust on freight, [and] $700,000 in the hands of passengers."[126] At the same time, the remarkable volume of immigrant arrivals from Europe into New York was reported nationally as well. For example, 20,000 arrived in one week in May 1849, and over a period of six months that year, 163,000 newcomers disembarked in that city.[127] Two years later Gloucester (and other urban areas throughout the nation) learned that in the month of June "112 emigrant vessels arrived at New York . . . from foreign ports, bringing 24,000 persons, not including cabin passengers."[128]

Some of the energy and confusion of mid-nineteenth-century New York, with the dramatic inflows of capital and population (and outflows of eager miners), is evident in Lane's *New York Harbor*. Such works describe and argue for a global view of the marine and economic activities suggested in Lane's canvases depicting the largest port cities as well as in his views of Gloucester. Even Lane's seemingly defensive views validating a New England ethos of community-centered localism include clues to a broad understanding of cultural and spatial disruption and point to Lane's understanding of the links between ports and therefore also ties between institutions of power, economic forces, social practices, and wildly disparate places. Lane knew that Cape Ann was a fenced landscape where boundaries and order were well understood; his works argue for the usefulness of a bounded worldview. However, they also point, often slyly and obliquely, to powerful links to such very different places as Europe, Dutch Guiana, and California, places that internationalized and seriously impacted life in the small town as well as in cosmopolitan centers in the United States. What we learn from Lane's paintings is that Surinam and California (and to a lesser extent Europe) were not peripheral but central to life in Gloucester, and to the way Gloucesterites like Lane and his patrons understood their world.

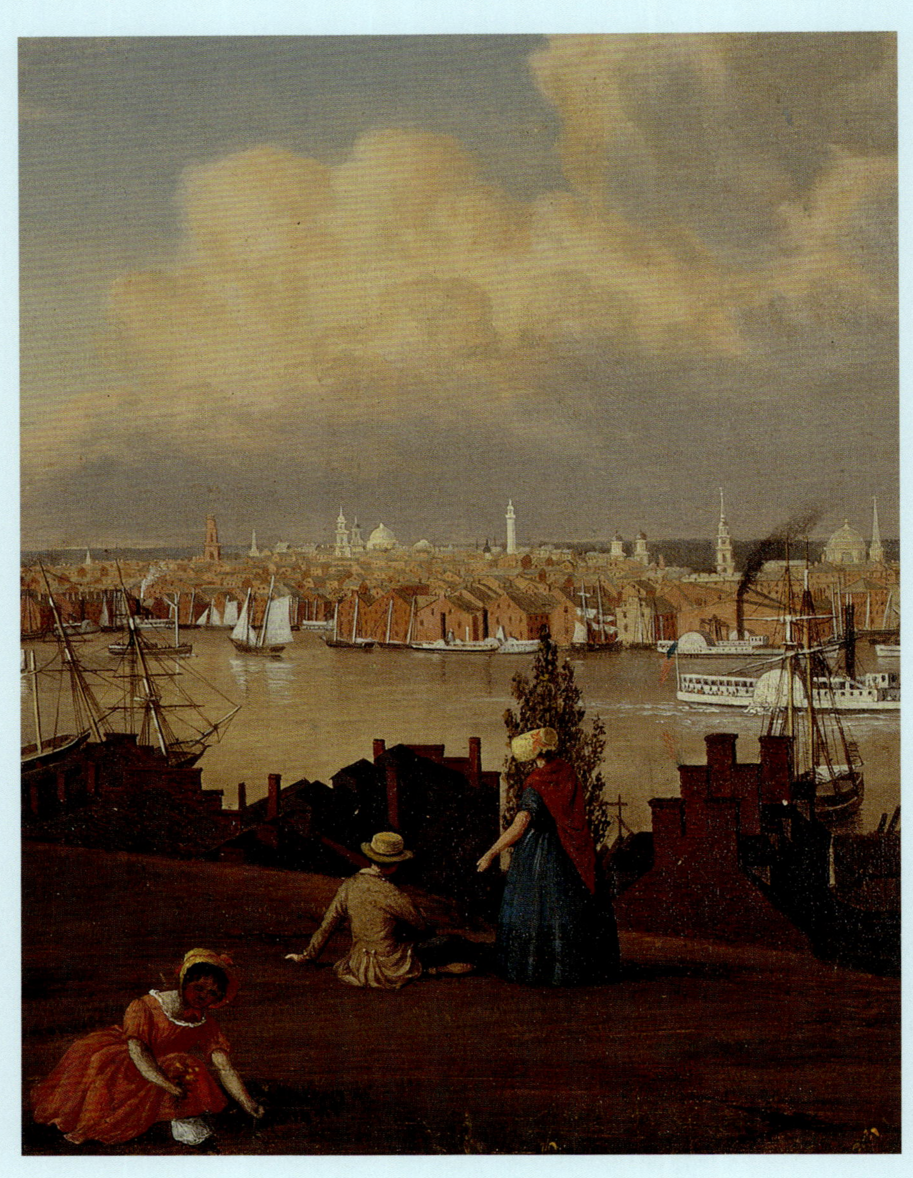

CHAPTER 8

TRAVELERS II

Ireland, China, Puerto Rico

Two of Fitz H. Lane's most important repeat customers, Robert Bennet Forbes and Sidney Mason, spent many years abroad, Forbes in China and Mason in Puerto Rico, then a Spanish colony. Forbes patronized Lane as a lithographer in the 1840s, as an artist who could enliven his publications with accurate ship portraits, and he may well have extended his patronage to help Lane establish himself as a producer of fine art. Mason, on the other hand, after decades focused on international business, in the 1850s commissioned a group of paintings from the artist recording foreign and domestic sites that had been important in his life, constructing a kind of visual memoir. As in the case of Surinam and California considered in chapter 7, traces of these distant places are evident in the works that Lane created for these much-traveled New Englanders. The projects for Forbes were very different from those Lane executed for Mason, making clear in that fact alone what a versatile artist he was.

LITHOGRAPHIC PORTRAITS: FRIGATE, PACKET, CLIPPER, TUG

Fitz Henry Lane worked as a lithographer for sixteen years in Boston, between 1832 and 1848, before he identified himself as a painter. These were important journeyman years during which he developed his drawing skills, joined the community of print artisans and aspiring fine artists, learned and practiced the trade of lithographer, comanaged his own lithography establishment, and met

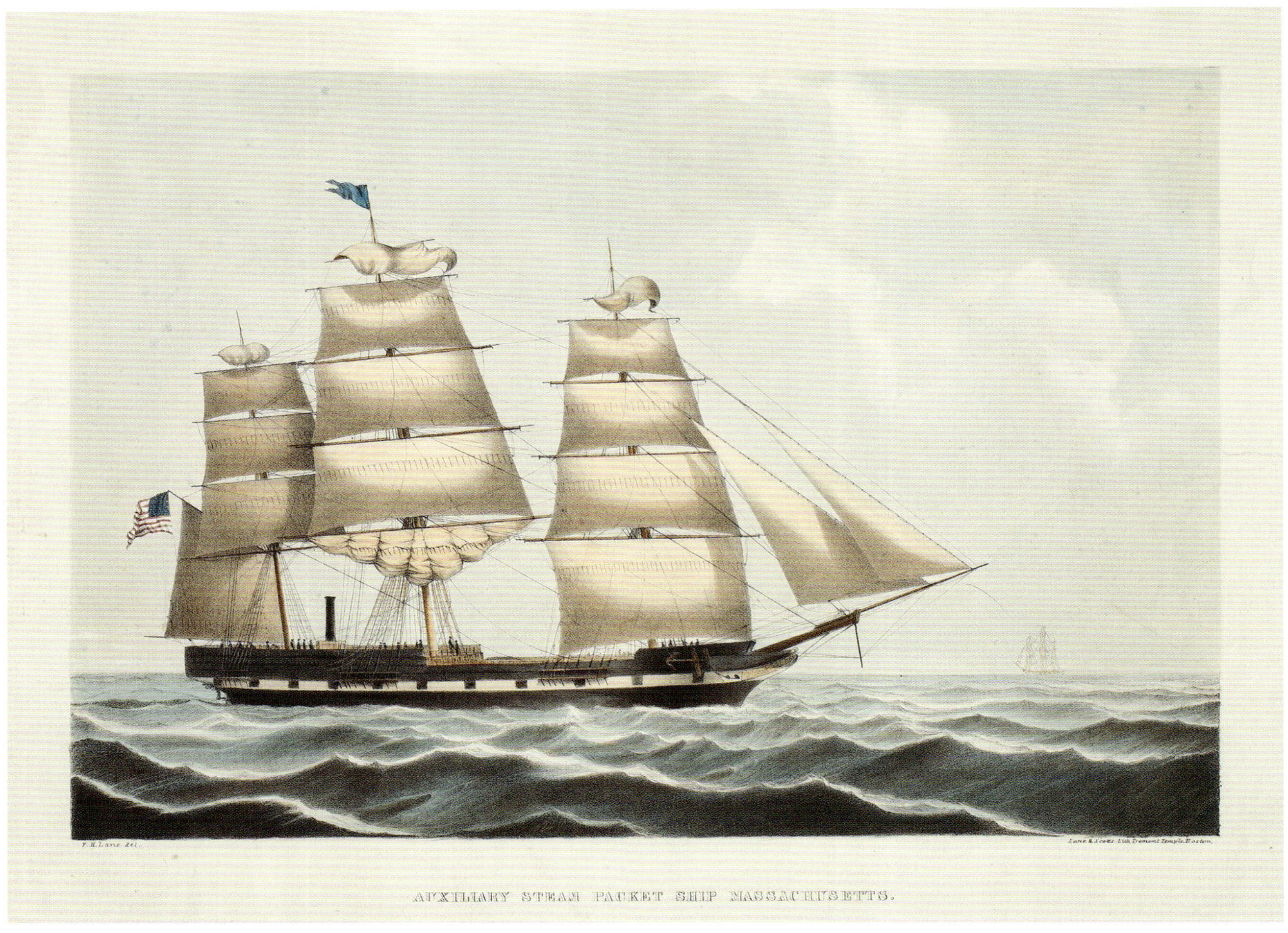

FIGURE 143
Fitz H. Lane del., *Auxiliary Steam Packet Ship* Massachusetts, n.d. [1844–48]. Lithograph on paper, 10½ × 14 3/16 in. (26.67 × 36.04 cm). Probably commissioned by Robert B. Forbes. Lane & Scott's Lith., Tremont Temple, Boston. Courtesy, American Antiquarian Society.

important patrons. Then, in 1848, he returned to his native Gloucester, where he settled in as a landscape painter, marine painter, and the town's go-to artist for parade floats, political banners, murals, and other public projects. Key to the important transition in his self-identity in 1848 were the lithographic commissions he executed in connection with high-profile projects for Robert Bennet Forbes, who in 1844 had returned to Massachusetts after his second long sojourn in Canton (Guangzhou). The prints this wealthy China trader commissioned from Lane date from 1845 to 1855.

Unlike the majority of Lane's lithographs, which were created as individual sheets to publicize businesses, to embellish sheet music, to capitalize on dramatic newsworthy incidents, and to reinforce civic pride in the citizens of Gloucester, Boston, Baltimore, Washington, New Bedford, and Castine, Lane's lithographs for Forbes were created to punctuate books, journal articles, and pamphlets authored by that redoubtable ship designer and merchant. Forbes, born in 1804, the same year as Lane, had risen from youthful mariner to clipper-ship captain, and partner in America's premier trade house in China,

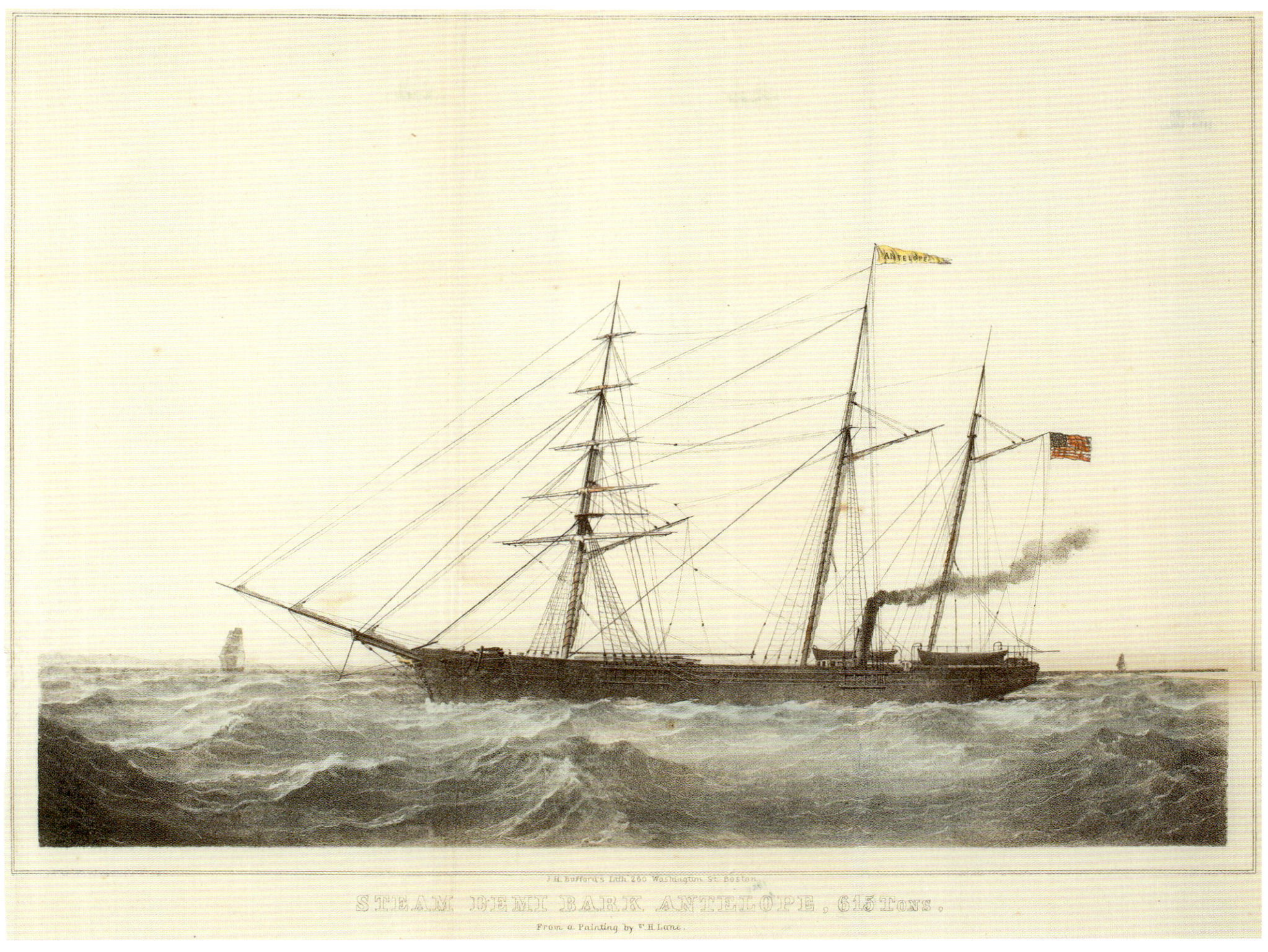

FIGURE 144
Fitz H. Lane, *Steam Demi Bark* Antelope [2], *615 Tons: From a Painting by F. H. Lane*. Colored lithograph on paper, 11 7⁄16 × 14 in. (29 × 38 cm). Lithographed expressly for the *Nautical Magazine*, 1855, by J. H. Bufford's Lith., 260 Washington Street, Boston. Courtesy, American Antiquarian Society. Gift of Charles Henry Taylor.

Russell & Co.[1] He was also a pioneer designer and owner of boats and ships of all descriptions and undoubtedly chose Lane because of the artist's reputation for knowledgeable precision in depicting marine subjects. Records of the transactions between Forbes and Lane have been lost—indeed, almost no direct records of Lane's life have survived except his artworks—but some of the stories behind this set of lithographs may be gleaned from Forbes's diary, his published reports, and other records, providing a sense of Lane's usefulness to Forbes and suggesting the usefulness of Forbes to Lane.

Even though evidence of the financial arrangements is lacking, it is probable that these seemingly modest, small-scale lithographic ship portraits commissioned by Forbes in association with his publication projects were well remunerated and thus had far-reaching results for Lane, putting him on a sound financial footing and enabling him to undertake the painting career for which he is better known. The three lithographed ship portraits that Lane produced for Forbes are *Boston, March 28th, 1847 / Departure of the* Jamestown *for Cork, Ireland, R. B. Forbes, Commander* (1847); *Auxiliary Steam Packet Ship* Massachusetts

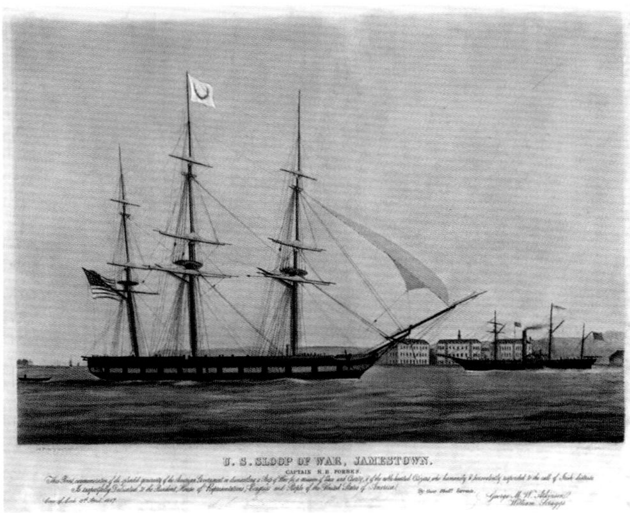

FIGURE 145
George M. W. Atkinson and William Scraggs, *U.S. Sloop of War,* Jamestown, *Captain R. B. Forbes*, 1847. Colored lithograph on paper, 16½ × 20½ in. (42 × 52 cm); sheet 18 × 22½ in. (46 × 57 cm). Made for Robert B. Forbes. Courtesy, American Antiquarian Society. Gift of Jay Last.

(1844–48); and *Steam Demi Bark* Antelope [2], *615 Tons: From a Painting by F. H. Lane* (1855) (figs. 16, 143, and 144). These are characteristic broadside views of three ships associated with the professional skills and public roles of Forbes, a prolific writer as well as one of the wealthiest and most active men of his generation.

Ship portraits may seem to modern viewers an unexciting assignment with unexciting results, but in the antebellum period, a ship portrait was not just a picture of a ship, it was a visual gateway to a complex, far-reaching, and often emotional narrative the importance of which would have been commonly understood at the time. These ships were extremely valuable, they displayed the era's most advanced technology, and their voyages, while often profitable, were always dangerous. For those who owned or sailed on them, shipped goods on them, or bought goods transported in them, these ships were not generic but individual vessels with specific rigging, hull shapes, and personal histories. As noted in chapter 1, a mariner understood his ship to be "his home, his theme of constant, and frequently of painful interest, his tabernacle, and often his source of pride and exultation."[2] Lane's lithographed ship portraits had audiences well beyond ship owners, however, including fellow mariners and the local populace, as all were conscious that their prosperity depended on the global reach of coastal New England's maritime trade. Ship portraits were the visible descriptive entry points to far-reaching tales with serious private, and often public, import.

Lane's lithographic portrait of the frigate *Jamestown* embarking from Boston harbor on March 28, 1847, with eight hundred tons of supplies served as frontispiece to Forbes's published account of what was probably the United States' first large-scale international relief effort—the delivery of food donated by New Englanders for the starving Irish at the height of the great famine.[3] One of two relief ships loaded with donated food that spring, the *Jamestown*, a navy sloop-of-war, was loaned to Forbes by act of Congress for this humanitarian mission.[4] Making the Atlantic crossing, Forbes reports, in "just fifteen days and three hours from Boston—which considering that the ship was [riding] very deep [in the water], [t]he crew rather light, and the season very unpropitious . . . was a very remarkable passage"; they anchored off Cork on April 12.[5] The following week, as the food was being unloaded and dispersed, the graphic memorializing of this historic voyage began. As Forbes reports, "Messrs Atkinson & Scraggs, artists, did me the great pleasure of presenting a beautiful [lithographed] likeness of the Jamestown. . . . The likeness is good" (fig. 145).[6] As in the portraiture of people, portraits of ships were valued for their exact likeness—that is, the recognizability of the subject and hence the character of the image as a document and as an appropriate trigger to memory.

On May 16 Forbes arrived back in Boston, and two days later he "entertained [the Committee of Relief] on New England mutton and poultry taken out in the ship in ice, and consequently killed over fifty-one days previous," and read his report on the undertaking to the committee.[7] Forbes's intention in publishing this report on the voyage of the *Jamestown* shortly after his return to Boston was to use "the proceeds of the sale of this narrative," paying its production costs himself, to procure and transport "another cargo for Ireland" to relieve the "suffering Irish." So the report was not just a public account of what he termed "the happiest event of my life," it was a key aspect of a strategy to enlarge the humanitarian project of famine relief.[8] One can imagine, then, that Forbes pressed Lane for a handsome drawing and prompt execution of this commission to frontispiece his narrative. The printing as well as the design of the lithograph of the *Jamestown* was in Lane's hands, as the report was published at the Lane & Scott firm. Lane's lithograph is characteristically precise in its details of rigging, the Boston skyline, and the harbor's buoyant waves at the outset of a propitious voyage (fig. 16).

In gratitude for Forbes's organizational skill and generosity, the Irish had a large silver salver crafted, engraved, and presented to him a few months after his return, and the English participants engaged the young British marine painter George M. Atkinson (who had seen the ship and drawn it in Ireland) to render in oils the Lane print of the *Jamestown* departing from Boston as a present for Forbes (one of the rare instances in which a painting is documented as having derived from a print) (fig. 146).[9]

In Lane's lithograph of the *Jamestown* (and in the Atkinson painting after it), the majestic warship is escorted out of Boston Harbor by a little steam tug (figs. 16 and 146). This was a new and valuable type of boat that safely maneuvered large oceangoing vessels through crowded harbors with a power source not dependent on winds and tides. Lane's lithograph of that vessel very closely follows his preparatory pencil drawing, although the "Tow Boat" is animated by a plume of smoke from its twin stacks in the finished image (fig. 17). Very few Lane drawings of vessels survive, but there must have been many of them, and this instance suggests a careful, straightforward working method. This tug was named the *R. B. Forbes*, and thus its presence here constitutes a sort of witty aquatic portrait of the temporary master of the stately *Jamestown*.

As Forbes relates in *Personal Reminiscences*, he was "instrumental in building the first iron vessels in New England, the most notable of which was the iron twin-screw tug-boat named after me, in 1842, . . . for many years . . . the most powerful and successful tug in American waters."[10] A very hands-on sort of entrepreneur, Forbes himself captained this powerful and novel tugboat when he was not otherwise engaged. For instance, in November 1847, when a new propeller was being tried, he took the tug out; and in April 1848, when a packet ship went ashore at Scituate, he "fired up the R. B. Forbes . . . & proceeded to her. . . . We took hold and brought her to the City [of Boston]."[11] Others had predicted that "the propeller would not tow as well as the paddle-wheel," but he bet on propeller propulsion in this and most of his steamships.[12] In response to the gold rush, Forbes, "having become somewhat infected with gold fever," as he put it, in 1849 designed and had built in New York an iron steamship seventy-five feet long, which he shipped to California on the deck of one of his square riggers with a view to transporting gold miners and their equipment up the Sacramento River toward the gold fields in the Sierra foothills, the first such vessel on that river.[13] He had other steamships for river and harbor navigation built and shipped to China, but Forbes was also interested in steam power for blue-water navigation.[14]

The forty-two entries in Forbes's "List of Vessels Built Under My Order or Supervision, or in Which I Have Had an Interest" includes vessels he classifies as bark, brig, ship, schooner, yacht, steam schooner, steam bark, steam tug, steamship, iron paddle steamer, and propeller steamer—of which fully half, in other words, are by category coal-burning, mostly propeller-driven vessels.[15] While he is known for his development of new rigs for, and skillful captaining of, sailing vessels, Forbes's life and his narratives make clear that he had a vigorous interest in steam propulsion for vessels of all kinds and wished to share his novel ideas with the public. He did not patent his innovations but rather published them, augmenting his verbal descriptions with Lane's careful lithographs.

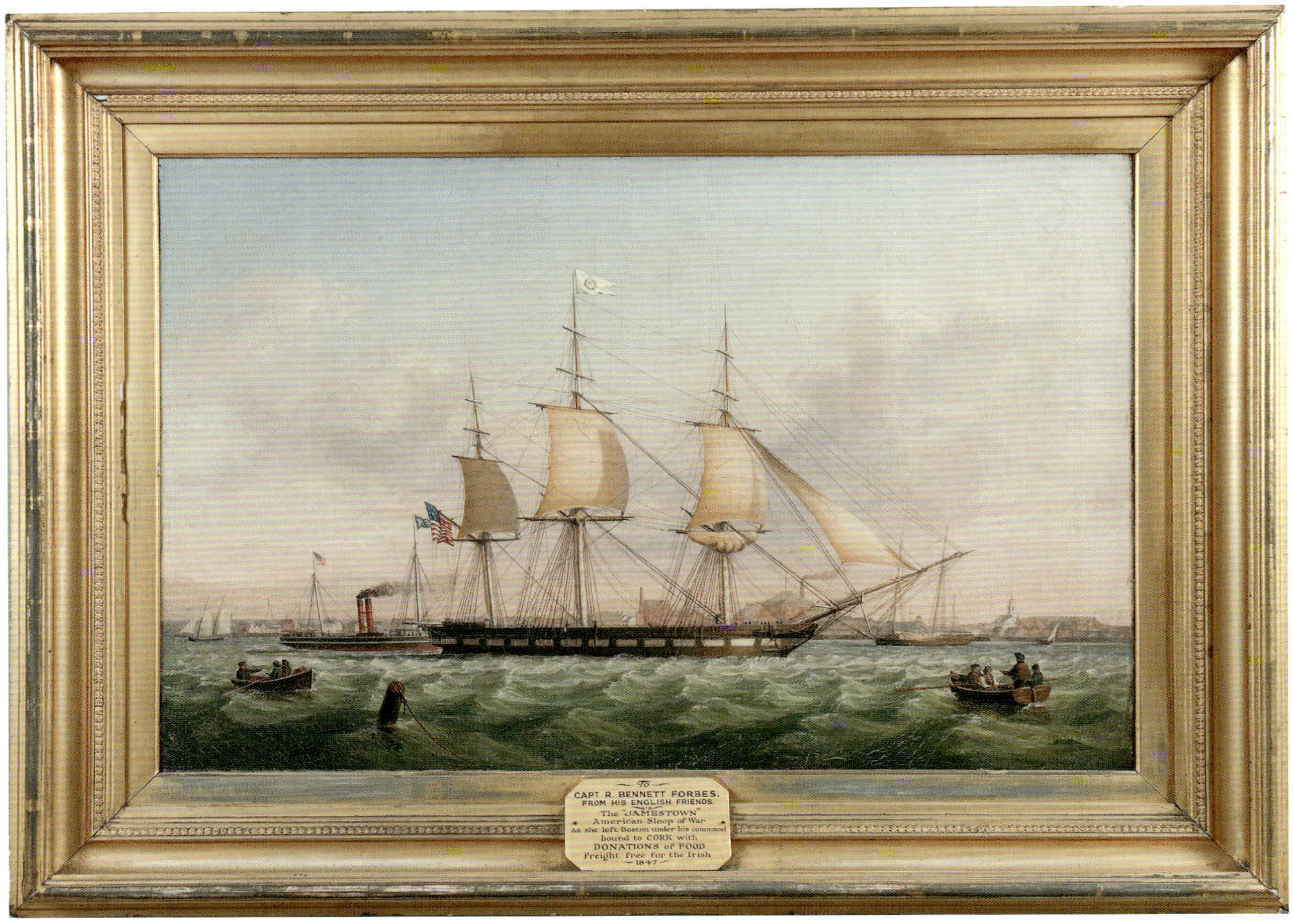

FIGURE 146
George M. Atkinson, *The USS* Jamestown, ca. 1847. Oil on canvas, 28 × 38 in. (71.12 × 96.52 cm). On the picture-frame plaque: "To / Capt R. Bennett [*sic*] Forbes / from his English friends. / The "Jamestown" / American Sloop of War / as she left Boston under his command / bound to Cork with / donations of food / freight free for the Irish. / 1847." Courtesy of Forbes House Museum, Milton, Massachusetts.

Probably Lane's earliest lithographic project for Forbes was in connection with the *Massachusetts*, an experimental vessel the entrepreneur designed and had built in 1845 in East Boston by Sam Hall, whose firm he frequently patronized, with engines built by a New York City firm and a novel sail rig designed by Forbes to make the ship easier to manage by fewer seamen and more resilient in foul weather (fig. 143). The *Massachusetts* was a three-masted ship with auxiliary steam capacity (note the black smokestack toward the stern of the ship) intended as a packet ship making scheduled Atlantic crossings. It was launched in late July, and Forbes decided to take his family and friends on its maiden voyage to England, leaving New York on September 15 and arriving in Liverpool October 3 with eight first-class passengers and thirty in steerage.[16] The return crossing, at twenty-nine days, took almost twice as long. Safely back, Forbes recorded in his diary on November 20: "Arrived at home & found all well. . . . We have had a rough & trying passage, only a day or two of fair winds."[17] It is a dramatic, particularly harrowing event in this "rough & trying passage" that Lane pictures in a two-toned tinted lithograph entitled *Steam Packet Ship* Mass. *in a Squall, Nov. 10, 1845*—almost

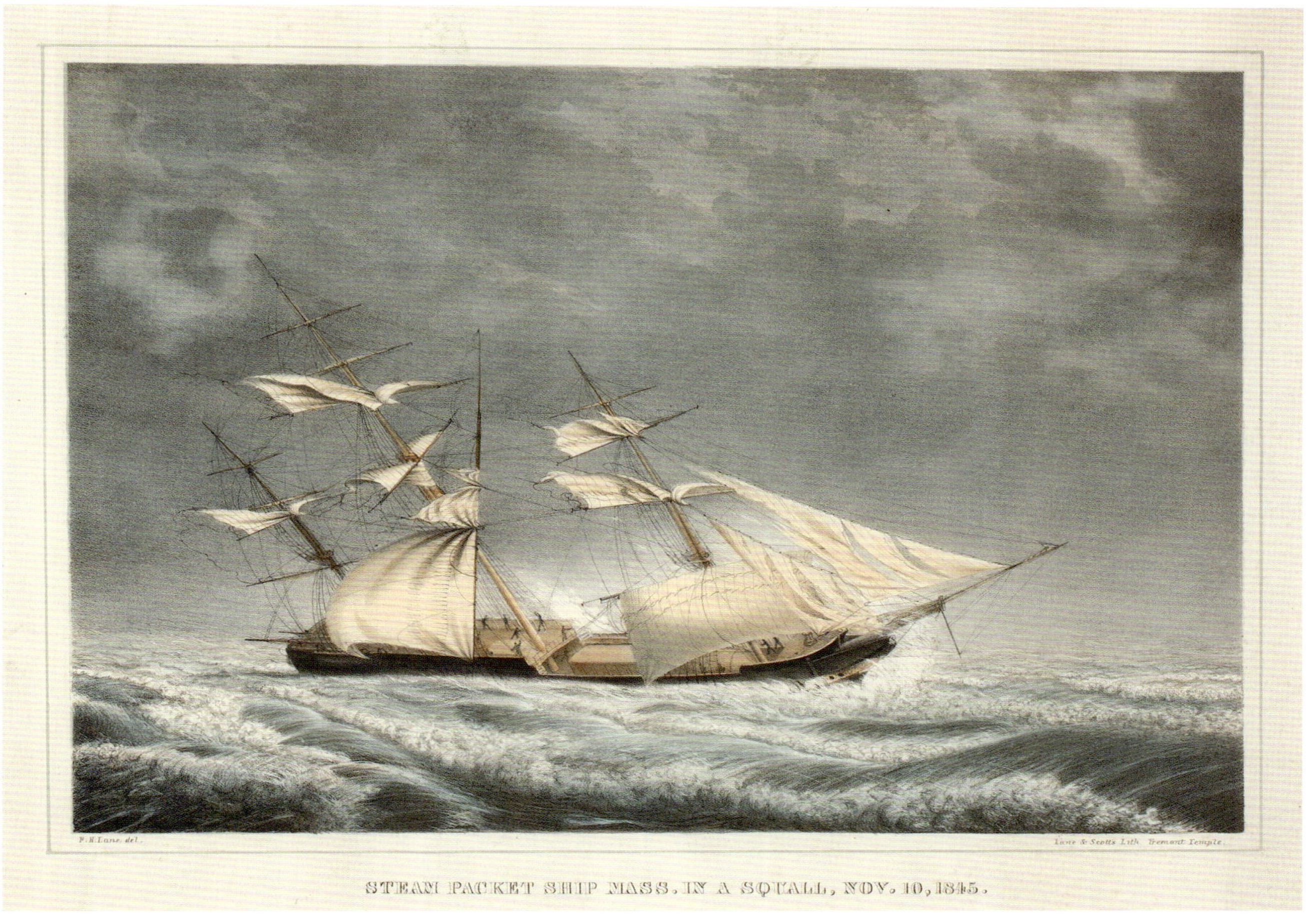

FIGURE 147
Fitz H. Lane, *Steam Packet Ship* Mass. *in a Squall, Nov. 10, 1845*, n.d. [1845–48]. Colored lithograph on paper, 10½ × 14³⁄₁₆ in. (26.67 × 40.64). Probably commissioned by Robert B. Forbes. Lane & Scott's Lith., Tremont Temple, Boston. Courtesy, American Antiquarian Society.

certainly derived from Forbes's verbal description (fig. 147). Caught off guard by a sudden violent wind, the crew had not had time to furl or even reef enough sails, creating an exceptionally dangerous situation.

Forbes's published account of the near disaster is couched in terms of the specialized sails that provided the ship's primary propulsion. It reads in part:

> In the ship Massachusetts, coming from Liverpool when I came in her as passenger, we had . . . a sudden and severe squall,—the ship had been under royals, jibs, and spanker, fore and main topmast studding sails, heading westerly. . . . About 8 A.M., squally; took in studding sails, royals . . . flying jib and spanker; 8:30, took in mizzen topgallant sail; at 9 . . . a sudden and dense blackness came over [us. Despite having furled half her sails,] . . . we were caught with too much canvass set. [The ship heeled over dangerously, and] everything forward excepting the foresail was torn to tatters.

Lane's print depicts this perilous situation, with the dark sky and turbulent sea, sails, yards, and spars in serious disarray, the crew safely on deck but helpless to mitigate the damage. Perhaps surprisingly, Forbes understood the event to have had, however disquieting, a positive outcome, an endorsement of his new rig: "Not a spar [was] injured in any way. . . . Had such a squall struck any other ship with whole topsails, of the old rig, she would have lost her topmasts, at least. . . . There never could have been a more awful and beautiful illustration of the value of the rig" that Forbes developed to make the management of the sails easier for the crew.[18] The frontispiece of the book describing this rig is a large-format, clear foldout diagram of the recommended rig, which may have been drawn by Lane.

Unlike other lithographs commissioned by Forbes that were intended as descriptive images to accompany descriptive text, Lane's *Steam Packet Ship* Mass. *in a Squall, Nov. 10, 1845* appears to have been issued as a standalone print, offered as an aesthetic artwork to a public well aware of and interested in the emotional impact of such terrifying—and potentially sublime—misadventures on the high seas. As the unit cost of a hand-colored print at this time was about 90¢ (about the price of a pair of inexpensive shoes) and the cost of a lithograph's production about $100 (eight months' wages for Forbes's "outdoor man" on his Milton property), it is probable that Lane (and possibly Forbes) imagined that a nautical scene of high drama would have broad appeal, selling more than a hundred hand-tinted lithographs of this "awful and beautiful" scene to New Englanders knowledgeable about and sensitive to the perils of the sea.[19]

The *Massachusetts* made one more transatlantic crossing as a passenger ship early in 1846 but could not compete with either the sailing packets or the first generation of British transatlantic steamships, so it was leased and then later sold to the U.S. government and reliably served the navy in the Pacific until 1871.[20] Its auxiliary steam power made it particularly agile near shore, where it scouted sites for federal lighthouses; and on one occasion, under steam, it towed a navy sloop that had been baffled by head winds and unable to get through the Straits of Magellan for twelve weeks.[21] Forbes remained convinced of the virtues of the *Massachusetts*'s novel rig and hybrid nature as a sailing ship with steam capacity for certain uses, as we will see.

When the navy was refitting the *Massachusetts* in Norfolk with gunports in 1853, Forbes wrote a long letter to the editor of the *Nautical Magazine* about its "double topsail rig," designed so that "the sails are more easily managed, set better on a wind, can be furled snugger in a gale, and are much less subject to wear out," yielding a vessel that "can be taken care of in bad weather by the [few men on] watch as well or better than the ship rigged after the ordinary fashion by all hands."[22] In connection with this effort to share with others involved in maritime affairs his enthusiasm for the *Massachusetts*'s unusual rig and steam capacity, Forbes reused the lithograph of the ship by Lane in which both the sail arrangement and the smokestack are prominent, a print that was executed a decade earlier, for the article published in the *U.S. Nautical Magazine and Naval Journal* concerning the value of steam-assisted navigation (fig. 143).[23] So two very different lithographs of this same vessel were executed from drawings by Fitz H. Lane, printed by the Lane & Scott firm between 1845 (when the *Massachusetts* was launched) and 1848 (when the Lane & Scott firm dissolved), one upbeat, descriptive, and matter-of-fact to accompany a text about an improved arrangement of sails and the benefits of auxiliary steam power, the other a stand-alone print suitable for framing and full of drama—prompting narratives of fear and excitement. Both promoted Forbes's acumen as a designer of vessels and their propulsion systems.

R. B. FORBES AND THE PIRATES OF THE SOUTH CHINA SEA

The third Forbes ship that Lane lithographed was the steam demi-bark *Antelope* (which, for convenience, I shall call *Antelope 2*), but he also depicted another Forbes vessel with the same name, the brig *Antelope* (which, for convenience, I shall call *Antelope 1*) (figs. 144 and 148). Both these *Antelope*s were designed by Forbes and built

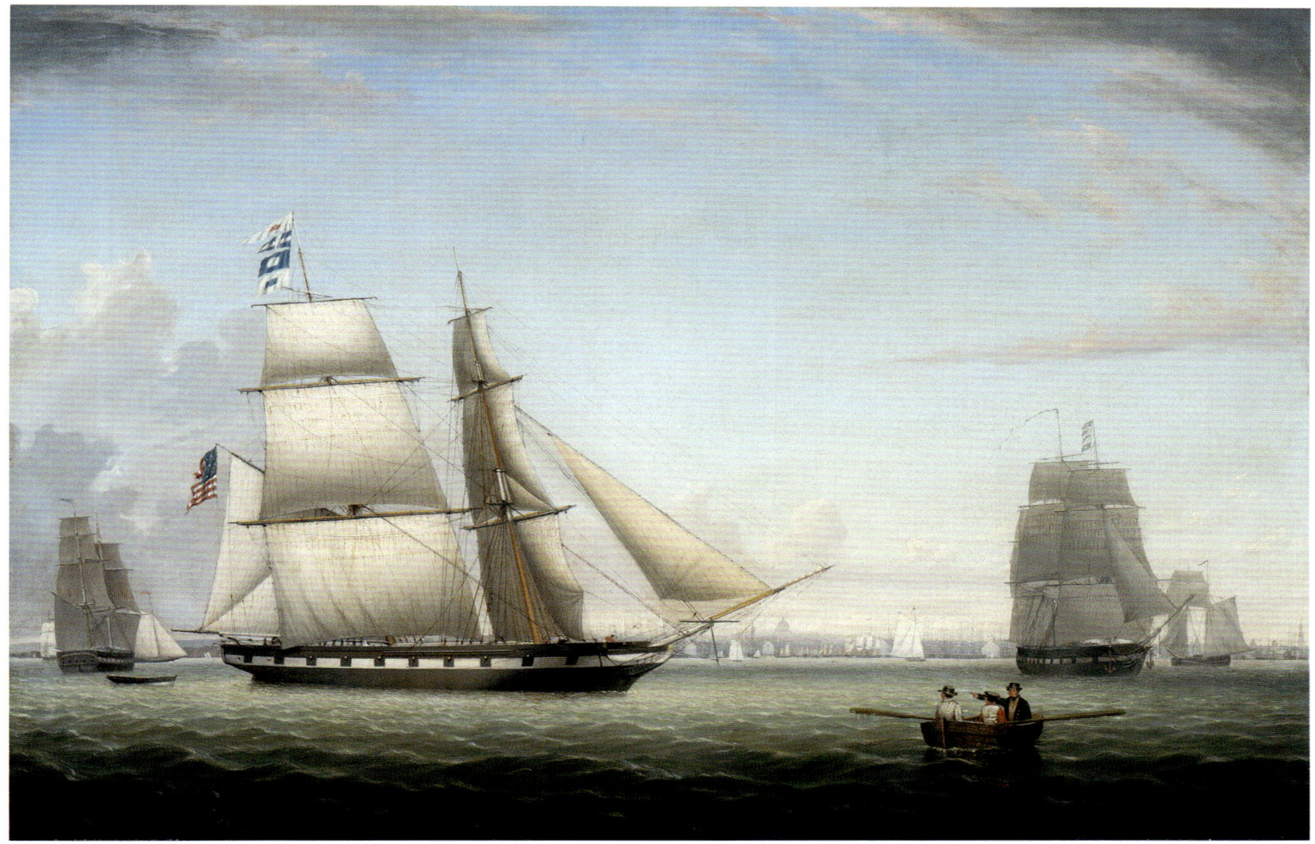

FIGURE 148
Fitz H. Lane, *Brig* Antelope [1] *in Boston Harbor*, probably 1843 (possibly 1863). Oil on canvas, 24¼ × 36 in. (61.59 × 91.44 cm). Possibly commissioned by Robert B. Forbes. Museum of Fine Arts, Boston. Bequest of Martha C. Karolik for the M. and M. Karolik Collection of American Paintings, 1815–1865 (48.449). Photo © 2022 Museum of Fine Arts, Boston.

by Samuel Hall in East Boston for the firm in which Forbes was a partner from 1839 to 1844 and 1849 to 1854, Russell & Co., headquartered in China. Lane portrayed *Antelope 1* in an oil painting probably in 1843, and *Antelope 2* in a lithograph of 1855.[24] *Antelope 1* was built in 1843, dismasted in a typhoon in 1848, rerigged as a bark, and finally wrecked in 1852 off the coast of China.[25] *Antelope 2* was built in 1855 in the same shipyard, but it was larger and incorporated nautical strategies for resiliency that Forbes had experimented with on the *Massachusetts*.[26]

The Lane painting of *Antelope 1*—a handsome brig with forward-raking bow and masts raking aft—pictures a scene in Boston harbor when Forbes returned from taking the just-launched *Antelope 1* on trials during July 1843 (fig. 148). It sailed as far as Norfolk, Virginia, that month and the press in that city spoke of it as a "splendid vessel . . . new and beautiful. . . . She is intended for the China trade and is fitted out with unsurpassed neatness. She is pierced for sixteen guns." In New York the press reported that "her neat and rakish appearance . . . excited no little speculation."[27] As majority owner as well as master of vessels competing with the *Antelope*, Forbes noted its superior sailing qualities, that it was swifter and more agile than competitors, including other ships he had designed and ships he was commanding.[28] When captained by Philip Dumaresq, who was Forbes's uncle by marriage and, like Forbes and Lane, was also born in 1804,

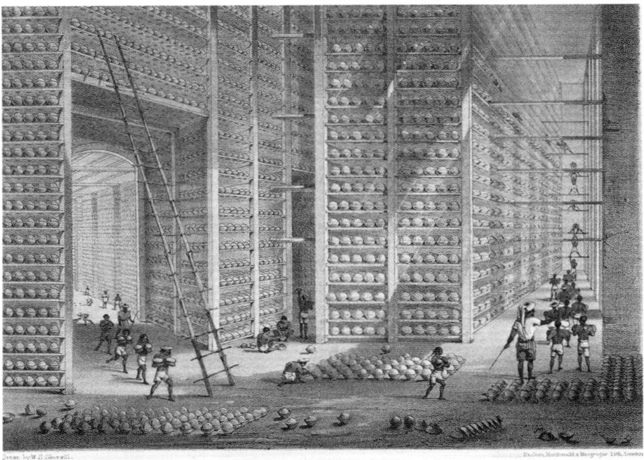

FIGURE 149
Walter Stanhope Sherwill, *One of the Stacking Rooms*. Tinted lithograph. From W. S. Sherwill, *Indian Opium, Its Mode of Preparation for the Chinese Market* (London: James Madden, 1851), 9. Courtesy of the Yale Center for British Art.

Antelope did hard and profitable service for its owners in the difficult opium trade.[29]

Antelope 1 and *Antelope 2*, like other opium clippers, were well armed and swift, as they were considered prizes. In 1828, when he was twenty-four years old, Forbes served as master on the *Danube*; its first port of call was Smyrna, in Turkey, carrying a cargo of coffee, $20,000 in specie (Spanish dollars), and bank credit for £60,000, "the principal object being to procure Turkey opium for China."[30] The cargo of Turkish opium he then took around Africa, through the Indian Ocean to China, would have been worth almost $200,000 in the Mediterranean and yielded a great deal more on delivery in China.[31] What was at stake in these journeys was a considerable profit on a substantial outlay.[32] Whether China-bound with opium or homebound with silver (Spanish or Mexican minted dollars or bars), these vessels were attractive marks for pirates.

By the 1840s most American opium clippers were picking up their valuable cargo in India rather than Turkey—in Bombay (Mumbai) or Calcutta (Kolkata)—and delivering it to Hong Kong.[33] The opium trade was highly organized, highly capitalized, and dominated by a handful of firms: the British firms Jardine Matheson & Co. and Dent & Co.; the Sassoon family (Sephardic Jewish-Indian, originally from Persia); the Indian Parsee family of Bonajee; and the American firm Russell & Co. Of about one hundred vessels importing opium to China in the mid-nineteenth century, seventeen, including the clipper-brig *Antelope 1*, were American built and owned.[34]

Opium, the single most valuable commodity being traded in the world by the 1830s and reaching its peak in the 1870s, was shipped in balls (liquid opium contained within a protective shell of poppy leaves) weighing about three pounds each, packed in chests weighing about 120 to 140 pounds (fig. 149).[35] The standard shipload was from 500 to 1,000 chests, or 20,000 to 40,000 balls; during 1848, when *Antelope 1* was engaged in this trade, about 42,000 chests were imported into China annually; this figure would double by 1874.[36] *Antelope 1* made the run with this cargo from Calcutta to Hong Kong in as little as twenty-six days, and because of its superior sailing abilities, it could beat to windward against prevailing winds, even monsoon winds, and thus in a year deliver to China three cargoes rather than one.[37] The success of Russell & Co. was, in large part, due to their alliance with Houqua II (Wu Bingjian, 1769–1843), the Chinese leader of the Cohong, the powerful guild of Chinese merchants authorized by the Chinese government to oversee the business activities of Western merchants at Canton (Guangzhou), the only port at which these outsiders were permitted to trade.[38] Houqua was esteemed by Western traders as a fair, intelligent, and generous partner; his personal worth was estimated at $26 million, and his portrait, in recognition of his alliance with Forbes, hangs in the Forbes House Museum in Milton, Massachusetts.[39]

Opium was legal, unregulated, readily available, and used medicinally in liquid form in the United States and Britain, where it was the principal ingredient (together with alcohol) in patent medicines and broadly used for a wide variety of ailments as laudanum.[40]

Forbes, for instance, recommended it to Oliver Wendell Holmes Sr. prior to that noted physician's embarkation on a transatlantic voyage.[41] In India, where opium was introduced by the Mughals in the seventh century, it was legal, and its trade was a state monopoly (until that monopoly was taken over by the British East India Company in 1757); it was widely available and used in ritual, social contexts.[42] In China, opium had been introduced in the eighth or ninth century by traders from the Middle East, but in the early eighteenth century pipe smoking, a Native American delivery system for tobacco, crossed paths with opium, and its consumption in China became addictive, individual rather than social, and debilitating both to individuals and to the economy, so it was outlawed by imperial edict, under punishment of death, in 1729.[43] But since such wide segments of the Chinese civil service, business community, populace, and especially the coastal gentry were deeply invested in the opium trade ("the mandarins, lesser officials, linguists [translators], merchants, money changers, pilots, seamen, smugglers, opium smokers, waterborne prostitutes and even the pirates"), the trade continued largely unabated.[44] Attempts by the Chinese government to curtail the trade in 1839–42 and 1856–57 resulted in English aggression, the forced continuation of the trade, and the legalization (and government taxation) of opium.[45] Other important commodities were traded for American furs and silver—tea, silks, and porcelain prominent among them—but opium was the most profitable for all parties handling it.

A seaman who shipped aboard *Antelope 1* during 1844, its first year in the opium trade, wrote of it admiringly: "With her low, black hull, tall rakish masts, and square yards, she was a regular beauty" (fig. 148).[46] "[It had] two guns on a side besides a Long Tom amidships. Boarding pikes [to repel those attempting to board] were arranged in great plenty on a rack around the main mast, and the large arms chest on the quarter-deck was well supplied with pistols and cutlasses. . . . Our topsails were fully large enough for a vessel of double her tonnage. . . . Our little craft could go to windward. . . . Our crew consisted of seventeen men, all stout able fellows. . . . It was sometimes neck-breaking work to shin up the tall royal mast when skysails were to be furled."[47]

This crew member then goes on to describe what happened when the wind died as *Antelope 1* approached the Ladrone Islands, "the great stronghold of Chinese pirates" off the Chinese coast: "We lay becalmed [near] land. The little vessel was perfectly unmanageable, drifting at the mercy of the current," and Chinese pirates in "long mandarin boats" headed "toward us. With the immense force they have at the oars it did not take them long to get within gun-shot range" of the becalmed and unmaneuverable brig.[48] This description brings to mind a curious Lane drawing titled *Sooloo Pirate's Proa* among the drawings preserved and annotated by Lane's close friend Joseph Stevens (fig. 150). Note the hooked boarding plank on its bow. Forbes probably described this sort of vessel for Lane, and there may have been a project, never realized, to add such images to Forbes's *Reminiscences* or another narrative entirely. Singly, the Sooloo pirate's proa, even noting that it has thirty-six rowers, does not look formidable, but pirate navies were highly organized and numbered as many as two hundred of these "centipede" boats working in teams to plunder shipping. The unnamed seaman's account continues: After initially keeping the pirates at a distance with its broadside guns, *Antelope 1* was set upon by "four large boats containing from sixty to a hundred men each."[49] They closed on the brig and "directly twenty or thirty leaped upon the low bowsprit."[50] The crew was able to repulse the attack with pistols and pikes, and the cook, armed with bucketfuls of scalding water, until a fortuitous stiff breeze facilitated *Antelope*'s escape. He goes on to report that "on his next passage Captain Watkins [again at the helm of *Antelope 1*] was attacked. This time he made a regular example of the mandarin boats, and after running down two of them, and drowning their crews, sailed into Macao Roads with a Chinaman hanging at each yardarm as a warning."[51]

Antelope 1 never returned to the Atlantic, and after nine years in the opium trade, it was wrecked in 1852.

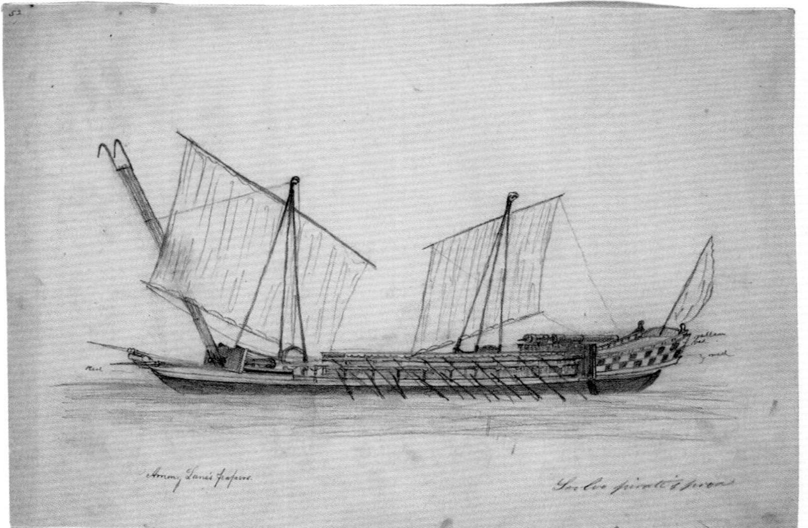

FIGURE 150
Fitz H. Lane, *Sooloo Pirate's Proa*, 1850s. Graphite on paper, 9½ × 14 in. (24.1 × 35.6 cm). Probably commissioned by R. B. Forbes. Cape Ann Museum, Gloucester, Massachusetts. Gift of Samuel H. Mansfield, 1927 (485.52).

Within months, Forbes had plans for *Antelope 2*, but mindful of the pirate problem and the Achilles' heels of *Antelope 1*, he equipped it with swivel guns, which could protect its bow and stern, as well as broadside guns, and he equipped it with an auxiliary steam engine like that on the *Massachusetts* to remedy the problem of a wind-dependent vessel under attack while becalmed. This significant use of auxiliary steam power was overlooked by historians of steamship design, one of whom, commenting on Robert Bennet Forbes's enthusiasm for this hybrid type of vessel, opined: "The auxiliary steamship could command little or no advantage over a sailing ship."[52] Certainly it cost more to build and probably to maintain, and it necessitated turning valuable cargo-hold space into storage for coal (*Antelope 2* carried seventy-five tons of coal); but given the specific dangers of the pirates of the South China Sea, auxiliary steam power was an invaluable advantage, and Lane describes with care the bark's bow swivel gun, unusual rigging, and prominent smokestack (fig. 144).[53] Such matters as its coal-bunker size and overall cost (over $50,000) were covered by the editors of the *U.S. Nautical Magazine and Naval Journal*, who in 1855 produced a long and thorough article about the vessel, detailing the exact specifications of all its parts, illustrating with diagrams its hull and scarf joints, and including a foldout lithograph by Lane of the proud vessel, *Antelope 2*, under way under steam, puffs of coal smoke issuing from the stack between the second and third mast (fig. 144).[54] The essay specifies where the cutlasses were stored, the exact bore of its deck-mounted swivel guns, and an antipirate innovation: "she can throw hot water from her boilers to a distance of one hundred yards from her side," improving on the cook's buckets that helped drive pirates off the stern of the becalmed and beleaguered *Antelope 1* when boarded fore and aft by hundreds of pirates.[55] *Antelope 2* also carried two metal self-bailing lifeboats, which Lane portrays prominently in silhouette, as Forbes was intensely interested in testing, using, and writing about lifeboats and other rescue equipment intended to preserve life during marine catastrophes.[56]

The lithograph of *Antelope 2*, drawn on the stone by J. P. Newell at J. H. Bufford's Lithography in Boston "from a painting by F. H. Lane," as noted on the face of the image, was issued in several forms: Its two primary forms were that of a folded enclosure in the 1855 article featuring the vessel's innovations in the *U.S. Nautical Magazine and Naval Journal*, and as a stand-alone print on heavier paper. Some of the prints evidencing two vertical folds were printed with a blue-tinted sea and with the figurehead and pennant "Antelope" and national flag prominently hand painted. It was also printed in different size formats, allowing more "sky" in some of the images. Some include "Lithographed expressly for the Nautical Magazine." This variety suggests that the publishers of that journal, Forbes, or the firm of Bufford's, where it was printed, felt there was a wide and varied audience for the image both within the descriptive article and as a stand-alone artwork.[57]

The caption on the print gives *Antelope 2*'s tonnage as 615 tons, while Forbes's "List of Vessels Built" indicates that it was rated at 450 tons, an indication of the difficulties in record keeping caused by the revision in tonnage-measurement systems at midcentury.[58] The subtitle of the lithograph indicates that it was reproduced "from a painting by F. H. Lane." That painting could be a lost work or the almost-identical oil painting, a somewhat larger grisaille, *The* Antelope (private collection). Lane is not known to have worked in this manner—that is, employing the eighteenth-century practice in which, when a print was wanted, a painting was first made, usually at the same scale as the print to guide the printmaker in producing a copy drawing and often to solicit subscribers to underwrite the cost of producing the print. But little is known about Lane's manner of working or his shifting practices as he identified himself increasingly as a painter rather than a lithographer in the mid-1850s.

A few years before *Antelope 2* was launched and featured in the marine press, advertisements appeared throughout the summer of 1850 in the *Gloucester Telegraph* for a Mr. George F. Lane, "who is now giving instructions in Mono-Chromatic Painting, a new and beautiful art." He promises that "persons entirely ignorant of the rules of drawing and perspective, are taught in the short term of 12 hours to paint pictures superior in effect to any penciling or water colors,—that will not fade,—and would ordinarily be worth ten dollars." It is possible, then, that this other Lane, about whom little is known, or one of Fitz H. Lane's skillful pupils made this grisaille painting, copying the Lane lithograph.[59] The artist had many Lane relatives on Cape Ann, but none is known to have been an artist, so this is probably an out-of-town visitor eager to support himself over the summer by instructing amateurs in a novel genre. Since the grisaille painting of *Antelope 2* is so proficiently done, it seems likely it is by F. H. Lane, perhaps inspired by the presence and example of this other Lane doing grisaille ("monochrome") painting in Gloucester.

Forbes was a millionaire (as were his Chinese collaborators and American business partners).[60] He chose to pour energy and cash not only into his own and Russell & Co.'s ventures but also into publication projects to advance and popularize novel rigging of sails, innovative steamboats for harbor tasks, experimental lifeboats, and job-specific hybrid ships tailored to preserve labor, life, cargo, and vessels on the high seas. To this end he partnered with Fitz H. Lane, commissioning lithographs aimed at informing the maritime public about his projects. Far from keeping the secrets of his successes to himself, Forbes sought to popularize his experiments and innovations at a time when marine matters were of primary importance both domestically and globally. A ship's portrait—whether in a print or a painting—is never just a well-described vessel; it is always an image invested with memory, a sense of history, achievement, possibly instruction (in picturing innovation) or poignancy (in memorializing ships lost). For Forbes these lithographed ships represented not just personal narratives and successes or losses but narratives of vessels with impact on others: the starving Irish, able seamen who needed safer and more efficient rigging systems, and the crews of ships who needed steam power to supplement wind power to avoid deadly confrontations with pirates. He did not commission parlor pictures of the many ships and boats "built under his order or supervision" but rather small-scale lithographic portraits to accompany long and detailed explanatory texts. He clearly saw these publications as important aspects of his formidable legacy.

For Lane, Forbes was a repeat customer with good reason to be grateful and encouraging to the artist. The four lithographs illustrated here, two drawings, and possibly both oil paintings were Lane's responses to Forbes's successive commissions. In 1849 Lane bought land on Duncan Point, in Gloucester; he designed and had built a large stone house on this prominent knob overlooking the harbor. While at this time he was beginning to get painting commissions, it is improbable that the capital necessary for such an ambitious building project came from the sale of paintings, averaging as they did $50 to $100 each. And it is unlikely that his wage work for several lithography firms or his three-year partnership with John W. A. Scott was, in itself, sufficiently remunerative to suggest substantial profits. So where did the resources come from that enabled him effectively to begin his painting career in Gloucester on such a solid foundation? My hypothesis is that it was Lane's wealthy Boston patron, Robert Bennet Forbes, whose repeat patronage in commissioning these lithographs, in conjunction with important publication projects, generously bankrolled Lane's house (valued with its land and gardens in 1852 at $1,500 and in 1860 at $3,200) and his turn to the ambitious career of fine artist.[61]

Just as distant Surinam and California are resonant in Lane's work for George H. Rogers and Nathaniel Babson, in the vessels and activities included in the paintings commissioned by those patrons, elements in his work for Robert Bennet Forbes also pointedly reference distant ports and specific cargoes and maritime threats. Contemporaries looking at the oil painting of *Antelope 1*, with its narrow prow, raking masts, and many gunports, would have understood that this vessel was fast, agile, and ready to defend itself vigorously. In other words, they would easily have read "China trader" in the physical features of *Antelope 1*. In particular, the ten black squares punctuating a broad white band on each of the vessel's long flanks purported to cover the business end of twenty cannons. Although only two of those ports on each side actually covered cannons, while eight were faux cannon ports, the look is one of serious military defensiveness and hence a readiness for the known character of the South China Sea. *Antelope 2* delivered the same message by different means: swivel-mounted cannons at the bow and stern appear in silhouette, as does the darkly active smokestack driving the vessel smartly through choppy waters with a purposefulness and straight-line direction rarely possible under sail. Forbes designed these vessels to travel halfway around the world with valuable cargo, traversing dangerous seas unscathed. Lane dramatized the aspects of their designs that made those journeys possible and profitable.

NEW ENGLANDERS IN THE TROPICS

While the Lane images Robert Bennet Forbes commissioned were outward-facing, intended to accompany and help explain to a broad public his designs for ships and humanitarian projects, those made for Sidney Mason were private works, directed at personal memory and destined for domestic space. Representing Mason's complex geographic and economic itinerary, Lane's known paintings for him include images of Gloucester, San Juan (Puerto Rico), New York Harbor, Buzzard's Bay, and probably Baltimore. They all date to the early 1850s, when Mason was a very successful businessman living in New York, and they show a wide range of Lane's skill at portraying aspects of these cities, harbors, and marine activities, and a sense of that vibrant, competitive, and sometimes nostalgic midcentury moment.

Mason's Lane commissions include at least five (and likely as many as eight) canvases depicting specific locales associated with episodes in his life and the lives of family members. Most of these city views are of a uniform size, about 24 × 36 inches. The *Gloucester Harbor* of 1852 is larger and painted in the same stretched format as two canvases depicting the New York Yacht Club races that Lane also painted for Mason, approximately 28 × 50 inches (fig. 10). This uniformity suggests that these two groups of works—all painted between 1850 and 1856—were conceived as a set and perhaps hung together in the Fifth Avenue marble mansion Mason shared with his

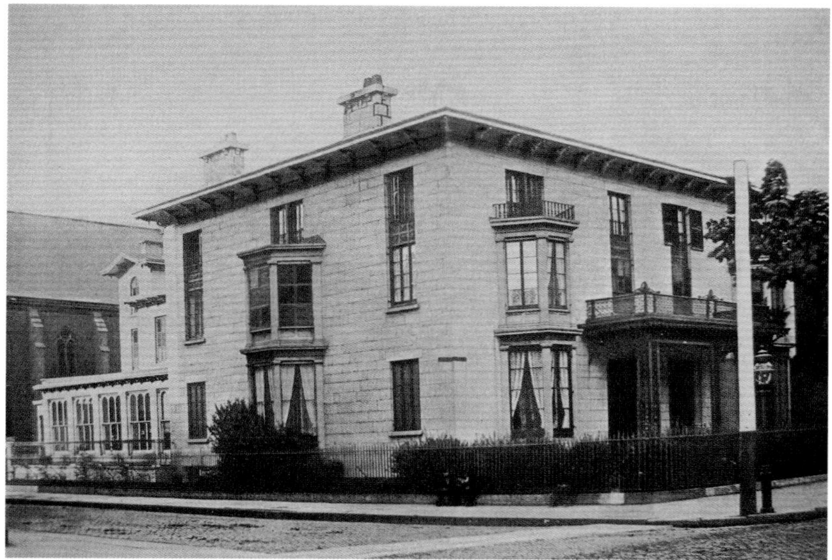

FIGURE 151
Home of Sidney Mason, 132 Fifth Avenue at 18th Street, New York City, 1847–71. From Cassie Mason Myers Julian-James, *Biographical Sketches of the Bailey-Myers-Mason Families, 1776 to 1905: Key to a Cabinet of Heirlooms in the National Museum, Washington* [Smithsonian Institution] (n.p.: privately printed, 1908), opposite p. 119. Courtesy, American Antiquarian Society.

second wife, daughter, son-in-law, and two grandchildren from 1850 (fig. 151).

When thirty years earlier, in 1820, Sidney Mason was sent to the West Indies as supercargo for Wheeler & Gay, the Boston mercantile company for which he had worked since a child, he had had an excellent education in business but little else.[62] From the age of twelve he had worked his way from janitorial assignments through clerkship posts, and was, at twenty-one, acting as the company's agent and, on the side, making business decisions on his own behalf with a part interest in a schooner.[63] Settling in Puerto Rico in 1821, he displayed unusual cultural pliancy in obeying the stringent regulations for foreigners in this, one of Spain's two remaining colonies in the Western Hemisphere: converting immediately to Catholicism and swearing an oath of allegiance to the "enlightened despot" Fernando VII and the Spanish Crown.[64] He learned Spanish with sufficient fluency that he admitted to a friend in 1831 that he in fact preferred speaking Spanish to English.[65]

Puerto Rico, unlike polyglot places like Surinam and international entrepôt islands like neighboring St. Croix and St. Thomas, was monocultural, developed by the Spanish Crown as a military base using transported convict labor. It was, therefore, economically speaking, underdeveloped when Mason arrived, with little to export, a population with little capital, education, or expertise, and much of its territory (3,515 square miles) mountainous forests and verdant, uncultivated valleys. Compared to other Caribbean islands, it lacked roads, capital, and government initiative.

Lane's painting of San Juan (or St. Johns), painted for Mason in the early 1850s, describes the fortress city from a vantage point looking north across the broad bay that for four centuries provided safe harbor for provisioning Spanish fleets (figs. 152 and 153).[66] This is the prospect Mason had when traveling from his plantation, near Bayamon, back to his home and business office in San Juan. It is a cityscape that in many respects is the counterpart to Lane's *Gloucester Harbor* painted for Mason at the same time (fig. 10). That San Juan was primarily a military outpost of empire is clear from the formidable gray stone walls encircling the two-mile-long island town—from El Morro Castle, on a high bluff guarding the bay's entrance, on the left, to the battlements at the right edge of Lane's view. In the words of New Englander Edward Bliss Emerson, who worked for Mason and was resident in the city from 1831 to 1834, "imagine to yourself then a well fortified city,—with lofty walls encircling its entire extent

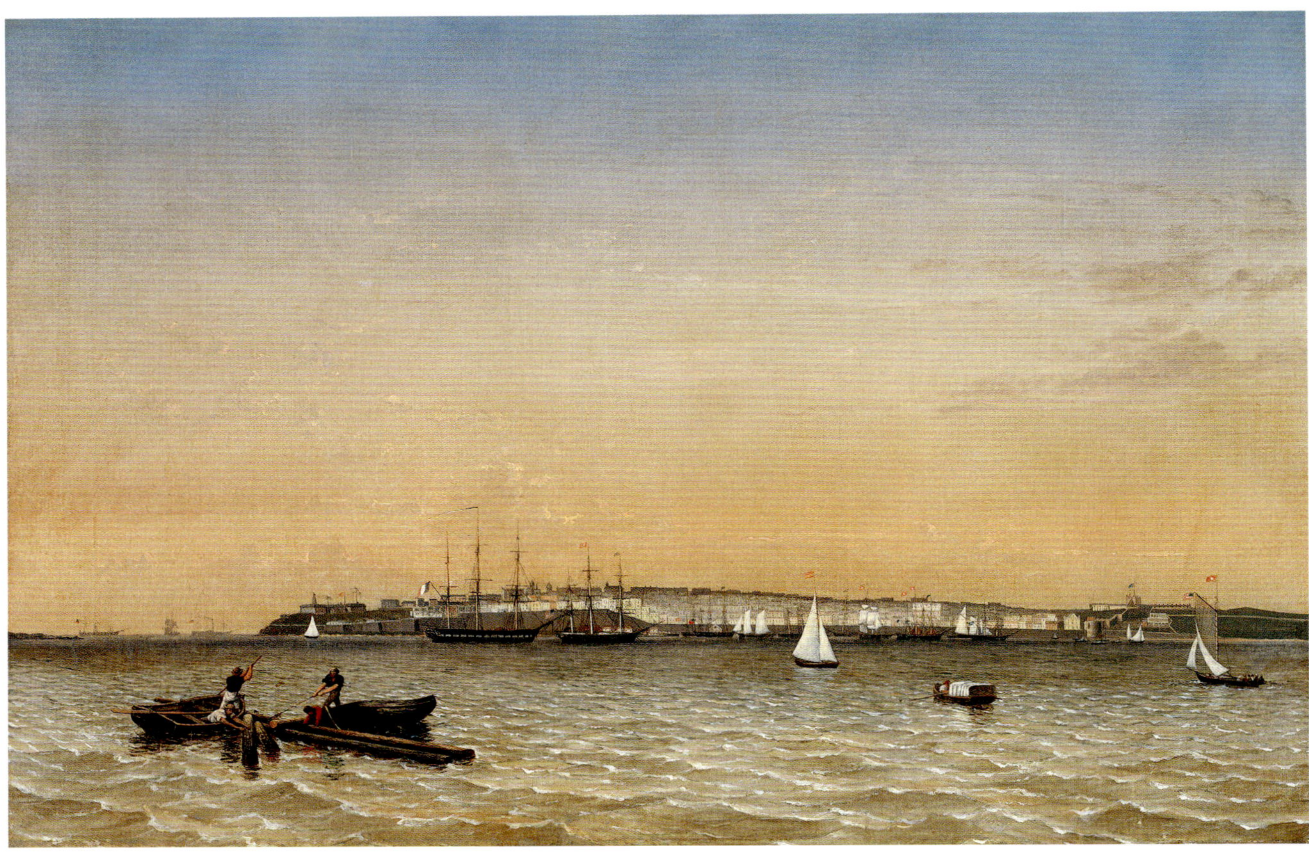

FIGURE 152
Fitz H. Lane, *San Juan, Porto Rico* (*St. Johns, Porto Rico*), ca. 1850. Oil on canvas, 23¾ × 36¼ in. (60.3 × 92.1 cm). Commissioned by Sidney Mason. The Mariners' Museum and Park, Newport News, Virginia (1947.0790.000001 / QO 0718).

supporting ramparts from which, at due intervals, jut forth round sentry boxes, and huge cannons peep through the embrasure[s]."[67] This wall was, in the nineteenth century, patrolled day and night by a formidable military force and accessed through six gates that were closed at sundown.[68] Designed by Spanish engineer Juan de Helí in 1554, these massive fortifications, which in places have forty-foot-thick walls, were built and maintained by convict labor, as Puerto Rico was for more than three centuries a penal colony, an island prison where malefactors from Spain and its possessions were sentenced to involuntary migration and hard labor.[69] Lane's painting takes in the breadth of the whole city, so it appears miniaturized but is quite accurately portrayed, emphasizing the effect of a militarized, tightly walled-in urban space.

This particular prospect of the excellent deepwater harbor was well known, so it is possible that Lane based his view on a preexisting print by another artist rather than journey to the site himself, but even if this is the case here, the artist has labored to carefully tailor the image to his patron and to the years of Mason's residence in Puerto Rico (1821–38).[70] Because the population of the island (about 267,837 in 1828 and 319,163 in 1835) was largely composed of former convicts who had served their time, former soldiers, military deserters, and others with little property or expertise, Puerto Ricans farmed small subsistence lots that did not bring the island the kind of prosperity or the government the kind of tax revenue that

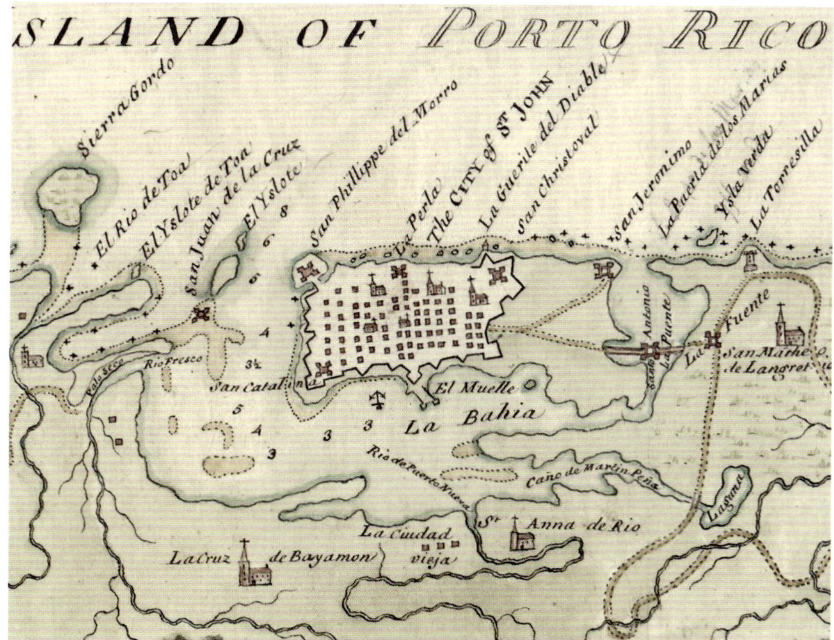

FIGURE 153
The Island of Porto Rico, 1760–69, detail. Ink and watercolor on paper, 9 ⅞ × 24 in. (25 × 61 cm); sheet 19 ⅜ × 26 in. (50 × 66 cm). Library of Congress, Geography and Map Division, Washington, DC (73691519).

the Spanish Crown observed on neighboring English and Danish sugar islands.[71] Puerto Rico as a military bastion lacked a business and planter elite, so the Crown made efforts in 1815 and 1828 to attract Catholic loyalists from Spain's and France's rebellious New World colonies, who were encouraged to bring their capital, technical expertise, and African slaves to enable Puerto Rico to become a profitable plantation-based colony.[72] But leery of liberation-minded troublemakers, on the one hand, and slave insurrections, on the other, the military autocracy governing Puerto Rico remained nervous about foreigners even as they realized that openness to foreign capital was necessary to achieve their economic goals and that the primary market for the staple crops they encouraged—sugar, coffee, tobacco—would be North America.[73]

When Sidney Mason arrived from New England in 1821, his enterprise was exactly what the governments of Spain and Puerto Rico thought they wanted, but he was an outsider within a formidable monocultural and military walled fortress. He acculturated quickly and in 1823 shrewdly married Mariquita Benito Dorado, one of the daughters of Don José Dorado and Señora Doña Catalina Dorado, originally from Cadiz, who had emigrated to Venezuela but became exiled royalists when that country declared its independence from Spain, and fled to Puerto Rico, where Señora Dorado's kinsman was a Spanish general and the island's governor.[74] Until 1837 Puerto Rico's governors were recruited exclusively from the Spanish nobility, and Mrs. Mason's aunt was a marchioness.[75] But even as anchored as he was then to the Spanish power elite, Sidney Mason and his brother John (who came to Puerto Rico to join him in business) were reminded of their precarious outsider position when, on January 2, 1832, "the Capt. of the Port grossly insulted Messrs. S. & J. Mason & struck the latter, who reflected on his position & interest enough to abstain from returning the blow."[76] As late as 1856 it was noted that Puerto Rico's "immense uncultivated plains," lack of good roads, and shortage of labor could be mended by a more hospitable attitude toward outsiders, but "it has ever been the policy of the government to discourage the introduction and settlement of foreigners."[77]

Where others saw obstacles, Mason saw opportunity and applied the business acumen he had gained in Boston

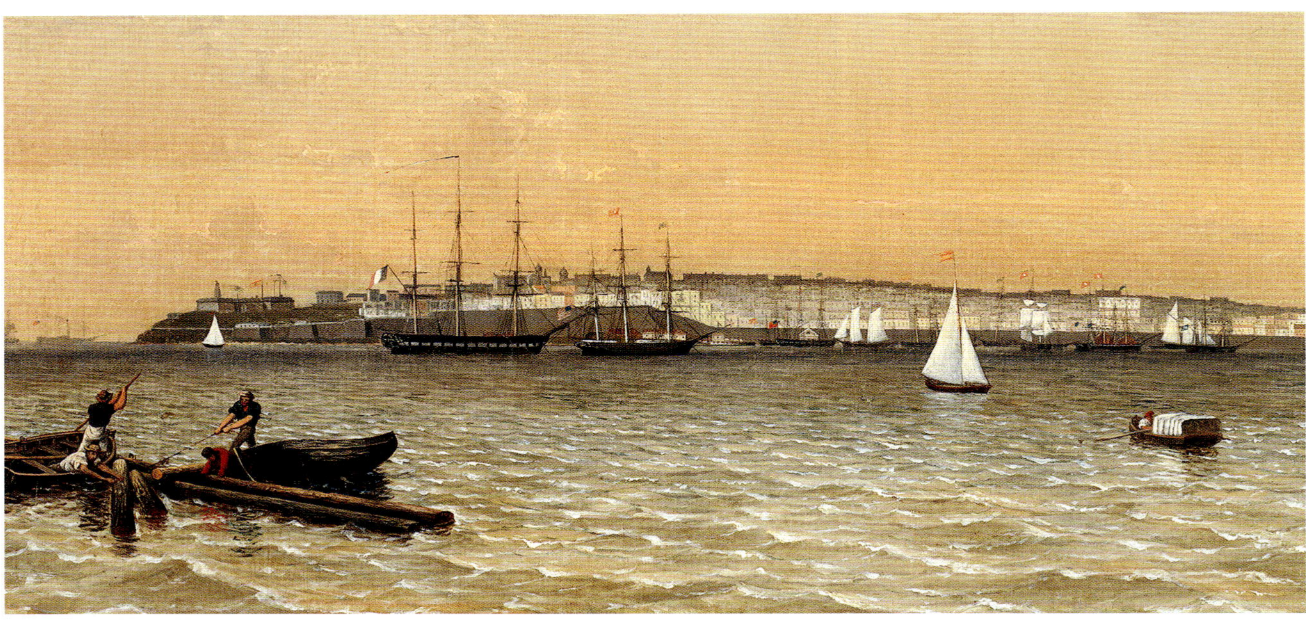

FIGURE 154
Fitz H. Lane, *San Juan, Porto Rico* (*St. Johns, Porto Rico*), ca. 1850 (fig. 152), detail.

to this new situation. From 1824 he advertised in the New England newspapers for the commission business of merchants, noting that he possessed "a knowledge of the language, and [had the] credit of the commercial community" in Puerto Rico.[78] Through the 1820s notices appear in the *Gloucester Telegraph* praising Puerto Rican sugar and coffee, listing Puerto Rican produce for sale in Gloucester shops, noting when ships arrived in Boston-area ports from Puerto Rico, and mentioning that while American ships were shut out from Britain's West Indian islands, they were welcome to trade in Puerto Rico and Cuba.[79] It is likely that Mason and family members in Gloucester were active in placing these notices and facilitating this trade.

By September 1829 the U.S. government felt there was sufficient commercial and national interest in Puerto Rico to appoint a consul in that capital, charged with assisting American citizens (including the relief and protection of American seamen), researching commercial opportunities, gathering statistics related to trade for the State Department, communicating to the U.S. Treasury the commercial law of Puerto Rico, and generally furthering the interest of the United States in trade with the Spanish colony. President Andrew Jackson appointed Sidney Mason.[80] The post came with no salary but with the capacity to levy fees from each American ship for safeguarding the vessel's papers while in port and looking after the interests of American citizens on board.[81] Mason reported that during 1830 eighty-four U.S. vessels entered the port of San Juan; by 1834 that number had risen to three hundred.[82] The responsibilities of consul also came with the dignity of an "Esq." and a certain amount of power. Within weeks of his appointment Mason investigated a suspicious ship and its cargo that had landed in San Juan from Connecticut. The ship and its cargo had been appropriated by what the newspapers called the "villainy" of a crooked captain who sought to sell both cargo and ship as his own in Puerto Rico. Restoring both the ship and the proceeds of the sale of its cargo to their rightful owner, Mason received widespread praise in the U.S. press.[83]

Mason was also trading on his own account. He formed a partnership first with his brother John—Mason & Co., the first American commercial firm in Puerto Rico—around 1824, and second a firm based in New York City with William David Thompson, who was later U.S. consul in Ecuador.[84] Lane's painting of San Juan includes no fewer than five vessels of different sizes and types flying the Mason & Thompson firm's flag—a red field with a central white disc—as well as the stars and stripes (fig. 154).[85] The largest ship in the painting flies the French flag, and the sloop in the middle of the picture flies the Spanish civil ensign used on merchant ships from 1828 to the present—a yellow field flanked by red stripes. But the majority of the ships and boats pictured, from the excursion party at the far right to the sleek ship anchored toward the center, are Mason & Thompson's. So successful was this firm that when Sidney Mason died decades later, a cryptic obituary in the *Alexandria (VA) Gazette* summed up his enterprise thus: "He was formerly the senior partner in the commercial house of Mason & Co., which at one time controlled the Porto Rico trade."[86] Both Mason & Co. and Mason & Thompson traded coffee, sugar, and molasses from South American and Caribbean ports and branched out to the San Francisco trade with the California Gold Rush.[87] Sidney Mason became very wealthy.

The second largest of the vessels, the three-master flying the Mason & Thompson flag and moored close to shore toward the center of Lane's painting, points with its bowsprit at a pink house overlooking the city wall, and immediately under the bowsprit stands a large structure on the skirt of land between the city walls and the water. In her account of her visit to the site as a teenager in 1867, Mason's granddaughter describes this pink house, which remained in family hands through the nineteenth century, as "a large house almost overhanging the city wall."

> It was built in Spanish fashion round a patio in which were bright flowers and a fountain. . . . The long drawing room windows opened upon a gallery extending the length of the house, overlooking the bay. Below the wall, near the water stood my grandfather's old counting house of Mason & Thompson. . . .
>
> [The Mason] house, now known, I am told, as the Pink Palace was formerly the home of my grandfather and here my dear mother was born.[88]

A visitor in 1831 described the house as "an extensive building, running . . . from one street to another, . . . [with] square lofty, roughfinished rooms, & long passages & a court yard . . . & every thing reminds you of baronial states. All the floors & stairs are of brick or stone."[89] There were steps leading from a gate in the city wall near this house down to the water's edge just at this point, making the proximity of Mason's home and counting house very convenient.[90]

Sidney Mason's younger brother John and his wife, Mary Eliza Babson, were also in Puerto Rico at this time (1829–40), John in partnership in the early years with Sidney. Their eldest brother, Alphonso, who remained in Gloucester, lost his wife in 1829 and sent his two young daughters, Lydia Ann and Harriett Tryphena, to live with John Mason in Puerto Rico, where they stayed for three years, until he remarried in 1832. Both girls became artists. Lydia Ann credited her years in Puerto Rico with developing her musical talent. As an adult, she became a teacher and keen biologist, collaborating with Lane on temperance projects, and was praised for her paintings of birds and flowers; she married Gloucester historian and Lane patron John James Babson.[91] Harriett is reputed to have been a pupil of Lane's when the Mason family returned to Gloucester. One of the brothers of Joseph Stevens Jr., Lane's closest friend, was named after the senior John Mason.[92] So while the circumstances of the arrangements between the artist and Sidney Mason are undocumented, beyond the survival of a corpus of paintings from the early 1850s, there were multiple links between Lane and Mason family members.

The two Mason couples, Sidney's and John's, each had two children born during their years in San Juan, while

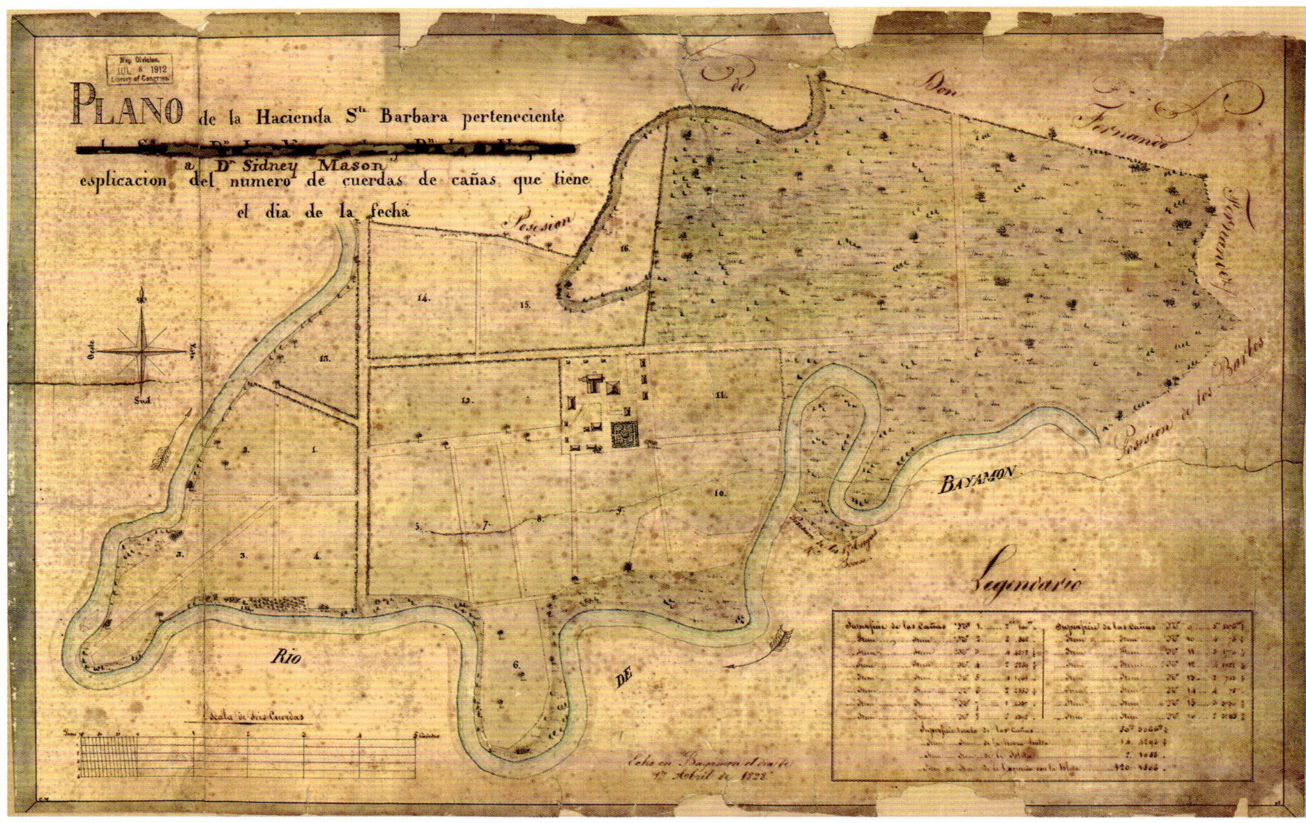

FIGURE 155
Plano de la Hacienda Sta. Barbara perteneciente a Sidney Mason (Plan of the Hacienda Santa Barbara belonging to Sidney Mason), 1828. Ink and watercolor on paper, 13¾ × 21¼ in. (35 × 54 cm). Library of Congress, Geography and Map Division, Washington, DC (98687136).

they were also looking after the two eldest children of their widower brother, Alphonse, who was back in Gloucester and deeply involved in starting a savings bank.[93] At this time Puerto Rico had no such institutions, hampering the ability of the business community and householders there to borrow or save money, so the Masons are credited with developing banking in San Juan.[94]

A good deal is known about Puerto Rico in the 1830s, and especially about Sidney Mason and his enterprises, because two of the brothers of Ralph Waldo Emerson—Edward Bliss Emerson and Charles Chauncy Emerson, both in their twenties and both suffering from tuberculosis—came to Puerto Rico in hopes that the tropical climate would cure their lungs and there kept journals and wrote home copiously about their experiences on the island.[95] Edward, who had previously graduated from Harvard at the top of his class, traveled in Europe, suffered a nervous breakdown, and studied law, landed in St. Croix early in 1831 and, finding himself "sick, in debt," and unwilling to continue drawing on the "slender means" of his brothers, was casting about for employment when he met Sidney Mason and was persuaded to come to Puerto Rico to work for this fellow New Englander.[96] He lived in Mason's household and worked in his business and consular offices for three years, until his death in 1834. Charles C. Emerson came for a long visit in the winter of 1831–32. They both frequently accompanied Mason when he traveled to the nearby plantation he had surveyed and purchased in 1828, Sta. Barbara, on the Bayamón River south of San Juan (figs. 153 and 155).

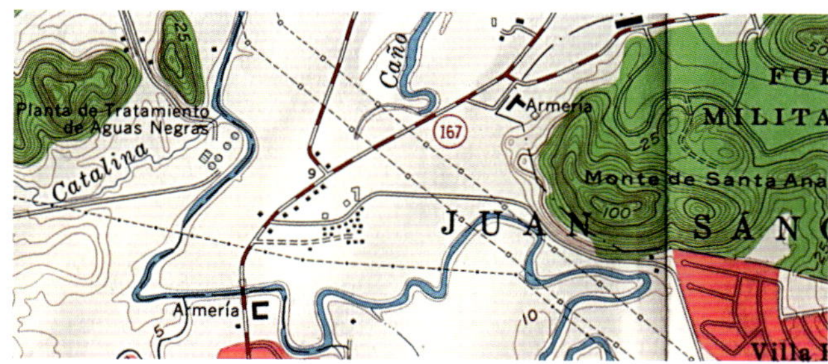

FIGURE 156
Bayamón topographical map, Puerto Rico, 1963, detail. US Geological Survey, https://www.gifex.com/puerto_rico_maps/Bayamon_Topographic_Map_Puerto_Rico_2.htm.

With the buildings clustered at the center of the property, the western portion comprised sixteen partitioned fields planted in sugar cane. The eastern part—steeply hilly, as is clear in a mid-twentieth-century United States Geological Survey topographical map of the area—was undeveloped and forested (fig. 156). Visitor Charles Chauncy Emerson made an ascent of this prominent hill early in 1832:

> Yesterday I came out to Santa Barbara, Mr. Mason's plantation, about 5 miles from St. Johns. This morning before breakfast, I rode to the top of a steep hill which commands a view of several miles round about and oh the beauty & fatness of the land! I feasted on it as on some delicious fruit. Spread out beneath my feet, was a valley of thousands of acres—cane-fields & pasture-lands, a sheet of living green. . . . This valley was bounded by ridges of hills . . . rough with precipices & chalky rocks glaring out from under a tangled & matted vegetation.[97]

Family documents indicate that "much of the furniture in [the residence to which Sidney Mason moved in New York City in the early 1840s] was made from wood brought from the plantation in Porto Rico, from designs drawn for Mr. Mason in Europe."[98] In 1847 Mason built a Fifth Avenue home, later described by his niece: "The interior was filled with works of art, and beautiful furniture, some of which was made of mahogany from Porto Rico, and grown on his plantation Santa Catalina, San Juan [aka Sta. Barbara], and fashioned from designs selected during his visits to Europe."[99]

It is probable that the mahogany for this furniture was harvested from the forested eastern hillside section of the property and floated on the Bayamón River to the bay, where, in Lane's version of this narrative, two men in small boats wrangle a group of long straight logs (fig. 157). While the eastern portion of Mason's property was wild and undeveloped, the "plan" drawn at the time the hacienda changed hands makes clear that the main business of the property was the production of sugar (fig. 155).[100] Mahogany trees grow only in a widely dispersed pattern in climax tropical forests, still very much intact in inland Puerto Rico in the 1830s, although these trees were long gone in the other Caribbean islands by that date.[101] Although Puerto Rico is not known for the export of mahogany, these trees were valued and used by locals for building when they could be extracted from the inland forests in which they grew in remote isolation.[102] As late as 1856 a report relates: "The island abounds in excellent timber. . . . Different kinds of the more valuable woods for cabinet-makers . . . repose undisturbed amid the ravines of the mountains."[103] By foregrounding a vignette of log moving in his painting *San Juan, Porto Rico*, Lane is pointing to the physical evidence of Mason's years in the tropics, to the literal furniture in proximity to which the painting was hung in New York City, memorializing his life in that very different city two decades earlier.

Mason's granddaughter, Cassie Mason Myers Julian-James, the last in direct line from Sidney Mason, died in 1922 and willed the two Washington, DC, houses she owned (hers and that of her deceased brother) and their contents to two cousins, one of whom was Robert Trail Spence Lowell.[104] His son, the future poet Robert Lowell, remembered the arrival in his family's Boston household of what he called "nervous" Victorian furniture from Cousin Cassie, "mahogany, cherry, teak," confusing

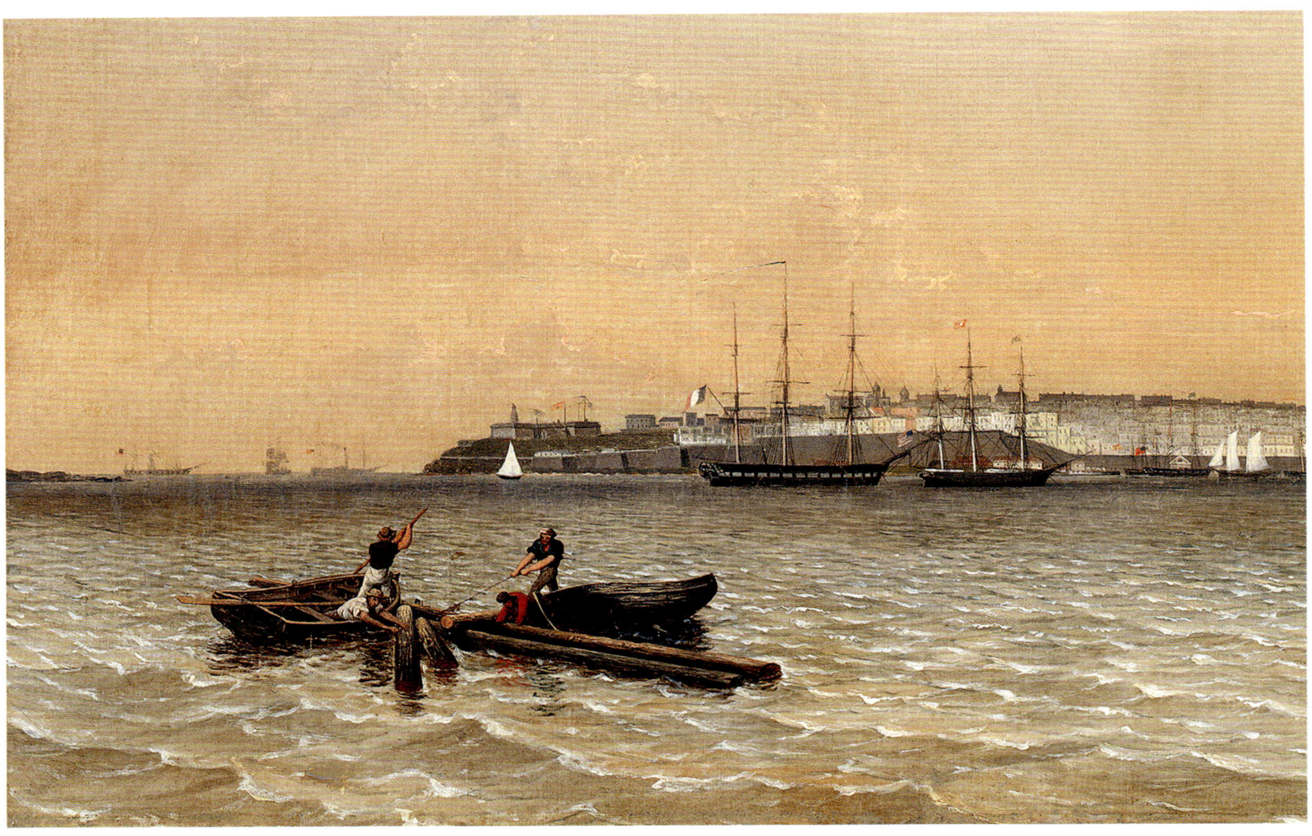

FIGURE 157
Fitz H. Lane, *San Juan, Porto Rico (St. Johns, Porto Rico)*, ca. 1850 (fig. 152), detail.

Mason objects (with heraldic mermaids) with objects inherited from the Myers family.[105] Thereafter the trail of the descent of the Puerto Rican furniture, made from logs like those Lane displays so conspicuously in his painting of San Juan, grows cold.

While the Emerson brothers found much to admire in Puerto Rico, they found it difficult to understand a community in which there were "no lectures, no sermons . . . no reading rooms, no public libraries," no bookstores, no participatory government, no literature, no independent press, and no educational institutions, as these, to them, constituted the attributes of a good society.[106] As Edmund Emerson put it, "Men do not strive [in Puerto Rico] as in New England after [becoming] the perfect man. It is present pastime or gainful industry or chance which they follow as their stars."[107] Finding themselves in such a very unfamiliar culture and desperately ill, both brothers were inclined to philosophy, to brooding on the meaning and purpose of human existence. As Charles put it in a letter to brother Waldo written at Mason's hacienda Santa Barbara (fig. 158): "If we are not immortals, all of life is wasted . . . yet does this world seem . . . a fit school for candidates for the Kingdom of Heaven? . . . This brewing of porter, & filling of writs & passports, this ship-building & trafficking, & ball-dressing, is [this] the discipline ordained under Providence to educate souls for a spiritual state—where . . . the society of angels is to be our employment & bliss? Is it not a Paradox beyond the Stoics?"[108]

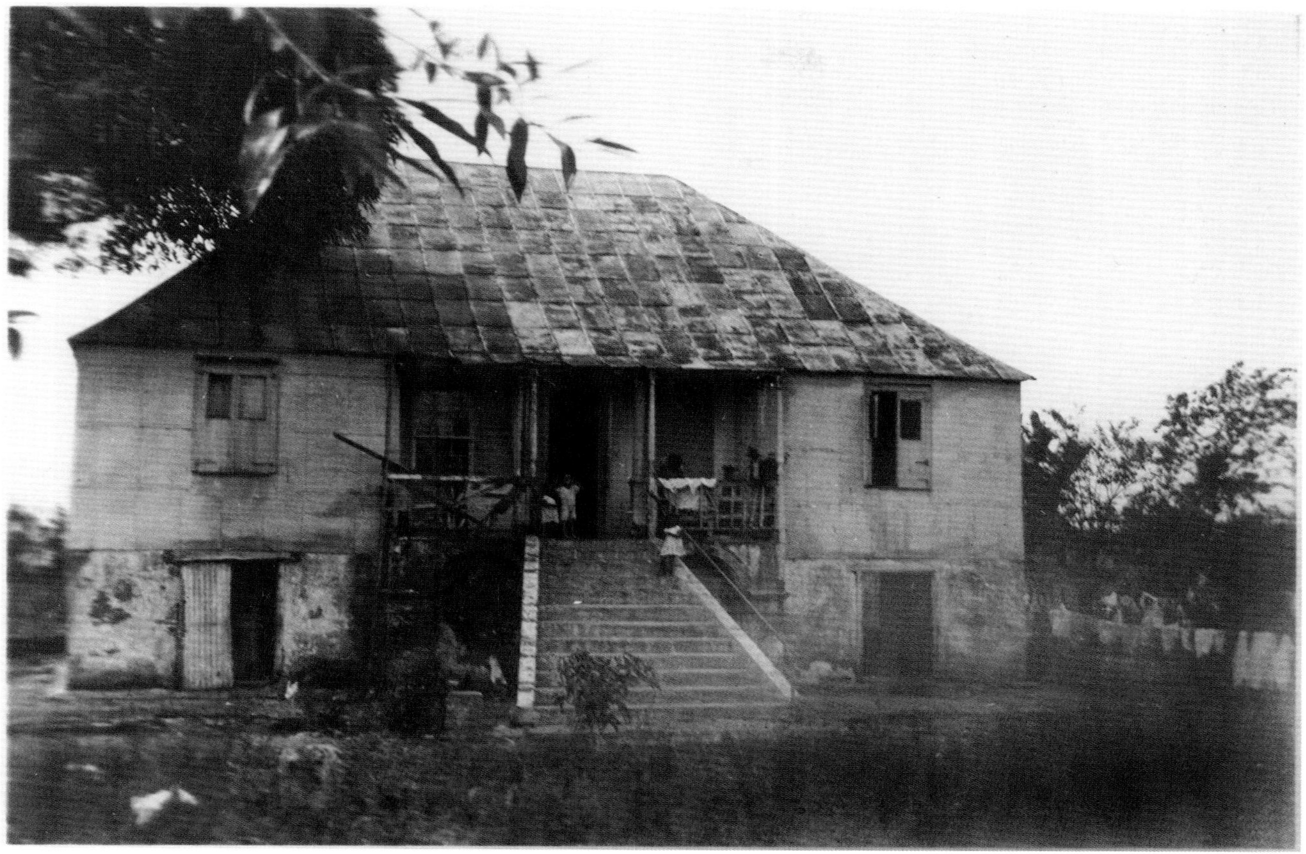

FIGURE 158
Sylvester Baxter, *Hacienda Santa Barbara at Bayamón* (plantation home of Sidney Mason in Puerto Rico), ca. 1925. Photograph. Ralph Waldo Emerson Memorial Association deposit, Houghton Library, Harvard University, bMsAm 1280.235 (706.32).

Edmund—who had had a classical education and read avidly in literature, philosophy, and history, spoke Italian, French, Greek, and Spanish, and meditated frequently on the meaning and purpose of human existence—daily offered an alternative model to Sidney Mason, whose own education had been curtailed so early and channeled so completely into business.[109] When Mason decided to leave Puerto Rico, his articulated reason for doing so was to seek educational opportunities for his children, suggesting that the Emersons had had an important influence on his thinking and his life: his children would have the kind of opportunity for a broad-based education in Western history, philosophy, literature, and languages that the Emersons instantiated and that he had not been given but had learned to value during his association with them.[110]

Sidney was, no doubt, attentive to the Emerson brothers' comments about art as well as education in the Western tradition in general—Charles thought a lot about art and aesthetics. He tended to evaluate landscapes—both literal and in prints—with reference to Washington Allston; he had written a thoughtful college essay on the relationship between art and happiness and wondered in a passage in his Puerto Rican journal why "in Architecture, in poetry, in eloquence, the recurrence of similar forms or cadences and sounds produces an effect which to us is ultimate . . . [why] human taste is thus soothed by Repetition."[111] Edmund must have told his host about the art and architecture he had seen in Europe, and when

Mason had an opportunity to import objects from New England to Puerto Rico, he elected to bring engravings and plaster casts—that is, reproductions—of celebrated Greek and Roman artworks.[112] Given Mason's subsequent European sojourn and his patronage of Lane (and other artists), it is apparent that the consul/businessman was listening when the Emersons talked about art.

Frequently remarked on by the Emerson brothers in their letters and journals was the institution of slavery. Never accounting for more than 12 percent of the island's population, slaves in Puerto Rico were on a footing different from that of slaves elsewhere in the Caribbean, but they and their situation loomed large in both Edmund's and Charles's commentary.[113] Charles watched the slaves at Sta. Barbara given their new clothing and remarked: "[The slaves] are treated humanely in this island. . . . [But] slavery affords a frightful illustration [that] . . . the most lovely spots on our earth seem fated to be nests of suffering & wrong." He pointed to the fact that in the 1830s slavery was a cultural given in virtually every tropical country in the Western Hemisphere and much of the rest of the world.[114] Edmund noted in June 1831 that "70 or 80 negroes were landed [in Puerto Rico] from a Guinea man [transatlantic slave ship]; the illicit trade being still connived at" despite vigorous English interdictions and growing public sentiment in Denmark, England, New England, and elsewhere concerning abolishing both the transatlantic slave trade and slavery.[115] It would be more than forty years before the Spanish government abolished slavery in Puerto Rico.[116]

SIDNEY MASON'S LANE PAINTINGS

By 1834 Sidney Mason began the complex process of moving himself, his business interests, and his family to the United States. His powerful father-in-law had died (in 1831); his consular appointment and U.S. passport were revoked because he had taken an oath of allegiance to the Spanish Crown (even though that oath was a criterion of his residence in Puerto Rico and therefore of his service as consul); and he wished his children to be educated in America.[117] It is also possible that he wanted to distance himself from slavery and equally from the forced labor of the island's free population (those farming less than four acres) under the *libreta* system, used earlier but formalized in 1838, when the population of slaves proved insufficient to produce the prosperity and tax revenue desired by the large landowners and the government.[118]

Mason's primary port in the United States for his business in Caribbean goods was Baltimore, and in this city he registered many of the vessels he owned or part-owned, including the schooners *Frances Jane*, which he registered in November 1834, and *Catalina*, in November 1837.[119] Many of Mason's and the Emersons' extensive communications also went through Baltimore.[120] It was in the schooner *Frances Jane*, especially fitted out for the purpose, that in 1834 he transported his family (his wife, two children, and probably the two daughters of his brother Alphonso), first to Baltimore and then to Gloucester.[121] It is possible that Lane's detailed painting of Baltimore's inner harbor, recently deaccessioned by the Shelburne Museum and now in a private collection, reenacts and memorializes this first step in Mason's remigration north (fig. 159). Catalina would have been ten in 1834, and possibly she is memorialized in the dark-haired child picking flowers in the center foreground of the painting. Her brother was five, about the age of the boy in green with a hoop on the right; the dapper couple facing toward the harbor at the center are perhaps Sidney and Mariquita. Another boy plays with a dog, and a tight-knit Black family at the far left completes the group of figures on Federal Hill, a greensward public park overlooking the busy city, with its shipping, warehouses, shot towers, houses, lumber yards, and churches. In the print derived from this painting, the cityscape and the vessels are taken exactly from the painting, but the figures are more numerous and quite different, suggesting perhaps that the painting was

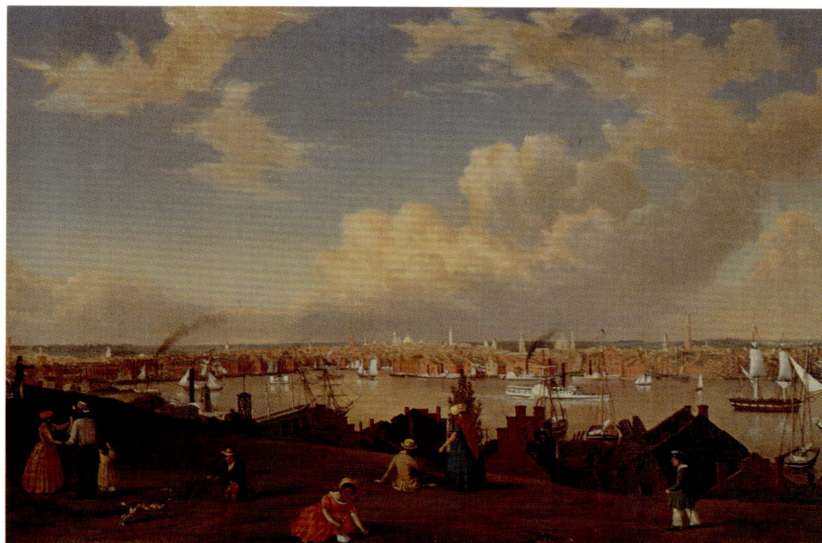

FIGURE 159
Fitz Henry Lane, *Baltimore from Federal Hill*, ca. 1850. Oil on canvas, 19¼ × 28½ in. (48.26 × 71.12 cm). Possibly commissioned by Sidney Mason. Private collection.

private, intended for one household, and the print public, intended for wide circulation. The print title includes the notation "Sketched from Nature by F. H. Lane," indicating that he undertook the trip to Baltimore to fulfill this commission, possibly en route to or from Puerto Rico in one of Mason's vessels.

Another Lane painting of Baltimore Harbor that might have been painted for Mason—this one in the characteristic 24 × 36 inch format—includes prominent portraits of a handsome schooner in the foreground, perhaps the *Frances Jane*, and of a young man dramatically warping a raft of logs toward a dock, perhaps alluding to Mason's mahogany unloaded from a freighter and en route to cabinetmakers in Baltimore, New England or New York (private collection).[122] After a quick stop in Baltimore, the family moved on to New England, where Mason established himself in the town of his childhood, Gloucester.

In 1852 Mason "gave . . . to Mr. Lane" "an order for the painting" of Gloucester, the town for which, his granddaughter recounts, he had "ever cherished a love."[123] Eighteen fifty-two is the year his father died, and that may have been the event that precipitated the retrospective suite of paintings discussed here. *Gloucester Harbor*, the largest of these canvases, summarizes the town's historical landmarks (such as the Revolutionary-era fort), its shipping (the ubiquitous "Surinamers"), its major industry (fishing), and its newest buildings, which included the Pavilion Hotel (figs. 10, 63, and 93). This establishment, intended to attract summer visitors, was first envisioned in 1827 and eventually built by Sidney Mason in 1849; it is visible at the harbor edge on the extreme left of the image.[124] It was newly built on the site of a former windmill, land that had been owned by Mason's father.[125]

Mason appears to have been ready to settle into Gloucester on his return from Puerto Rico in 1834, when he brought his family north, but a number of misfortunes unsettled him, and by 1840 he was living in New York City, although he continued to visit, own property in, invest in, and donate to philanthropic causes in Gloucester.[126] He placed his daughter Catalina, together with her two cousins Lydia Ann and Harriett Tryphena Mason, in the Ursuline convent school at Mount Benedict in Charlestown (now Somerville), which was beset a few weeks later by an anti-Catholic mob and burned in August 1834. The girls survived, Catalina having been rescued by the father of Oliver Wendell Holmes.[127] Mason's

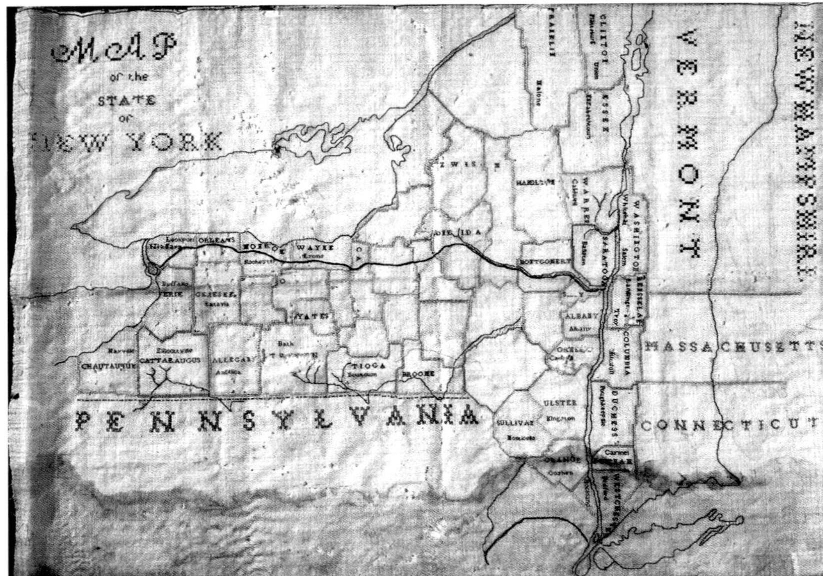

FIGURE 160
Catalina Mason, *County and River Sampler Map of New York State*, ca. 1837–40. Silk embroidery on wool ground, 18⅛ × 27 in. (46.0375 × 68.58 cm). Division of Cultural and Community Life, National Museum of American History, Smithsonian Institution. Estate of Cassie Mason Myers Julian-James (70138).

wife died the following year, and in response to this unforeseen uprooting of the family core, Mason traveled between 1836 and 1840, closing out his business interests in Puerto Rico in 1838 (but retaining both his San Juan house and business property throughout his life).[128] He visited Europe while his children were in boarding school.[129] Catalina was placed at Emma Willard School in Troy, New York, where, among other accomplishments, she learned embroidery and continued the cartographic tradition for which her grandfather, Gloucester town surveyor John Mason, was well known (figs. 9 and 160).[130]

Late in 1839 Mason's son, then a twelve-year-old at boarding school in New York City, died, and in December of that year three hurricanes hit Gloucester Harbor, in which hundreds of vessels had sought refuge, causing the destruction of 86 vessels (and another 213 badly damaged) and the loss of more than 150 lives in this port alone.[131] A Committee of Relief was immediately formed, including Lane patron George H. Rogers and Mason's brother Alphonso, to relieve the suffering of the families of those so "suddenly hurried into eternity."[132] A fortnight after the last of these catastrophic storms hit, Alphonso Mason, returning to New England from the funeral of his namesake nephew, Sidney's son, died in the disastrous fire on the steamer Lexington in Long Island Sound.[133]

Perhaps it is no surprise then that Lane's painting recording the New York City chapter in Mason's life, which began in 1840, soon after the deaths of his wife, brother, and only son, tempers the buoyancy of the busy harbor scene with an exceptionally turbulent sea (fig. 161). A majestic clipper ship outbound with calm confidence upstages paddle wheelers, a stolid merchantman, and other vehicles of commerce and transportation in heavy seas that render the smaller vessels almost unmanageable. Overall, however, despite his personal sorrows, Mason prospered in New York. Based at South Street, he continued in business as a commission merchant with William D. Thompson, building vessels and shipping internationally in ships and steamers, but he also moved into insurance, banking, and railroads.[134]

Mason began the New York chapter in his life with the purchase of a home at 3 College Place, where his sixteen-year-old daughter Catalina joined him while continuing her schooling as a day pupil nearby.[135] By the time the "memory set" of Lane paintings was commissioned, around 1850, Mason had built a marble mansion on Fifth

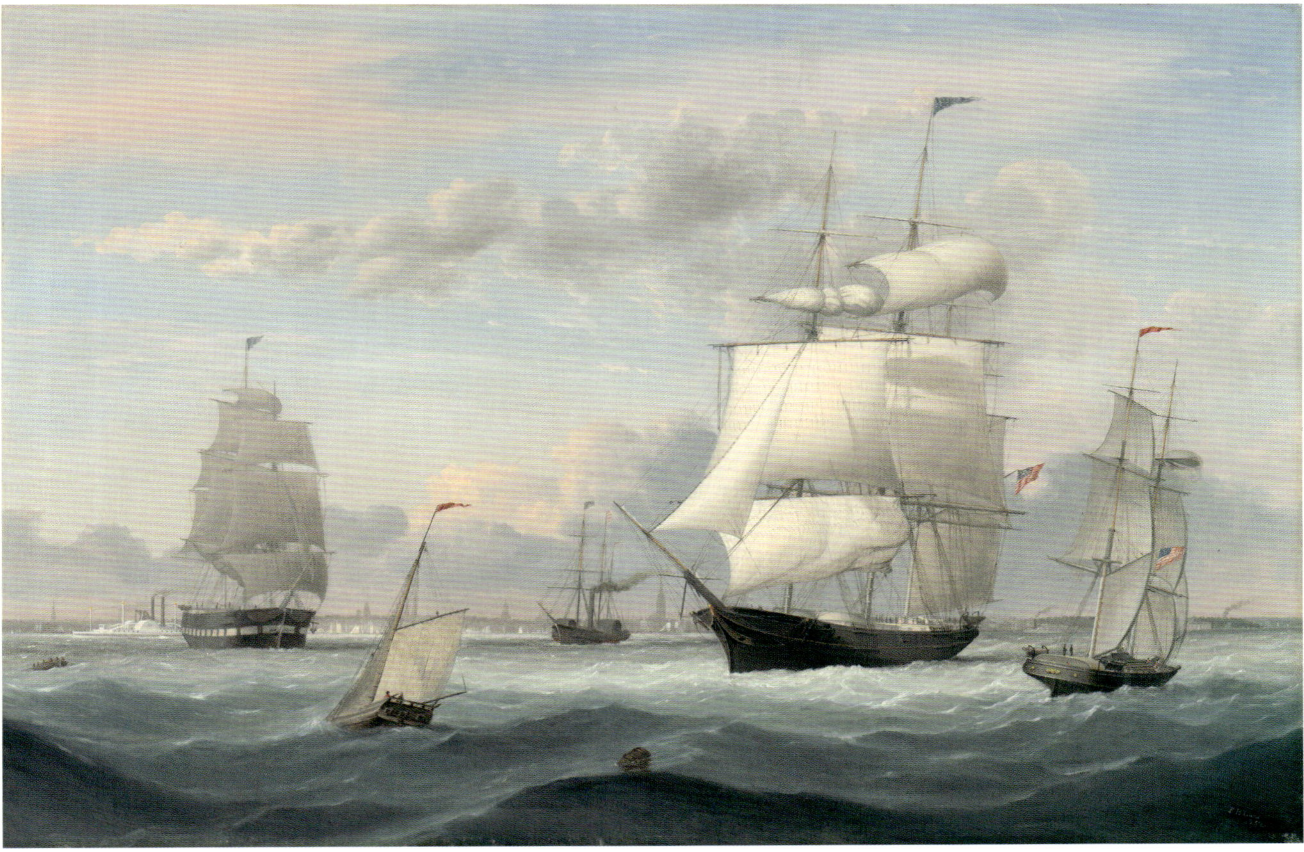

FIGURE 161
Fitz H. Lane, *New York Harbor*, 1852. Oil on canvas, 23½ × 35 in. (59.7 × 88.9 cm). Commissioned by Sidney Mason. National Gallery of Art, Washington, DC. Gift of Frances Elizabeth Smith (1994.100.1).

Avenue (with a stable and carriage house behind it on Eighteenth Street), to accommodate himself, his daughter, his growing collection of furniture and art, his second wife, and, after 1847, his son-in-law Col. Theodorus Bailey Myers, a lawyer and collector of historical manuscripts, and, from 1848, his two grandchildren (fig. 151).[136] Mason's commissioning of Lane paintings picturing places important in his life decades earlier makes clear his nostalgic tendency, also evident in the fact that, while he moved from place to place, he did not sell the "old" real estate in Puerto Rico or in Gloucester or in New York City.[137] Like viewing the paintings, visiting these sites of earlier chapters in his life was probably linked to his (thwarted) hope to establish a dynasty conscious of its roots.

Probably because of the death of his only son, Mason kept his daughter and son-in-law close and requested that his grandson take the "Mason" name. Son-in-law Myers was associated in business with Mason, most significantly in the Sixth Avenue horse railway—Mason was president and Myers was secretary of this successful enterprise.[138] The idea of an urban rail system to move New Yorkers efficiently on the north-south axis of Manhattan was inspired by Baltimore's success in this respect, first broached with the city council in 1830, and permitted in 1831 despite "frightful predictions of steam-carriages furiously propelled through the street . . . overturning and demolishing travelers and carriages."[139] Mason made his entry into urban transit at an auspicious moment when the city, no longer a compact "walking city" concentrated

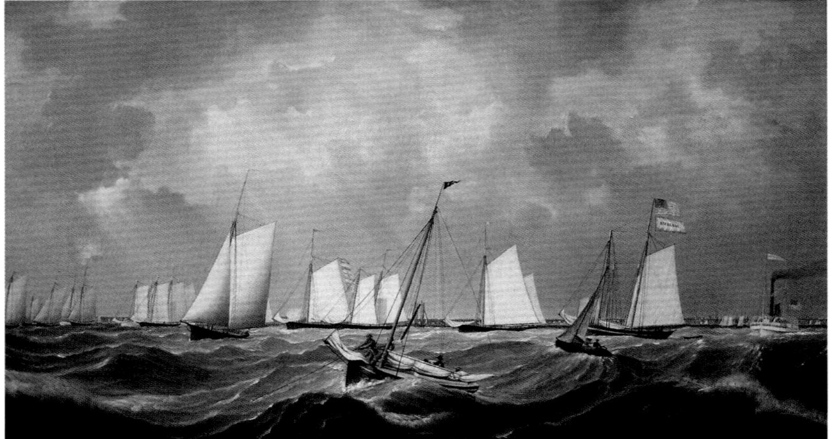

FIGURE 162
Fitz H. Lane, *New York Yacht Club Regatta, Buzzards Bay off the Coast of New Bedford*, 1856. Oil on canvas, 28 × 50¼ in. (71.1 × 127.6 cm). Commissioned by Sidney Mason. Newport Art Museum. Gift of Mrs. Elizabeth Morris Smith in memory of her mother, Nathalie Bailey Morris, wife of Lewis Gouverneur Morris of Newport and New York (1991.007.001).

below Fourteenth Street, was expanding northward: in 1840 only 10 percent of Manhattan's population lived north of Fourteenth Street; by 1860 42 percent did.[140] The sixty cars in the Sixth Avenue line, inaugurated in 1851 and one of the first public rail-transit systems in New York, were drawn by mules and horses and eventually powered by electricity.[141] These cars were ornamented "with small oil paintings over the windows and on the panel of the swinging door. . . . Often painted by artists of merit, as pot-boilers . . . [they were] little landscapes with . . . blue skies, purple mountains, placid lakes and inevitable boats with white sails faithfully reflected."[142] Perhaps Mason saw these little landscapes as a way to share with the public his growing interest in art. He was president of the Sixth Avenue horsecar line for seventeen years, a role in which he was succeeded by his son-in-law.

During this midcentury period the rural character of the small ornamental paintings on the horsecar interiors was brought to Manhattan quite literally by the construction of Central Park, with its hillocks, grassy fields, woodsy dells, and miniature sailboat pond. According to Clarence Cook (the only art critic to take notice of Lane during his lifetime), Central Park was first sketched out in an essay by A. J. Downing in 1849 where he proposed the idea of "a large public park [to] . . . foster the love of rural beauty, and increase the knowledge of, and taste for, rare and beautiful trees and plants . . . where people could walk, and drive, and ride, and skate, and row; where baseball . . . could be played, and all classes of the community find rest and recreation."[143] The city began to acquire the land (7,500 lots at a cost of more than $5 million) in 1853, and Mason, an avid horseman, frequently rode with his grandchildren to see this extraordinary public amenity under construction.[144] Historian George Bancroft and the park's designer, Frederick Law Olmsted, sometimes joined the Masons on these rides.[145]

Mason's son-in-law Theodorus Bailey Myers, a navy recruiter during the Civil War, was the nephew of a rear admiral (Theodorus Bailey, for whom he was named) and the father of another navy officer, so it is not surprising that his sporting interests included the new sport of yachting. Myers joined the fledgling New York Yacht Club in 1852, and this new maritime activity in his household may have prompted Sidney Mason to commission Lane to paint two views of New York Yacht Club races, probably in 1856 (figs. 162 and 163).[146] These paintings were given to the club by Mason or by Myers. However, early in the twentieth century, understanding that they were undervalued in that institution, Mason's granddaughter, Cassie Mason Julian-James, as the last direct descendant

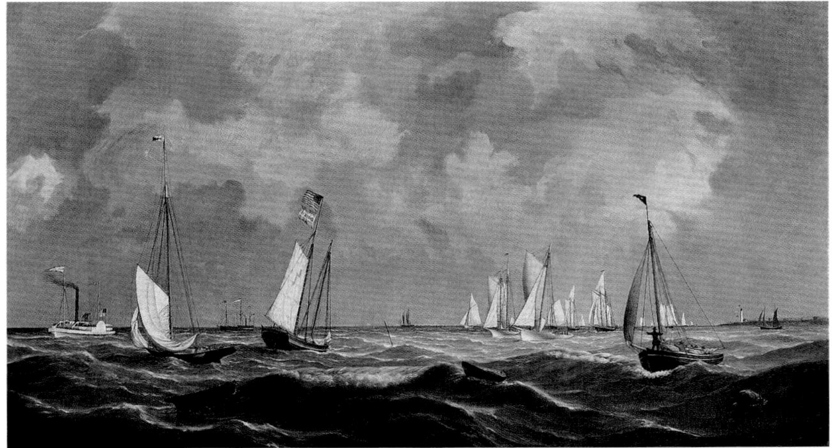

FIGURE 163
Fitz Henry Lane, *First Regatta of the New York Yacht Club*, 1856. Oil on canvas, 31½ × 50 in. (71.1 × 127 cm). Commissioned by Sidney Mason. Preservation Society of Newport County / Collection at Chepstow, Rhode Island. Bequest of Mrs. Alletta Morris McBean to The Preservation Society of Newport County, Newport, Rhode Island (PSNC.8727).

of Sidney Mason, in her project to carefully place family objects in appropriate hands toward the end of her life, retrieved them. She then gave them, together with other Mason-commissioned Lane paintings, including *Near Reef of Norman's Woe* and *New York Harbor*, to her cousin Alletta Nathalie Lorrillard Bailey, wife of Lewis Gouverneur Morris of New York and Newport (figs. 72, 73, and 161).[147] In the 1990s Alletta's daughters placed the two New York Yacht Club paintings and the Norman's Woe work at three institutions in Newport, Rhode Island, the yachting capital of the United States and venue of many the club's summer regattas.

It was at the New York Yacht Club regattas in the 1850s that the paths of Sidney Mason, Fitz Henry Lane, Robert Bennet Forbes, and Theodorus Bailey Myers crossed. Yachting was the play form of the global maritime competitions for trade in which Forbes and Mason participated on the larger scale of the world's oceans most of their lives. In yachting, purpose-built ultraswift boats traversing controlled home-seas race courses tested the technical limits of hull and rigging designs and the canniness of their skippers against one another. Speed and strategy, knowledge of winds, tides, and navigation, and the performance limits of the vessels were tested and validated in these very competitive club regattas. To up the stakes beyond pride in equipment and personal prowess, substantial cash prizes were offered. Forbes is credited with introducing yachting to the United States, and he attended and wrote accounts of New York Yacht Club races for the press.[148] In light of the widely celebrated victory of the yacht *America*, owned by a consortium of club members, winning the Royal Yacht Squadron's One Hundred Sovereign Cup (subsequently the America's Cup) off the Isle of Wight in 1851, the sport blossomed in the United States. Lane was commissioned to paint multiple portraits of *America* and at least two views of early New York Yacht Club regattas for Sidney Mason.[149]

While yachting was the play form of the deadly serious business of moving vessels, people, and goods on the world's oceans, it had positive real-world outcomes. Beyond developing new technical strategies for moving over water swiftly, it appears to have fostered the exchange of ideas and inventions for moving over water safely. Sidney Mason's grandson, Theodorus Bailey Myers Mason, who became a lieutenant commander in the U.S. Navy and founder of the Office of Naval Intelligence, wrote a slim book, entitled *The Preservation of Life at Sea*, that gathered known techniques, materials, and practices, including cork life preservers, ring life buoys, metal lifeboats with watertight air-pocket bulkheads, night lighting conventions on ships and boats, the construction of lifesaving stations, and buoy designs. It also copied a drawing, perhaps by Lane, of the operation of lifeboat davits designed and sent to Mason by Robert Bennet Forbes, who had vigorously pursued these many lifesaving strategies himself and published his own text on the subject, *Life-Boats, Projectiles, and Other Means for Saving Life*, a few years earlier.[150] While Lane did not paint these devices in operation (such as the breeches buoy and novel lifeboats launched from shoreline lifesaving stations), an artist who followed him to Gloucester, Winslow Homer, did.

When Sidney Mason died, in 1871, his obituaries praised his business acumen and his leadership positions in banking, insurance, and rail transportation. They also remarked that "he possessed a cultivated taste, which was evinced not only in a well-selected library, but in numerous paintings and objects of art that adorn his late residence."[151] Mason's selection of works for this library, collection of objets d'art, and purchase and commission of paintings from Lane and perhaps other artists reflect the long shadow of the Emerson brothers, with their eager enthusiasm for books and literature and their musings on art and its uses so many decades earlier, and so many miles away in Puerto Rico.

Mason's granddaughter Cassie, her father, and Alletta Bailey's mother were all notable collectors, and together with many others, all three lent dozens of artworks to a major exhibition of art objects and historical materials at the National Academy of Design in New York in 1878.[152] Col. Theodorus Bailey Myers served on the Committee on Reception and Arrangement for this exhibition, with Louis Comfort Tiffany, Samuel Colman, Worthington Whittredge, and other art-world notables.[153] In keeping with post–Civil War taste among American collectors, Myers and his kin did not loan (or highly value) the American landscape paintings on their walls. Rather, they lent fifteenth-century Spanish tiles, fourteenth-century French tapestries, a Gilbert Stuart portrait of Lafayette, English ceramic wares, a Sèvres bust of Marie Antoinette, Dutch pictorial tiles, eighteenth-century Dresden vases, and the manuscript survey of Mt. Vernon drawn by George Washington. None of these three Mason family-linked collectors lent Lane paintings. And in 1922, when Cassie, last of the direct descendants of Sidney Mason, died, she had placed ceremonial clothing in the National Museum of American History (now part of the Smithsonian Institution) in Washington, DC, and she left laces to the Metropolitan Museum of Art in New York City but gave no paintings to either institution.[154] The set of five or more Lane paintings memorializing the important geographies and activities in the life of her grandfather, Sidney Mason, she had given the previous year to relatives or, in the case of the big *Gloucester Harbor*, to the city of his birth, a city that had no art museum. Even if she had sought to place the Lane paintings in an important urban museum, Lane's reputation was at such a low ebb in the 1920s that it is doubtful such an institution would have accepted them.

In sum, the Lane works discussed in this chapter and chapter 7 were created for four New Englanders whose horizons were geographically expansive. They constitute a special case in patronage of this artist. These men were repeat customers who saw in Lane's skills a means to gratify strong and repeated desires they had for clarity of communication (Forbes), constructing elastic home ties (Babson), recording business and real-estate investments (Rogers), and creating a personal pictorial memoir (Mason). Their personal activities and memories were tied up in long-term engagement with distant places and very different kinds of communities. While thoroughly embedded in the culture and society of antebellum Massachusetts, they were also sojourners in foreign worlds, hints of which bleed through the localism of Lane's canvases and his own Gloucester-bound experience of the world.

Three of these men were merchants, self-made men skilled at moving goods from where they were plentiful and cheap to where they were rare and expensive, so they were necessarily outward-facing in their approach to people and places. The fourth was a father eager to maintain contact with, and cultural intimacy alive in, his only surviving children, thousands of miles away. They selected Lane to create artworks and documents to carry their messages to contemporaries and to posterity: some poignant, some explanatory, some evocative of longing, and all rooted in the immediate capacity of an image (or a set of images) to transport the imagination, clarify a concept, or trigger memory. Lost are the conversations between Lane and his patrons that resulted in these carefully orchestrated works, but the pictures themselves bear the eloquent residue of these exchanges and of the distant places they obliquely reference: Surinam, California, China, Puerto Rico.

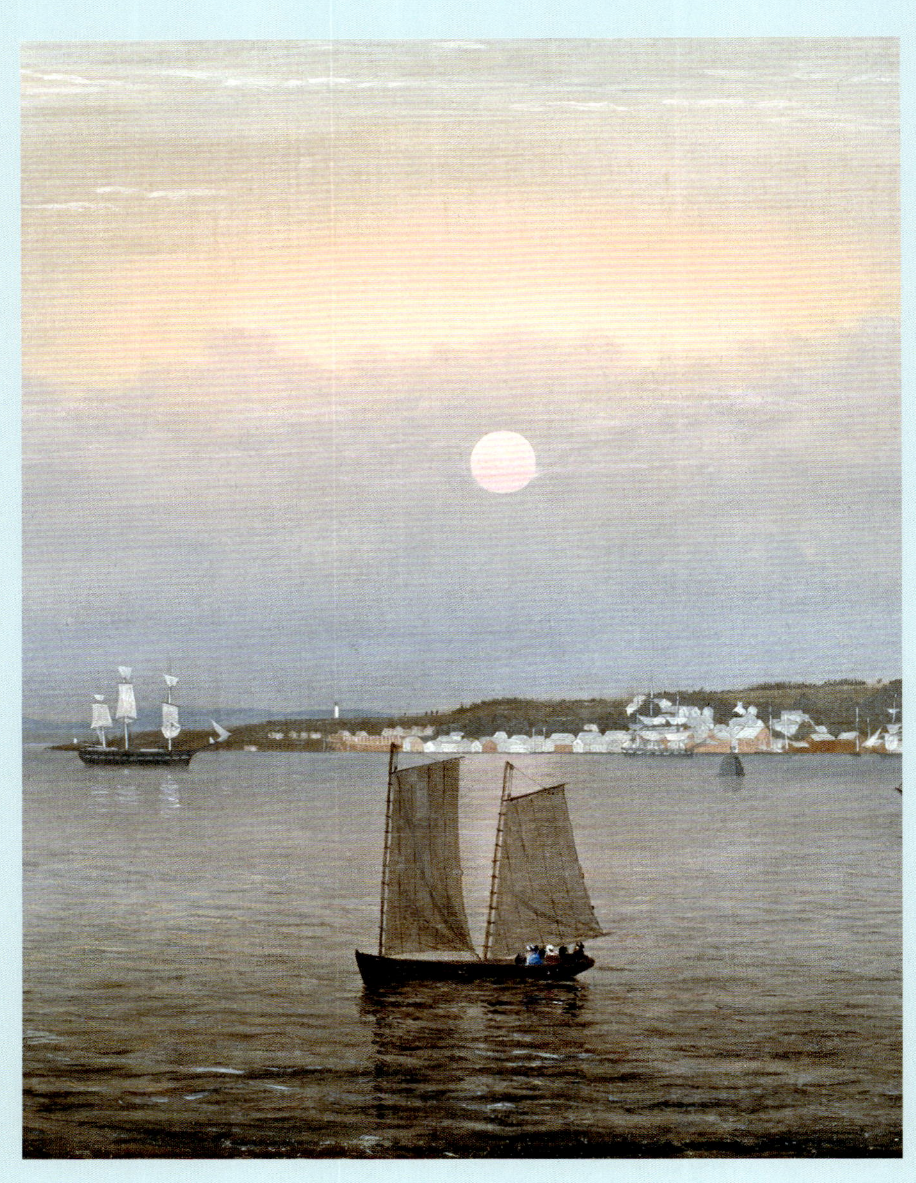

CONCLUSION

Looking at an image such as *Castine Harbor and Town* of 1851, it is easy to see why Lane's contemporaries admired his work and how audiences today find his paintings stunning (figs. 103 and 164). Two-thirds of this canvas is a meteorologically dramatic sky; pearlescent clouds frame the oculus of a sun setting behind a fog bank above a shimmering harbor. Vessels of all sizes punctuate the quiet of evening, their white sails catching the last sun. Most discussions of such Lane works draw on abstract words like "serenity," "calm," and "harmony" and reference both abstract geometry and the Transcendentalism of Ralph Waldo Emerson to gloss the scene, dodging or apologizing for the specific objects—buildings, vessel types, cargoes, human figures, hillsides—on view.

Without denying the extraordinary power of Lane's poetic mastery of cloud, tone, and atmospheric light, the project of this book has been to do readings of the paintings of Fitz Henry Lane that are rather different from the interpretive structures so popular in the literature. I am conscious that the emphasis in this study on environment, community, labor, and economic relations runs against the grain of commentary on Lane to date. My emphasis on human communities in relation to the natural world and on the conversion of that natural world into products of exchange evolved out of close looking at the works. This study takes the "incidental detail" of such a painting as *Castine Harbor and Town*, as well as its "harmony," seriously—the mariners managing sails and

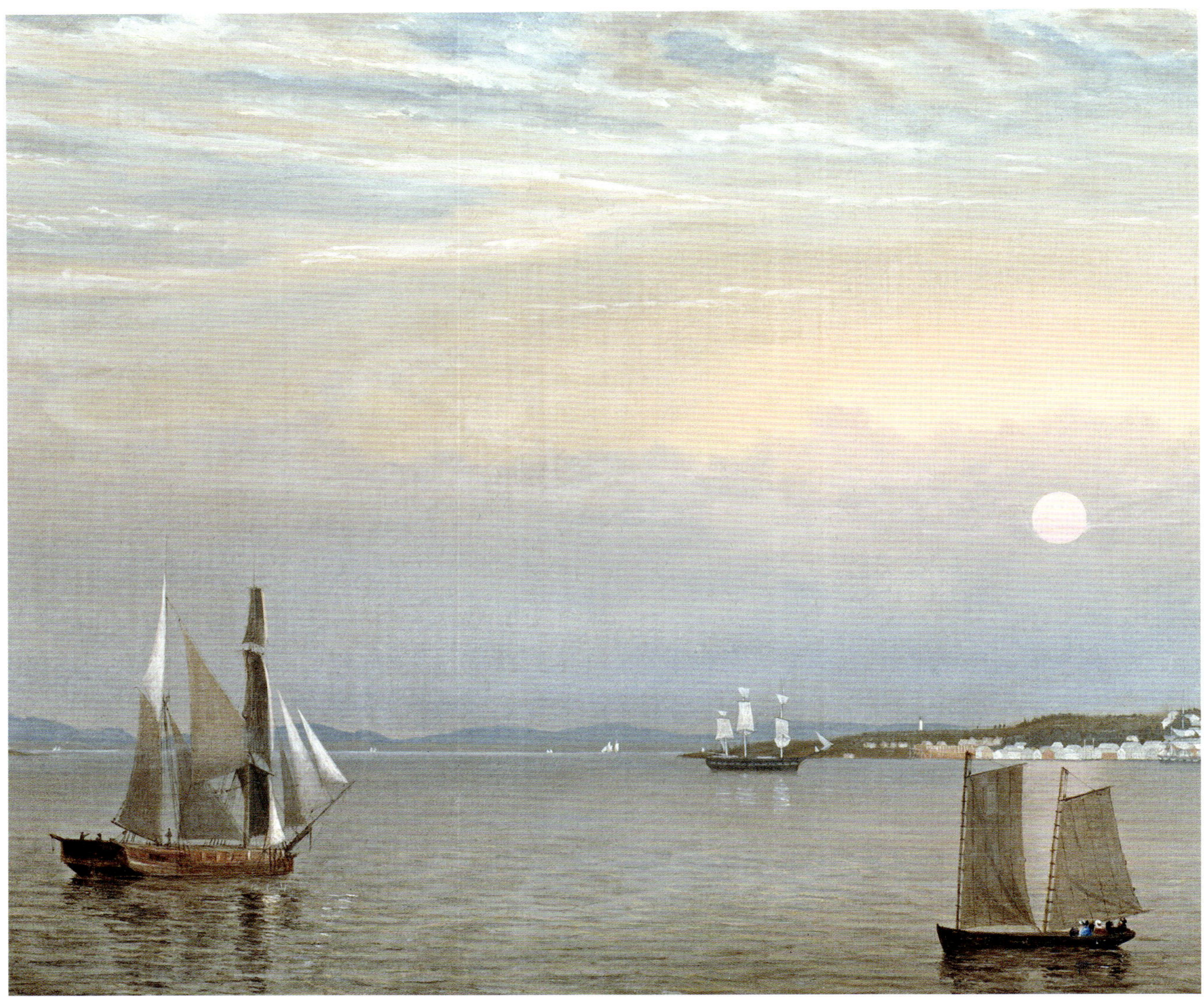

FIGURE 164
Fitz H. Lane, *Castine Harbor and Town*, 1851 (fig. 103), detail.

cargo, the lumber loaders' impressive superstructure of dimensional wood on the brig heading out into the Atlantic, the day-trippers on the foreground schooner admiring the evening light, and the gathered sense of community evident in the distant townscape that defines this harbor. I understand these to be visual events that matter. They mattered to the artist who constructed them as essential elements in his fiction, and they matter today as factoids of a past era in which the artist and his audience were embedded.

It is useful to try to recover what Lane's patrons admired in his work and what they thought they were purchasing when they commissioned paintings. And it is useful to try to understand how Lane's contemporaries understood their physical, social, and economic world as they saw it interpreted in his canvases. What they spoke about was his "accuracy": "We have never seen any paintings equal to his in *perfect accuracy* in all the details of marine architecture ... [similarly in] the whole details of the seacoast, the harbor or haven with its many or few vessels in storm or in calm, at sunset or sunrise; the rock bound coast with its gigantic boulders lashed by the surges of the storm, or gently washed by the still waters of a summer sea; the pebbly shore or the smooth sand beach, with the adjacent cliffs, light-houses and cottages."[1]

But this study is not a plea for a simpleminded endorsement of Lane's contemporaries' admiration for his "accuracy"; it is rather a plea for an enlarged context in which to see his work. It is also a critique of the contextualization of these works and their author in solely formalist terms, and it is an attempt to put that "Luminist"/ Emersonian interpretive slant in its own period-specific mid-twentieth-century High Modernist context. Part of the project here is to underline the fact that meaning is not "singular, lucid, and recoverable" but changes over time, and perhaps enlarges with successive generations.[2] Because of the moment in which I study these works, I am interested in the material world Lane pictures, on the one hand, and in the global reach of Lane's Gloucester, on the other. The project here is to open up the interpretive range to include consideration of all the elements pictured and all the elements that are implied by the lumber, cannon, baskets, rocks, fences, fish heads, "Surinamers," patched sails, loads of hay, Gothic gables, looming promontories, and laboring men that Lane so carefully describes.

Perhaps most emphatically, this study emphasizes the material basis of social, economic, and aesthetic experience in Lane's life, work, and culture. It takes seriously the raw materials of antebellum New England (granite, lumber, fish) as elements in Lane's fictions, and it attends to the roles of labor, knowledge, and social experience as he pictures them. It foregrounds *things*, the artisanal labor employed to make things, and it takes a particular interest in geographies of distance, cultural difference, and linkage. It takes account of Lane's interest in history, and time. It understands social contexts to have economic dimensions and looks closely at the strong links between his culture and distant parts of the globe.

The material evidences of human effort, intention, and achievement that are everywhere in Lane's canvases underline an important difference between his work and that of the Hudson River School painters, whose preference (and whose patrons' preference) was for the uninhabited landscapes of the wild parts of the continent. They painted, and were celebrated for painting, the superscaled unique features of Niagara, the Rocky Mountains, Yellowstone—Nature at its grandest, Nature making promises of imminent national prosperity. Lane's subjects are smaller in scale and more ambiguous in meaning. They picture inhabited places, such as Castine, with centuries of violent history, chameleon sovereignty in the world of clashing empires, and evidence of an uneasy coexistence between formerly hostile populations. A pearly sky suggests a pacific present, but everywhere Lane intimates that he also acknowledges the past, that he sees human history as an integral element of place.

The study offered here is also a departure in that it attends to the ways Lane made a living, built a reputation, and developed patrons. It uses Lane as a case study in canon formation, tracking the shifts in American culture as they dramatically affected the valuing, devaluing, and revaluing of his work.

The book's argument is that Lane's paintings were created as actors, responsive to their audiences, instructing viewers, through mime and fiction, how to see Gloucester and coastal Maine, to recognize in those places commerce, work, extraction industries, history, and the curious eye of tourism. The paintings express attitudes, create alliances, conjure memories and identities. They are works of the imagination that do cultural work: they say things that language cannot say, or that language says in different terms. Although fictions, they speak truths about community, commerce, death, and time through modest utterances focused on quotidian, even radically inconsequential, visual events. Although he painted nature and economic life, Lane is not an illustrator of Ralph Waldo Emerson on nature or John Ruskin on political economy. He is an artist who speaks to us as he did to his contemporaries, but distance makes it a little harder for us to hear. In order to begin to understand Lane's world from inside, I read contemporary accounts—in diaries, letters, tracts, memoirs, census records, maps, and court records, but especially in the Gloucester newspapers. Here one can read the almost-daily account of the time and place Lane knew so well, an account that Lane probably read, and doing that has been an education in itself. As the editor of the *Gloucester Telegraph* put it in May of 1850: "Some sagacious person has aptly styled newspapers the daily history of the world. They catch the living manners as they rise, record the hopes, and doubts, and fears, which agitate the public mind, the changes in law, morals, politics, trade. They chronicle facts for future historians, astronomers, geologists, statesmen, theologians. Taken together they form a complete abstract of the times in which they flourish."[3]

One could say equally that Lane's paintings offer an account of the daily history of his world, vignettes of everything important but spoken through the language of the incidental and quotidian. It is a world that, on canvas, evokes not narratives of national destiny but local knowledge and the threads that bind the local with the global. This is a strategy very different from that of his New York City contemporaries.

Lane's paintings elicit powerful responses from their viewers—recognition, memory, grief, terror, sorrow, longing, joy, and contemplative contentment. These responses register somewhat differently for different generations, but of these perhaps the most important to Lane and his immediate audience was memory. Memory is a portal to contemplation, sometimes to pain, and often to pleasure. Lane painted sites as they had appeared in his childhood (such as the fort in Gloucester Harbor); he painted places at which family and public events had occurred more than a century before his birth (Owl's Head); and he painted workers engaged in practices that had been supplanted by the time of his maturity (beachside fish cleaning). In these and many other instances, he designed his paintings to trigger double recognitions—of both time and place.

While by some measures long, this book still leaves much unsaid and underdeveloped, and it is my hope that others will expand questions broached here and will in this study find seeds of new questions for exploration and analysis. In terms of reading paintings and culture in tandem, there is much still to learn—for instance, about Lane—in uncovering and studying the patrons and the provenance of Lane's works. Object biographies speak eloquently about the variability of value and the disparate preoccupations of disparate decades, individuals, communities, and generations. By what steps, for instance, did dreamy *Castine Harbor and Town* move from the Castine chimneypiece of Noah Brooks, a prolific writer of biographies, travel guides, and boys' fiction—including romping adventures in the Wild West illustrated by Thomas Moran and Frederic Remington—and end up in San Diego?

Opportunities for further research include attentive study of Lane's pupils and their work. At least six men and women sought his tutelage, but little (beyond some research on Mary Mellen) is known about what they learned from him or how their work builds on his instruction and model.[4] While this line of inquiry has thus far been focused on separating Lane's work from Mellen's, investigation of the larger questions of Lane as a teacher may help explain how painting, outside of established centers such as New York and Boston, was taught to and learned by amateurs like the Mason sisters and aspiring professionals like William Bradford.[5] These are part of the Lane story as yet untold.

Fitz Henry Lane had a relatively short career as an artist—just twenty years—a modest education, and an outwardly circumscribed life, but his canvases make clear exactly what a canny observer, recorder, interpreter, and communicator he was of the salient aspects of his time and place. And he was alert to how the distant past and the globally remote resonated with that localness and temporal immediacy. Both modest and worldly patrons came to his granite studio and trusted him to express their understanding of their place in the world, to show them what they saw and how they saw, to remind them and perhaps to exhort them. Tumultuous and precarious or calm and expressive of reconciliation, his paintings speak to us today somewhat differently but nevertheless powerfully. Just sixty when he stretched his last canvas, I suspect Lane would have agreed with his ruminating and mortally ill contemporary Charles C. Emerson: "I am pleased to find how sufficient is life for the purposes of life. It is long enough to let us look about ourselves, examine our chart, determine our true place & destination in the universe and it comes to an end before the oil of Hope runs dry."[6]

APPENDIX A

EXHIBITIONS AND SALES THAT INCLUDED FITZ H. LANE PAINTINGS DURING HIS LIFETIME

Note: Catalogue numbers, when known, precede titles. Measurements bearing asterisks were originally given with width before height, as nineteenth-century lists tend to give them.

AMERICAN ART-UNION

1841 97. *Ship in a Gale*. For sale. [Apollo Association]

1847 114. *Marine View*. To P. P. Bradish, Lyons, NY. [In lottery]

1848 59. *Ipswich Bay*. To Major Philip Kearny, U.S. Army, New York. [In lottery]
204. *Landscape—Rockport Beach*. To Ebenezer Collamore, New York. [In lottery]

1849 197. *View in Boston Harbor*. *27 × 34 in. "A Merchant vessel with a lighter alongside. On the right a man-of-war. Beyond is the city of Boston." To A. B. Smith, Madison, IN. [In lottery]
245. *New York from Jersey City, New Jersey*. *16 × 25 in. "The bay with ships and steam boats; in the blue distance the spires of the city." To F. Falkland, New York. [In lottery]
344. *Twilight on the Kennebec*. *20 × 30 in. "The western sky is still glowing in the rays of the setting sun. In the foreground is a vessel lying in the shadow. The river stretches across the picture." To W. H. Wheeler, Lynn, MA. [In lottery]
411. *View on the Penobscot*. To Mrs. Alex. Stott, New York. [In lottery]

1850 36. *New York Harbor*. *28 × 42 in. "Vessels of all kinds lying at anchor or sailing. In the distance the spires of the city." To Joseph Johnson, New York. [In lottery]

Source: Mary Bartlett Cowdrey, *American Academy of Fine Arts and American Art-Union, 1816–1852* (New York: New-York Historical Society, 1953), 2:220–21.

AMERICAN ART-UNION DISPERSAL SALE

1852 206. *Marine View—Coast of Maine*. *23 × 34 in. "A Sunset scene. On the left are a promontory and light-house, and on the right a ship lying at anchor." $50.00. [To] A. Edwards.

Source: Mary Bartlett Cowdrey, *American Academy of Fine Arts and American Art-Union, 1816–1852* (New York: New-York Historical Society, 1953), 2:221. See also *New York Times*, December 17, 1852.

BLEECKER SALE

A. J. Bleecker Son & Co., over Goupil's, 772 Broadway, corner 9th Street, New York City, February 22 and 23, 1861.

1861 7. *Cod Fishing on the Bank*

59. *After Storm*

92. *~~Storm~~ Calm at Sea* [correction in 1961 list, possibly copied from source]

100. *View in New York Harbor*

127. *View of Boston Harbor*

Source: Frick Art Reference Research Sheet, January 1961. Typescript at CAM.

THE BOSTON ARTISTS' ASSOCIATION

1842 *Britannia in a Gale*

1844 *Lying To for a Pilot in Boston Bay*

1845 *The Voyage* [series]: *The Departure, Fine Weather, Stiff Breeze, Storm and Wreck, Calm After the Storm*

1850 *View of Gloucester*

Sources: Leah Lipton, "The Boston Artists' Association, 1841–1851," *American Art Journal* 15, no. 4 (Autumn 1983): 45–57. Lipton reports that the Boston Artists' Association exhibitions were housed at Harding's Gallery at 22 School Street 1841–46, then from 1846 at 37 Tremont Row; see also Travers Newton and Marcia Steele, "The Series Paintings of Fitz Henry Lane: From Field Sketch to Studio Painting," in *Emil Bosshard, Paintings Conservator (1945–2006): Essays by Friends and Colleagues*, ed. Maria de Peverelli, Marco Grassi, and Hans-Christoph von Imhoff (Florence: Centro Di, 2009), 198.

BOSTON ATHENAEUM

1841 85. *Sea Beach*. For sale.

104. *Scene at Sea*. For sale.

1845 3. *View of the Town and Harbor of Gloucester*.

85. *Marine View in Boston Harbor*. For sale.

1846 51. *View of the Navy Yard—in Charlestown*. For sale.

168. *View of a Steam-Vessel (The Cutter McLane)*. Capt. Howard.

1847 116. *Marine View*.

1848 20. *View of Little Good Harbor Beach, Cape Ann*.

1850 261. *Marine View*. J. Burnett.

1855 218. *Mt. Desert Light House*.

1857 329. *Manchester Harbor*. T. J. Herring.

1858 232. *Boston Harbor*. For sale.

1859 278. *The Outward Bound*. For sale.

138. *Sunset in the Bay*. For sale.

197. *Sunset After a Storm*. For sale.

1860 230. *Approaching Storm*. For sale.

1864 247. *Boston Harbor*. G. B. Upton.

300. *A (Foggy) Morning*. T. Wigglesworth.

1865 262. *Egg Rock, Nahant*. G. W. Wales.

Sources: Robert F. Perkins Jr. and William J. Gavin III, eds., Mary Margaret Shaughnessy, asst. ed., *The Boston Athenaeum Art Exhibition Index, 1827–1874* (Boston: Library of the Boston Athenaeum, 1980). F. H. Lane, "Address: 1841, 1842, Boston; 1845–47, Tremont Temple," 90. See also Frederic Alan Sharf, "Fitz Hugh [*sic*] Lane Re-considered," *Essex Institute Historical Collections* 96 (January 1960), 77.

BOSTON MECHANICS' ASSOCIATION

1847 1109. One marine painting and one framed print. "The painting is very well drawn, but wanting in coloring and aerial perspective."

Source: Catalogue through Smithsonian Institution Research Information System, Pre-1877 Art Exhibition Catalogue Index, http://siris-artexhibition.si.edu/ipac20/ipac.jsp?, accessed April 28, 2010.

FAIR AT GLOUCESTER TOWN HALL

1850 *Stiff Breeze in NY Harbor*. Exhibited.

Source: Sarah Dunlap and Stephanie Buck, *Fitz Henry Lane, Family and Friends* (Gloucester, MA: Church & Mason Publishing and Cape Ann Historical Museum, 2007), 56.

NATIONAL ACADEMY OF DESIGN

1859 269. Glouces*ter Fish[in]g Sch[oone]r on Georges Bank*. H. Hitchins. "By Fritz [*sic*] H. Lane."

Source: *National Academy of Design Exhibition Record, 1826–1860* (New York: New-York Historical Society, 1943), 1:283.

NEW ENGLAND ART UNION

1851 27. *Ship of the Line* Ohio. For Sale, $35.00.

49. *Gloucester Harbor, Hazy Afternoon*. For Sale, $87.00

Source: *Catalogue of Paintings Now on Exhibition in the Free Gallery of the New England Art Union* (Boston: Dutton & Wentworth, 1851), 6 and 7.

APPENDIX B

INVENTORIES AND LISTS OF LOCATED LANE PAINTINGS, 1865–1961

GLOUCESTER ART AND LOAN EXHIBITION PICTURE CATALOGUE, 1892

Excerpts from *Memorial of the Celebration of the Two Hundred and Fiftieth Anniversary of the Founding of Gloucester in 1642* (Boston: Alfred Mudge & Son, 1892), 247–66. This exhibition of 314 items was held at the high school; it included "quaint old furniture," cradles, "shoes worn by a Chinese Lady," photos of Copley portraits, etc., as well as the artworks listed in the picture catalogue.

Lane works:

Title	Lender
3 Marines	C. W. Trask
A Marine	S. A. Stacy
A Smart Blow	S. A. Stacy
A Marine	S. A. Stacy
View of Gloucester	J. J. Healy
Coffin's Beach	D. W. Low
Scene in Maine	Mrs. Chas. P. Thompson
View of Gloucester	F. W. Tibbets
Mount Desert	Mrs. David Plumer [Elizabeth C. Procter]
Portrait	Mrs. J. J. Babson
Harbor View	Mrs. J. J. Babson
Riverdale	Mrs. E. P. Ring
Marine	Allan Rogers
View of Gloucester	Dr. Conant
Portrait	Fred L. Stacy
Last of the Surinam Fleet	Mrs. J. M. Todd
Sketch	George J. Marsh
Schooner	John Lloyd
Baker's Island	William Gardner

Selected related non-Lane works:

Title	Artist	Lender
Copy from Lane	[Salisbury] Tuckerman	C. E. Grover
Canal Beach, Stage Fort, and Norman's Woe	M. B. Mellen after FHLane	Mrs. Edward Grover
Old Fort & Ten Pound Island	[no artist listed]	Mrs. Edward Grover
Artist Brook, White Mountains	Champney	C. E. Grover
View of Gloucester, 1817	Capt. John Beach Jr.	Mrs. Asa G. Andrews
Portrait	Major John Mason	[no owner listed]
After the Storm	J. M. Barnsley	Alex Pattillo
Portrait	[no artist listed]	Master Moore
Study of the Loaf, Coffin's Beach	William Morris Hunt	Miss Hovey
Century Room, Hovey Mansion, Fresh Water Cove	[no artist listed]	Miss Hovey

PUBLISHED INVENTORY OF LANE PAINTINGS, *GLOUCESTER DAILY TIMES*, FEBRUARY 24, 1916

From Susan Babson, "Fitz H. Lane," C. A. S. & L. A. Weekly Column on Matters of Local History: "The historical department of the CAS&LA have gathered the following facets in regard to the life and work of Fitz H. Lane, marine painter and would be glad of any further information which may be sent to the *Gloucester Daily Times*."

We have located in town the following paintings:
Gloucester in 1844 from Rocky Neck
On a Lea Shore
An Old Clipper Ship
Old Wharf, Scene with Surrinamer [*sic*] *Brig at Anchor*
Moon Rise, Mt. Desert, Me.
Fresh Water Cove and the Harbor, Vessel in Ice
Owl's Head, Me. (3 paintings of this subject)
Fresh Water Cove
Marshes in Annisquam River
City of Gloucester
Manchester Beach
Ship Cadette [*sic*], *Edward Babson, Master*
Gloucester Harbor
Norman's Woe and Coast
Pavilion Beach
Bear Island off Maine Coast
Maine Coast, Taken from Castine
Composition
View Half Moon Beach and Stage Rocks
Bouquet of Flowers
View from the Harbor of the Old Fort
Brook-bank
Vessel at Sea
Brace's Cove and Rocks
Rough Water
Salt Island
Annisquam River (lower part)
Little River

Paintings that have gone out of town are:
Half Way Rock
Steamship in a Rough Sea
Half Moon Beach
Church Green
View of the Low-Babson House, Taken from Town Landing
Ship in a Storm
Square Rigged Ship in Gloucester Harbor
Brace's Cove and Rock
Sunset Scene

Indian Bar, Castine
Sunset in Camden, Me.
A View of Half Moon Beach and Stage Fort
A View of the Inner Harbor
Yacht Race off Cape Ann
Also a picture of a wreck on a beach (*Dream Painting*)

MANUSCRIPT PARTIAL INVENTORY IN CAM LIBRARY/ARCHIVES, MARCH 1916

The author of this partial inventory is unknown, but probably Susan Babson.

Sunset and [??] off Mt Desert 1859 given to Lizzie Plummer [by F. H. Lane] as wedding present. [See *Gloucester Daily Times*, March 2, 1916.]
Small picture of him at my home.
Two in town hall destroyed by fire.
1 given by John Trask. Council Chamber (advertising Sign) *California* owned by late George Rogers.
Painting [*Gloucester Harbor*, 1852] given by Mrs. [Cassie Mason Myers] Julian-James. Mayor[']s office.
Lchang [?] Old Surinamer given by Mrs. John Tod. [Judith M. Todd gave *Old Surinamer in Gloucester Harbor* to the Sawyer Free Library, according to the *Gloucester Daily Times*, March 2, 1916.]
. . .
Mr. [Joseph] Stevens [Jr.] owned several fine pictures among which he loaned the view of Gloucester.
Common-wealth club and the *Yacht America* loaned to the Business[?] Men's club (at one time interested admirers tried to buy the view of the city for Gloucester but could not raise the money for which Mr. Stevens was willing to sell).
In 1858 Mr. L was engaged in painting 'Landing at Cape Ann in 1623['] inspired by a visit from [J. Wingate] Thornton . . . for frontispiece to new edition [of his book]. [See GDT March 1, 1916.]

INVENTORY KNOWN TO THE FRICK ART REFERENCE LIBRARY, 1938

This list is derived from a letter from Frick reference librarian Miss Ethelwyn Manning, December 8, 1938, to Alfred Mansfield Brooks in the Brick House, Middle Street, Gloucester, Massachusetts, describing five Lane paintings of which the library had photographs (CAM files). Manning: "One of them is signed F. H. Lane 1852. They are all marines and the artist may have come from Gloucester as four of them were originally owned by a Mr. Sidney Mason of Gloucester and New York. . . . If the artist you are interested in is the same as the one whose works we have listed . . . , we shall like to know the whereabouts of any other pictures by him."

Title	Owner
Gloucester Harbor, Massachusetts	Mrs. John Rutherfoord [*sic*] 1602 Twentieth St. NW Washington, DC
San Juan Harbor, Porto Rico	Mrs. John Rutherfoord [*sic*] 1602 Twentieth St. NW Washington, DC
New York Harbor	Mr. Lewis Gouverneur Morris Union Club, New York City
First regatta of NY Yacht Club	Mr. Lewis Gouverneur Morris Union Club, New York City B. Bogart, photographer
First regatta of NY Yacht Club	Mr. Lewis Gouverneur Morris Union Club, New York City B. Bogart, photographer

LOCATIONS OF PAINTINGS BY INDIVIDUAL OWNER, COMPILED BY SUSAN BABSON, 1938

This list combines the handwritten and typewritten lists compiled by Susan Babson of the Cape Ann Scientific Literary and Historical Association.

George B. Stevens—Gloucester [annotation: Alice Stevens]
1. Bear Island, Maine
2. Twilight over the water with Light-House building on point of land at right boat at left.
3. Pencil drawing of Groups of Ships
   Square rigger in center, 3 other ships.
4. Small oil study of Boats in smooth water
5. Small oil study of single storm tossed ship
6. Lithograph of Gloucester Harbor

Miss Mary L. Stacy (deceased), James Stacy,
Middle St. Gloucester [annotation: Lewis]
1. Owl's Head
2. Rough Sea
3. Salt Island—very lovely
4. Little River (large painting—figures in foreground)
5. Lower part of Squam River. Large painting
6. Bouquet of flowers—Painted for Catalina Davis' mother and given to James Stacy, small picture.

Miss Isabel Lane—Gloucester [annotation: C. A. S.]
1. Ship Cadette 16 × 24 in. (Edward Babson Master)
2. Gloucester Harbor
3. Norman's Woe Coast 22¼ × 35 in.

Mr. Samuel Mansfield
1. and 2. Owl's Head Maine in two pictures (framed in 2 separate frames)
3. Manchester Beach
4. Lithograph of Gloucester Harbor
5. Gloucester Harbor

Pierpont E. Johnson—New York
1. South West Harbor, Maine

Miss Alice Woodbury—Winter Park, Florida
1. Calm Sea

Mrs. George B. Stevens, Manthorn Rd., West Roxbury.
1. Two pictures of ships (one a steamship in rough sea at twilight)
2. Brace's Cove [annotation: CA?] [annotation: deceased]

Mrs. Leary Swan—40 Manthorn Rd. West Roxbury
1. One painting not named

Mrs. John Whistler 517 Howard St., Santa Rosa Cal.
(Delhi, Calif.)
1. Sunset in Camden Hills [annotation: ?]

Mrs. John Graham Brooks (deceased) Cambridge, Mass.
Son: Judge Lawrence Brooks, 8 Francis Ave., Cambridge
1. Gloucester Harbor [annotation: Medford]

Mr. John N. Estabrook, Morris D. 26, Soldier's Field
Boston Mass.
1. The Fort [annotation: CA]
2. Sea Scene with boat [annotation: CA]

Gilbert L. Patillo—673 Boylston St., Boston
1. Painted Lithograph of Gloucester Harbor

Alfred M. Brooks—Gloucester
1. Somes' Sound [annotation: CA]

Mrs. J. Everett Garland (deceased) [annotation: children of]
Mr. Kimball Garland—Newton, Mass. [annotation: Mrs. Lewis Swamscott]
1. Owl's Head
2. Half Way Rock

Miss Adeline Procter—Gloucester
1. Fresh Water Cove

Mr. Edward Babson Stanwood, Marysville, Cal.
1. View of Gloucester Harbor with 10 L [Pound] Island.

Mr. William Gardner, deceased
1. Norman's Woe [annotation: unable to trace]

Mrs. James H. Mansfield, deceased
1. Ship in a Storm [annotation: unable to trace]

Mrs. Helen Kimball—Concord, N. H.
1. View of Half Moon Beach & Stage Fort
2. View of the Inner Harbor [annotation: not verified]

Mrs. Louise S. Campbell—206 Inwood Ave., Upper Montclair, N. J.
1. Boats on Ice
2. Fresh Water Cove, 1848
3. Owls Head, Penobscot Bay, 1862 [annotation: sold (Karolik)]

Mrs. Harriet G. Whitman—Augusta, Maine
1. & 2. Vessel owned by Mr. Geo. Rogers returning from Surrinam [*sic*] and a vessel owned by Mr. Homans sailing for same port
3. View of Samuel E Sawyer's Estate, located in Gloucester, including the woods & coast line at Fresh Water Cove [annotation: Karolik]
This last picture is in Mrs. Whitman's house on Mason St, Gloucester

Mrs. J. F. Locke (deceased)
Son: 7 Elmore St., Dorchester, Mass
1. Indian Bar, Castine, Me.
2. Sunset in Gloucester Harbor
3. Pencil Sketch, Castine Harbor [annotation: (*not found*)]

Richard Fisher—Gloucester
1. Norman's Woe

Sargent Murray Gilman Hough House—Gloucester
1. Old Fort, foot of Commercial Street, 1853

City Hall—Gloucester
1. Vessel on Railway said to be the California Commanded by Capt. Solomon Center [annotation: CA]
2. View of Gloucester, painted 1852, Gift of Mrs. Cassie James [annotation: CA]

Sawyer Free Library—Gloucester
1. Portrait of himself [annotation: unaccountably lost]
2. Brookbank
3. View from old fort
4. Ship picture [annotation: ?]

Addison Gilbert Hospital—Gloucester
1. Old Fort and 10 Pound Island From Fr Healys estate

Cape Ann Scientific Literary & Historical Assoc.
1. Owls Head, By will from Catalina Davis
2. Half Moon Beach, ditto
3. Church Green with view of hills beyond
4. Town Landing & Gambrel roof house (Babson House) Gift of Roger W. Babson
5. Rough Sea, Gift of Mr. & Mrs. Brooks
6. Half Moon Beach, Gift of Mrs. Thos. M. Babson
7. Painted lithograph of Gloucester Harbor, From Fred. Tibbets Esq.
8. Storm at Sea, Gift of [?] Trask
9. Box of drawings—important Gift of Samuel H. Mansfield

Mrs. David Low, [98 Pedrson Drive, Ashville, NC]
1. Braces Cove

New York Yacht-club
1. Yacht race off Cape Ann 1848 or '50

Presented by Mrs. James, Washington D.C.
Peabody Museum Salem
1. Yacht America winning the international race in 1851

This painting belonged to Tyler family and was taken over by the Fine Art Museum of Boston, later it was transferred to the Peabody Museum.

Judge Sumner D. York, Rockport
1. Painting

PHOTOGRAPHS AT THE FRICK ART REFERENCE LIBRARY, 1961

"Fitz Hugh Lane Photographs at the Frick Art Reference [Library], New York City January 1961" (typescript in the CAM Library files).

Title, Size & Inscription	Owner
1. *The Packet* Boston *of Gloucester [Burning]* 20 × 28 in.	Cape Ann Association, Gloucester, MA
2. *Two Ships in Harbor* ca. 16 × 24¼ in.	Cape Ann Association
3. *Southwest Harbor, Maine* 30? × 40 in. Signed lower right: "F. H. Lane 1852"	Pierrepont E. Johnson Collection
4. *Shore Near Gloucester, Massachusetts* ca. 22¼ × 36 in.	Miss Isabel Lane
5. *Ship* Cadet ca. 16 × 24 in.	Miss Isabel Lane
6. *First Regatta of the New York Yacht Club* no measurements "Painted by Fitz H. Lane, 1856, for Sidney Mason of Gloucester and New York"	Lewis G[ouverneur] Morris
7. *First Regatta of the New York Yacht Club* no measurements, different scene "Painted by Fitz H. Lane, 1856, for Sidney Mason of Gloucester and New York"	Lewis G[ouverneur] Morris
8. *New York Harbor* ca. 24 × 36 in. Signed and dated lower right: "F. H. Lane, 1852"	Lewis Gouverneur Morris

Title, Size & Inscription	Owner
9. *Gloucester Harbor* ca. 24 × 39 in.	Old Print Shop
10. *Yacht Racing*	Mrs. John Rutherford, Washington, DC (cousin of Sidney Mason's granddaughter)
11. *Gloucester Harbor, Mass.*	Mrs. John Rutherford, Washington, DC (cousin of Sidney Mason's granddaughter)
12. *San Juan Harbor, Porto Rico* 24 × 36 in.	Mrs. John Rutherford
13. *Two Ships* 6¼ × 9½ in., cardboard Inscribed on back: "Fitz H. Lane to his friend Joseph L. Stevens, Jr., Gloucester February, 1857."	George B. Stevens, Gloucester

NOTES

INTRODUCTION

1. Franklin Kelly, "Lane and Church in Maine," in *Paintings by Fitz Hugh Lane*, exh. cat., ed. John Wilmerding (Washington, DC: National Gallery of Art, 1988), 144, 153; John Wilmerding, *Fitz Hugh Lane* (New York: Praeger, 1971; repr., with the title *Fitz Henry Lane*, Gloucester, MA: CAM, 2005), 27, 31, 46, 61.
2. For instance, Thomas Moran's painting *The Grand Canyon of the Yellowstone* (1872) and the mammoth plate photographs by Carleton Watkins; see Richard A. Grusin, *Culture, Technology, and the Creation of America's National Parks* (Cambridge: Cambridge University Press, 2004), 25, 63; and Alan C. Braddock and Karl Kusserow, "Introduction" in Karl Kusserow and Alan C. Braddock, *Nature's Nation: American Art and Environment* (Princeton: Princeton University Press, 2018), 15–17.
3. David C. Huntington, *Landscapes of Frederic Edwin Church: Vision of an American Era* (New York: Braziller, 1966), 1, 9, 10, 17, 34, 39, and passim. Coining the term "Manifest Destiny," journalist John L. O'Sullivan was specifically discussing Texas and Oregon. See O'Sullivan, "Annexation," *United States Magazine and Democratic Review* 17, no. 85 (July–August 1845): 5–10, and *New York Morning News*, December 27, 1845.
4. W. J. T. Mitchell, "Imperial Landscape," in *Landscape and Power*, ed. W. J. T. Mitchell (Chicago: University of Chicago Press, 1994), 10.
5. Rebecca Bedell, *The Anatomy of Nature: Geology and American Landscape Painting, 1825–1875* (Princeton: Princeton University Press, 2001); Rachael Ziady DeLue, *George Inness and the Science of Landscape* (Chicago: University of Chicago Press, 2005); Jennifer Raab, *Frederic Church: The Art and Science of Detail* (New Haven: Yale University Press, 2015).
6. See, for instance, Barbara Novak, *American Painting of the Nineteenth Century: Realism, Idealism, and the American Experience* (New York: Praeger, 1969), 96–99, 105, 110–11, 122–23; Barbara Novak, "On Defining Luminism," in *American Light: The Luminist Movement, 1850–1875; Paintings, Drawings, Photographs*, exh. cat., ed. John Wilmerding (Washington, DC: National Gallery of Art, 1980), 28; Earl A. Powell III, "Luminism and the American Sublime," in ibid., 72, 78; and John Wilmerding, "The Luminist Movement: Some Reflections," in ibid., 97, 98.
7. John Wilmerding, "The Master of the Silvery Mist," *Wall Street Journal*, April 5–6, 2014, C13; Karen E. Quinn, Sandra Kelberlau, and Jean Woodward, "Rediscovering Fitz Henry Lane's *View of Coffin's Beach* on Cape Ann," *Antiques* 170, no. 1 (July 2006): 69.
8. For the facts of Lane's life, see Sarah Dunlap and Stephanie Buck, *Fitz Henry Lane, Family and Friends: Nathaniel Rogers Lane–Fitz Henry Lane, December 19, 1805–August 13, 1865* (hereafter *FHL*) (Gloucester, MA: Church & Mason Publishing and Cape Ann Historical Museum, 2007) and http://fitzhenrylaneonline.org/page/?name=biography.
9. Joseph Moore, kin to notable British mathematician Sir Hamilton Moore, taught Stephen and Edward Lane, but his account book contains no record of his having taught the future artist. Dolliver/Moore Papers, Archive Collection 34 / Document Box P 23, CAM; Dunlap and Buck, *FHL*, 10–11, 14, 16; *GT* 5, no. 44 (Saturday, October 29, 1831).
10. According to a contemporary, "At the age of eighteen months, while playing in the yard or garden of his father, he ate some of the seeds of the apple-peru [tomato]; and was so unfortunate as to lose the use of his lower limbs in consequence." John J. Babson, *History of the Town of Gloucester, Cape Ann, Including the Town of Rockport* (Gloucester, MA: Procter Brothers, 1860; repr., Gloucester, MA: Peter Smith, 1972), 258.
11. Lane's partner, J. W. A. Scott, is quoted at length in an undated, incomplete newspaper clipping concerning the early years of lithography in Boston and especially his own and Lane's years at Pendleton's shop. AAS clipping collection of Charles Henry Taylor. See Dunlap and Buck, *FHL*, 36–47; David Tatham, "The Pendleton-Moore Shop: Lithographic Artists in Boston, 1825–1840," *Old-Time New England* 62, no. 2, serial no. 226 (October–December 1971): 38–42; Frederic Alan Sharf, "Fitz Hugh Lane Re-considered," *Essex Institute Historical Collections* 96 (January 1960): 76; Edward H. Lane, "Early Recollections of Artist Fitz H. Lane," C. A. S. & L. A. Weekly Column on Matters of Local History, *GDT*, March 23, 1916, "Clippings," CAM: "Before he became an artist he worked for a short time making shoes, but after a while, seeing that he could draw pictures better than he could

make shoes he went to Boston and took lessons in drawing and painting and became a marine artist"; *Stimpson's Boston Directory* of 1840, in which Lane is listed as "marine painter," as he is on a business card stored at CAM; and J. J. Babson, *History of the Town of Gloucester*, 258: "He . . . received no instruction in the rules [of art] till he went to Boston, at the age of twenty-eight, to work in Pendleton's lithographic establishment."

12. See http://fitzhenrylaneonline.org/catalog/entry.php?id=268, accessed August 5, 2019, catalogue entry for *The Yacht* Northern Light *in Boston Harbor*.
13. Lane is referenced with "Esq.," for instance, in the newspaper accounts of his participation in the town's 1849 "Floral Procession" (*GT*, July 4, 1849, and July 7, 1849, "Clippings," CAM), and in the account of one of his works (*CAA*, August 1, 1857, "Clippings," CAM). The butchering of sheep took place at Joseph Shepherd's building just behind the Burnham Railways. Fred W. Tibbets, "Fitz H. Lane," C. A. S. & L. A. Weekly Column on Matters of Local History, *GDT*, March 9, 1916, "Clippings," CAM.
14. This skewed gender demographic is reported in *GT* 3, no. 11 (May 16, 1829); by midcentury Gloucester's demographics had achieved a more even distribution with in-migration from abroad, but equilibrium was still not achieved, due to the loss of men in the fisheries, the Civil War, and California migration. See, for instance Joseph C. G. Kennedy, comp., *Population of the United States in 1860* (Washington, DC: Government Printing Office, 1864), 221.
15. The notations made, probably after his death, by his friend Joseph L. Stevens Jr. on his topographic drawings—105 of which are at CAM—constitute the best documentation of his commissions.
16. "He painted two yacht races of Newport and received five hundred dollars for each of them." From "Notes on the Life of Fitz Henry Lane as Given by John Trask of Gloucester to Emma Todd (now Mrs. Howard P. Elwell) about 1885," transcribed by Todd's daughter L. Elwell, CAM. F. E. Church sold *Heart of the Andes* in 1859 for $10,000; see Kevin J. Avery, *Church's Great Picture, "The Heart of the Andes"* (New York: Metropolitan Museum of Art, 1993), 32.
17. John C. Gray, *Essays: Agricultural and Literary* (Boston: Little, Brown, 1856), 40. Francis Bennett Jr., diary, 1852–54, unpaginated MS, AAS, noted in March 1853 that he received $110 that year working for Samuel Stevens in Gloucester as a sixteen-year-old and the following year noted that he earned $251 working for Charles F. Hovey in Boston as a seventeen-year-old (August 3). W. P. Tilden, an experienced minister, earned $700 in 1854 and by the time he commissioned a painting by Lane, in 1864, was earning $1,500/year. William Phillips Tilden, *Autobiography and Personal Tributes* (Boston: Press of George H. Ellis, 1891), 125, 145.
18. Annette Babson (1815–1884), unpaginated diary, entry for September 23, 1848, CAM; this event is reported in *CAL & GT* for September 23, 1848: an estimated five hundred vessels in the harbor that night, at times more than a hundred of them under sail, entering the harbor "four and six abreast." The population of Gloucester was estimated to be 8,000 in 1829 (*GT* 3, no. 11 [March 7, 1929]), 6,000 in 1848 (*CAL & GT* 22, no. 15 [April 8, 1848]), and was counted at 7,416 in the 1850 census (*GT* 14, no. 60 [July 27, 1850]). The population of the Cape Ann peninsula was estimated at 10,000 in 1848 (*CAL & GT* 22, no. 15 [April 8, 1848]).
19. *CAL & GT*, April 8, 1848.
20. Rich Edward C. Hoyt, "Industrial Statistics of Gloucester [. . .] for the Year Ending May 1, 1865," *CAA*, August 25, 1865.
21. In 1865 Gloucester produced 420,000 pounds of dressed beef and 29,500 pounds of dressed pork; it manufactured 6,000 casks to ship this meat. *CAA*, August 25, 1865.
22. Reprinted from "John Neal's Yankee," *GT* 2, no. 46 (Saturday, November 8, 1828).
23. *GT* 4, no. 24 (June 12, 1830).
24. *GT* 4, no. 33 (August 14, 1830).
25. "Yankee Enterprise," repr. from the *Pawtucket (RI) Chronicle* in *GT* 4, no. 3 (January 16, 1830).
26. Most of these items are preserved at the Cape Ann Museum (formerly the Cape Ann Historical Association), for the most part in "Fitz H. Lane: Notes & Clippings from Authors & Artists of Cape Ann Scrapbook and other Sources," CAM 759.13 L24, gift of Mrs. Carrie Mason Myers Julian-James, granddaughter of Lane's principal patron, Sidney Mason. Five of the drawings were sold by CAM in the 1960s to the Farnsworth Museum in Rockland, Maine, and to a pair of private collectors. A few letters from F. H. Lane to Joseph L. Stevens Jr. (n.d.) and to Joseph L. Stevens Sr. (January 29, 1851; February 9, 1853; and n.d.), and others concerning him (e.g., Helen Stevens Babson to Susan Babson, June 10, 1929), are also preserved at CAM. An account by William Howe Witherle of an excursion by Lane and friends to Maine is at the Wilson Museum in Castine, ME.
27. The Day Book of George W. Floyd, 1848–49, CAM, contains entries for "F. H. Lane" for livery rentals January 3 ($5.00), June 25 ($2.00), and October 2 ($5.00), 1849.
28. The painting in the Huntington Library and Art Gallery collection now known as *Sailing Ships off the Coast of New England* (83.8.31) was, according to curatorial files, exhibited and illustrated in the 1960s and 1970s variously as *Scene on the New England Coast*, *Ships off Cape Ann*, *Ships off the Marine Shore*, *Off the New England Coast*, *Sailing Ships off the New England Coast*, *Ships off Cape Ann Shore*, *Ships off the Maine Shore*, and *Sailing off Cape Ann*, finally getting its generic and current title in 1977.
29. Those instrumental in preserving Lane's drawings, his paintings, and his memory were Joseph Stevens Jr. (1865–1908), Samuel H. Mansfield

(in the early twentieth century), Fred Tibbets (in the 1920s), Alfred Mansfield Brooks (in the 1930s and '40s), and John I. H. Baur (in the 1950s).

30. The CAM's partial but richly annotated online catalogue raisonné, *Fitz Henry Lane Online*, http://fitzhenrylaneonline.org, was launched in March 2016; key figures in this project were Sam Holdsworth, Erik Ronnberg, and Melissa Trafton.

31. Documentation concerning students and copyists of Lane: Mary Mellen (Alfred Mansfield Brooks, "Communication," *Essex Institute Historical Collections* 96, no. 1 [January 1960]: 73–74; Dunlap and Buck, *FHL*, 87–99; John Wilmerding, *Fitz Henry Lane and Mary Blood Mellen: Old Mysteries and New Discoveries*, exh. cat. [New York: Spanierman Gallery, 2007]); Salisbury Tuckerman (see "Gloucester Art and Loan Exhibition Picture Catalogue," in *Memorial of the Celebration of the Two Hundred and Fiftieth Anniversary of the Founding of Gloucester in 1642* [Boston: Alfred Mudge & Son, 1892], 247–66); Harriett Mason (noted in CAM object label for *Gloucester Harbor*); Ada C. Bowles (Ada C. Bowles, C. A. S. & L. A. Weekly Column on Matters of Local History, *GDT*, March 16, 1916, as cited in Dunlap and Buck, *FHL*, 117); William Bradford (Trask, in "Notes on the Life," CAM); D. Jerome Elwell (Wilmerding, *Lane and Mellen*, 41); F. L. Palmer (Wilmerding, *Lane and Mellen*, 45n62, 55); Henry J. Pierce (John Wilmerding, "Fitz Hugh Lane: Imitations and Attributions," *American Art Journal* 3, no. 2 [Autumn 1971], 36, with an illustration of an 1865 Pierce copy of Lane's *Ships in Ice* [MFA]).

32. For *Salem Harbor*, see chapter 2. *Gloucester Inner Harbor* is signed in pencil on the back of the stretcher. Letter from Charles D. Childs to Francis W. Robinson at Detroit Institute of Art, February 21, 1942, Archives of American Art, Albert Duveen Files, reel NDu2 (no frame numbers on reel).

33. See Quinn, Kelberlau, and Woodward, "Rediscovering," concerning the discovery of an inscription—"View of Coffin's Beach, from the rocks at / the Loaf, after a sketch taken, August, 1862. / by Fitz H. Lane. / Presented to Dr H.E. Davidson, and Lady / by the Artist"—on the verso of this work.

34. James Elkins, "The Art Seminar," in *Landscape Theory*, ed. Rachael Ziady DeLue and James Elkins (New York: Routledge, 2008), 91.

35. James Brinkerhoff Jackson, "Jefferson, Thoreau, and After," in *Landscape in Sight: Looking at America*, ed. Helen Lefkowitz Horowitz (New Haven: Yale University Press, 1997), 182, first published in *Landscape* 15, no. 2 (Winter 1965–66): 25.

36. John S. Springer, *Forest Life and Forest Trees: Comprising Winter Camp-Life Among the Loggers [...] with Descriptions of Lumbering Operations on the Various Rivers of Maine and New Brunswick* (New York: Harper & Brothers, 1851), 222.

37. *GDT*, August 10, 1913.

38. Charlotte Bailey Myers Jackson, "Sketch of the Life of Theodorus Bailey Myers, 1821–1888," in *Biographical Sketches of the Bailey-Myers-Mason Families, 1776 to 1905: Key to a Cabinet of Heirlooms in the National Museum, Washington*, ed. Mrs. Cassie Mason Myers Julian-James (n.p.: privately printed, 1908), 25; Frances Alice Jackson, "Catalina Juliana Mason, Afterward Mrs. Theodorus Bailey Myers, 1824–1905," in ibid., 37–38; and Helen Mason, "Sidney Mason, 1799–1871," in ibid., 113–20.

39. Kelly, "Lane and Church," 134.

40. Tim Barringer, "A White Atlantic? The Idea of American Art in Nineteenth-Century Britain," *19: Interdisciplinary Studies in the Long Nineteenth Century* 9 (2009): 8, http://doi.org/10.16995/ntn.507.

41. William Howe Witherle, "A Cruise with Fitz Hugh Lane" (diary, August 16–21, 1852), *Wilson Museum Bulletin* 2, no. 2 (Winter 1974–75), 2–3.

42. Ibid., 2.

43. Margaretta M. Lovell, "Fitz Henry Lane, spectateur de l'histoire," in *Refaire l'Amérique: Imaginaire et histoire des États-Unis*, ed. Didier Aubert and Hélène Quanquin (Paris: Presses Sorbonne nouvelle, 2011), 47–61.

CHAPTER 1

1. Robert F. Perkins Jr. and William J. Gavin III, eds., Mary Margaret Shaughnessy, asst. ed., *The Boston Athenaeum Art Exhibition Index, 1827–1874* (Boston: Library of the Boston Athenaeum, 1980), 90; *National Academy of Design Exhibition Record, 1826–1860* (New York: New-York Historical Society, 1943), 1:283; Mary Bartlett Cowdrey, *American Academy of Fine Arts and American Art-Union, 1816–1852*, vol. 2, *Exhibition Record* (New York: New-York Historical Society, 1953), 220–21.

2. Campbell Gibson, "Population of the 100 Largest Cities and Other Urban Places in the United States: 1790–1990," U.S. Census Bureau Working Paper Series no. 27, 1998.

3. For articles about items on view in Lane's studio, see, for instance, *CAL & GT* 23, no. 39 (September 29, 1849); *CAA*, February 8, 1861; and, in "Clippings," CAM, untitled newspaper clippings of August 4, 1849, and September 22, 1849, and an untitled newspaper clipping dated only 1850.

4. On shop signs in general in antebellum America, see "Signboards, Vision, and Commerce in the Antebellum City," chap. 4 in Peter John Brownlee, *The Commerce of Vision: Optical Culture and Perception in Antebellum America* (Philadelphia: University of Pennsylvania Press, 2019), 111–34.

5. *CAA*, August 1, 1857, "Clippings," CAM.

6. Capt. Isaac Somes was one of fifty-eight Gloucester landholders whose real estate was taxed at more than $50 in 1850 and one of seventy paying more than $100 in 1860. *GT* 14, no. 74 (September 14, 1850); *GT* 34, no. 74 (September 15, 1860).

7. Pictorial advertisements, on the other hand, often matter-of-factly centered the featured object; see, for instance, M. M. Tidd's lithograph *Simpson's Patent Dry Dock* [...] *East Boston*, dated between 1854 and 1864 (AAS R57/SubB/Dr9), for an obverse view of a similar subject.
8. Dunlap and Buck, *FHL*, 122n508.
9. Trask, "Notes on the Life." Dunlap and Buck, *FHL*, 33, 149–51. Trask was also active in the Gloucester Lyceum. Bennett, diary, March 6, 1854, AAS.
10. *CAWA*, March 10, 1876, as quoted in Dunlap and Buck, *FHL*, 123; and, in "Clippings," CAM, an undated, unattributed newspaper clipping after 1876 as well as an undated *GDT* clipping by Fred Tibbets from the 1920s. For George H. Rogers, see the tax list in *CAL & GT*, September 2, 1848. Using the Gloucester Marine Railway was expensive: in 1860 hauling up and one-day use for a vessel less than one hundred tons (four thousand cubic feet) cost $10. *GT* 34, no. 74 (September 15, 1860).
11. For Hogarth and shop signs, see Ronald Paulson, "The Signboard and Its Painter," in *Popular and Polite Art in the Age of Hogarth and Fielding* (Notre Dame: University of Notre Dame Press, 1979), 31–48, esp. 37–38; for Garrard, see Michel Serres, "Turner Translates Carnot," in *Calligram: Essays in New Art History from France*, ed. Norman Bryson, trans. Stephan Bann (New York: Cambridge University Press, 1988), 154–65, with thanks to Mary Pardo for bringing this article to my attention; see also Jonathan Conlin, "'At the Expense of the Public': The Sign Painters' Exhibition of 1762 and the Public Sphere," *Eighteenth-Century Studies* 36, no. 1 (Fall 2002): 1–21.
12. E. Lane, "Early Recollections."
13. *GT*, July 4 and 7, 1849, "Clippings," CAM; Sharf, "Fitz Hugh Lane Re-considered"; "The Ball of the Mechanic Engine Co.," *CAA*, January 3, 1862. Lane's contemporary Edward Hicks also painted banners on silk, one of which survives: see Carolyn J. Weekley, *The Kingdoms of Edward Hicks* (Williamsburg, VA: Colonial Williamsburg Foundation, Abby Aldrich Rockefeller Folk Art Center, 1999), 164, fig. 157. Lane the pageant designer was working in a tradition of public art dating from at least the Renaissance. See Dennis Geronimus, *Piero di Cosimo: Visions Beautiful and Strange* (New Haven: Yale University Press, 2006), 28–30.
14. A. Babson, diary, entry for September 23, 1848.
15. Tax list, *GT*, July 4, 1849.
16. James R. Pringle, *History of the Town and City of Gloucester, Cape Ann, Massachusetts* (Gloucester, MA: self-published, 1892; repr., Gloucester, MA: Gloucester Archives Committee, 1997), 108–10, as cited in Dunlap and Buck, *FHL*, 46–47; Martha Oaks, *Gloucester at Mid-Century: The World of Fitz Hugh Lane*, exh. cat. (Gloucester, MA: CAHA, 1989), 19. For the history of the Sea Serpent in Gloucester, see Chandos Michael Brown, "A Natural History of the Gloucester Sea Serpent: Knowledge, Power, and the Culture of Science in Antebellum America," *American Quarterly* 42, no. 3 (September 1990): 402–36.
17. *GT*, July 4 and 7, 1849, "Clippings," CAM. See also Sharf, "Fitz Hugh Lane Re-considered," 78–79, and Gene E. McCormick, "Fitz Hugh Lane, Gloucester Artist, 1804–1865," *Art Quarterly* 15 (Winter 1952): 291–306.
18. Manuscript journal of Hannah S. Babson, as cited in Dunlap and Buck, *FHL*, 59; Massachusetts, Wills and Probate Records, 1635–1991, Case No. 44960, http://search.ancestry.com/cgi-bin/sse.dll?indiv=1&db=USProbateMa&h=709757, accessed October 27, 2016.
19. *CAL & GT*, March 3, 1853, "Clippings," CAM. Addison Center was also an artist/designer (Dunlap and Buck, *FHL*, 122). See also "Gloucester Art and Loan Exhibition."
20. J. J. Babson, *History of the Town of Gloucester*, 258; *CAA*, August 18, 1865.
21. April 26, 1856, "Clippings," CAM.
22. *GT*, June 30, 1860.
23. *GT* clipping dated only 1865, "Clippings," CAM. The Gloucester Bank was "open every [week]day from 9 A.M. to 1 o'clock P.M." *CAL & GT* 23, no. 24 (July 14, 1849). During these years Gorham Parsons Low (whose wife commissioned a painting from Lane) was president of the bank and director of the Gloucester Marine Insurance Co. *The Gloucester Directory* [...] *Business Directory* [...] *and Almanac for 1860* (Gloucester, MA: Procter Brothers, 1860); *CAL*, May 12, 1849; J. J. Babson, *History of the Town of Gloucester*, 11–12; *GT*, September 14, 1850; *Paintings and Drawings by Fitz Hugh Lane Preserved in the Collections of the Cape Ann Historical Association, Gloucester, Massachusetts* (Gloucester, MA: CAHA, 1974), fig. 80. This painting was destroyed (as were unsold copies of Lane's lithographic views of the town) with the burning of the town hall in 1869 (undated, untitled clipping, "Clippings," CAM); for a copy of Lane's will and an account of the fire, see Dunlap and Buck, *FHL*, 159–60 and 161–63. Jerome Elwall's elegiac painting *Burnt Ruins of Town House on Dale Avenue* was, in turn, "on exhibition at the store of Procter Brothers for a few days" (*CAA*, June 18, 1869). As late as 1913, when a Lane painting was given to the city by the granddaughter of his principal patron, it was housed not in an art venue but in the mayor's office. See the March 1916 inventory of Lane paintings, appendix B.
24. Undated, unattributed clipping, "Clippings," CAM, reprinted with slight differences in *GDT*, April 6, 1916; *CAA* 3, no. 22 (March 16, 1860); *GT* 34, no. 74 (September 15, 1860). An undated, unattributed clipping at CAM notes that "the fine painting by Lane, recently on exhibition at the store of Procter Bros., has been purchased by Mr. Collector Webber [*sic*]." Whether this is the same painting or another is not known. Two Penny Loaf is a promontory framing Coffin's Beach directly north of town.
25. *CAL & GT* 25, no. 29 (July 19, 1851); *GT* 34, no. 74 (September 15, 1860).

26. Dunlap and Buck, *FHL*, 49–53; unattributed newspaper clipping, August 4, 1849, "Clippings," CAM.
27. Unattributed newspaper clipping, September 22, 1849, "Clippings," CAM.
28. Undated, unattributed clipping with pen notation "1850," "Clippings," CAM.
29. *Gloucester Telegraph and News*, April 26, 1856, "Clippings," CAM.
30. Ibid.; A. Babson, diary, entry for September 23, 1848.
31. He showed paintings at the Boston Athenaeum in 1841, 1845, 1846, 1847, 1848, 1850, 1855, 1857, 1858, 1859, 1860, 1864, and 1865. Perkins and Gavin, *Boston Athenaeum Art Exhibition Index*, 90; see also *A Climate for Art: The History of the Boston Athenaeum Gallery, 1827–1873*, exh. cat. (Boston: Boston Athenaeum, 1980), 6–8, 14–18. Lane exhibited at the Boston Artists' Association in 1842, 1843, and 1844. See Leah Lipton, "The Boston Artists' Association, 1841–51," *American Art Journal* 15, no. 4 (Autumn 1983): 45–57. In 1841 his painting of the *Britannia* in a storm, commissioned by its captain, was exhibited in a music-store window (Sharf, "Fitz Hugh Lane Re-considered," 76–77); *Catalogue of Paintings Now on Exhibition in the Free Gallery of the New England Art Union* (Boston: Dutton & Wentworth, 1851), 6–7. In 1847 he also exhibited two works at the Boston Mechanics' Association (http://siris-artexhibition.si.edu/ipac20/ipac.jsp?session=1272M041R9361.11337&menu=search&aspect=alpha&npp=50&, accessed April 28, 2010) and at the Albany Gallery of Fine Arts (Alfred Mansfield Brooks, "The Fitz Lane House in Gloucester," *Essex Institute Historical Collections* 78, no. 3 [July 1942]: 281–83).
32. Cowdrey, *American Academy of Fine Arts*, 2:220–21. See also Malcolm Goldstein, *Landscape with Figures: A History of Art Dealing in the United States* (New York: Oxford University Press, 2000), 20–26.
33. Cowdrey, *American Academy of Fine Arts*, 2:220–21. With membership at $5 a year, the Art-Union did much to encourage the taste for American art among the middle class as well as the elites, but the lottery was investigated, deemed illegal, and the institution dissolved and its collection sold in 1852. See Amanda Lett, Patricia Hills, Peter John Brownlee, and Randy Ramer, *Perfectly American: The Art-Union and Its Artists*, exh. cat. (Tulsa, OK: Gilcrease Museum, 2011).
34. Gloucester members were friends and patrons of Lane: Mrs. Joseph L. Stevens Jr. (#50), David Dennison (#51), John S. E. Rogers (#1275), Samuel Stevens (#1276), Capt. Harvey C. Mackay (#1827), T. Sewall Lancaster (#1828), Frederic Norwood (#2487), Nathaniel Babson (#2488), William Babson (#3489), Franklin K. Woodbury (#5296), C. S. Stevens (second subscription, #11446), and T. Sewall Lancaster (second subscription, #11447). A "list of members whose subscriptions [had] been received and entered . . . , with their numbers annexed," was regularly published in the *Bulletin of the American Art-Union*: 2 (May 10, 1848): 9; 3 (May 25, 1848): 9–10; 4 (June 10, 1848): 11–12; 5 (June 25, 1848): 11–12; 4 (July 1850): 67–68; 5 (August 1850): 85–86; 6 (September 1850): 104; 7 (October 1850): 121–22; 8 (November 1850): 141–42; 9 (December 1850): 159–62. FirstSearch@oclc.org, accessed June 6, 2008.
35. *GT* 14, no. 30 (May 15, 1850).
36. *National Academy of Design Exhibition Record*, 283: *Gloucester Fishing Schooners*, owned by H. Hitchings. The *Boston Directory* for 1850 lists Henry Hitchings, clerk, at 13 Tremont Row, home at Dedham.
37. *GT*, January 21, 1835; August 15, 1835; December 19, 1835; and March 16, 1836; as quoted in Tibbets, "Fitz H. Lane," March 9, 1916.
38. Letter from Joseph L. Stevens Jr. in Boston to Samuel H. Mansfield in Gloucester, October 17, 1904, later given by Mansfield to CAM and received by his cousin Alfred Mansfield Brooks, president, September 19, 1949.
39. *GT*, November 5 and 25, 1846.
40. Alexander Pattillo comment to Fred Tibbets, in "Fitz H. Lane," March 9, 1916; *CAA*, February 8, 1861; undated, untitled newspaper clipping about "the recent [1869] disastrous fire," "Clippings," CAM.
41. Alexander Pattillo comment to Fred Tibbets, in "Fitz H. Lane," March 9, 1916.
42. *GDT* undated clipping, "Clippings," CAM.
43. "The State and Prospects of Lithography," *Art-Union* (London) 1, no. 6 (July 15, 1839): 97–98. Lane was a lifelong subscriber to this London publication. See the letter from Joseph L. Stevens Jr. to S. H. Mansfield, October 17, 1904, CAM.
44. In a letter of January 29, 1851, from Dr. Joseph L. Stevens Sr. to F. H. Lane in Gloucester, the father of Lane's friend noted that "several [Castine] gentlemen have . . . expressed a desire to have a drawing from you of our town similar to yours of Gloucester which they much admire, and, if lithographed, I have no doubt copies enough would be disposed to remunerate you" (CAM).
45. These drawings were given by Stevens to Samuel H. Mansfield, who, in turn, gave them to CAM in 1927, and except for five of the most beautiful, which were sold in 1964, they are preserved there; 105 are illustrated in *Paintings and Drawings*. See also Alfred Mansfield Brooks, "Fitz Lane's Drawings," *Essex Institute Historical Collections* 81, no. 1 (January 1945): 83–86. Also preserved at CAM is Alfred Brooks's manuscript notebook, with some of these inscriptions transcribed in 1944 and additions in 1947, and a typescript made from this notebook in 1959; in the notebook Brooks notes that "almost everything written on the drawings is in Stevens' hand." See Dunlap and Buck, *FHL*, 159–60, for Lane's will. For a discussion of Lane's possible use of a camera lucida to execute the drawings and aid in their enlargement and transfer to canvas, see Quinn, Kelberlau, and Woodward, "Rediscovering."

46. Travers Newton and Marcia Steele, "The Series Paintings of Fitz Henry Lane: From Field Sketch to Studio Painting," in *Emil Bosshard, Paintings Conservator (1945–2006): Essays by Friends and Colleagues*, ed. Maria de Peverelli, Marco Grassi, and Hans-Christof von Imhoff (Florence: Centro Di, 2009), 203. In the preserved set of drawings are images of four sloops, a schooner wreck, three ancient or Asian sailing vessels, a steam tug, and only two very sketchy drawings of ships; the rest are topographical. Twenty-six are 10 ½ inches high, and half are 10 ¼ to 10 ¾ inches high, suggesting a preferred stock size, but they vary greatly in length, as many are composed of glued sheets, suggesting the importance of horizontal extension to the artist; see http://fitzhenrylaneonline.org concerning the corpus of these drawings and their annotations.

47. Letter fragment, n.d., CAM P31A FF11.

48. "Sketch of supposed 'oldest house in town,'" fig. 133 in *Paintings and Drawings* (FHLo inv. 199), is reproduced in J. J. Babson, *History of the Town of Gloucester*, 452; and "Parson White [House] Town Parish," fig. 134 in *Paintings and Drawings* (FHLo inv. 200), is reproduced in ibid., 230. See ibid., 258, for Babson's acknowledgment of Lane.

49. *GT* 14, no. 74 (September 14, 1850); *Gloucester Directory* (1860), 102; *The Boston Directory, for the Year Commencing July 1, 1864* (Boston: Adams, Sampson, 1864), 25.

50. Charles C. Smith, "A Memoir [of John James Babson]," typescript prepared for the Massachusetts Historical Society, 1886, Authors and Artists Scrapbook, 2:1–4, CAM; *GT* 4, no. 33 (August 14, 1830).

51. The image is marked "F. H. Lane, del." and "Lane & Scott, Lith., Tremont Temple Boston"—indicating it is a product of Lane's short-lived business partnership with painter and lithographer John W. A. Scott—and "Published in Boston by Eastburn's [*sic*] Press, 1847."

52. For a quick précis of Forbes's career and his patronage of Lane, see James A. Craig, *Fitz H. Lane: An Artist's Voyage Through Nineteenth-Century America* (Charleston, SC: History Press, 2006), 62–64; for a list of some of the vessels built under Forbes's direction, see app. 1 (unpaginated) in Robert B. Forbes, *Personal Reminiscences, to Which Is Added Rambling Recollections Connected with China*, 3rd ed., rev. (Boston: Little, Brown, 1892).

53. Robert Forbes, *Personal Reminiscences*, 95; "Diary of Robert Bennet Forbes," vol. 3, entry for April 8, 1841, Massachusetts Historical Society.

54. For friendship between the men, see, for instance, "Diary of Robert Bennet Forbes," vol. 3, entries for April 21, August 6, and November 18, 1841; December 11, 1847; October 19 and November 14, 1848; and April 7, 1849. For Upton biography, see Walter Allen, *A Memoir of George Bruce Upton* (Boston: David Clapp & Son, 1875) (repr. from the *Historical and Genealogical Register* for January 1875). For reference to Upton's ownership of the Lane painting, see the Boston Athenaeum's 1864 exhibition list: Perkins and Gavin, *Boston Athenaeum Art Exhibition Index*, 247.

55. Newton and Steele, "Series Paintings," 200; the drawing of the Boston skyline is fig. 92 in *Paintings and Drawings*, FHLo inv. 158.

56. *Reminiscences of Ralph B. Forbes: Notes Regarding the Picture of the Schooner* Coquette *Hanging in the Lower Room at Milton* (Boston: Cotter, [1887]) concerns events recorded in the first two decades of the nineteenth century in the Atlantic and Caribbean.

57. "Capt. R[obert] B[ennet] Forbes was born in Jamaica Plain Sept 18, 1804. . . . At the age of 13 he went to sea before the mast; at 16 he was third mate, at 20 Captain, at 26 he owned a ship and commanded her; at 28 he left the sea, and at 36 was head of the largest American house in China." From the *Boston Traveller*, September 18 (no year noted), loose clipping in the Massachusetts Historical Society copy of *Reminiscences of Ralph B. Forbes*.

58. See Margaretta M. Lovell, "Fitz H. Lane's Marine Lithographs, Robert Bennet Forbes, and the Pirates of the South China Sea," in *Laid Down on Paper: Printmaking in America, 1800–1865*, ed. Caroline Sloat (Gloucester, MA: CAM, 2020). For more on the narrative of Forbes's involvement in the China trade, see chapter 8 below.

59. "Diary of Robert Bennet Forbes," vol. 3, entries for May 9, 10, 11, 14, and 17, 1842.

60. R. B. Forbes, newspaper article, n.d., no newspaper name, loose clipping inserted into ibid., vol. 4.

61. One of Lane's paintings of *America* was reported to have been owned by his friend Joseph Stevens Jr., but it is likely that the other was painted for a New York Yacht Club patron. *GDT*, March 2, 1916. For a thorough account of *America*'s career and the many paintings and prints it inspired, see Alan Granby and Jessica Hyland, with William I. Koch, *The Holy Grail of Yachting: The Art of the America's Cup*, vol. 1, *1851: Race for the Squadron Cup* (West Palm Beach, FL: America 3 Foundation, 2013).

62. According to Peabody Essex Museum object records, "this was painted from a lithograph by T. Dutton of the *America* winning the royal Yacht Club Cup at Cowes, 21 Aug. 1851." Originally given to the Museum of Fine Arts, Boston, this painting was deposited by that institution at the Essex Institute in 1932 (object files for 4696); see chapter 2.

63. See Erik Ronnberg's entry concerning Lane's omission of elements on *America*'s deck at FHLo inv. 255.

64. Trask, "Notes on the Life." Three Lane paintings recording New York Yacht Club races are illustrated in Wilmerding, *Paintings by Fitz Hugh Lane*, 78, 79, 80. By contrast, Lane was commissioned by Samuel Sawyer to paint Brook Bank, the Sawyer family home, in 1857 for $100, and in 1860 Sawyer bought a view of Mount Desert Light for $41. Sam Sawyer

expense account, as communicated by Molly Hardy to Georgia Barnhill by email, April 1, 2016.

65. *New York Times*, September 20, 1851; March 28, 1896; and February 16, 1947.

66. Sharf, "Fitz Hugh Lane Reconsidered," 77. Benjamin K. Hough, for whom Lane painted *Southern Cross*, was a repeat customer; he ordered a second portrait of *Southern Cross*, in which the vessel figures in a double portrait, in company with another of Hough's ships, *Winged Arrow*. Hough was one of eleven Gloucesterites paying more than $300 in taxes (*GT*, September 15, 1860). The inscription on the second painting, now at the Cincinnati Art Museum, reads: "Southern Cross / by Fitz Lane / Winged Arrow / of Gloucester / Father's Ships / Sargent Murray Gilman House / from the Misses Hough."

67. Lane exhibited forty-one paintings at these "fine arts" venues (excluding those sent to the American Art-Union), of which thirteen have listed owners (see appendix A and note 1 above).

68. *CAL*, January 17, 1862; *Gloucester Directory* (1860), 99.

69. Newton and Steele, "Series Paintings," 208.

70. Josiah Quincy Jr. (1802–1882) was mayor of Boston and chair of the Committee of Relief for the Suffering Irish at the time of the *Jamestown* expedition, in which Robert B. Forbes was instrumental, an event memorialized in Lane's lithograph, figure 16.

71. Goldstein, *Landscape with Figures*, 15–46.

72. See figs. 09 and 115 in *Paintings and Drawings*; FHLo inv. 175, 181.

73. Letter from Joseph L. Stevens Jr. to Samuel H. Mansfield, October 17, 1903, CAM.

74. According to curatorial files at CAM, one painting in their collection appears to have its original William Y. Balch frame, *New England Harbor at Sunrise*, ca. 1850.

75. "List of Members," *Bulletin of the American Art-Union*, November 17 and December 25, 1848; letter from Honorary Secretary William Y. Balch to Andrew Warner, November 5, 1850, Letters to Art-Union File, Manuscript Collection, New York Historical Society, as cited in Jane Aldrich Dowling Adams, "A Study of Art Unions in the United States of America in the Nineteenth Century" (MA thesis, Virginia Commonwealth University, Richmond, VA, 1990), 47, 170.

76. William Balch does not appear in the Boston city directory for 1864, but Susan Balch does; William Y. Balch died in 1882. *The Boston Directory*, no. 79, *For the Year Commencing July 1, 1883* (Boston: Sampson, Davenport, 1883), 84.

77. *Art Journal*, no. 12 (1840): 5.

78. "Wealth of Boston," *CAL & GT* 25, no. 17 (April 26, 1851), lists only four Bostonians wealthier than Josiah Quincy Jr.

79. Goldstein, *Landscape with Figures*, 26; C. L. Beaumont, "The Picture Sales of New York—A Retrospective History," *New York Times*, December 11, 1897. I thank Shelley Bennett for this reference.

80. J[oseph] L. Stevens Jr. to Samuel H. Mansfield, October 17, 1903; Dunlap and Buck, *FHL*, 51. Lane bought land from Eban Hough Stacy for the stone house in October 1849 (Dunlap and Buck, *FHL*, 59), and Lane sold paintings to many of the Stacys. Eli Stacy was a liquor retailer (*GT*, July 14, 1827; August 2, 1828); Eli F. Stacy was customs collector, bank trustee, and merchant dealing in fish, "pork, lard, and hams," and men's clothing (*CAL & GT*, February 3, 1849; *CAL*, June 9, 1849; *GT*, March 12, 1831; *GT*, January 12, 1850); George O. Stacy built hotels (Alfred Mansfield Brooks and Ruth Steele Brooks, *Gloucester Recollected: A Familiar History*, ed. Joseph E. Garland [Gloucester, MA: Peter Smith for CAHA, 1974], 15, 25, 35, 119–20); Samuel A. Stacy was an insurance agent, director of the Gloucester Lyceum, and an American Art-Union member (obituary, October 21, 1895, CAM bio file); see also *GT*, September 2, 1859, as cited in Elizabeth Garrity Ellis, "Cape Ann Views," in Wilmerding, *Paintings by Fitz Hugh Lane*, 23. Eli T. Stacy, Samuel A. Stacy, and J. R. Stacy were Boston-based members of the American Art-Union ("List of Members").

81. "*Marine View—Coast of Maine* (F. H. Lane) [bought by] A. Edwards [for] $50" ("American Art-Union: Second Day's Sale," *New York Times*, December 17, 1852); of numbers 7, 59, 92, 100, and 127 in Bleecker's sale in New York in February 1861, apparently only one sold (for $20) (correspondence of Florence C. Lamb, Frick Art Reference Library in New York, to A. M. Brooks at CAHA, January 30, 1961, CAM files).

82. Francis Bennett records attending several evening book auctions in Gloucester in the 1850s (diary, February 24, 1854, and ff.); significant sales of paintings in Boston occurred on January 30, 1829; October 12, 1840; and April 5, 1844 (Harold Lancour, comp., *American Art Auction Catalogues, 1785–1942* [New York: New York Public Library, 1944), 28, 30, 32.

83. Massachusetts Charitable Mechanic Association, *Catalogue of Paintings by Mr. [Alvan] Fisher Exhibited at the [Mechanic Association] Fair, to be sold at Faneuil Hall, on Monday, Oct. 9, 1837, at 12*, pamphlet, AAS.

84. Joseph Stevens's notes on the drawings FHLo inv. 80 (2), 104, 107, 114, 178. Insofar as extant records indicate, the buying of paintings and the amassing of art collections were predominantly male activities in the nineteenth century. See, for instance, Frederick Baekeland, "Collectors of American Painting, 1813 to 1913," *American Art Review* 3, no. 6 (November/December 1976): 120–66, and Melissa Geisler Trafton, "Critics, Collectors, and the Nineteenth-Century Taste for the Paintings of John Frederick Kensett," PhD diss., University of California, Berkeley, 2003, app. C, "List of Owners," 402–65.

85. Assessments, *GT* 14, no. 74 (September 14, 1850).

86. "Property in Art," *Art Journal* (London) 11 (May 1849): 133–36.
87. *GT*, August 15, 1835, and November 5, 1846; *CAA*, August 1, 1857.
88. May 1850, as cited in *GT* 14, no. 39 (Wednesday, May 15, 1850).
89. *GT*, August 19, 1865; Craig, *Fitz H. Lane*, 162.
90. "Junior," on the brig *Cronstadt*, *CAA* 3, no. 2 (January 13, 1860).
91. "Junior," *CAA* 3, no. 3 (January 20, 1860).
92. *CAL & GT* 23, no. 39 (September 29, 1849).
93. Stephen Willard Phillips, ed., *Ship Registers of the District of Gloucester, Massachusetts, 1789–1875* (Salem, MA: Essex Institute, 1944), 23; Capt. Edward Babson, log of the brig *Cadet*, 1837–41, Ships Log Book Collection, CAM; *CAL & GT*, May 6, 1848.
94. A. Babson, diary, entry for January 30, 1848.
95. Ibid., July 12, 1849.
96. *GT* 2, no. 23 (Saturday, May 31, 1828).
97. Edward Babson, like many former captains, became a successful merchant, moving his business to Boston but continuing to live in Gloucester, on Summer Street, where his tax assessment in 1850 was one of the sixteen highest in the town and in 1860 one of the eleven highest. *The Gloucester Directory* [. . .] *Business Directory* [. . .] *and Almanac for 1860* (Gloucester, MA: Procter Brothers, 1860); *Gloucester and Rockport Directory* [. . .] *Business Directory* [. . .] *and Almanac for 1861* (Gloucester, MA: Procter Brothers, 1861); *Gloucester and Rockport Directory* [. . .] *Business Directory* [. . .] *and Almanac for 1869* (Gloucester, MA: Sampson, Davenport; Procter Brothers, 1869); *Boston Directory* (1864); *GT* 14, no. 74 (September 14, 1850); and *GT* 34, no. 74 (September 15, 1860). A brig named *Cadet*, possibly the same vessel, left Boston for the Pacific in the 1860s, its cabin "finished in mahogany and oak, the dark panels being embellished with a small painting." Lucy Brown Reynolds, "The Brig Cadet," chap. 4 in *Drops of Spray from Southern Seas* (Waterville, ME: Mail Publishing, 1896), 26–35, quotation on 18.
98. Roger Ward Babson, *Actions and Reactions: An Autobiography* (New York: Harper & Brothers, 1935); Ann Theopold Chaplin, *The Babson Genealogy, 1606–1997: Descendants of Thomas and Isabel Babson* (Baltimore: Gateway Press, 1999), 60–61. The best map of property in this part of Gloucester is G. M. Hopkins, *Atlas of the City of Gloucester and Town of Rockport, Massachusetts* (Philadelphia: G. M. Hopkins, 1884) (Sawyer Free Library, Gloucester), plate 16.
99. *Gloucester Directory* (1860), 86; American Art-Union member #2488 ("List of Members").
100. *CAA*, February 8, 1861.
101. Joseph S. Wood, with a contribution by Michael P. Steinitz, *The New England Village* (Baltimore: Johns Hopkins University Press, 1997), 2–8.
102. [Alfred Mansfield Brooks], attrib., "Historical House Adds Paintings by Fitz Lane," *GDT*, 1937, "Clippings," CAM.
103. *Paintings and Drawings*, figs. 44 and 46; FHLo inv. 126.
104. *GT*, August 15, 1835.
105. *GT*, June 30, 1860. For a discussion of the idea of the Revolution in Lane's paintings, see Lovell, "Fitz Henry Lane, spectateur."
106. *GT*, March 16, 1836; *CAA*, Friday, August 18, 1865.
107. Clarence Cook, "Letters on Art.—No. IV," *Independent* (New York), September 7, 1854, 281, from which the quotations in the following paragraphs come; see William H. Gerdts and C. C., "'The Sea Is His Home': Clarence Cook Visits Fitz Hugh Lane," *American Art Journal* 17, no. 3 (Summer 1985): 44–49; Clarence Cook obituary, *New York Times*, June 2, 1900. See also John P. Simoni, "Art Critics and Criticism in Nineteenth-Century America" (PhD diss., Ohio State University, 1952), 120–39, and Jo Ann Weiss, "Clarence Cook: His Critical Writings" (PhD diss., Johns Hopkins University, 1977).
108. Joseph L. Stevens Jr.'s letter to Samuel Mansfield, October 17, 1903, CAM.
109. We do not know when Lane began to subscribe, but the journal was in production from 1839 (with monthly circulation of that issue reported to be three thousand); articles on art matters in the United States included one in 1851 on the success of the American Art-Union (n.s., 3 [February]: 63) and one in 1856 on the death of Thomas Doughty (n.s., 2 [September]: 289).
110. "British Artists: Their Style and Character, No. 1—John Constable," *Art Journal*, n.s., 1 (1855): 9–12, quotation on 9.
111. *Art Journal*, n.s., 1 (1855): 275.
112. "The Brook by the Way," *Art Journal* 11 (March 1849): 72.
113. Examples of Turner engravings and discussions in the *Art Journal* include *The Grand Canal* (1, no. 3 [April 1839]: 52), *Venice—The Dogana* (11 [August 1849]: 260), *Venice* (12 [March 1850]: 92), *Golden Bough* (3 [February 1851]: 132), and a series of articles about Turner's gift of one hundred works to the British nation (n.s., 2 [April 1856]: 126 and [August 1856]: 257).
114. "A" of New York City, *Art Journal*, n.s., 3 (July 1851): 191–92; *Art Journal* 10 (June 1848): 195.
115. On Cook's acquaintance with Downing, see Simoni, "Art Critics," 138.
116. Alexander J. Downing, *The Architecture of Country Houses* (Philadelphia: G. S. Appleton, 1850; repr., New York: Dover, 1969), 262–63. Downing's ultimate model may have been Aristotle's ranking of the liberal man and the magnificent man (*Nicomachean Ethics*, IV.3).
117. See Michael Baxandall, *Painting and Experience in Fifteenth Century Italy: A Primer in the Social History of Pictorial Style* (Oxford: Oxford University Press, 1972), 87; Baxandall, *The Limewood Sculptors of Renaissance Germany* (New Haven: Yale University Press, 1980), 142; and Baxandall, "Truth and Other Cultures: Piero Della Francesca's *Baptism of Christ*," in *Patterns of Intention: On the Historical Explanation of Pictures* (New Haven: Yale University Press, 1985), 105–37.
118. *Journal of Captain Solomon H. Davis, a Gloucester Sea-Captain, 1828–1846* (Norwood, MA: Plimpton Press,

1922), 12. Novels that Davis recorded reading include *Hobomok*, by "Miss Francis of Duxbury"; *Emily, or a Wife's Affection*; *Love Without a Doubt*; *Flirtation*; *Westbrook Village*; and *Three Perils of Woman* (ibid., 12–13). He also read the Bible. En route to Hawaii during a voyage in 1845 (then aged forty-eight), he read *Texas and Mexico*, by Mrs. Houston; *Amy Herbert*; and Ellis's *Polynesian Researches* (ibid., 13, 65, 67, 93).

119. Ibid., 13. See Peter de Bolla, *The Education of the Eye: Painting, Landscape, and Architecture in Eighteenth-Century Britain* (Stanford: Stanford University Press, 2003), concerning training to see.

120. *Journal of Captain Solomon H. Davis*, 67.

121. Letter of February 11, 1849, from Clarence C. Cook, aged nineteen, to Jared Sparks, newly appointed Harvard president, requesting response "to the care of Hon. Israel Trask, Gloucester," his stepmother's father, a state senator (Houghton Library, Harvard, MS Am 800.13 [153]; *GT* 1, no. 14 [March 31, 1827]), state lyceum representative (*GT* 4, no. 8 [February 20, 1830]), vice president of Gloucester's Saving Bank (*GT* 5, no. 11 [March 12, 1831]), and one of the eight wealthiest taxpayers in Gloucester (*GT* 14, no. 74 [September 14, 1850]). See also Simoni, "Art Critics," 125. For a discussion of the Tremont Temple area of Boston, see Lipton, "Boston Artists' Association."

122. Letter from Fitz Henry Lane to Caroline and Joseph Stevens Jr., ca. 1857, CAM.

123. U.S. Supreme Court: New England Insurance Company v. the Brig *Sarah Ann*, involving the claim of Obadiah Woodbury and others dating from 1834 (http://supreme.justia.com/us/38/387/index.html). Around 1854 Woodbury commissioned *A Rough Sea*, a painting of a ship anchored in a storm (photocopy of newspaper article ca. 1938, n.d., "Clippings," CAM), given to CAM before 1937 by Mr. and Mrs. Alfred Mansfield Brooks (Susan Babson's notes on paintings, in appendix B).

124. Ann Bermingham, "System, Order, and Abstraction: The Politics of English Landscape Drawing Around 1795," in W. J. T. Mitchell, *Landscape and Power*, 77–101. It would be interesting to speculate on whether Lane had read the standard theorists of the picturesque—William Gilpin or Uvedale Price and Richard Payne Knight—or, more likely, the drawing books by Craig, but it appears that Lane is using the term in this letter in a general or vernacular sense. See also Kim Ian Michasiw, "Nine Revisionist Theses on the Picturesque," *Representations* 38 (Spring 1992): 76–100.

125. Horace Mann, *A Few Thoughts for a Young Man: A Lecture, Delivered Before the Boston Mercantile Library Association, on Its 29th Anniversary* (Boston: Ticknor, Reed & Fields, 1850), 12–13, repr. in *GT*, March 2, 1850.

CHAPTER 2

1. The reputation of John Frederick Kensett, for instance, and the value of his works "soared" on his death in 1872. See Alan Wallach, "A Note on Aestheticizing Tendencies in American Landscape Painting, 1840–1880," in *Renew Marxist Art History*, ed. Warren Carter, Barnaby Haran, and Frederic J. Schwarz (London: Art/Books, 2014), 148–49, and John K. Howat, "Kensett's World," in *John Frederick Kensett: An American Master*, exh. cat., ed. John Paul Driscoll and John K. Howat (Worcester, MA: Worcester Art Museum; New York: W. W. Norton, 1985), 15–47.
2. "Fitz H. Lane, Esq.," obituary, *CAL*, August 1865, "Clippings," CAM.
3. Benjamin W. Labaree, "The Making of an Empire: Boston and Essex County, 1790–1850," in *Entrepreneurs: The Boston Business Community, 1700–1850*, Massachusetts Historical Society Studies in American History and Culture, no. 4, ed. Conrad Edick Wright and Katheryn P. Viens (Boston: Massachusetts Historical Society, 1997), 342–63. See, for a sense of the scale of the postwar fish business, *The Boston Almanac and Business Directory*, vol. 45, *1880* (Boston: Sampson, Murdock, 1879), 273–75; *The Boston Almanac and Business Directory*, vol. 53, *1888* (Boston: Sampson, Murdock, 1888), 301–3; *The Boston Almanac and Business Directory*, vol. 59, *1894* (Boston: Sampson, Murdock, 1894), 393–94.
4. For example, among Lane's patrons and friends Sidney Mason had moved his capital and household to New York City by 1840; in 1864 Samuel E. Sawyer, Joseph L. Stevens Jr., and J. J. Babson are listed at business addresses in Boston, but in each case their "house [is] at Gloucester." *Boston Directory* (1864).
5. For an album of photographs of the homes of Mason kin, 1876–88, through whom Lane paintings descended, see Julian-James, *Biographical Sketches*, unpaginated photographs. Although apparently not hung in the principal rooms, the Mason family's Lane paintings appear to have been well cared for. Alfred Mansfield Brooks described Fitz H. Lane paintings hanging in the front and back parlors of the Gloucester homes of his grandmother, his great aunt, and neighbors during his boyhood in the 1870s and '80s. Brooks and Brooks, *Gloucester Recollected*, 6, 15, 26, 35, 57, 120.
6. Beaumont, "Picture Sales of New York"; Goldstein, *Landscape with Figures*, 26. My thanks to Shelley Bennett for bringing these sources to my attention.
7. John K. Howat, "Private Collectors and Public Spirit: A Selective View," in *Art and the Empire City: New York, 1825–1861*, exh. cat., ed. Catherine Hoover Voorsanger and John K. Howat (New York: Metropolitan Museum of Art, 2000), 83–107; see also Linda Henefield Skalet, "The Market for American Painting in New York: 1870–1915" (PhD diss., Johns Hopkins University, 1980), and Sarah Burns, *Inventing the Modern Artist: Art and Culture in Gilded Age America* (New Haven: Yale University Press, 1996), 27 and passim.

8. Baekeland, "Collectors of American Painting."
9. Ibid., 120–35; Beaumont, "Picture Sales of New York," passim.
10. Baekeland, "Collectors of American Painting," 136. F. E. Church maintained a studio in New York City from 1847 to 1888 and used dealers as middlemen for at least two important paintings. John K. Howat, *Frederic Church* (New Haven: Yale University Press, 2005), 73–74. Sanford Robinson Gifford had studios in New York City from 1847 until after 1877. Eleanor Jones Harvey, "Tastes in Transition," in *Hudson River School Visions: The Landscapes of Sanford R. Gifford*, exh. cat., ed. Kevin J. Avery and Franklin Kelly (New Haven: Yale University Press, 2003), 34. And John Frederick Kensett maintained studios in New York from 1848 until his death in 1872, and he used the services of at least six New York dealers to sell his paintings. Annette Blaugrund, "'Up Through the Snow' to Kensett's Studio," *Archives of American Art Journal* 23, no. 3 (1983): 31–32; Christine I. Oaklander, "Studios at the YMCA, 1869–1903," *Archives of American Art Journal* 32, no. 3 (1992): 14–22; and Trafton, "Critics, Collectors."
11. Beaumont, "Picture Sales of New York." For a discussion of the overall picture of the art business in late nineteenth-century New York and the taste for European works, see John Ott, "How New York Stole the Luxury Art Market: Blockbuster Auctions and Bourgeois Identity in Gilded Age America," *Winterthur Portfolio* 42, nos. 2–3 (Summer–Autumn 2008): 133–58.
12. Beaumont, "Picture Sales of New York"; Arnold Lewis, James Turner, and Steven McQuillin, eds., *The Opulent Interiors of the Gilded Age* (New York: Dover, 1987), 23. The Turner painting, having failed to find a buyer when offered at auction in London in 1869, was sent to America for auction sale. Martin Butlin and Evelyn Joll, *The Paintings of J. M. W. Turner* (New Haven: Yale University Press, 1977), 1:214.
13. "Picture Sales: The Stewart Collection and Others Since the [Civil] War—Only Three That Have Surpassed the Stewart Total of Prices," *New York Times*, February 12, 1898; see also "1885–1897—Statistics from Samuel P. Avery, Jr.," *New York Times*, December 11, 1897. I thank Shelley Bennett for bringing these articles to my attention.
14. "Fitz Hugh Lane Photographs at the Frick Art Reference [Library], New York City, January 1961," list, CAM file.
15. Exceptions may include two Lane works, *Pic-Nic near Camden, Maine* and *Landscape View of Gloucester*, offered at auction by Samuel Hatch & Co., Boston, in 186? (date obscured), but it is not known whether they found buyers (lots 62 and 155, Archives of American Art reel D152, "Catalogues from the Boston Public Library," frames 139 and 141); one Lane painting was reportedly sold at auction in Boston in 1868 for $62.50 (*CAWA*, May 29, 1868, as cited in Dunlap and Buck, *FHL*, 75n279), and four changed hands at auction in Gloucester in May 1871 (*CAWA* May 12, 1871; a detailed description of what was sold appears in an undated clipping in Sawyer Free Library Scrapbook—as cited in fitzhenrylaneonline entry for George H. Rogers, http://fitzhenrylaneonline.org/historical_material/?type=People§ion=Rogers%2C+George+H., accessed July 9, 2017).
16. *American Art Sales* 7, no. 7 (June 1927): 12–15; 11, no. 2 (January 1931): 18; 10, no. 5 (April 1930): 23. A colored lithograph was offered at Ritter-Hopson Galleries May 17, 1933 (Archives of American Art, reel N421, frame 576). Two Lane lithographs were offered at auction March 30 and 31, 1921, by Thomas E. Kirby in New York City, but it is not known whether they found buyers (Archives of American Art, "American Art Auction Catalog Collection, 1785–1962," reel N186, lot 112 / frame 670; lot 114 / frame 673).
17. Henry T. Tuckerman, *Book of the Artists: American Artist Life, Comprising Biographical and Critical Sketches of American Artists; Preceded by an Historical Account of the Rise and Progress of Art in America* (New York: G. P. Putnam & Son, 1867). Similarly, Boston-based James Jackson Jarves discussed Kensett, Gifford, Martin Johnson Heade, and others in *The Art-Idea* (originally published 1864; repr., Cambridge: Belknap Press of Harvard University Press, 1960) and *Art Thoughts: The Experiences and Observations of an American Amateur in Europe* (New York: Hurd & Houghton, 1869), 190, but omits Lane.
18. Dunlap and Buck, *FHL*, 126–27, 151; Tuckerman, *Book of the Artists*, 56, 551–56; Thomas Patrick Hughes, *American Ancestry: Giving the Name and Descent, in the Male Line, of Americans Whose Ancestors Settled in the United States Previous to the Declaration of Independence, A.D. 1776*, vol. 4 (Albany, NY: Joel Munsell's Sons, 1889), 76; John Lathrop, reporter, "Peter Wainwright and Another vs. S. Salisbury Tuckerman & Others, Suffolk [Co.], Nov. 17, 1875, March 18–April 18, 1876," in *Massachusetts Reports*, vol. 120, *Cases Argued and Determined in the Supreme Judicial Court of Massachusetts, March–September 1876* (Boston: Houghton Mifflin, 1877), 232–39.
19. *Harper's* 59, no. 353 (October 1879): 673–89, as cited in Dunlap and Buck, *FHL*, 126n529.
20. C. Cook, "Letters on Art"; C. Cook, *Art and Artists of Our Time*, 6 vols. (New York: Selmar Hess, 1888; repr., New York: Garland, 1978). See Gerdts and C. C., "'The Sea Is His Home,'" and *New York Times*, June 2, 1900; see also Simoni, "Art Critics," 120–39, and Jo Ann Weiss, "Clarence Cook."
21. Clarence Cook, "John F. Kensett," in *Art and Artists of Our Time*, 4:292–94.
22. Trask, "Notes on the Life"; also Dunlap and Buck, *FHL*, 149.
23. Letter from Joseph L. Stevens Jr. in Boston to Samuel H. Mansfield in Gloucester, October 17, 1904 (CAM P31A FF11), annotated in another

hand: "Received from Samuel H. Mansfield and given to the CASL & HA [Cape Ann Scientific, Literary, and Historical Association] September 19, 1949. Alfred Mansfield Brooks."

24. *Memorial of the Celebration*, 247–66.
25. "Painting by Lane of Town in 1852 Presented by Washington Lady as Memento of Her Grandfather Mason," *GDT*, June 15, 1913, "Clippings," CAM. Other family relics related to Sydney Mason and his descendants she gave to the Smithsonian (Julian-James, *Biographical Sketches*).
26. "Lane Painting Formally Presented to City on Behalf of Donor," *GDT*, July 15, 1913.
27. Susan Babson, "Fitz H. Lane," C. A. S. & L. A. Weekly Column on Matters of Local History, *GDT*, February 24, 1916, "Clippings," CAM.
28. Tibbets, "Fitz H. Lane"; this Mount Desert painting had been lent to the 1892 exhibition.
29. Arthur Williams Jr., of Arthur Williams Jr. & Co., Boston (importers of Turkish, Indian, and Persian carpets), wrote on December 10, 1914, to William Dickerman Straight, cofounder of India House in Manhattan, indicating that he had amassed "a great collection of American clipper ship pictures . . . [which he offered] to sell to the India House": "Some are painted by Fitz Hugh Lane, who was about the best American painter. . . . For two years I have advertised in the *Boston Transcript* every day for old ship pictures." The advertisements from January 1913 indicated "Paintings by Fitz Hugh Lane preferred." Eleanor Gustafson, ed., "Collectors' Notes," *Antiques* 172, no. 2 (August 2007): 44.
30. "Lane Held in High Rank," *GDT*, March 2, 1916, "Clippings," CAM.
31. Bowles, C. A. S. & L. A. Weekly Column.
32. *GDT*, April 6, 1916, "Clippings," CAM.
33. Helen Stevens Babson in Brookline in 1929 to Susie [Babson] in Gloucester: "[A]fter my death, you [Cape Ann Scientific and Literary Association] shall have my large picture . . . painted by Mr. Fitz H. Lane and given to father & mother when they went West,—where they planned to make there [*sic*] home but things were disappointing so they returned to Gloucester bringing the picture with them. We all loved it. It remained in our home till we went to Boston to live when father gave it to me for a wedding gift. Now it please[s] me to put it back in Gloucester." Stevens/Lane papers, box P31A, FF10, CAM; carbon copies of correspondence from G. H. Edgell, MFA director, to Miss Caroline Trask of Wellesley Hills, December 2 and 4, 1935, MFA object file for Lane, *Antelope*. Probably the first non-Gloucesterite who deliberately collected Lane paintings (and lithographs) was Charles H. Taylor, a marine painting enthusiast who donated a portrait of two ships by Lane to the Peabody Museum in 1933 (Peabody Essex Registrar's records re LC 3936); see also Lawrence W. Jenkins, comp., *A Catalogue of the Charles H. Taylor Collection of Ship Portraits in the Peabody Museum of Salem* (Salem: Peabody Museum, 1949), and Clarence S. Brigham, "Charles Henry Taylor," Obituaries, *Proceedings of the American Antiquarian Society* 51, pt. 2 (October 1941): 237–41.
34. Dunlap and Buck, *FHL*, 121–28. It was possibly the Boston antiques dealer Arthur Williams (see note 29 above) who, as a non-Gloucesterite and a dealer familiar with Asian objects (including prized "Fitzhugh" porcelain), was responsible for the erroneous renaming of the artist; he was among the first to use the "Hugh."
35. Joseph E. Garland, editor's preface, in Brooks and Brooks, *Gloucester Recollected*, ix–xvi.
36. Brooks and Brooks, *Gloucester Recollected*, 14, 15, 34, 54, 57; [Brooks], "Historical House."
37. Samuel H. Mansfield to A. M. Brooks, 1944. In 1949 Mansfield turned over to Brooks Stevens's 1904 letter giving his account of the artist. Brooks Papers, CAM.
38. Alfred M. Brooks, "Catalogue of the Drawings by Fitz H. Lane & given to CASL & HA by Samuel H. Mansfield, made by A. M. Brooks 1944. Added to 1947" (CAM); Brooks, "Fitz Lane's Drawings."
39. Letter from Frick Art Reference Librarian to A. M. Brooks, December 8, 1938, Scrapbook #86, CAM.
40. Forbes Watson, "My Country 'Tis of Thee," *Magazine of Art*, June 1939, 324–25, 334–35. *Life* magazine for June 19, 1939, included a six-page color spread about the exhibition entitled "Life in America: Artists Have Loved and Painted It for 300 Years" (26–31), which noted: "The Metropolitan Museum in New York has assembled a summer show of 291 paintings . . . in nine cool galleries, where visitors to the Fair can find refuge from the World of Tomorrow" (26). *Life*'s labels for the images emphasize American ingenuity, commerce, and homespun values in a historical context. The *Official Guide Book of the New York World's Fair, 1939* (New York: Exposition Publications, 1939) makes clear the emphasis at that event on ingenuity and commerce within the context of modernity and the future. I thank Kathleen Moran for bringing these publications to my attention.
41. Watson, "My Country," 324, 334, 335.
42. Ibid., 324. Harry B. Wehle, *Life in America: A Special Loan Exhibition of Paintings Held During the Period of the New York World's Fair, April 24 to October 29*, exh. cat. (New York: Scribner Press, 1939), 104–5.
43. Wehle, *Life in America*, 104; this painting is illustrated on p. 105.
44. Bruce Robertson, "The Tipping Point: Museum Collecting and the Canon," *American Art* 17, no. 3 (Autumn 2003): 2.
45. John I. H. Baur, "Unknown American Painters of the 19th Century," *College Art Journal* 6, no. 4 (Summer 1947): 277–82.
46. Ibid., 280. Baur was curator at the Brooklyn Museum (where he acquired a Lane for the collection in 1947 [Robertson, "Tipping Point,"

11n10]) and later one for the Whitney Museum as director of the latter institution during a career that spanned 1934–74 (Grace Glueck, "John I. H. Baur, Art Scholar: Headed the Whitney Museum," obituary, *New York Times*, May 16, 1987). Carol Troyen, "The Incomparable Max: Maxim Karolik and the Taste for American Art," *American Art* 7, no. 3 (Summer 1993): 64–87; between 1938 and 1945 the Karoliks bought more than two hundred paintings they gave to the MFA by 1949 (Robertson, "Tipping Point," 4, 11); see also Aline B. Louchheim, "Forgotten Men of American Art," *New York Times*, September 30, 1951 (illustrating Lane's *Ships in Ice off Ten Pound Island*); "230 U.S. Paintings in Boston Display," *New York Times*, September 30, 1951; Stuart Preston, "Americans Yesterday and Today," *New York Times*, May 9, 1954 (illustrating Lane's *Owl's Head, Penobscot Bay, Maine*); "Maxim Karolik, Art Patron, Dies: Collector Gave Americana to Boston Museum," *New York Times*, December 21, 1963.

47. "Pierrepont E. Johnson," obituary, *Newport Daily News*, May 7, 1963; "Fleet of 29 Sails from New London in 650-Mile Yacht Race to Bermuda," *New York Times*, June 25, 1934; class-A yachts are those longer than forty feet.

48. Edward W. Forbes, "Report of the William Hayes Fogg Art Museum, 1938–39," in *Fogg Art Museum Annual Report, No. 1938/1939*, 20 ("Appendix II: Loans"). Johnson was a Williams College, not a Harvard, alumnus, although the former husband of his divorcée bride had graduated from Harvard. "Miss Lilias Moriarty Snow to Wed Pierrepont E. Johnson Here Saturday," *Newport Mercury and Weekly News*, July 13, 1934. While the *Newport Mercury* reported that the couple "will reside in Boston," the *New York Times* (July 15, 1934) announced that "[t]hey are contemplating making their future home in Westchester N.Y."; in fact, according to the *Newport Daily News* Pierrepont Johnson obituary, they appear to have divided their time between Bar Harbor, Maine, and Newport, Rhode Island.

49. In 1899 they both attended a Bar Harbor moonlight canoe parade and dance ("Bar Harbor Canoe Parade," *New York Times*, August 22, 1899); in 1902 they were married in Bar Harbor ("Miss Julia Edwards Weds R. M. Johnson," *New York Times*, July 3, 1902).

50. William Richard Cutter, ed., *Genealogical and Personal Memoirs Relating to the Families of the State of Massachusetts* (New York: Lewis Historical Publishing, 1910), 36–37, 40–41; *CAL & GT*, June 4, 1859. It is not known whether C. F. Hovey or his wealthy Gloucester kin patronized Lane, but the Hovey house, Pine Cottage on Freshwater Cove, appears in several Lane canvases (including *Stage Fort Across Gloucester Harbor*, at the Metropolitan Museum). Hovey hired Francis Bennett, clerk in the Gloucester dry-goods store of Lane's close friend Joseph L. Stevens Jr., when the Stevens store closed in July 1854. Bennett, diary, entries for July 29, 1854, and August 3, 12, and 27, 1854.

51. *New York Times*, December 17, 1852.

52. P. E. Johnson's grandmother, Antoinette L. Waterbury Edwards Burden, was worth, it was reported in the newspaper, $1,275,418 when she died in 1930. *New York Times*, October 24, 1931.

53. Pierrepont Edwards Johnson and his wife, Lilias Moriarty Snow Johnson, were resident on an "estate near Boston," probably at Newport, Rhode Island (Ethne Clark, *Hidcote: The Making of a Garden* [1989; repr., New York: W. W. Norton, 2009], 132), but they were also extremely peripatetic, traveling frequently to Europe. Charles D. Childs to Francis W. Robinson at the Detroit Institute of Art, February 21, 1942, Archives of American Art, reel NDu2 (no frame numbers). It is also possible that Johnson and Karolik, both resident in Newport, knew one another and encouraged each other in their admiration of Lane's work; Troyen, "Incomparable Max," 80.

54. Childs mentioned *Somes Sound* in his offer of Lane's *Gloucester Harbor* (now known as *Gloucester Inner Harbor*, in the collection of the Mariners' Museum, Newport News, VA) to the Detroit Institute of Art. Childs to Robinson, Archives of American Art, reel NDu2 (no frame numbers).

55. Glueck, "John I. H. Baur."

56. Robertson, "Tipping Point," 4–5; "About Art and Artists," *New York Times*, May 3, 1954; Preston, "Americans Yesterday and Today" (illustrated by Lane's *Owl's Head*); Sharf, "Fitz Hugh Lane Re-considered," 75.

57. John I. H. Baur, *American Painting in the Nineteenth Century: Main Trends and Movements* (New York: Frederick A. Praeger, 1953), 9, 10. Baur included Lane's *Off Mount Desert Island* (Brooklyn Museum) and *Sunrise in Fog* (now known as *Sunrise through Mist*) (Karolik collection) in an exhibition he organized that toured Germany in 1953 (John I. H. Baur, *Hundert Jahre amerikanische Malerei, 1800–1900* [Munich: Prestel, 1953]), where the two Lane works appeared as #58, *Landschaft um Mt. Desert Island*, 1856 (Brooklyn Museum), and #57, *Sonnenaufgang bei Nebel*, 1852 (Karolik), 29.

58. John I. H. Baur, "Trends in American Painting, 1815 to 1865," in *M. and M. Karolik Collection of American Paintings, 1815 to 1865* (Boston: Museum of Fine Arts, Boston, 1949), xli; Baur illustrates nine works by Lane in this essay.

59. Baur, *American Painting*, 9; John I. H. Baur, "American Luminism: A Neglected Aspect of the Realist Movement in Nineteenth-Century American Painting," *Perspectives USA* 9 (Autumn 1954): 90–98. For a thoughtful New York–oriented reading of the nineteenth-century social context of artists later called luminists, see Alan Wallach, "Rethinking 'Luminism': Taste, Class, and Aestheticizing Tendencies in Mid-Nineteenth-Century American Landscape Painting," in *The Cultured*

Canvas: New Perspectives on American Landscape Painting, ed. Nancy Siegel (Durham: University of New Hampshire Press, 2011), 115–47.

60. Baur, *American Painting*, 10; Baur, "Trends," xli.

61. John Wilmerding paid $3,500 for *Stage Rocks and Western Shore of Gloucester Outer Harbor* (1857), according to Carol Vogel, "National Gallery Enriched by Gift," Inside Art, *New York Times*, May 7, 2004. The Shelburne Museum featured a Lane by 1960 (*New York Times*, August 21, 1960), as did the White House collection by 1966 (*New York Times*, February 3, 1966). The average cost of a new car in the United States in 1960 is reported to have been $2,600 (http://www.thepeoplehistory.com/1960s.html, accessed August 20, 2011); a *Boston Harbor Sunset* sold at auction in 1962 for $8,900 (Sotheby's, April 14, 1962, lot 185 [email from Laura West at Sotheby's, July 23, 2018]).

62. The drawings were sold to John Wilmerding and Philip Hofer; the sale took place despite institutional policy established fifteen years earlier: "As a matter of policy, the Association shall not sell any of its historical or artistic objects" (board meeting, July 5, 1951); Ruth Brooks, widow of the donor, protested the sale, and perhaps to mollify her, Wilmerding promised to will his Lane drawings to the Cape Ann S. L. & H. Association, reuniting at least part of this unique body of work (CAM records).

63. *Ship in a Fog off Ten Pound Island, Gloucester*, $42,000, Christie's, New York, 5/23/1979, lot 39; *Blue Hill, Maine*, $352,000, Christie's, New York, 6/3/83, lot 50; *The Annisquam River Looking Toward Ipswich Bay*, $825,000, 12/1/1989, Christie's New York, lot, 7; *View of West Beach, Beverly*, $3,852,500, Skinner Inc., 5/9/1997, as reported by Ken Shulman, "A Master Re-emerges from the Attic," *New York Times*, June 15, 1997; *Manchester Harbor*, $5,506,000, Skinner Inc., 11/19/2004, lot 370, as reported by Jeanne Schinto, "Skinner's Latest Fitz Hugh Lane Sale Sets a Record," *Maine Antiques Digest*, January 2005. The prices estimated and paid for rough-water paintings were considerably lower; for instance, *Sunset After Storm* (1859) sold for $30,000 in 1989 (Sotheby's, 11/30/1989, lot 12), and *Ships in a Squall off the Coast of Gloucester* (1842) sold for $281,000 in 2006 (Northeast Auctions, 08/19–20/2006, lot 1055); see askART. See also Richard Hislop, ed., *Auction Prices of American Artists, 1977–94*, 9 vols. (Weybridge, Surrey: Art Sales Index, 1978–94). This disparate valuation persists: two paintings of the same schooner, of the same size, with the same provenance, both signed and dated, were sold June 26, 2020: the "stormy sea" one brought $93,750, while the "calm sea" portrait brought $312,500, https://www.sothebys.com/en/buy/auction/2020/american-art/fitz-henry-lane-schooner-loo-choo-in-a-stormy-sea?locale=en; https://www.sothebys.com/en/buy/auction/2020/american-art/fitz-henry-lane-schooner-loo-choo-in-a-calm-sea?locale=en.

64. The relatively new field of the economics of the art market considers many factors in its models, but interestingly, scholarship and exhibitions do not figure centrally; see, for instance, the very thought-provoking work by Robert B. Ekelund Jr., John D. Jackson, and Robert D. Tollison, *The Economics of American Art: Issues, Artists, and Market Institutions* (Oxford: Oxford University Press, 2017).

65. J. Carter Brown, foreword, in Wilmerding, *Paintings by Fitz Hugh Lane*, 6. Some attributed the meteoric rise in the value of Lane paintings in the second half of the twentieth century to a rise in yachting culture. Steven K. Bursten, "Marine Art Is Riding Wave of Success," *New York Times*, August 16, 1970.

66. Earl A. Powell, "The Boston Harbor Pictures," in Wilmerding, *Paintings by Fitz Hugh Lane*, 54; Ellis, "Cape Ann Views," 19, 36.

67. Ellis, "Cape Ann Views," 36.

68. Wilmerding, *Fitz Hugh Lane* (1971), 46, 70, 76.

69. Robert Rosenblum, as quoted in a press release for the exhibition *The Natural Paradise: Painting in America, 1800–1950* (Museum of Modern Art, September 29, 1976), 4.

70. Kelly, "Lane and Church," 144, 153; Franklin Kelly, "The Paintings of Fitz Hugh Lane," *Antiques* 134 (July 1988): 119, 121; Wilmerding, *Fitz Hugh Lane* (1971), 30.

71. Kelly, "Lane and Church," 151; Wilmerding, "Master of the Silvery Mist."

72. Quinn, Kelberlau, and Woodward, "Rediscovering," 69.

73. Clement Greenberg, "'American-Type' Painting," 1955, rev. 1958, in *Art and Culture: Critical Essays* (Boston: Beacon Press, 1961), 226.

74. Ibid., 208; Clement Greenberg, "Abstract and Representational," *Art Digest*, November 1, 1954, repr. in *Clement Greenberg: The Collected Essays and Criticism*, ed. John O'Brian (Chicago: University of Chicago Press, 1993), 3:191.

75. Clement Greenberg, "Abstract, Representational, and So Forth" (originally given as a Ryerson Lecture at Yale, May 12, 1954), in *Collected Essays and Criticism*, 3:137; Greenberg, "Abstract and Representational," 192. See also Alfred Barr's comment in which he proposes the Mondrian look of Whistler's *Arrangement in Grey and Black No. 1 (Portrait of the Artist's Mother)* with the figure erased. Alfred H. Barr Jr., *What Is Modern Painting?* (New York: Museum of Modern Art, 1943), 10–11.

76. Clement Greenberg, "Abstract Art," *The Nation*, April 15, 1944, repr. in *Collected Essays and Criticism*, 1:203; Greenberg, "'Feeling Is All,'" *Partisan Review*, January–February 1952, repr. in ibid., 3:99, 100, 101, 104; Greenberg, "Abstract, Representational, and So Forth," 134; Greenberg, "'American-Type' Painting," 208, 217, 218, 225.

77. Greenberg, "Abstract Art," 199, 201; Clement Greenberg, "The Present Prospects of American Painting and Sculpture," *Horizon*, October 1947, repr. in *Collected Essays and Criticism*,

2:160–61, 165; Clement Greenberg, "Review of an Exhibition of Arshile Gorky," *Partisan Review*, April 1948, repr. in ibid., 2:222; Greenberg, "'Feeling Is All,'" 104; Clement Greenberg, "Some Advantages of Provincialism," *Art Digest*, January 1, 1954, repr. *Collected Essays and Criticism*, 3:163; Greenberg, "Abstract and Representational," 190, 193; Greenberg, "'American-Type' Painting," 209–14, 219, 224.

78. For an excellent account of the intersecting narratives of luminism, nationalism, modernism, and the market, see J. Gray Sweeney, "Inventing Luminism: 'Labels Are the Dickens,'" *Oxford Art Journal* 26, no. 2 (2003): 93–120.

79. Wilmerding, *Fitz Hugh Lane* (1971), 13, 56; Wilmerding points to occasions on which Lane's works appeared in exhibitions in which other "Luminists" participated (ibid., 79).

80. Ibid., 69; for thoughtful comments on the context of the invention of luminism, see John Davis, "Only in America: Exceptionalism, Nationalism, Provincialism," in *A Companion to American Art*, ed. John Davis, Jennifer A. Greenhill, and Jason D. LaFountain (Hoboken, NJ: John Wiley & Sons, 2015), 323–24.

81. Powell, "Boston Harbor Pictures," 48.

82. Ibid., 53; however common the (market) ground they stand on today, Church could in his lifetime command $10,000 for a single work, while Lane never received more than $500, suggesting that, for these artists and their patrons, their works were hugely disparate.

83. Greenberg, "Present Prospects," 165; Clement Greenberg, "Our Period Style," *Partisan Review*, November 1949, repr. in *Collected Essays and Criticism*, 2:325; Greenberg, "Some Advantages of Provincialism," 3:162; Greenberg, "Abstract Art," 199; Greenberg, "'American-Type' Painting," 216, 228; Robert Rosenblum, "The Primal American Scene," in *The Natural Paradise: Painting in America, 1800–1950*, exh. cat., ed. Kynaston McShine (New York: Museum of Modern Art, 1976), 15–18.

84. Rosenblum, "Primal American Scene," 15, 18, 22; John Wilmerding, "Fire and Ice in American Art: Polarities from Luminism to Abstract Expressionism," in McShine, *Natural Paradise*, 46; Roberta Smith, "A Youthful Land in All Its Glory," *New York Times*, June 14, 2002; Elizabeth Johns, "Histories of American Art: The Changing Quest," *Art Journal* 44, no. 4 (Winter 1984): 343; Michael Kimmelman, "Art/Architecture: Ambition and Rapture Add Up to Joy," *New York Times*, May 12, 2002 ("Imagine [Eva] Hesse extending the nineteenth-century American Luminist tradition").

85. Andrew Wilton and Tim Barringer, eds., *American Sublime: Landscape Painting in the United States, 1820–1880* (London: Tate, 2002), 192; Kelly, "Paintings of Fitz Hugh Lane," 121. Echoing this established rhetoric, a conservator musing on Lane's underdrawing suggested in 2007 that some drawn elements were painted out "to eliminate clutter." Cape Ann Museum, *Report on Scholars' Gathering in Association with the Exhibition "Fitz Henry Lane and Mary Blood Mellen: Old Mysteries and New Discoveries"* (New York: Terra Foundation, 2007), 6.

86. Wilmerding, *Fitz Hugh Lane* (1971), 34–35; Powell, "Boston Harbor Pictures," 48; Wilton and Barringer, *American Sublime*, 194.

87. Kelly, "Lane and Church," 144, 153. For the dating of the Sawyer Homestead paintings, see the Sawyer diary entry of August 25, 1864, as cited in Wilmerding, *Paintings by Fitz Hugh Lane*, 61, and that of November 8, 1857, in Samuel Sawyer Papers (Notebooks and Diaries #20), Expense Accounts of Samuel Sawyer, 1851–60, A63 Series II and III, Box 2, CAM. I thank Molly Hardy and Mary Rhinelander McCarl for this CAM reference.

88. Baur, in *M. and M. Karolik Collection*, 398.

89. Kelly, "Lane and Church," 144, 154; see also John Wilmerding, *Compass and Clock: Defining Moments in American Culture, 1800, 1850, 1900* (New York: Harry N. Abrams, 1999), 108–14.

90. Greenberg, "Abstract Art," 200, also 201–4; Greenberg, "Present Prospects," 160; Greenberg, "Review of an Exhibition," 222; Greenberg, "'Feeling Is All,'" 104; Theodor W. Adorno, "Late Style in Beethoven," in *Essays on Music*, ed. Richard Leppert, trans. Susan H. Gillespie (Berkeley: University of California Press, 2002), 564–68.

91. Greenberg, "Abstract and Representational," 191.

92. Kelly, "Paintings of Fitz Hugh Lane," 121.

93. The original building lot cost him $368 in October 1849, to which (taking out mortgages) he added garden plots in 1853 and 1856 for a further $763; in 1860 his real estate was valued at $4,000, and embroiled in a lawsuit, he sold the property in 1862 to his friend and executor Joseph L. Stevens Jr. for $6,000. Stevens sold the property in 1866 for $5,000. Dunlap and Buck, *FHL*, 152, 153, 154, 156, 160, 165.

94. Ralph Waldo Emerson, "Nature," in *Essays: Second Series* (Boston: James Munroe, 1844), 183, 184, 186, 187.

95. Novak, *American Painting*, 110, 123.

96. Ellis, "Cape Ann Views," 19; Wilmerding, "Luminist Movement," 98.

97. Powell, "Luminism and the American Sublime," 71, and Powell, "Boston Harbor Pictures," 59.

98. The most recent extended discussion of this theory is Barbara Novak's "Emerson and Lane: Luminist Time and the Transcendental Aboriginal Self," chap. 2 in *Voyages of the Self: Pairs, Parallels, and Patterns in American Art and Literature* (Oxford: Oxford University Press, 2007).

99. Baxandall, *Patterns of Intention*, 76–78; Baxandall, *Limewood Sculptors*, 142; see also Barbara Novak, "Self, Time, and Object in American Art: Copley, Lane, and Homer," in *American Icons: Transatlantic Perspectives on Eighteenth- and Nineteenth-Century*

American Art, ed. Thomas W. Gaehtgens and Heinz Ickstadt (Los Angeles: Getty Center, 1992), 64.

100. Tilden, *Autobiography and Personal Tributes*, 73, 77.
101. Barbara Novak, "Fitz Hugh Lane: A Paradigm of Luminism," chap. 6, in *American Painting*, 110–24, esp. 301n2; Marshall W. S. Swan, "Emerson and Cape Ann," *Essex Institute Historical Collections* 121, no. 4 (October 1985): 257–68; Elizabeth Garrity Ellis, "Fitz Hugh Lane and the American Union of Associationists," *American Art Journal* 17, no. 2 (Spring 1985): 89; Mary Foley, "Fitz Hugh Lane, Ralph Waldo Emerson, and the Gloucester Lyceum," *American Art Journal* 27, nos. 1–2 (1995–96): 99–101. One could add to this list of "overlaps" the fact that one of Lane's most important patrons employed R. W. Emerson's brother Edward in the 1830s, but in surviving correspondence there is no evidence that aesthetic/philosophical issues were discussed or reconveyed to Lane. Correspondence of Edward Bliss Emerson, Houghton Library, Harvard, bMS AM 1280.235 (349).
102. Sharon Worley, "Mapping the Metaphysical Landscape off Cape Ann: The Reception of Ralph Waldo Emerson's Transcendentalism Among the Gloucester Audience of Reverend Amory Dwight Mayo and Fitz Hugh Lane," *Historical Journal of Massachusetts* 29, no. 2 (2001): 137–69.
103. Ralph Waldo Emerson, "Spirit," in *Nature*, facsimile edition of 1836 first edition, ed. Jaroslav Pelikan (Boston: Beacon Press, 1985), 80.
104. For more on Lane's background, see chapter 3.
105. Ellis, "Lane and the American Union of Associationists."
106. Ralph Waldo Emerson, "Nominalist and Realist," in *Essays: Second Series* (Boston: James Munroe, 1844), 268.
107. John Trask's long retrospective account of Lane includes the comment: "He was a strong spiritualist." Trask, "Notes on the Life."
108. *CAL*, February 8, 1861.
109. *CAL & GT* 23, no. 45 (Saturday, November 10, 1849), and 23, no. 48 (Saturday, December 1, 1849); *CAA*, Friday, February 22, 1861.
110. *GT* 14, no. 14 (Saturday, February 16, 1850).
111. *CAL & GT* 23, no. 9 (March 3, 1849); 23, no. 13 (March 31, 1849).
112. *GT* 14, no. 22 (Saturday, March 16, 1850).
113. *GT* 14, no. 30 (Saturday, April 13, 1850); 14, no. 49 (June 19, 1850); and 14, no. 77 (September 25, 1850).
114. Powell, "Luminism and the American Sublime," 78; Powell, "Boston Harbor Pictures," 48.
115. *GT* 4, no. 33 (Saturday, August 14, 1830).
116. A. Babson, diary, entry for Thursday, August 16, 1849.
117. Ibid., August 28, 1841, as cited in Worley, "Mapping the Metaphysical," 160.
118. Caroline Blinder, "'The Transparent Eyeball': On Emerson and Walker Evans," *Mosaic: An Interdisciplinary Critical Journal* 37, no. 4 (December 2004): 149–63; Walker Evans, *American Photographs*, with an essay by Lincoln Kirstein (New York: Museum of Modern Art, 1938); William Carlos Williams, "Sermon with a Camera," *New Republic*, October 11, 1938, 282–83.
119. Vernon Louis Parrington, "Ralph Waldo Emerson: Transcendental Critic," chap. 2 in *Main Currents in American Thought: An Interpretation of American Literature from the Beginnings to 1920* (New York: Harcourt, Brace, 1927), 2:386–99. On the mid-twentieth-century uses of Emerson, see also Samuel Otter, "*American Renaissance* and Us," *Journal of Nineteenth-Century Americanists* 3, no. 2 (Fall 2015): 228–35.
120. Blinder, "'Transparent Eyeball,'" 150.
121. Ralph Waldo Emerson, introduction to *Nature* (1836), 5.

CHAPTER 3

1. Wilmerding, "Luminist Movement," 111.
2. Kelly, "Lane and Church," 144; Wilmerding, "Luminist Movement," 111.
3. Although many Lane paintings are on plain-weave canvas, those on twill are a notable group, including, besides *Salem Harbor, Gloucester Harbor* (fig. 10).
4. Salem's harbor was home base to more large vessels than Gloucester's—in 1830, 32 ships, 7 barks, 87 brigs, and 87 schooners. *GT* 4, no. 2 (January 9, 1830).
5. John G. B. Hutchins, *The American Maritime Industries and Public Policy, 1789–1914: An Economic History* (Cambridge: Harvard University Press, 1941), chaps. 10 and 11, 287–370, especially 294–96; Samuel Eliot Morison, *The Maritime History of Massachusetts, 1783–1860* (Boston: Houghton Mifflin, 1921), 339–64.
6. Morison, *Maritime History*, 362–64.
7. A label on the back of *Salem Harbor* reads: "Belonged to my great-grandparents / Nathaniel Silsbee Jr. / Dec. 18, 1804–July 1881 / and Marianne [aka Mary Anne] C[abot] D[evereaux (1812–1889)] /—/ Marianne M. Beach / sa—" (MFA object files). Silsbee's father was ship captain for Salem nabob Elias Haskett Derby and later became Derby's son-in-law and a U.S. senator for Massachusetts; he was a descendant of Salem's wealthiest dynasties—the Crowninshields and Derbys. John Frayler, "Pickled Fish and Salted Provisions: Historical Musings from Salem Maritime NHS," *Pepper and Providence* (a publication of the National Park Service, Salem Maritime National Historic Site) 7, no. 2 (July 2005): 3.
8. MFA object file.
9. Frayler, "Pickled Fish," 3; William Marsden, *The History of Sumatra* (repr. of the 3rd ed., 1811, Oxford: Oxford University Press, 1966), v–viii (1st ed. published London, 1783).
10. Herman Moll, inscription detail of "A Map of the East-Indies and the adjacent countries; with the Settlements, Factories and Territories, explaining what belongs to England, Spain, France, Holland, Denmark, Portugal &c.," n.d., probably 1709, map 5 in Herman Moll, *The World Described; or, A New and Correct Sett of Maps* [...] (London: I Bowles, [1709–20]), twenty-seven two-sheet maps, AAS.

11. The firm of Stone, Silsbee, and Pickman owned five clipper ships and was in business from 1798 to 1898. Glenn A. Knoblock, *The American Clipper Ship, 1845–1920* (Jefferson, NC: McFarland, 2014), 166.
12. For explanation of the types of ships and boats in Lane paintings, see http://fitzhenrylaneonline.org/historical_material/?type=Vessel+Types.
13. *GDT*, July 1913, in "Clippings," CAM, as cited in Dunlop and Buck, *FHL*, 125.
14. *GDT*, October 15, 1915, in "Clippings," CAM, as cited in Dunlop and Buck, *FHL*, 125.
15. Letter of December 1914 from Arthur Williams Jr. and Co. of Boston offering a "Fitz Hugh Lane" painting to a party in New York City (Eleanor H. Gustafson, ed., "Collector's Notes," *Antiques* 172, no. 2 [August 2007]: 44) and an advertisement, probably dating from 1938, placed by Richard Nichols Co. of Boston for a lithograph "drawn by Fitzhugh Lane" (in "Clippings," CAM, as cited in Dunlop and Buck, *FHL*, 128).
16. Elinor Gordon, *Collecting Chinese Export Porcelain* (Pittstown, NJ: Main Street Press, 1984), 117–29; J. B. S. Holmes, "Fitzhugh and FitzHughs in the China Trade," in *Chinese Export Porcelain: An Historical Survey*, ed. Elinor Gordon (New York: Main Street / Universe Books, 1975), 155–56. A well-known turn-of-the-century English art collector, Sir Hugh Lane, has also been proposed as another possible source for the erroneous name. Gustafson, "Collector's Notes," 44.
17. Sarah Dunlap and Stephanie Buck, "Fitz Henry/Hugh Lane," chap. 7 in *FHL*, 121–37.
18. Trask, "Notes on the Life." Emma Todd's daughter, testifying to her verbatim transcription, indicated: "I have not 'edited' these notes. They are merely converted from my mother's long hand."
19. John Wilmerding, *Fitz Hugh Lane, 1804–1865: American Marine Painter* (Salem, MA: Essex Institute, 1964), 49.
20. Franklin Kelly, "The Westervelt Warner Museum of Young America," *Antiques* 166, no. 2 (August 2004): 61.
21. Lewis I. Sharp, "American Paintings and Sculpture," *Notable Acquisitions (Metropolitan Museum of Art)*, 1965–75, 13. The painting has evidently been relined, so that this inscription is no longer visible.
22. See http://www.mcny.org/Collections/paint/Painting/pHcat26.htm, accessed February 24, 2005; the information on *Sweepstakes* includes a notation that J. Wilmerding looked at the work in 1993 and concluded that it was indubitably by Lane, but "felt that [Joseph L.] Stevens or someone else might have been involved in the ['peculiar'] signature"; Knoblock, *American Clipper Ship*, 197.
23. Massachusetts Archives, *Laws of the Commonwealth of Massachusetts*, chap. 74, March 13, 1832; *List of Persons Whose Names Have Been Changed in Massachusetts, 1780–1883* (Boston: Wright & Potter Printing, 1885), 68, as cited in Dunlap and Buck, *FHL*, 40n148; see also Eleanor H. Gustafson, ed., "Collectors' Notes," *Antiques* 157, no. 6 (June 2005): 48, and Dunlap and Buck, *FHL*, 39–41. Changing one's name was apparently not unusual—long lists of official name changes appear frequently in the local papers (e.g., *GT* 3, no. 13 [March 21, 1829]); the city fathers were also busy at this time renaming Gloucester's streets (*GT* 3, no. 14 [March 28, 1829]).
24. Trask, "Notes on the Life."
25. Dunlap and Buck, *FHL*, 40.
26. Mackay was illegitimate, and named at birth Joshua Gee Whittemore Jr; he renamed himself in 1815, at the age of thirty-seven. Dunlap and Buck, *FHL*, 40n, 51, 157n. The patronage by Mackay and his wife of Lane is recorded in Brooks, "Catalogue of the Drawings," 12, 18, 19, 40, 77. Mackay received a $500 reward from one of the passengers on the *Boston*, education pioneer Admiral Sir Isaac Coffin, in June 1830 and probably commissioned the picture in memory of his windfall as much as in memory of the disaster. *GT* 4, no. 24 (June 12, 1830). The ship and cargo (cotton bound for Liverpool) were lost, but among crew and passengers only one was lost. In the year of Mackay's death, the painting was in the hands of E. D. Knight, first officer on the *Boston*, who gave it to Joseph L. Stevens Jr. Letter from Knight to Stevens, August 18, 1869, CAM. See *GT* 14, no. 74 (September 14, 1850), and 34, no. 74 (September 15, 1860), for Mackay's position in Gloucester's tax list.
27. David Tatham, "The Lithographic Workshop, 1825–50," in *The Cultivation of Artists in Nineteenth-Century America*, ed. Georgia Brady Barnhill, Diana Korzenik, and Caroline F. Sloat (Worcester, MA: AAS, 1997), 45–54.
28. "F. H. Lane / Marine Painter / 7 Summer St. Boston" (copper plate at CAM).
29. I am using "self-fashioning" here in the sense that Stephen Greenblatt employs the term in *Renaissance Self-Fashioning: From More to Shakespeare* (Chicago: University of Chicago Press, 1980), 1–9 and passim.
30. In 1820, the year Lane turned sixteen (and in subsequent years), the taxes on his mother's property were abated because she "supports a lame child / ought not to be taxed." Dunlap and Buck, *FHL*, 26. Gloucesterites were sensitive to the "Esq." designation. See *GT* 3, no. 36 (August 29, 1829). See chapter 1 above for Lane's recognition as "Esq."
31. The journal of Charles A. Homans, second mate on the bark *Izette* from Gloucester to Surinam in 1848–49, Nathaniel Rogers, master, is preserved at CAM. Capt. Nathaniel Rogers stands equal to F. H. Lane in Gloucester's 1860 tax list. *GT* 14, no. 77 (September 15, 1860). Nathaniel Peabody Rogers (1794–1846) of New Hampshire took on the editorship of *Herald to Freedom* only in 1838. Parker Pillsbury, "Nathaniel Peabody Rogers," *Granite Monthly* 4, no. 7 (April 1881). Nathaniel Rogers

(1598–1655), the Ipswich minister, was reported in the Gloucester paper to have been of "slender constitution and feeble health." *GT* 1, no. 49 (December 1, 1827).

32. William Dunlap, *A History of the Rise and Progress of the Arts of Design in the United States* (New York: G. P. Scott, 1834; repr., New York: Dover, 1969), vol. 2, pt. 1, 251–53.
33. Ibid.
34. *GT* 3, no. 7 (Saturday, February 7, 1829). See also Joel Hawes, "Formation and Importance of Character," lecture 4 in *Lectures Addressed to the Young Men of Hartford and New-Haven* (Hartford, CT: Oliver D. Cooke, 1828), 91–116, quotation on 95–96.
35. Phillips, *Ship Registers*, 36; *GT* 5, no. 2 (January 8, 1831), and 14, no. 26 (March 30, 1850); *CAL & GT* 33, no. 23 (June 4, 1859); *Gloucester Directory* (1860); *CAL & GT* 45, no. 35 (September 2, 1871). Lane's contemporaries also included Fitz E. Riggs, Fitz W. Elwell, Fitz E. Oakes, and Fitz Norwood; Aaron Fitz, Capt. Charles Fitz, and Daniel Fitz.
36. In *An Address Delivered Before the Newburyport [MA] Mechanic Association [. . .] Oct. 28, 1812*, Henry Fitz, a member of that association, exhorted his fellows to charitable benevolence and warned them about the danger of overweening ambition and self-love; it is unlikely that Lane picked his name in emulation of this individual or the pieties of his published tract.
37. Authored by Lady Scott (Caroline Lucy), edited by Lady Bury (Charlotte Campbell), *Fitzhenry* was erroneously credited to Louis Fitzgerald Tasistro. It was first published in London by Henry Colburn in 1828, and subsequent editions were published in London, Paris, Dublin, and Boston.
38. Lady Caroline Lucy Scott, *Fitzhenry* (Boston: F. Gleason, 1847), 8, 23.
39. Ibid., 24, 28.
40. Ibid., 39–47.
41. *Journal of Captain Solomon H. Davis*, 12, 13. On voyages in the 1840s he continued reading in this vein (93).
42. *GT* 3, no. 43 (October 17, 1829).
43. Trask, "Notes on the Life," discussed in Dunlap and Buck, *FHL*, 33–35; E. Lane, "Early Recollections."
44. Dunlap and Buck, *FHL*, 28, 33.
45. Trask, "Notes on the Life," and Dunlap and Buck, *FHL*, 149–51.
46. Repr. from the *Courier* in *GT* 4, no. 17 (April 24, 1830).
47. Barbara M. Solomon, "The Growth of the Population in Essex County, 1850–60," in *Essex Institute Historical Collections* 45, no. 2 (April 1959): 83.
48. *GT* 14, no. 8 (January 26, 1850).
49. *GT* 1, no. 18 (April 28, 1827); Dunlap and Buck, *FHL*, 34.
50. *GT* 2, no. 14 (March 29, 1828).
51. *GT* 4, no. 38 (September 18, 1830), and 4, no. 47 (November 20, 1830).
52. *GT* 14, no. 16 (February 23, 1850), and 34, no. 74 (September 15, 1860). It should be noted that by the date of these midcentury ads, Haskell is a "Dealer in Boots, Shoes . . . ," rather than a shoemaker.
53. *GT* 2, no. 4 (January 19, 1828); 4, no. 14 (April 3, 1830); 3, no. 22 (May 23, 1829); 4, no. 33 (August 14, 1830); 4, no. 16 (April 17, 1830). This aphorism persists today among horsemen, who generally prefer farrier hot-worked shoes.
54. *GT* 3, no. 51 (December 12, 1829); see also *GT* 3, no. 44 (October 24, 1829).
55. *GT* 4, no. 47 (November 20, 1830); 2, no. 29 (July 12, 1828); 4, no. 21 (May 22, 1830); 2, no. 30 (July 19, 1828); 2, no. 34 (August 16, 1828); 3, no. 30 (July 18, 1829).
56. "Diseases of Painters," repr. from the *New York Journal of Commerce* in *GT* 1, no. 47 (November 17, 1827).
57. The Stuart portrait was reported in *GT* 1, no. 31 (July 28, 1827). Nollekens's estate was discussed in *GT* 2, no. 13 (March 22, 1828). In 1831, 43,000 prints and drawings as well as 928 pictures were apparently detained on bond in London; *GT* 5, no. 46 (November 12, 1831).
58. Ad for the *New York Mirror, a Repository of Polite Literature and the Arts*, in *GT* 4, no. 24 (June 12, 1830); see also Cynthia Lee Patterson, *Art for the Middle Classes: America's Illustrated Magazines of the 1840s* (Jackson: University Press of Mississippi, 2010).
59. *GT* 4, no. 29 (July 17, 1830), and 4, no. 47 (November 20, 1830). Other periodicals that advertised their lavishly illustrated numbers in the Gloucester newspapers in this decade included the *Philadelphia Album and Ladies' Literary Gazette* (*GT* 4, no. 24 [June 12, 1830]), *Atkinson's Casket* (*GT* 5, no. 6 [February 12, 1831]), and *The Token* (*GT* 5, no. 52 [December 24, 1831]).
60. *GT* 2, no. 33 (August 9, 1828), and 2, no. 34 (August 16, 1828).
61. *GT* 1, no. 9 (February 24, 1827).
62. *GT* 3, no. 52 (December 19, 1829).
63. *GT* 4, no. 40 (October 2, 1830). The painting tour brought in $8,886 for Peale. Goldstein, *Landscape with Figures*, 18. See also the letter from Joseph L. Stevens Jr. to Samuel H. Mansfield, October 17, 1904, CAM, in which he recounts the impact on him as a child of hearing about the exhibition of *Death on the Pale Horse*, probably William Dunlap's painting of this name, which toured in the 1820s.
64. *CAA* 3, no. 27 (July 7, 1860).
65. *GT* 2, no. 6 (February 2, 1828), and 4, no. 16 (April 17, 1830).
66. *GT* 1, no. 27 (June 20, 1827).
67. Samuel W. Rogers: *GT* 1, no. 3 (January 13, 1827), and 3, no. 51 (December 12, 1829); Harrington Hatch: *GT* 1, no. 8 (February 17, 1827); Gloucester Bookstore: *GT* 1, no. 43 (October 20, 1827); G. H. Rogers: *GT* 2, no. 52 (December 20, 1828); 3, no. 29 (July 11, 1829); and 3, no. 38 (September 12, 1829). Also, a Miss M. Whittemore sought through an advertisement to recover a missing bundle that included her "Paint Boxes and Brushes": *GT* 1, no. 30 (July 21, 1827).
68. *GT* 3, no. 11 (March 27, 1829).
69. *GT* 4, no. 4 (January 23, 1830). As late as 1850 Sherman and his shoemaker's bench figured in Gloucester sermons and newspaper articles. *GT* 14, no. 11 (February 9, 1850).
70. *GT* 2, no. 30 (July 19, 1828).
71. *GT* 3, no. 20 (May 9, 1829), repr. from the *Evening Bulletin*.
72. Ibid.

73. *GT* 2, no. 50 (December 6, 1828).
74. Ibid., from an uncited work by "Burton."
75. *GT* 4, no. 43 (October 23, 1830), quoted from an uncited source by C. C. Felton.
76. *GT* 2, no. 34 (August 16, 1828), and 4, no. 32 (August 7, 1830).
77. A brief article reported on the development of a "machine for cutting out boots . . . [up to] twenty pair at the same stroke of the knife . . . [manageable by] a person unacquainted with the business" (*GT* 5, no. 46 [November 12, 1831]); another reports on a machine that saved the necessity to hammer the leather (*GT* 4, no. 33 [August 14, 1830]).
78. *GT* 2, no. 7 (February 9, 1828).
79. *GT* 5, no. 52 (December 24, 1831). By 1850 Massachusetts factories were producing $20 million worth of "coarse" shoes alone. *GT* 14, no. 26 (March 30, 1850).
80. On printing, see *GT* 3, no. 20 (May 9, 1829), and 2, no. 10 (March 1, 1828). On self-fashioning, *GT* 3, no. 28 (July 4, 1829). Similarly singled out is Capt. H. Clipperton, "The African Traveller," *GT* 2, no. 30 (July 19, 1828).
81. *GT* 5, no. 46 (November 12, 1831).
82. Dunlap and Buck, *FHL*, 37.
83. *GT* 4, no. 36 (September 5, 1830).
84. Tatham, "Pendleton-Moore Shop," 30–32.
85. Edward Hazen, *The Panorama of Professions and Trades* (Philadelphia: Uriah Hunt, 1836), 175–76.
86. Hazen, *Panorama*, 176; "State and Prospects of Lithography."
87. Obituary for William S. Pendleton, *Advertiser* (Boston), February 15, 1874, clipping from Charles Henry Taylor collection, AAS.
88. Ibid.
89. Ibid.
90. Benjamin Champney, *Sixty Years' Memories of Art and Artists* (Woburn, MA: self-published, 1900), 10–15, as cited in Tatham, "Lithographic Workshop," 48.
91. Pendleton's establishment became T. Moore's after 1836 and J. H. Bufford & Co. after 1844. Tatham, "Lithographic Workshop," 47, 54.
92. Elliot Bostwick Davis, "American Drawing Books and Their Impact on Fitz Hugh Lane," in Barnhill, Korzenik, and Sloat, *Cultivation of Artists*, 55–80. Davis makes a strong case for the particular importance to Lane of John Gadsby Chapman's *American Drawing Book* (appearing serially in 1847). See also Elliot Bostwick Davis, "Training the Eye and the Hand: Fitz Hugh Lane and American Drawing Books," in *Training the Eye and the Hand: Fitz Hugh Lane and Nineteenth Century American Drawing Books*, exh. cat. (Gloucester, MA: CAHA, 1993), 7–25, 33–36.
93. The Menil Collection holds a set of these illustrations: http://50.201.124.17/people/1408/charles-c-green;jsessionid=AD3B34A6E9F89AABAFEBB08F850E166B/objects, accessed August 28, 2020.
94. Craig, *Fitz H. Lane*, 56–61. See the inscription on the back of *The Yacht* Northern Light *in Boston Harbor* (1845): "From a Sketch by Robert Salmon" (Shelburne Museum, Shelburne, VT).
95. *GT* 14, no. 1 (January 2, 1850).
96. Dunlap and Buck, *FHL*, 29, 42.
97. For Lane's lithographs, see http://fitzhenrylaneonline.org; John Wilmerding, "The Lithographs of Fitz Hugh Lane," *Old-Time New England* 54, no. 2 (October–December 1963): 31–39; and Clifford Geertz, *Local Knowledge: Further Essays in Interpretive Anthropology* (New York: Basic Books, 1983).
98. Most of the Boston Athenaeum works were apparently done on spec and offered for sale. Perkins and Gavin, *Boston Athenaeum Art Exhibition Index*, 90. See appendix A.
99. *CAL & GT*, September 30, 1848; *CAL & GT*, October 21, 1848; *CAL & GT* 23, no. 1 (January 6, 1849); *GT* 14, no. 3 (January 9, 1850); *GT* 14, no. 14 (February 16, 1850); *CAL & GT* 23, no. 29 (July 21, 1849); *GT* 14, no. 63 (August 7, 1850); *GT* 14, no. 65 (August 14, 1850); *BET*, October 23, 1850; *GT* 14, no. 66 (August 17, 1850).
100. *CAL & GT*, May 13, 1848; *CAL & GT* 23, no. 36 (September 8, 1849); *CAL & GT* 25, no. 26 (June 28, 1851); Bennett, diary, entry for June 16, 1854.
101. *GT* 14, no. 52 (June 29, 1850).
102. *BET*, February 4, 1851.
103. *GT* 14, no. 27 (April 3, 1850); *CAL & GT*, July 1, 1848; *BET*, May 10, 1850; *CAL & GT* 23, no. 39 (September 29, 1849); *GT* 14, no. 26 (March 30, 1850).
104. This sum was in addition to the costs of the tour ($100,000). *GT* 14, no. 21 (March 13, 1850), and 14, no. 33 (April 24, 1850). Tickets for her first concert alone were reported to have netted $24,618.87½ *GT* 14, no. 74 (September 14, 1850).
105. Brooks and Brooks, *Gloucester Recollected*, 15, 22, 25–26, 26–27, 35, 51, 58.
106. *GT* 14, no. 74 (September 14, 1850).
107. "Dusseldorf Paintings at New York, May 8, 1850," *BET*, May 10, 1850.
108. Letter from Joseph L. Stevens Jr. to Samuel H. Mansfield, October 17, 1904, CAM.
109. "Dusseldorf Paintings."
110. *CAL & GT* 23, no. 23 (June 9, 1849).
111. Witherle, "Cruise with Fitz Hugh Lane," 2–3.
112. Dominic Serres and John Thomas Serres, *Liber Nauticum* [*sic*] *and Instructor in the Art of Marine Drawing*, pt. 1 (London, 1805), as cited in Eleanor Hughes, "Vessels of Empire: Eighteenth-Century British Marine Painting" (PhD diss., University of California, Berkeley, 2001), chap. 4, 1–2; see also Eleanor Hughes, ed., *Spreading Canvas: Eighteenth-Century British Marine Painting*, exh. cat. (New Haven: Yale University Press, 2016), 221, 270.
113. Francis A. Durivage, "The Career of an Artist" (1850), in *Life Scenes, Sketched in Light and Shadow from the World Around Us* (Boston: Sanborn, Carter & Bazin, 1856), 99–111, quotations on 104 and 105.
114. *Bulletin of the American Art-Union* 2, no. 5 (August 1849): 10–12. This article was puffed in a notice in the Gloucester paper, also informing locals that among the paintings purchased by the organization for the 1849 prizes was "a 'View of Boston Harbor,' 34 × 27 inches in size, from the easel of F. H. Lane, Esq.,

of this town." *CAL & GT* 23, no. 32 (August 11, 1849).

115. *Bulletin of the American Art-Union* 2, no. 5 (August 1849): 10–12.
116. *View of Coffin's Beach* (MFA object file); Quinn, Kelberlau, and Woodward, "Rediscovering."
117. James Craig believes this painting may depict Portsmouth harbor rather then Salem (*Fitz H. Lane*, 169, 171–72).
118. The mid-nineteenth-century application of insignia of ownership at large scale directly on sails (in addition to pennants) has been recorded, for instance, in a painting illustrated in Knoblock, *American Clipper Ship*, 161.
119. Object files, CAM; see also John R. Parker, *The New Semaphoric Signal Book* [...] *The United States Telegraph Vocabulary* [...] *to Which Is Annexed the Boston Harbor Signal Book* (Boston: Kidder & Wright, 1842), ixff.
120. For comments on the Boston pilot schooner and identifying flags, see Erik Ronnberg: http://fitzhenrylaneonline.org/catalog/entry.php?id=35.
121. Robert Bennet Forbes puzzles for several paragraphs in his memoir over why, in the painting of the ship his father captained, "*Coquette* carries the red flag of the Barbary States" and why his father sailed out of New York in 1808 "under the Swedish flag" but in the Caribbean "anchored flying American colors." *Reminiscences of Ralph B. Forbes*, 11–12.
122. Signal flags in Lane's portrait of the brig *Antelope*, for instance, were identified by Lt. Com. M. V. Brewington, Arlington, VA, and Earnest S. Dodge, Peabody Museum, Salem, MA (MFA object file; see Federick Marryat, *The Universal Code of Signals* [London: Richardson, 1869], at the Peabody Museum, Salem).
123. *GT* 14, no. 41 (May 22, 1850).
124. This clipper takes its name from the constellation by which mariners navigated south of the equator. Lawrence Kramer, ed., *Hart Crane's "The Bridge"* (New York: Fordham University Press, 2011), 89n1.
125. W, "J. M. W. Turner," *Bulletin of the American Art-Union*, no. 3 (June 1, 1851): 37. Lane and his friend J. L. Stevens Jr. were impressed by published images and discussions of clouds in the work of John Constable and John Ruskin as well as Turner. Letter from Joseph L. Stevens to Samuel H. Mansfield, October 17, 1904, CAM P31A FF11.
126. T. B. Butler, *The Philosophy of the Weather and a Guide to Its Changes* (New York: D. Appleton, 1856).
127. Advertisement for Thorne's Photographic Gallery, 75 Front Street, *GT* 34, no. 74 (September 15, 1860).
128. Daniel Vickers, *Farmers and Fishermen: Two Centuries of Work in Essex County, Massachusetts, 1630–1850* (Chapel Hill: University of North Carolina Press, 1994), 311, 319.
129. "For the Telegraph," *GT* 14, no. 25 (March 27, 1850). The Rockport Steam Cotton Mill was built of granite, employed 175 operatives, and principally produced "cotton duck for vessels' sails" but also sheeting and heavy cotton fabric for waterproof "India rubber cloth." *GT* 14, no. 37 (May 8, 1850).

CHAPTER 4

1. *CAA*, Friday, April 12, 1861.
2. "Along Shore, Down East, September 12," repr. in *GT* 2, no. 4 (Saturday, September 27, 1828).
3. *GT* 2, no. 21 (Saturday, May 17, 1828).
4. Bryant F. Tolles Jr., *Summer by the Seaside: The Architecture of New England Coastal Resort Hotels, 1830–1950* (Hanover: University Press of New England, 2008), 103.
5. P, letter to the editor, *CAL & GT* 25, no. 24 (June 14, 1851).
6. *BET*, June 29, 1849, as cited in James F. O'Gorman, *This Other Gloucester: Occasional Papers on the Arts of Cape Ann, Massachusetts* (Boston: self-published, 1976), 35. The architectural drawings for the Pavilion Hotel, in which Sidney Mason apparently had a hand, are at CAM. The similarity of the Pavilion Hotel to the Wawona Hotel in Yosemite, CA (1876), in which the Bugbees may have had a hand, is notable.
7. *CAL & GT*, April 8, 1848.
8. *GT* 2, no. 32 (Saturday August 2, 1828); "Description of the Cod Fish," repr. from *The American Encyclopedia* in *GT* 5, no. 37 (September 10, 1831); Francis J. Bremer, *The Puritan Experiment: New England Society from Bradford to Edwards* (Hanover: University Press of New England, 2013), 39.
9. *CAL & GT* 23, no. 29 (July 21, 1849).
10. *CAL & GT* 23, no. 32 (August 11, 1849). Perhaps surprisingly, Gloucester shipped fish overland by cart to Vermont and Montreal and westward via the Erie Canal long before the railroad made most of the route reasonable. *GT* 1, no. 3 (January 13, 1827); 1, no. 18 (April 28, 1827); 1, no. 46 (November 10, 1827); 4, no. 4 (January 23, 1830). For a discussion of the relationship of early railroad ventures to business and "nature," see David Schley, "A Natural History of the Early American Railroad," *Early American Studies* 13, no. 2 (Spring 2015): 443–66.
11. *CAL & GT*, March 4, 1848; *CAL & GT*, April 8, 1848; *CAL & GT* 23, no. 32 (August 11, 1849).
12. *GT* 14, no. 52 (June 29, 1850); see also "The Salt Trade of Boston," *CAL & GT* 45, no. 35 (September 2, 1871), for foreign trade in salt, and *GT* 1, no. 43 (October 20, 1827), and 2, no. 46 (November 8, 1828), for Massachusetts-produced salt.
13. The U.S. census indicated that Gloucester's population was 6,394 in 1840 and 7,416 in 1850; the Gloucester paper reported these figures and noted that much of this increase was due to immigration from the Canadian Maritime provinces and Maine by those seeking jobs in the fisheries (*GT* 14, no. 45 [June 5, 1860]); by 1860 Gloucester had grown to 10,904, of which 2,188 were foreign born (1,099 from Canada, 544 from Ireland, 179 from Portugal, and the rest from England, Sweden, Scotland, Norway, Denmark, and less than a dozen each from France, Germany, Holland, Italy, Russia, Spain, Switzerland, and Wales. Solomon, "Growth of the Population."

14. *CAA*, January 18, 1861.
15. George H. Procter, *The Fishermen's Memorial and Record Book: Containing a List of Vessels and Their Crews, Lost from the Port of Gloucester from the Year 1830 to October 1, 1873, Embracing a Period of Nearly Half a Century; Comprising Fourteen Hundred and Thirty-Seven Names, and Two Hundred and Ninety-Six Vessels, Including Those Lost in the Gale of August 24, 1873; It Also Contains Valuable Statistics of the Fishing Business, Off-Hand Sketches, Big Trips, Tales of Narrow Escapes, Maritime Poetry, and Other Matters of Interest to These Toilers of the Sea* (Gloucester, MA: Procter Brothers, 1873), 69–70, 77. For ice harvesting from Cape Ann's ponds, see *CAA*, January 4, 1861. An excellent record of the icehouses on every freshwater body in the area is to be seen in Hopkins's 1884 *Atlas of the City of Gloucester*, plates 2, 8, 11, 21, etc.
16. The schooner *Bernice* sold for $1,515 the week John Somes bought the Plumer house for $1,595; both were auction transactions. *CAA* 3, no. 5 (February 3, 1860). Thirteen years later Procter states that the schooners for use on St. George's Bank had an average value of $2,800 (*Fishermen's Memorial*, 69).
17. Procter, *Fishermen's Memorial*, 82.
18. *CAA* 3, no. 30 (July 27, 1860).
19. Ibid.; *CAL & GT* 23, no. 36 (September 8, 1849); *CAA*, November 2, 1860.
20. Procter, *Fishermen's Memorial*, 65–66, 73.
21. *CAL & GT* 23, no. 32 (August 11, 1849).
22. W. Jeffrey Bolster, *The Mortal Sea: Fishing the Atlantic in the Age of Sail* (Cambridge: Belknap Press of Harvard University Press, 2012), 103; Hoyt, "Industrial Statistics of Gloucester."
23. Salt was made at Barnstable on Cape Cod, but apparently not enough. Gloucester shops offered salt from Liverpool and Cadiz. *GT* 2, no. 18 (April 26, 1828); 1, no. 43 (October 20, 1827); 2, no. 46 (November 8, 1828); 34, no. 74 (September 15, 1860).
24. *CAA*, August 25, 1865.
25. *GT* 2, no. 37 (September 6, 1828); Hoyt, "Industrial Statistics of Gloucester," *CAA*, August 25, 1865. The isinglass manufactory at Rockport opened in 1824. *GT* 14, no. 25 (March 27, 1850).
26. *CAA*, August 25, 1865; an Our Town article in the *Telegraph* of June 6, 1846, explicitly links new wharves and houses that year to fishing success (green notebook of photocopied Fitz Henry Lane material, CAM).
27. *GT* 14, no. 48 (June 15, 1850); 5, no. 11 (March 12, 1831); 14, no. 19 (March 6, 1850). Bounties were paid, for instance, for 828 crows' heads in 1850. *GT* 14, no. 20 (March 9, 1850).
28. *GT* 3, no. 33 (August 8, 1829), and 3, no. 34 (August 15, 1829); *CAL & GT*, March 4, 1848; *CAA* 3, no. 30 (July 27, 1860); *CAL & GT*, January 27, 1849; Procter, *Fishermen's Memorial*, 72.
29. Brian Fagan, *Fish on Friday: Feasting, Fasting, and the Discovery of the New World* (New York: Basic Books, 2006), xiii, as cited in Bolster, *Mortal Sea*, 27.
30. Bolster, *Mortal Sea*, 23–26, 41–46.
31. Oaks, *Gloucester at Mid-century*, 12–13. Third-grade fish were on the whole "called *Jamaica fish*, because such are generally sold in that island, for the use of the slaves" (Edward Hazen, "The Fisherman," in *Panorama*, 95); they were also known as "West India dry fish" ("Fish," broadside, 1792, AAS BDSDS/1792).
32. *CAL & GT*, September 9, 1848; log of the brig *Amazon*, July 6 to December 2, 1854, acc. #2549, Ships Log Book Collection, CAM.
33. Our Town, *GT*, June 6, 1846 ("Clippings," CAM); *GT* 14, no. 47 (June 12, 1850); Procter, *Fishermen's Memorial*, 76.
34. Procter, *Fishermen's Memorial*, 73.
35. "Inspection of Mackerel for 1862," *CAL & GT* 36, no. 3 (January 17, 1863), lists thirty-three owners of mackereling schooners.
36. "Big Trips," *CAA* 3, no. 19 (May 11, 1860): 2.
37. Procter, *Fishermen's Memorial*, 83.
38. Bolster, *Mortal Sea*, 67–86.
39. Vickers, *Farmers and Fishermen*, 264; Bolster, *Mortal Sea*, 106.
40. Tilden, *Autobiography and Personal Tributes*, 46, 49, 56.
41. "Fish Market," *CAL & GT* 23, no. 36 (September 8, 1849); Procter, *Fishermen's Memorial*, 65.
42. "Good Harbor Beach," no newspaper noted, October 23, 1850, "Clippings," CAM (vol. 2).
43. "Description of the Cod Fish."
44. Ibid.; "Sketch of Rockport," *GT* 14, no. 25 (March 27, 1850); "Rockport," *GT* 14, no. 37 (May 8, 1850).
45. Hazen, *Panorama*, 95.
46. *Lowell Daily Citizen and News* 22, no. 4843 (February 13, 1872); *CAWA*, February 9, 1872; January 5, 1866; September 14, 1866.
47. Procter, *Fishermen's Memorial*, 66–70, quotation on 66.
48. Ibid., 70. While most fish were preserved with salt and/or drying, news of the theft of a substantial quantity of halibut from a smokehouse at the head of the harbor indicates that smoking was also practiced. *GT* 14, no. 62 (August 3, 1850).
49. Procter, *Fishermen's Memorial*, 69–70.
50. Letter to Mr. Samuel H. Mansfield in Gloucester from Joseph L. Stevens in Boston, postmarked October 17, 1904, "given to CAM Sept. 19, 1949" (notation on document). See Katherine Haskins, *"The Art-Journal" and Fine Art Publishing in Victorian England, 1850–1880* (Burlington, VT: Ashgate, 2012).
51. See Lovell, "Fitz Henry Lane, spectateur."
52. *GT* 5, no. 20 (May 14, 1831).
53. *CAA* 3, no. 11 (March 16, 1860).
54. Lane would have seen "low-life" activities in Dutch seventeenth-century seascapes owned, exhibited, and sold at auction in Boston from the 1820s. See Ronni Baer, *The Poetry of Everyday Life: Dutch Painting in Boston*, exh. cat. (Boston: Museum of Fine Arts, 2002), 6–13.
55. *GT*, August 15, 1835, "Clippings," CAM BR Box 23.
56. *GT* 14, no. 47 (June 12, 1850).
57. *CAL & GT* 23, no. 24 (June 16, 1849).
58. *CAA* 3, no. 11 (March 16, 1860); Dunlap and Buck, *FHL*, 72; *CAL*, January 17, 1862; Procter, *Fishermen's Memorial*, 3–4.

59. *CAA* 3, no. 30 (July 27, 1870).
60. Procter, *Fishermen's Memorial*, 4.
61. Bennett, diary, entry for May 25, 1854.
62. A. Babson, diary, entry for Thursday, January 22, 1847.
63. *CAA* 3, no. 11 (March 16, 1860).
64. *CAA* 3, no. 16 (April 20, 1860).
65. Joseph E. Garland, *Boston's North Shore: Being an Account of Life Among the Noteworthy, Fashionable, Wealthy, Eccentric, and Ordinary, 1823–1890* (Boston: Little, Brown, 1978), 116.
66. Procter, *Fishermen's Memorial*, 53.
67. Ibid., 26.
68. Ibid., 7.
69. Ibid., 52.
70. *GT* 5, no. 1 (January 1, 1831).
71. *GT* 4, no. 38 (September 18, 1830).
72. Ibid.
73. Mrs. Nowell, "Gloucester," *CAL & GT* 23, no. 36 (September 8, 1849).
74. Procter, *Fishermen's Memorial*, 115–16.
75. Ibid., 116.
76. *CAL & GT* 23, no. 41 (October 13, 1849).
77. Powell, "Luminism and the American Sublime," 81; David C. Miller, "The Iconology of Wrecked or Stranded Boats in Mid to Late Nineteenth-Century American Culture," in *American Iconology: New Approaches to Nineteenth-Century Art and Literature*, ed. David C. Miller (New Haven: Yale University Press, 1993), 189, 196–97. Martin Berger notes this tendency among scholars to associate images produced between 1861 and 1865 as consciously or unconsciously referencing the Civil War. Martin A. Berger, *Sight Unseen: Whiteness and American Visual Culture* (Berkeley: University of California Press, 2005), 22.
78. J. J. Babson, *History of the Town of Gloucester*, 529–30.
79. Those commissioning paintings of the Brace's Rock site were Mrs. H. Davidson, Mrs. G. P. Low, Mr. J. Whipple, James Houghton, and James Mansfield, as J. Stevens noted on the drawing *Brace's Rock, Eastern Point* (fig. 13).
80. Procter, *Fishermen's Memorial*, 6.
81. Bolster, *Mortal Sea*, 139.
82. Procter, *Fishermen's Memorial*, 105.
83. Garland, *Boston's North Shore*, 115.
84. *CAL & GT* 26, no. 31 (August 2, 1862).
85. *CAL & GT* 23, no. 36 (September 8, 1849) (fifteen deaths by cholera in twenty-four hours), and 23, no. 24 (June 16, 1849). I use the idea of tourism, or "looking," in a somewhat broader sense than that developed by Dean MacCannell in his landmark work *The Tourist: A New Theory of the Leisure Class* (New York: Schocken Books, 1989) as the "ideological framing of history, nature, and tradition . . . that has the power to reshape culture and nature to its own needs," but his insights are fundamental to the whole issue.
86. *GT* 2, no. 26 (June 21, 1828); "Cape Ann," *GT* 4, no. 33 (August 14, 1830); "From the Journal of Health: Country Air," *GT* 4, no. 29 (July 17, 1830).
87. *GT* 4, no. 32 (August 7, 1830).
88. "For Sale," *GT* 1, no. 13 (March 24, 1827).
89. "Sloop *Evelina*," *GT* 5, no. 24 (June 11, 1831); *CAL & GT* 33, no. 23 (June 4, 1859); "Round the Cape," *CAA* 3, no. 30 (July 27, 1860); *CAA* 3, no. 27 (July 7, 1860).
90. *GT* 5, no. 20 (May 14, 1831); Garland, *Boston's North Shore*, 116–17; re camping, see "Camping Out," *CAA*, August 18 and 25, 1865.
91. Garland, *Boston's North Shore*, 106.
92. Ibid.
93. Ibid. Another Sawyer-commissioned painting is *Gloucester from Brookbank* (1848, MFA).
94. Mrs. Nowell, "Gloucester," *CAL & GT* 23, no. 36 (September 8, 1849).
95. Bennett, diary, entries for August 16 and 22, 1854; A. Babson, diary, entries for July 27 and 28, 1849 (p. 63 second series).
96. Mrs. Nowell, "Gloucester."
97. Dona Brown, *Inventing New England: Regional Tourism in the Nineteenth Century* (Washington, DC: Smithsonian Institution Press, 1995), 1–31; Edward Halsey Foster, *The Civilized Wilderness: Backgrounds to American Romantic Literature, 1817–1860* (New York: Free Press, 1975), 3–25.
98. Thomas Cole, "Essay on American Scenery," *American Monthly Magazine* 1, no. 3 (January 1836): 4–5, repr. in Sarah Burns and John Davis, *American Art to 1900: A Documentary History* (Berkeley: University of California Press, 2009), 266.
99. "Strangers," *GT* 2, no. 33 (August 9, 1828).
100. "Cape Ann," *GT* 4, no. 33 (August 14, 1830).
101. "Take a Trip to Gloucester," *Lynn Mirror*, repr. in *GT* 5, no. 34 (August 20, 1831).
102. *GT* 5, no. 29 (July 16, 1831); Francis A. Durivage, "Sketches of Cape Ann," *Pictorial National Library* 2 (March 1849): 143–47.
103. Durivage, "Sketches of Cape Ann," 146.
104. Lane probably accessed such sites in a rented gig (see note 27 to the introduction), often in company with the Stevens family, as notations on the drawings make clear.
105. Ralph Waldo Emerson, "Nature," in *The Annotated Emerson*, ed. David Mikics (Cambridge: Belknap Press of Harvard University Press, 2012), 27–71, esp. 31: "There is a property in the horizon which no man has but he whose eye can integrate all the parts"; and Henry D. Thoreau, *Walden*, ed. Jeffrey S. Cramer (New Haven: Yale University Press, 2004), 80: "I have frequently seen a poet withdraw, having enjoyed the most valuable part of a farm [by looking at it]."
106. Eric T. Freyfogle, *On Private Property: Finding Common Ground on the Ownership of Land* (Boston: Beacon Press, 2007), 29–60.
107. A. Babson, diary, entries for September 22 and 23, 1848 (p. 50 second series); Bennett, diary, entries for May 26, July 5, and August 11, 1852, and July 5, 23, and 30, 1854.
108. Bennett, diary, entry for January 27, 1854.
109. Ibid., entry for August 24, 1854.
110. Ibid., entry for September 5, 1854.
111. The Day Book of George W. Floyd, 1848–49, contains entries for livery rentals to "F. H. Lane" January 3 ($5.00), June 25 ($2.00), and October 2 ($5.00) in 1849; evidence of

those accompanying Lane on many of his sketching excursions is provided by Joseph Stevens Jr., who recorded the initials of the excursionists on the face of the drawings (see, for instance, fig. 13).

112. Garland, *Boston's North Shore*, 100, 104, 114.
113. *GT* 5, no. 12 (March 19, 1831).
114. Garland, *Boston's North Shore*, 114–15.
115. Ibid., 108; *CAL & GT*, September 2, 1848.
116. "Trustee's Sale of Real Estate in Gloucester—Under the Will of the late Mr. James Gaffield," *BET*, May 10, 1850.
117. Quoted in Garland, *Boston's North Shore*, 92.
118. Ibid., 107–8.
119. *CAL & GT* 25, no. 24 (June 14, 1851).
120. Garland, *Boston's North Shore*, 108.
121. The others are the two versions of *Stage Rocks* (1857), at CAM and the National Gallery of Art.
122. Letter from F. H. Lane to Joseph L. Stevens Jr., CAM Library and Archive. The inventory of items mentioned in the letter—the beach between Stage Fort and Steep Bank, Hovey's Hill, the lone pine tree on the point, the "old vessel stranded on the beach with 2 or 3 figures," the overcast sky—and the size of the canvas (20 × 33 inches), together with the ownership by Stevens's daughter, make it very likely that *Dolliver's Neck* is the painting Lane is describing in such detail. See also note 33 to chapter 2.
123. For Lane's extant drawings, see http://fitzhenrylaneonline.org/catalog/index.php?pageNum=0, accessed May 14, 2017.

CHAPTER 5

1. Ellis, "Cape Ann Views," 34; Powell, "Boston Harbor Pictures," 47; Kelly, "Lane and Church," 144, 151. An exception is Erik Ronnberg, who is very focused on vessel types; see Erik A. R. Ronnberg Jr., "Imagery and Types of Vessels," in Wilmerding, *Paintings by Fitz Hugh Lane*, 61–104.
2. Kelly, "Lane and Church," 144.
3. Frederic Alan Sharf, "Fitz Hugh Lane: Visits to the Maine Coast, 1848–1855," *Essex Institute Historical Collections* 98, no. 2 (April 1962): 113; Dunlap and Buck, *FHL*, 79, 94; *GT* 14, no. 73 (September 11, 1850).
4. *GT* 14, no. 73 (September 11, 1850). The diary of shipbuilder William Howe Witherle, one of the participants in a subsequent cruise Lane took with friends in August 1852, conveys more-detailed information. Witherle, "Cruise with Fitz Hugh Lane." See also Francis W. Hatch, "Maine Diary Describes Fitz Lane Art Cruise," *GDT Supplement*, November 23, 1974, n.p.
5. Springer, *Forest Life*, 43; David Clayton Smith, *A History of Lumbering in Maine, 1861–1960*, University of Maine Studies, no. 93 (Orono: University of Maine Press, 1972), 37.
6. On "the feeling of emptiness," the "moody sense of emptiness," of Lane's late work, see Kelly, "Paintings of Fitz Hugh Lane," 121–22, 125, 126.
7. Smith, *History of Lumbering*, 140.
8. These rafts were generally composed of thirty to a thousand logs. Alfred Geer Hempstead, *The Penobscot Boom and the Development of the West Branch of the Penobscot River for Log Driving*, University of Maine Studies, second series, no. 18 (Orono, ME: Printed at the University Press, 1931), 18.
9. James Elliott Defebaugh, *History of the Lumber Industry of America* (Chicago: American Lumberman, 1906–7), 1:489 and 2:22.
10. *GT* 2, no. 48 (November 22, 1828).
11. John C. Gray, "Essay on Forest Trees," in *Essays: Agricultural and Literary* (Boston: Little, Brown, 1856), 83–89.
12. Ibid.
13. Defebaugh, *History of the Lumber Industry*, 2:73.
14. *GT* 14, no. 11 (February 6, 1850), reported 400,000 feet of milled lumber sailing for California from New Hampshire that day.
15. Edward Hazen, "The Shipwright," in *Panorama*, 102. A single clipper ship in 1855 required 1,500,000 board feet of pine and 986,000 of white oak. Charles F. Carroll, "Wooden Ships and American Forests," *Journal of Forest History* 25, no. 4 (October 1981): 213.
16. Kelly, "Lane and Church," 151.
17. *GT* 5, no. 25 (June 18, 1831); *CAL & GT* 33, no. 23 (June 4, 1859).
18. *GT* 1, no. 26 (June 23, 1827).
19. Letter from Joseph L. Stevens in Maine to Zachariah Stevens in Gloucester, May 5, 1836, CAM P31A FF12.
20. Curtis Family Journals, 1829–1847, Manuscript Collections, folio vol. C, AAS.
21. Michael Williams, "Industrial Impacts on the Forests of the United States, 1860–1920," *Journal of Forest History* 31, no. 3 (July 1987): 109. Gloucester's lumberyards sold cordwood as well as lumber of all kinds. *GT* 14, no. 76 (September 21, 1850). An advertisement in *CAL & GT*, March 25, 1848, lists "2000 cords of Pine Wood and 100 cords Hard do. such as Black Birch, Oak, Maple."
22. Williams, "Industrial Impacts," 110.
23. Springer, *Forest Life*, 182.
24. Huntington, *Landscapes of Frederic Edwin Church*, 1, 9, 10, 17, 34, 39, and passim.
25. Henry David Thoreau, *The Maine Woods*, ed. Jeffrey S. Cramer (New Haven: Yale University Press, 2009), 74.
26. *GT* 4, no. 3 (January 16, 1830). According to one authority, the lumber industry catered more to markets abroad than to domestic markets: "The pine was sawed mostly into boards and shipped to the West Indies, where it was exchanged for Spanish gold, molasses and rum [resulting in] flush times generally for everyone connected with the business." Defebaugh, *History of the Lumber Industry*, 2:55. According to another, "the island of Cuba alone consumes forty millions of feet per annum for the one article of sugar-boxes." Springer, *Forest Life*, 223.
27. Henry David Thoreau, "Chesuncook," *Atlantic Monthly*, June 1858, http://www.theatlantic.com/unbound

/flashbks/fall/chesunk.htm, accessed February 18, 2009. Church did include a small sawmill in his prospective view of Mount Ktaadin (1853), since he imagined the inland mountain as a site of settlement some years hence (Yale University Art Gallery).

28. John Wilmerding, "The Lure of Mount Desert and the New England Coast," Wilmerding, *Paintings by Fitz Hugh Lane*, 118.
29. Nathaniel Hawthorne, *The Marble Faun: or, The Romance of Monte Beni* (New York: Houghton Mifflin, 1890), 1:15.
30. For a harrowing account of the transport of hay into the forest, see Springer, *Forest Life*, 82–90; see also Gray, "Essay on Forest Trees," 107–9.
31. From April 1827, when two trips a week were initiated between Boston, Portland, Owl's Head, Castine, and other Maine destinations, there was regular steamship travel in the region. *GT* 1, no. 17 (April 28, 1827).
32. For instance, Thomas Cole, *Kaaterskill Falls* (1826, Wadsworth Atheneum), and John Neal, *Little Moccasin; or, Along the Madawaska: A Story of Life and Love in the Lumber Region* (New York: Beadle, 1866).
33. Stephanie Francis and Scott Francis, eds., *Baskets of the Dawnland People* (Old Town, ME: Maine Indian Basketmakers Alliance, 2008), 1–7.
34. George A. Wheeler, *History of Castine, Penobscot, and Brooksville, Maine* (Cornwall, NY: Cornwall Press, 1923), 346.
35. *GT* 4, no. 2 (January 16, 1830).
36. The Wabanaki Confederacy comprised multiple tribes in Maine, including the Penobscot.
37. John Stevens, teenage brother of Joseph L. Stevens Jr., reported visiting five Indian camps on the Back Cove near Castine in the summer of 1852. Stevens, journal, entry for September 22, 1852, Box 2, F1 [A00772], Wilson Museum, Castine, ME, as cited at http://fitzhenrylaneonline.org/catalog/entry.php?id=52, accessed June 1, 2017.
38. *GT* 14, no. 76 (September 4, 1850).
39. Hempstead, *Penobscot Boom*, 28–30.
40. *CAL & GT* 23, no. 38 (September 22, 1849).
41. *GT* 14, no. 34 (April 27, 1850).
42. See note 71 to chapter 4.
43. Bennett, diary, entry for Friday, August 25, 1854.
44. Defebaugh, *History of the Lumber Industry*, 2:93.
45. *Report of State Prisons for 1829*, Massachusetts General Court Documents (n.p., 1830), 263 (AAS); *CAL & GT* 23, no. 31 (August 3, 1849).
46. James H. Merrell, "'The Customes of Our Countrey': Indians and Colonists in Early America," in *Diversity and Unity in Early North America*, ed. Philip D. Morgan (London: Routledge, 1993), 77.
47. *CAL & GT*, May 20 and 27, 1848.
48. Reports of the Committees of the House of Representatives, nineteenth Congress, first session, 1826, H.R. Rep. No. 209, U.S. docs. / Serial Vol. / 0142 / Doc. 204, AAS.
49. *GT* 2, no. 2 (January 5, 1828).
50. *GT* 2, no. 19 (May 3, 1828).
51. *GT* 4, no. 33 (August 14, 1830). Another very sympathetic, articulate argument against Indian removal was reprinted in *GT* 3, no. 22 (September 5, 1829) (from the *Lancaster Gazette*); and a surprisingly long, detailed *GT* account of Native Americans seen in a historical light suggested that, in fact, it was those interested in the fur trade who resisted helping Indians become "enlightened, temperate, industrious, and above all agricultural." *GT* 4, no. 27 (July 3, 1830).
52. *GT* 5, no. 4 (January 22, 1831).
53. *GT* 5, no. 16 (April 16, 1831).
54. *GT* 14, no. 26 (March 30, 1850) (Mormons peacefully coexisting); 14, no. 58 (July 20, 1850) (Yumas punished by U.S. troops for murder of Glanton's party); 14, no. 64 (August 10, 1850) (military expedition to Clear Lake and Russian River [CA] quells "Indian troubles" so "miners are no longer interrupted in their occupations"); *CAL & GT* 23, no. 31 (August 3, 1849) ("brutal massacre of Indians . . . by white men" in California).
55. Sybil Noyes, Charles Thornton Libby, and Walter Goodwin Davis, *Genealogical Dictionary of Maine and New Hampshire* (1928–29; repr., Baltimore: Genealogical Publishing, 1996), 411.
56. Mary Beth Norton, "Pannick at the Eastward," in *In the Devil's Snare: The Salem Witchcraft Crisis of 1692* (New York: Alfred A. Knopf, 2002), 95–96 and 353n34.
57. Noyes, Libby, and Davis, *Genealogical Dictionary*, 411; Norton, "Pannick at the Eastward," 99.
58. See also Andrew Lipman, *The Saltwater Frontier: Indians and the Contest for the American Coast* (New Haven: Yale University Press, 2015), 80–81, 216–17.
59. J. J. Babson, *History of the Town of Gloucester*, 111–12; John T. Hull, *York Deeds* (Bethel, ME: Maine Genealogical Society, 1907), 742, 743; William Richard Cutter, ed., *New England Families, Genealogical and Memorial*, 3rd ser., vol. 1 (New York: Lewis Historical Publishing, 1915), 448–49.
60. See https://archive.org/details/thurstongenealog01thur/page/60/mode/2up, accessed March 1, 2022; James P. Lane, ed., "James Lane of North Yarmouth, ME, and His Descendants," *New England Historical and Genealogical Register* 42 (April 1888): 141–44 (accessed through ProQuest). In 1755 a Captain Cargyle killed nine Indians at Owl's Head for bounty. Federal Writers' Project, *Maine: A Guide "Down East"* (Boston: Houghton Mifflin, 1937), 223 (Maine State Library, Augusta).
61. J. J. Babson, *History of the Town of Gloucester*, 112.
62. Bruce J. Bourque, *Twelve Thousand Years: American Indians in Maine* (Lincoln: University of Nebraska Press, 2001), 147–97. Details of this trade in 1742 suggest the relative desirability of European goods to Native Americans: "a pound of gunpowder for four beavers, a pound of shot for one, an ell of coarse cloth for fifteen, a blanket for twelve, two fish-hooks or three flints for one; a gun for twenty-five, a pistol for ten; a common hat for seven, an ax for four, a check-shirt for seven, a bill-hook for one, and a gallon

of brandy for four; all of which is said to have brought in a profit of 2000 per cent" for the traders. *The History of the British Dominions in North America: From the First Discovery* [. . .] *to Its Present Glorious Establishment as Confirmed by the Late Treaty of Peace in 1763* (London: W. Strahan, 1773), pt. 2, pp. 217–18.

63. Harald E. L. Prins, "Chief Rawandagon, Alias Robin Hood: Native 'Lord of Misrule' in the Maine Wilderness," in *Northeastern Indian Lives, 1632–1816*, ed. Robert S. Grumet (Amherst: University of Massachusetts Press, 1996), 93–115; Daniel R. Mandell, *King Philip's War: Colonial Expansion, Native Resistance, and the End of Indian Sovereignty* (Baltimore: Johns Hopkins University Press, 2010), 77–85.
64. *GT* 1, no. 14 (March 31, 1827); see also *GT* 4, no. 17 (April 24, 1830).
65. *GT* 1, no. 14 (March 31, 1827). Lane and both Joseph Stevenses had antiquarian interests, as did George B. Stevens, son of Joseph Stevens Jr. Wheeler, *History of Castine*, 360.
66. Wilmerding, "Lure of Mount Desert," 118.
67. Letter from Dorothy Stevens in Castine to Lane in Gloucester, October 14, 1851, CAM.
68. According to MFA curatorial records, there are six known Lane paintings of Owl's Head.
69. The lighthouse was built in 1826, a scant twenty-six feet high, but equipped with a fourth-order Fresnel lens in 1856, it was visible sixteen miles away. Federal Writers' Project, *Maine*, 224.
70. Richard McLanathan, *The American Tradition in the Arts* (New York: Harcourt, Brace & World, 1968), 264; Wilmerding, *Fitz Hugh Lane* (1971), 55–56; Christopher Knight, "Is There a California School?," *Portfolio* 3, no. 5 (September–October 1981): 59; Wilton and Barringer, *American Sublime*, 198; Michaela Keck, *Walking in the Wilderness: The Peripatetic Tradition in Nineteenth-Century American Literature and Painting* (Heidelberg: Universitätsverlag Winter, 2006), 260–61.
71. MFA curatorial notes. Lane's lithograph *Castine from Hospital Island*, published by Joseph L. Stevens Jr. in 1855, is almost exactly the same size as the three Castine paintings (figs. 104, 105, 112).
72. Benson J. Lossing, *Pictorial Field-Book of the War of 1812* (New York: Harper & Brothers, 1868), 909.
73. Ibid., 908.
74. Wheeler, *History of Castine*, 187. A letter from Joseph Stevens in Castine to F. H. Lane in Gloucester, January 29, 1851, praises the latter's "Drawing of the 'Siege'" evolving out of their earlier conversation (CAM); the interest in associations devoted to history, especially the gathering of primary documents, oral histories, and historical objects with a view "to rescue the true history of this country from the ravages of time, and the effect of ignorance and neglect," had begun in Massachusetts with the establishment of the Massachusetts Historical Society in 1791, the Boston Athenaeum in 1805, and the American Antiquarian Society in 1812. Louis Leonard Tucker, "Massachusetts," in *Historical Consciousness in the Early Republic*, ed. H. G. Jones (Chapel Hill: North Caroliniana Society, 1995), 7.
75. J. B. Calvert, "Cannons and Gunpowder," at http://mysite.du.edu/~jcalvert/tech/cannon.htm#C, accessed June 1, 2017.
76. Ibid.
77. Defebaugh, *History of the Lumber Industry*, 2:50.
78. Warren Boeschenstein, *Historic American Towns Along the Atlantic Coast* (Baltimore: Johns Hopkins University Press, 1999), 56–65; Felicia Smuts, "Shipbuilding and the Mast Trade in Colonial New England," *Revere House Gazette*, no. 89 (Winter 2007): 1–4.
79. Lossing, *Pictorial Field-Book*, 908.
80. Boeschenstein, *Historic American Towns*, 62.
81. Lossing, *Pictorial Field-Book*, 908.
82. Joseph Williamson, "Castine and the Old Coins Found There," printed for the Maine Historical Society, 1859; repr., *Wilson Museum Bulletin* 4, no. 24 (Spring 2003): 1–8; Alaric Faulkner and Gretchen Faulkner, *The French at Pentagoet, 1635–1674: An Archaeological Portrait of the Acadian Frontier* (Augusta, ME: Maine Historic Preservation Commission, 1987), 1–3, 11, 15.
83. Williamson, "Castine," 3–4.
84. Faulkner and Faulkner, *Pentagoet*, 3.
85. Ibid., 4.
86. Ibid.
87. George J. Varney, *A Brief History of Maine* ([Portland, ME]: McLellan, Mosher), 201, 204.
88. Defebaugh, *History of the Lumber Industry*, 2:49.
89. *GT* 1, no. 14 (March 31, 1827).
90. Gideon Lane, autobiography, written soon after 1857, CAM.
91. Williamson, "Castine," 4; Wheeler, *History of Castine*, 162.
92. William Hutchings, "Narrative of the Siege of Penobscot [of 1779]" (narrated to Mr. Joseph L. Stevens Jr. in August 1855), in Wheeler, *History of Castine*, 271–76. George J. Varney notes that Dr. G. A. Wheeler succeeded to the practice of Dr. Joseph L. Stevens in *A Gazetteer of the State of Maine* (Boston: B. B. Russell, 1886), 168, http://history.rays.place.com/me/castine-me.htm, accessed March 24, 2005.
93. Lovell, "Fitz Henry Lane, spectateur."
94. Capt. Edward Johnson, *Wonder Working Providence of Sion's Saviour in New England* (London, 1654), as cited in Defebaugh, *History of the Lumber Industry*, 2:181.
95. Franklin Kelly, in Wilmerding, *Paintings by Fitz Hugh Lane*, 134. Other scholars opine that Lane painted "uninterrupted harmony between man and nature." Carol Troyen, *The Boston Tradition: American Paintings from the Museum of Fine Arts, Boston*, exh. cat. (New York: American Federation of Arts, 1980), #45, p. 114.

CHAPTER 6

1. Quoted in Thomas Hutchinson, *The History of the Colony of*

Massachuset's Bay, from the First Settlement Thereof in 1628, Until [. . .] *1691* (London: M. Richardson, 1765), 484.

2. Edward Hitchcock, *Final Report on the Geology of Massachusetts* (Northampton: J. H. Butler, 1841), 147 (Huntington Library RB477575). See also Robert L. Herbert, "The Sublime Landscapes of Western Massachusetts: Edward Hitchcock's Romantic Naturalism," *Massachusetts Historical Review* 12 (2010): 70–99.
3. H. C. L. Haskell, "Looking Out over the Sea" ("Here"), quoted in Procter, *Fishermen's Memorial*, 6. Technically, the rocks of Gloucester, called granite in the vernacular and in this text, are mixed with syenite, a rock of the same composition but lacking quartz.
4. Mr. Hubbard, 1680, quoted in Hutchinson, *History of the Colony*, 484.
5. Hitchcock, *Geology of Massachusetts*, 147.
6. Lane's contemporary Nancy Prince described subsisting on and selling "strawberries, raspberries, blackberries and whortleberries . . . [she found] in abundance, in the stony environs, growing spontaneously" that she gathered, and fish her brother caught during one summer of their impoverished childhood in Gloucester. Nancy Prince, *A Narrative of the Life and Travels of Mrs. Nancy Prince Written by Herself*, 2nd ed. (Boston: self-published, 1853), 8.
7. *GT* 14, no. 37 (May 8, 1850), repr. from the *Salem Register*.
8. *GT* 2, no. 7 (February 9, 1828).
9. Marc Simpson, "Noble Rock Portraits: Haseltine's American Work," in *Expressions of Place: The Art of William Stanley Haseltine*, exh. cat. (San Francisco: Fine Arts Museums of San Francisco, 1992), 15–30. Contemporary knowledge of and debates concerning geology were available on a vernacular level in Gloucester in such media as the local newspaper, where a substantial article on Charles Lyell's *Principles of Geology* appeared shortly after the first volume was published (*GT* 5, no. 4 [January 8, 1831]); on this general subject of landscape and geology, see Bedell, *Anatomy of Nature*.
10. Tuckerman, *Book of the Artists*, 553; see note 31 to the introduction.
11. Hitchcock, *Geology of Massachusetts*, 265.
12. R. Hunt, "Granite," *Art Journal* (London), n.s., 2 (September 1856): 264–65.
13. Hitchcock, *Geology of Massachusetts*, 269–70.
14. Durivage, "Sketches of Cape Ann," 146.
15. Hitchcock, *Geology of Massachusetts*, 270.
16. *GT* 4, no. 30 (August 14, 1830), repr. from the *Boston Patriot*; "Fences," *GT* 3, no. 22 (May 23, 1829).
17. "Survey of Sandy Bay," *GT* 4, no. 17 (April 24, 1830); *CAL & GT*, January 22, 1848; "Mammouth Barn," *GT* 5, no. 3 (August 20, 1831).
18. *GT* 3, no. 4 (January 17, 1829); 3, no. 30 (July 18, 1829).
19. "Blowing Rocks," *GT* 1, no. 38 (September 15, 1827). These experiments continued; three years later "about three kegs of powder," being used to prepare the site of a bank in town, threw a three-hundred-pound rock through the roof of a distillery "60 or 70 yards" away. *GT* 4, no. 44 (October 30, 1830).
20. Dunlap and Buck, *FHL*, 25n, 30, 130; Prudence Paine Fish, *Antique Houses of Gloucester* (Charleston, SC: History Press, 2007), 47–52.
21. *GT* 1, no. 38 (September 15, 1827).
22. Harley J. McKee, *Introduction to Early American Masonry: Stone, Brick, Mortar, and Plaster* (Washington, DC: National Trust for Historic Preservation, 1973), 14.
23. *GT* 1, no. 10 (April 28, 1827); 1, no. 43 (October 20, 1827).
24. This vessel is identified as a "stone sloop" by Charles Olson, quoting Gordon Thomas, in a letter of June 12, 1960, to "Mr. [Alfred M.] Brooks," CAM correspondence files.
25. *CAL & GT* 23, no. 38 (September 22, 1849).
26. "Sketch of Rockport." Another account reports that three hundred men were employed on the ledges and twenty-five sloops engaged in carrying the granite. *CAL & GT*, April 8, 1848.
27. *GT* 14, no. 55 (July 10, 1850).
28. *GT* 14, no. 16 (February 23, 1850).
29. Massachusetts's new state prison, for instance, started in 1826, was a four-story structure containing 304 cells, with walls four feet thick using eleven thousand tons of Quincy granite at a cost of $84,995.88. *Report of State Prison*, Massachusetts General Court Documents (Boston: Dutton & Wentworth, 1830), 1–6.
30. *GT* 14, no. 25 (March 27, 1850).
31. *Report of Survey of Rail Road Boston to Lowell*, Massachusetts General Court Documents (Boston: Dutton & Wentworth, 1830), 14.
32. *Pictorial Views of Massachusetts* (Worcester, MA: Warren Lazell, 1845), 47; unknown artist, *A View of the Massachusetts Prison and Workshops Taken from the Center of the Yard* (1829), watercolor, in Harriet Ropes Cabot, *Handbook of the Bostonian Society* (Boston: Bostonian Society, 1979), 50.
33. E. H. Cameron, "Of Yankee Granite, Part I," *Technology Review* 54, no. 7 (May 1952): 359–64; Cameron, "Of Yankee Granite, Part II, *Technology Review* 54, no. 8 (June 1952): 419–22.
34. Roger G. Reed, *Building Victorian Boston: The Architecture of Gridley J. F. Bryant* (Amherst: University of Massachusetts Press, 2007), 11.
35. Lane's lithograph is dated 1840 by its inclusion of the Concord Monument, completed in 1836 and dedicated in 1837; its printing by Thayer's Lithography, which operated in Boston between 1840 and 1847 (Sally Pierce and Catharina Slautterback, *Boston Lithography, 1825–1880* [Boston: Boston Athenaeum, 1991], 155–56); and its advertisement by printer Elbridge Jefts in the July 4, 1840, issue of the *Yeoman's Gazette* (personal communication from Bob Gross, June 17, 2017).
36. There was a third obelisk in this conversation—the Washington Monument in Washington, DC. See Kirk

Savage, "The Self-Made Monument: George Washington and the Fight to Erect a National Memorial," *Winterthur Portfolio* 22, no. 4 (Winter 1987): 225–42.

37. John S. Keyes notes that Lane's drawing was made before Concord citizens planted an allée of trees to the site in 1838 or '39 (probably in 1839), and as observed in note 35 above, the lithograph was published and offered for sale in 1840. "Autobiography of Hon. John S. Keyes" (b. September 19, 1821) at Concord Library, p. 48 ½, https://concordlibrary.org/uploads/scollect/doc/Autobiography_final.pdf, accessed June 17, 2017. My thanks to Bob Gross for calling this document (and much else) to my attention.
38. Ibid.
39. Douglass Shand-Tucci, *Built in Boston: City and Suburb, 1800–1950* (Amherst: University of Massachusetts Press, 1988), 16; S. Willard, *Plans and Sections, of the Obelisk on Bunker's Hill, with the Details of Experiments Made in Quarrying the Granite* (Boston: Charles Cook's Lithography, 1843).
40. Shand-Tucci, *Built in Boston*, 17.
41. Reed, *Building Victorian Boston*, 10.
42. Ibid.
43. *CAL & GT* 23, no. 36 (September 8, 1849).
44. *CAL & GT* 23, no. 39 (September 29, 1849). For the fire, see note 51 to chapter 3. Among the buildings "totally destroyed" was the "dwelling house of Z. Stevens with five buildings in the rear. . . . Store in front occupied by Samuel Stevens, and wharf destroyed." *GT* 4, no. 38 (September 18, 1830); Dunlap and Buck, *FHL*, 28–29.
45. See chapter 1 above. See also Hopkins, *Atlas of the City of Gloucester*, plate 2, where just below Lane's house are identified a soap factory, the local gas company, the Atlantic Halibut Co., a sail loft, a "lumber yard," etc.
46. Margaretta M. Lovell, *Art in a Season of Revolution: Painters, Artisans, and Patrons in Early America* (Philadelphia: University of Pennsylvania Press, 2005), 220–23. See Wanda M. Corn, "Artists' Homes and Studios: A Special Kind of Archive," *American Art* 19, no. 1 (Spring 2005): 2–11.
47. C. Cook, "Letters on Art," as quoted in full in Gerdts and C. C., "'The Sea Is His Home,'" 47.
48. S. Babson, "Fitz H. Lane." Ignatius is listed as a "[window-]sash manufacturer" in the 1860 *Gloucester Directory*, 169.
49. Fred Tibbets speaks of beacons lit here celebrating the Declaration of Independence in 1776 (*GDT*, March 2, 1916), and Alfred Mansfield Brooks speaks of an illumination staged on this knoll October 22, 1783, on the signing of the Treaty of Paris ("Fitz Lane House," 281).
50. Brooks, "Fitz Lane House," 281, 283; C. Cook, "Letters on Art," in Gerdts and C. C., "'The Sea Is His Home,'" 47.
51. Sarah Burns, *Painting the Dark Side: Art and the Gothic Imagination in Nineteenth-Century America* (Berkeley: University of California Press, 2004), xv.
52. C. Cook, "Letters on Art," in Gerdts and C. C., "'The Sea Is His Home,'" 48; Downing, *Architecture of Country Houses*, 305, 311.
53. Brooks, "Fitz Lane House," 282. In the mid-1950s this third floor was occupied by Mr. and Mrs. John Sawyer and their six children, so the space had been partitioned. "Fitz Hugh Lane, Self-Taught Artist, Now Recognized Here and Nationally," *GDT*, August 12, 1953, clipping from CAM Authors and Artists Scrapbook, vol. 2. There are no complete plans of this house, and it has not achieved National Register status; it is used today by several nonprofits.
54. Tibbets, "Fitz H. Lane," March 2, 1916, comments on Lane's "[s]tone house . . . [with] a large glass roof for getting the right light for painting."
55. Concerning impromptu studio visits, see "Louise," "Our Artist at Home," [*Telegraph and News*], April 26, 1856 (MFA object file for Lane, *Fishing Party*).
56. Abbott Lowell Cummings, *The Framed Houses of Massachusetts Bay, 1625–1725* (Cambridge: Harvard University Press, 1979), 37, 135.
57. A rare early house of uncertain date surviving into the twentieth century was built by James Babson, who arrived in Gloucester in 1637 with his mother, Isabel; a cooper and farmer, James built a small one-cell stone house on the road between Gloucester and Rockport. R. W. Babson, *Actions and Reactions*, 5.
58. Jane Holtz Kay, *Lost Boston*, expanded and updated ed. (Amherst: University of Massachusetts Press, 2006), 80.
59. A view of the facade of Oak Hall is owned by the Bostonian Society and reproduced in ibid., 81, 329.
60. See also William Pendleton, *Essay on Gothic Architecture*, booklet, n.d., AAS Lith/Pend/Essa.
61. E. B. Davis, "Training the Eye and the Hand," 13–14. Edwards authored the *Juvenile Drawing Book* (1830) and *Juvenile Drawing Book, or Instructions in Landscape Drawing, and Painting in Water-Colours* (1844). Tatham, "Pendleton-Moore Shop," 35, 36, 37–38.
62. Reed, *Building Victorian Boston*, 23; E. Lane, "Early Recollections."
63. The Eastern Railroad Station in Salem, MA, 1847, is illustrated as figure 2.9 in Reed, *Building Victorian Boston*, 49.
64. Scott's novels were advertised in *GT* 3, no. 45 (November 21, 1829), and *GT* 5, no. 4 (January 22, 1831). "Annisquam Meeting House to Have Three Gothic Windows," *GT* 4, no. 22 (May 29, 1830); "Sandy Bay Meeting House . . . Approaches the Gothic [. . .] Mr. David White the Architect," *GT* 3, no. 42 (October 10, 1829). Moreover, a new Gothic cottage on Water Street, "in all respects an eligible residence for a genteel family," was offered for sale in *CAL & GT*, December 2, 1848. Beyond Lane's probable engagement with romantic novels (discussed in chapter 3), his taste in literature is unknown, but scholars have asserted, in general, a persuasive argument for a link between romantic literature and Gothic architecture in the United States. Kerry Dean Carso, *American*

Gothic Art and Architecture in the Age of Romantic Literature (Cardiff: University of Wales Press, 2014), esp. 51–68, 95–113.

65. Cook, "Letters," in Gerdts and C. C., "'The Sea Is His Home,'" 47.
66. "The Studio and Garden of F. H. Lane," *Boston Traveler*, August 28, 1857.
67. Haskell, "Looking Out," in Procter, *Fishermen's Memorial*, 6.
68. *GT* 4, no. 17 (April 24, 1830).
69. Paul H. Sherman, *Shipwrecks of Cape Ann from 1635*, map printed at Rockport, MA, 1964, CAM 082 Drawer 3.
70. For a philosophical and literary approach to the metaphor of shipwreck as a kind of natural outcome of greed and blasphemous transgressing of boundaries, see Hans Blumenberg, *Shipwreck with Spectator: Paradigm of a Metaphor for Existence*, trans. Steven Rendall (Cambridge: MIT Press, 1997), 9–46.
71. Newton and Steele, "Series Paintings," 198; *Catalogue of Paintings, of the Third Exhibition of the Boston Artists' Association, 1844, at Harding's Gallery, 22 School Street* (Boston: Clapp & Son, 1844), numbers 102 through 106 (BA call # N 521.B67 C37 1844). I thank Melissa Trafton for reminding me of this series and for her central contributions to fitzhenrylaneonline.org.
72. Blumenberg, *Shipwreck with Spectator*.
73. Dunlap and Buck, *FHL*, 5.
74. *GT* 14, no. 63 (August 7, 1850).
75. "Collisions in the Harbor," *CAA*, October 26, 1860.
76. *Awful Calamities, or the Shipwrecks of December 1839, Being a Full Account of the Dreadful Hurricanes of Dec. 15, 21, & 27 on the Coast of Massachusetts; in Which Were Lost More Than 90 Vessels, and Nearly 200 Dismasted, [. . .] More Than 150 Lives Destroyed* (Boston: Press of J. Howe, 1840), 12 (Pams/ A966/ Awfu/ 1840/ 3rd ed. AAS).
77. Ibid., 7.
78. Lane, describing *Dolliver's Neck*, says, "[A]n old vessel lies stranded on the beach." Letter from Lane to Joseph and Caroline Stevens, 1857, CAM.
79. *CAL & GT*, January 22, 1828.
80. Ibid.
81. *Awful Calamities*, 23–24.
82. Longfellow would later be an officer in the New England Art Union, of which Lane was a charter member, and William Y. Balch, Lane's Boston dealer, was honorary secretary. Boston Artists' Association, Charter and Roster, December 1841, 1–4, Manuscript Collection, Athenaeum Library, Boston; "New England Art Union," *Literary World* 3, no. 16 (May 20, 1848): 310; letter from Balch to Andrew Warner, November 5, 1850, Letters to Art-Union File, Manuscript Collection, New-York Historical Society.
83. In one version, the folk saying is "Last night the sun went pale to bed; / The moon in halos hid her head," which bespeaks foul weather. Percy Society, *Early English Poetry, Ballads, and Popular Literature of the Middle Ages* (London: Printed for the Percy Society, 1847), 20:72.

CHAPTER 7

1. John Piper, editor of the *Gloucester News and Semi-weekly Messenger* (1848–51), ordered paintings from two drawings: *View at Bass Rocks Looking Eastward* and *Stage Rocks and the Western Shore of Gloucester Outer Harbor* (1857) (Martha Oaks, fitzhenrylaneonline, accessed July 8, 2018); James Mansfield, listed in the 1860 *Gloucester Directory* as "grocer," bought a view "of a barque dismasted, and rolling in heavy sea" (*GDT*, March 2, 1916); Henry Hitchings, listed in the 1850 *Boston Directory* as a clerk, lent Lane's *Gloucester Fishing Schooner on Georges Bank* to the 1859 National Academy of Design exhibition; Benjamin H. Smith, listed as a lawyer in *GT* 34, no. 74 (September 15, 1860), ordered a painting from drawing #28, *Norman's Woe* (1861); Rev. William P. Tilden of Milton ordered a painting of Ten Pound Island from drawing #12; Lane painted several works for his friend Dr. Herman Davidson and his wife from drawings #21 and #87 and sold him the *Dream Painting* (Susan Babson, *GDT*, n.d., photocopy at CAM). Drawing numbers refer to *Paintings and Drawings*.
2. *CAL & GT*, June 10, 1848; *GT* 34, no. 74 (September 15, 1860); Gray, *Essays*, 27.
3. Wigglesworth is the only Lane patron listed in the Archives Directory for the History of Collecting at the Frick Museum Center for the History of Collecting (http://research.frick.org/directoryweb/browserecord.php?-action=browse&-recid=6233, accessed July 1, 2018). He is listed in the 1864 Boston Athenaeum list as the owner of Lane's painting *A (Foggy) Morning*. Perkins and Gavin, *Boston Athenaeum Art Exhibition Index*, 90. Nathaniel Babson, housepainter, ordered four paintings from Lane. See http://fitzhenrylaneonline.org/historical_material/?type=People§ion=Babson%2C+Nathaniel, accessed July 16, 2018.
4. See https://research.frick.org/directory/detail/299.
5. Stephen Greenblatt, "Cultural Mobility: An Introduction," in *Cultural Mobility: A Manifesto*, ed. Stephen Greenblatt et al. (Cambridge: Cambridge University Press, 2009), 1–23, quotation from 1.
6. Edward Hazen, "The Mariner," in *Panorama*, 104.
7. James W. Cook, "Antebellum Cultural History," in *A Companion to American Cultural History*, ed. Karen Halttunen (Hoboken, NJ: John Wiley & Sons, 2008), 74.
8. Greenblatt puts it somewhat differently: "[M]obility studies should shed light on hidden as well as conspicuous movements of peoples, objects, images, texts, and ideas." Stephen Greenblatt, "A Mobility Studies Manifesto," in Greenblatt et al., *Cultural Mobility*, 250.
9. Greenblatt, "Cultural Mobility," 2.
10. William Vans Jr., *A Short History of the Life of William Vans, a Native Citizen of Massachusetts* (Boston: self-published, 1825), 7, as cited in Frayler, "Pickled Fish and Salted Provisions," 2.

11. The Babson brig *Cadet* was built in 1821 (Phillips, *Ship Registers*), so this is a different vessel.
12. *GT* 2, no. 46 (November 8, 1828).
13. *GT* 2, no. 48 (November 22, 1828).
14. *GT* 2, no. 51 (December 13, 1828).
15. *GT* 2, no. 52 (December 20, 1828).
16. *GT* 3, no. 22 (May 23, 1829).
17. Stephanie Buck, "George H. Rogers," http://fitzhenrylaneonline.org/historical_material/?type=People§ion=Rogers%2C+George+H, accessed July 17, 2018.
18. His wharf was extended in 1849 (*CAL & GT*, April 21, 1848); his brig *Pleiades* set a record for the largest cargo ever, with 590 hogsheads, 28 tierces, and 20 barrels of molasses (*GT*, March 7, 1846, as cited in Alfred Mansfield Brooks, "Gloucester and the Surinam Trade," *Essex Institute Historical Collections* 89, no. 3 [July 1953], 291).
19. *CAL & GT*, September 2, 1848; *GT* 34, no. 74 (September 15, 1860); Brooks, "Surinam Trade," 289.
20. Lovell, "Fitz Henry Lane, spectateur."
21. *GDT*, March 2, 1916, newspaper clippings, CAM. Fred Tibbets, *GDT*, n.d., recounts the January 18, 1857, storm that drove the *California* and its lightering schooner out of the harbor, to be washed up at Scituate, as a result of which they were being refurbished by Trask in the Lane shop sign.
22. Woodbury, a partner of G. H. Rogers who commissioned a Surinam brig in a rough sea (*A Rough Sea* [1854], CAM), is listed in the 1860 *Gloucester Directory* as in the Surinam trade; James Mansfield, who ordered one of the Brace's Rock paintings, was a grocer dealing in Surinam goods in bulk, offering, for instance, "2000 lbs Prime Green Surinam Coffee" in the newspaper (*CAL & GT* 23, no. 13 [March 31, 1849]).
23. "Painting by Lane of Town in 1852."
24. The *California* was built at Medford, MA, in 1830 and was registered to George H. Rogers in 1855. Phillips, *Ship Registers*, 23.
25. Obituary for harbor pilot William Sayward, *CAL & GT* 23, no. 17 (April 28, 1849).
26. *CAWA*, May 12, 1871, a newspaper clipping in the Sawyer Free Library Scrapbook, as quoted at http://fitzhenrylaneonline.org, accessed July 16, 2018.
27. Brooks and Brooks, *Gloucester Recollected*, 108. Piper and Rogers were business partners from 1848 to 1857. See also note 115 to chapter 4 concerning Rogers's buying up of coastal land and "cow rights" in the area of Good Harbor Beach and Bass Rocks.
28. See note 18 above. Sample imports are noted in *CAL & GT*, March 18, 1848, and June 10, 1848; Peter Tharp, *A New and Complete System of Federal Arithmetic* [. . .] *for the Use of Schools* (Newburgh, NY: D. Denniston for the author, 1798), 23; Albert von Sack, *A Narrative of a Voyage to Surinam; of a Residence There During 1805, 1806, and 1807; and of the Author's Return to Europe by the Way of North America* (London: Printed for G. and W. Nicol by W. Bulmer, 1810), 77 .
29. William H. Noyes opened an ice cream saloon and confectionary bakery on Front Street in Gloucester in June 1849 (*CAL & GT* 23, no. 23 [June 9, 1849]); the U.S. Commissioner of Patents Report estimated consumption of sugar worldwide at a million tons in 1850 (*GT*, May 22, 1850); "The Medicine Business in Philadelphia," *CAL & GT* 23, no. 36 (September 8, 1849).
30. For teaching two of his sons, Jonathan Lane paid Joseph Moore with molasses (1 gal. = 60¢) and coffee (6 lb. = $1). Dolliver/Moore Papers, Archive Collection 34 / Document Box P 23, CAM.
31. *GT* 2, no. 21 (May 17, 1828), and 1, no. 43 (October 20, 1827).
32. *GT* 4, no. 38 (September 18, 1830).
33. *GT* 4, no. 44 (October 30, 1830).
34. The number of "retailers" comes from records of the clerk of the Court of Sessions. *GT* 2, no. 32 (August 2, 1828).
35. *GT* 14, no. 52 (June 29, 1850).
36. Tilden, *Autobiography and Personal Tributes*, 57.
37. *CAL & GT*, September 23, 1848.
38. *CAL & GT*, July 14, 1849. Some citizens took issue with John S. E. Rogers, the editor of the *CAL & GT*: "You take the most violent and ultra temperance ground. Because a useful member of society, who pays taxes, buys goods, employs his fellows, and supports the gospel happens to sell rum, you will not allow that he is a Christian, as if piety could not be found among decanters and toddy sticks." *CAL & GT* 23, no. 13 (March 31, 1849).
39. Marcis Kempe, "New England Water Supplies—A Brief History," *Journal of the New England Water Works Association* 120, no. 3 (September 2006): 35, 86, 152; Paul E. Osborne, *Water Franchise Areas in Commonwealth of Massachusetts* (Massachusetts Department of Public Utilities, March 2016), n.p.; "Gas and Water," *Engineering News* 7 (January–December 1880), March 20, 1880, 109, 144; "Personal," ibid., April 24, 1880, 144; Anthony R. Wilbur and Fara Courtney, "The Environmental History and Current Characteristics of Gloucester Harbor," in *Gloucester Harbor Characterization: Environmental History, Human Influences, and Status of Marine Resources*, ed. Anthony R. Wilbur, Fara Courtney, and Robert P. Glenn (Boston: Massachusetts Office of Coastal Zone Management, 2004), 9.
40. *GT* 2, no. 23 (June 14, 1828).
41. *CAA* 3, no. 11 (March 16, 1860). This establishment is frankly called "the bar-room" of the Gloucester House in a notice of 1828. *GT* 2, no. 16 (April 19, 1828).
42. Bennett, diary, entries for January 7 and 16, 1854.
43. Ibid., entry for May 3, 1854.
44. Rev. William George Hawkins, *Life of John H. W. Hawkins, Compiled by His Son, Rev. William George Hawkins, A.M.* (Boston: John P. Jewett, 1859), 144, 154, 157, 177, 259, 353; Tilden, *Autobiography and Personal Tributes*, 89.
45. "Sugar Plantations," *GT* 1, no. 14 (March 31, 1827); Vickers, *Farmers and Fishermen*, 284. Von Sack, *Narrative*, 66, indicates that the North American traders were only permitted to import molasses, but the notices of

arrivals in Gloucester make clear that they also took cacao, coffee, cotton, vanilla, and many other products in exchange for their fish and lumber. Stiff regulations (with eighty-two articles) make clear that at Surinam a guard had to be put on each ship to prevent the unauthorized landing or stowing of any forbidden cargo. *GT* 5, no. 26 (June 2, 1831).

46. Thomas Wentworth Higginson, *Travellers and Outlaws: Episodes in American History* (Boston: Lee & Shepard, 1889), 152.
47. Edward Sullivan, *Rambles and Scrambles in North and South America* (London: Richard Bentley, 1852), 356; Capt[ai]n J. G. Stedman, *Narrative of a Five Years' Expedition Against the Revolted Negroes of Surinam, in Guiana, on the Wild Coast of South America; from the Year 1772 to 1777: Elucidating the History of That Country, and Describing Its Productions, Viz. Quadrupeds, Birds, Fishes, Reptiles, Trees, Shrubs, Fruits, & Roots; with an Account of the Indians of Guiana & Negroes of Guinea, Illustrated with 80 Elegant Engravings from Drawings Made by the Author* (London: J. Johnson, 1796), 1:33. Some Gloucesterites, apparently those suffering from tuberculosis, went to Surinam in an attempt to recover health. See, for instance, the letter from Edward Parrott in Surinam to Miss Elizabeth E. Parrott in Gloucester sent "per *Cadet*" July 25, 1834 (CAM BR Box P 24 Folder).
48. David Eltis and David Richardson, *Atlas of the Transatlantic Slave Trade* (New Haven: Yale University Press, 2010), 18–19, 30, 226, 240–41; John Gimlette, *Wild Coast: Travels on South America's Untamed Edge* (New York: Alfred A. Knopf, 2011).
49. *Oroonoko* is a very early English novel set in Surinam in the 1660s, when Behn may or may not have been in what was then English Guiana.
50. Stedman, *Narrative*, 1:30, 44; Richard Price, *Representations of Slavery: John Gabriel Stedman's "Minnesota" Manuscripts* ([Minneapolis]: Associates of the James Bell Ford Library, University of Minnesota, 1989), 6, 13, 22, 24–26.
51. Stedman, *Narrative*, 1:292. Population figures a century later were estimated at "eighty thousand blacks to four thousand whites"—many of the latter having abandoned the sugar plantations when slavery was outlawed, in 1863. Higginson, *Travellers and Outlaws*, 156.
52. Stedman, *Narrative*, 1:288.
53. Ibid., 1:289.
54. Ibid., 1:287, 289.
55. Ibid., 2:55.
56. Ibid., 1:319. One observer notes that slaves taunted free negroes with a song suggesting that the latter only ate mackerel, while they themselves had a more varied diet. Von Sack, *Narrative*, 114.
57. Ibid., 103, 104.
58. Stedman, *Narrative*, 2:205n.
59. *CAA* 3, no. 13 (March 30, 1860).
60. Obituary for Charles A. Homans, *New-York Daily Tribune*, November 11, 1901; Charles A. Homans, Journal of a Voyage from Gloucester to Surinam in the Bark *Izette*, 1848–49, Nathaniel Rogers, Master, CAM; Phillips, *Ship Registers*, 87.
61. Price, *Representations of Slavery*, 10; von Sack, *Narrative*, 117.
62. Log of the brig *Amazon*.
63. "Slaves in the Northern States," *CAL & GT*, December 2, 1848, notes the number of slaves in the North in the 1840 census; twenty-three slaves in New England had apparently, owing to "incapacitude [*sic*] for service," declined to accept freedom papers. *BET*, October 23, 1850; *CAL & GT* 23, no. 23 (June 9, 1849).
64. *CAL & GT* 23, no. 17 (April 28, 1849), and 23, no. 31 (August 3, 1849); Eltis and Richardson, *Transatlantic Slave Trade*, 284–85; *GT* 14, no. 31 (April 17, 1850).
65. Bennett, diary, entries for March 8, 1854, and August 6, 1854.
66. *GT* 14, no. 15 (February 20, 1850). It is possible that this is the same "Backus . . . stolen from Africa," a slave of Capt. Winthrop Sargent (of Gloucester), whose granddaughter Nancy Prince published a remarkable account of her life in 1850 (*A Narrative of the Life and Travels of Mrs. Nancy Prince Written*, quotation on p. 5 of the 2nd ed.).
67. Bennett, diary, entry for June 2, 1854.
68. Ibid., entry for June 8, 1854.
69. *CAA*, February 8, 1861.
70. Individual states, and within them municipal jurisdictions, were given specific quotas of soldiers to recruit. *CAL & GT* 26, no. 31 (August 2, 1862).
71. Dunlap and Buck, *FHL*, 65–68, 78.
72. Gloucester, then, singularly refutes the claim by Brian Roberts that most East Coast newspapers paid little attention to reports of gold in California in 1848 or treated such reports with skepticism. Roberts, *American Alchemy: The California Gold Rush and Middle-Class Culture* (Chapel Hill: University of North Carolina Press, 2000), 19. On October 7, 1848, *CAL & GT* reported the gold strike, on December 2 the extraction of $64,000 a day from the diggings, on December 9 the desertion by ship's crews, and during December the hurried preparation and departure of four vessels from Boston, four from New York City, three from Philadelphia, four from Baltimore, and one from New Orleans for San Francisco. Literally every week from the discovery of gold to the onset of the Civil War the Gloucester papers contained fulsome news of California.
73. *CAL & GT* 23, no. 36 (September 8, 1849). Equal exoduses occurred from other regions and nations, as noted, for instance, in Malcolm Rohrbough, "The California Gold Discoveries: The French View of Themselves and the World," *Commonplace* 6, no. 3 (April 2006), http://common-place.org/book/the-california-gold-discoveries, accessed July 18, 2016.
74. Reprinted in *GT* 14, no. 66 (August 17, 1850).
75. *CAL & GT* 23, no. 24 (June 16, 1849), and 23, no. 45 (November 10, 1849).
76. *CAL & GT* 23, no. 23 (June 9, 1849); *GT* 14, no. 40 (May 18, 1850).
77. *GT* 14, no. 64 (August 10, 1850); J. S. Holliday, *The World Rushed In:*

The California Gold Rush Experience (New York: Simon & Schuster, 1981), 303.

78. See Stephen Mihm, *A Nation of Counterfeiters: Capitalists, Con Men, and the Making of the United States* (Cambridge: Harvard University Press, 2007).

79. Jane Kamensky traces the belief that "industry plus economy equaled prosperity" to the Revolution. Kamensky, *The Exchange Artist: A Tale of High-Flying Speculation and America's First Banking Collapse* (New York: Viking, 2008), 4–5, 11.

80. "Mercantile Integrity," *CAA*, February 22, 1861.

81. "California Items," *CAL & GT* 23, no. 4 (January 27, 1849).

82. Nathaniel Babson was also a store owner, a bank director, a painter, and a member of the American Art-Union.

83. Emeline (Emma) Babson emigrated in 1869 on one of the first transcontinental trains, followed in 1870 by her sister, both bearing Lane paintings. *Past and Present of Alameda County, California*, ed. Joseph E. Baker (Chicago: S. J. Clarke, 1914), 2:472–73.

84. [Brooks], "Historical House"; John C. Gray, "Remarks on New England Agriculture," in *Essays: Agricultural and Literary*, 3, 6, 10–18.

85. H. D. Jr., Rockport, "Industry," *GT* 14, no. 16 (February 23, 1850).

86. *GT* 14, no. 46 (June 8, 1850); see also "Industry," *GT* 14, no. 22 (March 23, 1850); H. S., "Habits of Study Written by a Student," *GT* 14, no. 45 (June 5, 1850); Kamensky, *Exchange Artist*, 4–5, 11.

87. "Times Gone By," *GT* 5, no. 10 (March 5, 1831); *GT* 1, no. 52 (December 22, 1827).

88. "From the *Salem Observer*," *GT* 3, no. 36 (August 29, 1829).

89. *Companion to the United States Census of 1850*, as cited in Gray, "New England Agriculture," 54.

90. Gray, "New England Agriculture," 62.

91. Gray, *Essays: Agricultural and Literary*, viii.

92. *CAL & GT* 23, no. 29 (July 21, 1849). The subversion of patriarchal authority by bands of young men forming companies and heading to the gold fields was a dramatic version of the general tendency toward greater youth autonomy described by Karen Halttunen as a characteristic of antebellum America. Halttunen, *Confidence Men and Painted Women: A Study of Middle-Class Culture in America, 1830–1870* (New Haven: Yale University Press, 1982), 13.

93. *GT* 1, no. 18 (April 28, 1827).

94. *CAL & GT* 23, no. 48 (December 1, 1849). Elsewhere in this issue a two-sentence article asserts that two million turkeys were consumed in the fourteen states that celebrated Thanksgiving three days earlier.

95. Roberts, *American Alchemy*, 5.

96. See, for instance, *CAL & GT* 23, no. 29 (July 21, 1849).

97. *CAL & GT* 23, no. 36 (September 8, 1849).

98. Ibid.

99. Complete hotels were shipped from New York as well. *CAL & GT* 23, no. 5 (February 3, 1849).

100. For some accounts of misery en route to California, see *GT* 14, no. 77 (September 25, 1850); *CAL & GT* 23, no. 15 (April 14, 1849); *GT* 14, no. 66 (August 17, 1850); and *CAL & GT* 23, no. 38 (September 22, 1849). For a thoughtful historical and psychological study of gambling, see Jackson Lears, *Something for Nothing: Luck in America* (New York: Penguin, 2003).

101. *CAL & GT* 23, no. 41 (October 13, 1849). *CAL & GT* in March had reported on the scarcity and high prices of milled lumber in San Francisco. *CAL & GT* 23, no. 13 (March 31, 1849). Conversely, in 1855 Rogers bought the serviceable but slow *California*, which had been engaged in the hide trade in the 1830s, and put it on the Surinam route, as the premium among vessels bound for the Golden State was on speed, even for freight. Erik Ronnberg, *California*, http://fitzhenrylaneonline.org, accessed June 9, 2018.

102. *CAL & GT* 23, no. 16 (April 21, 1849). Susan Haskell Burnham's sister, Elizabeth A. Haskell Gabcar (or Galacar, Galacer, Gallicor, or Gallagher), was in California with her husband, Charles Gabcar, by 1853 but returned to Gloucester by 1863; widowed in 1864, she probably became Lane's housekeeper; she received a bequest in his will. Dunlap and Buck, *FHL*, 109–11.

103. Robert Forbes, *Personal Reminiscences*, app., "List of Vessels Built Under My Order or Supervision, or in Which I Have Had an Interest"; "Diary of Robert Bennet Forbes," vol. 3, entries for January 27 and March 22, 1849; Forbes's friend and Lane patron George Upton had five ultrafast clipper ships built specifically for the California trade. Allen, *George Bruce Upton*, 11.

104. *CAL & GT*, December 2 and December 9, 1848; 23, no. 9 (March 3, 1849); 23, no. 32 (August 11, 1849); 23, no. 38 (September 22, 1849); S. Augustus Mitchell, *Description of Oregon and California, Embracing an Account of the Gold Regions* (Philadelphia: Thomas, Cowperthwait, 1849), 43.

105. George Babson (1818–1853) was the son of John Babson, so first cousin to Lane customers Nathaniel Babson, John J. Babson, and Capt. Edward Babson. *CAL & GT* 23, no. 39 (September 29, 1849).

106. Ibid.

107. Stephanie Buck, "Edward Babson," http://fitzhenrylaneonline.org, accessed August 23, 2019.

108. U.S. Census Reports for 1860, 1880. https://search.ancestry.com/search/db.aspx?dbid=6742, accessed August 10, 2018.

109. Joseph Sayward Friend was the brother of Babson's second wife, Julia Friend (1834–1864).

110. U.S. Census Reports for 1860, 1870. In the census report of 1860, J. S. Friend reports real estate worth $2,000 and personal estate worth $4,000; in the 1870 census he reports real estate worth $20,000 and personal estate of $30,000. In both cases his occupation is "lumber merchant."

111. Anonymous text on *Map of the Gold Regions of California* [...], published by Ensigns & Thayer, New York (AAS). By the time of the 1880

census, Joseph S. Friend had died, and his widow Elizabeth (who was not from Gloucester) had moved to Marysville, California, with her two children.

112. Marysville continued to prosper in the 1860s and '70s as the port at which heavy goods from San Francisco were transshipped from river boats to wagons to supply Virginia City, where the Comstock Lode added silver to the mineral boom.
113. It is also possible that the Lane painting Edward Babson Stanwood reported having in 1961 is the one ordered in 1864 by Joseph Sayward Friend, whose widow moved to Marysville by 1880. As both Friend and Stanwood were in the lumber business, lived near one another, and were kin through Edward Babson, it is possible that Friend's widow Elizabeth, who came from New York, gave the painting to the elder Stanwood because, as someone familiar with Gloucester, he could appreciate it better.
114. *GT* 14, no. 73 (September 11, 1850).
115. *CAL & GT* 25, no. 28 (July 12, 1851); *GT* 34, no. 74 (September 15, 1860); *CAL & GT* 23, no. 48 (December 1, 1849): ad by Geo. L. Ford at 32 Front Street for California Charts; *CAL & GT* 23, no. 45 (November 10, 1849).
116. *CAL & GT* 23, no. 23 (June 9, 1849). Capt. Oliver Gideon Lane's detailed manuscript ledger covering the years 1860–66 is at CAM. Admirable prefabricated houses were also imported into San Francisco from China. *GT* 14, no. 66 (August 17, 1850).
117. *GT* 14, no. 12 (February 1850).
118. *CAL & GT* 23, no. 13 (March 31, 1849).
119. Ibid.
120. Dunlap and Buck, *FHL*, 109. For the various spellings of the name Gabcar, see note 102 above.
121. Ibid., 109–10.
122. Ibid., 109–11.
123. *CAL & GT*, March 25, 1848.
124. Fitzhenrylaneonline, accessed June 9, 2018. The inscription on the *Golden State* canvas was recorded as "Painted by Fitz Henry Lane. / Gloucester. / Mass. / A.D. 1854" before lining.
125. *GT* 14, no. 38 (May 11, 1850).
126. *GT* 14, no. 45 (June 5, 1850), and 14, no. 64 (August 10, 1850).
127. *CAL & GT* 23, no. 19 (May 12, 1849), and 23, no. 48 (December 1, 1849).
128. *CAL & GT* 25, no. 28 (July 12, 1851).

CHAPTER 8

1. In the words of the *Boston Traveller*, "At the age of 13 [Forbes] went to sea before the mast [i.e., as a common seaman]; at 16 he was third mate, at 20 Captain, at 26 he owned a ship and commanded her; at 28 he left the sea, and at 36 was head of the largest American [trading] house in China." September 18 (no year) clipping inserted into the copy of *Reminiscences of Ralph B. Forbes* at the Massachusetts Historical Society.
2. "The Mariners Secret Tie" (excerpt from James Fenimore Cooper's *Red Rover*), *GT* 2, no. 23 (May 31, 1828).
3. [Robert B. Forbes], *The Voyage of the* Jamestown *on Her Errand of Mercy* (Boston: Eastburn's Press, 1847).
4. Forbes notes that on March 11, 1847, he "received authority from the Secretary of the Navy to command the U.S. ship of War, the *Jamestown* . . . for the purpose of carrying out (as a private Ship) the private donation[s] of Boston & the vicinity." On March 28 the *Jamestown* sailed for Cork. "Diary of Robert Bennet Forbes," vol. 3, December 10, 1840, to March 28, 1847; Robert Forbes, *Personal Reminiscences*, 188–89.
5. Robert Forbes, *Personal Reminiscences*, 188.
6. [Robert Forbes], *Voyage of the* Jamestown, 13.
7. Ibid., 27; "Diary of Robert Bennet Forbes," vol. 4, October 3, 1847, to July 22, 1854.
8. [Robert Forbes], *Voyage of the* Jamestown, 25–27.
9. On November 24, 1847, Forbes noted in his diary the arrival of a "splendid [silver] salver and an address from the Citizens of Cork." The Atkinson painting is at the Forbes House Museum in Milton, MA. I am grateful to Eugene Sullivan for providing me access.
10. Robert Forbes, *Personal Reminiscences*, 296.
11. "Diary of Robert Bennet Forbes," vol. 4, entries for November 10, 1847, and April 22, 1848.
12. Robert Forbes, *Personal Reminiscences*, 296.
13. Ibid. and app., "List of Vessels." This was the iron paddle steamer *Mint*, which Forbes co-owned with S. Hooper and W. Delano.
14. Ibid.
15. Ibid., app., "List of Vessels."
16. Cedric Ridgely-Nevitt, "The *Massachusetts*," in *American Steamships on the Atlantic* (Newark: University of Delaware Press, 1980), 94; "Diary of Robert Bennet Forbes," vol. 3, entries for July 22 and September 14, 1845. Although scheduled to sail on September 1, the ship's departure was delayed to accommodate Forbes's party, as they arrived in New York City only on September 14; the party included Forbes's uncle Thomas H. Perkins and his sister Emma. Robert Forbes, *Personal Reminiscences*, 214.
17. "Diary of Robert Bennet Forbes," vol. 3, entry for November 20, 1845. I thank Georgia Barnhill for this reference.
18. Robert B. Forbes, *A New Rig for Ships and Other Vessels, Combining Economy, Safety, and Convenience* (Boston: Wier & White, 1849), 10–11.
19. Helena E. Wright, "The Image Makers: The Role of the Graphic Arts in Industrialization," *Journal of the Society for Industrial Archeology* 12, no. 2 (1986): 10 (I thank Georgia Barnhill for this reference); Bennett, diary, entry for August 26, 1854, records the purchase of shoes; R. B. Forbes noted in his diary entry for November 14, 1847: "Abner Fisk came to live with me as out of door man at $12 pr mo [plus room and board]."
20. "Diary of Robert Bennet Forbes," vol. 3, entry for Thursday, June 11, 1846; Ridgely-Nevitt, *American Steamships*, 94–96.
21. Ridgely-Nevitt, *American Steamships*, 96.

22. Robert B. Forbes, *The Auxiliary Screw Packet Ship* Massachusetts*: Forbes's New Rig*, pamphlet (London: Nautical Magazine, 1853), 2, repr. from a February 16, 1853, letter to the editor, *Nautical Magazine*, April 1853 (Phillips Library, Peabody Essex Museum).
23. John W. Griffiths, "Japan and China Packet Propeller *Antelope*," *U.S. Nautical Magazine and Naval Journal* 3 (October 1855): 11–17.
24. Either the oil-on-canvas *Antelope* is misinscribed, or, less likely, it is a retrospective reimagining of the brig's debut, in 1843, as the MFA reports that it is inscribed on the back "Painted by F. H. Lane / July 1863." By that date *Antelope 1* had been lost, its remarkable first captain, Philip Dumaresq (in whose family the painting descended), had died, Lane was approaching his last productive months, and Forbes was busy supervising the building of gunboats for the U.S. Navy and other Civil War urgencies.
25. Letter of February 19, 1948, from Charles Copeland, Assistant Curator of Marine Rooms at Peabody Museum, to Richard McLanathan, in MFA object file for *Antelope*.
26. Robert Forbes, *Personal Reminiscences*, 296 and app., "List of Vessels." Confusing the record, there was also a New York–based *Antelope*, which was in the West African trade (owned by Charles Peter Clark, in business 1857–60), and a fourth *Antelope*, a medium clipper in the China trade built at Medford, MA, for William Lincoln & Co. of Boston in 1851, sold to a New York firm, and lost near Bangkok in 1858 (Octavius T. Howe and Frederick C. Matthews, *American Clipper Ships, 1833–1858* [Salem, MA: Marine Research Society, 1926], 1:13; Knoblock, *American Clipper Ship*, 162), as well as an extreme clipper of that name, of 1,055 tons, built in Long Island in 1852 for the China trade, sold to British owners in 1864, and still at sea in 1870 (Howe and Matthews, *American Clipper Ships*, 1:14–15, 2:668, 745). Identifying vessels by their tonnage is difficult, as three different tonnage-measurement systems were used between 1775 and 1875: "Old Measurement" until 1835, "New Measurement" between 1835 and 1854, and yet another system from 1854 until 1875. Hunt Janin, *The India-China Opium Trade in the Nineteenth Century* (Jefferson, NC: McFarland, 1999), 10.
27. Reprinted in the *Boston Advertiser* of July 27, 1843. On July 28 the *Antelope* had arrived at Holmes Hole, and on the twenty-ninth, in Boston. On August 8, 1843, it sailed for China. In my view, the inscription on the back of Lane's painting is probably in error; there is also a handwritten paper label on the painting with another mistaken date: "Brig 'Antelope' / built in the '30s / painted by Lane" (MFA curatorial files).
28. Robert Forbes, *Personal Reminiscences*, 211.
29. *Other Merchants and Sea Captains of Old Boston* (Boston: State Street Trust, 1919), 21–25. According to MFA records, this *Brig* Antelope *in Boston Harbor* includes on its stretcher an inscription in pencil—"Mr. Dumaresq. 35 Broad St."—indicating that it once belonged to a member of the Dumaresq family. See also http://genealogyfinds.com/documents/bostondumaresq.htm, accessed October 2, 2017.
30. Robert Forbes, *Personal Reminiscences*, 124. American traders acquired their opium in Turkey from 1805 until the British East India Company allowed other traders into Indian markets from the 1830s. Janin, *Opium Trade*, 62.
31. Janin, *Opium Trade*, 23, 67.
32. Robert Forbes, *Personal Reminiscences*, 124. The vessels themselves also represented a substantial investment; a clipper built in Baltimore in 1844, for instance, cost $20,000. Janin, *Opium Trade*, 17. When *Bald Eagle*, owned by Forbes's friend and Lane patron George B. Upton, was lost in 1861 under ghastly circumstances, the insurance payout was $300,000. Howe and Matthews, *American Clipper Ships*, 1:35; Basil Lubbock, *The China Clippers* (Glasgow: James Brown & Son, 1914), 44–47.
33. Bombay and Calcutta were the headquarters of the East India Company, which established opium plantations and held a near monopoly in Indian opium. Janin, *Opium Trade*, 36.
34. Ibid., 62, 66, 67, 71; Lubbock, *China Clippers*, 7.
35. Janin, *Opium Trade*, 17, 23, 31.
36. Donald Matheson, *What Is the Opium Trade?* (Edinburgh: Constable, 1857), 7–8, as cited in Janin, *Opium Trade*, 1; see also 32, 35. Each chest cost about 400 rupees to produce and sold in Calcutta for 1,400 rupees. Janin, *Opium Trade*, 38.
37. Copeland letter cited in note 25 above; Janin, *Opium Trade*, 81.
38. Josephine C. Dobkin, "Chinnery and Houqua: Questions of Attribution," *Metropolitan Museum Journal* 48 (2013): 205–16.
39. William C. Hunter, *The "Fan Kwae" at Canton Before Treaty Days, 1825–1844* (London: Kegan, Paul, Trench, 1882), 37, 38, as cited in Janin, *Opium Trade*, 65; see also Robert B. Forbes, *Remarks on China and the China Trade* (Boston: Dickinson, 1844), 14.
40. Opium was legal in the United States until the passage of the Harrison Act in 1914. Richard Harvey Brown, "The Opium Trade and Opium Policies in India, China, Britain, and the United States: Historical Comparisons and Theoretical Interpretations," *American Journal of Social Science* 30, no. 3 (2002): 624, 626, 639–46. Opiates (except in patent medicines) were regulated in Britain after 1868. Brown, "Opium Trade," 634, 637; Janin, *Opium Trade*, 26, 33.
41. Robert Bennet Forbes to Oliver Wendell Holmes Sr. [Ap?], 1886, Houghton Library, Harvard University, bMS Am 1241.1 (278): "I recommend you put on a cork jacket and wear it by night and by day, take an opiate on clearing Boston Light and wake up off Cape Clear [Ireland]."
42. Janin, *Opium Trade*, 34; Brown, "Opium Trade," 625–26, 629.
43. Janin, *Opium Trade*, 39, 40; Brown, "Opium Trade," 629, 232. According

to a contemporary, "those [in China] who at present smoke opium are the relatives and dependents of the officers of Government. . . . Those who do not smoke are the common people of the villages." F. S. Turner, *British Opium Policy and Its Results to India and China* (London: Sampson, Low, Marston, Searle & Rivington, 1876), 253, as cited in Janin, *Opium Trade*, 51–52. But others held that regular users were predominantly rural peasants. Brown, "Opium Trade," 630.

44. Matheson, *Opium Trade*, as cited in Janin, *Opium Trade*, 1; Janin, *Opium Trade*, 7, for the quotation; Brown, "Opium Trade," 628.
45. Janin, *Opium Trade*, 28. On American neutrality in this war, take note of Robert B. Forbes, "Relations with China," *National Era* (Washington, DC) 11, no. 62 (April 16, 1857).
46. Lubbock, *China Clippers*, 25. The vessel was captained during this voyage by "a lank West Indian," according to this unnamed able seaman. Ibid., 26.
47. Quoted in ibid., 25–28.
48. Ibid., 28–30.
49. Ibid., 30.
50. Ibid., 31.
51. Ibid., 32.
52. Cedric Ridgely-Nevitt, "Auxiliary Steamships and R. B. Forbes," *American Neptune* 1, no. 1 (January 1941): 52.
53. Griffiths, "Japan and China Packet Propeller *Antelope*," 14.
54. Ibid., 11; the Lane print is inserted with two folds at p. 18.
55. Ibid., 15.
56. Ibid., 16. See Robert B. Forbes, *The Life Boat, and Other Life-Saving Inventions* (Boston: A. Williams, 1880), and R. B. Forbes's correspondence with Dorothea Lynde Dix, 1853–60, Houghton Library, Harvard bMS AM 1838 (233), about lifeboats for Cunarders and for land-based rescue units.
57. It is difficult to tell which prints were originally bound into Forbes's publications, because most have been removed and framed as wall-appropriate artworks, although it is probable that those with traces of fold marks were originally bound within books and pamphlets.
58. On the different measurement systems, see note 26 above.
59. *GT* 14, no. 60 (July 27, 1850). It is also possible that this is George Phineas Lane, born 1828, the son of Fitz H. Lane's brother Edward. Dunlap and Buck, *FHL*, 30n109.
60. Hunter, *"Fan Kwae,"* 37, 38, as cited in Janin, *Opium Trade*, 65.
61. Dunlap and Buck, *FHL*, 156. R. B. Forbes built Masconomo, a summer home, on a promontory on the coast of Manchester a few miles from Lane's residence in Gloucester and summered there with his family from 1855 to 1866, so they were part-time neighbors as well as collaborators.
62. Edward Bliss Emerson, journal, entry for July 16, 1831, Houghton Library, Harvard University, bMS AM 1280.235 (576), p. 5.
63. H. Mason, "Sidney Mason," 113–14; Sidney Mason, deposition, December 1838, Southern District of New York, National Archives, RA M1372, images of handwritten letters and application forms for U.S. passports, 1795–1905, roll 0007, catalog Id 566612, p. 2; https://www.fold3.com/image/1/85072098, accessed July 21, 2019.
64. John Bassett Moore, "Oaths of Allegiance," sect. 468 of *A Digest of International Law* (Washington, DC: Government Printing Office, 1906), 3:718; Frederick Van Dyne, *A Treatise on the Law of Naturalization of the United States* (Washington, DC: self-published, 1907), 338; S. Mason, deposition, December 31, 1838; Edmund Flagg, ed., *Report on the Commercial Relations of the United States with All Foreign Nations* (Washington, DC: Cornelius Wendell, 1856), 208; Donald Thompson, "Notes on the Inauguration of the San Juan (Puerto Rico) Municipal Theater," *Latin American Music Review* 11, no. 1 (June 1990): 84.
65. E. B. Emerson, journal, entry for April 10, 1831, p. 11.
66. Thomas Jefferys, *The West-India Atlas* [. . .] (London, 1776), 15.
67. Edward Bliss Emerson, untitled account of San Juan [ca. 1832], Houghton Library, Harvard University, bMS AM 1289.235 (249) and bMS 1280.235 (350).
68. Edward E. Crain, *Historic Architecture in the Caribbean Islands* (Gainesville: Library Press at the University of Florida, 2017), 31.
69. Fernando Picó, *History of Puerto Rico* (Princeton, NJ: Markus Wiener, 2006), 141–42, 188; Kelvin Santiago-Valles, "Forced Labor in Colonial Penal Institutions Across the Spanish, U.S., British, French Atlantic, 1860s–1920s," in *On Coerced Labor: Work and Compulsion After Chattel Slavery*, ed. Marcel van der Linden and Magaly Rodríguez García (Boston: Brill, 2016), 86–87; Jorge L. Chinea, "Fissures in El Primer Piso: Racial Politics in Spanish Colonial Puerto Rico During Its Pre-plantation Era, c. 1700–1800," *Caribbean Studies* 30, no. 1 (January–June 2002): 175–76.
70. See Augustus de Vaudricourt, *Puerto-Rico*, ca. 1842, a lithograph that Melissa Trafton proposes might be the source for Lane's view: http://fitzhenrylaneonline.org/catalog/entry.php?id=239, accessed July 22, 2019. See also chapter 1 for an instance in which Lane based a painting on a print by another artist.
71. The population breakdown in 1835 was given as 180,783 white, 104,044 free colored, 34,336 slaves. David Turnbull, *Travels in the West: Cuba, with Notices of Porto Rico and the Slave Trade* (London: Longman, Orme, Brown, Green & Longmans, 1840), 555–57; Frank Moya Pons, *History of the Caribbean: Plantations, Trade, and War in the Atlantic World* (Princeton, NJ: Markus Wiener, 2007), 231; John Disturnell, *Emigrant's Guide to New Mexico, California, Oregon* (New York: self-published, 1849), n.p.; Picó, *History of Puerto Rico*, 141, 189; Chinea, "Racial Politics," 175–76.
72. Moya Pons, *History of the Caribbean*, 220, 223–24, 230–33; Flagg, *Commercial Relations*, 208; Chinea, "Racial Politics," 194, 195; Picó, *History of Puerto Rico*, 145–50, 175–76, 187–88.

73. E. B. Emerson, journal, entry for February 23, 1831, p. 8.
74. F. A. Jackson, "Catalina Juliana Mason," 37; Cassie Mason Myers Julian-James, "Early Recollections of Cassie Mason Myers Julian-James," in Julian-James, *Biographical Sketches,* 90; H. Mason, "Sidney Mason," 114.
75. Puerto Rico Reconstruction Administration and the Writers' Program of the Work Projects Administration, *Puerto Rico: A Guide to the Island of Boriquén* (New York: University Society, 1940), 111, 175.
76. E. B. Emerson, journal, entry for January 2 and 3, 1832, n.p.
77. Flagg, *Commercial Relations,* 207–8. By 1899 a military road had been built across the island, but nonmilitary roads were still insufficient for transport beyond loaded mules. Amos Kidder Fiske, *The West Indies* (New York: G. P. Putnam's Sons, 1899), 280–81.
78. "Sidney Mason," *Newburyport Herald* 27, no. 83 (January 13, 1834).
79. *GT* 1, no. 14 (March 31, 1827); 2, no. 32 (August 2, 1828); 2, no. 51 (December 13, 1828); 3, no. 35 (August 22, 1829); 4, no. 27 (May 29, 1830); 4, no. 33 (August 14, 1830).
80. "Foreign Posts at Home," *American Foreign Service Journal* 2, no. 2 (February 1925): 66, "Porto Rico"; *Journal of the Executive Proceedings of the Senate of the United States of America,* vol. 4, *From March 4, 1829, to March 3, 1837, Inclusive* (Washington, DC: Government Printing Office, 1887), 51–52; *An Account of the Receipts and Expenditures of the United States for the Year 1836* (Washington, DC: Blair & Rives, Printers, 1837), 60. By 1840 there were 327 English and North American citizens resident in Puerto Rico. Turnbull, *Travels in the West,* 558; E. B. Emerson, journal, entry for November 17, 1831. For a summary of Sidney Mason's report to the State Department for 1830, see Charnel Anderson, "Nineteenth-Century Historical Background," in *The American Presence in Puerto Rico,* ed. Lynn-Darrell Bender (Hato Rey, PR: Publicaciones Puertorriqueñas, 1998), 3–4, 6–7.
81. "From the *Journal of Commerce,*" *GT* 3, no. 11 (March 7, 1829). Some consuls reported considerable earnings from these fees: the consulates at London and Rio de Janeiro were reputed to be worth nearly $10,000 a year at midcentury. *CAL & GT* 23, no. 19 (May 12, 1849).
82. Edward Bliss Emerson, "Statistics &c P.R.," miscellaneous notes, Pocket Memorandum Book, Houghton Library, Harvard University, MS Am 1280.235 (333), n.p.
83. *Spectator* (New York), January 12, 1830; *Georgian* (Savannah) 12, no. 51 (January 25, 1830); Puerto Rico Reconstruction Administration, *Puerto Rico: A Guide,* 85.
84. John Bassett Moore and Hamilton Fish, "Consuls," chap. 16 in *A Digest of International Law as Embodied in Diplomatic Discussions, Treaties,* [. . .] *and the Decisions of Courts, Federal and State,* H.R. Doc. No. 551, 56th Cong. (Washington, DC: Government Printing Office, 1906), 5:713; *Official Proceedings of the International Commercial Congress* [. . .] *1899* ([Philadelphia]: Press of the Philadelphia Commercial Museum, 1899), 394.
85. Joe McMillan, House Flags of U.S. Shipping Companies, from Charles C. Gifford, "Private Signals of the Merchants of New York and San Francisco," ca. 1858, broadside, Bancroft Library, https://www.crwflags.com/fotw/flags/us~hfma.html#masonthompson, accessed July 19, 2019, and https://calisphere.org/item/ark:/13030/tf429008x61, accessed February 3, 2022.
86. *Alexandria (VA) Gazette,* May 12, 1871.
87. Kenneth J. Blume, *Historical Dictionary of the U.S. Maritime Industry* (Lanham, MD: Scarecrow Press, 2012), 308–9. Sidney Mason's nephew Capt. John Sidney Mason, son of Alphonso, whether in collaboration or competition with Mason & Thompson, took the clipper schooner *Loo Choo* to San Francisco early in 1850. *GT* 14, no. 24 (March 23, 1850).
88. Julian-James, "Early Recollections," in Julian-James, *Biographical Sketches,* 89–90.
89. Letter from Charles C. Emerson to R. W. Emerson, December 23, 1831, Houghton Library, Harvard University, bMS AM 1280.229 (100).
90. F. A. Jackson, "Catalina Juliana Mason," 37.
91. "[Lydia] Ann Mason Babson—Feb 19, 1822–Jan. 11, 1907," newspaper clipping, no date or name of newspaper noted, CAM.
92. Grave marker for John Mason Stevens (1836–1857), Gloucester.
93. *GT* 5, no. 11 (March 12, 1831).
94. Annie Santiago de Curet, *Crédito, moneda y bancos en Puerto Rico durante el siglo XIX* (Río Piedras: Editorial de la Universidad de Puerto Rico, 1989), 62–63.
95. These letters, journals, and memoranda books are at the Houghton Library at Harvard. For published selections, see Ronald A. Bosco and Joel Myerson, *The Emerson Brothers: A Fraternal Biography in Letters* (Oxford: Oxford University Press, 2006), and José G. Rigau-Pérez, ed., *Edward Bliss Emerson: The Caribbean Journal and Letters, 1831–1834* (Privately printed, 2013).
96. Letter from E. B. Emerson to C. C. Emerson, July 27, 1833, Houghton Library, Harvard University, MS Am 1280.226 (173). E. B. Emerson had met Mason's father-in-law a few years earlier on board a ship crossing the Atlantic to Gibraltar. E. B. Emerson, journal, entry for April 24, 1831, p. 14.
97. Letter from Charles Chauncy Emerson to Ezra Ripley, January 15, 1832, Houghton Library, Harvard University, MS Am 1280.226 (161).
98. F. A. Jackson, "Catalina Juliana Mason," 40.
99. H. Mason, "Sidney Mason," 118. It is possible that the designer of this furniture was one Heilbruner of Paris. Ibid., 52–53.
100. Mason, with others, bought information on a new sugar-refining process in 1831. E. B. Emerson, journal, entry for April 7, 1831, p. 9. By 1840 there were 1,555 sugar estates and 124 coffee estates on Puerto Rico. Turnbull, *Travels in the West,* 558–59.

101. See Jennifer L. Anderson, *Mahogany: The Costs of Luxury in Early America* (Cambridge: Harvard University Press, 2012), and William Farquhar Payson, ed., *Mahogany, Antique and Modern* (New York: E. P. Dutton, 1926).
102. In his journal entry of July 22, 1831, Edward Bliss Emerson describes the use of dense tropical hardwoods "uninflammable as stone" in San Juan buildings.
103. Flagg, *Commercial Relations*, 207.
104. "Last Will and Testament of Cassie Mason Myers Julian-James," *Washington, D.C., Wills and Probate Records, 1737–1952* [online database], ancestry .com. Original data: Washington, DC, District and Probate Courts: Wills, boxes 0723 Gilmore–0734 Pierce, 1922, images 372–81.
105. Robert Lowell, *Life Studies* (New York: Farrar, Straus & Giroux, 1959), 41, 43, 45.
106. E. B. Emerson, journal, entries for April 7, April 8, and June 26, 1831, pp. 9, 14; letter from E. B. Emerson to Mary Moody Emerson, April 5, 1834, Houghton Library, Harvard University, bMS Am 1280.226 (182); Frank Otto Gatell, "Puerto Rico Through New England Eyes, 1831–1834," *Journal of Inter-American Studies* 1, no. 3 (July 1959): 282. As late as 1899 Puerto Rico had no general system of public instruction, and illiteracy predominated. Fiske, *West Indies*, 282; Puerto Rico Reconstruction Administration, *Puerto Rico: A Guide*, 135, 160.
107. E. B. Emerson, journal, entry for July 1, 1831, p. 18.
108. Letter from Charles C. Emerson to Rev. R. W. Emerson, February 2, 1832, Houghton Library, Harvard University, MS Am 1280.229 (102).
109. Charles C. Emerson was, at times, reconciled. C. C. Emerson, diary of 1831–36, entry for August 1, 1831, Houghton Library, Harvard University, folder 1 of 5 bMS Am 1280.220 Series IV.
110. Sidney Mason, deposition concerning passport application, December 31, 1838, Southern District of New York, https://www.fold3.com /image/85072099, accessed July 22, 2019; F. A. Jackson, "Catalina Juliana Mason," 37.
111. Charles Chauncy Emerson, prose fragment found in a notebook dated September 11, 1831, Houghton Library, Harvard University, bMS Am 1280.235 (294); letter from E. B. Emerson to Ezra Ripley, October 30, 1831, Houghton Library, Harvard University, bMS Am 1280.226 (259); letter from C. C. Emerson to R. W. Emerson, December 23, 1831, Houghton Library, Harvard University, MS Am 1280.229 (100); C. C. Emerson, "Whether an extreme sensibility to the beauties of the Fine Arts be conducive to happiness. Negative" [1826–28], Houghton Library, Harvard University, bMS Am 1280.235 (300); C. C. Emerson, journal fragment, Porto Rico, December 15, 1831, Houghton Library, Harvard University, bMS Am 1280.235 (268).
112. Edward Bliss Emerson, "Scraps of My Journal in Europe 1826," Houghton Library, Harvard University, bMS AM 1280.235 (327); E. B. Emerson, "Memorandum Book" [1831–34], list of items to bring back to Puerto Rico from New England: "clocks, Paper, . . . Jams, Pictures, . . . canes, Mus[ic] boxes, Glass ware . . . plaster casts, Engravings," Houghton Library, Harvard University, bMS Am 1280.235 (333).
113. Annette B. Ramírez de Arellano, "Encountering the Viper: Edward Bliss Emerson and Slavery," *Qualitative Report* 19, no. 16 (2014): 61, https://nsuworks.nova.edu/tqr/vol19 /iss16/4/, accessed July 29, 2019.
114. Letter from C. C. Emerson to Ezra Ripley, January 15, 1832, Houghton Library, Harvard University, MS Am 1280.226 (161).
115. E. B. Emerson, journal, entries for March 9 and June 26, 1831, pp. 1, 15.
116. At the abolishment of slavery in 1873, slaves constituted 4.2 percent of Puerto Rico's population. Ramírez de Arellano, "Encountering the Viper," 67.
117. Letter from Mr. [John] Forsyth, secretary of state, to Mr. [William] Emerson, January 23, 1839, as quoted in Moore, "Oaths of Allegiance," in *A Digest of International Law* 3:718–19; Van Dyne, *Treatise*, 338. Sidney Mason's brother and former partner in business, John Mason, remained in Puerto Rico until 1840, when he moved with his family and Caribbean import-export business to Philadelphia. Edna Warren Mason [Mrs. Mason Pfizenmayer], *Descendants of Capt. Hugh Mason in America* (New Haven: Tuttle, Morehouse & Taylor, 1937), 552; *Official Proceedings*, 394.
118. Moya Pons, *History of the Caribbean*, 233–35; Picó, *History of Puerto Rico*, 176–77.
119. J. H. W. Cullohy, attachment, dated December 20, 1838, to Sidney Mason, deposition concerning passport, December 31, 1838.
120. Letters from Charles C. Emerson to Rev. R. W. Emerson, December 23, 1831, and January 9, 1832 (MS Am 1280.229 [100, 101]); E. B. Emerson, "Memorandum Book," bMS AM 1280.235 (349), October 15, 1831, p. 11; E. B. Emerson, journal, entry for August 9, 1831.
121. F. A. Jackson, "Catalina Juliana Mason," 37.
122. This second painting of Baltimore is illustrated in Wilmerding, *Paintings by Fitz Hugh Lane*, 103.
123. Letter from Cassie Mason Myers Julian-James to Mr. [Harry C.] Foster, mayor of Gloucester, and Council [early in 1913], published in *GDT*, July 15, 1913, giving the provenance of Sidney Mason's *Gloucester Harbor*.
124. A letter to the editor of the *Gloucester Telegraph* states that "our townsmen are pretty well agreed, that a spacious Hotel, with suitable pleasure grounds, and placed in an eligible and pleasant situation, is greatly needed . . . to make our healthy, and delightfully situated town a summer resort." *GT* 1, no. 18 (April. 28, 1827); *CAL & GT* 23, no. 15 (April 14, 1849).
125. "Windmill!," *GT* 2, no. 43 (October 18, 1820).
126. S. Mason's property value placed him tenth on the Gloucester tax list in 1848 (*CAL & GT*, September 2, 1848); he was criticized for not paying enough attention to the Pavilion Hotel in 1860 (*CAA* 3, no. 28 [July 13, 1860]); he contributed $500 of $3,000

collected for "Gloucester sufferers" in 1862 (*Lowell Daily Citizen and News* 12, no. 1821 [April 8, 1862]); and in 1871 he donated both money and land for the building of the [Civil War] Soldiers and Sailors Monument on Boston Common, completed 1877 (*CAWA*, May 12, 1871).

127. F. A. Jackson, "Catalina Juliana Mason," 38–39.
128. Sidney Mason, last will and testament, *New York, Wills and Probate Records, 1659–1999* [online database], p. 151, ancestry.com. Original data: New York County, District and Probate Courts: Wills, vol. 0203–0204, 1869–1874, images 415–21.
129. H. Mason, "Sidney Mason," 115.
130. John Mason's completed lithographic map, "the first map of Cape Ann ever made from actual survey," "shewing the roads, rivers, harbours, coves, islands, and ledges [as well as] . . . the soundings and best anchorage," was previewed in *GT* 4, no. 36 (September 5, 1830), and announced for sale in *GT* 5, no. 6 (February 5, 1831).
131. See chapter 6.
132. *Awful Calamities*, 16. On George H. Rogers, see chapter 7.
133. "Loss of the Steamer Lexington," in ibid., on the inside cover of the 6th ed.; H. Mason, "Sidney Mason," 115; E. W. Mason, *Descendants of Capt. Hugh Mason*, 551–52; J. J. Babson, *History of the Town of Gloucester*, 561.
134. H. Mason, "Sidney Mason."
135. F. A. Jackson, "Catalina Juliana Mason," 40–41; H. Mason, "Sidney Mason," 115.
136. H. Mason, "Sidney Mason."
137. Sidney Mason obituary, *Commercial Advertiser* (New York), May 11, 1871; S. Mason, last will and testament, p. 151.
138. C. B. M. Jackson, "Theodorus Bailey Myers," in Julian-James, *Biographical Sketches*, 9, 25.
139. John Mason, *A Statement of Facts in Relation to the Origin, Progress, and Prospects of the New-York and Harlem Rail Road Company* (New York: George P. Scott, 1833), pamphlet, 4, 12.
140. Edward K. Spann, *The New Metropolis: New York City, 1840–1857* (New York: Columbia University Press, 1981), 103–4; Eric Homberger, *The Historical Atlas of New York City: A Visual Celebration of Nearly 400 Years of New York City's History* (New York: Henry Holt, 1994), 76–77.
141. E. W. Mason, *Descendants of Capt. Hugh Mason*, 551. The Sixth Avenue Railroad, operational from 1851, was four miles long and carried more than four million passengers a year (1855). *Annual Report of the Railroad Commissioners of the State of New-York, and of the Reports of the Railroad Corporations, Made to the Board, for the Year Ending September 30, 1855* (Albany, NY: C. Van Benthuysen, 1856), 683–94; D. T. Valentine, *Manual of the Corporation of the City of New-York, 1862* (New York: Corporation of New-York, 1862), 384–85; H. Mason, "Sidney Mason," 119.
142. H. Mason, "Sidney Mason," 121.
143. Clarence Cook, *A Description of New York Central Park* (New York: F. J. Huntington, 1869), 15–17.
144. C. Cook, *Central Park*, 20–22; Julian-James, "Early Recollections," in Julian-James, *Biographical Sketches*, 85; H. Mason, "Sidney Mason," 115.
145. H. Mason, "Sidney Mason," 117–19.
146. *Constitution, By-Laws, Sailing Regulations, &c. of the New York Yacht Club* (New York: F. H. Biglow, 1871), 31; Theodorus Bailey Myers obituary, *New York Times*, June 17, 1888.
147. Curatorial records, Preservation Society of Newport County, object accession number PSNC.8727, accessed June 2016. For Lewis Gouverneur Morris, blueblood deadbeat, and his marriage to Cassie's cousin Alletta Nathalie Lorrillard Bailey, see *New York Times*, January 17, 1908; September 29, 1921; January 14, 1935; March 23, 1946; and August 15, 1967. The location of Lane's *San Juan, Porto Rico* after Mason's death, in 1871, and before 1947, when it was given by Mrs. I. G. Redpath to the Mariner's Museum in Norfolk, is not known (she had purchased it and *Gloucester Inner Harbor* [fig. 6], perhaps also a Mason painting, from the Old Print Shop, New York City, at an unknown date).
148. R. B. Forbes, undated newspaper article inserted as a loose clipping into "Diary of Robert Bennet Forbes," vol. 4, and reprinted as Robert Bennet Forbes, "Regatta at New Bedford, Massachusetts, 8 August, 1856," *American Neptune* 10 (1950): 231–34 (document contributed by Llewellyn Howland), as cited in Erik Ronnberg, entry for *The Yacht* America *Winning the International Race*, fitzhenrylaneonline, accessed August 5, 2019.
149. There is at least one other New York Yacht Club regatta Lane painting; it is currently in private hands.
150. Theodorus Bailey Myers Mason, *The Preservation of Life at Sea* (New York: American Geographical Society, 1879), 17–19; Robert B. Forbes, *Life-Boats, Projectiles, and Other Means for Saving Life* (Boston: Wm. Parsons Lunt, 1872), 117.
151. "Funeral of the late Sidney Mason," *Commercial Advertiser* (New York), May 11, 1871.
152. *Catalogue of the Loan Exhibition, 1878, in Aid of the Society of Decorative Art* (New York: E. Wells Sackett & Bro., 1878), 15, 16, 19, 25, 31, 32, 61. The other collections have been dispersed, but the Theodorus Bailey Myers collection of historical manuscripts is at the New York Public Library: https://digitalcollections.nypl.org/collections/theodorus-bailey-myers-collection#/?tab=about.
153. *Catalogue of the Loan Exhibition, 1878*, 3.
154. Julian-James, "Last Will and Testament."

CONCLUSION

1. *BET*, August 19, 1865.
2. Berger, *Sight Unseen*, 21.
3. *GT* 14, no. 35 (May 1, 1850).
4. Wilmerding, *Fitz Henry Lane and Mary Blood Mellen*.
5. H. Travers Newton Jr., Marcia Steele, Peter John Brownlee, et al., *Fitz Henry Lane's Series Paintings of "Brace's Rock": Meaning and Technique* (privately printed, 2010), 40–44.
6. C. C. Emerson, diary of 1831–36, entry for August 1, 1831.

BIBLIOGRAPHY

N.B. I have included only the more substantial period newspaper articles here—references to many one-sentence untitled news items appear in the notes.

MANUSCRIPTS AND UNPUBLISHED SOURCES

Babson, Annette. Diary, 1841, 1847–49. CAM.

Babson, Capt. Edward. Log of the brig *Cadet*, 1837–41. Ships Log Book Collection, CAM.

Bennett, Francis, Jr. Diary, 1852–54. AAS.

Boston Artists Association, Charter and Roster, December 1841, 1–4. Manuscript Collection, Athenaeum Library, Boston.

Brooks, Alfred M. "Catalogue of the Drawings by Fitz H. Lane & given to CASL & HA [Cape Ann Scientific, Literary & Historical Association] by Samuel H. Mansfield, made by A. M. Brooks 1944. Added to 1947." CAM.

Curtis Family Journals, 1829–1847. Manuscript Collections, folio vol. C, AAS.

Dolliver/Moore Papers. Archive Collection 34 / Document Box P 23, CAM.

Emerson, Charles Chauncy. Diary of 1831–36, folder 1 of 5, bMS Am 1280.220 Series IV and bMS Am 1280.235 (268). Houghton Library, Harvard University.

———. Letter to Ezra Ripley, January 15, 1832, MS Am 1280.226 (161). Houghton Library, Harvard University.

———. Letters to R. W. Emerson, December 23, 1831, and January 9, February 2, 1832, bMS AM 1280.229 (100, 101, and 102). Houghton Library, Harvard University.

———. Prose fragment found in notebook dated September 11, 1831, bMS Am 1280.235 (294). Houghton Library, Harvard University.

———. "Whether an extreme sensibility to the beauties of the Fine Arts be conducive to happiness. Negative" [1826–28], bMS Am 1280.235 (300). Houghton Library, Harvard University.

Emerson, Edward Bliss. Correspondence with family members, bMS AM 1280.235 and MS Am 1280.226 (173); bMS Am 1280.226 (182); bMS Am 1280.226 (259); MS Am 1280.226 (161). Houghton Library, Harvard University.

———. Journal, bMS AM 1280.235 (576). Houghton Library, Harvard University.

———. "Memorandum Book" [1831–34], bMS Am 1280.235 (333, 349). Houghton Library, Harvard University.

———. "Scraps of My Journal in Europe 1826," bMS AM 1280.235 (327). Houghton Library, Harvard University.

———. "Statistics &c P.R.," MS Am 1280.235 (333). Miscellaneous notes, Pocket Memorandum Book. Houghton Library, Harvard University.

———. Untitled account of San Juan [ca. 1832], bMS AM 1289.235 (249) and bMS 1280.235 (350). Houghton Library, Harvard University.

"Fitz H. Lane: Notes & Clippings from Authors & Artists of Cape Ann Scrapbook and Other Sources," CAM 759.13 L24. Gift of Mrs. Carrie Mason Myers Julian-James, granddaughter of Lane's principal patron, Sidney Mason. CAM.

"Fitz Hugh Lane Photographs [List] at the Frick Art Reference [Library], New York City January 1961." File. CAM.

Floyd, George W. Day Book, 1848–49. CAM.

Forbes, R[obert] B[ennet]. Correspondence with Dorothea Lynde Dix, 1853–60, bMS AM 1838 (233). Houghton Library, Harvard University.

———. "Diary of Robert Bennet Forbes." Massachusetts Historical Society.

Homans, Charles A. Journal of a Voyage from Gloucester to Surinam in the Bark *Izette*, 1848–49, Nathaniel Rogers, Master. CAM.

Lane, Gideon. Autobiography. CAM.

Letters from F. H. Lane to Joseph L. Stevens Jr. (n.d.) and to Joseph L. Stevens Sr. (January 29, 1851; February 9, 1853; and n.d.), and others concerning him (e.g., Helen Stevens Babson to Susan Babson, June 10, 1929), CAM.

Log of the brig *Amazon*, July 6 to December 2, 1854, acc. #2549. John A. Pulcifer, master. Ships Log Book Collection, CAM.

Mason, Sidney. Deposition, December 31, 1838, Southern District of New York, National Archives, RA M1372, images of handwritten letters and application forms for U.S. passports, 1795–1905, roll 0007, catalog Id 566612, p. 2; https://www.fold3.com/image/85072099, accessed July 22, 2019.

Moore, Joseph. Account book. Dolliver/Moore Papers. Archive Collection 34 / Document Box P 23, CAM.

Samuel Sawyer Papers. Series II (Notebooks and Diaries #20) and III (Expense Accounts, 1851–60), Box 2, Archive Collection 63, CAM.

Smith, Charles C. "A Memoir [of John James Babson]." Typescript prepared for the Massachusetts Historical Society, 1886. Authors and Artists Scrapbook, 2:1–4, CAM.

Stevens, John. Journal, 1852, Box 2, F1 [A00772]. Wilson Museum, Castine, ME.

Taylor, Charles Henry. Clipping collection. AAS.

Trask, John. "Notes on the Life of Fitz Henry ["Henry" struck out and replaced with "Hugh"] Lane as Given by John Trask of Gloucester to Emma Todd (now Mrs. Howard P. Elwell) about 1885." Typescript of a manuscript transcribed by Todd's daughter L. Elwell. CAM.

INTERNET SOURCES

Archives Directory for the History of Collecting at the Frick Museum Center for the History of Collecting. Accessed July 1, 2018. http://research.frick.org/directoryweb/browserecord.php?-action=browse&-recid=6233.

Calvert, J. B. "Cannons and Gunpowder." http://mysite.du.edu/~jcalvert/tech/cannon.htm#C.

Fitz Henry Lane Online. Online catalogue raisonné launched March 2016. CAM. Authors include Sam Holdsworth, Erik Ronnberg, and Melissa Trafton. http://fitzhenrylaneonline.org.

Green, Charles C. Works. Menil Collection. http://50.201.124.17/people/1408/charles-c-green;jsessionid=AD3B34A6E9F89AABAFEBB08F850E166B/objects.

Julian-James, Cassie Mason Myers. "Last Will and Testament of Cassie Mason Myers Julian-James." *Washington, D.C., Wills and Probate Records, 1737–1952* [online database], ancestry.com. Original data: Washington, DC, District and Probate Courts: Wills, boxes 0723 Gilmore–0734 Pierce, 1922, images 372–81.

Keyes, John S. "Autobiography of Hon. John S. Keyes." Concord [MA] Library. https://concordlibrary.org/uploads/scollect/doc/Autobiography_final.pdf.

Massachusetts, Wills and Probate Records, 1635–1991, Case No. 44960. http://search.ancestry.com/cgi-bin/sse.dll?indiv=1&db=USProbateMa&h=709757.

McMillan, Joe. "Private Signals of the Merchants of New York." https://www.crwflags.com/fotw/flags/us~hfma.html#masonthompson.

New York, Wills and Probate Records, 1659–1999 [online database], ancestry.com. Original data: New York County, District and Probate Courts.

Pre-1877 Art Exhibition Catalogue Index, Smithsonian Institution. http://siris-artexhibition.si.edu/ipac20/ipac.

Theodorus Bailey Myers Collection, New York Public Library. https://digitalcollections.nypl.org/collections/theodorus-bailey-myers-collection#/?tab=about.

U.S. Census Reports for 1860, 1880. https://search.ancestry.com/search/db.aspx?dbid=6742.

U.S. Supreme Court. New England Insurance Company v. The Brig *Sarah Ann*, 38 U.S. 387 (1839), involving the claim of Obadiah Woodbury and others dating from 1834. http://supreme.justia.com/us/38/387/index.html.

ATLASES

Eltis, David, and David Richardson. *Atlas of the Transatlantic Slave Trade*. New Haven: Yale University Press, 2010.

Homberger, Eric. *The Historical Atlas of New York City: A Visual Celebration of Nearly 400 Years of New York City's History*. New York: Henry Holt, 1994.

Hopkins, G. M. *Atlas of the City of Gloucester and Town of Rockport, Massachusetts*. Philadelphia: G. M. Hopkins, 1884.

Jefferys, Thomas. *The West-India Atlas* [...]. London, 1776.

Moll, Herman. *The World Described; or, A New and Correct Sett of Maps* [...]. London: I Bowles, [1709–20].

PUBLISHED SOURCES

"About Art and Artists." *New York Times*, May 3, 1954.

Adams, Jane Aldrich Dowling. "A Study of Art Unions in the United States of America in the Nineteenth Century." MA thesis, Virginia Commonwealth University, Richmond, VA, 1990.

Adorno, Theodor W. "Late Style in Beethoven." 1937. In *Essays on Music*, edited by Richard Leppert, translated by Susan H. Gillespie, 564–68. Berkeley: University of California Press, 2002.

Allen, Walter. *A Memoir of George Bruce Upton*. Boston: David Clapp & Son, 1875. (Reprinted from the *Historical and Genealogical Register* for January 1875.)

"American Art Auction Catalog Collection, 1785–1962." Archives of American Art, reel N186, lot 112/frame 670; lot 114/frame 673.

"American Art-Union: Second Day's Sale." *New York Times*, December 17, 1852.

An Account of the Receipts and Expenditures of the United States for the Year 1836. Washington, DC: Blair & Rives, Printers, 1837.

Anderson, Charnel. "Nineteenth-Century Historical Background." In *The American Presence in Puerto Rico*, edited by Lynn-Darrell Bender, 1–29. Hato Rey, PR: Publicaciones Puertorriqueñas, 1998.

Anderson, Jennifer L. *Mahogany: The Costs of Luxury in Early America*. Cambridge: Harvard University Press, 2012.

Annual Report of the Railroad Commissioners of the State of New-York, and of the Reports of the Railroad Corporations, Made to the Board, for the Year Ending September 30, 1855. Albany, NY: C. Van Benthuysen, 1856.

Artistic Houses: Being a Series of Interior Views of a Number of the Most Beautiful and Celebrated Homes in the United States, with a Description of the Art Treasures Contained Therein. 2 vols. New York: D. Appleton, 1883–84. Reprinted as *The Opulent Interiors of the Gilded Age*. Edited by Arnold Lewis, James Turner, and Steven McQuillin. New York: Dover, 1987.

Avery, Kevin J. *Church's Great Picture, "The Heart of the Andes."* New York: Metropolitan Museum of Art, 1993.

Avery, Kevin J., and Franklin Kelly, eds. *Hudson River School Visions: The Landscapes of Sanford R. Gifford*. New

Haven: Yale University Press, 2003. Exh. cat.
Awful Calamities, or The Shipwrecks of December 1839, Being a Full Account of the Dreadful Hurricanes of Dec. 15, 21, & 27 on the Coast of Massachusetts; in Which Were Lost More Than 90 Vessels, and Nearly 200 Dismasted, [...] More Than 150 Lives Destroyed. Boston: Press of J. Howe, 1840. Pams/ A966/ Awfu/ 1840/ 3rd ed. AAS.
Babson, John J. *History of the Town of Gloucester, Cape Ann, Including the Town of Rockport*. Gloucester, MA: Procter Brothers, 1860. Reprint, Gloucester, MA: Peter Smith, 1972.
Babson, Roger Ward. *Actions and Reactions: An Autobiography*. New York: Harper & Brothers, 1935.
Babson, Susan. "Fitz H. Lane." C. A. S. & L. A. Weekly Column on Matters of Local History. *GDT*, February 24, 1916. "Clippings," CAM.
Baekeland, Frederick. "Collectors of American Painting, 1813 to 1913." *American Art Review* 3, no. 6 (November/ December 1976): 120–66.
Baer, Ronni. *The Poetry of Everyday Life: Dutch Painting in Boston*. Boston: Museum of Fine Arts, 2002. Exh. cat.
"Bar Harbor Canoe Parade." *New York Times*, August 22, 1899.
Barr, Alfred H., Jr. *What Is Modern Painting?* New York: Museum of Modern Art, 1943.
Barringer, Tim. "A White Atlantic? The Idea of American Art in Nineteenth-Century Britain." *19: Interdisciplinary Studies in the Long Nineteenth Century* 9 (2009). http://doi.org/10.16995/ntn.507.
Baur, John I. H. "American Luminism: A Neglected Aspect of the Realist Movement in Nineteenth-Century American Painting." *Perspectives USA* 9 (Autumn 1954): 90–98.
———. *American Painting in the Nineteenth Century: Main Trends and Movements*. New York: Frederick A. Praeger, 1953.
———. *M. and M. Karolik Collection of American Paintings, 1815 to 1865*. Boston: Museum of Fine Arts, Boston, 1949.
———. "Trends in American Painting, 1815 to 1865." In *M. and M. Karolik Collection*, xv–lvii.
———. "Unknown American Painters of the 19th Century." *College Art Journal* 6, no. 4 (Summer 1947): 277–82.
Baxandall, Michael. *The Limewood Sculptors of Renaissance Germany*. New Haven: Yale University Press, 1980.
———. *Painting and Experience in Fifteenth Century Italy: A Primer in the Social History of Pictorial Style*. Oxford: Oxford University Press, 1972.
———. *Patterns of Intention: On the Historical Explanation of Pictures*. New Haven: Yale University Press, 1985.
Beaumont, C. L. "The Picture Sales of New York—A Retrospective History." *New York Times*, December 11, 1897.
Bedell, Rebecca. *The Anatomy of Nature: Geology and American Landscape Painting, 1825–1875*. Princeton: Princeton University Press, 2001.
Behn, Aphra. *Oroonoko: or, The Royal Slave: A True History*. London: Will. Canning, 1688.
Berger, Martin A. *Sight Unseen: Whiteness and American Visual Culture*. Berkeley: University of California Press, 2005.
Bermingham, Ann. "System, Order, and Abstraction: The Politics of English Landscape Drawing Around 1795." In W. J. T. Mitchell, *Landscape and Power*, 77–101.
Blaugrund, Annette. "'Up Through the Snow' to Kensett's Studio." *Archives of American Art Journal* 23, no. 3 (1983): 31–32.
Blinder, Caroline. "'The Transparent Eyeball': On Emerson and Walker Evans." *Mosaic: An Interdisciplinary Critical Journal* 37, no. 4 (December 2004): 149–63.
"Blowing Rocks." *GT* 1, no. 38 (September 15, 1827).
Blume, Kenneth J. *Historical Dictionary of the U.S. Maritime Industry*. Lanham, MD: Scarecrow Press, 2012.
Blumenberg, Hans. *Shipwreck with Spectator: Paradigm of a Metaphor for Existence*. Translated by Steven Rendall. Cambridge: MIT Press, 1997. (Originally published in German as *Schiffbruch mit Zuschauer: Paradigma einer Daseinsmetapher*, 1979.)
Boeschenstein, Warren. *Historic American Towns Along the Atlantic Coast*. Baltimore: Johns Hopkins University Press, 1999.
Bolster, W. Jeffrey. *The Mortal Sea: Fishing the Atlantic in the Age of Sail*. Cambridge: Belknap Press of Harvard University Press, 2012.
Bosco, Ronald A., and Joel Myerson. *The Emerson Brothers: A Fraternal Biography in Letters*. Oxford: Oxford University Press, 2006.
The Boston Almanac and Business Directory. Vol. 45, *1880*. Boston: Sampson, Murdock, 1879.
The Boston Almanac and Business Directory. Vol. 53, *1888*. Boston: Sampson, Murdock, 1888.
The Boston Almanac and Business Directory. Vol. 59, *1894*. Boston: Sampson, Murdock, 1894.
Boston and the China Trade: A Massachusetts Historical Society Picture Book. Boston: Massachusetts Historical Society, 1970.
The Boston Directory. No. 79, *For the Year Commencing July 1, 1883*. Boston: Sampson, Davenport, 1883.
The Boston Directory, for the Year Commencing July 1, 1864. Boston: Adams, Sampson, 1864.
Bourque, Bruce J. *Twelve Thousand Years: American Indians in Maine*. Lincoln: University of Nebraska Press, 2001.
Bowles, Ada C. C. A. S. & L. A. Weekly Column on Matters of Local History. *GDT*, March 16, 1916.
Bremer, Francis J. *The Puritan Experiment: New England Society from Bradford to Edwards*. Hanover: University Press of New England, 2013.
Brigham, Clarence S. "Charles Henry Taylor." Obituaries. *Proceedings of the American Antiquarian Society* 51, pt. 2 (October 1941): 237–41.
"British Artists: Their Style and Character, No. 1—John Constable." *Art Journal*, n.s., 1 (1855): 9–12.
"The Brook by the Way." *Art Journal* 11 (March 1849): 72.
Brooks, Alfred Mansfield. "Communication." *Essex Institute Historical Collections* 96, no. 1 (January 1960): 73–74.
———. "The Fitz Lane House in Gloucester." *Essex Institute Historical Collections* 78, no. 3 (July 1942): 281–83.
———. "Fitz Lane's Drawings." *Essex Institute Historical Collections* 81, no. 1 (January 1945): 83–86.

———. "Gloucester and the Surinam Trade." *Essex Institute Historical Collections* 89, no. 3 (July 1953): 288–91.

[———], attrib. "Historical House Adds Paintings by Fitz Lane." *GDT*, [no day indicated] 1937. "Clippings," CAM.

Brooks, Alfred Mansfield, and Ruth Steele Brooks. *Gloucester Recollected: A Familiar History*. Edited by Joseph E. Garland. Gloucester, MA: Peter Smith for CAHA, 1974.

Brown, Chandos Michael. "A Natural History of the Gloucester Sea Serpent: Knowledge, Power, and the Culture of Science in Antebellum America." *American Quarterly* 42, no. 3 (September 1990): 402–36.

Brown, Dona. *Inventing New England: Regional Tourism in the Nineteenth Century*. Washington, DC: Smithsonian Institution Press, 1995.

Brown, Richard Harvey. "The Opium Trade and Opium Policies in India, China, Britain, and the United States: Historical Comparisons and Theoretical Interpretations." *American Journal of Social Science* 30, no. 3 (2002): 623–56.

Brownlee, Peter John. *The Commerce of Vision: Optical Culture and Perception in Antebellum America*. Philadelphia: University of Pennsylvania Press, 2019.

Burns, Sarah. *Inventing the Modern Artist: Art and Culture in Gilded Age America*. New Haven: Yale University Press, 1996.

———. *Painting the Dark Side: Art and the Gothic Imagination in Nineteenth-Century America*. Berkeley: University of California Press, 2004.

Bursten, Steven K. "Marine Art Is Riding Wave of Success." *New York Times*, August 16, 1970.

Butler, T. B. *The Philosophy of the Weather and a Guide to Its Changes*. New York: D. Appleton, 1856.

Butlin, Martin, and Evelyn Joll. *The Paintings of J. M. W. Turner*. 2 vols. New Haven: Yale University Press, 1977.

Cabot, Harriet Ropes. *Handbook of the Bostonian Society*. Boston: Bostonian Society, 1979.

Cameron, E. H. "Of Yankee Granite, Part I." *Technology Review* 54, no. 7 (May 1952): 359–64.

———. "Of Yankee Granite, Part II." *Technology Review* 54, no. 8 (June 1952): 419–22.

Cape Ann Museum. *Report on Scholars' Gathering in Association with the Exhibition "Fitz Henry Lane and Mary Blood Mellen: Old Mysteries and New Discoveries."* New York: Terra Foundation, 2007.

Carroll, Charles F. "Wooden Ships and American Forests." *Journal of Forest History* 25, no. 4 (October 1981): 213–15.

Carso, Kerry Dean. *American Gothic Art and Architecture in the Age of Romantic Literature*. Cardiff: University of Wales Press, 2014.

Catalogue of Paintings Now on Exhibition in the Free Gallery of the New England Art Union. Boston: Dutton & Wentworth, 1851.

Catalogue of Paintings, of the Third Exhibition of the Boston Artists' Association, 1844, at Harding's Gallery, 22 School Street. Boston: Clapp & Son, 1844.

Catalogue of the Loan Exhibition, 1878, in Aid of the Society of Decorative Art. New York: E. Wells Sackett & Bro., 1878.

Champney, Benjamin. *Sixty Years' Memories of Art and Artists*. Woburn, MA: self-published, 1900.

Chaplin, Ann Theopold. *The Babson Genealogy, 1606–1997: Descendants of Thomas and Isabel Babson*. Baltimore: Gateway Press, 1999.

Chinea, Jorge L. "Fissures in El Primer Piso: Racial Politics in Spanish Colonial Puerto Rico During Its Pre-plantation Era, c. 1700–1800." *Caribbean Studies* 30, no. 1 (January–June 2002): 169–204.

Clark, Ethne. *Hidcote: The Making of a Garden*. 1989. Reprint, New York: W. W. Norton, 2009.

A Climate for Art: The History of the Boston Athenaeum Gallery, 1827–1873. Boston: Boston Athenaeum, 1980. Exh. cat.

Cole, Thomas. "Essay on American Scenery." *American Monthly Magazine* 1, no. 3 (January 1836): 1–12. Reprinted in Sarah Burns and John Davis, *American Art to 1900: A Documentary History*, 264–71. Berkeley: University of California Press, 2009.

Conlin, Jonathan. "'At the Expense of the Public': The Sign Painters' Exhibition of 1762 and the Public Sphere." *Eighteenth-Century Studies* 36, no. 1 (Fall 2002): 1–21.

Constitution, By-Laws, Sailing Regulations, &c. of the New York Yacht Club. New York: F. H. Biglow, 1871.

Cook, Clarence. *Art and Artists of Our Time*. 6 vols. New York: Selmar Hess, 1888. Reprint, New York: Garland, 1978.

———. *A Description of New York Central Park*. New York: F. J. Huntington, 1869.

———. "John F. Kensett." In *Art and Artists of Our Time*, 4:292–94.

———. "Letters on Art.—No. IV." *Independent* (New York), September 7, 1854, 281.

Cook, James W. "Antebellum Cultural History." In *A Companion to American Cultural History*, edited by Karen Halttunen, 65–78. Hoboken, NJ: John Wiley & Sons, 2008.

Corn, Wanda M. "Artists' Homes and Studios: A Special Kind of Archive." *American Art* 19, no. 1 (Spring 2005): 2–11.

Cowdrey, Mary Bartlett. *American Academy of Fine Arts and American Art-Union, 1816–1852*. 2 vols. New York: New-York Historical Society, 1953.

Craig, James A. *Fitz H. Lane: An Artist's Voyage Through Nineteenth-Century America*. Charleston, SC: History Press, 2006.

Crain, Edward E. *Historic Architecture in the Caribbean Islands*. Gainesville: Library Press at the University of Florida, 2017.

Cummings, Abbott Lowell. *The Framed Houses of Massachusetts Bay, 1625–1725*. Cambridge: Harvard University Press, 1979.

Cutter, William Richard, ed. *Genealogical and Personal Memoirs Relating to the Families of the State of Massachusetts*. New York: Lewis Historical Publishing, 1910.

Davis, Elliot Bostwick. "American Drawing Books and Their Impact on Fitz Hugh Lane." In *The Cultivation of Artists in Nineteenth-Century America*, edited by Georgia Brady Barnhill, Diana

Korzenik, and Caroline F. Sloat, 55–80. Worcester, MA: AAS, 1997.

———. "Training the Eye and the Hand: Fitz Hugh Lane and American Drawing Books." In *Training the Eye and the Hand: Fitz Hugh Lane and Nineteenth Century American Drawing Books*, 7–25, 33–36. Gloucester, MA: CAHA, 1993. Exh. cat.

Davis, John. "Only in America: Exceptionalism, Nationalism, Provincialism." In *A Companion to American Art*, edited by John Davis, Jennifer A. Greenhill, and Jason D. LaFountain, 317–35. Hoboken, NJ: John Wiley & Sons, 2015.

Davis, Solomon Haskell. *Journal of Captain Solomon H. Davis, a Gloucester Sea-Captain, 1828–1846*. Norwood, MA: Plimpton Press, 1922.

de Bolla, Peter. *The Education of the Eye: Painting, Landscape, and Architecture in Eighteenth-Century Britain*. Stanford: Stanford University Press, 2003.

Defebaugh, James Elliott. *History of the Lumber Industry of America*. 2 vols. Chicago: American Lumberman, 1906–7.

DeLue, Rachael Ziady. *George Inness and the Science of Landscape*. Chicago: University of Chicago Press, 2005.

DeLue, Rachael Ziady, and James Elkins, eds. *Landscape Theory*. New York: Routledge, 2008.

"Description of the Cod Fish." Reprinted from *The American Encyclopedia* in *GT* 5, no. 37 (September 10, 1831).

"Diseases of Painters." Reprinted from the *New York Journal of Commerce* in *GT* 1, no. 47 (November 17, 1827).

Disturnell, John. *Emigrant's Guide to New Mexico, California, Oregon*. New York: self-published, 1849.

Dobkin, Josephine C. "Chinnery and Houqua: Questions of Attribution." *Metropolitan Museum Journal* 48 (2013): 205–16.

Downing, Alexander J. *The Architecture of Country Houses*. Philadelphia: G. S. Appleton, 1850. Reprint, New York: Dover, 1969.

Dunlap, Sarah, and Stephanie Buck. *Fitz Henry Lane, Family and Friends: Nathaniel Rogers Lane–Fitz Henry Lane, December 19, 1805–August 13, 1865*. Gloucester, MA: Church & Mason Publishing and Cape Ann Historical Museum, 2007.

Dunlap, William. *A History of the Rise and Progress of the Arts of Design in the United States*. 2 vols. New York: G. P. Scott, 1834. Reprint, New York: Dover, 1969.

Durivage, Francis A. "The Career of an Artist." 1850. In *Life Scenes, Sketched in Light and Shadow from the World Around Us*, 99–111. Boston: Sanborn, Carter & Bazin, 1856.

———. "Sketches of Cape Ann." *Pictorial National Library* 2 (March 1849): 143–47.

"Dusseldorf Paintings at New York, May 8, 1850." *BET*, May 10, 1850.

"1885–1897—Statistics from Samuel P. Avery, Jr." *New York Times*, December 11, 1897.

Ekelund, Robert B., Jr., John D. Jackson, and Robert D. Tollison. *The Economics of American Art: Issues, Artists, and Market Institutions*. Oxford: Oxford University Press, 2017.

Ellis, Elizabeth Garrity. "Cape Ann Views." In Wilmerding, *Paintings by Fitz Hugh Lane*, 19–44.

———. "Fitz Hugh Lane and the American Union of Associationists." *American Art Journal* 17, no. 2 (Spring 1985): 89.

Emerson, Ralph Waldo. *The Annotated Emerson*. Edited by David Mikics. Cambridge: Belknap Press of Harvard University Press, 2012.

———. "Nature." In *Essays: Second Series*, 183–213. Boston: James Munroe, 1844.

———. "Nominalist and Realist." In *Essays: Second Series*, 262–75. Boston: James Munroe, 1844.

———. "Spirit." In *Nature*, facsimile edition of 1836 first edition, edited by Jaroslav Pelikan, 76–81. Boston: Beacon Press, 1985.

Evans, Walker. *American Photographs*. New York: Museum of Modern Art, 1938.

Fagan, Brian. *Fish on Friday: Feasting, Fasting, and the Discovery of the New World*. New York: Basic Books, 2006.

Faulkner, Alaric, and Gretchen Faulkner. *The French at Pentagoet, 1635–1674: An Archaeological Portrait of the Acadian Frontier*. Augusta, ME: Maine Historic Preservation Commission, 1987.

Federal Writers' Project. *Maine: A Guide "Down East."* Boston: Houghton Mifflin, 1937. Maine State Library, Augusta.

"Fish." Broadside. 1792. AAS BDSDS/1792.

Fish, Prudence Paine. *Antique Houses of Gloucester*. Charleston, SC: History Press, 2007.

Fiske, Amos Kidder. *The West Indies*. New York: G. P. Putnam's Sons, 1899.

Fitz, Henry. *An Address Delivered Before the Newburyport [MA] Mechanic Association [. . .] Oct. 28, 1812*. Pamphlet.

"Fitz H. Lane, Esq." Obituary. *CAL*, August 1865. "Clippings," CAM.

"Fitz Hugh Lane, Self-Taught Artist, Now Recognized Here and Nationally." *GDT*, August 12, 1953. Clipping from CAM Authors and Artists Scrapbook, vol. 2.

Flagg, Edmund, ed. *Report on the Commercial Relations of the United States with All Foreign Nations*. Washington, DC: Cornelius Wendell, 1856.

"Fleet of 29 Sails from New London in 650-Mile Yacht Race to Bermuda." *New York Times*, June 25, 1934.

Foley, Mary. "Fitz Hugh Lane, Ralph Waldo Emerson, and the Gloucester Lyceum." *American Art Journal* 27, nos. 1–2 (1995–96): 99–101.

Forbes, Edward W. "Report of the William Hayes Fogg Art Museum, 1938–39." In *Fogg Art Museum Annual Report, No. 1938/1939*, 1–24.

Forbes, Ralph B. *Reminiscences of Ralph B. Forbes: Notes Regarding the Picture of the Schooner* Coquette *Hanging in the Lower Room at Milton*. Boston: Cotter, [1887]. Massachusetts Historical Society.

Forbes, Robert B. *The Auxiliary Screw Packet Ship* Massachusetts: *Forbes's New Rig*. Pamphlet. London: Nautical Magazine, 1853. Reprinted from a February 16, 1853, letter to the editor, *Nautical Magazine*, April 1853. Phillips Library, Peabody Essex Museum.

———. *The Life Boat, and Other Life-Saving Inventions*. Boston: A. Williams, 1880.

———. *Life-Boats, Projectiles, and Other Means for Saving Life*. Boston: Wm. Parsons Lunt, 1872.

———. *A New Rig for Ships and Other Vessels, Combining Economy, Safety,*

and Convenience. Boston: Wier & White, 1849.
———. *Personal Reminiscences, to Which Is Added Rambling Recollections Connected with China*. 3rd ed., rev. Boston: Little, Brown, 1892.
———. "Regatta at New Bedford, Massachusetts, 8 August, 1856." *American Neptune* 10 (1950): 231–34. Document contributed by Llewellyn Howland.
———. "Relations with China." *National Era* (Washington, DC) 11, no. 62 (April 16, 1857).
———. *Remarks on China and the China Trade*. Boston: Dickinson, 1844.
[———]. *The Voyage of the* Jamestown *on Her Errand of Mercy*. Boston: Eastburn's Press, 1847.
"Foreign Posts at Home." *American Foreign Service Journal* 2, no. 2 (February 1925): 66, "Porto Rico."
Foster, Edward Halsey. *The Civilized Wilderness: Backgrounds to American Romantic Literature, 1817–1860*. New York: Free Press, 1975.
Francis, Stephanie, and Scott Francis, eds. *Baskets of the Dawnland People*. Old Town, ME: Maine Indian Basketmakers Alliance, 2008.
Frayler, John. "Pickled Fish and Salted Provisions: Historical Musings from Salem Maritime NHS." *Pepper and Providence* (a publication of the National Park Service, Salem Maritime National Historic Site) 7, no. 2 (July 2005): 2–4.
Freyfogle, Eric T. *On Private Property: Finding Common Ground on the Ownership of Land*. Boston: Beacon Press, 2007.
"From the Journal of Health: Country Air." *GT* 4, no. 29 (July 17, 1830).
"Funeral of the Late Sidney Mason." *Commercial Advertiser* (New York), May 11, 1871.
Garland, Joseph E. *Boston's North Shore: Being an Account of Life Among the Noteworthy, Fashionable, Wealthy, Eccentric, and Ordinary, 1823–1890*. Boston: Little, Brown, 1978.
"Gas and Water." *Engineering News* 7 (January–December 1880).
Gatell, Frank Otto. "Puerto Rico Through New England Eyes, 1831–1834." *Journal of Inter-American Studies* 1, no. 3 (July 1959): 281–92.
Geertz, Clifford. *Local Knowledge: Further Essays in Interpretive Anthropology*. New York: Basic Books, 1983.
Gerdts, William H., and C. C. "'The Sea Is His Home'; Clarence Cook Visits Fitz Hugh Lane." *American Art Journal* 17, no. 3 (Summer 1985): 44–49.
Geronimus, Dennis. *Piero di Cosimo: Visions Beautiful and Strange*. New Haven: Yale University Press, 2006.
Gibson, Campbell. "Population of the 100 Largest Cities and Other Urban Places in the United States: 1790–1990." U.S. Census Bureau Working Paper Series no. 27, 1998.
Gimlette, John. *Wild Coast: Travels on South America's Untamed Edge*. New York: Alfred A. Knopf, 2011.
Gloucester and Rockport Directory [...] *Business Directory* [...] *and Almanac for 1861*. Gloucester, MA: Procter Brothers, 1861.
Gloucester and Rockport Directory [...] *Business Directory* [...] *and Almanac for 1869*. Gloucester, MA: Sampson, Davenport; Procter Brothers, 1869.
"Gloucester Art and Loan Exhibition Picture Catalogue." In *Memorial of the Celebration of the Two Hundred and Fiftieth Anniversary of the Founding of Gloucester*, 247–66.
The Gloucester Directory [...] *Business Directory* [...] *and Almanac for 1860*. Gloucester, MA: Procter Brothers, 1860.
The Gloucester Directory, Number 24, 1915: Comprising Also the Towns of Rockport and Manchester. Boston: Sampson & Murdock, 1915.
Glueck, Grace. "John I. H. Baur, Art Scholar: Headed the Whitney Museum." Obituary. *New York Times*, May 16, 1987.
Goldstein, Malcolm. *Landscape with Figures: A History of Art Dealing in the United States*. New York: Oxford University Press, 2000.
Gordon, Elinor. *Collecting Chinese Export Porcelain*. Pittstown, NJ: Main Street Press, 1984.
Granby, Alan, and Jessica Hyland, with William I. Koch. *The Holy Grail of Yachting: The Art of the America's Cup*. Vol. 1, *1851: Race for the Squadron Cup*. West Palm Beach, FL: America 3 Foundation, 2013.
Gray, John C. *Essays: Agricultural and Literary*. Boston: Little, Brown, 1856.
Greenberg, Clement. "Abstract and Representational." *Art Digest*, November 1, 1954. Reprinted in *Collected Essays and Criticism*, 3:186–93.
———. "Abstract Art." *The Nation*, April 15, 1944. Reprinted in *Collected Essays and Criticism*, 1:199–204.
———. "Abstract, Representational, and So Forth." In *Collected Essays and Criticism*, 3:133–38. Originally given as a Ryerson Lecture at Yale, May 12, 1954.
———. "'American-Type' Painting." 1955, rev. 1958. Reprinted in *Art and Culture: Critical Essays*, 208–29. Boston: Beacon Press, 1961.
———. *Clement Greenberg: The Collected Essays and Criticism*. 4 vols. Edited by John O'Brian. Chicago: University of Chicago Press, 1993.
———. "'Feeling Is All.'" *Partisan Review*, January–February 1952. Reprinted in *Collected Essays and Criticism*, 3:99–106.
———. "Our Period Style." *Partisan Review*, November 1949. Reprinted in *Collected Essays and Criticism*, 2:322–26.
———. "The Present Prospects of American Painting and Sculpture." *Horizon*, October 1947. Reprinted in *Collected Essays and Criticism*, 2:160–70.
———. "Review of an Exhibition of Arshile Gorky." *Partisan Review*, April 1948. Reprinted in *Collected Essays and Criticism*, 2:218–25.
———. "Some Advantages of Provincialism." *Art Digest*, January 1, 1954. Reprinted in *Collected Essays and Criticism*, 3:161–64.
Greenblatt, Stephen. "Cultural Mobility: An Introduction." In *Cultural Mobility: A Manifesto*, edited by Stephen Greenblatt et al., 1–23. Cambridge: Cambridge University Press, 2009.
———. "A Mobility Studies Manifesto." In *Cultural Mobility: A Manifesto*, edited by Stephen Greenblatt et al., 250–53. Cambridge: Cambridge University Press, 2009.
———. *Renaissance Self-Fashioning: From More to Shakespeare*. Chicago: University of Chicago Press, 1980.

Griffiths, John W. "Japan and China Packet Propeller *Antelope*." *U.S. Nautical Magazine and Naval Journal* 3 (October 1855): 11–17.

Grusin, Richard A. *Culture, Technology, and the Creation of America's National Parks*. Cambridge: Cambridge University Press, 2004.

Gustafson, Eleanor H., ed. "Collector's Notes." *Antiques* 157, no. 6 (June 2005): 48.

———, ed. "Collector's Notes." *Antiques* 172, no. 2 (August 2007): 44.

Halttunen, Karen. *Confidence Men and Painted Women: A Study of Middle-Class Culture in America, 1830–1870*. New Haven: Yale University Press, 1982.

Haskins, Katherine. *"The Art-Journal" and Fine Art Publishing in Victorian England, 1850–1880*. Burlington, VT: Ashgate, 2012.

Hatch, Francis W. "Maine Diary Describes Fitz Lane Art Cruise." *GDT Supplement*, November 23, 1974.

Hawes, Joel. "Formation and Importance of Character." Lecture 4 in *Lectures Addressed to the Young Men of Hartford and New-Haven*. Hartford, CT: Oliver D. Cooke, 1828.

Hawkins, Rev. William George. *Life of John H. W. Hawkins, Compiled by His Son, Rev. William George Hawkins, A.M.* Boston: John P. Jewett, 1859.

Hawthorne, Nathaniel. *The Marble Faun: or, The Romance of Monte Beni*. 2 vols. New York: Houghton Mifflin, 1890. Originally published in Boston by Ticknor & Fields, 1860.

Hazen, Edward. *The Panorama of Professions and Trades*. Philadelphia: Uriah Hunt, 1836.

Hempstead, Alfred Geer. *The Penobscot Boom and the Development of the West Branch of the Penobscot River for Log Driving*. University of Maine Studies, second series, no. 18. Orono, ME: Printed at the University Press, 1931.

Herbert, Robert L. "The Sublime Landscapes of Western Massachusetts: Edward Hitchcock's Romantic Naturalism." *Massachusetts Historical Review* 12 (2010): 70–99.

Higginson, Thomas Wentworth. *Travellers and Outlaws: Episodes in American History*. Boston: Lee & Shepard, 1889.

Hislop, Richard, ed. *Auction Prices of American Artists, 1977–94*. 9 vols. Weybridge, Surrey: Art Sales Index, 1978–94.

The History of the British Dominions in North America: From the First Discovery [. . .] *to Its Present Glorious Establishment as Confirmed by the Late Treaty of Peace in 1763*. London: W. Strahan, 1773.

Hitchcock, Edward. *Final Report on the Geology of Massachusetts*. Northampton: J. H. Butler, 1841.

Holliday, J. S. *The World Rushed In: The California Gold Rush Experience*. New York: Simon & Schuster, 1981.

Holmes, J. B. S. "Fitzhugh and FitzHughs in the China Trade." In *Chinese Export Porcelain: An Historical Survey*, edited by Elinor Gordon, 155–57. New York: Main Street / Universe Books, 1975.

Howat, John K. *Frederic Church*. New Haven: Yale University Press, 2005.

———. "Kensett's World." In *John Frederick Kensett: An American Master*, exh. cat., edited by John Paul Driscoll and John K. Howat, 15–47. Worcester, MA: Worcester Art Museum; New York: W. W. Norton, 1985.

———. "Private Collectors and Public Spirit: A Selective View." In *Art and the Empire City: New York, 1825–1861*, exh. cat., edited by Catherine Hoover Voorsanger and John K. Howat, 83–107. New York: Metropolitan Museum of Art, 2000.

Howe, Octavius T., and Frederick C. Matthews. *American Clipper Ships, 1833–1858*. 2 vols. Salem, MA: Marine Research Society, 1926–27.

Hoyt, Rich Edward C. "Industrial Statistics of Gloucester [. . .] for the Year Ending May 1, 1865." *CAA*, August 25, 1865.

Hughes, Eleanor, ed. *Spreading Canvas: Eighteenth-Century British Marine Painting*. New Haven: Yale University Press, 2016. Exh. cat.

———. "Vessels of Empire: Eighteenth-Century British Marine Painting." PhD diss., University of California, Berkeley, 2001.

Hughes, Thomas Patrick. *American Ancestry: Giving the Name and Descent, in the Male Line, of Americans Whose Ancestors Settled in the United States Previous to the Declaration of Independence, A.D. 1776*. Vol. 4. Albany, NY: Joel Munsell's Sons, 1889.

Hunt, R. "Granite." *Art Journal* (London), n.s., 2 (September 1856): 264–65.

Hunter, William C. *The "Fan Kwae" at Canton Before Treaty Days, 1825–1844*. London: Kegan Paul, Trench, 1882.

Huntington, David C. *Landscapes of Frederic Edwin Church: Vision of an American Era*. New York: Braziller, 1966.

Hutchings, William. "Narrative of the Siege of Penobscot [of 1779]" (narrated to Mr. Joseph L. Stevens Jr. in August 1855). In Wheeler, *History of Castine*, 271–76.

Hutchins, John G. B. *The American Maritime Industries and Public Policy, 1789–1914: An Economic History*. Cambridge: Harvard University Press, 1941.

Hutchinson, Thomas. *The History of the Colony of Massachuset's Bay, from the First Settlement Thereof in 1628, Until* [. . .] *1691*. 2nd ed. 2 vols. London: M. Richardson, 1765–68.

Jackson, Frances Alice. "Catalina Juliana Mason, Afterward Mrs. Theodorus Bailey Myers, 1824–1905." In Julian-James, *Biographical Sketches*, 37–58.

Jackson, James Brinkerhoff. "Jefferson, Thoreau, and After." In *Landscape in Sight: Looking at America*, edited by Helen Lefkowitz Horowitz, 175–82. New Haven: Yale University Press, 1997. First published in *Landscape* 15, no. 2 (Winter 1965–66): 25–27.

Janin, Hunt. *The India-China Opium Trade in the Nineteenth Century*. Jefferson, NC: McFarland, 1999.

Jarves, James Jackson. *The Art-Idea*. 1864. Reprint, Cambridge: Belknap Press of Harvard University Press, 1960.

———. *Art Thoughts: The Experiences and Observations of an American Amateur in Europe*. New York: Hurd & Houghton, 1869.

Jenkins, Lawrence W., comp. *A Catalogue of the Charles H. Taylor Collection of Ship Portraits in the Peabody Museum of Salem*. Salem, MA: Peabody Museum, 1949.

Johns, Elizabeth. "Histories of American Art: The Changing Quest." *Art Journal* 44, no. 4 (Winter 1984): 338–44.

Journal of the Executive Proceedings of the Senate of the United States of America.

Vol. 4, *From March 4, 1829, to March 3, 1837, Inclusive*. Washington, DC: Government Printing Office, 1887.

Julian-James, Mrs. Cassie Mason Myers, ed. *Biographical Sketches of the Bailey-Myers-Mason Families, 1776 to 1905: Key to a Cabinet of Heirlooms in the National Museum, Washington*. N.p.: privately printed, 1908. Smithsonian Institution.

"'Junior,' on the Brig *Cronstadt*." *CAA* 3, no. 2 (January 13, 1860).

Kamensky, Jane. *The Exchange Artist: A Tale of High-Flying Speculation and America's First Banking Collapse*. New York: Viking, 2008.

Kay, Jane Holtz. *Lost Boston*. Expanded and updated ed. Amherst: University of Massachusetts Press, 2006.

Keck, Michaela. *Walking in the Wilderness: The Peripatetic Tradition in Nineteenth-Century American Literature and Painting*. Heidelberg: Universitätsverlag Winter, 2006.

Kelly, Franklin. "Lane and Church in Maine." In Wilmerding, *Paintings by Fitz Hugh Lane*, 129–56.

———. "The Paintings of Fitz Hugh Lane." *Antiques* 134 (July 1988): 116–28.

———. "The Westervelt Warner Museum of Young America." *Antiques* 166, no. 2 (August 2004): 54–66.

Kempe, Marcis. "New England Water Supplies—A Brief History." *Journal of the New England Water Works Association* 120, no. 3 (September 2006).

Kimmelman, Michael. "Art/Architecture: Ambition and Rapture Add Up to Joy." *New York Times*, May 12, 2002.

Knight, Christopher. "Is There a California School?" *Portfolio* 3, no. 5 (September–October 1981): 54–61.

Knoblock, Glenn A. *The American Clipper Ship, 1845–1920*. Jefferson, NC: McFarland, 2014.

Kramer, Lawrence, ed. *Hart Crane's "The Bridge."* New York: Fordham University Press, 2011.

Kennedy, Joseph C. G., comp. *Population of the United States in 1860*. Washington, DC: Government Printing Office, 1864.

Kusserow, Karl, and Alan C. Brraddock, eds. *Nature's Nation: American Art and Environment*. Princeton: Princeton University Press, 2020.

Labaree, Benjamin W. "The Making of an Empire: Boston and Essex County, 1790–1850." In *Entrepreneurs: The Boston Business Community, 1700–1850*, Massachusetts Historical Society Studies in American History and Culture, no. 4, edited by Conrad Edick Wright and Katheryn P. Viens, 342–63. Boston: Massachusetts Historical Society, 1997.

Lancour, Harold, comp. *American Art Auction Catalogues, 1785–1942*. New York: New York Public Library, 1944.

Lane, Edward H. "Early Recollections of Artist Fitz H. Lane." C. A. S. & L. A. Weekly Column on Matters of Local History. *GDT*, March 23, 1916. "Clippings," CAM, p. 58.

"Lane Held in High Rank." *GDT*, March 2, 1916. "Clippings," CAM.

"Lane Painting Formally Presented to City on Behalf of Donor." *GDT*, July 15, 1913.

Lathrop, John, reporter. "Peter Wainwright and Another *vs*. S. Salisbury Tuckerman & Others, Suffolk [Co.], Nov. 17, 1875, March 18–April 18, 1876." In *Massachusetts Reports*, vol. 120, *Cases Argued and Determined in the Supreme Judicial Court of Massachusetts, March–September 1876*, 232–39. Boston: Houghton Mifflin, 1877.

Lears, Jackson. *Something for Nothing: Luck in America*. New York: Penguin, 2003.

Lett, Amanda, Patricia Hills, Peter John Brownlee, and Randy Ramer. *Perfectly American: The Art-Union and Its Artists*. Tulsa, OK: Gilcrease Museum, 2011. Exh. cat.

"Life in America: Artists Have Loved and Painted It for 300 Years." *Life*, June 19, 1939, 26–31.

Lipman, Andrew. *The Saltwater Frontier: Indians and the Contest for the American Coast*. New Haven: Yale University Press, 2015.

Lipton, Leah. "The Boston Artists' Association, 1841–1851." *American Art Journal* 15, no. 4 (Autumn 1983): 45–57.

"List of Members." *Bulletin of the American Art-Union*, November 17 and December 25, 1848.

Lossing, Benson J. *Pictorial Field-Book of the War of 1812*. New York: Harper & Brothers, 1868.

Louchheim, Aline B. "Forgotten Men of American Art." *New York Times*, September 30, 1951.

"Louise." "Our Artist at Home." [*Telegraph and News*], April 26, 1856. MFA object file for Lane, *Fishing Party*.

Lovell, Margaretta M. *Art in a Season of Revolution: Painters, Artisans, and Patrons in Early America*. Philadelphia: University of Pennsylvania Press, 2005.

———. "Fitz Henry Lane, spectateur de l'histoire." In *Refaire l'Amérique: Imaginaire et histoire des États-Unis*, edited by Didier Aubert and Hélène Quanquin, 47–61. Paris: Presses Sorbonne nouvelle, 2011.

———. "Fitz H. Lane's Marine Lithographs, Robert Bennet Forbes, and the Pirates of the South China Sea." In *Laid Down on Paper: Printmaking in America, 1800–1865*, edited by Caroline Sloat, 99–119. Gloucester, MA: CAM, 2020.

Lowell, Robert. *Life Studies*. New York: Farrar, Straus & Giroux, 1959.

Lubbock, Basil. *The China Clippers*. Glasgow: James Brown & Son, 1914.

MacCannell, Dean. *The Tourist: A New Theory of the Leisure Class*. New York: Schocken Books, 1989.

Mandell, Daniel R. *King Philip's War: Colonial Expansion, Native Resistance, and the End of Indian Sovereignty*. Baltimore: Johns Hopkins University Press, 2010.

Mann, Horace. *A Few Thoughts for a Young Man: A Lecture, Delivered Before the Boston Mercantile Library Association, on Its 29th Anniversary*. Boston: Ticknor, Reed & Fields, 1850.

Marryat, Federick. *The Universal Code of Signals*. London: Richardson, 1869. Peabody Museum, Salem.

Marsden, William. *The History of Sumatra*. Reprint of the 3rd ed., 1811, Oxford: Oxford University Press, 1966. First edition published London, 1783.

Mason, Edna Warren [Mrs. Mason Pfizenmayer]. *Descendants of Capt. Hugh Mason in America*. New Haven: Tuttle, Morehouse & Taylor, 1937.

Mason, Helen. "Sidney Mason, 1799–1871." In Julian-James, *Biographical Sketches*, 113–22.

Mason, John. *A Statement of Facts in Relation to the Origin, Progress, and Prospects of the New-York and Harlem Rail Road Company*. Pamphlet. New York: George P. Scott, 1833.

Mason, Theodorus Bailey Myers. *The Preservation of Life at Sea*. New York: American Geographical Society, 1879.

Massachusetts Charitable Mechanic Association. *Catalogue of Paintings by Mr. [Alvan] Fisher Exhibited at the [Mechanic Association] Fair, to be sold at Faneuil Hall, on Monday, Oct. 9, 1837, at 12*. Pamphlet. AAS.

Matheson, Donald. *What Is the Opium Trade?* Edinburgh: Constable, 1857.

"Maxim Karolik, Art Patron, Dies: Collector Gave Americana to Boston Museum." *New York Times*, December 21, 1963.

McCormick, Gene E. "Fitz Hugh Lane, Gloucester Artist, 1804–1865." *Art Quarterly* 15 (Winter 1952): 291–306.

McKee, Harley J. *Introduction to Early American Masonry: Stone, Brick, Mortar, and Plaster*. Washington, DC: National Trust for Historic Preservation, 1973.

McLanathan, Richard. *The American Tradition in the Arts*. New York: Harcourt, Brace & World, 1968.

Memorial of the Celebration of the Two Hundred and Fiftieth Anniversary of the Founding of Gloucester in 1642. Boston: Alfred Mudge & Son, 1892.

Merrell, James H. "'The Customes of Our Countrey': Indians and Colonists in Early America." In *Diversity and Unity in Early North America*, edited by Philip D. Morgan, 75–112. London: Routledge, 1993.

Michasiw, Kim Ian. "Nine Revisionist Theses on the Picturesque." *Representations* 38 (Spring 1992): 76–100.

Mihm, Stephen. *A Nation of Counterfeiters: Capitalists, Con Men, and the Making of the United States*. Cambridge: Harvard University Press, 2007.

Miller, David C. "The Iconology of Wrecked or Stranded Boats in Mid to Late Nineteenth-Century American Culture." In *American Iconology: New Approaches to Nineteenth-Century Art and Literature*, edited by David C. Miller, 186–208. New Haven: Yale University Press, 1993.

"Miss Julia Edwards Weds R. M. Johnson." *New York Times*, July 3, 1902.

"Miss Lilias Moriarty Snow to Wed Pierrepont E. Johnson Here Saturday." *Newport Mercury and Weekly News*, July 13, 1934.

Mitchell, Samuel Augustus. *Description of Oregon and California, Embracing an Account of the Gold Regions*. Philadelphia: Thomas, Cowperthwait, 1849.

Mitchell, W. J. T., ed. *Landscape and Power*. Chicago: University of Chicago Press, 1994.

Moore, John Bassett. *A Digest of International Law*. 8 vols. Washington, DC: Government Printing Office, 1906.

Moore, John Bassett, and Hamilton Fish. *A Digest of International Law as Embodied in Diplomatic Discussions, Treaties, [...] and the Decisions of Courts, Federal and State*. H.R. Doc. No. 551, 56th Cong. 8 vols. Washington, DC: Government Printing Office, 1906.

Morison, Samuel Eliot. *The Maritime History of Massachusetts, 1783–1860*. Boston: Houghton Mifflin, 1921.

Moya Pons, Frank. *History of the Caribbean: Plantations, Trade, and War in the Atlantic World*. Princeton, NJ: Markus Wiener, 2007.

National Academy of Design Exhibition Record, 1826–1860. 2 vols. New York: New-York Historical Society, 1943.

Neal, John. *Little Moccasin; or, Along the Madawaska: A Story of Life and Love in the Lumber Region*. New York: Beadle, 1866.

"New England Art Union." *Literary World* 3, no. 16 (May 20, 1848).

Newton, Travers, and Marcia Steele. "The Series Paintings of Fitz Henry Lane: From Field Sketch to Studio Painting." In *Emil Bosshard, Paintings Conservator (1945–2006): Essays by Friends and Colleagues*, edited by Maria de Peverelli, Marco Grassi, and Hans-Christof von Imhoff, 195–215. Florence: Centro Di, 2009.

Norton, Mary Beth. "Pannick at the Eastward." In *In the Devil's Snare: The Salem Witchcraft Crisis of 1692*, 82–111. New York: Alfred A. Knopf, 2002.

Novak, Barbara. *American Painting of the Nineteenth Century: Realism, Idealism, and the American Experience*. New York: Praeger, 1969. Third edition 2007.

———. "Emerson and Lane: Luminist Time and the Transcendental Aboriginal Self." Chap. 2 in *Voyages of the Self: Pairs, Parallels, and Patterns in American Art and Literature*. Oxford: Oxford University Press, 2007.

———. "On Defining Luminism." In Wilmerding, *American Light*, 23–29.

———. "Self, Time, and Object in American Art: Copley, Lane, and Homer." In *American Icons: Transatlantic Perspectives on Eighteenth- and Nineteenth-Century American Art*, edited by Thomas W. Gaehtgens and Heinz Ickstadt, 61–91. Los Angeles: Getty Center, 1992.

Noyes, Sybil, Charles Thornton Libby, and Walter Goodwin Davis. *Genealogical Dictionary of Maine and New Hampshire*. 1928–29. Reprint, Baltimore: Genealogical Publishing, 1996.

Oaklander, Christine I. "Studios at the YMCA, 1869–1903." *Archives of American Art Journal* 32, no. 3 (1992): 14–22.

Oaks, Martha. *Gloucester at Mid-Century: The World of Fitz Hugh Lane*. Gloucester, MA: CAHA, 1989. Exh. cat.

Obituary for Charles A. Homans. *New-York Daily Tribune*, November 11, 1901.

Obituary for Sidney Mason. *Commercial Advertiser*, May 11, 1871.

Obituary for William S. Pendleton. *Advertiser* (Boston), February 15, 1874. Clipping in Charles Henry Taylor collection, AAS.

Official Guide Book of the New York World's Fair, 1939. New York: Exposition Publications, 1939.

Official Proceedings of the International Commercial Congress [...] 1899. [Philadelphia]: Press of the Philadelphia Commercial Museum, 1899.

O'Gorman, James F. *This Other Gloucester: Occasional Papers on the Arts of Cape Ann, Massachusetts*. Boston: self-published, 1976.

Osborne, Paul E. *Water Franchise Areas in Commonwealth of Massachusetts*. Massachusetts Department of Public Utilities, March 2016.

O'Sullivan, John L. "Annexation." *United States Magazine and Democratic Review* 17, no. 85 (July–August 1845).

Other Merchants and Sea Captains of Old Boston. Boston: State Street Trust, 1919.

Ott, John. "How New York Stole the Luxury Art Market: Blockbuster Auctions and Bourgeois Identity in Gilded Age America." *Winterthur Portfolio* 42, nos. 2–3 (Summer–Autumn 2008): 133–58.

Otter, Samuel. "*American Renaissance* and Us." *Journal of Nineteenth-Century Americanists* 3, no. 2 (Fall 2015): 228–35.

P. Letter to the editor. *CAL & GT* 25, no. 24 (June 14, 1851).

"Painting by Lane of Town in 1852 Presented by Washington Lady as Memento of Her Grandfather Mason." *GDT*, June 15, 1913. "Clippings," CAM.

Paintings and Drawings by Fitz Hugh Lane Preserved in the Collections of the Cape Ann Historical Association, Gloucester, Massachusetts. Gloucester, MA: CAHA, 1974.

Parker, John R. *The New Semaphoric Signal Book* [. . .] *the United States Telegraph Vocabulary* [. . .] *to Which Is Annexed the Boston Harbor Signal Book*. Boston: Kidder & Wright, 1842.

Parrington, Vernon Louis. "Ralph Waldo Emerson: Transcendental Critic." Chap. 2 in *Main Currents in American Thought: An Interpretation of American Literature from the Beginnings to 1920*, 2:386–99. New York: Harcourt, Brace, 1927.

Past and Present of Alameda County, California. Edited by Joseph E. Baker. 2 vols. Chicago: S. J. Clarke, 1914.

Patterson, Cynthia Lee. *Art for the Middle Classes: America's Illustrated Magazines of the 1840s*. Jackson: University Press of Mississippi, 2010.

Paulson, Ronald. "The Signboard and Its Painter." In *Popular and Polite Art in the Age of Hogarth and Fielding*, 31–48. Notre Dame: University of Notre Dame Press, 1979.

Payson, William Farquhar, ed. *Mahogany, Antique and Modern*. New York: E. P. Dutton, 1926.

Pendleton, William. *Essay on Gothic Architecture*. Booklet. N.d. AAS Lith/Pend/Essa.

Percy Society. *Early English Poetry, Ballads, and Popular Literature of the Middle Ages*. Vol. 20. London: Printed for the Percy Society, 1847.

Perkins, Robert F., Jr., and William J. Gavin III, eds., Mary Margaret Shaughnessy, asst. ed. *The Boston Athenaeum Art Exhibition Index, 1827–1874*. Boston: Library of the Boston Athenaeum, 1980.

Phillips, Stephen Willard, ed. *Ship Registers of the District of Gloucester, Massachusetts, 1789–1875*. Salem, MA: Essex Institute, 1944.

Picó, Fernando. *History of Puerto Rico*. Princeton, NJ: Markus Wiener, 2006.

Pictorial Views of Massachusetts. Worcester, MA: Warren Lazell, 1845.

"Picture Sales: The Stewart Collection and Others Since the [Civil] War—Only Three That Have Surpassed the Stewart Total of Prices." *New York Times*, February 12, 1898.

Pierce, Sally, and Catharina Slautterback. *Boston Lithography, 1825–1880*. Boston: Boston Athenaeum, 1991.

"Pierrepont E. Johnson." Obituary. *Newport Daily News*, May 7, 1963.

Pillsbury, Parker. "Nathaniel Peabody Rogers." *Granite Monthly* 4, no. 7 (April 1881).

Powell, Earl A., III. "The Boston Harbor Pictures." In Wilmerding, *Paintings by Fitz Hugh Lane*, 47–59.

———. "Luminism and the American Sublime." In Wilmerding, *American Light*, 69–94.

Preston, Stuart. "Americans Yesterday and Today." *New York Times*, May 9, 1954.

Price, Richard. *Representations of Slavery: John Gabriel Stedman's "Minnesota" Manuscripts*. [Minneapolis]: Associates of the James Bell Ford Library, University of Minnesota, 1989.

Prince, Nancy. *A Narrative of the Life and Travels of Mrs. Nancy Prince Written by Herself*. 2nd ed. Boston: self-published, 1853.

Pringle, James R. *History of the Town and City of Gloucester, Cape Ann, Massachusetts*. Gloucester, MA: self-published, 1892. Reprint, Gloucester, MA: Gloucester Archives Committee, 1997.

Prins, Harald E. L. "Chief Rawandagon, Alias Robin Hood: Native 'Lord of Misrule' in the Maine Wilderness." In *Northeastern Indian Lives, 1632–1816*, edited by Robert S. Grumet, 93–115. Amherst: University of Massachusetts Press, 1996.

Procter, George H. *The Fishermen's Memorial and Record Book: Containing a List of Vessels and Their Crews, Lost from the Port of Gloucester from the Year 1830 to October 1, 1873, Embracing a Period of Nearly Half a Century; Comprising Fourteen Hundred and Thirty-Seven Names, and Two Hundred and Ninety-Six Vessels, Including Those Lost in the Gale of August 24, 1873; It Also Contains Valuable Statistics of the Fishing Business, Off-Hand Sketches, Big Trips, Tales of Narrow Escapes, Maritime Poetry, and Other Matters of Interest to These Toilers of the Sea*. Gloucester, MA: Procter Brothers, 1873.

"Property in Art." *Art Journal* (London) 11 (May 1849): 133–36.

Puerto Rico Reconstruction Administration and the Writers' Program of the Work Projects Administration. *Puerto Rico: A Guide to the Island of Boriquén*. New York: University Society, 1940.

Quinn, Karen E., Sandra Kelberlau, and Jean Woodward. "Rediscovering Fitz Henry Lane's *View of Coffin's Beach* on Cape Ann." *Antiques* 170, no. 1 (July 2006): 66–69.

Raab, Jennifer. *Frederic Church: The Art and Science of Detail*. New Haven: Yale University Press, 2015.

Ramírez de Arellano, Annette B. "Encountering the Viper: Edward Bliss Emerson and Slavery." *Qualitative Report* 19, no. 16 (2014): 57–69.

Reed, Roger G. *Building Victorian Boston: The Architecture of Gridley J. F. Bryant*. Amherst: University of Massachusetts Press, 2007.

Report of State Prison. Massachusetts General Court Documents. Boston: Dutton & Wentworth, 1830.

Report of State Prisons for 1829. Massachusetts General Court Documents. N.p., 1830. AAS.

Report of Survey of Rail Road Boston to Lowell. Massachusetts General Court Documents. Pamphlet. Boston: Dutton & Wentworth, 1830.

Reynolds, Lucy Brown. "The Brig Cadet." Chap. 4 in *Drops of Spray from*

Southern Seas, 26–35. Waterville, ME: Mail Publishing, 1896.

Richards, Leonard L. *The California Gold Rush and the Coming of the Civil War*. New York: Alfred A. Knopf, 2007.

Ridgely-Nevitt, Cedric. "Auxiliary Steamships and R. B. Forbes." *American Neptune* 1, no. 1 (January 1941): 51–57.

———. "The *Massachusetts*." In *American Steamships on the Atlantic*, 89–96. Newark: University of Delaware Press, 1980.

Rigau-Pérez, José G., ed. *Edward Bliss Emerson: The Caribbean Journal and Letters, 1831–1834*. Privately printed, 2013.

Roberts, Brian. *American Alchemy: The California Gold Rush and Middle-Class Culture*. Chapel Hill: University of North Carolina Press, 2000.

Robertson, Bruce. "The Tipping Point: Museum Collecting and the Canon." *American Art* 17, no. 3 (Autumn 2003): 2–11.

Rohrbough, Malcolm. "The California Gold Discoveries: The French View of Themselves and the World." *Common-place* 6, no. 3 (April 2006). Accessed July 18, 2016. http://common-place.org/book/the-california-gold-discoveries.

Ronnberg, Erik A. R., Jr. "Imagery and Types of Vessels." In Wilmerding, *Paintings by Fitz Hugh Lane*, 61–104.

Rosenblum, Robert. "The Primal American Scene." In *The Natural Paradise: Painting in America, 1800–1950*, exh. cat., edited by Kynaston McShine, 15–37. New York: Museum of Modern Art, 1976.

Santiago de Curet, Annie. *Crédito, moneda y bancos en Puerto Rico durante el siglo XIX*. Río Piedras: Editorial de la Universidad de Puerto Rico, 1989.

Santiago-Valles, Kelvin. "Forced Labor in Colonial Penal Institutions Across the Spanish, U.S., British, French Atlantic, 1860s–1920s." In *On Coerced Labor: Work and Compulsion After Chattel Slavery*, edited by Marcel van der Linden and Magaly Rodríguez García, 73–97. Boston: Brill, 2016.

Savage, Kirk. "The Self-Made Monument: George Washington and the Fight to Erect a National Memorial." *Winterthur Portfolio* 22, no. 4 (Winter 1987): 225–42.

Schinto, Jeanne. "Skinner's Latest Fitz Hugh Lane Sale Sets a Record." *Maine Antiques Digest*, January 2005.

Schley, David. "A Natural History of the Early American Railroad." *Early American Studies* 13, no. 2 (Spring 2015): 443–66.

Scott, Lady Caroline Lucy. *Fitzhenry, or A Marriage in High Life: A Story of the Heart*. Edited by Lady Bury (Charlotte Campbell). Boston: F. Gleason, 1847. Originally published in London by Henry Colburn, 1828.

Serres, Michel. "Turner Translates Carnot." In *Calligram: Essays in New Art History from France*, translated by Stephan Bann, edited by Norman Bryson, 154–65. New York: Cambridge University Press, 1988.

Shand-Tucci, Douglass. *Built in Boston: City and Suburb, 1800–1950*. Amherst: University of Massachusetts Press, 1988.

Sharf, Frederic Alan. "Fitz Hugh Lane Re-considered." *Essex Institute Historical Collections* 96 (January 1960): 75–83.

———. "Fitz Hugh Lane: Visits to the Maine Coast, 1848–1855." *Essex Institute Historical Collections* 98, no. 2 (April 1962): 111–20.

Sharp, Lewis I. "American Paintings and Sculpture." *Notable Acquisitions (Metropolitan Museum of Art)*, 1965–75, 11–19.

Shulman, Ken. "A Master Re-emerges from the Attic." *New York Times*, June 15, 1997.

"Sidney Mason." *Newburyport Herald* 27, no. 83 (January 13, 1834).

Simoni, John P. "Art Critics and Criticism in Nineteenth-Century America." PhD diss., Ohio State University, 1952.

Simpson, Marc. "Noble Rock Portraits: Haseltine's American Work." In *Expressions of Place: The Art of William Stanley Haseltine*, exh. cat., 15–30. San Francisco: Fine Arts Museums of San Francisco, 1992.

Skalet, Linda Henefield. "The Market for American Painting in New York: 1870–1915." PhD diss., Johns Hopkins University, 1980.

"Sketch of Rockport." *GT* 14, no. 25 (March 27, 1850).

Smith, David Clayton. *A History of Lumbering in Maine, 1861–1960*. University of Maine Studies, no. 93. Orono: University of Maine Press, 1972.

Smith, Roberta. "A Youthful Land in All Its Glory." *New York Times*, June 14, 2002.

Smuts, Felicia. "Shipbuilding and the Mast Trade in Colonial New England." *Revere House Gazette*, no. 89 (Winter 2007): 1–4.

Solomon, Barbara M. "The Growth of the Population in Essex County, 1850–60." *Essex Institute Historical Collections* 45, no. 2 (April 1959): 82–103.

Spann, Edward K. *The New Metropolis: New York City, 1840–1857*. New York: Columbia University Press, 1981.

Springer, John S. *Forest Life and Forest Trees: Comprising Winter Camp-Life Among the Loggers* [. . .] *with Descriptions of Lumbering Operations on the Various Rivers of Maine and New Brunswick*. New York: Harper & Brothers, 1851.

"The State and Prospects of Lithography." *Art Journal* (London) 1, no. 6 (July 15, 1839): 97–98.

Stedman, Capt[ai]n J. G. *Narrative of a Five Years' Expedition Against the Revolted Negroes of Surinam, in Guiana, on the Wild Coast of South America; from the Year 1772 to 1777: Elucidating the History of That Country, and Describing Its Productions, Viz. Quadrupeds, Birds, Fishes, Reptiles, Trees, Shrubs, Fruits, & Roots; with an Account of the Indians of Guiana & Negroes of Guinea, Illustrated with 80 Elegant Engravings from Drawings Made by the Author*. 2 vols. London: J. Johnson, 1796.

Stimpson's Boston Directory. Boston: C. Stimpson, 1840.

"The Studio and Garden of F. H. Lane." *Boston Traveler*, August 28, 1857.

Sullivan, Edward. *Rambles and Scrambles in North and South America*. London: Richard Bentley, 1852.

"Survey of Sandy Bay." *GT* 4, no. 17 (April 24, 1830).

Swan, Marshall W. S. "Emerson and Cape Ann." *Essex Institute Historical Collections* 121, no. 4 (October 1985): 257–68.

Sweeney, J. Gray. "Inventing Luminism: 'Labels Are the Dickens.'" *Oxford Art Journal* 26, no. 2 (2003): 93–120.

"Take a Trip to Gloucester." *Lynn Mirror*. Reprinted in *GT* 5, no. 34 (August 20, 1831).

Tatham, David. "The Lithographic Workshop, 1825–50." In *The Cultivation of Artists in Nineteenth-Century America*, edited by Georgia Brady Barnhill, Diana Korzenik, and Caroline F. Sloat, 45–54. Worcester, MA: AAS, 1997.

———. "The Pendleton-Moore Shop: Lithographic Artists in Boston, 1825–1840." *Old-Time New England* 62, no. 2, serial no. 226 (October–December 1971): 29–46.

Tharp, Peter. *A New and Complete System of Federal Arithmetic* [. . .] *for the Use of Schools.* Newburgh, NY: D. Denniston for the author, 1798.

Thompson, Donald. "Notes on the Inauguration of the San Juan (Puerto Rico) Municipal Theater." *Latin American Music Review* 11, no. 1 (June 1990): 84–91.

Thoreau, Henry David. "Chesuncook." *Atlantic Monthly*, June 1858. http://www.theatlantic.com/unbound/flashbks/fall/chesunk.htm.

———. *The Maine Woods.* 1864. Edited by Jeffrey S. Cramer. New Haven: Yale University Press, 2009.

———. *Walden.* 1854. Edited by Jeffrey S. Cramer. New Haven: Yale University Press, 2004.

Tibbets, Fred W. "Fitz H. Lane." C. A. S. & L. A. Weekly Column on Matters of Local History. *GDT*, March 2, 1916. "Clippings," CAM.

———. "Fitz H. Lane." C. A. S. & L. A. Weekly Column on Matters of Local History. *GDT*, March 9, 1916. "Clippings," CAM.

Tilden, William Phillips. *Autobiography and Personal Tributes.* Boston: Press of George H. Ellis, 1891.

Tolles, Bryant F., Jr. *Summer by the Seaside: The Architecture of New England Coastal Resort Hotels, 1830–1950.* Hanover: University Press of New England, 2008.

Trafton, Melissa Geisler. "Critics, Collectors, and the Nineteenth-Century Taste for the Paintings of John Frederick Kensett." PhD diss., University of California, Berkeley, 2003.

Troyen, Carol. "The Incomparable Max: Maxim Karolik and the Taste for American Art." *American Art* 7, no. 3 (Summer 1993): 64–87.

"Trustee's Sale of Real Estate in Gloucester—Under the Will of the Late Mr. James Gaffield." *BET*, May 10, 1850.

Tucker, Louis Leonard. "Massachusetts." In *Historical Consciousness in the Early Republic*, edited by H. G. Jones, 1–28. Chapel Hill: North Caroliniana Society, 1995.

Tuckerman, Henry T. *Book of the Artists: American Artist Life, Comprising Biographical and Critical Sketches of American Artists; Preceded by an Historical Account of the Rise and Progress of Art in America.* New York: G. P. Putnam & Son, 1867.

Turnbull, David. *Travels in the West: Cuba, with Notices of Porto Rico and the Slave Trade.* London: Longman, Orme, Brown, Green & Longmans, 1840.

Turner, F. S. *British Opium Policy and Its Results to India and China.* London: Sampson, Low, Marston, Searle & Rivington, 1876.

"230 U.S. Paintings in Boston Display." *New York Times*, September 30, 1951.

Valentine, D. T. *Manual of the Corporation of the City of New-York, 1862.* New York: Corporation of New-York, 1862.

Van Dyne, Frederick. *A Treatise on the Law of Naturalization of the United States.* Washington, DC: self-published, 1907.

Vans, William, Jr. *A Short History of the Life of William Vans, a Native Citizen of Massachusetts.* Boston: self-published, 1825.

Varney, George J. *A Brief History of Maine.* [Portland, ME]: McLellan, Mosher, 1888.

———. *A Gazetteer of the State of Maine.* Boston: B. B. Russell, 1886.

Vickers, Daniel. *Farmers and Fishermen: Two Centuries of Work in Essex County, Massachusetts, 1630–1850.* Chapel Hill: University of North Carolina Press, 1994.

Vogel, Carol. "National Gallery Enriched by Gift." Inside Art. *New York Times*, May 7, 2004.

von Sack, Albert. *A Narrative of a Voyage to Surinam; of a Residence There During 1805, 1806, and 1807; and of the Author's Return to Europe by the Way of North America.* London: Printed for G. and W. Nicol by W. Bulmer, 1810.

W. "J. M. W. Turner." *Bulletin of the American Art-Union*, no. 3 (June 1, 1851): 37–39.

Wallach, Alan. "A Note on Aestheticizing Tendencies in American Landscape Painting, 1840–1880." In *Renew Marxist Art History*, edited by Warren Carter, Barnaby Haran, and Frederic J. Schwarz, 140–50. London: Art/Books, 2014.

———. "Rethinking 'Luminism': Taste, Class, and Aestheticizing Tendencies in Mid-Nineteenth-Century American Landscape Painting." In *The Cultured Canvas: New Perspectives on American Landscape Painting*, edited by Nancy Siegel, 115–47. Durham: University of New Hampshire Press, 2011.

Watson, Forbes. "My Country 'Tis of Thee." *Magazine of Art*, June 1939, 324–25, 334–35.

Weekley, Carolyn J. *The Kingdoms of Edward Hicks.* Williamsburg, VA: Colonial Williamsburg Foundation, Abby Aldrich Rockefeller Folk Art Center, 1999.

Wehle, Harry B. *Life in America: A Special Loan Exhibition of Paintings Held During the Period of the New York World's Fair, April 24 to October 29.* New York: Scribner Press, 1939. Exh. cat.

Weiss, Jo Ann. "Clarence Cook: His Critical Writings." PhD diss., Johns Hopkins University, 1977.

Wheeler, George A. *History of Castine, Penobscot, and Brooksville, Maine.* Cornwall, NY: Cornwall Press, 1923. Originally published in Bangor by Burr & Robinson, 1875.

Wilbur, Anthony R., and Fara Courtney. "The Environmental History and Current Characteristics of Gloucester Harbor." In *Gloucester Harbor Characterization: Environmental History, Human Influences, and Status of Marine Resources*, edited by Anthony R. Wilbur, Fara Courtney, and Robert P. Glenn, 3–16. Boston: Massachusetts Office of Coastal Zone Management, 2004.

Willard, S. *Plans and Sections, of the Obelisk on Bunker's Hill, with the Details of Experiments Made in Quarrying the Granite.* Boston: Charles Cook's Lithography, 1843.

Williams, Michael. "Industrial Impacts on the Forests of the United States,

1860–1920." *Journal of Forest History* 31, no. 3 (July 1987): 108–121.

Williams, William Carlos. "Sermon with a Camera." *New Republic*, October 11, 1938, 282–83.

Williamson, Joseph. "Castine and the Old Coins Found There." Printed for the Maine Historical Society, 1859. Reprint, *Wilson Museum Bulletin* 4, no. 24 (Spring 2003): 1–8.

Wilmerding, John, ed. *American Light: The Luminist Movement, 1850–1875; Paintings, Drawings, Photographs.* Washington, DC: National Gallery of Art, 1980. Exh. cat.

———. *Compass and Clock: Defining Moments in American Culture, 1800, 1850, 1900.* New York: Harry N. Abrams, 1999.

———. "Fire and Ice in American Art: Polarities from Luminism to Abstract Expressionism." In *The Natural Paradise: Painting in America, 1800–1950*, exh. cat., edited by Kynaston McShine, 40–56. New York: Museum of Modern Art, 1976.

———. *Fitz Henry Lane and Mary Blood Mellen: Old Mysteries and New Discoveries.* New York: Spanierman Gallery, 2007. Exh. cat.

———. *Fitz Hugh Lane.* Westport, CT: Praeger, 1971. Reprint, with the title *Fitz Henry Lane*, Gloucester, MA: CAM, 2005.

———. *Fitz Hugh Lane, 1804–1865: American Marine Painter.* Salem, MA: Essex Institute, 1964.

———. "Fitz Hugh Lane: Imitations and Attributions." *American Art Journal* 3, no. 2 (Autumn 1971): 32–40.

———. "The Lithographs of Fitz Hugh Lane." *Old-Time New England* 54, no. 2 (October–December 1963): 31–39.

———. "The Luminist Movement: Some Reflections." In Wilmerding, *American Light*, 97–152.

———. "The Lure of Mount Desert and the New England Coast." In Wilmerding, *Paintings by Fitz Hugh Lane*, 107–28.

———. "The Master of the Silvery Mist." *Wall Street Journal*, April 5–6, 2014, C13.

———, ed. *Paintings by Fitz Hugh Lane.* Washington, DC: National Gallery of Art, 1988. Exh. cat.

Wilton, Andrew, and Tim Barringer, eds. *American Sublime: Landscape Painting in the United States, 1820–1880.* London: Tate, 2002.

Witherle, William Howe. "A Cruise with Fitz Hugh Lane" (diary, August 16–21, 1852). *Wilson Museum Bulletin* 2, no. 2 (Winter 1974–75): 1–4.

Wood, Joseph S., with a contribution by Michael P. Steinitz. *The New England Village.* Baltimore: Johns Hopkins University Press, 1997.

Worley, Sharon. "Mapping the Metaphysical Landscape off Cape Ann: The Reception of Ralph Waldo Emerson's Transcendentalism Among the Gloucester Audience of Reverend Amory Dwight Mayo and Fitz Hugh Lane." *Historical Journal of Massachusetts* 29, no. 2 (2001): 137–69.

Wright, Helena E. "The Image Makers: The Role of the Graphic Arts in Industrialization." *Journal of the Society for Industrial Archeology* 12, no. 2 (1986): 5–18.

INDEX

Italicized page references indicate illustrations. Endnotes are referenced with "n" followed by the endnote number.

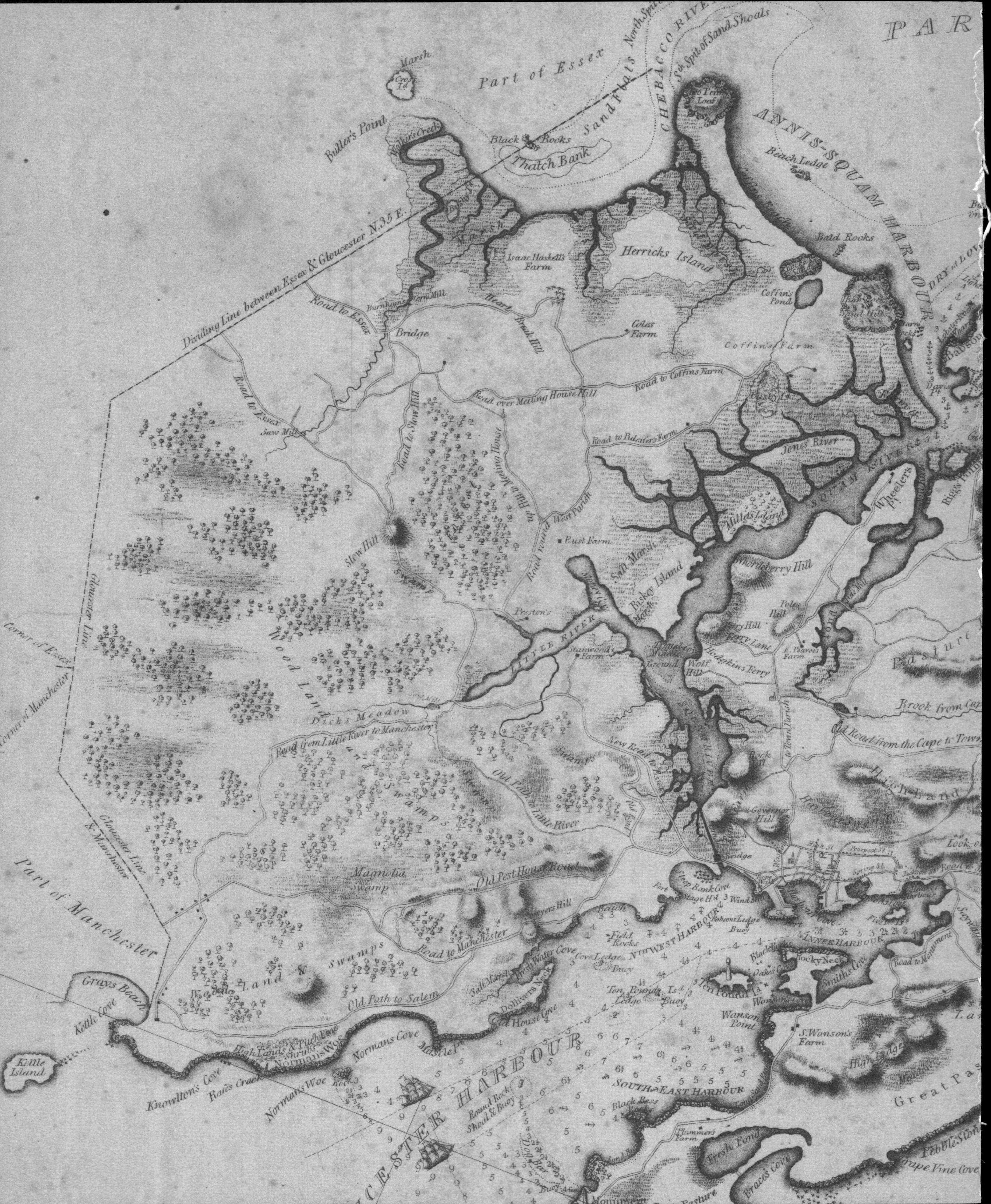